CAMP COUNSELING:
Leadership and Programming for the Organized Camp

CAMP COUNSELING: Leadership and Programming for the Organized Camp

Sixth Edition

A. Viola Mitchell, A.B., M.A.

Former Assistant Professor, Hanover College, Winthrop College and University of Maryland

Joel F. Meier

Professor of Recreation Management, University of Montana

This is a volume in the
SAUNDERS SERIES IN RECREATION

Geoffrey C. Godbey, *Consulting Editor*

Professor
The Pennsylvania State University

SAUNDERS COLLEGE PUBLISHING

Philadelphia New York Chicago
San Francisco Montreal Toronto
London Sydney Tokyo Mexico City
Rio de Janeiro Madrid

Address orders to:
383 Madison Avenue
New York, NY 10017

Address editorial correspondence to:
West Washington Square
Philadelphia, PA 19105

This book was set in Palatino by University Graphics, Inc.
The editors were John Butler, Michael Fisher, Merry Post, and Mary Agre.
The art & design director was Richard L. Moore.
The text design was done by Nancy E. J. Grossman.
The cover design was done by Larry Didona.
The artwork was drawn by Barbara Marsac.
The production manager was Tom O'Connor.

Cover credit: Photograph by Joel F. Meier.

Library of Congress Cataloging in Publication Data

Mitchell, A. Viola, 1904–
Camp counseling.

Bibliography: p.
Includes index.

1. Camp counselors. 2. Camps. I. Meier, Joel F.
II. Title.

GV198.C6M5 1982 796.54 81-53092
ISBN 0-03-058398-5

Camp Counseling ISBN 0-03-058398-5

Library of Congress catalog card number 81-53092.

345 016 98765432

CBS COLLEGE PUBLISHING
Saunders College Publishing
Holt, Rinehart and Winston
The Dryden Press

To
The Modern Camping Movement

May it continue to enhance our love and appreciation of the outdoors.

Table of Contents

Preface

Camp Counseling: Leadership and Programming for the Organized Camp presents a fresh, contemporary view of the trends, philosophies and practices of the organized camping movement. To reflect these changes, parts of the text have been expanded, while others have been reduced or revised. This edition continues the original intent of *Camp Counseling*—to serve as a useful tool for persons who are or will be engaged in positions of camp leadership.

The text can be used by at least five different groups of people: (1) students enrolled in college or university courses in camp counseling or outdoor leadership; (2) agency or organization personnel responsible for sponsoring camps, for use in their own training courses or as recommended reading for their prospective counselors; (3) camp directors conducting precamp or in-camp training courses; (4) counselors who want to work independently to prepare themselves to do their jobs more adequately; and (5) individuals who want to improve their skills in order to enjoy and benefit more from their own camping experiences. In short, *Camp Counseling* presents a ready resource of things to do with campers and ways of doing them.

Working in an organized camp offers many opportunities to make a contribution to society. In the modern camp, adequate training and skill are required of staff members who fill important leadership roles. A staff member must, first of all, build a professional philosophy of organized camping, including an understanding of its purposes, objectives, background, present status, and future trends. To these ends, Part I was written.

Further, a counselor or program leader must work closely with people, and consequently must have the ability to understand them and to devise ways to lead them successfully. This is actually more important than the skills that are taught. Part II was designed to help in this area. Working intimately with campers in a rustic setting is, of course, not everyone's cup of tea. Therefore, Part II also presents a rather detailed picture of the type of person most likely to be a successful counselor/leader and the duties he or she will be expected to perform, along with hints for doing them.

Campers want action and excitement and expect plenty of it in a variety of forms. Part III describes a number of activities and programming techniques especially suited for use in the informal, rustic atmosphere of a modern camp. The chapter on outdoor adventure programs introduces a whole new group of challenging activities.

Part IV treats in some detail the skills that are necessary for living comfortably in the out-of-doors. These skills represent the basic core of the camping experience. They are essential because they distinguish the camping experience from other forms of recreational or educational activities.

The reader will find countless ideas for a "program" throughout the book. A wide range of information about all aspects of camp programming and leadership is covered so that the book may serve as a handy reference; however, in order to save space and avoid repetition, only brief descriptions are given of some specialized activities. For those desiring additional information on any of these topics, please refer to the Selected General Bibliography in Appendix A. Other handy references are available in Appendices B, C, D, and E, where you will find updated directories of magazines, organizations, publishers and commercial films concerned with camping and related activities. In addition, those persons involved in conducting leadership training programs will find Appendices F and G to be particularly helpful. They present suggestions for conducting courses in camp counseling and CIT training programs.

This new edition points the way to some of the more successful outdoor/environmental education techniques and adventure programs used today. Also, emphasis is placed on understanding and appreciating the natural environment and how to reduce human impact on the land. *Camp Counseling: Leadership and Programming for the Organized Camp* brings a modern perspective to our concern for the fragility of the environment and suggests ways to enjoy the outdoors without spoiling it for future generations.

In recent years our environmental values have undergone radical change. As a result, certain traditional activities or skills once considered essential in any camp program are no longer appropriate in the modern organized camp. This is particularly so in respect to some forms of camp crafts and construction projects, such as building wood-burning fires and using elaborate cooking devices. However, material relating to some of these traditional skills is included in this book, since these activities may still be worthwhile if done in suitable locations under the guidance of leaders who have proper environmental awareness. Obviously, discretion and care must always be applied in respect to potential impact on the natural environment. Throughout the book, new emphasis is placed on these considerations, along with suitable alternative program suggestions.

Hopefully you will find this edition to be a valuable resource and of practical use.

JOEL MEIER

Acknowledgments

So many organizations and people have helped with the previous five editions of *Camp Counseling* over the years that it would be impossible to thank them all for their assistance. Many of their ideas and a few of their photographs can still be found among the many new ones in this book.

Sincere appreciation also goes to those who provided figures, illustrations and new photographs for this current edition. I am especially grateful to Barbara Marsac for her many hours at the drawing board sketching the illustrations. Appreciation is also expressed to the following people and organizations who kindly submitted photographs: Art Cosgrove of Camp Spalding, Spokane, Washington; Mrs. J. C. David of the National Oceanic and Atmospheric Administration, Rockville, Maryland; Lorene Drapalla of Camp Summer Life, Odessa, Texas; Dudley Improta and the Outdoor Program, University of Montana; Glenn Job of the American Camping Association; Dick Peterson of Camp Mishawaka, Grand Rapids, Minnesota; Janet Rohracher of Camp Kingsmont, West Stockbridge, Massachusetts; and Rick Tangeman of the Willamette Council of Camp Fire, Salem, Oregon. Photographs were also received from the following: Bikecentennial, Inc., Missoula, Montana; Columbine Girl Scout Council, Inc., Pueblo, Colorado; Evergreen Section of the American Camping Association (thanks to Betsy Lewis of Seattle, Washington for forwarding the many pictures that were submitted to the Evergreen Section's photo contest); Pacific Peaks Girl Scout Council, Olympia, Washington; and Silva, a division of Johnson Company, Inc., Binghamton, New York.

Sincere thanks to Bill Wildprett, Director of Orienteering Services, USA, for reviewing the manuscript dealing with map and compass and Orienteering in Chapter 21. His suggestions were most valuable in bringing the material up to date. Grateful acknowledgment is also given to the individuals and publishers who gave kind permission to use quoted materials.

Many of the ideas included in this edition have derived from association with various individuals. Special thanks should be given to Reynold Carlson, Professor Emeritus of Recreation, Indiana University, for the privilege of knowing him and the opportunities to gain a true appreciation of the outdoors. The same goes for Cal Tassinari, U.S. Forest Service Wilderness Ranger of the Flathead National Forest of Montana, who has shared his wisdom with many of us over the past years.

It would be remiss not to recognize just a few others, including my wife, Patti, who has shown love and tolerance throughout the many hours I've spent on this book. She has been the real backbone for my staying power. I should also thank the members of the editorial and production staff of Saunders College Publishing, especially John Butler, whose patience and assistance has been deeply appreciated.

Last, but certainly not least, I would like to express appreciation to Viola Mitchell for letting me join her team as a co-author. Over the years there have been thousands of people, including myself, who literally grew up with one or more of the first five editions of *Camp Counseling*. The knowledge and skills that she has passed on to so many cannot fail to have an impact on our attitudes about the great outdoors and the organized camping movement.

JOEL MEIER

one
Growth, Structure and Values of Organized Camping

one

Organized Camping—What Is It?

Millions of us have participated in camping experiences of one type or another, from short overnight excursions in nearby rural areas to extended outings of several weeks or more with friends or family. The term "camping," in fact, creates a variety of different images in our minds, depending upon the extent and nature of our experiences. To some, camping means pulling a mobile shelter behind a car and spending the evenings sleeping in it in a forest, park, or private campground. Many associate camping with agency- or organization-sponsored outings at established group sites, where nature-oriented programs are offered on a scheduled basis. To others, camping means carrying essential belongings in a backpack and hiking long distances into wilderness or backcountry areas far away from civilization.

WHY WE CAMP

Whatever the extent of our camping experience, it usually is associated with a chance to get away from our normal routines and an opportunity to refresh ourselves or relax in the natural world of the great outdoors. There are numerous other reasons why interest is growing rapidly in outdoor life and in living somewhat as our forefathers had. In fact, each person probably has many reasons for enjoying camping.

As our society has evolved, we have grown less reliant upon nature and therefore less familiar with it. The need for us to reacquaint ourselves with the outdoor world becomes particularly critical as more of us move into suburbs and cities. Camping allows us to satisfy our nomadic urge to escape the routine of everyday existence and the daily grind, and to experience our cultural heritage first hand.

For some of us, camping provides a chance to break away from the softness and ease that are so much a part of today's lifestyle. Camping is appealing because it provides us with an opportunity to rough it, to improvise and make do, to test our wits against the forces of nature, to discover our own potential, and to exercise personal initiative. Camping also helps to develop desirable physical, mental, social, and spiritual qualities. For instance, studies indicate that the effects of camping on an individual often include a positive measurable outcome in terms of self-concept (including self-reliance and self-confidence), development of environmental awareness, aesthetic appreciation, cooperation, physical fitness, ability to deal with stress, and tenacity.* Thus, camping experiences can help people acquire many valuable skills and attitudes that they do not necessarily gain in school or from their usual daily routine.

Many people look upon camping as a prime means of maintaining close family and friendship ties. In fact, very basic concepts of sociology and psychology come into use as we mingle with different people in diverse camping situations. Camping offers us opportunities for developing companionship with others, for sharing joys and hardships, for learning the meaning of humility, and for understanding the importance of open dialogue. Camping is a total experience in itself and unique because it consists of a 24-hour-a-day adventure outdoors. Since campers live together in a small group, there are many opportunities for each individual to assume a share of the work, for cooperative give and take, for group decision making, and for building lifelong friendships.

There is no doubt that many who camp do so because it is the current popular fad and is so widely discussed in the media, including magazines, movies, and television, and also by friends and acquaintances. Luckily, many who are first motivated to try camping for this reason quickly learn to enjoy it and are transformed into outdoor enthusiasts.

Some people say that camping provides a way to "get away from it all," while others prefer to think that it offers possibilities for personal involvement, enrichment, and renewal. Camping is a unique experience that provides an opportunity for reestablishing our roots, bringing us into harmony with our outdoor heritage, and giving us a perspective beyond that obtained in the narrow confines of a crowded society.

*Howard Lynn Dickey: *The Influence of an Outdoor Survival Experience Upon the Self Concept of Adolescent Boys and Girls* (Master's thesis, University of Montana, 1974), pp. 52–54; Minorv Lida: Adventure-Oriented Programs—A Review of Research. In Betty van der Smissen (ed.): *Research Camping and Environmental Education* (Penn State HPER Series No. 11, 1975), pp. 219–241; Joel F. Meier: "Risk Recreation: Philosophical Issues." *Trends.* vol. 17, no. 1 (Winter 1980), pp. 14–17.

ORGANIZED CAMPING

What Is Organized Camping?

The previous discussion centered around the variety of camping experiences available. In informal camping, people come and go as they please; however, since this book is primarily concerned with *organized* camping, we will need to understand more about the nature, design, function, and types of *organized camps.*

What are the key characteristics of an organized camp that differentiate it from other forms of outdoor recreation, including camping in general? Organized camping can be defined and some of its components identified.* We may define an organized camp as being comprised of a community of persons living together as an organized, democratic group in an outdoor setting. The related educational and recreational activities or programs are supervised by trained staff so as to meet the personal needs and interests of the participants. The camp program consists of the *total* of all experiences or events in the camp, whether structured or not. In as much as possible, however, the activities of the camp program should focus on the natural environment and should take advantage of experiences that are inherent to living in the out-of-doors. Thus, the natural surroundings should contribute significantly to the mental, physical, social, and spiritual growth of the camper.

From this definition we can easily identify four components or principles that apply to the basic philosophy of organized camping. These are:

1. *Organized camping focuses on the natural environment in an outdoor setting.* The camp experience concentrates on those activities that are

*Hedley S. Dimock (ed.): *Administration of the Modern Camp,* Association Press, 1948, pp. 22–31; Dennis A. Vinton and Elizabeth M. Farley (ed.): *Camp Staff Training Series, Module 1, An Orientation to Camping and the Camp,* a joint publication of Project REACH, University of Kentucky, The American Camping Association, and Hawkins and Associates, Inc., 1979, pp. 25–27; American Camping Association, Inc.: *Camp Administration Course Outline for Colleges and Universities.* The American Camping Association, Inc., 1961, p. 1; American Camping Association: *Camp Standards with Interpretations,* The American Camping Association, Inc., 1972, p. 12.

natural to the camp environment, including campcrafts, hiking, nature appreciation, and other skills for living simply in the out-of-doors. Similarly, the camp facility usually focuses on the beauty with which nature has endowed it rather than on manmade additions dictated by urban standards. In other words, the campsite should be somewhat rustic and free of the modern conveniences and contrivances found in an urban environment.

2. *The program consists of the total of all experiences that take place throughout the length of the camp.* The organized camp offers a broad and varied range of activities, and the program consists of every experience each camper has on a 24-hour-a-day basis throughout the total life of the camp, including participation in unstructured or informal aspects of camp life as well as in the more structured and formal activities that more readily come to mind. Thus, the camper is participating in camp life whether he or she is on a group day-hike in the woods or washing dishes after the evening meal. Living fully in a camp community leads participants into a complete range of relationships, experiences, and activities that are part of social and educational growth.

3. *The organized camp revolves around group living experiences in an organized community.* The basic unit of camp life consists of campers and staff who work and live together in small groups. Cooperation and teamwork is necessary in order to successfully meet the requirements of daily life. There is probably no better opportunity for such complete participation in meeting these daily requirements since the camp structure represents a microcosm of a true democratic society. Through this group process campers develop skills in cooperating, sharing, decision making, and assuming leadership and citizenship responsibilities.

4. *The organized camp relies on trained and well-qualified staff.* The staff consists of the camp director and camp counselors, as well as other personnel who might be involved in the operation of the camp, such as program specialists, maintenance personnel, medical aides, and cooks. People who want to work at an organized camp must be mature, must respect and care for others and be interested in working with them. They must usually have a wide range of interests and skills, including an understanding of the campers themselves, and a commitment to the goals of the camp. Because campers and staff associate with one another over an extended period of time, it is essential that camp personnel be capable of providing guidance and support to campers so that their personal needs and problems receive the very best attention.

Types of Camps

Organized camps commonly are established for young people, usually from 7 to 16 years old, although some camps now offer programs for older people as well. Regardless of age group, all camps offer opportunities for participants to dwell more or less in a world of their own, and to work, recreate, and carry on the daily business of living together under the guidance of a staff of counselors and camp personnel. Organized camps are of many types and are conducted in various ways and for many purposes.

Camps may be classified into five types: (1) resident or established camps, (2) trip or travel camps, (3) day camps, (4) special camps, and (5) school camps.

RESIDENT OR ESTABLISHED CAMPS. A *resident* or *established camp* is one in which campers live for a period of time, usually from a few days to eight or more weeks. There are usually several permanent buildings surrounded by a broad expanse of woods and meadows that are left as much as possible in their natural state. The camps are located away from the main roads to provide privacy and freedom from intrusion by those without legitimate camp connections.

Resident camps are of many types, with many points of similarity, yet differing in certain aspects so that each has a distinct personality of its own. Some are purposely kept primitive and rustic, and feature a more rugged and simple way of life that is quite different from the average camper's home environment. Others go to the opposite extreme, and provide most of the refinements and conveniences of modern urban life. These camps might better be termed summer resorts, for they often contribute little of what is generally considered a good camping experience. All good camps, no matter how rustic, maintain the qualities essential for good, safe and healthful living.

A typical large camp contains quantities of

(Camp Summer Life, Odessa, Tex.)

woodland and meadows, often with brooklets meandering through and crisscrossed by several trails traced by the feet of scores of adventuresome counselors and campers. Here, all types of plant and animal life abound, for the attitude of camp people toward wildlife is one of friendliness and appreciation rather than indifference or destructiveness. These unspoiled natural surroundings provide the background for a real organized camp experience.

Campers and staff may live in rustic cabins, teepees or tents on wooden platforms, which usually are grouped into separate units of from 12 to 24 campers with their counselors. Each unit is somewhat segregated from the others to promote a feeling of solidarity and privacy. In some camps each living unit is entirely self-sufficient; however, most camps feature centrally located buildings, including a common dining room and kitchen, a large lodge or recreation room, an arts and crafts shop, washrooms, showers, toilets, laundry facilities, a camp office, tool houses and sheds for camp storage and the caretaker's equipment, a health center, trading post, counselors' retreat, nature museum, camp library and a center to house equipment and supplies for cook-outs or trips away from camp.

Some camps have fields and courts for such sports as tennis, archery, softball, badminton, horseshoes, riflery and golf, an amphitheater, an outdoor chapel and a council ring. Located at the ends of certain trails and at some distance from the main camp will probably be outposts or campsites where those with sufficient campcraft skills can go to break the monotony of camp life and experience the thrill of living comfortably and simply under more primitive conditions. There may be a stable, tack room, riding ring and riding trails. A popular spot is the waterfront on a lake, river or seashore with an array of rowboats, canoes, sailboats and possibly even power boats. Most camps also have a swimming pool, for few are fortunate enough to possess natural bodies of water still free enough from contamination to be safe for swimming and lifesaving activities. Some camps specialize in certain activities, such as tennis, horseback riding or water sports; while others offer a wide variety of activities, from woodworking and ballet dancing to tutoring subjects ranging from electronics to nuclear physics. Most camp programs, however, lie somewhere in between.

This description of a more or less typical camp depicts a busy, thriving community, and

(Camp Mishawaka, Grand Rapids, Minn.)

that is exactly what camp is. A large camp represents a big investment and may be populated by as many as a hundred or even several hundred lively youngsters and a fairly large staff of counselors and other personnel.

TRIP OR TRAVEL CAMPS. Those participating in *trip* or *travel camping* start from a common base, then travel by foot, canoe, bicycle, horseback, sailboat, a horse-drawn "covered wagon" or almost any other conceivable means of transportation. They make camp each night at a new location and may use a map and compass to find their way over a predetermined route. Some travel groups consist of older campers from a resident camp who have won this privilege by demonstrating their knowledge and skills in camping techniques; other groups are made up of individuals who come together for the express purpose of making the trip, which is often commercially sponsored and led by an experienced guide or guides.

Wilderness, pioneer or *survival camping* is a specialized form of primitive camping undertaken by older campers specially trained for it. Participants are usually transported to a takeoff spot where they set out with only rudimentary equipment and supplies. They may obtain some of their food and other necessities from what nature provides along the way. One or more skilled counselors or guides are in charge, and the trip may last from a week to an entire summer.

DAY CAMPS. A *day camp* is one set up to accommodate campers who commute from home each day. The camps ordinarily operate from one to five days a week, with the children arriving by bus or private car soon after breakfast and returning home in the late afternoon, although some camps lengthen the hours to accommodate the children of employed mothers. The children spend the day participating in various camping activities and may cook part or all of their lunch using ingredients brought from home.

Day camping is most common in or near metropolitan areas, and often the camp utilizes parks or other public recreational facilities. A city or town or some service organization such as the Boy Scouts, Girl Scouts, Camp Fire Inc., Boys' or Girls' Clubs, YMCA or YWCA, may sponsor the camp. Privately owned day camps, operated for profit from fees paid by those attending, are now on the increase. Nearly all the activities of a resident camp are possible in a day camp, except for those conducted in the early morning or nighttime and, of course, sleeping on the campgrounds. However, some camps, do sponsor overnight sleep-outs and occasional trips for those able to participate, using borrowed tents or a park shelterhouse in case of inclement weather. Programming in a day camp is especially challenging since campers will choose to return or stay away each day depending upon how appealing the previous day's activities were. Day camps make an important contribution to camping by extending their benefits to those who are too young or who are financially unable to attend resident camps. They also prepare beginning campers for later participation in a resident or travel camp.

SPECIAL CAMPS. Most organized camps offer a well-rounded program, including such activities as woodcraft, campcraft, aquatics, nature study and arts and crafts; however, some concentrate on only one or a few activities in order to serve those with special interests or needs. Examples of special interest camps include salt water camps, ranch camps, farm camps, mountain climbing camps and trip and pioneering camps, which develop their programs around their particular environments. Others stress specific activities such as field hockey, tennis, aquatics, basketball, horseback riding, nature or science study, dramatics, music, dance, religious education, tutoring or language study. Some camps are referred to as "special purpose camps," since they serve those with special problems, such as diabetics, the deaf, the mentally retarded, cardiac cases, epileptics, the physically handicapped or the socially mal-adjusted. Some camps are coed, and others accommodate special groups such as families, adults or senior citizens (those over age 60).

OUTDOOR EDUCATION AND SCHOOL CAMPING. Although people sometimes use these terms interchangeably, they are not the same. *Outdoor education* includes all types of experiences that improve our knowledge, attitudes or skills in the out-of-doors and help make us more appreciative of it and better able to enjoy it. Outdoor education may involve anyone, of any age, at any time and in various situations. In school the first experience may come as a teacher takes a class out on the playground to observe cloud formations, soil erosion or the activities of the surprisingly large number of plants and animals living there. Outdoor education may consist of a trip to a farm, zoo, museum, dam, wildlife refuge, fish hatchery or municipal or state park. It may include viewing films and slides about nature and ecology or growing plants or caring for pet animals in the classroom. It may involve instruction in fishing, hunting, hiking or camping techniques.

School camping, on the other hand, consists of a camping trip to a regular campsite by one or more school classes and their teachers and other personnel. The trip may last from a few days to several weeks. Neither school camping nor outdoor education is new, for progressive teachers have always tried to acquaint their students with the world around them. However, in recent years interest in this field has grown, and more and more school districts and states are now incorporating school camping into their programs. As their experience grows, school camping practices will improve.

Objectives of School Camping. Although the objectives of school camping are somewhat similar to those of general organized camping, a definite effort is made to closely correlate the camping experience with what is occurring in the classroom. Thus, when properly carried out, it supplements and makes more meaningful certain phases of the regular school curriculum. Throughout recent years it has become evident that society is making progressively greater demands on the school to accept increasing responsibility for rounding out and totally educating the child, not only in the new subject matter necessitated by our increasingly complex society, but also in other areas of learning formerly taught by the neighborhood, church and family. When this country was largely agricultural, each child had chores to perform and did them under the close supervision of the family and neighbors. Families and friends conversed for long hours, uninterrupted by radio, television, movies or other modern forms of entertainment. Now children have few, if any, chores to do, and family members often make little effort to instruct the child in even rudimentary tasks. Consequently, the school has been asked to provide more and more of the training needed to help children become healthy, happy citizens having the knowledge and skills to earn a living and the attitudes and abilities to use wisely our rapidly increasing leisure time.

Some parents do not send their child to summer camp because they fail to recognize its values and so do not encourage attendance. Others feel they cannot afford even the modest fees charged by organization camps, while some fear interference with family vacations. Therefore, the logical solution seems to be for the school to take on this added responsibility.

Most educators now recognize that a good camping experience can make an important contribution in the educational process. Consequently, many schools provide every child with this opportunity. The school's approach to camping should be educational rather than merely recreational, for usurping school time can scarcely be justified unless the results make a definite contribution to general school objectives. However, even though school camping is not specifically designed to entertain children, they usually enjoy it thoroughly because,when the program is well administrated, every waking hour is filled with novel, exciting things to do, that seemingly are expressly designed to stimulate and enchant youngsters. They often become so completely absorbed in what they are doing that previous discipline problems, psychosomatic allergies and antagonistic attitudes are dispelled, since they are no longer needed to fulfill personal needs or to gain attention. Since most children possess great curiosity, and are naturally observant and eager to know, learning in the outdoors takes place unconsciously. Children who were previously lackadaisical in the classroom may discover for the first time just how much fun it is to learn.

A school camping trip should not be a spree or a vacation trip. Instead, it should be carefully planned to correlate with what takes place in the classroom and, like the laboratory experience it really is, it should develop more meaningful attitudes and knowledge in such fields as health, housekeeping, woodworking, arts and crafts, ecology and nature study, history, language arts, arithmetic, dramatics, music, social studies and moral and spiritual values. The aim is to retain for the classroom those activities and studies best handled there while transferring to the camping situation those that are especially suitable for that environment. This necessitates careful planning before the trip as well as a thoughtful analysis and evaluation upon returning, so that the next trip will be even more successful.

The children's learning might begin as they study maps to trace the school bus route to the campsite, and continues as they plan nutritional menus, consult with classmates on such matters as what individual and group equipment will be needed and decide what types of information can be gained and what questions can be answered by observation and experimentation while at camp.

Camping offers an unparalleled opportunity to develop social skills. Children who have seldom if ever been away from home learn to depend on themselves and to make their own decisions with the help of accompanying adults. Here they must assume responsibility for washing and dressing themselves and caring for their own clothing. They must keep their own quarters neat and also share in caring for group facilities. Campers learn to be punctual in performing assigned chores and come to realize that there are several ways of doing a given task. Children who come from disadvantaged or poorly supervised homes may absorb much from the teaching and example of others in such areas as personal grooming, cleanliness, proper setting of tables, dishwashing, table manners, proper eating habits, saying of grace before meals and appropriate conduct at such ceremonies as flag raising and lowering. Teachable moments occur frequently for leaders skilled enough to see them. Camp living is democratic and a child learns how group decisions are made, why a certain number of rules and guidelines are necessary to safeguard the welfare and rights of all, and that privileges are always accompanied by responsibilities. Campers also learn the roles of the leader and followers in a group. By close association with others, they recognize that no two individuals are precisely alike and that, in order to be happy in a group, they must learn to appreciate the good qualities of each person while accepting individual shortcomings. Thus, campers might see how a slow learner excels at the waterfront, or how a problem child might efficiently plan and carry out the details of a campfire program. Here is a golden opportunity to acquire the social graces and amenities necessary to live happily and cooperatively with others.

Youngsters can experience the satisfaction of serving others and helping those with less skill. They can act as good citizens while helping with a camp or community project such as planting trees or controlling erosion in order to benefit future campers. Ecology and nature study, carried on in natural surroundings, assume new importance to the student and elicits enthusiastic support for wise conservation methods. Also, valuable skills and lifelong interests may be acquired in such forms of recreation as camping, hiking, water sports, hunting, fishing, geology and nature study.

Educators have long realized that greater progress is made when students and teachers work in an informal but controlled situation in which they learn to know and appreciate each other as individuals. The school camp, where campers eat, work, study and play together 24 hours a day, presents an ideal opportunity for this to occur.

Organization and Administration. Most schools enter school camping on a modest basis, starting with a weekend camping trip by one or

(Willamette Council of Camp Fire, Salem, Oreg.)

two classes in the fall. As enthusiasm, support and momentum grow the program most likely will expand to where the same classes camp for a week or two, while additional grades are introduced to the program. School camping may eventually extend into the winter months, necessitating the use of winterized facilities. Some school systems even extend school camping into the summer months.

The fourth, fifth and sixth grades are most commonly included, although often programs are provided for those of high school age. It seems best not to have more than two classes, or a total of 30 youngsters, present at one time, since a larger group tends to lose the feelings of intimacy and solidarity that are so desirable. If there are more youngsters, they should be separated into smaller groups, with each group functioning as independently as possible.

Each class should be accompanied by its own teacher to allow for better integration of camp life and classroom work and also to provide opportunities for informal association between students and instructor. This sometimes presents a problem, because many classroom teachers have had little, if any, training or experience in camping and outdoor living and are reluctant to try it, since they may lose confidence when away from the familiar classroom environment.

To overcome this difficulty, many colleges and universities now offer courses, workshops and institutes in outdoor education for teachers. These usually take place on a campsite and include instruction in camping techniques as well as in planning programs tailored for the teacher's particular class. They are designed to show how to integrate the camp experience with what is done in the classroom in order to improve both. For instance, teachers might realize how practical such a subject as arithmetic can be when they use it in teaching students how to measure the ingredients for recipes, the height of a tree, or the width and depth of a river.

A school camp might have a professional camp director as well as cooks and persons trained in campcraft techniques. Schools with an extended program may hire a permanent camp staff to serve on an annual basis. In addition, resource personnel, such as astronomers, conservationists, foresters, geologists, agriculturalists and nature study experts may be invited to assist with the program.

Financing the Program. The school district usually pays for instruction, equipment and supplies just as it does for other school activities and also assumes the cost of capital improvements and maintenance for the campsite. Grounds and buildings may be available in a state or local park, a summer resident camp may be rented, or the school district may build its own campsite.

Local service clubs or the PTA may supply financial aid to help support school camps. As the federal government has become more interested in outdoor education, environmental education, and school camping programs, it has provided substantial help in several areas.

Children often pay for their own food and lodging by starting a Camp Fund Bank early in the year in which each child deposits small amounts in a personal account. This system provides a valuable lesson in economics and banking procedures as the children note how rapidly their nickels and dimes, earned by doing odd jobs or set aside from their allowances, add up. Clubs or other service organizations can be enlisted to provide aid for indigent children. A class may also raise money through such projects as paper drives, class carnivals, cookie sales or chili suppers. Insurance is often provided in the comprehensive insurance policies of the school or sometimes through the family policies carried by the parents.

Planning. For the school camping experience to be valuable, careful and cooperative planning by teachers, parents and children is essential. When introducing school camping to a community, a first step may well be to call a meeting of all interested parties for a general discussion of the goals of camping and to appoint committees to handle various phases of the project. The purpose and procedures must be interpreted to the entire community as well as to parents so that all come to regard camping as a valuable educational experience rather than just another frill on which to spend school time and taxpayers' money. As enthusiasm increases, individuals will begin to help by giving suggestions and providing such tangible services as aid with finances, facilities, supplies, work needed at the campsite, transportation and proper physical and psychological preparation of the youngsters.

Sponsorship of Camps

ORGANIZATION OR AGENCY CAMPS. Many youth organizations or independent organizations with branches designed to serve youth find camping an excellent way to further their own objectives and consequently conduct their own camps, that are tailored to meet their specific purposes. These organizations are supported largely by the public through the United Fund, government funds, public taxation, fund-raising projects and private subscription. Campers pay only nominal fees, bringing camping well within the reach of even those from low income groups. There often are camperships* available for those unable to pay even this small sum. Since the facilities are limited and the camp must accommodate large numbers, a child's stay is often limited to a week or two. Fortunately, this is not necessarily as great a handicap as it may seem, for the camping experience is often merely an extension of what the child has been doing in the organization's regular city program, and under the supervision of the same leaders. An organization camp is usually located near the campers it serves and this reduces transportation costs. These camps often have high standards, follow excellent camping practices, and have been instrumental in introducing many worthwhile practices into camping. Since they handle so many children from so many social strata, they play an important role in the attempt to bring camping to all.

So many organizations now promote camping as a part of their programs that it is next to impossible to list all of them. The following, however, are noteworthy:

American Red Cross
Associations for handicapped children and adults
Big Brother Association
Boy Scouts
Boys' Clubs of America
Camp Fire, Inc.
Church groups
Easter Seal Society for crippled children and adults
Four-H Clubs
Girl Scouts
Girls' Clubs of America
Pioneer Girls
Salvation Army
Settlement houses
Volunteers of America
Woodcraft Rangers
YMCA
YMHA
YWCA
YWHA

Independent or Private Camps. *Independent* or *private camps* are owned by an individual or individuals and are usually run for profit. They are often incorporated, and some sell stock. Since they receive no public moneys, they must usually charge a supportive fee of from $500 to $1,000 or more a season. This tends to limit their patronage to children of the upper-middle or high income groups, although many have camp-

*A "campership" is a grant or scholarship given to deserving children to enable them to attend camp.

erships that are available to selected children from lower income families. Private camps often draw their clientele from widespread areas, a practice that gives many campers the benefit of seeing a new part of the country and mingling with children whose customs and ways of life may be different.

The greater financial resources of private camps sometimes enable them to provide somewhat more in the way of equipment and facilities; this, of course, does not necessarily mean that they offer a better program, since those in charge may lack the wisdom and will to make good use of these material things. This, fortunately, is seldom the case, for most private camp directors are public spirited and sincerely dedicated to conducting their camps in the best interests of children.

A camper in a private camp ordinarily remains four to eight weeks, which allows enough time to thoroughly acclimate the child and make real progress toward achieving camp objectives.

Throughout their history, private camps have generally been quite progressive and have made many valuable contributions to the camping field. Unfortunately, there have been a few that have put monetary gains above the welfare of the children or that have catered too much to the whims of parents and children, giving them what they want rather than what would be most beneficial. Thus, they sponsor city-type activities or activities that are glamourous and prestigious rather than activities that would make maximum use of their wonderful outdoor enironment, which often is unavailable to most of the children elsewhere.

Government-Sponsored Camps. Various government agencies, acting on behalf of the public, use tax funds to support camp programs. Government sponsorship means that camp services usually are either free of charge or have a minimum fee to help defray expenses. Sponsorship may come from federal, state, or local levels of government. In some cases, financial support is allocated by the federal govenrment to a local agency that assumes responsibility for carrying out the program. Examples of government sponsors are municipal recreation and park departments, school systems, welfare departments, and state-owned hospitals or rehabilitation centers. The Youth Conservation Corps (YCC) is an example of federal government involvement in camping. Today, more than 400 YCC programs teach environmental education and resource conservation while providing opportunities for youth to work in an outdoor setting.

Length of the Camp Season

Summer camps ordinarily operate during the months of July and August, which is called the *camp season.* In some camps, the season may be divided into several shorter periods known as *camp sessions.* In *long-term camps,* campers may stay for a half or the entire camp season of four to eight weeks. In others, their stay may be limited to one session that lasts a week, ten days or two weeks. These are known as *short-term camps.*

(Willamette Council of Camp Fire, Salem, Oreg.)

Because they must serve a large number of campers, most camps sponsored by agencies or organizations are short-term camps.

Some Figures Revealed by the ACA and National Surveys

A 1969 national survey conducted on the American Camping Association (ACA) member camps*, showed that 48 percent of camps were agency sponsored, 35 percent were private independent camps, 13 percent were church affiliated, 1 percent were school sponsored and 3 percent of camps were in the miscellaneous category. The survey showed that 79 percent of camps were resident, 20 percent were day and 1 percent were travel camps, although there were several combinations of resident and day camps and travel camps. Of every 31 ACA camps, 12 were for girls, 9 were for boys and 10 were coed.

Although records indicate that the total number of camps is shrinking, the number of children in camps has grown by as much as 40 percent over a 10-year period of time. More recently, the ACA reports that approximately 10,000 organized camps are in operation and serve approximately 10 percent of the children and youth in the United States.† A majority of these campers are between the ages of 9 and 13. During an average year, approximately 2 million children and adults attend 2,400 camps (approximately 25 percent of all camps) that have been officially accredited by the ACA.‡

A 1973 study revealed that the average ACA camp encompassed 286.4 acres and represented an average investment of $403,081. Of course, these figures are only averages, and many camps vary markedly from them. Using extrapolated data from the state of Maine, a 1978 report* indicated that organized camping might well generate over 2 billion dollars in economic activity in the United States, including an estimated payroll of 185 million dollars to 3,500,000 employees. From these figures, it is obvious that organized camping is a thriving business that touches the lives of many people.

*Ernest F. Schmidt: "An Accounting to ACA Members," *Camping Magazine*, May, 1969, p. 5.

†Ernest F. Schmidt: "What is the Future of Camping for Handicapped Children as We Know It?" In J. Nesbitt, and others (ed.), *Training Needs and Strategies in Camping for the Handicapped* (University of Oregon Press, 1972), pp. 70–72; Dennis A. Vinton and others: *Camping and Environmental Education for Handicapped Children and Youth*, Hawkins and Associates, 1978, p. 1.

‡American Camping Association: *1980 Parents' Guide to Accredited Camps* (The American Camping Association, 1980), p. 7 and p. 28.

*F. M. Levine: "Maine Study Indicates Organized Camping is $2 Billion U.S. Industry," *Camping Magazine*, Mar. 1978, pp. 16–20.

ADDITIONAL READINGS

(For an explanation of abbreviations and abbreviated forms used, see page 13.)

Church Camping

Davis, Robert Pickens: *Church Camping*. Knox, 1969, 140 pp., paper.
Ensign, John and Ruth: *Camping Together as Christians*. Knox, 1958, 148 pp.
Genne, Elizabeth and William: *Church Family Camping and Conferences*. Judson Press, 1979, 77 pp. Available from ACA.
MacKay, Joy: *Creative Counseling for Christian Camps*. Scripture, 1966, 128 pp., paper.
Purchase, Richard and Betty: *Let's Go Outdoors With Children*. Westminster, 1972, 32 pp.
Springer, James C.: *Boys, Girls and God*. Vantage, 1971, 82 pp.
Todd: *Camping for Christian Youth*.

Day Camping

MAGAZINE ARTICLES

Camping Magazine:
Hall, Mrs. William, and Grant Southwell: "Keep 'Camp' in Day Camping." June, 1967, p. 12.
Melamed, Monte: "Day Camp Busing." May, 1970, p. 17.
Papich, Robert: "Real Camp Program in a City Park Day Camp? Of Course You Can!" Feb., 1971, p. 20.
Recreation:
Musselman, Virginia: "Factors Affecting the Day Camp Program." Mar., 1963, p. 131.

Miscellaneous

Ball, Armand B. and Beverly H: *Basic Camp Management*. ACA, 1979, 156 pp., paper.
Broome, Harvey: *Faces of the Wilderness*. Mountain Press, 1972, 271 pp.
Camp Job Packet: ACA, 1978.
Camp, The Child's World, ACA, 1962, 32 pp., paper.
Hartwig, Marie D. and Bettye B. Myers: *Camping Leadership: Counseling and Programming*. C. V. Mosby Co., 1976, 156 pp.

Leopold, Aldo: *A Sand County Almanac (and Sketches Here and There).* Order from ACA, 1966, 226 pp., paper.
Levine, Frank M.: *Children's Summer Camps: Their Economic Value to Maine.* ACA, 1976, 107 pp.
Meier, Joel F.: *Backpacking.* W. C. Brown, 1980, ch. 1, pp. 1–6.
Meier, Joel F., et al.: *High Adventure Outdoor Pursuits.* Brighton Publishing Co., 1980, 232 pp., paper.
Parents' Guide to Accredited Camps, 1980. ACA, 1980, 30 pp.
Rodney and Ford: *Camp Administration,* ch. 1, pp. 1–12 and 21–24; ch. 16.
Shivers: *Camping,* chs. 1 and 16.
van der Smissen, Betty: *Bibliography of Research in Camping, Environmental Education and Interpretative Services.* ACA, 1979.
Vinton, Dennis A., et al.: *Camping and Environmental Education for Handicapped Children and Youth.* Hawkins and Associates, 1978, 170 pp.
Webb: *Light From a Thousand Campfires.*
Webb, Kenneth B.: *Summer Camps—Security in the Midst of Change.* ACA, 1968, 52 pp.

MAGAZINE ARTICLES

Camping Magazine:
Levine, Frank: "Maine Study Indicates Organized Camping is $2 Billion U.S. Industry." Mar. 1978, p. 16.
Webb, Kenneth B.: "Camps Can Set New Lifestyles." Jan. 1976, p. 10.
Webb, Kenneth B.: "So You Want to Start a Camp." May, 1964, p. 23.

School Camping and Outdoor Education

Donaldson, George W. (ed.): *Perspectives on Outdoor Education—Readings.* Brown, 1972, 233 pp., paper.
Garrison, Cecil: *Outdoor Education: Principles and Practice.*
Hammerman and Hammerman (eds.): *Outdoor Education: A Book of Readings.*
Hammerman and Hammerman: *Teaching in the Outdoors.*
Mand: *Outdoor Education.*
Outdoor Education. AAHPERD, rev., 1970, 32 pp., paper.
Sanford, Jean: *Bibliography of School Camping and Outdoor Education.* ACA, 1962, 29 pp., paper.
Schramm, Wilbur: *Classroom Out-of-Doors—Education Through Camping.* Sequoia, 1969, 192 pp.
Smith et al.: *Outdoor Education.*
Swan, Malcolm D. (ed.): *Tips and Tricks in Outdoor Education.* (Compiled by members of the Department of Outdoor Education at Northern Illinois University's Lorado Taft Field Campus) Interstate, 1970, 184 pp., paper.
van der Smissen, Dr. Betty (Chairman): *Use of Resident Camps for School Programs.* ACA, 1972, 22 pp., paper.

EXPLANATION OF ABBREVIATED FORMS USED IN BIBLIOGRAPHIES

The reader will note that the bibliographies sometimes contain only skeleton information about a book and author. This practice has been followed for those books deemed of special interest to the reader or for those cited in several chapters. You will find complete data about these books in the *Selected General Bibliography* in Appendices A and B. Likewise, abbreviated forms are sometimes given for publishers; their complete names and addresses will be found in the *Director of Publishers and Organizations,* located in Appendix D.

Order books through your local bookstore, directly from the publisher or from the following professional organizations: National Recreation and Park Association (NRPA), the American Camping Association (ACA), or the American Alliance for Health, Physical Education, Recreation and Dance (AAHPERD). These organizations carry a rather extensive list of publications in the fields of camping and recreation and offer the convenience of ordering books from a single source. They sell these books at list price; however, the American Camping Association offers a discount to members. Catalogues of their selections are free upon request. Their addresses are:

American Alliance for Health, Physical Education, Recreation and Dance
1900 Association Drive
Reston, Virginia 22091

American Camping Association
Bradford Woods
Martinsville, Indiana 46151

National Recreation and Park Association
3101 Park Center Drive
Alexandria, Virginia 22302

two

History of Organized Camping

The nice thing about this world is that it has a past and a present as well as a future; and so it is with camping. To understand why an oak tree bears acorns we must recall that it originally came from an acorn. Similarly, to comprehend the camping movement we must know something of its past, for only then can we understand its present status and prepare ourselves for its potential development.

EARLY CAMPERS

Camping is as old as human existence, for early people were often nomadic, moving with the changing seasons in search of food or better climate, or in pursuit of or flight from their enemies. Some lived in caves, while others constructed temporary, and sometimes portable, shelters.

The American Indians were among this country's early campers, and experts they were, for we still marvel at the vast amount of wood lore and camping know-how they acquired and passed on from one generation to the next. From the first moment the Pilgrims landed, they also became campers, for their long ocean voyage had depleted their supplies and they needed to supplement them with whatever game and vegetation they could find while hurrying to construct shelters against the weather. Regardless of how history and movies have pictured them, many of the Indians were friendly and gave invaluable help; without them, our problem-ridden ancestors probably could not have survived.

Almost every growing thing was of interest to these early settlers. Many plants were valuable as sources of food, tools, medicine, clothing or shelter, while others were a hindrance to be gotten rid of to make room for crops, buildings or cattle. These people *had* to know nature intimately, for there was no time for mistakes when selecting the proper wood for a box or axe handle or finding food to eat or herbs to relieve illness and pain. Hunting and trapping animals for fur, food, leather and clothing required cunning and a thorough knowledge of animal life.

The history of America is rich in the lore of early explorers and frontiersmen who matched wits with nature in a constant struggle for survival. We are spellbound at the courage and high adventure of such early American campers as Lewis and Clark, Daniel Boone, and Kit Carson, and outdoorsmen such as Theodore Roosevelt, Daniel Beard and Ernest Thompson Seton. But it is human nature to recall the pleasant and forget the painful and distasteful; thus we bask in the glamour and excitement of the exploits of the early settlers and explorers while glossing over the privations, dangers and hardships that formed the very core of their daily lives.

Early Rural Life

At the time of the signing of the Constitution, 98 percent of the population lived in rural areas. With the coming of the machine age, industries developed in the larger towns and cities, and as more lucrative employment opportunities appeared in the more populated areas, people left the farms and turned the settlements into towns and the towns into cities. This movement still continues, so that now, a little over 200 years later, only about 8 percent of our population lives on farms as defined by the 1977 census. This exodus from the farm to the city, with its mechanization and gadgetry, has affected our way of life greatly, especially that of young people.

In the farm environment of several generations ago, boys and girls grew up with a knowledge of nature, for nearly every plant, tree and animal was of interest, since if it was not useful, it needed to be controlled or eliminated. Children grew up as jacks-of-all-trades, for most things were grown or made at home and repaired by the user. Thus, shop or manual training, arts and crafts and homemaking were learned and practiced from an early age, under the close supervision of parents or grandparents. Formal school training in "readin', writin' and 'rithmetic" was confined to a few winter months when the children could be spared from their farm duties.

Farm chores furnished vigorous exercise and the whole countryside served as a natural outlet in which to release pent-up emotions. There was no lack of social contacts, for families were large and closely knit and children enjoyed the companionship of brothers and sisters as they worked and played together. Guests provided welcome diversion and were urged to make an extended stay, for distances were too great and traveling too hazardous and uncomfortable to warrant brief overnight or casual evening visits. For those living nearby, there were numerous social affairs such as corn huskings, bellings, house and barn warmings, taffy pulls, spelling bees and singing schools. Attendance at church services was regular, and camp meetings drew people from great distances.

All this changed as people moved to cities and began to specialize in one trade or occupation, and to earn wages that they used to buy services or commodities from other specialists. People began to lose the intimate contact with nature they had experienced while tilling the soil or rambling over woods and fields.

Modern Urban Life

Today, children spend a long nine or ten months in a school that is often overcrowded, and for many, the school year may be even longer if they attend summer school to catch up on work missed or to forge ahead in the struggle for college acceptance. Although there have been improvements, school is still too often geared mainly to meet college entrance requirements, and classes are sometimes so large that little attention can be given to individuals and their particular difficulties and needs. Also, children constantly are regulated by schedules and bells and subjected to the formality of teaching methods that are necessary when large numbers of students must meet course and credit requirements.

Another problem of our age is that many children get very little exercise. Except for a few perfunctory physical education periods each week, little more than lip service is paid to this extremely important aspect of their development. They ride to and from school, and their out-of-school hours are crammed with band practice, dramatics, trips to the movies or long periods of time in front of the television set.

Today, children often live entirely with adults in a small house or apartment where there is no room to run, jump, or climb. When children feel a perfectly normal craving for action, their antics are likely to end unhappily in a severe scolding or even in physical punishment for their misbehavior. Can we wonder that children are puzzled and sometimes rebellious? Our knowledge of children shows us how irritating and damaging it can be to live among the constant "do's" and "don'ts" of a crowded society.

In today's society, both parents often are employed outside the home and spend their free time in pursuits that continue to segregate them from their offspring and reduce the family's time for being together. Instead of providing their children with companionship, understanding and sympathy, parents try to substitute with liberal allowances for movies and comic books, baby sitters, television shows and other makeshifts that are supposed to supply happiness.

Children now have a great deal of leisure time, but unfortunately, they quickly fall into the pattern set by their parents and become afflicted with "spectatoritis," the result of depending on commercial organizations to supply them with ready-made entertainment that is all too often merely time-consuming busywork. With all the problems facing children today, it is easy to understand the elation a child derives from participating in camping activities that provide meaningful and constructive opportunities.

THE BEGINNINGS OF ORGANIZED CAMPING

As early as the latter half of the nineteenth century, some of those who had rushed to the city for its advantages found that the life there was not as idyllic as anticipated. Problems immediately arose, as they do when many people live in close proximity to one another, and some were plagued with nostalgic memories of the peace and quiet of the old days and the buoyant good health that resulted from their vigorous lives in the open. Perhaps of even greater concern to people was the manner in which their children were growing up. Although children from poorer families were kept busy with household chores and apprenticeships at trades or other outside jobs, those from well-to-do families had servants to satisfy their every need, which left them with time on their hands to loaf about and perhaps get into mischief or serious trouble. Camping seemed to offer an acceptable solution; thus, in this way, organized camping began in the United States as devoted men and women organized groups of young people for outings in the woods. As will be seen in the following discussion, organized camping was originally a "Yankee notion," conceived and fostered in New England before quickly spreading across the country and throughout many parts of the world.

The First School Camp (1861)

Frederick William Gunn, who generally is regarded as the Father of Organized Camping, was the founder and head of the Gunnery School for Boys in Washington, Connecticut. With the coming of the Civil War, his students, like typical boys, wanted to live like soldiers and sometimes were permitted to march, roll up in their blankets and sleep outdoors. The school operated through part of the summer and in 1861, yielding to the wishes of the boys, Mr. and Mrs. Gunn packed all of them up for a gypsy trip to Milford on the Sound, 4 miles away. There they spent two weeks boating, sailing, hiking and fishing. The experiment proved so successful that it was repeated in 1863 and 1865, with some former students returning to join in the excursion.

Later, a new site was selected at Point Beautiful on Lake Waramauge, 7 miles from the school, and the name was changed from Camp Comfort to Gunnery Camp; the camp continued to exist until 1879. Although Mr. Gunn's camp might be considered as the beginning of school camping (he simply moved his school program outdoors for a brief session), the objectives and procedures of today's school camping are quite different from those of Mr. Gunn's camp. However, his camp was the first organized camp in the world and so established the United States as the birthplace of organized camping.

The First Private Camp (1876)

Dr. Joseph Trimble Rothrock was a practicing physician in Wilkes-Barre, Pennsylvania, who combined his hobbies of forestry and conservation with his desire to do something for frail boys by establishing the North Mountain School of Physical Culture. Here he felt that the children's health would improve since they could live, out-of-doors in tents while continuing their education. The school was located on

(U.S. Forest Service)

North Mountain in Luzerne County, Pennsylvania, and lasted from June 15 to October 15; there were 20 pupils and 5 teachers. Each student paid $200 tuition, but income failed to meet expenses, and Dr. Rothrock abandoned the idea in favor of spending the next year on an Alaskan expedition. Various attempts to revive the school under different leadership proved similarly unprofitable and it was permanently closed within a few years.

The First Church Camp (1880)

The Reverend George W. Hinckley of West Hartford, Connecticut, was the next to try an established camp, for he saw in its informal atmosphere an opportunity to get to know the boys of his congregation more intimately and so perhaps to influence them more permanently. Consequently, in 1880 he took seven members of his church on a camping trip to Gardner's Island, Wakefield, Rhode Island. The results must have been gratifying, for he later founded The Good Will Farm for Boys at Hinckley, Maine. His schedule called for a "sane and sensible" religious and educational morning program, with afternoons spent in such activities as swimming, baseball and tennis, and evenings devoted to singing, talks and various other forms of entertainment.

The First Private Camp Organized to Meet Specific Educational Needs (1881)

In 1880, while Ernest Berkely Balch was traveling on Asquam Lake near Holderness, New Hampshire, he chanced upon Burnt Island, which seemed to be unowned and appeared to be an ideal spot on which to realize his aspiration to give boys from well-to-do families a summer of adventure instead of letting them idle away their time in resort hotels. Consequently, in 1881 he returned with five boys and erected a small frame shanty that they christened "Old '81." The campers were surprised by the unexpected appearance of a man who claimed to own the island, but their offer of $40 as complete payment for the entire island was accepted, and so they bought it. They called their retreat Camp Chocorua because of its superb view of Chocorua Mountain, 30 miles away, and the camp continued to exist for eight years until 1889.

The boys wore camp uniforms of gray flannel shorts and shirts with scarlet belts, caps and shirt lacings. All work was done by the boys, who were divided into four crews, each with a leader called the "stroke." One crew was off duty each day while the other three spent about five hours as kitchen, dish or police crews. Spiritual life was planned carefully and the services must have been quite impressive as the boys came singing through the woods, dressed in cotta and cassock (a short surplice over a long garment reaching to the feet), to the altar of their chapel, which was set deep in a grove of silver maples.

The camp had an average of five staff members and 25 boys who competed in tennis, sailing, swimming, diving and baseball. Winners were awarded ribbons bearing their names, the event and the date. Mr. Balch was the first to formulate definite objectives for his camp, which included instilling in each boy a sense of responsibility, both for himself and others and an appreciation of the value of work. The Camp Chocorua silver pin was given annually to the two or three campers who best demonstrated the qualities of "manliness, justice, truth and conscientiousness." The pin symbolized recognition of innate qualities and was not a reward to be worked for; in fact, those who consciously set out to win it were said to stand little chance of doing so, and no award at all was made in the years when none were judged worthy of receiving it.

The First Institutional Camp (1885)

Sumner F. Dudley, a young resident of Brooklyn, was associated with his father and brother in the manufacture of surgical instruments. His first venture in camping was to take seven members of the Newburgh, New York, YMCA on an eight-day fishing, swimming and boating trip to Pine Point on Orange Lake, 6 miles away. Since the boys had had their heads shaved close in what they deemed proper preparation for the trip, their camp was appropriately dubbed Camp Bald Head.

Dudley spent the next several years conducting other camping trips for boys and entered the YMCA as a full-time worker in 1887. He died in 1897 at the age of 43. His last camp on Lake Champlain near Westport, New York, was renamed Camp Dudley in his honor and is the oldest organized camp still in existence.

Camping for Girls (1890, 1892 and 1902)

In 1890, Luther Halsey Gulick opened a private camp for his daughter and her friends. He later founded the Camp Fire Girls.

In 1891, Professor Arey of Rochester, New York, established Camp Arey as a natural science camp and a year later he lent it for a month's use by girls. Mr. and Mrs. Andre C. Fontaine took over the camp in 1912 and from that time on conducted it as a camp exclusively for girls.

Laura Mattoon founded what generally is regarded as the first camp exclusively for girls in 1902 at Wolfeboro, New Hampshire, calling it Camp Kehonka for Girls.

The Developmental Periods of Camping

Early organized camping has been classified by Dimock* into three stages of development, according to the main emphasis at the time. These include (1) the recreational stage, (2) the educational stage and (3) the stage of social orientation and responsibility. As with any movement, no precise dates can be demarcated for these periods, for the changes have been gradual and overlapping and at no time was there perfect unanimity among leaders or uniformity as to the programs and practices of the various camps.

The Recreational Stage (1861–1920)

Early camps were sponsored mainly by conscientious, public-spirited men who saw in them a chance to get boys out into the open and away from potentially harmful pursuits in the city. They believed that the rugged, outdoor life would strengthen the boys physically and keep them engaged in wholesome, enjoyable activi-

*Hedley S. Dimock: *Administration of the Modern Camp.* Association Press, 1948, p. 24.

ties. Bible study often played a prominent part in the program; high moral and spiritual values were held in esteem, and it was believed that values, like mumps or measles, could be contracted merely by association with the right people. There was no thought of financial gain from the project, and the lack of adequate monetary backing caused the early demise of many camps.

It was common for one or two adults to start out on a trip with as many as 40 or 50 boys and a meager supply of equipment. The expeditions were, almost without exception, built around the strong personality of a man who kept the respect and admiration of the boys by his unselfish motives, sympathetic understanding, tactful leadership and sound principles concerning the roles of work and play. Ralph Waldo Emerson's statement that "Every institution is but the lengthened shadow of a man" certainly applies to these early camps.

The camping movement was slow starting: there were probably no more than 25 to 60 camps in existence in 1900.

The Educational Stage (1920–1930)

Great changes and exciting developments often follow wars, and the years after World War I were no exception. The number of organized camps increased rapidly and there were marked changes in their methods and programs. "Progressive education," with its foundations in psychology and mental hygiene, was coming to the fore, fostering increased emphasis on satisfying the needs of each child instead of trying to fit all children into a preconceived mold. In response to this trend, camps added activities such as dramatics, arts and crafts, dancing and music that were designed to supplement the expanding school curriculum. Almost every hour of a camper's day was regimented strictly and campers were enrolled in scheduled classes much as they had been at school. Competition, often with an elaborate system of awards was stressed. One reason for this change in philosophy was the development of new testing methods that demonstrated that personality, character and spiritual growth were *not* inevitably acquired through association with the right people but must be taught and planned for to obtain optimum results.

The Stage of Social Orientation and Responsibility (1930–)

Continued research in testing methods and evaluation showed that camps were not always measuring up to the high aspirations associated with them, but, as always, ever-resourceful camp directors proved equal to the occasion and continued to forge ahead.

Camping enthusiasts had assumed that the active outdoor life invariably was invigorating and healthful and were shocked when a 1930 study of over 100 camps showed that camping was sometimes detrimental to health and that the longer children stayed in camp the more likely their health was to suffer. In an attempt to remedy the situation, camp directors added physicians, nurses and trained dietitians to their staffs and instituted more healthful practices in their programs. Campers were allowed more freedom of choice in activities and the hectic tempo of camp life was reduced.

The strength of a society can be only as great as that of its individual citizens, and we in the United States, as well as citizens of other parts of the world, are well aware that the best way to strengthen and preserve our forms of government is to give each citizen a solid foundation in the principles of democracy. Early in camping's development, camping leaders realized that they had not only the opportunity but also the responsibility to foster the cause of democracy, since they were dealing with young people in their formative years. Consequently, progressive camps have tried to offer young people a chance to experience democratic living in a democratic atmosphere. Ideally, camping is an experience in group living at its best, as campers are encouraged to develop independence, self-control and self-reliance as they help plan and accept responsibility for their own way of life through the friendly guidance and example of adults who maintain high personal standards. Camp personnel are becoming ever more aware of the necessity for adapting programs to the needs of individuals rather than trying to fit them into the system.

In recent years, many people who are concerned about camping have begun to reevaluate camping's past purposes and to plan new directions it might take. There is more awareness now of what has been happening between various groups of people, and corresponding changes have been made in the conduct and organization of the modern camp. (These changes will be discussed in more detail in Chapter 3.)

THE ORGANIZATION OF THE CAMPING PROFESSION

Each early camp was a highly individualized project that was conducted largely according to the beliefs, past experiences and particular ideals and aspirations of the person or organization sponsoring it. Before long, however, some of the more progressive camp directors and other interested individuals began to recognize the values of meeting informally with others both for fellowship and for a chance to discuss common successes, problems and failures. These gatherings proved so helpful and inspirational that a formal meeting was held in Boston in 1903 with about 100 people in attendance.

Additional meetings followed and, in 1910, a decision was made to form an organization to be known as the *Camp Directors' Association of America,* with 11 charter members. Charles R. Scott served as its first president. The *National Association of Directors of Girls Camps* was formed in 1916, with Mrs. Luther Halsey (Charlotte V.) Gulick as president. The *Mid-West Camp Directors' Association* followed in 1921. These three organizations joined forces as the *Camp Directors' Association of America* in 1924, with George L. Meylan serving as president. In 1926 the Association began publication of a magazine called *The Camp Directors' Bulletin,* later changed to *Camping.*

The American Camping Association (ACA)

The Camp Directors' Association was renamed the *American Camping Association* in 1935, and since that time the organization has continued to grow steadily in both membership and influence. It is a nationwide, nonprofit professional organization dedicated to the promotion and improvement of organized camping for children and adults, with more than 5,000 members in 50 states and 10 foreign countries. Among its members are camp owners, camp directors and staff, educators, clergymen, commercial firms supplying camps, family camping leaders and others with diverse training and experience who are interested in camping. It has nine categories of membership, providing for an equitable system of dues for individual members. (Students enjoy a special reduced rate.)

OBJECTIVES. The objectives of the American Camping Association are:

1. To extend the educational and recreational benefits of out-of-doors living.
2. To give emphasis in camping to citizenship training, in keeping with the principles and traditions of American democracy.
3. To provide opportunities for developing awareness and appreciation of the interdependence of all living and nonliving resources and a sense of responsibility for them.
4. To give emphasis to spiritual opportunities through camping.
5. To provide opportunities for fellowship among camp leaders.
6. To stimulate high professional standards of camp leadership.
7. To provide for exchange of experiences and successful practices and for development of materials, standards and other aids for the progress of camping.
8. To interpret camping to related groups and to the public.

ORGANIZATION. The American Camping Association is composed of five regions that are subdivided into 32 sections. National conventions are held annually and the sections also hold meetings. Much of the work of the organization is carried on by volunteers; however, a team of full-time staff members that includes an executive vice president works directly with an elected National Board of the ACA from the national headquarters at Bradford Woods, near Martinsville, Indiana. Serving on the executive committee of the board are the national president, the vice presidents for development, field service, private/independent camping, and for programs as well as the president-elect, and the executive vice president.

PUBLICATIONS. Since 1926, the ACA's official publication has been *Camping Magazine,* which is published eight times a year (monthly January through June and bimonthly September through December). The publication covers topics on education, guidance, and legislative developments, as well as on programming, business management, and other important subjects. The ACA also publishes an annual *Parents' Guide to Accredited Camps.* In the *Guide* the country is divided into four sections—northeast, south, midwest, and west—with a separate edition listing the accredited camps in each section along with information about them. These publications are valuable references for those seeking camp employment as well as for parents seeking a good camp for their children.

ACA members also receive the *Leadership Catalog,* which outlines certification programs in leadership development, outdoor living skills, ecology, camp intergrouping, and standards, as well as lists training events for the year.

The ACA encourages studies and research pertaining to camping and fosters the writing and publication of worthwhile literature in the field. Its National Publications Services has in stock several hundred publications pertaining to camping and recreation that are available to members at a 10 percent discount from the list price. This service provides the convenience of ordering from one source, eliminating the need to contact numerous publishers and bookstores. A catalogue of publications available is free upon request.

LEADERSHIP TRAINING. The ACA provides leadership training course outlines in camp counseling and administration that can serve as guides for colleges, camp directors and others offering such courses. It also has developed the First national programs in camp director certification, camp ecologist training and outdoor living skills (OLS) training. The latter program leads to certification on five levels: campcrafter, advanced campcrafter, tripcrafter, OLS instructor, and director of instructors. These courses are given on a sectional basis and are directed by a leadership chairman and OLS instructors. Areas covered are firecraft, food, toolcraft, ropecraft, gear and shelter, campsite, maps and compass, health and safety, nature and conservation, trips, and leadership. Interested parties can obtain details from their local sections of the ACA or by consulting the *Leadership Catalog* referred to earlier.

Camp director institute training programs are conducted on a regional basis in cooperation with certain colleges and universities. Participants in these programs can earn certification as certified camp directors. The ACA also has developed curricula to train staff in such specialized areas as camp ecology and naturalist training, and training for camp health directors; these courses are offered periodically at various places around the country.

Figure 2-1 ACA logo of the national headquarters and chartered sections.

ACCREDITATION AND OTHER SERVICES. One of the outstanding accomplishments of the ACA has been its contribution to the general upgrading of camp operation and performance. Since 1948, it has carried on a program of camp accreditation that it constantly reevaluates and revises. To be accredited by ACA, a camp must be visited by official ACA Standards Visitors, who rate the camp in Four areas of overall operation: administration, program, personnel and site. Nearly one-fifth of the camps checked by ACA Visitors in recent years have failed to meet the standards and were denied accreditation. During an average year, approximately two million children and adults attend 2,400 camps that have been visited by trained ACA Standards teams and officially accredited.* Accredited camps are permitted to display and otherwise use the insignia and emblem shown in Figures 2-1 and 2-2. The accreditation program is of great value to camp directors and other camp personnel because it

*American Camping Association: *1980 Parents' Guide to Accredited Camps.* (The American Camping Association, 1980), p. 24.

Figure 2-2 Only camps accredited by the ACA may display this emblem.

provides a method of evaluating the quality of their camp. It also is useful as a guide to prospective camp staff members and parents seeking a quality camp for their children.

Among its other services, the ACA sponsors meetings, conventions and workshops in which participants can exchange ideas, learn of new developments, and receive instruction and information from experts in the field while enjoying good fellowship. The ACA keeps abreast of proposed legislation that would affect camping and provides guidance and counseling to lawmakers at local, state and federal levels. Through consultation, the ACA helps camp personnel to solve professional, legal or other problems they may encounter. It also conducts an ongoing public relations program that includes issuing news releases and newspaper articles, and developing radio and television spot announcements. The ACA also provides a Camp Job Packet, that is designed to help summer staff job applicants. Since the ACA has no placement service on a national level, the packet provides valuable information to help students seeking summer jobs.

The Fund for Advancement of Camping (FAC)

The Fund for Advancement of Camping (FAC) is part of the Development Division of the American Camping Association and works cooperatively with it. Its purpose is to raise funds to support needed and worthwhile projects in camping that cannot be included in the regular ACA budget. FAC began as an outgrowth of a private camp "cracker-barrel" session in 1962, and was first known as the American Camping Association Foundation. In 1966, its headquarters were moved to Chicago and its name was changed to the Fund for Advancement of Camping. Its general management is the responsibility of an elected board of trustees, and it depends entirely upon voluntary contributions from individuals, sections of the ACA, foundations and other sources.

FAC has contributed to the publication of various books and pamphlets, and it has funded many new and innovative projects in such areas as camp standards and evaluation, research, leadership training, the use of government funds for the purchase of camping services, a survey of the values of camping, a study of the history of camping and a study on acclimatization. A recent project, Camping Unlimited, has as its objective the promotion of integrated camping for those of different religious, racial and cultural backgrounds. This program is being conducted in many existing camps under the auspices of various ACA sections.

Other Professional Organizations

The following is a brief summary of several other professional or public organizations involved in one or more aspects of camping and outdoor adventure programming, which includes provision of technical assistance, leadership training, and publications.

ASSOCIATION OF EXPERIENTIAL EDUCATION. This professional association represents the efforts of diverse groups to collaborate in the creation of a formal, international network that provides both support and impetus to the development of experience-based teaching and learning techniques and to their application to the traditional aims of education and human development. The organization has grown from the need for persons who conduct programs that use camping, outdoor pursuits and other experiential approaches to learning to be in touch with each other. Among the Association's major undertakings are sponsorship of the Annual Conference on Experiential Education and publication of the professional journal, *The Journal of Experiential Education,* and its more informal *Newsletter.* The office of the AEE is Box 4625, Denver, Colorado 80204.

THE OUTDOOR EDUCATION COUNCIL. The Council, a unit of the American Alliance for Health, Physical Education, Recreation and Dance, (AAHPERD) was formed to provide a national leadership base for educators from all disciplines who have a common interest in educating in the out-of-doors. The scope of the Council's interests ranges from camping and adventure programs to biological field research. Membership in the Council is open to all members of AAHPERD who, by experience or training, have demonstrated a professional interest in outdoor education. The address of the Outdoor Education Council is AAHPERD, 1900 Association Drive, Reston, Virginia 22091.

ADDITIONAL READINGS

(For an explanation of abbreviations and abbreviated forms used, see page 13.)

Hammerman and Hammerman (eds.): *Outdoor Education: A Book of Readings,* Gibson, H. W.: "The History of Organized Camping," pp. 62–76.

Mand: *Outdoor Education,* ch. 2.

Rodney and Ford: *Camp Administration,* pp. 21–24.

Shivers: *Camping,* pp. 11–20.

Todd: *Camping for Christian Youth,* chs. 1 and 2.

Webb: *Light From a Thousand Campfires:* Sinn, Mrs. B. A., and Kenneth Webb: "A Brief History of the American Camping Association," p. 371.

The American Camping Association (ACA)

Camp Job Packet. ACA, 1978.

Camp Standards With Interpretations for the Accreditation of Organized Camps. ACA, 1980, 78 pp., paper.

OLS Instructor's Manual. ACA, 1979, 84 pp., paper.

Parents' Guide to Accredited Camps. ACA. (Issued annually).

Rodney and Ford: *Camp Administration,* pp. 21–24.

MAGAZINE ARTICLES

Camping Magazine:

"ACA Interracial-Interfaith Policy." Jan., 1972, p. 19.

Burns, Gerald A.: "A Short History of Camping." Feb., Mar. and Apr., 1949.

Eels, Eleanor P.: "Fund for Advancement of Camping." Nov./Dec., 1973, p. 16.

———: "Ernest Balch and Camp Chocuroa (1881–88)." Mar., 1979, p. 9.

———: "Hedley Seldon Dimock: 1891–1958." June, 1979, p. 7.

———: "Church Camping has Colorful Past." Jan., 1980, p. 7.

three

Values and Trends in Organized Camping

I Wonder

I wonder, when you pack away this week
The things you've used at camp and need no more.
Whether in fancy you will put away
Some other treasures gained, among your store.

I wonder, if within the garment folds,
The scent of new-learned flowers may be laid.
Or hidden in the corner of your trunk
A bird wing or a bit of pine tree shade.

I wonder if perhaps when you unpack,
Attempting to shake out a stubborn fold,
There may come tumbling out before your eyes
A sunset sky or tiny star of gold.

I wonder if, when you can do no more,
And all the tray is packed quite firm and tight,
You'll softly step and o'er it gently lay
A moonlight mist you saw, some lovely night.

I wonder if the very last of all,
Because your trunk is locked to go away,
You might just slip within your heart's small wall,
Some of the peace and love you learned at Onaway.

—Frances M. Frost,
Director, Camp Onaway.

CAMPING IS EDUCATION

What are the objectives of organized camping and why do we believe that the camping environment is particularly well-suited for accomplishing them? Why has interest in camping grown so rapidly and why is it considered to be worth all the time and money that camping personnel and parents have devoted to it? The ultimate aim of all education is, of course, to help people develop into happy, healthy, and well-adjusted contributing members of society. Unfortunately, to many people, education is only what takes place within the confines of a classroom. However, it is obvious that every single experience we have during our waking and sleeping hours plays a part in making us what we are and what we will become. Every person we come in contact with leaves some impression. We are influenced also by the organizations we belong to as well as the books we read, the television programs we watch, and the movies we attend. While some influences are quite positive, there are others we might do better without.

Obviously, a well-conducted camp experience can be quite educational and beneficial in that learning becomes fun. A good camp will take advantage of its unique environment to strengthen the values instilled in campers by others and to teach new values that are particularly meaningful in the camp setting.

UNIQUE CHARACTERISTICS OF THE CAMPING ENVIRONMENT AND THEIR POTENTIAL BENEFITS

It is not the primary function of the summer camp to entertain children, but to provide a setting, an environment, a program and a leadership out of which children will find their own entertainment. With the proper motivation in an outdoors environment, children entertain themselves and acquire much of the kind of education they need most.*

—C. Walton Johnson
The Unique Mission of the Summer Camp.

*Used by permission of the author.

Camp Possesses a Camper Wholly

Camp possesses campers completely, for they eat, sleep, work, and play there 24 hours a day, seven days a week, with almost no outside influences or distractions. The campers live in their own world, associating closely with counselors and others in their cabin group, and often doing things with an entire unit or the camp as a whole. Not even parents spend as much time with a child each day as do counselors and fellow campers. In terms of hours, two months spent in camp are the equivalent of a whole year in school. Camp is at once home, school, friends, place of worship, and playground, all in an outdoor setting that contrasts strongly to the urban environment with which we are familiar.

The Out-of-Doors Setting

Most camps pride themselves on their large grounds of varied terrain, most of it left in a relatively primitive and unspoiled state. Here, campers spend most of their waking as well as an appreciable amount of their sleeping hours outdoors with only a tent or the sky for a roof. The many camp activities geared or adapted especially to outdoor living attune participants to a life in the open. All of their senses undergo constant stimulation by the smells, sights, sounds, textures and possibly even tastes of nature.

Some potential benefits of this out-of-door setting are:

1. An intimate knowledge of nature and a lasting love of the outdoors that can form the basis for a lifelong interest in outdoor activities and related hobbies.
2. A keen insight into nature's blueprint for keeping all things in balance and an appreciation of the interdependence of all living things and of man's proper place in the natural world.
3. A meaningful spiritual awakening as campers develop appreciation and concern for others as well as knowledge about the universe itself. A sense of awe and inspiration can overwhelm campers when they see the majesty of a high mountain, the peace of a quiet valley, the glory of a colorful sunset, the glint of sunlight on a lake, or dewdrops glistening on an intricate spider web.
4. An understanding of the urgent need to conserve our natural resources lest there be none left for future generations to enjoy after so many years of abuse and destruction. Observant campers will notice a good camp's practices of recycling, conservation, and ecology and will probably continue these practices at home.
5. The development of esthetic tastes as campers live with nature's panorama of unsurpassed beauty, largely unmarred by humans and their creations. Campers come to gain an appreciation of nature's peace and serenity, unbroken except for the occasional sound of some wild creature or the laughter and happy banter of their peers as they carry on their activities.

Living 24 Hours a Day with Others of Varied Backgrounds

Many youngsters spend much of their nonschool time with adults, and the children with whom they do associate often have very similar social backgrounds. In camp children live continuously with a variety of individuals having almost every conceivable personality and background.

Some potential benefits of this social diversity are:

1. Learning to accept those different from oneself, appreciating their good qualities and minimizing their idiosyncrasies, just as they will do in return.
2. Learning that flexibility, sharing, and consideration for others are essential for happy group living. Campers who do not learn this probably will not be accepted by the peer group. A trained and observant staff member will most likely come to the rescue in order to help remedy the situation.
3. Reinforcing good home training, or supplying it when lacking, in such areas as good grooming and manners, as well as satisfactory eating and health habits.
4. Developing deep and lasting friendships with both peers and older persons with whom campers have laughed and exchanged confidences while sharing the varied experiences of trail and camp living.
5. Assisting campers to mature by gradually leading them away from any overdependence on their families. This break must eventually be made if youngsters are ever to stand on

their own two feet and play their rightful role as adults in society.

Living in a Democratic Community

The usual camp method of handling problems and topics of general interest in a group is through group discussion with a counselor, or sometimes a camper, serving as leader. Matters concerning the whole camp similarly are handled through the Camp Council, which is composed of representatives and staff from each of the smaller groups. This gives campers an opportunity to share in formulating procedures and rules that are within their province.

Some potential benefits of democratic group living are:

1. Learning how the democratic process works, how to serve effectively as a leader or follower, and how to express oneself clearly without being obnoxious or usurping an undue amount of time and attention.

2. Understanding and accepting camp rules, since there is a necessity for having at least a few regulations in order to protect the rights of each individual and to make things run smoothly with a minimum of friction. Small group discussions help campers to become cooperative, law-abiding citizens since people rarely flout laws when they understand the reasons for them, especially if they have shared in making them.

3. Gaining the courage to take an active part in a meeting and to express honest opinions, even though they may not coincide with what is popular. Recognizing the right of others to differ and learning to listen and actually think about what they are saying.

4. Learning to abide by the will of the majority while still having concern for the rights and wishes of the minority. Being willing to compromise instead of insisting on having one's own way.

5. Learning to get the facts before making a decision, consulting knowledgeable people or reference sources if necessary, and then analyzing and evaluating all the pros and cons before making up one's mind.

6. Learning to bring problems and disputes out into the open instead of sulking, grumbling, becoming bitter, or discussing them only with those who are no better informed or in no better position to do anything about the situation.

7. Gaining experience in problem solving, for in the camp living situation questions frequently arise about what to do and how to do it.

A Broad Program of Activities

Most camps offer a wide variety of activities, with special emphasis placed on activities concerned with adventure and outdoor living. Many of these activities are unlikely to be available elsewhere, at least not in the same form, since they depend upon an outdoor environment and the general atmosphere of a typical camp.

Some potential benefits of a varied program are:

1. Developing lifetime hobbies, perhaps even a vocation. Participation in a wide variety of activities often discloses unsuspected interests and aptitudes, broadens perspectives, and enables campers to appreciate the interests and accomplishments of others. The average camp tries to develop general, all-around abilities rather than specialized ones, as is so often done in school sports and other activities in which only a few are chosen to participate and the majority are left to cheer on the sidelines.

2. Encouraging campers to try their best as they attempt to improve their own performance (in effect, competing against themselves). Although there is enough competition to challenge those with superior ability, the emphasis is on self-improvement. This is preferable to a highly competitive program in which a few consistently do well, while others become dejected and unwilling to try.

3. Being gracious losers by accepting defeat without rancor or excuses.

4. Having *fun* and enjoying the excitement and new experiences every child craves, but doing so in a wholly safe and sane way. Youngsters who learn to satisfy their desires for adventure and fun in wholesome ways never will need to resort to stealing, fighting or other less socially acceptable outlets in order to get their excitement.

(Camp Kingsmont, West Stockbridge, Mass.)

Every little boy has inside of him an aching void which demands interesting and exciting play. And if you don't fill it with something that is interesting and exciting and good for him, he is going to fill it with something that is interesting and exciting and isn't good for him.

—THEODORE ROOSEVELT, JR.

5. Satisfying curiosity and the desire to investigate and learn. The whole camp approach is "let's go together and find out."

6. Learning how to properly balance work, play, and rest; alternating vigorous activities with quieter ones, while observing regular hours for rest and sleep.

7. Learning the wise use of leisure time; choosing activities that give true enjoyment and satisfaction rather than merely kill time. This fulfills an increasingly pressing need as lessened working hours provide more leisure time. Many camp activities, such as canoeing, swimming, hiking, backpacking, boating, fishing, camping out, nature study and ecology, photography, tennis, and horseback riding, provide the lifelong interests and skills required to make full use of our rapidly expanding parks and other recreational facilities. In contrast, few individuals will continue as adults to participate in school sports.

8. Enjoying simple pastimes that cost little or nothing, and learning to be self-sufficient instead of depending on others or commercial entertainment.

9. Increasing feelings of patriotism and appreciation of our heritage through participation in such activities as flag-raising ceremonies, the Fourth of July celebration, studying local history, and living somewhat like our pioneers and early heroes.

10. Learning to appreciate seriousness and thoughtfulness through participation in vespers and campfire programs developed around thought-provoking themes and rituals.

Sufficient Free Time for Meditating and Dreaming and Regular Hours for Rest and Sleep

Modern society seems intent upon converting children into adults just as rapidly as possible. Youngsters' clothing, games, and social activities are patterned closely after those of adults, and their after-school hours are literally

(U.S. Forest Service)

crammed with activity. This greatly complicates the problem of setting aside regular hours for rest and sleep and leaving free time for simple relaxation. Even summer vacations no longer provide lazy, carefree days to spend in fishing, wading in a brook, browsing in a book, or just whiling away the hours in the hundreds of ways young people find enjoyable.

Camps long ago recognized the folly of cramming each day so full of a frenzy of activities that campers became completely exhausted. The pace and scheduling of today's camp provides opportunity for plenty of rest and relaxation.

Some potential benefits of sufficient free time are:

1. Having time to think and examine so that youngsters can come to better understand who and what they are as well as the world they live in.

2. Acquiring a sense of calmness and well-being. Children who have learned to solve their problems and live sanely, exercising enough to produce healthful physical fatigue then relaxing completely at something they enjoy, are unlikely to become one of the millions of adults who feel they must rely upon such crutches as aspirin, sleeping pills, and tranquilizers in order to keep going.

A High Ratio of Trained and Especially Selected Staff to Campers

The typical camp consists of a community of young persons and selected leaders, who live together in small groups. The American Camping Association recommends the following ratio of counselors to campers, according to age group.*

AGE SERVED	*NUMBER OF CAMPERS PER INDIVIDUAL COUNSELOR*
6 and under	5
7–8	6
9–14	8
15–18	10
19 and over	20

A staff usually is made up of a nucleus of older experienced persons that is supplemented by college students, younger counselors, teach-

**Camp Standards with Interpretations for the Accreditation of Organized Camps.* ACA, 1980, p. 25.

ers, and others who are specially trained and interested in youth work. This provides distinct advantages, since children who need or want advice or crave a sympathetic adult to whom they can express their hopes, frustrations, accomplishments, and problems almost always can find one.

Some potential benefits of a high ratio of staff to campers are:

1. Learning to regard adults in a new light. A cabin counselor acts as a sort of big brother or sister to the children and establishes a warm, friendly atmosphere by planning, working, sharing, laughing and having fun with the children. Other staff members play a similar role on occasion and present to the children, perhaps for the first time, a picture of adults as interesting, helpful people whom they can trust and enjoy.

2. Learning desirable traits and characteristics by example as well as by precept. It is a well-known fact that both desirable and undesirable traits are at least as likely to be acquired by association as taught. Informal camp living creates an atmosphere of closeness and camerаderie that is quite favorable for learning. Most campers are still in the stage of "hero worship" and a counselor or other staff member may well be chosen as the beloved model. Miracles can happen if the models chosen put their best foot forward on all occasions and use skill in handling situations.

Simple Living in Rustic Surroundings

Although camp buildings are often quite simple and rustic, they are fully equipped to serve their purposes, but without ornateness and unnecessary gadgetry. Such facilities as the health service and camp kitchen are strictly modern and are kept spotlessly clean and sanitary, but the attractiveness of the whole camp depends upon simplicity and ruggedness. "Do it yourself" is the usual motto as campers care for their own quarters and possessions and share in the upkeep of buildings and camp grounds used in common. They also share in such chores as washing dishes, setting tables, sweeping the lodge, and preparing and cooking outdoor meals. They learn to dress for the weather and pack and carry their own trip duffel, as well as a share of the group equipment.

Some potential benefits to campers of simple camp living are:

1. Acquiring new self-respect and self-confidence as campers learn to take care of themselves and do things others may previously have done for them.

2. Gaining a new and more realistic sense of values as campers note how relatively unimportant such things as money, material possessions, IQ and fine clothes are in assessing the true worth of an individual. In camp they find that the happiest, best liked and most respected counselors and campers have earned their status because of their character rather than their outward appearance and material possessions.

3. Gaining a feeling of community and camp pride and satisfaction from serving others as they share in maintaining the entire camp or assist in projects to improve it for the benefit of present and future campers.

4. Taking pride in their ability to improvise and make do with what they have, for at camp they cannot run to the store to replace something they have damaged or to satisfy a whim of the moment.

5. Acquiring a feeling of being at home in the out-of-doors as they learn the unique part each element plays in the make-up of the total environment.

6. Learning respect for the dignity of work and the satisfaction that comes from the sustained effort needed to complete individual or group projects.

7. Taking pride in the good health and physical fitness that vigorous outdoor life brings as it stimulates the lungs and heart, exercises the large muscles, and produces a healthy appetite for the simple, nutritious meals cooked outdoors or planned and served indoors by the dietitian and kitchen staff.

8. Acquiring skill in such household tasks as making beds, sweeping, washing dishes, planning and cooking well-balanced meals, setting tables, and constructing, repairing, and maintaining equipment and clothing.

9. Learning to appreciate our heritage, since camp life resembles that of the early pioneers. This appreciation may be enhanced

(Willamette Council of Camp Fire, Salem, Oreg.)

through appropriate programs that include dramatics, storytelling, reading, trips to nearby points of historical interest and many other similar endeavors.

REACHING GOALS

Camps can indeed accomplish many things, but not by being a camp in name only, coasting along on the good reputation of camping and relying on past merits. Worthy achievements are attained only when those who are in charge of a camp have made careful, intelligent plans that are based upon the sincere belief that their greatest accomplishment is to help campers develop to their highest potential. Organized camps therefore should have some general purposes, specifically stated, and the program of activities should be designed or directed toward attaining them. It is the task of the administration to lay the groundwork and unite the whole staff into a team that pulls together toward achieving these common goals.

The words purpose, goal, end, or aim are synonymous and connote the ultimate object to be sought or obtained. For instance, one common goal of camping is for campers to experience individual growth and development, while another is for campers to learn to live outdoors and become acquainted with the natural environment. Although these are admirable and worthy aims, such broad statements do not provide any specific guidelines on how to obtain them through the program offerings and services of the camp. Thus, definite directions are needed in order for a camp program to meet such stated goals. These directions can be developed through the formulation of objectives that serve as steppingstones toward the goal. An objective describes the way a goal can be achieved. In other words, the camp achieves its goals through specific program and activity objectives that are stated in detail. (This topic will be explored fully in Chapter 10.)

In actuality, camp sponsors and administrators place varying emphasis upon particular goals and objectives, depending on the individual camp's purposes and philosophy. For instance, a church camp probably will stress spiritual values, while a private camp might emphasize certain recreational skills. Although the goals and objectives may vary, all camps are established for the purpose of using the natural environment as an educational tool or training ground to create positive personal opportunities for the participants. Since camps offer unique living and learning experiences that draw upon a group living situation, they reflect the importance of transferring experiences learned in the out-of-doors to normal day-to-day living. Some of the common goals established by camps for their participants are illustrated in Figure 3-1.

As mentioned earlier, your camp probably will have already determined its goals and objectives (a requirement for any camp accredited by the ACA), which you will learn about during precamp training. These will provide the framework within which you will develop the specific activity objectives for your particular group. Take into consideration your own ideas and abilities as well as what your campers want for themselves and what their parents wish for their children. Assess campers' present status and build upon it. It is best to put your objectives in writing, and, in so doing, be specific but express them in simple terms in order to avoid high-flown generalities. Be sure objectives are realistic and attainable, then write out exact procedures for accomplishing them. Your objectives may well vary for each camper, depending on needs and personalities.

Try to be realistic and don't expect to accomplish miracles in the brief time you have available. Be prepared for disappointments and setbacks, for habits are hard to break and personality changes come slowly. Review your objectives frequently to refresh your memory and assess your progress, and don't hesitate to alter your goals as experience and a better un-

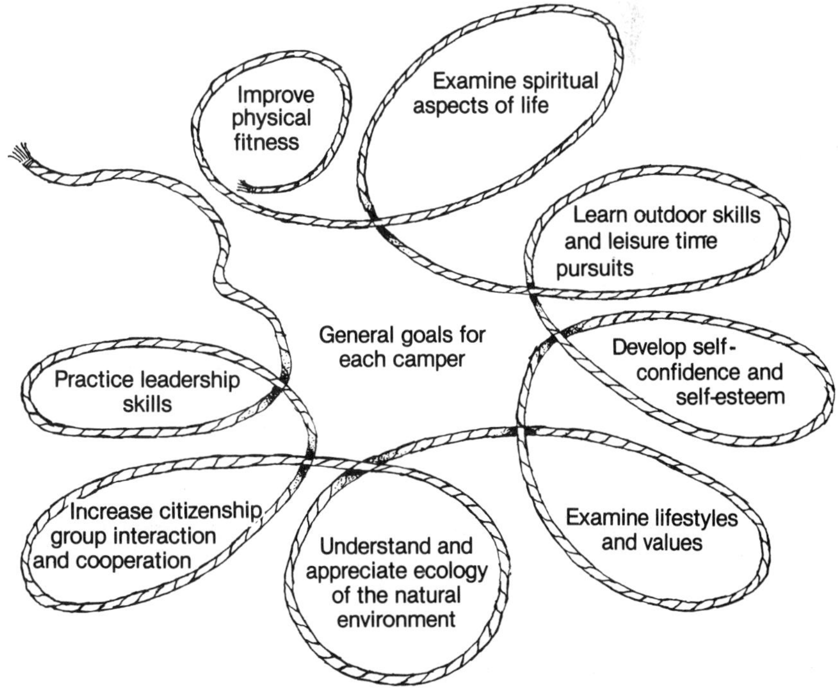

Figure 3-1 Some common goals of organized camps.

derstanding of your group dictate. Try hard to help each person to achieve at least a few constructive things as the season progresses; this will encourage each camper to try harder.

One of the best ways to change attitudes and instill new ideas is to present yourself as an example. Another is to recognize and take advantage of the "teachable moments" that arise during the activities of the day. These moments occur when campers are truly interested in what they are doing and recognize the need for guidance or information and are therefore alert and ready to look, listen, and learn. At these times, a brief anecdote (even if you have to make it up) is often an effective way to make your point.

Now and then, sit down and evaluate what has been accomplished with each individual and with the group. Informal chats with individuals and the group as a whole are helpful both in developing your initial objectives and in keeping tabs on how each camper feels about the progress that is being made.

Make a complete assessment for each camper at the end of the season; this will present a realistic picture of the value of your work during the summer. (There are several ways to do this; these will be discussed in later chapters.) Camps often request such an evaluation and also may ask campers to fill out a questionnaire about their accomplishments. Sometimes questionnaires also are sent to parents to learn what changes they have observed in their child and which seem likely to last.

TRENDS IN CAMPING

As in every other phase of American life, rapid changes are occuring in the field of camping. Many are necessary and desirable, but in our haste to accept each proposal just because it is new, we must take care to preserve and improve on what is good of the old and combine it with promising innovations. The following seem prominent among today's trends.

Number and Types of Camps

Although some decrease in the number of regular resident camps is apparent, especially among the smaller camps, some of the larger ones have become still larger so that even more campers can be accomodated. In fact, there are more children attending camps than ever before. As some camps close others are opening, many of which are purposely kept small in order to accomplish some specific purpose or goal. There are now more special camps such as day, trip, school, 4-H, and religious camps, as well as camps for particular groups, such as the retarded, the physically handicapped, older citizens, and the emotionally disturbed, and for particular activities, such as music, dramatics, weight gain or loss, conversational languages, sports, dance, and for almost any other type of activity or interest. Some of the latter would hardly qualify as camps as we interpret the name, but the term "camp" apparently has caught the American fancy and like an umbrella, it is used to cover everything, leaving anyone free to capitalize upon camping's good name and to apply it to situations not even remotely resembling true camping.

Size of Camps and Decentralization

The increase in the size of some of the larger camps is probably a response to a growing demand to accomodate more people or an attempt to use the economies of bigness to meet constantly spiraling expenses. However, as we have noted, a large group tends to lose the individuality and close intimacy so essential to achieving optimal objectives.

Early camps were laid out in the manner of army camps, with living quarters arranged in straight lines on either side of a central street or in the form of a hollow circle or square with common use buildings, such as the mess hall and camp lodge, centrally located. Multiple-occupant sleeping units, like army barracks, contained cots arranged in long rows. The emphasis was on all-camp activities or on various activities from which campers could choose, so that campers usually associated with either the entire camp group or with a constantly changing group of individuals who had chosen similar activities. This type of organization might be called *centralized camping*.

As camps grew larger, with some enrolling as many as a hundred or more campers, the participants often were lost in the shuffle and found themselves in an impersonal atmosphere that lacked the warmth, close intimacy, and personal attention that are so essential to a constructive camp experience. Some camps responded to this problem by dividing their entire enrollment into smaller camps that functioned more or less independently. Also, nearly all camps, even those of modest size, have now adopted what is known as a *decentralization* plan, which was pioneered by the Girl Scouts. Here the entire camp is divided into groups of 12 to 24 campers with each group living and functioning like an independent camp. Each group, which may be called a unit, section, division, or village, is fairly homogeneous, its members having been selected on some common basis, such as age, camping experience, general development, or interests. Each unit lives in a segregated area of its own that is situated close enough to the main dining room and lodge for convenience, yet sufficiently secluded to provide privacy and to allow the unit to function independently. Unit buildings usually consist of a unit house for group meetings, a latrine and bath house, and an outdoor kitchen. Unit members take most of their meals in the main dining room and occasionally participate in all camp activities in order to provide a happy blending of living in a small group while sharing in the life of the whole camp community.

Competition for Campers

Camps now are encountering more competition in their quest for camper patronage. One reason for this is the decreasing birth rate of the past few years, which means there is a constantly dwindling number of children of camp age. In addition, there are now more counterattractions to camp, such as Little League, extensive park and recreation programs, experimentation with the 12-month school year, tutoring in special subjects or summer school, driver education programs, band or baton instruction, summer travel, youth hosteling, social work, or summer jobs. Family camping now is becoming popular as longer weekends and vacations allow the time to travel and to camp and increased income furnishes the money for camping equipment and such accessories as recreational vehicles, boats, summer cottages, and horses.

Because today's youth are more sophisticated and often have substantial amounts of money at their disposal, they are disenchanted with those camps that still offer the dull, lackluster programs that sufficed previously. In response, many camps today are successfully promoting exciting, challenging programs that have real appeal for youngsters. In addition, many camps, particularly private independent camps, that once offered one six- or eight-week program during the summer now offer several short sessions of two or three weeks so that youngsters can attend camp and still have time for other summer activities.

Camp Facilities

Old camp buildings are being modernized and the new ones are sometimes more elaborate, largely because of camper or parent demands and more specific health, safety, and building regulations at all levels of government. Buildings frequently are winterized and pipe and sewer lines laid underground to permit camps to be used during cold weather.

Camp Personnel

The majority of camps now make a conscious effort to bring together both campers and staff from various social, religious, and economic backgrounds. Many counselors from foreign countries are being hired. Instead of remaining largely a middle class institution, camps are becoming true melting pots as those from minority and innercity groups receive camperships and other financial aid from many sources, such as foundations, government agencies, and the Camping Unlimited movement of ACA's Fund for the Advancement of Camping.

Ages of Campers

There was a period when the average age of campers grew progressively younger, as those who had previously attended stayed away in droves, preferring to stay at home rather than spend a boring summer repeating what was done the year before. Modern camps are successfully meeting this challenge by offering new activities each summer that are built upon techniques and skills acquired the previous summer. Teenagers now are returning in relatively large numbers, attracted by such challenging and exciting possibilities as wilderness camping (sometimes modeled after the Outward Bound program), mountain climbing, spelunking, travel and trip camping, and counselor-in-training (CIT) programs.

Camp Staff Are Better Qualified and More Professional

The first counselors were often college athletes who were selected because of their ability in sports, with their primary appeal derived from their prowess on field or court. They often knew little about the needs, desires, and personalities of children.

With the changes in camp philosophy and program has come a demand for counselors who not only love children but also know how to work with them in an atmosphere of mutual confidence and friendly rapport. Although program specialists still are needed in such areas as campcraft and trip camping, aquatics, health, crafts, and dramatics, the current tendency for campers and counselors to do most things together as a cabin or unit group has produced a need for more counselors with broad interests, versatility, and training and skills in group leadership.

Today's staff are much better trained for several reasons. Better and more diversified camping literature is available, and colleges and other organizations are offering more and better courses for training camp leaders. The precamp training period conducted by camps now is considerably longer and better planned and is used to *train* counselors, in contrast to the earlier custom of using the precamp period to get free help from incoming counselors in doing the physical work of getting the camp ready to open. Many camps are now "growing" their own counselors by conducting excellent CIT courses for older campers. The ACA has established standards and guidelines and is developing courses leading to certification as campcrafter, advanced campcrafter, trip crafter, and O.L.S. instructor. Staff members are taking courses in such specialized areas as ecology and aquatics. Increasing numbers of camp directors approach their jobs in a more professional manner as they study and acquire special training through such programs as the ACA-sponsored courses leading to a camp director certificate. More help is coming from such allied fields as health, psychology, sociology, and education. All of these factors combine to assure us that camping personnel are indeed becoming more professional.

Camp Program Is Changing

The program of an early centralized camp was rigidly scheduled; activities were planned like school classes and each camper was required to participate in most of the offerings. The program was planned by the camp or program director, sometimes with the assistance of a few chosen counselors, and was intended to fill every waking moment of the day. Tutoring in school subjects or special instruction in music, dramatics, or dancing often was included at the request of parents.

We no longer take the narrow view that the program is merely the schedule of activities offered each day or each week. Rather, we regard it as the sum total of every experience the children have from the time they enter camp until their final good-bye. There is now much more flexibility and the campers have more freedom to choose where they will go and what they will do, as campers, counselors, and general staff share in planning the program. The modern camp is child-centered and emphasizes what is happening to the campers as people rather than what physical skills they are developing.

The growing sophistication of campers has caused corresponding changes in the program, such as a greater variety of creative arts and more environmental study. Some of the traditional activities, such as woodcraft, no longer are emphasized in many camps. Instead, the emphasis is on conservation practices and development of an appreciation and understanding of nature. There also is more interest in adventure and challenge programs that stress self-reliance and competence in skills, such as mountaineering and whitewater kayaking. More common too is the development and use of facilities such as ropes courses and obstacle courses that are used for problem-solving activities and for instilling trust, confidence and initiative in the participants.

Camper Motivation

To motivate campers in the traditional program, an elaborate system of achievement charts and awards was devised. As a result, there was competition in almost every area, which was sometimes overstressed. Some modern camps have overreacted to competition so strenuously that they now refuse to use anything resembling a check list or awards of any type. Some of their reasons for this refusal are: (1) Campers become so intent on working for awards that they miss the real values inherent in the activities themselves. (2) Regardless of the care taken in planning any system of awards, for every winner there must be one or several losers. Since some campers or groups seldom win they may acquire a hopeless "what's the use of trying" attitude, while others win too frequently and become insufferably self-centered. (3) The desire to win sometimes becomes so keen that it leads to regrettable incidents. The extreme competitive spirit engendered results in petty bickering and jealousies that are in direct conflict with the atmosphere camps are trying to create.

Although modern camps may give awards, they minimize their importance and give them on the basis of doing one's best rather than attaining a specific goal. High camp morale, tradition, a word of commendation from sincere and enthusiastic counselors, the inner glow of self-satisfaction individuals feel at having done their best, and the impetus of group approval furnish enough reward to promote activities that have natural appeal for youngsters.

Utilizing Group Dynamics

The modern camp tries to ascertain the wishes and needs of each camper and develop a wide range of possibilities for meeting them. Units in a decentralized system usually plan their activities around their own living needs. The unit is small enough to permit the close-knit atmosphere of family life and each camper is recognized as a personality whose opinions are respected and whose needs are considered by understanding fellow-campers and counselors.

Today's youth are generally more aggressive and inclined to question authority, tradition, and the customary way of doing things. They deserve a greater role in planning their own programs and formulating their own rules of conduct. Successful leaders are using democratic methods to discover possible sources of conflict so that they can work jointly with campers to find acceptable solutions.

Health Practices

Health always has been an important objective of camping, but early camps deluded themselves into believing that good nourishing food plus an active life in the out-of-doors inevitably would produce good health. After a 1930 study exploded this theory, great changes took place in camp health practices and programs. A complete health examination for every camper and staff member immediately prior to camp opening was customary, but now an examination anytime within the preceding year is considered adequate to reveal any weaknesses needing correction, or at least protection, by a modified program. All campers are given a check-up on arrival at camp in order to find those with problems needing immediate attention. Trained nurses and doctors, and sometimes dietitians, are a part of the regular camp staff.

Camp personnel now realize that it is a serious error to schedule every moment so that campers engage in a feverish round of strenuous activities from reveille to taps. Camp programs now allow time for serenity and calm, and campers, with careful guidance, are more often permitted to pursue their own interests, even though these may occasionally involve nothing more strenuous than sitting under a tree daydreaming or watching a colony of ants at work. Often there is a rest hour following lunch, and campers are encouraged to balance active and inactive pursuits. Enough vigorous exercise should be provided in the camp program to keep campers strong and to produce a pleasant, healthful tiredness by nightfall.

Camp Standards and Government Involvement

There is a definite trend to develop and follow recognized camping standards, which are usually based upon those formulated by the camping profession itself, under the leadership of the ACA, as requirements for accreditation. There also has been more involvement by all levels of government in such areas as financial support, state licensing, and regulations concerning medical examination of food handlers and other personnel, sewage and garbage disposal, fire prevention, milk supply, licensing of the camp store, boating, fishing, and minimum wage laws. More recently, camps have been affected by regulations concerning the use of pesticides, solid waste disposal, air pollution produced by refuse burning and other types of fires, child welfare and day care, and legislation such as the Occupational Health and Safety Act. Further government participation seems imminent, as seen in a proposed Camp Safety Act that has been under consideration by Congress in recent years.

Research in Camping

Although there is still a great need for research in the field of camping, encouraging progress has been made. Financial support for research has come from such sources as the Fund for the Advancement of Camping, the ACA, various foundations, and the federal government.

Year-Round and Multiple Use of Camp Facilities

In an attempt to meet constantly spiraling costs and still maintain a reasonable return on a considerable investment, many camps are now promoting multiple and year-round use of their facilities. Among the positive results of this trend have been innovative programs and greater possibilities for year-round employment for those with camp program and administrative skills. As previously mentioned, buildings are being winterized and water and sewer lines placed underground to permit winter use.

Off-season usage may include such activities as winter sports, school camping and outdoor education, college camping and administration workshops, orientation programs, dude ranch experiences, senior citizen camping, family camping and family reunions. Camps also are used as retreats for conferences and vacations during the off-season.

Ecology and Conservation Influences

As land for camping becomes scarcer and more expensive, those responsible for operating camps have become more concerned about caring for what they have. Portable facilities now are used, and program activities are shifted about to provide rotation of land usage, minimizing the harmful effects of overuse. Primitive camping programs no longer depend largely upon natural resources but rely mainly upon manmade products (stoves for cooking and warmth, lanterns for light). The new philosophy embraces the concept that campers take everything they need to the campsite, then bring it all back again in order to disturb the environment as little as possible. Owners and users of land now feel a greater sense of stewardship or responsibility for its wise use and care, including planting trees to replace those lost to disease, accident, fire, or old age, controlling plant diseases, and preventing forest fires.

The use of wood for lashing elaborate camp facilities or for campfires often is discouraged, and is prohibited by law in some states and in federally owned areas. Additional legislation of this type no doubt will be more prevalent in the immediate future. We in camping who are interested in preserving our natural heritage should voluntarily support these conservation practices instead of waiting for legislation to force compliance.

Taxation of Camps

All levels of government, from local to federal, are reexamining their tax bases as they try to meet increasing demands for tax monies. Some camps that have been largely tax exempt now are being taxed and this practice seems likely to become much more widespread.

Demand for Urban Facilities

The growing desire among people, especially those with limited time, money, or transportation capabilities, for outdoor experiences of every kind is producing an increasing demand for facilities in or near population centers.

Small Group Camping

Camping expeditions often for short periods ranging from one to several days, by small groups such as a scout troop and its leader(s), are on the increase.

The Camping Profession Is Becoming More Sophisticated

As camping matures and its leaders become better trained and more experienced, we acquire greater ability to look at our profession objectively to see where we have been, the direction in which we should be going, and how best to get there.

ADDITIONAL READINGS

(For an explanation of abbreviations and abbreviated forms used, see page 13.)

Objectives

Camp Standards With Interpretations, pp. 16, 26, 30, and 58–59.
Camping Is Education.
Hammerman and Hammerman (eds.): *Outdoor Education: A Book of Readings:*
Donaldson, Lou and George: "A Camp Is a Children's Community." p. 33.
Hammerman, Donald R.: "A Case for Outdoor Education." p. 45.
Kilpatrick, W. H.: "The Role of Camping in Education Today." p. 16.
Masters, Hugh B.: "Values of School Camping." p. 21.
Miller, Paul S.: "The Summer Camp Reinforces Education." p. 77.
Mitchell, Elmer D.: "The Interests of Education in Camping." p. 80.
Partridge, E. DeAlton: "Some Psychological Backgrounds of Camping." p. 12.
Sharp, L. P., and E. DeAlton Partridge: "Some Historical Backgrounds of Camping." p. 57.
Vinal, William Gould: "The School Camp Line-Up for Nature Education." p. 28.
Johnson, C. Walton: *The Unique Mission of the Summer Camp.* ACA, 24 pp., paper.
Lowry, Thomas Power (ed.): *Camping Therapy: Its Uses in Psychiatry and Rehabilitation.* Thomas, 1974, 160 pp.
Rodney and Ford: *Camp Administration, pp. 12–21.*
Smith, et al.: *Outdoor Education,* chs. 1, 2.
Todd: *Camping for Christian Youth,* ch. 4.
Vinton, Dennis A., et al.: *Camping and Environmental Education for Handicapped Children and Youth.* Hawkins and Associates, 1978, 170 pp.
Vinton, Dennis A. and Elizabeth M. Farley: *Camp Staff Training Series, Module 3, Camp Program Planning and Leadership.* Available from ACA, 1979, 142 pp. paper.
Webb, Kenneth B.: *As Sparks Fly Upward.* Phoenix, 1973, 196 pp.
Webb, Kenneth B. (ed.): *Camping for American Youth—A Declaration for Action.* ACA, 1962, 26 pp., paper.
Webb: *Light From a Thousand Campfires:*
Gibson, H. W.: "Is It Worth While?" p. 41.
Hill, Ralph: "Creative Activity in Camping." p. 56.
Johnston, Margaret J.: "The Ministry of Nature." p. 260.
Kuebler, Clark G.: "Education for What?" p. 65.
Lorber, Max: "Give To Your Campers Work to Do." p. 311.
Reiley, Catharine C.: "Our Common Heritage." p. 67.
Roehrig, Gilbert H.: "There's a Reason for This Yearning." p. 51.
Vincent, E. Lee: "What a Piece of Work Is Man!" p. 59.
Webb: *Summer Camps—Security in the Midst of Change.*

MAGAZINE ARTICLES

Camping Magazine:
Brackeen, Margaret: "There's a Big Difference (and an Important One) Between Integration and Acceptance." Feb., 1971. p. 12.
Carlson, Reynold E.: "The Values of Camping." A monograph for the ACA. Insert, Nov./Dec., 1975, p.11.
Charpentier, Bruce and Helen: "Eight Values Camps Can Give." Sept./Oct., 1971, p. 14.
Cullen, William J.: "Foreign Counselors Come to Camp." Jan. 1971, p. 26.
Ford, Dr. Phyllis M.: "Two Modern Challenges for Every Camp Director." May, 1969, p. 12.
Goldsmith, Ann, and Robert Hellerson: "Our Commitment is to . . . Diversification of Campers." Mar., 1969, p. 19.
Kirk, John J.: "Camping Can Be Unique If We Only Let It." June, 1969, p. 8.
Konopka, Gisela: "How to Make Camping Significant in the 1970's." Jan., 1970, p. 8.
Krieger, William D.: "Study on Self-concept Changes in Campers." Apr., 1973, p. 16.
Liener, Martin: "Seven Step Program Helps to Integrate Camp." Sept./Oct., 1970, p. 14.
Mason, James A: "Uncertain Outposts: The Future of Camping and the Challenge of Its Past." An occasional paper issued by the Fund For Advancement of Camping. Insert, Sept./Oct., 1978, p. 13.
Penn, Matthew: "Learning in Camp: The Fourth Force in Total Education." June, 1970, p. 13.
Schmidt, Ernest F.: "How Parents Select a Camp." Mar., 1974, p. 4.
Tener, Dr. Morton: "Camp Can Be Much More Than Just 'Fun and Games'." Jan., 1970, p. 14.
Vankrevelen, Alice: "The Child at Camp: A Fresh Start." *Parents Guide to Accredited Camps, 1980.* ACA, p. 11.
Wylie, James A.: "How Camping Contributes to Educational Needs of Children." June, 1964, p. 10.

Trends

Gabel, Dr. Peter S.: *Camping Creates Community.* ACA, 1971, 17 pp., paper.
Rodney and Ford: *Camp Administration,* pp. 24–26.

MAGAZINE ARTICLES

Camping Magazine:
Baker, C. Woodson: "Year-Round Camping Through Adventure Education Programs." Jan., 1981, p. 17.
Ball, Armand: "A Hard Look at Camping—Today and Tomorrow." May, 1973, p. 12.
Buynak, Michael F.: "Facing the Camping Future With Confidence." Feb., 1972, p. 8.

Carlson, Reynold E.: "The Values of Camping." Nov./Dec., 1975, p. 11.

Catlin, Glenn: "Eminent Domain . . . the Common Good and Camps." Apr., 1972, p. 20.

Cowle, Irving: "Some Goals for the Seventies." Jan., 1969, p. 10.

Groves, David: "Future Trends in Camping." Mar., 1978, p. 24.

Hibbard, Roger: "What Criteria Must Be Met in Order to Make Camping a Profession?" Feb., 1973, p. 10.

"How to Think About the Extended School Year." ACA National Staff, Sept./Oct., 1971, p. 8.

Makoff, Stephen J.: "Preparing Groups for Weekend Camp Programs." Mar., 1970, p. 46.

Mason, James A: "Uncertain Outposts: The Future of Camping and the Challenge of Its Past." Sept./Oct., 1978, p. 13.

Melzer, Asher O.: "Camping—Where Do We Go From Here?" Jan., 1972, p.8.

Ramey, John H.: "Eminent Domain Is A Coin With Two Sides." Nov., 1972, p. 15.

Sanborn, Roger: "And What Do You Do In the Winter?" Nov./Dec., 1970, p. 8.

Smith, Ellis S., Jr.: "How To Use Your Camp All Year Long." Nov./Dec., 1969, p. 16.

two

The Camp Counselor's Role in Guidance

four

The Camp Counselor

Ideals are like the stars; you will not succeed in touching them with your hands, but like the seafaring man on the desert of waters, you choose them as your guides, and, following them, you reach your destiny.

—Carl Schurz*

*Reproduced by permission of Coronet Magazine.

Camp counseling provides a fascinating seasonal occupation for thousands of people who return to it year after year, but, as with any field of endeavor, not everyone is suited to it. Only when there is mutual admiration between the counselor, who likes almost everything about the camp, and the camp, which likes nearly everything about the counselor, can there be that happy blending that makes the days fly by all too quickly. Therefore, in this chapter, we shall try to consider some ways to predetermine how you would fit into the camping picture.

CHARACTERISTICS OF A GOOD COUNSELOR

Appreciation of and Liking for People

To enjoy the camp experience, you obviously must be a person who enjoys working with people rather than with things and ideas, although you will be called upon to do plenty of the latter, too. You must have a genuine interest in, liking for, and faith in people of all kinds and ages, since camp life involves associating with an assortment of personalities practically 24 hours a day. These qualities, or the lack of them, will quickly show up in your relationships with the campers as well as fellow staff members.

Your first consideration will be fitting in with other staff members; there will probably be a number of fellow counselors of approximately your own age, and older persons as well. All will have different personalities, interests, experiences, and camp duties. You must be versatile and adaptable, for, as you work, you will have frequent contacts with the camp nurse, in regard to your campers' health, the dietitian or head cook, in planning cookouts, and the waterfront director, the handy man, the camp director, and others. High camp morale and good working relationships do not necessarily develop automatically. Rather, they result when each staff member shows an enthusiastic willingness to combine with all others into a closely knit, harmonious camp family.

As a staff member, you must know and understand people and be able and willing to find good traits and qualities to appreciate in each of them, ungrudgingly accepting their quirks and peculiarities just as you hope they will accept yours. Basically, you must be aware of and able to seek out and acknowledge their intrinsic worth both to themselves and to society, while still realizing that each individual, like you, is unique and different from everyone else.

On the whole, you'll probably find your fellow counselors to be a pretty fine group, for they are the kinds of people who are ordinarily attracted to summer camp work. Among them you'll most likely find several who are very congenial and who may become lifelong friends.

Secondly, you must sincerely enjoy children, even when they are noisy, uncooperative, impulsive, or demanding. You must not like just some children but must extend your affection to the whole group. In fact, the shy, reticent, socially unattractive children need and hunger for the affection and appreciation you can give much more than those with outgoing personalities who, with little conscious effort on their part, almost instinctively attract others to them. You must be able to perceive the hidden possibilities in each individual, especially the ungifted child who seems to be "all thumbs"; you must be able to see behind the surface of the misfit and maladjusted who are trying in their immature way to find their place in a society that is too complex for them. Your sincere concern for each child as an individual will be evident to them, and will win their trust and good will and ideally will set the stage for you to help them gain acceptance by the group. You must be able to tolerate frequent and prolonged contact with children and maintain your patience and good humor, for you will be foster parent, teacher, friend, confidante, taskmaster, and model to them.

You must indeed like children, but you sometimes will have to be stern with them when their actions endanger their welfare or conflict with camp objectives and policies, yet you must maintain their good will and respect as you skillfully weld them into a peaceful and harmonious community.

Empathy

The ability to put yourself in the place of others and actually sense how they feel is called *empathy*. It is a rare and valuable quality that you are more likely to acquire if you have had many experiences and felt a variety of emotions yourself, such as joy, sadness, love, hate, anger, fear, depression, and loneliness. Such a broad background provides the basis for recognizing and correctly interpreting these emotions when you see them in others. In this way, you will be able to sense the problems and emotional needs of others as they see them, and only then can you determine how best to offer help.

Be an Example

You, as a leader, must exemplify by your own habits and conduct the ideals and objectives of the camp. An ability to attract youngsters is an almost priceless asset, but it would be much better for you to stay at home if the example you set is not of the best, for your very attractiveness then will make your influence more pernicious. Campers may pick up bad habits and become boisterous, vulgar, complaining, or boastful if you set such a pattern.

Pretense and sham soon are spotted in the intimacy of camp life. You might as well face it: everything you are and say and do will be carefully observed by bright-eyed youngsters who will be quick to detect and equally quick to dislike your hypocrisy. Youth is the period of hero worship and a child's heart is full of faith and love. Consequently, there is nothing in the world more painful or demoralizing to youngsters than to discover that a beloved idol is made of very common stuff and that the first favorable impression was a false one. All prospective counselors must ask themselves if they are prepared to inspire their campers. Counselors must try to be worthy of emulation, for they are the leaders who set the pattern, especially for younger, impressionable campers who may be away from parental authority for the first time.

Counselors must capitalize on opportunities that permit youngsters to develop and grow as well as help them recognize and develop their own potential. Furthermore, counselors must encourage campers to think through their own problems and, with minimal help, arrive at their own decisions.

Youthful in Spirit, Yet Mature in Judgment

The camp environment demands that counselors have mature judgment. In fact, as one of its requirements for accreditation, the American

(Camp Kingsmont, West Stockbridge, Mass.)

Camping Association has stated that at least 80 percent of a camp's counselors and program staff must be at least 18 years old, with the rest at least 2 years older than their campers, and at least 20 percent must have bachelor's degrees. However, mature judgment is not always a matter of age or experience, for some people attain it early, whereas others live a lifetime without ever having demonstrated a particle of it. Campers cannot be entrusted to those whose actions are determined by caprice and whim. Yet along with good judgment, counselors must retain a youthfulness of spirit and interest that keeps them forever curious and craving new experiences.

Love of the Out-of-Doors

Even the most luxurious camp usually has rustic surroundings and facilities, since these provide the basic setting necessary for accomplishing some of the main camping objectives. Counselors and campers spend many hours out in the open participating in a variety of activities and sharing many experiences in all types of weather. Therefore, you must have the ability to adapt to such an environment and hopefully you will come to thoroughly enjoy the outdoors. Often, counselors come to camp as green as the grass and trees only to find themselves completely captivated with outdoor living before the season is over. If you've never tried it, why not give it a chance?

Camping Skills

Having definite skills that can contribute to the camp program is of utmost importance to you as a counselor. You should be able to do at least a few things well since they play an important part in gaining the respect of your campers and establishing rapport with them. What can you do? Is there any area in which you excel? Is your tennis, camp cookery, swimming, or woodcraft of such quality that you can demonstrate and teach it to someone else? Can you step into a group that is unduly alarmed over a snake and, by looking at it, assure them that it is harmless and quite essential to nature's well-balanced plan? Can you start a fire in a steady downpour to dry out sopping campers? Can you oversee packing a canoe so that it rides properly in the water? Can you tell poison ivy from Virginia creeper? Can you tell stories, sing, play an instrument, or perform reasonably well in some phase of arts and crafts?

Even a program specialist needs a general background in camping skills, for camping is essentially an outdoor process, and a good modern camp coordinates the many facets of its program into one grand experience in out-of-door living. It isn't enough to just "love" nature; you must know something about it.

As a counselor, you may get along well with children, and the warmth of your personality may be evident to everyone, but unless you have at least a few basic outdoor skills, your charming smile will soon wear thin. However, do not despair if you do not already possess such skills; the main requirement is that you be willing to acquire them, for you will certainly not lack for opportunities to learn from others as well as from the many excellent printed materials now in existence. In fact, many of the best counselors have acquired their knowledge and "know-how" while on the job in camp.

Persistence

You must be able to find self-satisfaction in doing a job well and in serving others without thought of personal gain or self-aggrandizement. You must like hard work and plenty of it, because except for brief periods of free time, you will be on duty 24 hours a day. You must have enough persistence and will power to replace your "wishbone" with backbone, and you must realize that genius is but "1 percent inspiration mixed with 99 percent perspiration." If you really feel challenged by an opportunity to spend a summer in which you can do something and be someone worthwhile, then in you and those like you lie the hope and future of camping. Any director knows and will readily admit that, no matter how capable he or she may be or how elaborate the camp buildings and equipment, the real success of the camp depends upon the quality of the counselors.

(U.S. Forest Service)

Chart I

PHYSICAL HEALTH	1 Poor	2 Below Average	3 Average	4 Above Average	5 Superior
1. Stamina enough to last through a strenuous day					
2. Well-balanced meals eaten regularly					
3. Day planned well enough to get regular sleep in sufficient quantity					
4. Smoking, not at all or moderately, and in an appropriate place					
5. No intoxicating liquors or drug abuse (can't be tolerated at camp)					
6. Sufficient vigorous exercise each day					

GENERAL QUALITIES	1 Poor	2 Below Average	3 Average	4 Above Average	5 Superior
1. Curiosity (want to know about many things just for the sake of knowing)					
2. Cleanliness of person and clothing					
3. Pleasing appearance					
4. Graciousness and mannerliness					
5. Tact (speak truthfully, but without offending or hurting others)					
6. Cooperativeness (even when carrying out the plans of others)					
7. Cheerfulness (no sulking or moodiness)					
8. Sense of humor (even when the joke is on you)					
9. Ability to communicate well					
10. Warmth (a friendly personality that attracts others to you)					
11. Poise (even in emergencies or embarrassing situations)					
12. Appreciation of the beautiful in actions, nature, music, and literature					
13. Sincere liking for children (even unattractive and obnoxious ones)					
14. Ability to work well with a group of children					
15. Willingness to work hard even though it means getting dirty					
16. Skills and knowledge of outdoor living					

(Chart continued on following page.)

GENERAL QUALITIES *(Continued)*	Poor 1	Below Average 2	Average 3	Above Average 4	Superior 5
17. Adaptability (can happily change plans to fit in with others or the weather)					
18. Can follow as well as lead					
19. Love of fun (can see possibilities for enjoyment in almost any situation)					
20. Interested in many things					
21. Skill in at least one camp activity that children like to do					
22. Initiative (ability to start without outside prodding or suggestion)					
23. Promptness at all appointments and in performing all tasks					
24. Dependability (do *what* you say you will *when* you say you will)					
25. Persistence (finish what you start with dispatch and thoroughness)					
26. Good organization of your personal possessions					

WHAT IS YOUR SELF-CONCEPT?

Evaluate Yourself Realistically

As a counselor, you will be expected to zealously fulfill all your responsibilities, and hopefully you will volunteer in other areas in which there are needs that you can capably fill; therefore, it is essential that you seek out and recognize your own capabilities and limitations. When frankly assessing your own strengths and weaknesses, you must acknowledge each of your limitations as well as any special skills, talents, and competencies you may have. This open-minded and frank approach will be noted by others, and there will then be no need for you to go to extremes to either display or conceal what you really are—behavior that is almost universally disliked and would undoubtedly start you off on the wrong foot with your associates.

In order to better assess your potential for success and enjoyment as a counselor, it may be helpful to evaluate yourself using Chart I. Rate yourself by placing a dot in the appropriate column opposite each trait, then connect the dots with a line to achieve your "profile." Try to be honest and objective with each item. Now look at the profile and note your strengths and weaknesses as the line moves from left to right.

EMOTIONAL MATURITY

What is Emotional Maturity?

"When I was a child, I spake as a child, . . . but when I became a man, I put away childish things" is not necessarily true of adults, who sometimes unconsciously cling to childish ways of thinking and acting. Persons who harbor such childish traits are emotionally immature, and, though frequently at a loss to understand why, they are often unhappy, for their behavior keeps them constantly at odds with themselves as well as with their associates, and they often feel mistreated and deprived. Camp directors consider emotional maturity to be one of the surest indicators of a counselor's probable success, for a counselor cannot help campers to mature unless he or she can set an example for them.

Physical and intellectual maturity is not necessarily related to emotional maturity, for even older persons sometimes have not learned to face up to life squarely and to solve their own problems in an adult way. Indeed, a college student may be a straight "A" scholar but may still be unable to apply intelligence to solving his or her own problems or to dealing adequately with other people.

How often have we heard someone say in exasperation, "Why don't you grow up?" What actions and attitudes determine why one person is considered mature while another is not? First of all, mature people realize that every person has wants and needs similar to their own and that everyone cannot always have his or her own way. For instance, if a counselor is determined to do something with a particular friend on a day off, he or she does not sulk, try to get even, or throw a tantrum if unforeseen developments make it necessary for one of them to remain on duty in camp. Mature people try to persuade others to agree with their way of thinking by reasoning with them, not by pouting, wheedling, flattering, or being so disagreeable that others give in rather than suffer the consequences.

When someone with obviously good intentions criticizes us, we should be able to analyze the remark and profit by any truth there is in it instead of flaring up at the thought that another would even hint that we are anything less than perfect. Mature individuals realize that learning to accept criticism is a necessary part of growing up. They have pride and faith in themselves, yet are modest, and do not feel it necessary to excuse every shortcoming they may have. On the other hand, this doesn't mean that we should be a doormat and let everyone walk over us at will, for it is normal on occasion to express anger or resentment about things important enough to us to really matter.

UNDERSTANDING YOURSELF

Are you a well-integrated person who feels secure about yourself and adequate to carry on in your surroundings? Many psychologists believe that feelings of security come to people who from childhood have enjoyed many successful experiences. Eventually these people develop an increasing sense of competence and self-confidence sufficient to meet new circumstances.

Do you really know yourself? If you are an emotionally mature person, you will be able to realistically analyze your own behavior patterns and personality makeup so that you can better understand your own actions and reactions and your own motives and drives as you attempt to satisfy them. This will help you to gain keener insights into others as you recognize in them these same desires and needs and note the similar ways in which they attempt to satisfy them.

OTHER SIGNS OF MATURITY

If you are emotionally mature, you take pride in your ability to influence others, using it always to help them and lead them in the right direction and never misusing it to strengthen your own ego by making willing slaves of any hero-worshiping campers or younger counselors who might be willing to grovel at your feet. Your greatest satisfaction should come from watching young people become increasingly independent, and you don't want to encourage their dependence in order to feel powerful or superior. Instead of trying to run their lives, you concentrate on improving your own. You respect the rights of others and refrain from quarrels and undue anger or grudges. You readily and easily adapt yourself to the routines of camp living and cheerfully accept all camp rules, since you realize that without these rules for group living a few might take advantage and selfishly jeopardize the rights and privileges of everyone else. Most of all, you try your best to be thoughtful of others and considerate of their needs and wishes even though they sometimes conflict with your own.

Perhaps the surest indication of emotional maturity is that people's actions are governed by reason, not by emotions. Chart II can be used for a rough estimate of your overall emotional maturity. Total all scores and divide by 25 (the number of items rated). If you have proceeded objectively, an average of 4 or 5 is quite acceptable, 3 is average and 1 or 2 below average, perhaps indicating a low level of emotional maturity. People who recognize that they have a low level of emotional maturity also are capable of improving themselves. Honestly recognizing your own deficiencies means that you can re-

Chart II EMOTIONAL MATURITY	1 Poor	2 Below Average	3 Average	4 Above Average	5 Superior
1. Can you accept criticism without undue anger or hurt, acting upon it if justified, disregarding it if not?					
2. Are you tolerant of others and willing to overlook their faults?					
3. Do you feel genuinely happy at the success of others and sincerely congratulate them?					
4. Do you refrain from listening to and repeating gossip about others?					
5. Do you converse about other things and persons? Test this by checking your conversation to see how frequently you use "I."					
6. Are you altruistic, often putting the welfare and happiness of others above your own?					
7. Do you refrain from emotional outbursts of anger, tears, etc.?					
8. Do you face disagreeable duties promptly and without trying to escape by feigning sickness or making excuses?					
9. Can you stay away from home a month or more without undue homesickness?					
10. Can you weigh facts and make decisions promptly, then abide by your decisions?					
11. Are you willing to postpone things you want to do now in favor of greater benefits or pleasure later?					
12. Are you usually on good terms with your family and associates?					
13. When things go wrong, can you objectively determine the cause and remedy it without making excuses for yourself or blaming it on other people or things?					
14. When disagreeing with another, can you discuss it calmly and usually work out a mutually satisfactory agreement without hard feelings?					
15. Can you enter into informal social events of many types wholeheartedly?					
16. Do you really enjoy doing little things for others, even though you know they will likely go unnoticed and unappreciated?					
17. Do you dress appropriately for the occasion?					
18. Can you dismiss past mistakes that can't be remedied now without dwelling on them?					
19. Can you be objective about making decisions regarding others?					
20. Do you work democratically with others, neither dictating to nor forcing your will on others?					

(Chart Continued on following page.)

EMOTIONAL MATURITY *(Continued)*	1 Poor	2 Below Average	3 Average	4 Above Average	5 Superior
21. Are you loyal to your friends, minimizing or not mentioning their faults to others?					
22. Are you free from "touchiness," so that others do not have to handle you with kid gloves?					
23. Do you act according to your honest convictions regardless of what others may think or say?					
24. Do you have a kindly feeling toward most people, a deep affection for some, and no unhealthy attachments to any?					
25. Do you feel that you usually get what you deserve? Are you free from a feeling that others "have it in for" you?					

solve to acquire definite skills and interests that have social rather than selfish values.

THE COUNSELOR'S REWARDS

The satisfactions and rewards of camp counseling, as with any other occupation, will vary with the individual and the situation. The degree of effort you put into the job will largely determine what you will receive from the experience.

Although not always the case, camp counselors' salaries are sometimes quite low, especially for those with no experience or special training. On the other hand, lodging and food normally are provided, as well as the opportunity to live in the same environment as the campers who paid for the same privilege. You should not dismiss these benefits lightly. In addition to these benefits, camps sometimes pay for part or all of the staffs' transportation expenses and some provide free laundry as well. An increasing number of colleges and universities offer academic credit for experience as a summer camp staff member. Another advantage of working as a counselor is that there are few needs and little temptation to spend money in camp, making it easier to save whatever cash you do receive.

The value of many benefits, however, cannot be calculated, since they take nonmonetary and intangible forms. As a counselor, you will have almost unlimited opportunities to achieve the objectives of camping for yourself. You will not only spend your time in the out-of-doors, but you probably also will form some very close and lasting friendships with others of all ages, and you will have an unparalleled opportunity to acquire the techniques of successful group living while furthering your own development as an emotionally mature person. You also will

(Willamette Council of Camp Fire, Salem, Oreg.)

have a chance to improve your own skills in camp activities. In addition, counseling offers one of the best possible opportunities for learning the art of leadership and gaining experience in working with people.

As a counselor, you will enjoy helping youngsters grow and mature. In fact, you will experience the same deep and rewarding satisfaction that comes to all good leaders of youth—the knowledge that you have made a real contribution toward developing good citizens who will not only have more zest for living but also will be better prepared to become the leaders of the future.

GETTING A JOB OFFER

The Job Won't Come to You

This statement is important to bear in mind once you have decided you might like to become a camp counselor. Job hunting for camp positions is not always easy, and many people wonder where and how to start. One thing is certain, and that is that an early start is essential. Summer jobs usually are filled by late spring, so the position you want will probably open up sometime in the winter; that is the time when most camps start to advertise their jobs.

There are a number of possible sources for learning about positions, including the following:

1. School placement bureaus.
2. School departments of physical education or recreation, leisure services and park administration.
3. Local camping associations.
4. Municipal social, welfare, and youth-serving agencies, such as Boy Scouts, Girl Scouts, Camp Fire, Inc., YWCA and YMCA headquarters.
5. Private employment agencies and state and federal employment services.
6. Advertisements in newspapers and magazines that feature camp listings and job opportunities.
7. Personal contacts.
8. Current issues of the American Camping Association's *Parents' Guide to Accredited Camps,* which lists all ACA accredited camps in each geographical region.* Also, the ACA's *Camp Job Packet* should be considered.** This special collection of materials includes the center insert (from *Parents' Guide to Accredited Camps*) of the list of accredited camps by region, five camp staff application blanks, and a list of local ACA sections that have a summer placement service. Several ACA publications are also part of the *Packet* and cover topics such as interviewing and careers in camping.

It is important to learn as much as possible about specific camps that are of interest to you. You should read their booklets and, if possible, talk with current or former counselors and campers. Also, pay close attention to such things as location, length and dates of the camp season, general policies, programs, objectives, and types and ages of campers served. If you select camps which are accredited by the American Camping Association, you can be sure that they have met and continue to maintain high standards of camping practices in order to retain their accreditation.

Your Résumé or Data Sheet

All employers are interested in learning as much as possible about their prospective employees; therefore, it would be wise for you to provide such information in a neat and logical order. A one- or two-page summary can be developed along the lines of the sample résumé presented in Chart III, or you may wish to develop your own format. At any rate, be sure to reproduce copies if you anticipate a need for them.

Before filling out a data sheet, analyze your experience and ability by asking yourself:

1. What have I successfully accomplished and for what achievements have I been commended?
2. What jobs have I held?
3. What specific skills do I have that are appropriate for a camp leadership position?
4. What are the things I really like to do as well as those things I don't like to do?

---

*Available from ACA, Bradford Woods, Martinsville, Ind. 46151.

**Also available from ACA for $5.95.

Chart III

PERSONAL DATA SHEET (RÉSUMÉ)

IDENTIFICATION:

Name ____________________

Permanent address ____________________ Permanent phone number ____________________

Present address ____________________ Present phone number ____________________

Position(s) applied for (in order of preference) ____________________

VOCATIONAL OBJECTIVES:

(Describe your short- and long-range plans.)

PERSONAL DATA:

Date of birth ____________________ Height ____________ Weight ____________

Mo. Day Year

Father's name ____________________ Father's occupation ____________________

Mother's name ____________________ Mother's occupation ____________________

Ages of brothers ____________________ Ages of sisters ____________________

Religious preference ____________________

Physical limitations (if any) ____________________

EDUCATION:

(List in reverse chronological order.)

Colleges attended	Years attended	Graduated
____________________	____________	____________

High schools attended	Years attended	Graduated
____________________	____________	____________

Major field of study ____________________ Minor ____________________

Scholastic standing ____________________ School honors and activities ____________________

Special training (Include special courses you have taken, such as camp counseling, sociology, psychology, human relations, education, music, physical education, mental health, first aid, aquatics, arts and crafts, journalism, creative writing, geology, astronomy, dramatics, or ecology.)

____

WORK EXPERIENCE:

Present occupation ____________________ Years employed ____________

TYPE OF WORK PERFORMED:

(Start with present position and record employment data in reverse chronological order with dates employed and type of work.)

____

OTHER INFORMATION:

Special skills and hobbies ____________________

Travel, knowledge of foreign languages, etc. ____________________

Community activities ____________________ Other ____________________

REFERENCES:

(Give the names and addresses of three references [teachers, youth leaders, previous employers, and the like] who know you well and can speak authoritatively about you; be sure to secure their permission before listing them.)

____

Letter of Application

Since you should include the résumé or personal data sheet with any letter of application, it is neither necessary nor desirable for the letter to be lengthy; however, the personal letter should briefly explain why you are attracted to a particular camp and also describe those qualities you may have that will enable you to make a contribution to it.

A well-written (preferably typed) application letter is quite important and well worth your time and best efforts, since it may be influential in opening the door to future contacts and perhaps eventually may lead to a personal interview. Evaluate yourself honestly and avoid overstating your abilities or experience, for you, as well as the camp, will be the loser if you step into a job you can't adequately fill. Be specific in all your statements, especially as to the kind of job for which you are applying. Keep it brief, clear, concise, interesting, courteous and convincing. Address it to the proper person and enclose a stamped, self-addressed envelope to make it easy for a reply.

The Interview

Employers are as concerned about your personality as they are about the factual information you include in a résumé. When two applicants have approximately equal qualifications, the interview usually determines who will get the job. If you are invited for an interview, remember that you are presenting a valuable product: yourself. As with any merchandise, a product always sells better when it is attractively packaged. Thus, it is important to have a neat appearance as well as a clear and alert mind. Be prepared to talk about yourself in terms of the needs or requirements of the camp director. What do you have to offer that would make you an asset to the camp? Why do you want to be there, and why will the director be glad to have you? Have you thought of pertinent areas in which you want to obtain further information such as:

1. The philosophy and program structure of the camp.
2. The camp setting itself and its location.
3. The exact dates on which your job would begin and end.
4. General camp policies.
5. Does the camp specialize in particular activities such as aquatics, riding, or arts and crafts, or does it instead provide a balanced general program?
6. What living quarters and conditions are provided for staff? (Will you share a cabin with other staff members or be expected to live in the cabin with your campers?)
7. What is the age group with which you will be working?
8. What are the regulations regarding time off, smoking in camp, the use of alcohol in and out of camp, having your own car, etc?
9. What will be the remuneration, including possible transportation fare to and from camp, laundry services, use of camp equipment and extras such as riding and boating privileges?
10. What will be your definite responsibilities and duties on the job? Most reputable camps usually will be able to furnish you with such information through a definite and detailed written job description. Ask about it. (For a more detailed discussion of the job description, see Chapter 5.)

Throughout the interview the camp director will be evaluating your maturity, cooperativeness, physical and mental alertness, motivation, enthusiasm, and any other qualities that will help in assessing your willingness to work and your ability to get along with others (see Chart II).

ACCEPTING A POSITION

If you receive an offer of a position, do not accept it until you are reasonably sure that the camp's philosophy is sufficiently compatible with your own to enable you to give it your utmost loyalty and devotion. Now is the time for you to clear up all questions and doubts, for after having accepted a job, you have assumed obligations that you must fulfill. If you have applied to several camps, and receive an offer from one before you have heard from others in which you may be interested, it is entirely appropriate to call those camps that have not yet replied to determine the status of your application. Don't feel shy about inquiring; your honesty and initiative usually will be appreciated. Answer all correspondence promptly, since the director may lose

SOME DO'S AND DON'T'S IN SUCCESSFUL INTERVIEWING

DO'S	*DON'T'S*
1. Be prompt, neat, courteous, and appropriately dressed.	1. DON'T arrive late and breathless for the interview. Be a few minutes early to allow time to compose yourself.
2. Act naturally; be poised and friendly and remember to smile.	2. DON'T be extreme in mannerisms, grooming, or dress (no smoking or gum chewing).
3. Try to overcome nervousness or shortness of breath. (It may help to take a deep breath and sit back comfortably in your chair as you talk.)	3. DON'T display a passive or indifferent attitude.
4. Answer questions honestly and straightforwardly.	4. DON'T be overaggressive or inflexible.
5. An interview is a two-way street, so feel free to ask for information about the camp and its policies.	5. DON'T become impatient or emotional.
6. Recognize your limitations.	6. DON'T make claims if you can't deliver on the job.
7. Indicate your flexibility and readiness to learn.	7. DON'T be a "know-it-all" or a person who can't take instructions or suggestions.
8. Make yourself clear and be sure the interviewer understands what you mean; enunciate clearly and use good grammar and sentence structure.	8. DON'T speak indistinctly or in a muffled voice. Keep your head up and look directly at the employer as you talk.
9. Modestly point out the specific contributions you can make to the camp.	9. DON'T show undue concern about salary.
10. Give the employer an opportunity to express himself or herself and listen closely to what is said.	10. DON'T unnecessarily prolong the interview. Watch for signals that indicate that the interviewer is ready to conclude the interview, and leave promptly unless you have a reason for lingering.

other desirable applicants while you are trying to make up your mind. A signed contract is your word of honor that you will arrive on schedule, prepared to carry out your agreements to the best of your ability.

After returning the signed contract, you will, in all probability, receive various literature and correspondence from the camp. Read each carefully to better orient yourself and fix pertinent details in your mind, for this will help you to learn more about the camp. You should now prepare yourself to assume your duties. If possible, enroll in, or at least audit, helpful school courses and study any general camping books and materials in allied fields that are available in your school or community library. If you want to start your own camping library, you can find many worthwhile books, pamphlets, and articles available free or at modest cost. One of the most helpful things you can do is to start a camping notebook in which to jot down useful information and helpful ideas that come your way. A looseleaf cover, holding sheets 3¾ by 6¾ inches, is suggested, for it is a convenient size for recording and is small enough to carry with you on trips or at camp. Take advantage of opportunities to gain further experience in working with groups of children.

ADDITIONAL READINGS

(For an explanation of abbreviations and abbreviated forms, see page 13.)

A Guide for College Credit for Camp Field Experience. ACA, 1970, 6 pp., paper.

Camp Counseling Is Channel Number One. ACA, paper.
Camp Job Packet. ACA.
Camp Staff Job Descriptions. ACA.
Careers in Camping. ACA, 1972, paper.
Dudley, Geoffrey A.: *Your Personality and How to Use It.* Emerson, 1962.
MacKay: *Creative Counseling for Christian Camps,* ch. 2.
Parents' Guide to Accredited Camps. ACA, issued annually. (Lists all ACA accredited camps in each geographical region.)
Rodney and Ford: *Camp Administration,* chs. 6, 7, Appendices B, C, D, F.
Shivers: *Camping,* ch. 2, ch. 6 to p. 126.
Van Krevelen: *Children in Groups: Psychology and the Summer Camp,* ch. 9 to p. 123.
Webb: *Light From a Thousand Campfires:*
Allen, Hugh: "Let's Take Stock," p. 198.
Graham, Abbie: "On Being a Counselor," p. 150.
Joy, Barbara Ellen: "It's Fair to Expect," p. 157.
Link, Dr. Robert: "What Makes a Good Counselor?" p. 162.
Sharp, Dr. Lloyd B.: "The Campers' Prayer," p. 201.
Woal, S. Theodore: "Yours Is a Tough Assignment," p. 154.
Welch, Emily: *Its Fun to be a Counselor.* Ass'n Press, 1956, 63 pp.

Magazine Articles

Camping Magazine:
Bachert, Russel E.: "Quality of Program Depends on Preparedness of Staff." Jan., 1980, p. 8.
Ballentine, A. Cooper, and Lois Orr: "The Camp Leaders We Seek—And Those We Avoid." Jan., 1965, p. 17.
Brackeen, Margaret E.: "Some Questions Camp Directors Should Ask to Insure Good Staff Selection." Apr., 1973, p. 9.
Perry, Marion L.: "Camp Counselor Selection." Feb., 1964, p. 22.
Roberts, Kenneth: "The Fringe Benefits of Camp Counseling." June, 1964, p. 22.
Shelienberger, Don: "Strong Staff: The Key Ingredient." Apr., 1977, p. 6.
"Staff Recruitment." Jan. 1979, p. 38.
Steinman, Richard, Ph.D.: "From Campus to Camp—the Counter-Culture Is Imported." Feb., 1972, p. 12.

five
The Counselor on the Job

A great deal of the joy of life consists in doing perfectly, or at least to the best of one's ability, everything which he attempts to do. There is a sense of satisfaction, a pride in surveying such a work—a work which is rounded, full, exact, complete in all its parts—which the superficial man, who leaves his work in a slovenly, slipshod, half-finished condition, can never know. It is this conscientious completeness which turns work into art. The smallest thing, well done, becomes artistic.

—WILLIAM MATHEWS

In this chapter we shall survey some of the general aspects of a counselor's duties. Please study the chart in Figure 5-1 to gain an overall view of the general staff organization.

Figure 5-1 shows the lines of responsibility in the typical staff organization of a large camp. There may be many variations on it as each camp tailors its own plan, adapted to its own size, the capabilities of its staff, its individual program and facilities, and the objectives and personal preferences of the director or sponsoring agency; for instance, a director may prefer to assume some of the duties shown here as delegated to the assistant director.

The chart, however, does give an overall view of staff organization and indicates lines of authority and the particular staff member to whom each person is directly responsible. Note that there is one individual in charge of each of the five main areas of health, food, program, maintenance, and business, and that each is directly accountable to the director for the conduct of his or her particular area.

THE CAMP STAFF

Camp Director

You will note that the camp director is at the top of the chart. He or she is the highest authority in camp and is ultimately responsible for everything that occurs there. All staff members are accountable to the director, even though they may be under the immediate supervision of someone to whom the director has delegated responsibility. There will be general camp policies and rules to cover routine procedures, and those in charge of a certain area may be authorized to make important decisions in that area; however, every other decision of major importance must be referred to the camp director for final approval and consent.

The director basically is responsible for the welfare of each camper and staff member and carries out these responsibilities through the abilities and training of the staff, as well as through the camp rules, philosophy and objectives and the methods used to carry them out. Obviously the director must be a person of diverse abilities, since he or she serves simultaneously as an administrator, financial wizard,

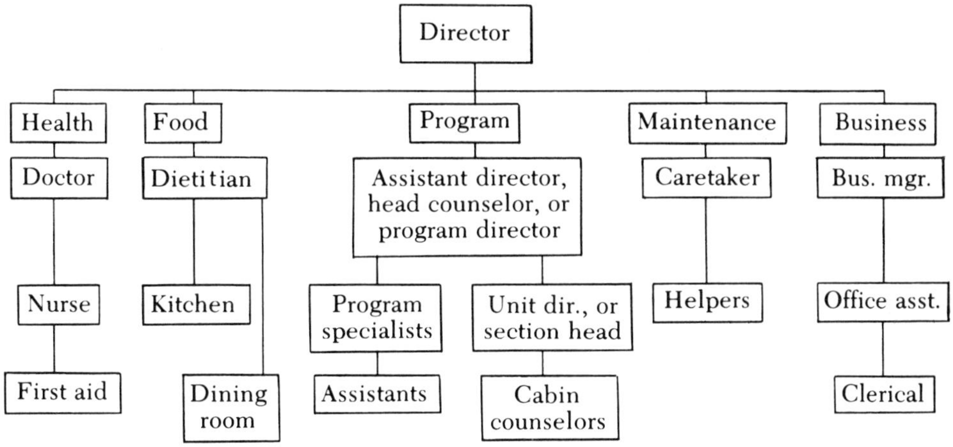

Figure 5-1 A camp staff organization chart.

child welfare expert, educator, recreation director, and advisor to counselors and other staff members.

Since the director realizes that a camp can be only as strong as its staff, he or she tries to obtain the best personnel available. Then, to obtain the optimum in total team performance, the director must recognize the inherent potential of each team member and help each to develop and use his or her abilities to best advantage in combination with whatever physical and natural resources the camp offers. At the same time, the director must realize that each staff member also has needs and desires that must be fulfilled.

The director, then, is the hub of the wheel, about which each staff member revolves.

Assistant Camp Director

The person second in position is called by various titles, such as assistant director, head counselor, or program director, and serves as the liaison or coordinator of the whole camp program. This person is accountable to the camp director and works directly with program specialists, unit directors, and sometimes their assistants. He or she is the mainspring of the whole camp, and the morale of both campers and staff is largely dependent upon this person. The specific duties of the assistant director will vary according to the size, philosophy, and general setup of the camp.

Program Specialists or Department Heads

Program specialists or department heads usually are available in larger numbers in long-term camps or those tending toward a more centralized system, though nearly every camp has a few, such as a riding instructor and a waterfront director. They head such specialized areas as equitation, tennis, campcraft, arts and crafts, ecology, sailing, trip camping, music, and dramatics; each may also have an assistant to help carry out the program.

Program specialists may perform their duties in a variety of ways. In some camps, the specialist keeps the work area open at definite hours for any who wish to come, whereas in others, each group is scheduled to come at a certain time. In camps that follow the recent trend of giving each group a freer hand in planning and carrying out its own activities, the group asks for the use of the services and facilities of the program specialist when they require them.

A program specialist may or may not be assigned regular cabin duties, depending on the philosophy of the camp and how demanding his or her special program is. In addition to instructing and advising, the program specialist's duties usually involve requisitioning the supplies needed and seeing that the work quarters and equipment are kept in good condition. He or she also will be held responsible for taking inventory, packing away supplies at the end of the season, and listing supplies needed for the following year.

Unit Directors and Counselors (Assistants)

A unit director, sometimes called a village or section head, presides over a living unit of four to six cabins or tents. Usually under this person are assistant unit heads or cabin counselors in direct charge of the cabins in the unit and the four to nine campers who live in each.

Prior to camp opening, the unit director works closely with the assistants in planning a skeleton unit program for the summer that is suited to the needs and interests of their particular campers. The details of the plan are then worked out and altered, if necessary, with the help of the campers after they arrive. The unit director also works with the assistants to decide such matters as the division of unit duties and time off, and serves as their liaison with the assistant director. He or she must see that the unit program coordinates with the overall program of the camp and with its general objectives and philosophy.

THE JOB DESCRIPTION

A job description is a written statement that spells out the exact terms of employment for a particular staff member and includes not only a detailed outline of a person's responsibilities to the camp, but also the obligations of the camp to the employee. The job description in a particular camp may develop in various ways and may be revised in succeeding years as experience or changing camp philosophy and customs dictate. At the end of a season, the camp administration usually reviews the job description with the employee in order to receive any suggestions he or she may have for ways to improve it.

When applying for a job, you may be shown the job description during your interview; if not, you should certainly ask for it before making your final decision to accept so that you will have a clear picture of what the job involves in specific and written form.

What a Job Description Includes

Job descriptions may be written in many different ways, but all should include the following information:

1. Title of the position.
2. To whom employee is accountable.
3. General responsibilities: degree of responsibility and performance expected.
4. Specific duties.
5. Qualifications: prior training and experience, skills and interests needed.
6. The relationship of the position to other positions in the camp as well as to the camp's total program.

Advantages of a Job Description

A job description aids the camp by (1) helping to recruit staff specifically suited for a particular position; (2) serving to remind an immediate supervisor of exactly what each of the subordinate's duties are in order to avoid having duties overlap or leaving important areas unassigned; (3) serving as an objective basis for evaluating an employee's performance during and at the end of the season; and (4) producing more satisfied and more confident staff members, since each knows just what he or she can expect and what is expected of that person before accepting the job. The job description also serves as a guide for the counselor to follow on the job.

The job description is important to the staff member because (1) it prevents the misunderstandings and confusion that often result from verbal discussions; (2) it informs the person of what his or her particular job entails, where to turn for help and guidance, to whom he or she is responsible, with whom he or she works, their positions in relation to his or hers and how they interrelate; (3) it lends status to a position and helps him or her to take pride in the job; (4) it assures him or her that the camp is efficiently administered and that concern for its personnel is a high priority; (5) it gives him or her something specific to refer to as questions arise on the job; and (6) it helps him or her to plan by supplying definite information about what and when things are expected to get accomplished (for instance, what reports are to be provided periodically and at the close of camp).

THE STAFF MANUAL

Most camps have a staff manual that will be either sent to you before camp opens or given to you soon after you arrive. It is a comprehensive reference book, with specific information and material, that should be studied thoroughly and kept for future reference. It probably will contain information concerning the camp's philosophy and objectives, the history of the camp, the camp staff organization chart, personnel policies and privileges, camp customs, sample record forms, a description of the camp layout with a map of the units and facilities, emergency procedures, policies regarding staff time off and staff use of equipment and facilities, staff meetings, in-camp training procedures, and, *hopefully*, a bibliography of camp library materials available for use when you need help in carrying out various phases of your job.

BEFORE THE CAMPERS ARRIVE

Precamp Training

Counselors and other staff personnel often are asked to report for duty several days to a week or more ahead of the campers. This precamp training session provides a very important orientation period for new counselors as well as a review for returning staff, and gives everyone a chance to get acquainted with one another and to become familiar with the camp site, routines, program, and customs and traditions. You will have a chance to do some planning for the summer, both individually and with various groups, and you probably will be learning or reviewing all sorts of campcraft skills as you go through some of the routines and activities your campers will be doing. You may be assigned some specific readings and may be asked to participate in discussions conducted by various members of the staff. Several unit staff meetings probably will be held in order to plan for your own unit program.

Previewing Campers

You will probably soon learn something of your incoming campers, if only their names and ages. Camp regulations usually require that each camper submit a personal record for use by the camp office and staff. This record contains a great deal of information about the camper, some of which may be of a highly personal nature, which is one of the reasons why the privilege of examining it is often denied to counselors. If you do receive this privilege, be professional and keep its contents strictly confidential, discussing it with no one except authorized persons. Use the information solely to gain a better understanding of the campers before you meet them face to face. If you study it objectively and with that purpose in mind, it may help you to anticipate and prevent future behavior problems and reveal the possible interests and abilities of the camper as well as provide an overall impression of your entire group.

Your wise handling of precamp evaluations will offer a real challenge to demonstrate your maturity and good judgment. Because these records contain only factual information, it is easy for a person examining them to jump to conclusions and form inaccurate judgments based upon single or isolated bits of information. It is also unwise and unfair to assume that episodes that may have occurred during one period of a camper's life necessarily forecast what he or she will do or be at a later period.

If a person previously attended the camp, records of earlier accomplishments and staff evaluations of his or her personality, social adaptability, adjustment to adult and peer groups, and general behavior may be available. Past health records and the health examination reports made prior to camp opening will also be of importance, since it is your responsibility to note any limitations regarding strenuous activities and any allergies or food idiosyncrasies and to see that recommendations regarding them are carried out.

RELATIONSHIPS WITH THE STAFF

It isn't your position that makes you happy or unhappy; it's your disposition.

—AUTHOR UNKNOWN

With the Camp Director

A camp director usually spends long months preparing for the approaching season and is naturally very concerned about its success. Though the director has delegated many duties and responsibilities to others, he or she still retains the primary responsibility for the administration of the camp, and is held accountable for any serious errors in judgment made by the staff. Obviously, the director has a comprehensive view of the whole camp situation, and there are a multitude of details and problems demanding attention. With this in mind, your actions should be directed toward helping to bear the load instead of unnecessarily adding to the director's burdens by making thoughtless, selfish requests or by failing to fully and efficiently carry out all tasks assigned to you.

Neither ask for nor expect special favors, for no administrator can afford to show partiality; you wouldn't like to have others receive privileges denied to you. Obey the spirit as well as the letter of camp rules and regulations. Turn in all required reports on time and be sure they are complete down to the last detail.

Keep the aims and objectives of the camp foremost in mind and direct all your efforts toward their accomplishment. Be conscious always that *camp is for the campers* and that their moral, spiritual, and physical welfare must take precedence over the self-centered desires of any individual or group.

Camp equipment is expensive so it is foolish to waste or abuse it. Since every camp has only a limited budget, the unnecessary destruction of equipment may mean that staff and campers must forego other things they might very much like to have.

Though it will often be difficult, you must be able to distinguish between problems and decisions you can handle yourself and those that you should refer to your superiors for their action or advice. On the one hand, you have been hired because you have a level head and mature judgment; these qualities will enable you to make minor decisions within your jurisdiction instead of passing responsibility along to someone else. On the other hand, you must be quick to recognize major problems that must be referred to the unit head, the camp nurse or doctor, or the head counselor. If the problem is of great urgency or importance, you may even need to take it directly to the camp director.

With Fellow Staff Members

Camping is not only a pleasant and satisfying way to spend the summer months, it is also a way of life and a valuable experience in adapting yourself to living harmoniously in close association with others 24 hours a day. The *esprit de corps* of the staff largely determines the spirit of the entire camp, for no person can be truly happy and do a good job when laboring under disharmony, tension, and vague feelings of insecurity and frustration. Thus, good staff morale almost invariably is the vital component found in every successful camp. Each person should make a conscientious effort to promote harmonious and cooperative relationships. This is essential not only for yourself but also for the well-being of the campers and for the attainment of camp objectives, since campers are quick to perceive any lack of staff unity and, like their elders, will discuss it among themselves and may even take sides in an open feud. A bit of petty gossip or a careless comment can cause the first break in staff morale. Therefore, it is essential to avoid being critical of other staff members.

Camp consists of a blending of many different activities and experiences, and most of the good that is accomplished results from this blending into a whole, rather than from the parts individually. At times this is hard for ambitious, conscientious counselors to remember, for they often become absorbed in trying to conduct their own particular part of the program and, consequently, lose sight of the camp picture *in toto*. Immature counselors often can be spotted by their attempts to vie with each other in attracting the greatest camper clientele; and this, of course, is very short-sighted and selfish and may seriously jeopardize the welfare of both the camp and the campers.

It is important to avoid forming cliques, for such exclusive friendships can damage camp morale and eventually the participants themselves will suffer as other staff members shun them. Returning counselors, who are reuniting after a winter's separation, must be especially careful about this, for in their joy at being together again they may unconsciously exclude new staff members, making them feel lonely and estranged from the rest of the camp family. Socialize in every way that you can, for mingling with many different people broadens your circle of friends and often exposes you to interesting, congenial personalities.

Like most people, you will, of course, want others to like you and seek out your companionship, but don't sacrifice your individuality or principles to gain acceptance. Such ill-gained popularity is shallow and fleeting, and such "friends" often desert you, leaving you lonely and disillusioned about people in general.

Take your job, but not yourself, seriously and be the first to acknowledge your mistakes and laugh at your blunders. Worthwhile personal relationships, *esprit de corps,* and good camp morale are the end products when staff members live by these principles.

WELCOMING YOUR CABIN GROUP

Planning For Their Arrival

If you are a cabin counselor, you will be living intimately with a small group of campers nearly 24 hours a day and will come to know them very well. Remember that decentralized camping came into being precisely to provide this experience of living in a small group in which each member plays an important role and enjoys the feeling of being an integral part of the group, sharing in its work, play, joys, and sorrows just as in a closely knit family. Hopefully, this living arrangement will give each camper a feeling of security and belonging.

Many activities will involve only the small group, yet, like any well-adjusted family, the group will frequently engage in "community" activities with other groups and the camp as a whole. It will be your job to teach your campers to function effectively in both their own and in larger groups, and the proceedings during the first few camp days will be instrumental in setting the stage for this undertaking.

First contacts are most important and largely will determine the attitude of the campers toward one another and you. It is therefore important to plan in some detail what you will do and how you will do it during these first crucial hours and days. Most camps feel that a large share of this time should be spent in the small group, so that the counselor can weld them together and build a climate of "oneness" and loyalty that will instill in each the courage to go out and take his or her place with larger groups.

Some camps wait until the campers arrive before assigning them to living quarters, preferring to wait until they have met and surveyed the entire assemblage. Others feel it is better to make assignments ahead of time, hoping to add to the youngsters' feeling of security by letting them know in advance that there is a definite bed and room ready and waiting for them.

Some camps ask the counselors to send brief notes to each of their campers a few days before they leave for camp. This is often helpful, for campers then can face the new experience more confidently knowing that there is definitely someone looking foward to his or her arrival. You will not want to do this, however, unless someone in authority has approved of it in advance.

When The Campers Arrive

The process of getting the campers settled will differ, depending on whether they arrive simultaneously, or come singly or in small groups. If all the campers arrive at one time, all staff members should be present together, for many hands will be needed to take care of a multitude of details. If campers dribble in a few at a time, one unit staff member may remain in the quarters as a host to greet the campers, show them their bunks, and help them to get settled. Program specialists and other staff may act as guides, receiving the newcomers, assigning them to quarters, and keeping an accurate record of who has checked in. Spare staff or returning campers may act as "runners" to help the new arrivals with their baggage and show them to their living units. A staff member may be assigned to meet those coming by train, bus, or plane at some central gathering place and to care for their needs during the trip to camp.

As a guide to your conduct at this time, imagine yourself as a small child leaving your parents, friends and familiar surroundings, perhaps for the first time. You probably would be overwhelmed by feelings of excitement and anticipation that are tempered by uncertainty and anxiety. At a time like this, it is reassuring to be greeted by a friendly counselor who tells you his or her name and makes a genuine attempt to help you get settled. Always remember that it is a boost to anyone's ego to be remembered and called by name. This is one of the secrets known and practiced by those who have the knack of quickly making friends and establishing rapport with them.

It is important for counselors to introduce campers to each other and see that each is provided with a name tag that can be read easily from a distance. Getting everyone started on a first-name basis breaks down barriers and helps to start things off in a spirit of friendliness.

Encourage a camper to unpack, put his or her belongings in a personal storage place, make up a bed, and get into comfortable camp clothes. All of these tasks help to make the camper feel at home and settled in for a long stay. This also helps to dispel the arrival's first instinct to turn away from the unknown and unfamiliar and run back home. As long as the bags are still packed, it is all too easy for the new camper to yield to his or her fears and latch onto any excuse to return to familiar surroundings.

The camp director probably will have provided each camper with an inventory of items to bring to camp. As the campers unpack their baggage, ask to check off each item when it is unpacked and, if there is a discrepancy, report it to the camp office. The inventories also should be filed in the camp office to use later when it is time to pack to return home. It is likely that the director also has requested that campers mark their belongings with their names prior to coming to the camp. You should check to see that this has been done, for children often leave things lying carelessly about, where they remain unidentified and unclaimed after all have departed at the end of the season.

Camp policies usually require that all campers' medicines and first aid equipment be collected and turned over to the nurse or doctor, for it is advisable to have anyone needing medical attention, no matter how minor, referred to the professional in charge. Unless specifically directed otherwise, you, the counselor, should not give any kind of medical treatment except first aid in a real emergency. Another common procedure is to collect return trip tickets, money, and other valuables for safekeeping in the camp office or other designated place.

All campers usually check in with the doctor or nurse soon after their arrival and then meet with the waterfront staff to be classified according to swimming ability and to receive a preliminary briefing about swimming procedures and the use of boats and canoes. Be sure to have your group report at the proper place and time during this unusually busy period.

Veteran campers placed in a cabin unit with neophytes can become a problem. If they are aggressive, the veterans may become bossy or dictatorial and may try to run the cabin for you, or they may try to play practical jokes on the newcomers. Such showing off might well be an attempt to gain what they consider to be their rightful recognition and to cover up underlying feelings of insecurity. Their needs often can be satisfied constructively by having these campers assume various responsibilities, such as helping newcomers unpack and get settled, showing them around the camp, preparing and passing out name tags, or running errands. Use discretion here, for delegating too much responsibility to some individuals can make them insufferably conceited, while others will experience feelings of failure if the responsibilities given them are more than they can handle. Keep yourself tactfully but firmly in charge and in full control of the situation, welcoming all campers and using the services of the returning campers as much as is reasonable.

When the parents do not bring the child to camp, it is a good idea to have the child write a card to go out in the first mail to tell them of the safe arrival. A worthwhile gesture on your part is to write the parents a short note within a day or two in order to establish rapport with them and to assure them that their child is in good hands.

As the occasion presents itself during the day, bring out some of the main points of camp life, such as mail call and basic camp rules, and discuss with your campers their importance to the general welfare of the camp family. Campers don't resent reasonable rules if they understand the reasons for them, so approach the subject from that angle. Ask them to figure out the reasons for the rules; you'll be surprised at how well they do. If possible, let youngsters help to formulate some of the rules that will affect them; this will help to give them a sense of responsibility for and participation in the camp community. Since the word "rules" often carries a negative connotation and may arouse antagonism and resentment in some, you may want to give them a more innocuous name, such as "guidelines," or "camp customs."

Developing Group Unity and Feelings of Acceptance

As soon as most of your campers are settled in and seem ready, proceed with some activities you have planned to break the ice and get them on easy terms with one another. This may be a good time to play some sure-fire fun games or to take them on a tour of the camp, and pointing out points of interest. You may want to pair them off, using the "buddy" system in which each camper stays close by a buddy for a designated period; this establishes stronger bonds with at least one other person.

When it seems appropriate, launch into a brief, informal group discussion, suggesting exciting adventures they may want to plan for the near future or long-term projects to think about now and decide on at a later date. Notice that we said *group* discussion, which means encouraging each and every one to contribute. Try to generate enthusiasm and present word pictures that will leave each camper starry-eyed and dreaming of the many happy times to come. This will help to keep their minds occupied and crowd out the feelings of homesickness and loneliness that are particularly likely to appear as night draws near. Work hard at this, for it also will give you a chance to establish yourself as a forceful, understanding leader who is as anxious as they to fill each day with excitement and fun. Keep your initial long-term plans flexible so that they can be altered as the group gets acquainted and becomes more aware of the possibilities of the camp, but make detailed and definite plans for the immediate future instead of waiting for chance inspiration.

Before the first meal, discuss dining room procedures and give campers an idea of what to expect. Later on, as the need arises, you can delve more deeply into dining room conduct and table manners. Stress the importance of cleanliness and being well groomed at all times, especially when in the dining room. Ask returning campers to volunteer to wait on tables and carry out other duties until newcomers have had a chance to observe operations and become familiar with procedures.

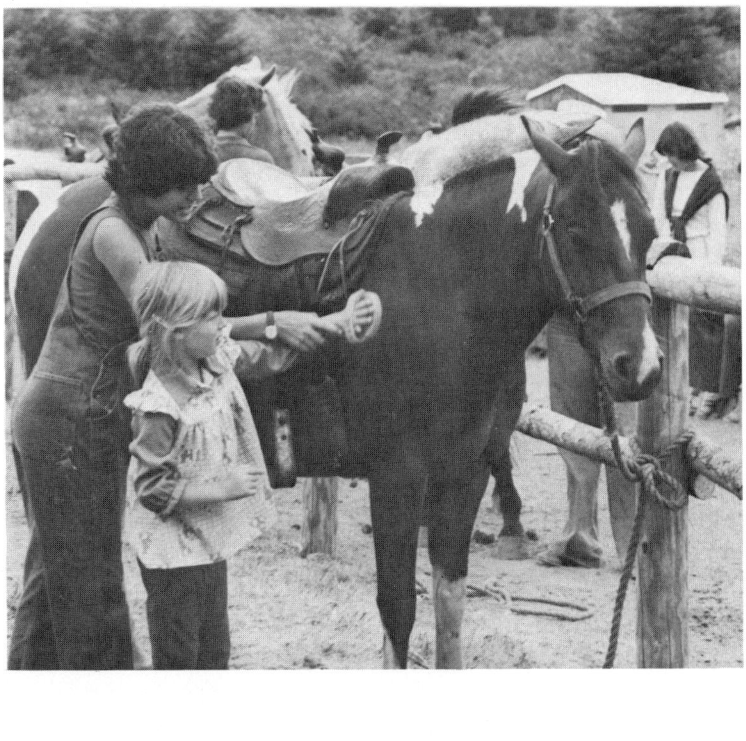

(Willamette Council of Camp Fire, Salem, Oreg.)

The First Night

Some camps have an all-camp council ring or other all-camp meeting on the first night to give everyone a chance to see the whole group and have the entire staff introduced to them. At this time, the staff may put on a skit or other entertainment to introduce themselves in a more informal way. Other camps prefer to arrange for unit or cabin programs, believing that a camper should become well acquainted with the small group before tackling the large one.

The time just before taps is a critical one, and that is when new campers need a little extra attention from you. Arrange for an early bedtime, for most of the group will be more tired than they realize from the day's emotional strain and excitement; it may be desirable to have them wash and perform other bedtime rituals before dark. Personally check to see that these chores are performed adequately. Leave some time for a short evening discussion or a bedtime story before lights out. Explain the procedure for morning rising and breakfast, and stress that taps is the signal for complete silence, with everyone in bed and ready for sleep, so that they can arise rested and fresh for a new day of fun and excitement. Take a little extra time this first night to show each of your campers that you are interested in them as individuals and to assure them that you will be nearby. Remember that these children may never have camped before, and even the small rustlings in the dark, such as a tree creaking in the wind, may be quite alarming in the unaccustomed stillness of an outdoor environment. Young children in camp for the first time often are encouraged to bring a precious, familiar toy or possession with them to give them a feeling of security at this crucial time.

Those Important First Days

Set a shining example from the start, for your charges will model their behavior on yours. Be the first out of bed in the morning to check on the weather, and advise campers how to dress accordingly; greet your sleepy-heads with a friendly "hello" and a smile as they arise, and, instead of dwelling on inconsequential irritations, keep yourself in a positive frame of mind by reminding yourself and your group of how fortunate you are to be spending this time in a wonderful outdoor setting. Maintain an outward optimism, even though it hurts sometimes, and try to see the funny side of things; joking and good-natured banter can help to start the day on a cheerful note. Perform the morning routines of washing, brushing teeth, and combing hair with dispatch. Campers and counselors who have gone to bed on time find it much easier to be cheerful and alert; if you find yourself with the disposition of a bear you need to decide whether those late evening hours are really worth it.

Campers like to have you join them in their morning routines, and this makes it easy for you to see that each practices proper habits of cleanliness and good grooming. Encourage those who awaken early to read or write letters so that they will not disturb others.

Homesickness is particularly likely to occur during the first few days of camp, and one of the best ways to forestall it is to get individuals deeply involved in things that absorb them. Constantly plan exciting adventures for the future so that there is always something to look forward to. If you spend some extra time with campers during the first few days and work hard to achieve a spirit of friendly camaraderie and cooperation, it will be easier to maintain this spirit throughout the summer.

Seize every available opportunity for informal chats, for there is no better way to get to know your campers and to find out why they came to camp, what their hobbies and interests are, and what they have looked forward to experiencing in camp. Listen attentively to campers' chatter, for, being wholly unplanned and uninhibited, it provides real insight into their current hopes, plans, interests, capacities, and ambitions. Initiate conversations with your campers, individually and in groups, so that you feel at ease with each other; make a special effort to include "loners" and "misfits." These conversations also will give you an opportunity to spot any camper who shows a tendency to stir up trouble or dissension within the group.

Don't try to tell your campers everything about camp customs at once, but gradually introduce them to such things as camp *kapers* (camper duties). Work out a rotation system for keeping cabins and unit quarters neat and clean, as well as planning for each camper to contribute his or her share to the upkeep of the whole camp. Pres-

(C. Coutellier, Detroit Area Council of Camp Fire)

ent information as the need for it arises; ears are much keener and minds more receptive when an individual sees that what is being presented can be put to use right away. As the days pass, appropriate occasions will arise to inform your group about such matters as camp traditions, programs, special events, camp government and how it works, waterfront procedures, fire drills, safety and health practices, and sick call.

Each unit or cabin should have its own bulletin board for posting timely material such as schedules, notices, "A Thought for the Day," and poems written by campers. A committee may supervise it, planning what is to appear, taking down outdated material, changing material frequently and seeing that it is arranged attractively.

One of the first things campers will want to do is to make their living quarters comfortable and attractive. By all means let them help with planning what is to be done, for the work then becomes more interesting and keeps them happily occupied. This is usually such a worthwhile project that some camps strip the cabins quite bare and tear down all the things the departing campers have built in order to give the incoming campers the thrill of planning their own cabin furnishings, decorations, and other camp trimmings, such as crate tables and chairs, lashed wooden clothes pegs and rustic clothes hangers, wall plaques and other objects. The campers can also devote their energies to cleaning the unit grounds. Safety may call for removing such hazards as glass, pieces of metal, and protruding tree roots. Stones make a decorative border for paths, and many other "improvements" will suggest themselves once the campers get started.

Before long, your group will probably want to plan a menu and program for a cookout and, if casually steered toward a good spot you have previously located, they will soon see its possibilities as a perfect place for a unit outpost camp. Such projects, interspersed with their other camp activities, will solve your program problems for some time to come.

CAMP HOUSEKEEPING

In General

Since many campers have learned virtually nothing of good housekeeping practices at home, you may need to demonstrate and give specific help with techniques. Right after breakfast is a good time for the whole group to straighten up the cabin and adjacent unit area; campers may also be expected to help out in cleaning up the entire camp. Make a check list for each job so that the camper will know how to proceed. Your attitude toward camp duties is important, for if you pitch in enthusiastically, your campers will follow suit and soon will learn the satisfaction of having done their work well and the pleasure of living in clean, orderly surroundings.

Most camps have tent or cabin inspection at least once a day, usually unannounced and at varying times, in order to encourage habitual orderliness rather than a periodic tidying up for an inspection. Cabins or units that have met high standards sometimes are recognized or given an award.

Toilet articles and towels should never be borrowed, and other borrowing should be discouraged and is permissible only with the express permission of the owner.

Campers usually are expected to help with various chores such as keeping unit showers, la-

	MARY	*HELEN*	*JEAN*	*SARAH*	*PEGGY*	*JOAN*	*RUTH*
Clean-up squad—sweep cabin floor	Su	M	Tu	W	Th	F	S
Woodsmen—clean out ashes in fireplace, bring in wood	M	T	W	Th	F	S	Su
Table setters—set tables and help prepare vegetables	Tu	W	Th	F	S	Su	M
Hoppers—wait on and clear tables	W	Th	F	S	Su	M	Tu
Ground keepers—clean up campsite	Th	F	S	Su	M	Tu	W
Kitchen police—help do dishes	F	S	Su	M	Tu	W	Th
Unit duty—help at the Unit house	S	Su	M	Tu	W	Th	F

Figure 5-12 A typical kapers chart.

trines, cabins, unit houses, and the main lodge in order, collecting and disposing of trash, helping to prepare vegetables and fruit, setting and waiting on tables, and washing dishes. Counselors should pitch in when their group is on duty to lend a hand and to see that the work is done properly. Cooperate in devising ways to complete the job more quickly and efficiently and discourage tendencies to dawdle.

Let campers help you work out some equitable way to share camp duties. You may work out a rotating kapers (duties) chart such as the one shown in Figure 5-2, or place slips with the names of duties or symbols for them (such as a fork for dishwashing or a broom for cleaning the cabin) in a hat and let each camper draw one out, or conceal them under the campers' plates at the table.

Dishwashing

After meals, some groups may be assigned certain duties such as washing dishes and cleaning up the dining room. These responsibilities usually are rotated among groups, or each table is held responsible for taking care of its own things. Dishwashing and cleanup needn't be dreaded chores. They often become enjoyable group experiences, with campers joking, singing, and telling stories while they work.

You will need to explain the dishwashing process favored at your camp and review it several times. Again, you will of course be there, helping as you check to see that the work is proceeding as it should. You probably will have learned your camp's procedures during precamp training, or you may have received written in-

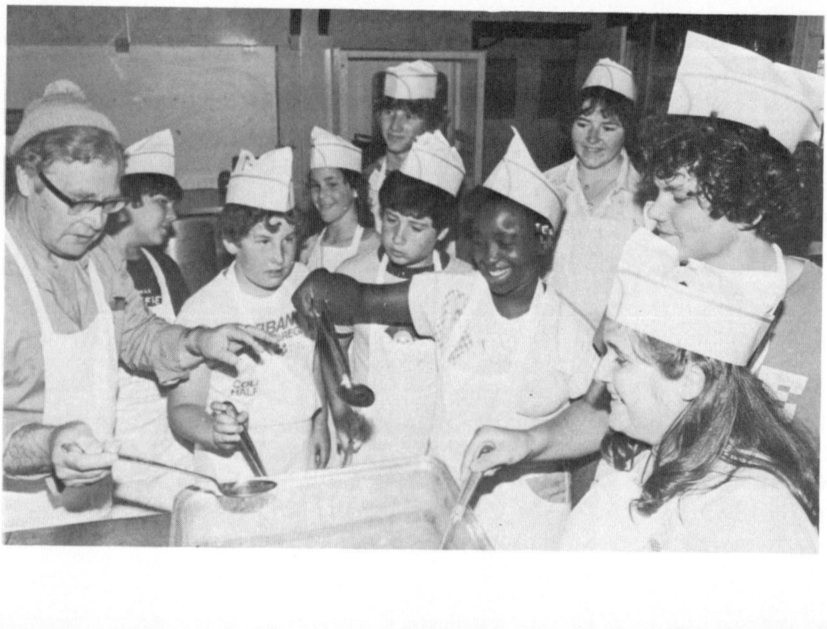

(Camp Kingsmont, West Stockbridge, Mass.)

structions or found them posted conveniently near the dishwashing area.

DISHWASHING ON COOKOUTS

On a cookout, one counselor, with camper help, should see that water is heating and ready for use as soon as the meal is over. Start washing immediately, for food comes off more easily before it has been allowed to dry. A counselor should always handle hot water when young campers are involved, for they could scald themselves or someone nearby.

Use hot, soapy water and wash in the following order: glassware, silver, dishes, and, finally, pots and pans. Keep enough water heating to replace the dishwater as it gets greasy or cold. Thorough washing and rinsing greatly decrease the number of bacteria on dishes, so, after the wash and rinse, sanitize them by one of the following methods:

1. Place dishes in a long-handled basket or net bag and immerse them in water at 170°F. or hotter. Leave them for at least 30 seconds, or longer if possible; merely pouring boiling water over them is definitely not sufficient.
2. Use a good chemical sanitizer and follow the directions that come with it. After sanitizing, remove the dishes from the hot solution with sterilized forceps, arrange them on a drying rack, cover them with clean cloths, and leave them to air dry. This is more sanitary than drying them with towels, for each swipe of the towel deposits more bacteria on all dishes dried subsequently. The less you handle dishes, the more sanitary they remain; however, you should towel dry silverware and pots and pans that might rust.

DISHWASHING KAPERS

1. *First scraper*—uses rubber scraper to remove food from dishes and places utensils that have held eggs or starchy or sticky foods in cold water to soak.
2. *Polisher*—supplements efforts of first scraper, using paper napkins. If facilities are available, polisher rinses the dishes and stacks them into piles.
3. *Dishwasher*—washes dishes in clean water and a detergent.
4. *Rinser*—arranges washed dishes in long-handled wire dishdrainers or net bags, ready for sterilization.
5. *Sterilizer* (always a counselor)—lowers the containers of dishes into the sanitizing agent and removes them at the prescribed time.
6. *Dish dryer and storer*—removes dishes and arranges them on the drying racks, covering them with clean cloths and leaving them to air dry. (When on a trip, you can place dishes in net bags to lower into the hot sterilizer and hang the bags on a convenient limb or bush to dry.) Wash out the used dishcloths and towels in hot, soapy water and hang them out to dry away from dust and other sources of contamination.
7. *General cleanup person*—cleans the tables and the area around them after the dishes have been covered or put away. Cleans dishpans, sinks and work surfaces.

Keep a close eye on your campers to make sure that the dishes are really clean and sanitary.

OTHER CAMP RESPONSIBILITIES

Dressing the Part

A well-groomed counselor usually sets an example for the campers. If you wear dirty clothes or fail to stow your extras away neatly, what can you expect from your campers? Like you, they should wear clothing appropriate for the weather and the activity. Since mornings and evenings usually are cool, extra clothing will be needed at these times.

For obvious reasons, campers should wear shoes at all times, and these should be appropriate for the activities in which campers are participating. In addition to keeping an eye out for proper shoes, you will also need to watch for the camper whose big toe is peeking out of an undarned sock or whose pants or shirts are missing buttons. Young campers may not have an inkling as to which end of a needle the thread goes through, and you will have to show them.

One of the greatest benefits of camp may be to show campers how pleasant it is to live among neat, clean people in rough and rustic surroundings. They will realize, too, that with so many living together in such close quarters, chaos will result if each person lets things stay where they have been dropped when he or she is through with them. The topic of an early group discussion may be how to utilize facilities efficiently, with each possession having a "home base" so that no time is wasted in looking for it.

Health

Being at camp is no excuse for disregarding personal health, especially in respect to cleanliness. For instance, it is not uncommon for various skin eruptions and infections to result directly from a camper's unhygienic practices while at camp. A swim is no substitute for a daily warm shower or bath. Even on backcountry trips, a wash pan can be used if no other facilities are available. Hair should be washed at least every week, and the counselor should help if necessary. See that campers use fresh towels and washcloths as needed and, of course, they should never use anyone else's. See that towels and washcloths are hung out to air and dry after use. Casually inspect campers daily for cleanliness, and inconspicuously call any deficiencies to their attention.

Impress upon your campers the importance of washing hands before eating and after going to the toilet and see that they brush their teeth each morning and again before retiring. Also see that they put on fresh clothing each day and collect and place soiled garments in the proper place. Youngsters are often inclined to stuff wet clothing or swimsuits in a corner, under the bed, or in a suitcase or laundry bag in their rush to get on to something else, so be sure that they hang them out to dry. Further, it is necessary to make sure your campers rotate wearing the clothing they have brought, for youngsters often have a few choice garments they put on day after day, never completely unpacking all the things they have brought with them.

Cabins, units, or whole camps often enjoy a special cleanup day when everyone washes clothes and helps to clean the cabins and grounds. These cleanup days can help foster a spirit of fun and camaraderie as each camper learns to be self-sufficient while lending a helping hand to others. Of course, you should be there too, helping with and enjoying these chores.

In addition to ensuring personal cleanliness, you must also work closely with the health staff to protect and maintain the health of your charges, since your proximity to them places you in an advantageous position to note many things of vital importance. What camping objective could be more important than keeping campers in the best of health?

During precamp training, you probably will have become familiar with the health facilities of your particular camp. Most camps have one or more nurses or health specialists on duty and a physician in residence or on call. These health officials have their headquarters in an infirmary that has ample space for campers who are ill or in need of special food, rest, or care. It is also likely that these specialists will provide the camp staff with special instructions or guidelines to assist them in identifying health problems.

Each morning, while campers are dressing, eating breakfast, or doing cabin cleanup, you should observe them for signs of illness or injury and note any symptoms or disorder, such as headache, sore throat, indigestion, sneezing, cough, fever, skin rashes, weight loss, paleness, swelling, cuts or other irritations, and signs of fatigue, such as listlessness, irritability, or excitability. If you suspect a child is injured or ill, send him or her to the nurse immediately. Better yet, escort the person there yourself, for a camper sometimes avoids the infirmary from fear that he or she will be prevented from pursuing a favorite activity, such as swimming. Show the camper the wisdom of taking a few moments now to prevent the development of an illness that could curtail future activities for days or even weeks. Some camps require counselors to turn in health reports each morning so that the nurse can note and call in any camper needing further attention.

When signs of fatigue are widespread in a group, it indicates an overly strenuous program, and a light schedule is advisable for a few days, with extra time provided for rest and sleep. Prevent fatigue by alternating quiet and active pursuits, and see that competition is not carried to the point of overstimulation. Insist on strict observation of hours for rest and sleep.

Most camps send a camper home or to the hospital if an illness is likely to last more than a few days or is of a serious nature. However, minor illnesses may detain the camper at the infirmary or Health Lodge for what may seem like many wearisome hours or days. If those in charge approve, the time will pass faster if a

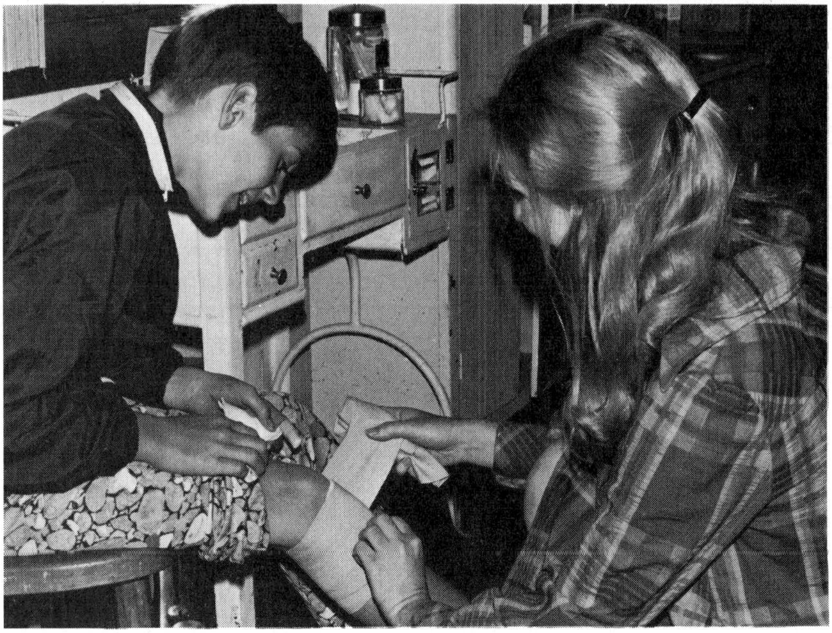

(Cheley Colorado Camps, Estes Park, Colo.)

camper's friends send a small token of remembrance, such as a round-robin letter, an informal diary of what they are doing, an original poem, a small arts and crafts gift, or present a personal serenade from outside. A visit is welcome if the nurse permits; if not, just waving to him or her through the window helps. The particular amusements you provide are not important as long as the camper knows that your group is thinking of him or her.

SAFETY

Your camp probably has established rules and guidelines regarding safety that you will need to interpret to your campers, and, most important of all, you also will need to develop in them a proper attitude toward the whole concept of safety and safe procedures. Camp safety standards are based upon long years of experience, as reflected in state and federal law and in the recommendations of such authoritative bodies as the American Camping Association and the American Red Cross. This again gives you an opportunity to demonstrate your ability as a leader, for if you invariably respect and observe good practices yourself, you will elicit a similar response from campers.

Safety doesn't end with merely obeying established rules, however, but also involves developing a proper state of mind so that you recognize potential hazards, such as bits of broken glass, tin cans with sharp edges, or a board with protruding nails, and are willing to pick them up and dispose of them properly.

Your campers also may show their awareness of good safety practices by spotting such hazards as a jagged stump near the path to the latrine that needs to be removed or tagged with a bit of phosphorescent paint or tape for the protection of sleepy nighttime travelers. Some low overhanging branches may need to be trimmed from a path, or the group may set aside an hour to pick up debris around the swimming area. Know where the fire extinguishers are and how to use them and conduct fire drills and fire prevention discussions with your group. Keep a careful eye on youngsters using knives, axes, or other possibly dangerous equipment, and see that they carry and use their own flashlight at night. When you are about to lead your group in an unfamiliar experience, try to anticipate any possible hazards and brief your campers as to what could happen and necessary precautions to take. Follow up by preventing needless risk-taking and correcting faulty techniques, and, if the welfare or safety of anyone is imperiled, be very firm and insist on immediate response to your directions. Of course, adventure and a certain amount of daring and trying the unknown are desirable adjuncts of the camping experience, and you must not err on the side of caution. As with many other camp problems, a group discussion may enable your campers to work out very creditable standards that they'll more willingly follow since they weren't imposed by someone else.

DINING ROOM PROCEDURES

Assembling in The Dining Room

Counselors and campers should arrive on time for meals, with hair combed and hands and faces washed. Those arriving early often enjoy singing while waiting to enter the dining room, and some camps have developed a tradition of assembling early to sing or carry on some other interesting activity.

Many different plans exist for seating in the dining area. In some cases, campers and counselors simply walk in and sit at previously assigned places, or a counselor will lead an assigned group to a table. The group may be the counselor's regular living unit, or a rotating system may be used to enable each individual to widen his or her circle of acquaintances. A less formal procedure consists of having campers enter the dining room first and fill in camper places at tables as they choose; the counselors then follow and seat themselves at tables, making it a point to choose a different one at each meal. All these methods avoid the melee that often occurs when counselors enter first, followed by the campers who often engage in a mad scramble to secure seats with the most popular counselors.

(Columbine Girl Scout Council, Inc., Pueblo, Colo.)

Meal Time Procedures

Counselors customarily occupy the places at the foot and head of a table, where they can act as hosts, serving the food, seeing that refills are provided as needed, giving second servings as requested, signaling for the tables to be cleared, and so forth. In some camps, campers stand quietly behind their benches or chairs until the counselors are seated, then the meal is opened with a grace, either sung, said in unison or by some individual, or observed silently. With younger campers it is better to serve plates family style, since heavy or hot platters often cause accidents when passed around.

Camps usually serve tasty, well-cooked, and nutritious meals that often have been carefully planned by a trained dietician. These efforts will be wasted, however, if campers are allowed to pick and choose what they eat. Although you must make allowances for food allergies or stipulated special diets, do not accept a camper's word about these, since he or she may be using them as an excuse to avoid eating certain foods. Consult the health staff about problems in this respect, and report a child who is absent from a meal to the proper person. You can allow an individual to ask for only a small portion if he or she really dislikes the item, but insist that something of it be eaten, for in this way the camper often learns to like something he or she has never tasted before or refuses in imitation of an admired older person who has made disparaging remarks about it. Serve small portions, especially to younger campers, encouraging them to clean up their plates before asking for seconds, instead of starting off with large quantities, much of which will go to waste. You can often invent games and otherwise use your ingenuity to encourage finicky or troublesome eaters by such tactics as forming a "Jack Spratt Club" that is open only to those who clean up their plates. You are doing campers a favor when you teach them to broaden their tastes and learn to eat a wide variety of foods. Seconds and even thirds usually are available for those who want them, but only after others, particularly slow eaters, have had their fair share. This encourages good table manners, since there is no incentive to gulp down food.

A crowd of girls usually includes a few "reducers," for, as Franklin P. Jones has said, "Women are never satisfied. They are trying either to put on weight, take it off, or rearrange it." Encourage overweight campers, either boys or girls, to cut down *sensibly* on their intake of fattening foods. Most reducers, however, should be discouraged in their attempts, for camp life is so strenuous that large quantities of energy-yielding foods are needed. Some camps maintain special diet tables for those with idiosyncrasies or those who need to gain or lose weight. In planning cookouts, it is easy to introduce good dietetic practices and to explain the necessity of maintaining a varied and well-balanced diet. When youngsters understand the importance of each item, they usually become quite cooperative about their eating.

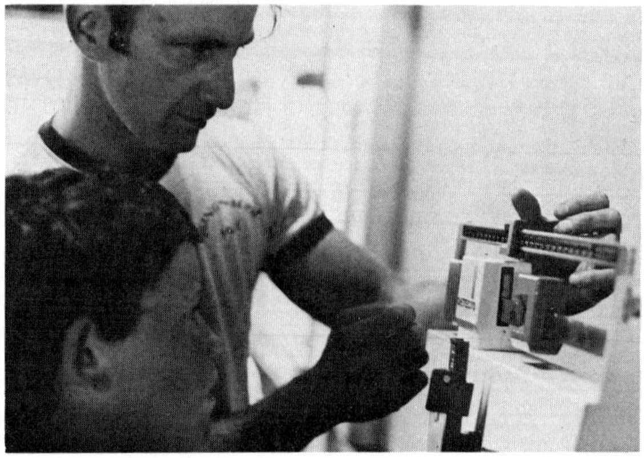

(Camp Kingsmont, West Stockbridge, Mass.)

Dining Room Atmosphere

The dining room atmosphere should be one of leisurely relaxation, with quiet, though sprightly, conversation. As host, you can set the pace for your table by keeping your voice well modulated and by trying to introduce topics of general interest instead of letting a few monopolize the conversation. These conversations can provide good social training, as each camper learns to respect the right of the person speaking to finish what is being said before adding his or her own comments. Keep your voice low as an example, for when a few individuals or a whole table becomes boisterous, others must raise their voices in order to be heard at all, and soon the whole dining room is in an uproar that is most unpleasant to hear. You may want to inconspicuously seat a shy or unpopular child next to you during the first few meals to draw that person out and give him or her self-confidence.

Everyone waits to eat until all are served and the host has taken the first bite. Talking to those at another table is always in poor taste; if you *must* communicate, ask to be excused and go over and speak quietly to the person. No one but "hoppers" leaves the table until all are ready to go; in case of emergency, campers should ask the host to be excused.

Camps have different ways of calling for silence when an announcement is to be made. Some have a pleasant chime, which is certainly better than banging loudly on glasses or the table. Another method that proves quite successful is for the person wanting attention to merely raise a hand; then each person in turn raises his or her own hand and stops talking as soon as the signal is seen. In almost no time at all the whole group is ready to listen.

Good Table Manners

Observe all the precepts of good table manners. Remind campers not to toy with their utensils while waiting to be served, not to talk when the mouth is full, to break bread slices into quarters and butter only one portion at a time, to cut meat a piece at a time as it is eaten, to handle knife and fork properly, to chew food with the mouth closed, and the like. Unfavorable comments about the food and bickering at the table create an unpleasant atmosphere and are strictly taboo. Do not make a public scene when a camper has violated good etiquette. It is usually better to discuss it with him or her privately, since such lapses are more likely to result from a lack of training, being ill at ease, or a desire for attention rather than willful misbehavior. In addition, consideration must be given to differences in children's cultural backgrounds.

After Eating

Each camp usually has a definite system for clearing tables: serving dishes are removed first, then when all have finished eating, campers pass their dishes to the counselor at the head of the table, who scrapes them, stacks them neatly, and signals the "hopper" to clear them from the table. Most camps forbid taking anything edible from the dining hall except on certain occasions when specific permission is given.

Singing songs, especially those requiring movements, distracts slow eaters and interferes with clearing tables, washing dishes, and putting food away. It also detracts from the quality of the singing, since some are still trying to eat and those singing tend to stress loudness instead of harmony and sweetness in an attempt to be heard above the noise of scraping dishes and clearing tables. It is probably better to wait until tables are cleared and then engage in a songfest led by a designated song leader. Obviously, no activity should be scheduled too soon after the meal to prevent campers from racing to get through.

Eating Between Meals

Camp meals are planned to include enough sweets to satisfy normal needs, and campers are consequently not encouraged to supplement them with between-meal soft drinks, candy, and other goodies that may offset the good effects of the carefully planned diet. When snacks are permitted at all, a limit is usually set on the daily amount and should be rigidly enforced.

Watch for the camper who tries to buy quantities of such contraband to bring back from a trip or other expedition, and guard against the promiscuous picking and eating of such things as green apples or berries while on a trip. This is not only a question of health, but also one of ethics when done on noncamp property.

No matter what steps the camp takes, it seems that many parents must demonstrate their love by sending their children treats from home. Some camps warn parents before camp that such food will be returned unless they want to send enough to substitute for a regular dessert for the whole cabin or table group; others simply save the individual packages until there are enough to make a treat for all. It is sometimes effective to encourage parents to substitute fruit or small items, such as a piece of camping equipment, when they feel they must send something to show their affection.

Campers readily understand the reasons for not keeping or eating food around living quarters when you point out to them that ants, flies, mice, and other unwelcome "guests" will be attracted by the crumbs.

(Camp Summer Life, Taos, N. Mex.)

REST AND SLEEP

Rest Hour

Busy camp life makes campers and counselors thankful for the rest hour, which usually comes right after lunch in order to rejuvenate them for the remainder of the day. It is a siesta in which everyone either sleeps or engages in some quiet activity that is restful. These activities can include reading, writing letters, telling stories, playing quiet games or working on a craft project. Stay with your campers to see that they observe this period, and set an example by observing it properly yourself, for you need to recharge your own batteries. Your camp may choose an individual name for the rest hour, such as Siesta or FOB (Feet on Bed and Flat on Back).* The camp that firmly insists upon a proper rest hour is a happier, healthier camp.

Sleep

Camp life is so strenuous that only those who get plenty of sleep can keep up and enjoy it to the fullest. Administering to this need constitutes one of your main responsibilities. As a general guideline, the following amounts of sleep (in addition to the one-hour rest period) are recommended:

AGES	*HOURS OF SLEEP*
6–8	11
9–11	10½
12–14	10
15–17	9
Staff	8

Children, like adults, differ in their reactions to the excitement and busyness of camp life, so some may need rest over and above this amount, while others can do with less.

As previously mentioned, a common mistake has been to try to crowd too many activities and periods of excitement into the camp day. This is especially true as the last weeks of camp draw near and each counselor grows intent on squeezing some highlight of his or her particular activity into a last round of water carnivals, arts and crafts exhibits, horse shows, and whatnot. The wise camp programmer tries to adopt the saner practice of spreading these special events over the entire summer so that campers can leave camp rested and healthy instead of completely frazzled.

*Smith, Billie F: "How 40 Camps Handle Rest Hour." *Camping Magazine*, Dec., 1952.

Children sleep better when healthily fatigued, but moderation is advisable, for too much excitement and tiredness cause fitful and restless sleep. A few individuals seem to run on sheer nerves, so watch for them and help them organize and distribute their time, saving enough for rest and sleep.

Bedtime

The period just before bedtime (taps) usually provides one of the best opportunities for developing group rapport. First come the routine procedures of washing, brushing teeth, and making the final trip to the latrine. Plan to have these taken care of in time to leave a few minutes for group activities, such as evening devotions, a discussion period, planning future activities, inactive games, a quiet bedtime story, stargazing, singing, or listening to soft music before lights out. It is quite important to create the right atmosphere just before your campers go to sleep, for when youngsters engage in roughhousing, horseplay, exciting games, or telling ghost stories, you will have difficulty in getting them to quiet down and go to sleep. Take time to participate with them wholeheartedly instead of hurrying them into bed in order to squeeze out more time for yourself.

Taps is the signal for lights out and absolute quiet. Enforce it from the first night in camp, for allowing exceptions usually leads to a never-ending bombardment of requests for further favors.

Unit counselors usually take turns on night duty in the unit so that some may get away for a little free time. When it is your turn to be on duty, stay there, for if you make a practice of leaving as soon as you think the campers are asleep, they'll "play possum" until you are gone and then bedlam will likely break loose. When on duty in the unit, you will probably be expected to stay in your counselor quarters, which are usually close by. Youngsters need assurance that you are near, ready to help if they become frightened or need you; this is especially important during a thunder and lightning storm. Youngsters should not get up again except for trips to the latrine, which should be quick and quiet, and there should be no disturbance of any kind until reveille. Impromptu moonlight excursions are definitely prohibited, unless planned and supervised as a part of the regular program.

Starting The Day

The rising signal should sound long enough before breakfast to allow ample time for a last stretch, washroom procedures, and putting bedding outside or turning it down to air. When the rising signal sounds, you should be the first out of bed and should see that all arise promptly. This will probably not be a problem during the first few days of camp, for some campers will be so excited they'll wake at the crack of dawn and will need to be restrained so others can sleep. You may need to help younger campers to manipulate buttons and hairbrushes, but encourage them to do these things for themselves as soon as they can.

VISITORS' AND PARENTS' DAYS

Policies

Each camp has its own policies regarding visitors' and parents' days, based upon its own philosophy, the length of the session, the nature of the camp, camp activities, and the ages of the campers. Visitors are always a disturbance to the smooth-running routines of a camp and, for this reason, some short-term camps discourage or prohibit visitors, or plan to carry on their regular activities so that interference is minimized and visitors get a better picture of regular camp operation. Long-term camps of six to eight weeks sometimes set aside specified hours and days for visitation and encourage family and friends to come in the belief that it boosts camper morale and satisfies natural parental concerns. Many camps plan special events for such occasions, such as horse shows, aquatic activities, campfire programs, and sightseeing tours around the camp grounds. If parents must travel a great distance, the camp sometimes sends them advance information about places nearby where they can stay overnight. Inviting parents to eat in the camp dining room or at an outdoor cookout helps to avoid the problem of parents who want to take their child out of camp to eat, a practice most camps disapprove of.

Some camps have several visiting days, so parents can choose the one they want to attend. This provides more flexibility and also avoids having too many visitors in camp at once. Children with no visitors need your attention so that they will not feel left out. Keep them busy by using them as guides to escort parents to their child's living unit or to help to prepare for the coming program.

Preparations for Visitors' Day

Successful visiting days require careful planning and preparation. Campers must be well-groomed and clean, ready to greet their guests and show off their camp and living quarters. You may need to explain to them some of the duties of a gracious host or hostess, such as introducing their guests to the camp administration, their counselors, and fellow campers and taking time to be pleasant to the guests of others. Encourage them to include friends without visitors in some of their activities, although they should reserve some time to be alone with their parents.

The Guests Arrive

Do not dread visiting day, for you probably will enjoy it thoroughly if you enter into it wholeheartedly. Meeting your campers' families lays the groundwork for better understanding on everyone's part. Since you have been serving as substitute parent, friend, and guide to each camper of your group, you will have at least one very important thing in common with parents—the welfare of their child. Step confidently into your role as host and be cordial and friendly to all and available for a short visit with each. Stay near your unit where they can find you, and be on your best behavior, courteous and considerate to all. Parents go home much happier and with a deepened sense of security when favorably impressed by their child's counselors. Be diplomatic in talking with them, remembering that the center of their attention is their child. Comment positively about any good points, achievements, or signs of improvement you have noticed, but be sincere in what you say, for most parents are fully aware that their children fall far short of being perfect, and will be quick to recognize insincerity. Never let yourself be drawn into long, involved discussions and never make unfavorable comments; if parents persist, refer them to the camp director or head counselor. Avoid being monopolized by a few, and share your time equally with all visitors. Since many camps wisely prohibit monetary and expensive gifts to camp personnel, you should closely adhere to the camp's policy on accepting tips from parents.

As guests leave at the end of the day, you often will be faced with severe emotional reactions by campers, some of whom may even want to return home with their families. It is important to plan exciting activities to follow parental departures in order to regain campers' attention and reestablish the normal tempo and atmosphere of camp life.

WRITING AND RECEIVING LETTERS

Each camp probably will have its own letter writing policy, which may require that campers write home regularly, although some leave this up to the discretion of the camper. No matter what guidelines are established, you will find it advantageous to encourage your group to set aside time for this activity. You may be called on for guidance, especially to help your younger campers spell difficult words and master the essentials of good letter writing. Suggest such topics as the activities they have been engaging in, the new skills acquired, new friends, the food, and the weather. Encouraging them to write about the positive side of camp life keeps them from recounting small grievances and unhappy incidents that often are only products of the moment and will be entirely forgotten by the time the letter reaches its destination. These complaints also may be attempts to get attention or sympathy, especially during the first few days of camp when feelings of homesickness and loneliness are common to nearly everyone. Whatever the camper's motivation for writing such letters, they often prove quite upsetting to parents, who magnify their importance out of all proportion and sometimes make long distance calls or come to camp to investigate and take the camper home.

See that envelopes are correctly and legibly addressed and that the letters are promptly mailed, for campers often misplace them and parents soon become concerned. It is often wise to elect a runner to post the letters at the camp post office or go there together as a group.

It can be heartbreaking to a child when he or she consistently receives nothing in the daily mail call. If necessary, bring the problem to the attention of the head counselor or camp director, who may write, or ask you to write, a tactful letter to the parents, suggesting how much it would boost the child's morale if they wrote more often.

RECORDS AND REPORTS

You may be asked to keep various records concerning your campers, including those previously mentioned. Although these often seem like odious chores and a waste of time, they actually are quite important and take only a few moments if you keep up with them. They serve to give the camp director and head counselor a composite picture of what is really happening throughout the camp, and this sometimes proves to be quite important later on.

Written reports mean different things to different people and you should never regard them as just busy work or an extra chore with no inherent value. Unfortunately, counselors are sometimes not told the ultimate purpose of these records and the exact information they should include, so ask for more information if you feel you need it. Here are a few simple, basic rules to follow in writing out reports:

1. Try to be *completely objective* and *impartial* in every statement you make.
2. Record all observations *accurately* and *correctly*. It is better to omit something than to risk being incorrect in important details.
3. If an incident with a camper has produced a strong emotional reaction in you, delay recounting it until you have had time to calm down and look at it objectively.
4. It often helps to include a brief description of the background or social setting in which certain actions took place.
5. Write down unusual behavior that you note frequently in an individual, together with the situations or circumstances that cause or accompany it. Note what you did about it and what resulted.
6. Make your report personal and reflective of your individuality. This conveys more meaningful information to those who read it than a dry, stereotyped report that reflects no real understanding of the child or situation.

You may want to keep records beyond those required by the camp just for your own benefit. Include such things as accounts of the individual camper's activities, reactions, growth, problems, and health. This helps to create a total picture of the camper that enables you or others to understand his or her needs and how to go about meeting and fulfilling them. The reports that the sponsoring agency, camp director, or head counselor send to parents or headquarters are based partially upon your evaluations; therefore, it is important to make your reports in an honest, objective and thorough manner.

Staff members are commonly asked to make a written report of any accident or injury to a camper, no matter how trivial. You usually will be furnished with a form on which to do this, which you should fill out as soon as possible before you have forgotten exactly what happened. Be accurate, and go into some detail and include what was done about it; this may be of the utmost importance if later complications or questions arise.

You may also be asked to submit certain reports at the end of the season, such as an inventory of the equipment and supplies in your unit or cabin or an activity with which you have worked, together with recommendations for additions or changes for next year. Again, devote time and thought to the procedure, for it will be instrumental in helping you or your successor to do a better job next season.

TIME OFF

All camps give counselors some time off—usually several hours each day, and a longer period each week or two weeks. This interlude can and should be of great benefit to both you and the camp. Dealing in such intimacy with many personalities can deplete physical and emotional energy and cause patience to grow short. Counselors sometimes are unaware of a gradual accumulation of emotional and nervous fatigue and become so attached to their jobs that they are reluctant to leave them, even when given time off. Such zealous overdevotion to duty can be a mistake, for sooner or later it will reduce job effectiveness.

It is important for camp staff to get away from their job responsibilities and their campers for an adequate time. The purpose of time off is for you to return rested and with renewed enthusiasm, and it is up to you to plan so that this purpose is accomplished.

If you hold your nose to the grindstone rough,
And hold it down there long enough,
You'll soon forget there are such things,
As brooks that babble and birds that sing;
These three things will your world compose,
Just you, and a stone and your darned old nose!

—AUTHOR UNKNOWN

During your daily breaks you may be allowed to use camp equipment and facilities for your own leisure time enjoyment. At other times you may plan to be away from the camp for a visit to a nearby community. When out in public, remember that you represent your camp and should dress and conduct yourself accordingly. Socially unacceptable conduct is completely out of order.

OTHER DETAILS

Personal Habits

Most camps request that counselors who smoke do so at designated times and in designated places, never in front of campers. Such requests are not based on moral issues, but reflect the example that a sincere counselor would want to present in view of recent medical findings concerning the health dangers of smoking as well as in recognition of the fire hazard created by indiscriminate smoking in rural areas. The use of alcoholic beverages is prohibited on the camp site and often on time off, for even parents who themselves indulge are likely to object to placing their children in charge of leaders who do, and it is probable that drinking will cause unfavorable community reaction toward the camp. Of course, the nonmedical use of drugs in camp is inappropriate as well as illegal.

Loyalty

You owe loyalty first, last, and always to your camp and camp director. You chose this camp above all others because it seemed to be most compatible with your objectives and ideals, but as in any situation, you will find things that are not just as you would wish them. When this occurs, keep your opinions to yourself and think them over for a few days, for you will probably see the situation in a different perspective as camp life unfolds and you get a better picture of the whole scene. If your problem still seems as important, don't complain about it or talk to others who are as unable as you to interpret things from a different perspective or to do anything about them; instead, go to someone who can give you the right answers, even the director if necessary. If you still cannot accept the situation and adjust happily to it, consider asking for a release from fulfilling the rest of your contract, for both you and the camp may be better off if you part company. Never, under any circumstances, criticize the camp to outsiders or other counselors, and, of course, never do so in front of campers. Even when started as good-natured small talk, griping will sooner or later prove ruinous to good morale and also will reflect unfavorably on you.

COUNSELOR-IN-TRAINING PROGRAMS

Conduct of The Program

Many camps conduct counselor-in-training (CIT) programs designed to prepare older campers for possible future positions as full-fledged counselors. Candidates are usually 17 or 18 years old and have had several seasons of successful camping experience. Although they sometimes admit outsiders, many camps use the training program as a means of "growing" some of their own future staff members by choosing outstanding campers with definite leadership qualities and abilities. It is a distinct honor to be chosen as a CIT, since stringent requirements usually are formulated and only those who are deemed worthy of consideration as future staff members are admitted. Each camp has its own standards, rules, regulations, fees, and course content, but most have similar objectives in mind.

The course is carried out on the camp site during the regular camp session and usually lasts over two seasons in order to do justice to all the material to be covered. It is conducted by one or more trained leaders who are familiar with the purposes of the program, their responsibilities as instructors, and proper course content and teaching methods.

Objectives and Values of The Program

A well-conducted CIT program provides an opportunity for the discussion of such topics as camp philosophy, history and development, objectives, program and activities, and the growth and behavior patterns of children at different ages, as well as their varying individual needs and how to understand and meet them.

The program also permits participants to enjoy satisfying experiences with peers while observing the workings of group dynamics. Further, it gives participants the opportunity to perfect or learn new skills and to increase their appreciation of and sense of security in the out-of-doors.

A good CIT program allows participants to work with campers so that they may apply and practice directly the techniques and skills they have been studying. As their skills develop, they are allowed to assume increasing responsibility as they assist in planning and carrying out such camp activities as evening programs, cookouts, song leading, initiating games, planning activities for rainy days, assisting in special areas such as aquatics or arts and crafts, and sometimes living with and working closely with counselors and their cabin group, always under close supervision and with the guidance of an older, more experienced person.

Although CIT training involves hard work, the trainees will find it quite enjoyable. They usually receive special privileges, such as living in their own cabin without a counselor, developing and enforcing their own codes of behavior, and planning their own social programs. Actually, CITs often set the tone of the whole camp, and attract others by their youthful enthusiasm and good cheer. Their special status in younger campers' eyes constantly challenges them to set a good example by adhering closely to all camp rules and regulations, for, because of their proximity in age, their young protégés often adopt them as models and try to emulate their behavior and attitudes. The CIT program is a very important professional undertaking and can be fun and rewarding to the individuals involved.

ADDITIONAL READINGS

(For an explanation of abbreviations and abbreviated forms, see page 13.)

Accident Report Form. ACA, 1 sheet.
Auld, Margaret E., and Graceann Ehlke: *Guide to Camp Nursing.* ACA, 1978, 44 pp., paper.
Bloom, Joel: *Camper Guidance—In the Routines of Daily Living.*
Camp Health Record Form. ACA.
Camp Staff Job Descriptions.
Camper Guidance—A Basic Handbook for Counselors. ACA, 1961, 24 pp., paper.
Ensign: *Camping Together as Christians,* Part I, ch. 3; Part II, ch. 1.
Ledlie and Holbein: *Camp Counselor's Manual.*
Rodney and Ford: *Camp Administration,* ch. 10; Appendices A and E.
Schmidt, Ernest F.: *Camping Safety.* ACA, 1971, 43 pp., paper.
Shivers: *Camping,* ch. 2 and pp. 126–139.
Todd: *Camping for Christian Youth,* pp. 140–144; 151–152.
Van Krevelen: *Children in Groups: Psychology and the Summer Camp,* chs. 6, 7; ch. 9 from p. 123.

Magazine Articles

Camping Magazine:
Borkowski, Richard P.: "A Camp Director Is—" Feb., 1972, p. 11.
Brower, Robert, and Mary Brower: "Group Experience: The Essence of Camping." Jan., 1980, p. 19.
Chenery, Mary Faeth: "Committing Yourself to The Camper." May, 1978, p. 18.
Ford, Dr. Phyllis M.: "Hireth Thou Me for I Shall Do Guidance," June, 1965, p. 14.
"14 Camp Accidents Which Could Have Been Avoided." Jan., 1970, p. 16.
Hansen, Robert H.: "A Structure for Counseling," May, 1966, p. 16.
Jones, Dr. Orville E.: "Does Staff Accept Campers or Just Tolerate Them?" June, 1965, p. 19.
Jordan, Lynn: "Turn-On Teaching at Camp." Apr., 1972, p. 16.
Kaufman, Abraham M.: "When Campers Write Home." June, 1963, p. 7.
Lomen, L. D.: "A Camp Experience Should Leave Time to Learn By Doing." June, 1973, p. 14.
Marley, Dr. William P.: "Sedentary Camper Syndrome." May, 1971, p. 14.
Northway, Mary L.: "Counselors Must Have Ability to *Camp* and to *Counsel.*" Apr., 1964, p. 16.

Putt, Arlene M.: "The Most Important Element in Camping Must Be Our Concern for Camper's Health and Safety." Feb., 1973, p. 20.

Scherer, Barbara, and Dan Heckenberger: "CIT." June, 1978, p. 9.

"Share These Tested Aids to Better Counseling." May, 1965, p. 22.

Shopper, Moisy: "Interpreting Camping to Parents." Mar., 1980, p. 21.

Stevenson, Dr. Jack L.: "Safety Is a Never-Ending Job." Apr., 1972, p. 22.

Thwing, Dr. Henry W.: "Campers Make More Friends If Your Dining Room Seating Is Scientifically Designed to Aid Them." June, 1970, p. 16.

Woal, S. Theodore: "Be Sure to Welcome Campers on That Important First Day." Apr., 1965, p. 16.

Woal, S. Theodore: "Get a Quieter Dining Room With These Practical Ideas." June, 1965, p. 21.

Parents Guide to Accredited Camps, 1980:

Cleaver, Nancy, and Richard Fransham: "Tune in—Learn Child's Feelings About Camp." p. 15.

Sloanaker, John: "Psychologist Suggests Ways to Build Bridge Between Camp and Home." p. 15.

chapter 6

Counselors Understand Human Nature

No one really understands humans except a dog and a sophomore psychology major

-Mary L. Northway

HOW WE INFLUENCE OTHERS

In order to be happy in this world, we must live in harmony with our associates. People who say they don't care what others people think of them are almost always covering up deep disappointment and frustration by pretending to scorn what they really desire—the respect and affection of others. Getting along well with others is most important to you as a counselor, for you will be neither happy nor successful in influencing campers unless you gain their respect, admiration, and cooperation.

The three main components of camp life that have a major effect on the camper's growth and improvement are the camp environment or facilities, the camp program or what is done in camp, and the camp personnel. The last component is by far the most important of the three, for not only do camp staff influence campers by their actions, words, and example, but also it is only through their skillful manipulation of the other two components that the potential of the whole camp experience can be realized. In order to function most effectively in this role, you must understand the needs of campers and how to satisfy them. Since you will be trying to promote the best in camper behavior and attitudes, you must consider the possible ways in which you can influence others.

Let us assume that you have a definite mental picture of what you want to accomplish and are trying to find a way to induce campers to act in accordance with your objectives. One way is to order the campers to do as you wish, and perhaps threaten punishment by withholding something they want, such as a regular swimming period, if they disobey. Although this may bring about the desired action, no lasting improvement in the campers' behavior is likely because as soon as the threat is removed, the campers probably will revert to their earlier behavior and may even resent the experience so much that they may behave worse than before. It may also teach them to dislike and resist authority and anyone who symbolizes it. Campers probably will rebel inwardly but from fear will keep their feelings bottled up inside, their bitterness gradually building until it eventually manifests itself in full force. It is possible that some individuals eventually may come to hate whatever activity you had ordered them to do, despite their initial feelings toward it, because of the unpleasantness of the whole experience.

A better method to accomplish your goals is to persuade people to act in a certain way because *they* want to. When you stop to think of it, almost everything we do is a response to a need or want. For instance, we go to bed because we need to rest; we eat because we want the taste of food or to satisfy hunger; we work because we want and need the things we can buy with the money earned; we practice long hours on a sports skill because we want to be a good athlete or because we seek the social prestige that comes from playing on a team. It therefore seems obvious that it is futile to try to persuade others to do something because we want them to, especailly if they have no interest in it; like everyone else, they primarily are interested in and motivated by their own needs and desires.

What we are saying is that a camp counselor must be able to recognize the genuine needs and interests of a child rather than simply impose his or her values on that child. Don't try to manipulate campers to get them to do what you want; instead, ask yourself how you can work together with the campers to achieve your mutual needs and aspirations. The relationship between camper and counselor requires feedback, including a two-way flow of information and ideas. This process allows the leader to recognize the wants and needs of the followers and then plan activities and programs that help to meet these needs. This quality in a leader can only come about if there is a real understanding and knowledge of people.

Nearly all of us are selfish to some degree and much more interested in ourselves than in anyone else. Therefore, lasting changes in other people's conduct can be made more successfully when we help them realize that such changes will satisfy their wants or needs. For instance, suppose a camper desires to pass an endurance test in swimming in order to qualify for a canoe trip. He or she probably will follow recommended guidelines for eating and rest if it is understood that these are essential for swimming endurance. How much better both the outcome and the attitudes of campers will be if generated by this process than they would have been if you had tried to force adherence to the requirements. Although this example is somewhat simplistic, it does illustrate the positive rather than the negative approach to a problem, and how to use self-motivation to accomplish objectives or achieve desired actions. This approach really works, but you must practice the technique and use it skillfully. Let us repeat this important point: *Help people to do those things that will satisfy their needs or desires.* Now let us consider some of the different kinds of needs and desires common to all people.

THE FUNDAMENTAL NEEDS

Though it is obvious that people are different, they nevertheless are also alike in many ways, and among the things they have in common are five needs (sometimes called desires or wishes) that are common to every normal person. Though these vary in intensity, they are usually so strong and compelling that we can understand almost anything a person does when we recognize it as an attempt to satisfy one of these needs. As we shall see, well-adjusted persons find ways to fulfill their wishes in a socially acceptable manner, but when they can't do so, they may resort to unacceptable ways, since compelling inner demands require fulfillment, no matter how this is accomplished. When these attempts to satisfy needs are carried to extremes, the person often is categorized as a social misfit, a delinquent, or even a hardened criminal.

The Need for Affection

One powerful wish is to be accepted and regarded affectionately by one's friends and associates. Fulfillment of this basic desire can come about when a camper feels his or her peers have accepted him or her in a friendly way. The longing to be loved, appreciated, needed, and missed is universal. When satisfied, people experience a feeling of wellbeing and contentment; when unsatisfied, people are lonely and unhappy. Therefore, we must be alert for the camper who shows dislike for the group or who doesn't want to mix with other campers. The chances are that this person really is miserable and desperately longs to be accepted. You may need to exercise the utmost tact and persistence to penetrate the "wall" that this person may erect, but when you

(Gnaw Bone Camp, Nashville, Ind.)

succeed, the happy, adjusted camper who will emerge will amply reward your efforts.

From the first day, your efforts to build group morale and a feeling of unity and camaraderie are aimed at helping each newcomer to feel wanted and accepted. You may need to take special pains with those who are shy and retiring or who aren't the type others readily take to. Pairing them off with a buddy or getting an experienced camper to take a newcomer in tow are often helpful. The naturally unattractive camper will especially challenge you to search for his or her good points and help that person to fit in. A wise father, consoling his befreckled little daughter said, "I love every one of your freckles because they are you." Find out why a camper is disliked or ignored, then set out diligently to help remedy the situation.

See that your program is broad and varies enough to provide for every youngster's interests and abilities, be he or she an athlete, a musician, a social introvert, a bookworm, or any other species of young human being. Be especially aware of the quiet, retiring youngster who tends to be overlooked and may be hiding a deep unhappiness and sense of loneliness.

A thoughtful counselor can find many ways to satisfy a camper's desire for affection. A friendly "hello," a willingness to listen to their achievements, a pat on the back and a "well done," a bedtime story, or a moment spent seeing that each is tucked in for the night will usually do the trick.

When you notice children who need help, it is best to spare their pride by using an indirect approach and unobtrusively devising ways to draw them into the group. Occasionally it may be best to approach the problem directly and have a frank talk with the isolated camper. Such conversation must be handled skillfully so that you can lead the person to realize that it is his or her own actions that cause others to dislike or shun his or her company. On some occasions, especially with more mature groups of children, it may be best to choose a time when the troubled camper is absent to discuss the situation with them, for they often can help by making a special effort to include him or her in the group. Most children basically are sympathetic and warmhearted and happily change their behavior when shown how their thoughtlessness is hurting someone else. Tolerating and forgiving the shortcomings of others are desirable traits to cultivate, and an alert counselor can do much to facilitate campers' awareness in this area.

A serious case of maladjustment or a continued failure to fit in may necessitate referral to the camp director or head counselor, since leaving the situation to those with insufficient training and experience often only compounds the problem. It may sometimes be best to transfer the camper to another cabin, but this should be a last resort, for much more satisfaction and good result if a counselor can help the child to confront and solve the problem rather than allow him or her to run away from it.

The Need for Achievement

Each of us would like to believe that we count for something in this world. In fact, the need to be successful and to have others believe that we are important is universal, as is the need to exercise control over ourselves and our circumstances. Campers achieve satisfaction when they learn to master a physical skill or to discipline themselves to see a project through to the end. Learning to master the backstroke, or catching and cooking one's own fish dinner are examples of such achievements. Opportunities to perform in a leadership role also provide campers with a constructive outlet for demonstrating control over a situation. Such satisfaction may be realized when a camper serves as chairperson of a committee, steering it to successful conclusion of its duties or persuading others to see his or her way of thinking during a group discussion. On the other hand, a bully may exercise misdirected power and try to control others through fear, or may try to dominate or do the thinking for weaker followers.

The need to achieve can be satisfied in part by an individual's selection and participation in activities that allow him or her a degree of success and personal enjoyment. A feeling of accomplishment gained from one task can be a powerful spur to further accomplishments. Consequently, broad and varied camp activities must be provided that are appropriate to the skill levels of different age groups. A camper can suffer frustration and disappointment when asked to compete with those who are older, who are more experienced, or who have more ability. This is the danger of carrying competition to extremes. One alternative is to deemphasize competition or to reasonably control it; another is to provide activities that are self-testing, thus allowing individuals to compete against themselves. For example, bettering a previous performance or passing standardized tests in activities such as

(Camp Kooch-I-Ching, International Falls, Minn.)

swimming or canoeing, are self-testing. Again, we can see the advisability of having a program that includes something in which *each* camper can experience a satisfactory degree of success.

The Need for Security

The need for security includes freedom from fear, apprehension, danger, insecurity and pessimism. We all want to feel safe and secure in our surroundings and with our associates. Campers, particularly those away from home for the first time, miss their familiar routines and ways of life. They are inexperienced in living with such a large number of other children their own age and associating with strange adults. In situations like this, a camper's security seems threatened, especially if others make unkind remarks, show outbursts of temper, or appear to be cross. Such responses from fellow campers or staff members can hurt a person's ego and reduce his or her confidence and optimism. A young camper may respond in kind, run to someone else for sympathy, or retreat into a shell and brood. The overall effect of a threat to a camper's security may be a bad case of homesickness or even more lasting problems. For instance, some children who are constantly worried and afraid may react by stuttering, wetting the bed, fighting back, criticizing others, or engaging in malicious gossip.

We previously discussed several responses you can make to add to the camper's sense of security. Be friendly and pleasant, but be firm when the need arises, and above all be consistent, for a counselor who is kindly and full of fun one minute and angry or temperamental the next will certainly not impart a sense of security to youngsters.

Encourage your campers to talk freely with you and feel flattered when they disclose their secrets, but never betray their confidences or let them overhear you discussing their personality or problems with others. Establish yourself as a never-failing friend to whom they can always feel free to communicate their hopes and dreams as well as their worries and concerns.

The Need for New Experiences

The desire for new experiences is basic to all humans, for we need opportunities in our lives for thrill, excitement and adventure. Although opposite to the need for security, the desire to do something different and to experiment in unconquered fields is often just as strong a drive, and when it is denied too long it can cause boredom, bad temper, and poor behavior. Varying camp routines and letting campers assist in planning their own programs, including suggesting new and exciting things that interest them, helps to satisfy this need.

Keeping campers busy at activities that give them a feeling of accomplishment is one of the secrets of a successful camp. Being in an outdoor environment naturally provides plenty of opportunities for this, but there are also many other activities to consider, such as camp plays, folk dancing, hobby displays, or a visit from a camp neighbor who has interesting experiences to relate.

Another consideration is to avoid unnecessary rules and regulations that retard or prohibit opportunities for campers to fulfill their need for adventure. In far too many cases, our programs are so formal or so structured that participants are not allowed adequate freedom to express aggressive behavior.

The Need for Recognition and Approval

The need for recognition includes our desire to be accepted by our fellows, to be noticed and gain attention, to receive praise, and to achieve status, prestige and distinction. Every person wishes for and seeks out ego support and social approval. Responses to this need include learning and demonstrating skills and abilities.

Like everyone else, a camper has a deep-seated wish to stand out as an individual and to do at least one thing better than anyone else. Campers will work diligently to run faster, swim better, swear more fluently, make more noise, or do whatever else it takes to get attention. From early childhood, this deep urge drives some people from one field of endeavor to another in search of activities in which they can excel.

Often a camper's reluctance to engage in an activity is based on a deep-seated fear that he or she cannot do it well. For instance, a person's reluctance to go in the water during a swimming period may stem from self-consciousness about a lack of ability that is heightened by the unthinking and unkind remarks of fellow campers or a counselor. The camper's attitude may well change to one of tolerance or even enthusiasm if a counselor wisely searches out some good point on which to compliment the person or offers help that may improve his or her technique. To work successfully with youngsters—or with persons of any age—you need to remember that praise produces better results than criticism. Praise your campers frequently, but avoid overdoing it or giving praise when none is deserved; others are quick to detect insincerity and consequently will lose faith in and respect for you.

Since youngsters desire to be accepted by their peers and receive recognition from them for their accomplishments, you may find it worthwhile to rearrange the program to make use of a talent not called for by the regular routines. For example, a quiet, socially inept child with a special ability, such as in art or music, may really shine when given a chance to demonstrate those special skills or talents. We are reminded of a story about a camper, Jean, whose lone outstanding trait seemed to be an ability to make more noise than anyone else. Her counselor, realizing that her frequently annoying breaches of good conduct were in reality an unconscious attempt to get the personal attention she could get in no other way, decided to stage a contest to see who could yell the loudest. Of course Jean won as anticipated, and thus achieved her place in the limelight.

Campers would prefer to have *favorable* distinction if they can get it. However, their desire for recognition is so strong that they will go to almost any length to satisfy it, and will settle for unfavorable attention if necessary. The actions of the constant troublemaker or camp mimic may be explained in this way, for he or she has at least achieved some distinction and would rather be known as bad than be treated as a nonentity. Nevertheless, persons like this have a gnawing sense of inadequacy and unhappiness, and you will render a real service by showing them how to achieve distinction in a more satisfactory way. No quick cure can be expected, however, and there will very likely be occasional discouraging relapses along the way.

Be especially eager to help the shy, retiring camper to achieve success and recognition. "The child who feels inferior can usually be helped to develop abilities which will in time make him truly superior along certain lines. Genuine superiority often grows out of a sense of inferiority which has served as a spur to unusual effort."*

When Wishes Are Thwarted

Children are a combination of a great deal of good spiced by a bit of bad, and those who long for the perfectly behaved child should remember this little poem:

Tommy does as he is told!
No one ever has to scold!
Quick! Drag him by the wrist
To see the psychoanalyst!

—Author Unknown

Let us summarize by recalling that, when children are "bad," it is usually because they have not found a satisfying and socially acceptable way to fulfill one or more of their basic needs. Therefore, when trouble arises, seek and eliminate the cause. Basic wishes are strong and will be fulfilled by fair means or foul, but children aren't anxious to sacrifice social approval to satisfy their desires, if they can avoid it.

MENTAL HEALTH

The wish for good mental health is universal, for although most of us would fail miserably if asked to tell just what the term means, we all recognize that it involves a general sense of wellbeing and of living at peace with oneself and the world. Well-adjusted individuals have stopped "reaching for the moon" by attempting things beyond their capabilities, yet, at the same time, they have recognized their strong points and have developed them to a high degree. They have learned to expect and accept a certain amount of disappointment in life but have kept their sense of humor and can laugh at themselves. They like people and have learned that it is wiser to emphasize the good traits of others than to look for faults and magnify them out of proportion. They are friendly and outgoing, yet

*Henry C. Link: *The Rediscovery of Man*, 1938, published by The Macmillan Company and used with their permission.

not backslappers whose shallowness soon shows through. They are cheerful and optimistic, yet recognize and meet problems and take constructive steps to solve them instead of wasting time in ineffective worry and indecision. What is perhaps most characteristic of well-adjusted people is that they have gone beyond exclusive, childish self-interest and have developed a concern for others and a desire to use their time and talents in ways that make the world a better place in which to live.

DEVELOPMENTAL CHARACTERISTICS

As previously pointed out, individuals are too different to classify and fit into pigeonholes, with instructions for understanding and handling each placed neatly in a nearby file. Each of us has a unique personality, created from our own genetic background and the totality of experiences and knowledge we have absorbed from our particular environment. We cannot truthfully say that there is such a thing as an average person, but only average characteristics of people. Nevertheless, it is helpful to understand these average characteristics, since they represent basic patterns upon which each person's own individual characterisitics are superimposed. As a counselor, it is essential that you understand the various stages of maturation and patterns of growth and development of children and older campers as well in order to counsel with and build a meaningful program for them.

The Camper from 6 to 8

This period might be termed the *individualistic period,* since a child's thoughts are still largely self-centered, with only a superficial and transitory interest in others. A friend may be completely spurned or disliked one minute and accepted again as a boon companion a short time later. In fact, children of this age show more interest in pleasing adults than in pleasing their contemporaries; thus, they can be easily motivated to demonstrate desirable conduct by a bit of praise or other signs of approval.

Children in this age group tend to be extremely active and cannot be restrained for very long. Their interests are keen but fleeting, and you must be prepared for them to suddenly drop a project or game in which they have been absorbed and clamor for something entirely new and different. They are impulsive, highly unpredictable, and also like to be first and to win. These children's imaginations know no bounds and much of what they do in play is make-believe or fantasy. They love to creep silently through the woods, stalking in the best manner of Daniel Boone or a fierce Cherokee brave, yet only moments later, a few touches of costume have transformed them into astronauts, piloting their rockets towards the moon.

It is very important to encourage campers of this age to try their skills in many areas and to sample everything in order to discover where their true interests and abilities lie. Although they are greatly excited about trying anything new, their physical coordination is not fully developed and their endurance is poor. Control over the finer muscle activities is so poor that concentrating on painstaking and exacting tasks is wearisome and unsatisfying. Simple, large-muscle activities such as running and jumping are therefore best. These children also need to be protected against overexcitement and fatigue, which tend to interfere with their getting sufficient rest and sleep.

The Camper from 9 to 11

Campers of this age are beginning to prize the approval of their peers above that of parents and other adults. At the same time, they are entering the age of hero worship and may adopt some adult, perhaps a famous athlete or even you as a model after whom to pattern their behavior. They seek an intimate relationship with one or two special buddies, perhaps in a club or gang, with whom closely-guarded secrets can be shared. These children are a bundle of energy in a constant whirlwind of activity, so you will need to watch them closely for signs of fatigue or overexcitement and see that they observe rest hour and get adequate amounts of sleep.

They have a good sense of humor, although it may be of the slapstick variety, and at times they may be effervescent and talk incessantly, sometimes imagining or exaggerating things. They love to collect things, be they nature specimens, trading stamps, or model airplanes. Their interests are so many and so varied and they are so intent on learning everything they can about the world that little time and interest are left for keeping themselves and their possessions clean and in good order. They want to know the "why" of everything and what makes things work, even if they have to tear them apart to find out. They like to read, but at the same time enjoy being out-of-doors.

Their improved coordination and muscle control enable them to acquire new skills in many fields, such as tennis, swimming, crafts, or the use of simple tools for camp construction. They enjoy working in a group on such activities as planning a campfire skit or program, an outdoor cookout or "gypsy" trip, or a cleanup project for their unit or cabin. They have a tendency to throw themselves wholeheartedly into a chosen task and work furiously, but often after a day or two, they will lose interest and abandon the project even though it is not yet finished.

Avoid using sarcasm or ridicule, even though the camper's boastfulness and braggadocio may irritate you, for these are often signs of an underlying lack of confidence and a desire for your attention. This age group is striving to grow up and exercise more independence, and consequently will resent it if you use a bossy, dictatorial approach, so try an understanding, friendly one and elicit their cooperation by a "let's" instead of by pressure or direct orders. Their imaginations are still strong and they find doing things much more fun when they can picture themselves as a "forty-niner," an Indian brave, or a beloved character from a history book or a favorite story.

The Camper from 12 to 15

This age is often referred to as the *gang age* because self-interests are now becoming subservient to a deeper loyalty to the group or gang. (This sense of gang loyalty is not usually quite so strong in girls as in boys.) Desire for the approval of the group is becoming so strong that to be different or to stand out from the rest is a major catastrophe. All want to act and dress as nearly alike as possible, even to the extent of engaging in minor acts of vandalism and disobedience, or wearing outlandish clothing of some sort. Don't forcibly try to stop this tendency, for adolescents of this age very much resent authoritative methods and their antagonism can be easily aroused; instead, try to employ this peer pressure in constructive ways to further camp objectives. A camper of this age is very anxious for independence but must be encouraged to recognize that more independence always brings with it increased responsibilities.

This loyalty to and enthusiasm for working as a group, plus a growing ability to discuss and see several sides of a question, make this an ideal time to give campers more responsibility for planning their own program and working out common problems. Rely on camper leadership whenever you can do so confidently and safely, and encourage individuals and committees to assume responsibilities and to develop a social consciousness, so that each camper realizes his or her own responsibility for and obligations to others.

This is the age of acute hero worship and "crushes," and the choice of the right models can be a very potent force for good. Campers are thrilled by examples of thoughtfulness, self-sacrifice, valor, and honesty in their models, and they themselves (even though loudly protesting) really want to be held to high standards, with reasonable rules and regulations consistently and fairly, but not over-rigidly, enforced. Above all, avoid the fatal error of striving for personal popularity by being overly lenient or by trying to be one of the gang, for these youngsters will take advantage of this mistake and will lose respect for you in the process.

This age group will vacillate between clowning around and showing off and moodiness and introspection, and it is often impossible to predict what any camper will do or say next. It is difficult to tell whether this period, with its rapid change of moods, interests, and general reactions to life, is harder on the individual or on those who associate with him or her. Rapid physical changes bring profound unrest, making the girls extremely self-conscious about their changing physical appearance and keeping the boys in constant anguish as their voices range without warning from treble to bass. Arms and legs are lengthening and hands and feet rapidly are increasing in size, leaving the owner embarrassed as he or she tries to maintain control over their changing proportions. Puzzled by these rapid physical, emotional, and social changes, the youngster often covers up self-consciousness by loud talk and laughter and general boisterousness. These persons very much need someone to confide in, and you can help to fulfull this need.

The Camper from 16 to 18

These older adolescents are nearing both physical and mental adulthood and the rapid changes taking place may both embarrass and puzzle them. They are both gregarious by nature, and now more than ever, are anxious to achieve a place of status and acceptance with their peers. They will go to almost any length to conform to whatever is currently popular in matters of dress, language, or behavior, and they sometimes may even be willing to sacrifice their own personal standards if group approval demands it. The combination of peer pressure and the older teenager's desire for new experiences often provides the impetus for experimentation with tobacco, drugs, or alcohol.

Their maturing sexual development intensifies their quest for sex information, and they are much more interested in the opposite sex and in seeking social contacts with them. Going steady is commonplace because it provides desired companionship, and also because it fulfills an increased need for security by providing someone who can be counted on.

Campers of this age want to be accepted as thinking, self-reliant adults by other adults, and bitterly oppose anyone who treats them otherwise; this is why they so often refuse to accept suggestions or advice from elders or those in positions of authority. They are in a transitional stage in which they are no longer children but not yet adults. Striving for identification as persons in their own right, they try to resolve the conflict between what adults expect of them, what they expect of themselves, and most of all, what their peers expect. They want adults, as well as their peers, to take them seriously, so that they can respect themselves as people of consequence, and if they fail to achieve this in a satisfactory way they may be inclined to find less desirable means to accomplish it.

This is a period of idealism and of wanting to participate in social causes to "save the world." There is interest in a wide variety of topics, including those of national and international scope as well as in topics of a religious and philosophical nature. Group discussions and informal discussion sessions are popular, and participation by older persons who have had interesting experiences is welcome. A sense of values and standards is rapidly taking form now, and this presents a distinct challenge to the sincere camp counselor.

A camper of this age craves adventure and activities that challenge his or her growing skills and ability to plan and think things out. In order to retain this interest, a progressive program is necessary that is free from repetition of activities of previous years. It is mandatory that you recognize the powers of self-direction in these campers by letting them play a major role in program planning and camp government. A minimum of guidance is still necessary, however, since these fledgling adults are inclined to fluctuate between their new-found maturity and their former immaturity. Enlist their help in planning longer and more rugged trips, more elaborate unit improvements and outpost activities, coed activities, and opportunities to explore and satisfy individual interests and developing skills. Many camps have found that a counselor-in-training (CIT) or junior counselor program is very effective with campers of this age.

BASIC EMOTIONS

Love can be of several types and is one of the deep basic needs in normal development. It begins in the very young child with self-love, and later grows to include affection for parents, brothers, sisters, and pets, then affection for persons of the same sex and, finally, love for a member of the opposite sex.

Fear is characterized by dread of impending harm to one's physical or emotional well being and makes the individual want to either fight or run away from whatever menaces him or her. Fears mostly are learned reactions, for few of those that later develop are present in a baby. The swimming instructor will be faced with the camper who is afraid of water yet wants to learn to swim, and you may have a camper who is afraid of the dark and loudly protests when lights go out at taps. A certain amount of fear is normal and important, since it causes us to temper our actions with caution and keeps us from taking foolhardy chances. However, children as well as adults sometimes have unreasonable or unduly magnified fears that may have developed from past traumatic experiences or from having others pass on their own fears to them. They may also result from exposure to too many ghost or horror stories, or from certain all-too-prevalent types of television programs and movies.

Worry is a form af anxiety about possible future happenings. Though sometimes related to dread of a specific thing or event, it is often quite vague and is merely a general feeling that something bad may happen. Some children are constant worriers, with such symptoms as insomnia, indigestion, nail-biting, or bed-wetting. Chronic worriers often have deep feelings of insecurity and inferiority, and therefore our efforts to make them feel wanted and approved of may result in rapid cessation of these often seemingly unrelated manifestations.

Inferiority feelings probably are present, at least occasionally, in everyone, for even some of the most outwardly composed, self-confident people confess to having shaky knees or butterflies in their stomachs even when doing something they have done repeatedly in the past. Some, however, experience such feelings almost constantly and in nearly everything they do, because they are convinced that they are inferior to their associates, either physically, mentally, or socially.

Anger usually results when one's plans or wishes are thwarted. A camper may respond to such frustration by throwing a temper tantrum or by screaming, biting, crying, or throwing things. The youngster may have found these tactics to be effective in getting his or her own way in the past and may have practiced them so often that they have become almost unconscious reaction patterns.

Jealousy results from the actual or feared loss of the affection of someone dear, such as a parent, friend, or pet, or the failure to attain some goal that the individual holds dear, such as winning a tennis match or being elected to an office. Naturally, this jealousy often is directed at the person who did win the thing coveted and may cause the jealous person to intensely dislike and even belittle him or her. This demonstrates the jealous person's effort to downgrade someone else while building up his or her own ego. Feelings of fear and inferiority usually accompany jealousy, and children with these feelings will respond in ways that promise the most satisfaction and pleasure. They may show some of the symptoms of a chronic worrier, or they may suck their thumbs, refuse to eat, pretend to be ill, run away, or even threaten to kill themselves in an effort to gain the sympathy and attention they crave.

CAMPERS ARE INDIVIDUALS

Although we have attempted to summarize the typical characteristics of children according to age, these are obviously generalizations, for changes take place gradually, and a youngster doesn't miraculously change from a 10 year old into an 11 year old on the eleventh birthday. Development proceeds at different rates in different individuals and even in the same individual, as in a child who suddenly increases in height and weight while remaining relatively immature emotionally and socially. A 12 year old might well have the physique of a 14 year old, a 10 year old's mentality, a social adaptability level of a 9 year old, and an emotional development of only an 8 year old.

Campers usually are placed in living groups according to such factors as chronological age, camping experience, and school grade in an attempt to obtain as homogeneous a grouping as possible, but you will undoubtedly still find quite a bit of diversity among them owing to the variations in personal development.

We have noted many points of similarity among individuals, and yet we know that there is no one in the whole world exactly like anyone else. Each person's unique personality results from his or her particular heredity, environment, and associates, for even in a young camper's short lifetime, he or she has been in contact with hundreds or even thousands of people, situations, and experiences, each of which has left its stamp of influence on the individual. The importance of developing what we call a good personality cannot be overestimated, for it opens many doors to an individual and helps him or her fit smoothly and happily into our society by fulfilling his or her basic needs and wishes in socially acceptable ways. All of us have a general idea as to what we mean

(Camp Fire, Inc., N.Y.)

by a pleasing personality, but we might find it hard to define in specific terms. In assessing it, we usually refer to the general impression the person makes, based upon such diverse qualities as posture and general appearance, facial expressions, voice, choice of vocabulary and manner of speaking, manners, and, most of all, the way a person reacts to others. Just as campers grow in height and weight, so too do they develop personalities for better or for worse.

It would be impossible as well as undesirable for us to try to eliminate campers' individual differences, for society needs a wide variety of personalities. You as a counselor must be mature enough to understand and accept each of your campers and encourage them to be individuals rather than try to change them to fit into a common mold, which indeed would result in monotony. It is true that we learn much by imitating others, but individuals attain a feeling of true fulfillment only when they assert their own individuality while still conforming and adapting enough to be acceptable to the group.

We tend to notice and perhaps give more attention to more confident, effervescent, outgoing children for they stand out through their capacity to successfully meet new and untried situations, their sense of security, and their eagerness to accept responsibility. For these reasons, we especially need to concentrate some of our attention on the quiet introvert who tends to shrink into the background and is often subservient to others in order to please them and gain reassurance. These kinds of children need your understanding and encouragement to help them develop and realize that their qualities and contributions are just as valuable as those of more extroverted children.

Not everyone is geared to the same speed, and constantly admonishing naturally slow persons to hurry may frustrate them. Similarly, campers differ in their vital capacity or stamina, and large, husky children may not necessarily be able to carry as heavy a pack or hike over as many miles as a small, wiry companion can with ease. Be careful not to confuse physical size with strength and endurance.

The problem, then, becomes one of determining just how much pressure to exert to bring campers to an acceptable level of performance. On the one hand, you must challenge them to reach their full potential, but at the same time, you must avoid overpressuring them to attempt attainments beyond their capacities. Thus, you must become adept at restraining with one hand while pushing with the other and must use all of your wits to determine the proper proportion of each.

HOW LEARNING TAKES PLACE

Over the years we have gained a tremendous amount of knowledge about behavior management and learning that has produced some psychological tools that counselors may use effectively in specific situations with campers. Edward L. Thorndike, along with other social scientists, is credited with discovering some of the principles of behavior and how learning takes place. These principles commonly are referred to as *the laws of learning.* Camp leaders who are aware of these principles are better prepared to understand camper behavior and to react to it appropriately for its effective management. For the most part, application of these principles involves common sense, but we must keep in mind that the theoretical area of human behavior is complex. In order to really master the techniques, they need to be practiced and studied in detail. The following discussion, as well as further reading in Chapters 8 and 9, will help you to better understand and apply these basic principles.

1. *The law of exercise* states that we learn by practice, since repetition produces habits. In other words, campers learn what they practice or repeat, including bad actions as well as good ones. We learn just what we practice, and each time we respond negatively our tendency to react in the same manner increases. Each time we exercise our bad habits we add to the difficulty in breaking them, so developing new and better ones also becomes difficult. Similarly, we should understand that simply discussing virtues such as kindness or honesty will not necessarily alter one's conduct if it is not accompanied by practice.

2. *The law of readiness* maintains that when someone is ready to act, doing so is satisfying; while not doing so is annoying. In other words, when a camper is not ready to learn an activity, forcing him or her to learn it will only cause displeasure and a lack of interest. We must remember that individuals differ greatly in what interests them; that is, they differ in their need structure. Consequently, learning will not take place unless there is a basic physiological or psychological need for the person to learn. This is important for counselors to remember, since campers will only be enthusiastic about an activity if it seems enticing, desirable, or necessary to them. Effective leaders can take advantage of those times when a camper is in a proper frame of mind for learning and is motivated and ready to learn. This time is often referred to as the 'teachable moment."

3. *The law of effect* states that people repeat those things that they find satisfying and avoid those that are dissatisfying. What this means is that if campers are to form good habits, they should experience satisfaction or enjoyment in the things they do. Fortunately, most of the things children do in an organized camp program are fun and, consequently, satisfying to the individual. Even so, counselors must do all they can to assure the internal satisfaction of each camper. Closely related to the law of effect is the law of reinforcement, which is discussed in the following paragraphs.

4. *The law of reinforcement* states that when satisfying conditions follow a response, then the bond between the stimulus and the response is strengthened, thus increasing the probability that the response will recur. In less technical terms, this means that behaviors that are positively reinforced or rewarded are more likely to recur. If the behavior is not rewarded, it is not likely to be repeated.

This is one of the most important principles for changing peoples' behavior, and yet it is not practiced often enough by those in leadership positions. Reinforcement can be used to maintain or increase appropriate behavior as well as to eliminate inappropriate behavior.

Another related point worth understanding is that performance will not improve unless an individual knows that what he or she has done is right or wrong. Without the knowledge (feedback) of results there can be no improvement in learning. Knowledge of the results of one's performance produces improvement and also functions to reinforce whatever behavior or action resulted in the improvement. For example, in archery, if a person were blindfolded while attempting to hit the target there would be no improvement in skill since there would be no visual clue as to where the arrow might land. The same idea applies to learning social behaviors. A youngster who wishes to make friends in camp might resort to making actions or comments that will gain attention and approval. If the results of an action elicit positive reactions such as smiles, friendly comments, and the like, positive feedback or reinforcement is provided that will probably encourage the camper to repeat the same actions or behavior. On the other hand, if the other campers pay no attention or respond negatively, such as by making derogatory comments or facial expressions that show disapproval, the original behavior might be altered until approval is received. In other words, if behavior is not rewarded with reinforcement acceptable to the individual, then the likelihood of the behavior being continued is reduced.

By now it should be obvious that reinforcement is based on human needs and their current state of fulfillment at any one time. (We are again speaking of the needs referred to earlier in this chapter, including the need for affection, achievement, security, and recognition.) Although our needs can be fulfilled through social reinforcement or rewards, it must be remembered that different individuals have different levels of need, and the same individual's needs vary from time to time. It can be difficult to know just what type of reinforcement to apply at any one time, yet counselors should make every attempt to understand the particular needs of campers in order to apply appropriate reinforcement.

Unfortunately, little has been done to inventory the reinforcers that may be used to shape the behavior of children, despite the fact that such a reference is sorely needed by camp counselors. There are probably wide individual differences in the reinforcers that are effective with different children, and the rewards used can take many different forms. We can recognize achievement through awards such as prizes or through a few words of praise or commendation for a task well done. In fact, supportive statements such as "good work," "well done," "fine effort," and other praise sometimes can be more meaningful than a tangible award. An additional method of reinforcement is to award special privileges to the camper, such as being allowed to participate in special activities or to demonstrate skills in personally selected projects.

You should also realize that campers can gain rewards from the simple satisfaction they get from carrying out a project from start to finish or from knowing that they have done something worthwhile. At any rate, it should be obvious that alert counselors can do much to discover opportunities in which campers may receive positive reinforcement.

Before leaving this subject, a few additional remarks should be made about the type of behavior to reinforce as well as the timing and frequency of rewards:

1. Keep in mind that any type of behavior that is reinforced will likely be repeated. Therefore, concentrate on rewarding only good behavior or performance.

2. Appropriate behavior should be reinforced *immediately* or as soon as possible after the behavior takes place. The effect of delay in offering reinforcement is a complex one, for under some conditions reinforcement may be delayed and still be effective. Immediate reinforcement, however, is more likely to be associated with the appropriate behavior for which it is given. It is important that the person receiving the reward be able to recognize what performance warranted it.

3. Initially, desired behavior should be reinforced each time it occurs. Once established, however, the best method for assuring that the behavior is sustained is to provide reinforcement at variable intervals or intermittently rather than each time the behavior takes place.

4. Keep in mind that you probably will not always be able to spend your time reinforcing subtle aspects of behavior, although it is desirable to do so when possible. In order to use your time wisely and function effectively, try to reinforce broad categories of behavior, such as work skills or general attitudes.

LEARNING ABOUT YOUR CAMPERS

Sources of Information

It becomes evident that in order to treat campers as the individuals they are you must learn as much as you can about each. Here are some of the possible sources of information:

1. The parental information blank filled in by parents before camp begins.

2. The camper information blank filled in by the camper.

3. Organizational records compiled by the sponsoring group, such as the Boy or Girl Scouts.

4. Records from the previous summer if he or she is a returning camper. These may include health records, activities records, and anecdotal or other profile records compiled by former counselors and other staff members.

5. The current health examination report from the camper's home physician.

6. Discussions with the camper. These should usually be informal and initiated by the counselor in a spontaneous way in order to put the camper at ease and in a mood to talk freely.

7. Observations of the camper as he or she participates in activities and the routines of group living.

8. Observations of the reactions of peers to the camper and comments gleaned by listening to their conversations.

THE SOCIOGRAM

As mentioned earlier in this chapter, one of our most important services in camping is to provide opportunities for children to meet their basic human need for affection, to be accepted as a member of a group, to be wanted and liked, and to be respected by others. There is merit in attempting to identify those campers who are accepted and those who are rejected by their peers. By successfully indentifying those who are rejected from the group we sometimes are able to isolate the cause for rejection and then take action to help change that behavior so that the youngster will be accepted by the group. Sociometry is a tool that can help us with this task.

Sociometry is an evaluative technique that can be utilized effectively to study the structure and organization of any group, including campers. It helps to identify general patterns of group integration or disintegration, including identifying those who are popular and those who are disliked, lonely or rejected. A *sociogram* is an instrument used to determine the relationships that exist among members of a group. Camp counselors or other members of the staff who understand the use of the sociogram can apply the results to improve the organization of a group, including overall relations and the social adjustment of individuals within the group.* This is done by developing a diagram that displays the predominant relationships among the members of the group. Once complete, the sociogram reveals potential leaders, mutual friendships, cliques, and those rejected by others.

How to Gather the Information

To illustrate the use of the sociogram, let us assume that you are the camp counselor for a group of children who have been under your guidance for the past week or two. In order to gather the necessary information for constructing the sociogram you should explain to the campers that during the remaining weeks in camp they will be participating in a number of new activities and that you would like to have their assistance in setting up small groups that work or play well together. If appropriate, you might point out that on overnight campouts several people will pack their clothing and equipment together and share the same tent. Whatever situation is used as an example, it should be realistic or highly probable.

The next step is to provide each of the campers with a sheet of paper on which they sign their own names and then list the names of a specified number of other persons in the group with whom each would most like to be for the activity previously described. The number of specified choices allowed should probably be limited to no more than five for older campers, while those eight years of age or younger should be limited to no more than three choices.*

How to Analyze the Results

Once the results are received from the campers they are summarized by developing a chart similar to the one shown in Figure 6-1. The following steps should be followed:

1. Four concentric circles are drawn and each one is labeled according to the number of choices made. For example, all children who are

*Howard G. Danford and Max Shirley: *Creative Leadership in Recreation.* Allyn and Bacon, second edition, 1970, pp. 361–362.

*Ibid., p. 363.

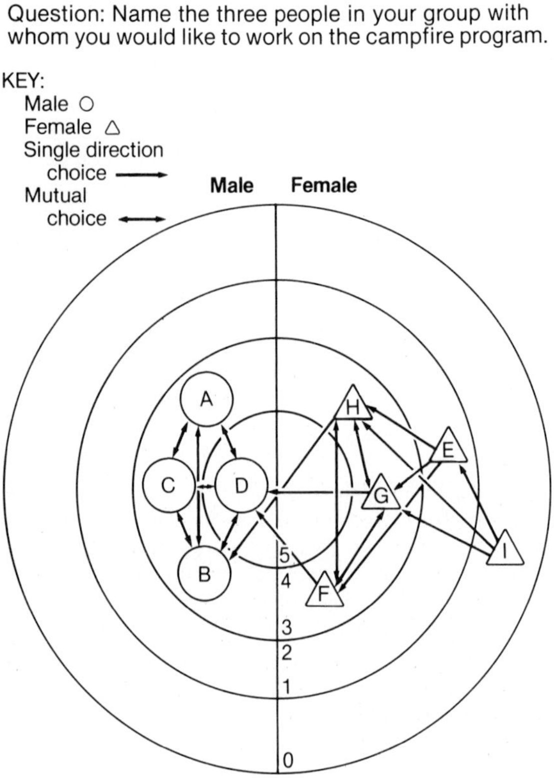

Figure 6-1 A sociogram.

mentioned either three or four times will be placed within the circle marked with a 3 or 4.

2. If both males and females are in the group, a vertical line is drawn through the center of the diagram to separate the sexes. Place the males on one side and the females on the other. Different symbols, such as triangles and circles, can be used to represent males and females.

3. Enter the campers' names onto the sociogram by placing them in the appropriate circle, based upon the number of times each was chosen. If adequate space is not available for full names, use either initials or an assigned number or letter to represent each child.

4. Draw arrows to connect the names of persons who have been chosen by others. Mutual choices should be indicated with double arrows. When possible, avoid crossing lines in order to make the chart easier to read.

As illustrated in the accompanying sociogram, the patterns of relationships are identified easily, including reciprocal and unreciprocal friendship choices. Camper *D* who is located in the center circle, is the most popular child in the group, having been chosen by five others as the one with whom they would like to work on the campfire program. On the other hand, camper *I*, who is located in the outer circle, appears to be the most isolated or neglected child since none of the others chose her as the one with whom they would like to work. *E* was also very unpopular. Further analysis reveals the formation of two small subgroups or cliques, as demonstrated by the reciprocal choices of boys *A*, *B*, *C*, and *D* and girls *F*, *G*, and *H*.

There are some obvious questions we might ask in respect to the sociogram. For instance, what are the basic reasons for *D*'s leadership position? Does he have a wholesome influence on the rest of the group? What do *F*, *G* and *H* have in common and what is the effect of this clique on the rest of the group? Is there something that can be done to help integrate these girls more completely in the group? Why are *E* and *I* isolated and neglected and what can the counselor do to help them be more accepted? Is there a need for a change in the isolates' behavior or is there a need to change the attitudes of the group? Is *I* unwanted or disliked because she is physically unattractive, lacks social skills, or has little athletic ability?

Although the sociogram does not portray the actual reasons for an individual's popularity or unpopularity, it does reveal definite patterns of relationships that can be studied by the trained observer. The sociogram affords helpful clues that may be analyzed to help reveal the various personal characteristics that might contribute to low or high social status. Once we understand the status of individuals in a group we can begin to implement programs and objectives to help overcome any problems that may be identified.

Precautions in Using the Sociogram

Before attempting to use the sociogram, you must allow sufficient time for the campers to get to know one another, otherwise the results will be meaningless. Also, it is not practical to use this technique for large groups since it will be difficult to interpret the results. As a general rule, no more than 15 or 20 campers should be involved at any one time; a smaller number is even more desirable.

Obviously, you should inform the group that all responses will be kept confidential and that they should not divulge their listings to anyone else. It is essential to exercise great tact and skill when using sociograms, for much harm can come from broadcasting or misinterpreting the information gained.

Bear in mind that the sociogram reveals only specific information about the individuals in a group in a single situation at a given time. You may want to repeat the procedure later in the season to determine any status changes as evidence of growth and development in individuals or changes in the opinions of others as they have become better acquainted.

ADDITIONAL READINGS

(For an explanation of abbreviations and abbreviated forms, see page 13.)

Ball, Edith L. and Robert E. Cipriano: *Leisure Services Preparation.* Prentice-Hall, 1978, Ch. 4

Bloom et al.: *Camper Guidance—A Basic Handbook for Counselors.*

Bossard, James H. S., and E S. Boll: *The Sociology of Child Development.* Harper & Row, 4th ed., 1966.

Coleman, James S.: *The Adolescent Society.* Free Press, 1971, paper.

Danford, Howard D. and Max Shirley: *Creative Leadership in Recreation.* Allyn and Bacon, 2nd ed., 1970, pp. 360–372.

Donaldson, Lou and George: *Teaching in the Field.* The Donaldsons, Box 203, Oregon, Ill. 61061, 1971, 31 pp.

Edginton, Christopher R., David M. Compton and Carol J. Hanson: *Recreation and Leisure Programming.* Saunders College Publishing, 1980, ch. 4.

Farrell, Patricia and Herberta M. Lundegren: *The Process of Recreation Programming.* John Wiley and Sons, 1978, ch. 2.

Gardner, Richard A., M.D.: *Understanding Children.* Jason Aronson, Inc., 59 Fourth Avenue, New York, N.Y. 10003, 1973, 258 pp.

Hauck, Paul A.: *The Rational Management of Children.* Libra, 2nd ed., 1972, 190 pp.

Hollander, Sandra, and Sox Saville: *Games People Ought to Play: Reality Games.* Macmillan, 1972, pp. 19–348.

James, Muriel, and Dorothy Jangeward: *Born to Win.* Addison-Wesley Publishing Company, Reading, Mass., 1971, pp. 1–433.

Jourard, Sidney M.: *The Transparent Self.* Van Nostrand, 1971, pp. 3–207.

Shea, Thomas M.: *Camping for Special Children.* C.V. Mosby, 1977, pp. 163–193.

Shivers: *Camping,* ch. 7 to p. 148; ch. 8.

Todd: *Camping for Christian Youth,* ch. 14.

Travers, Robert M.W.: *Essentials of Learning.* Macmillan, 2nd ed., 1967, 560 pp.

van der Smissen, Betty, ed.: *Research Camping and Environmental Education.* College of HPER, Penn State University, 1975, 508 pp. (paper):

Feldman, Ronald A.: "Socio-Behavioral Research in Camp Settings," p. 89.

Sherif, Carolyn W.: "Influencing Social Behavior," p. 149.

Van Krevelen: *Children in Groups: Psychology and the Summer Camp,* chs. 1, 2.

Vinton, Dennis A. and Elizabeth M. Farley: *Camp Staff Training Series, Module 2, Knowing the Campers.* Available from ACA, 1979, 127 pp. (paper).

———: *Camp Staff Training Series, Module 5 Dealing with Camper Behavior.* Available from ACA, 1979, 131 pp. (paper).

MAGAZINE ARTICLES

Camping Magazine:

"Camping for Older Girls." Mar., 1974, p. 11.

Gabel, Dr. Peter S.: "Teenage—The Best Age for Camping." Nov./Dec., 1973, p. 10.

Krieger, William, Ed. D.: "Study on Self-Concept Change in Campers Receives ACA's 1972 Research Award." Apr., 1973, p. 16.

McMaster, Robert: "Camp Rules for Adolescents," May, 1974, p. 11.

Solimine, Alexander, Jr.: "Seven-Year-Olds Meet Challenges of Real Wilderness Tripping." Sept., 1972, p. 19.

Witt, Ted: "The Teachable Moment." Feb., 1978, p. 14.

seven
The Counselor as a Leader

A Little Fellow Follows Me

A careful man I ought to be,
  A little fellow follows me.
I dare not go astray,
  For fear he'll go the self-same way.
I cannot once escape his eyes.
  Whate'er he sees me do he tries.
Like me, he says, he's going to be,
  The little chap who follows me.
He thinks that I am good and fine,
  Believes in every word of mine.
The base in me he must not see,
  That little chap who follows me.
I must remember as I go,
  Thru summers' sun and winters' snow,
I am building for the years to be,
  In that little chap who follows me.

—AUTHOR UNKNOWN

LEADERSHIP

Desirable Changes Do Not Automatically Occur

By now it should be clear that organized camping can provide participants with a number of social and therapeutic benefits that come from working, playing and living together in an out-of-doors setting. Note that although we have mentioned a number of positive outcomes resulting from the camping experience, we have not implied that they will happen automatically, for the quality of camps varies considerably. In fact, it is possible that some camps could offer few benefits to campers or actually could do them immense harm.

First and foremost, a camp's philosophy, organization, and personnel must be planned and utilized in such a way as to provide a favorable climate for desirable camper participation and growth if it is to reach its fullest potential. Therefore, you, the counselor, must make use of the opportunities provided, for they will be worthless opportunities unless you furnish the impetus to start things in motion. Your methods of dealing with individuals and groups will largely determine your success.

WHAT DYNAMIC LEADERSHIP INVOLVES

Every Group Has a Leader

Every group of individuals that acts together has a leader, either someone who spontaneously emerges as a leader or who is elected or appointed. Furthermore, it should be noted that the ability to demonstrate positive leadership skills is not automatic by virtue of the position. Though group members may feel duty bound to defer to a leader, they actually may be influenced to a much greater extent by someone who has no official leadership status at all. This unofficial leader is often a member of the group who, because of personality and behavior, is able to bring the group together and influence its members' point of view.

(Camp Mishawaka, Grand Rapids, Minn.)

Requirements for Leadership

As a counselor, you have a chance to demonstrate true leadership by guiding your group into constructive endeavors. Although you will be teaching skills and performing many other duties, your most important contribution will be your efforts to help your campers to develop a proper sense of values, together with desirable attitudes and ways of thinking.

Before becoming a good leader, one should learn to be a good follower. Dr. Joel W. Bloom and associates have defined *followership* as "the ability to serve in a democratic group situation under the leadership of a member of that group but still retain the capacity to suggest, criticize and evaluate, as well as serve in the project."* Through constant practice, you should have already acquired the skills of living congenially with a group. Heading the list of your attributes probably will be a spirit of cooperation and teamwork, for good group members work with their fellow members and often are called upon to willingly and unselfishly sacrifice their own wishes for the best interests of the group.

Whether in a camp setting or anywhere else, an ideal leader possesses the ability to weld a group into a well-coordinated team with each member contributing according to individual ability. In any group, however, personality clashes and dissension inevitably occur, since many personalities and individual desires are involved. Nonetheless, a leader must create an environment in which a spirit of harmony and goodwill prevail most of the time. In a camp setting, group spirit should deepen and strengthen as each successive project comes to fruition, but it must never be allowed to reach a point where it creates an unfriendly feeling or undue rivalry with other groups or a willingness to sacrifice the welfare of the whole camp.

As a leader, you will not only be learning to understand and counsel individuals, but you will also be mastering the techniques of dealing formally and informally with a group as a whole. We will now consider additional ways to increase your effectiveness in these areas.

*Bloom et al.: *Camper Guidance—A Basic Handbook for Counselors.* ACA, 1960, p. 16.

Leadership

The boss drives his men; the leader coaches them.
The boss depends upon authority; the leader on goodwill.
The boss inspires fear; the leader inspires enthusiasm.
The boss says, "I"; the leader says, "We."
The boss assigns the tasks; the leader sets the pace.
The boss says, "Get here on time"; the leader gets there ahead of time.
The boss fixes the blame for the breakdown; the leader fixes the breakdown.
The boss knows how it is done; the leader shows how.
The boss makes work a drudgery; the leader makes it a game.
The boss says, "Go"; the leader says, "Let's go."
The world needs leaders; but nobody wants a boss.*

TYPES OF LEADERS

There are three basic types of leaders: (1) *autocratic leaders* make all important decisions themselves and control a group mainly by force and fear; (2) *laissez-faire leaders* are almost the exact opposite, for they are overly lenient and allow their groups to decide everything for themselves, doing whatever they wish with a minimum of interference; and (3) *democratic leaders*, who are a combination of the two. They can assume control and apply discipline on the few occasions when it is necessary, but they ordinarily depend upon influencing their followers through the respect and confidence they engender in the group. Democratic leaders do this by the force of their personality and by what they stand for, as well as by demonstrating skills in planning and working cooperatively with the group. Most leaders fall somewhere within the last, broad category, between the extremes of the autocratic and the laissez-faire leaders.

The Autocratic Leader

Autocratic leaders single-handedly decide upon the activities, goals, and procedures for the group, then draw up step-by-step instructions for them to follow. They are apparently oblivious to the reactions of their campers and seldom consider their opinions or desires; such leaders seem to believe that their own judgments and decisions are so superior that they need no advice or help from anyone else. They feel that they know what is best for everyone and are therefore justified in enforcing their mandates on the campers. These "big stick" methods of control permit no lapse of discipline or questioning of authority, and the autocratic leader threatens drastic and certain punishment for all dissenters and nonconformists.

These high-handed tactics may accomplish little permanent good, for as we have previously noted, exemplary conduct evoked by fear or force lasts only while the leader is present. Some will respond to such a leader with passivity and subservience, often becoming so dependent that they lose the ability to make decisions for themselves. Others react by resisting or rebelling, and often develop an intense hatred for discipline and authority of any kind or from any source.

Under an autocratic leader, groups have a tendency to destroy more property when working, to be more aggressive, and to show much more hostility, often channeling their frustrations toward a scapegoat in the group, since they are afraid to direct tbem against the true target, the leader. On the whole, the members are more dependent and submissive and tend to show less individuality than those under other types of leadership. Although autocratic methods may sometimes be efficient or even necessary, as during an emergency, they should be the exception rather than the rule, since when used habitually, they reduce the initiative and creativity of those subjected to them as well as produce the undesirable results mentioned previously.

Unfortunately, an autocratic leader sometimes assumes these dictatorial qualities unconsciously, in a mistaken belief that such conduct is expected of a leader and indicates that he or she is forceful, aggressive, and strong. In reality, this type of leader is often covering up deep-seated feelings of insecurity and inadequacy for which bossing others seems to compensate. For such a person this technique may satisfy a desire for power over others in an unhealthy way.

The Laissez-Faire Leader

Laissez-faire leadership is almost the exact opposite of the autocratic leadership style, for it consists of no authority or leadership at all. Peo-

*Dodge, Dora E.: *Thirty Years of Girls' Club Experience.*

ple who use the laissez-faire leadership style mistakenly believe that a group can become independent and self-reliant only through *complete* self-direction. These leaders realize that a group of campers should be harmonious, but believe that harmony and happiness are produced only when people are entirely free to do as they please.

Counselors who use this wishy-washy method are either unconcerned about the campers' welfare or trying to be popular by going along with whatever the group suggests. Although the "leader" initially may be somewhat liked, the group will soon lose respect for such a leader when it recognizes his or her weakness and lack of direction. Children subconsciously expect their appointed leader to be stronger and wiser than they and to act in a dynamic and positive fashion. Although they frequently protest against it, studies have shown that children really want a certain amount of discipline.

When campers are left entirely on their own to work out a program, their inexperience and limited awareness of possibilities often result in a pointless and fragmented program with which they soon become bored. Groups under the guidance of a laissez-faire leader quickly deteriorate, sink into indifference and become apathetic. Obviously they accomplish very little, and even that is usually of poor quality.

The Democratic Leader

The democratic style of leadership strikes a balance between the autocratic and laissez-faire approaches. Someone who utilizes this style of leadership has mastered the art of working *with*, *for* and *in* the group without losing control of it. This person can be a good sport and believe in fun and good times, yet also can be firm and exercise control when necessary.

The democratic leader works cooperatively with the group by encouraging its members to express their views and to participate in camp government and in planning the program insofar as their ages and abilities permit. However, it must be realized that progress is made slowly using the democratic process, since explanations, discussions, and group action take more time than in an autocratic system. Even so, the democratic leader realizes that campers can grow and mature only by solving problems for themselves and that what campers learn is more important, in the long run, than the material things they accomplish.

In the best sense of the word, a democratic group is one that has learned to live together in comparative harmony while initiating, conducting and evaluating its own program; it is willing to accept and abide by the results of its own decisions. Citizens in a democracy must learn to be good "choosers" and each must be willing to accept group decisions and do his or her share to carry them out, even though they are not of one's own choice. The leader stays somewhat in the background, acting as an adviser and guide, helping when and where needed and seeing that responsibilities and privileges are distributed equitably.

Many counselors only give lip service to democratic planning with their group, holding perfunctory discussions with them but allowing them little real control over decisions. When true democratic procedures exist, all participants have a chance to express themselves and share in the decision-making processes of the camp, either directly, within a cabin group, or indirectly, through representatives on the unit council and all-camp council.

CHARACTERISTICS OF A GOOD LEADER

Leadership involves influencing and motivating a group to act, and therefore a good leader is someone who inspires a group to achieve goals that the group deems desirable and worthy. A leader must be capable of exerting positive influence on the group to help it conceptualize and formalize its goals and objectives, and also must serve as a motivating force in moving the group to meet those goals.

One of the basic functions of leaders becomes obvious here, namely, that leaders must be good at interacting and communicating with individual members of the group in order to persuade them to accept and move toward the established goals. Other leadership functions involve organizing, directing and coordinating efforts; helping to define situations and determine goals; and maintaining group happiness and cohesiveness. With these functions in mind, we now can look at a number of suggestions that

(National Music Camp, Interlochen, Mich.)

may be helpful to the camp counselor in developing leadership skills.

1. Good leaders lead by example. What they do coincides with what they say.

2. Leaders have a good sense of humor and exercise it to avert crises and to keep minor problems from becoming major ones.

3. The leader's thoughts are not always centered on the personal effect of each situation and decision, but instead extend out to consider the group as a whole.

4. In order to tactfully introduce worthwhile ideas or projects, leaders often rely upon the power of suggestion; they casually mention an idea without insisting that it be adopted and they suggest rather than command. In this way, the group is free to elaborate on the idea and improve or alter it, as so frequently happens when many minds work together toward a common goal. Often these suggestions are casual comments the campers make themselves, which gives the leader a clue as to their needs and interests.

5. Leaders tactfully avoid misunderstandings and feuds whenever they can and sincerely attempt to see things from others' viewpoints. They realize that when they arouse antagonism they diminish their ability to exert influence in the future.

6. When there is work to be done, leaders set the example by being in the midst of it, working side by side with the rest of the group.

7. Leaders understand the force of group pressure and group opinion, but also realize that there is danger in letting campers govern themselves entirely, since their judgment is still immature and they sometimes are carried away by their own enthusiasm.

8. Leaders are ever-mindful of the value of fun, for happy, self-motivated campers seldom become problems to themselves or others. When teaching new skills, leaders are thorough but patient and understanding, and proceed in an informal, friendly manner. They devise ways to make chores fun instead of drudgery.

9. Leaders know that campers, no matter how much they complain, do not really enjoy careless conduct or performance and that they will soon lose respect for leaders who tolerate laziness or haphazard performance. Leaders also

recognize that suggestions elicit a better response than orders, but they realize that there are occasions when orders are necessary, and that, once issued, orders must be enforced without exception.

10. Leaders give praise freely and can see some good in everybody, but they realize that when praise is insincere or overused it is quickly detected and discounted. They avoid squabbling and being excessively fussy about detail, for they know that this tends to destroy campers' enthusiasm and interest, and they seldom, if ever, resort to sarcasm or ridicule.

11. Leaders always are concerned with a camper's pride, and they know that emotional hurts are even more serious than physical ones. Scolding a camper before others and creating scenes in public are to be avoided. It often is better to give a camper a chance to preserve his or her dignity by ignoring an infraction committed in public, but discuss it with him or her privately at a later time. In other words, leaders reject bad conduct but not the camper who committed it and they avoid sending a camper away feeling dejected and hopeless.

12. Leaders seldom *tell* campers what to do, instead, they skillfully help guide them through discussion to analyze the situation and eventually arrive at their own solutions.

13. Leaders avoid the use of physical punishment, which seldom brings about the desired results. Such punishment usually is against camp policies and may involve the camp in legal difficulties.

14. Leaders use disciplinary measures sparingly and only when convinced that they will be of benefit, but they are never used vindictively. Punishment often is misused because it is so easy to administer and elicits such quick and sure results (at least outwardly). Superior counselors handle their groups so skillfully that serious disciplinary problems are reduced to a minimum, but even so, sooner or later a time will come when action can no longer be postponed. A leader will find that children usually are good sports about accepting punishment they deserve, if no partiality or spite is involved. When discipline is necessary, it should follow the misdemeanor as closely as possible and preferably should bear some relationship to it. For instance, depriving someone of participation in the day's waterfront activity would probably be appropriate only if one camper pushed another into the water. Using work as a punitive measure makes work an onerous task; however, it may sometimes be appropriately considered as punishment for a camper who causes unnecessary work for others, for example, by cluttering the grounds or throwing food in the dining room.

Of the best leaders, the people only know that they exist;
The next best, they love and praise;
The next, they fear;
And the next, they revile.
When they do not command the people's faith,
Some will lose faith in them,
And then they resort to recrimination,
But of the best, when their task is accomplished,
Their work done,
The people all remark: "We have done it ourselves."

—AUTHOR UNKNOWN

(Reprinted from Douglas Monahan, *Let's Look at Leadership.* Character Craft, 1958.)

WORKING WITH A GROUP

As mentioned previously, effective communication is an important aspect of leadership. There are several different skills and activities counselors can use as part of the regular program to facilitate communication, to improve their performance as group leaders, and to assist campers in expressing their own thoughts and feelings in order to better understand one another.

THE USE OF SOCIODRAMA

Sociodrama is a form of playacting in which individuals play the roles of certain people, creating the dialogue as they go along or using a previously prepared script; it is especially effective with older campers. It adds interest and variety to the program and can be useful as a teaching method and as a means of pinpointing and solving problems, especially when followed by a discussion of what took place and its implications. Sociodrama should be kept lively and never allowed to drift off into silliness or exaggeration, but some touches of humor can be allowed to creep in as actors inject their own personalities into the roles they are playing.

Sociodrama can serve many purposes, for example:

1. To instruct or get a point across. It is particularly useful in working with a CIT group or regular counselors during training sessions. A hypothetical situation is presented, with actors assigned to play such roles as camp director or other camp administrators, counselors, campers, or visiting parents. They may then act out proper (or improper) ways to behave on such occasions as visitors' day, the counselors' visit to the neighboring village on their day off, the counselor during rest hour or in the hour just before taps, and so forth. If desired, several others may act out their personal versions of proper procedures at these times, with the group then discussing and evaluating each presentation. In the same way, campers or staff may act out such topics as acceptable and unacceptable conservation practices (carving initials, strewing leftovers from a cookout around or dumping them in the lake, causing or controlling erosion, eliminating fire hazards), conduct in the dining room or kitchen, and so forth.

2. To solve a problem. The sociodrama may deal with a problem of campers, counselors, or both; possible topics might deal with the person who won't be quiet after taps or during rest hour; someone who has poor habits of personal cleanliness and neatness; someone who shirks cabin cleanup duties or who is bossy and always wants to run the show. This may provide a tactful way to allow campers to see themselves in a new light as they note how disagreeable some of their ways seem to others. (Be careful not to make the characterization so pointed that it hurts feelings.) The problem may be a real or imaginary one, with each acting out his or her idea of the best solution, followed by a general appraisal and discussion.

3. To develop *empathy* or attempt to put yourself in another's place, so that you understand how someone else feels. This might be illustrated by acting out a camper who won't observe quiet after taps and then discussing why the person acts that way and how others feel about being kept awake. Other examples may be concerned with the feelings of a member of a minority group, or the person who never gets letters at mail call. How does the busy dietician feel when campers are late for an appointment to plan the menu for a cookout, or the busy caretaker, when campers don't return tools promptly or damage them by careless use?

4. To learn desirable and undesirable ways to do something, such as launch a canoe, build a fire, act as leader of a discussion, serve as camper leader to organize an overnight, carry on cabin cleanup, or wash dishes. How can cabinmates help a camper who is painfully shy or who feels left out? The usual discussion and evaluation then follow.

5. To develop better communication within the camp and to give insights or awaken new emotions in people. After participating in such activities, campers will probably mull over what happened and their own and others' feelings about it and perhaps discuss it further with fellow campers or counselors.

Obviously, there are many possible variations, such as secretly selecting someone each day to play the role of a braggart, practical joker, or daredevil. The group then is asked to pick out the actor for the day and the good and bad qualities he or she was depicting. Another variation is to ask individuals to perform certain skills, such as building a fire, launching or docking a canoe, or packing for a trip, and deliberately make certain mistakes to see if the group observes them. You may want to ask the group to suggest topics, or leave it up to a committee or the cabin council to suggest problems they think might lend themselves well to such techniques.

LEADING GROUP DISCUSSIONS

> I dislike him because he only listens when he talks.
>
> —George Bernard Shaw

Group Discussions in Camp

Everyone enjoys taking part in a discussion, and campers are no exception. Discussion should be regarded as a valuable part of the camp experience, for the interchange of ideas and opinions is important to a camper's development as a person.

In addition to the usual spontaneous, informal discussions, there will probably be some of a more formal nature that are planned, either at your own instigation or in response to requests from campers. At other times, you may want to introduce a topic in a casual way so that the ensuing discussion is more spontaneous. Unless a situation calls for an immediate discussion, it is best to hold them on rainy days, late afternoons, or during the period just before taps. In the camp situation, a relaxed, informal atmosphere is usually most appropriate.

Reasons for Group Discussions

People often engage in discussions merely to exchange opinions or acquire information about almost anything under the sun. One of the most fascinating things about people of camp age is their insatiable curiosity and desire to know the how, where, what, and why of countless things, not only in their own environment, but also in far-away times and places. They often enjoy discussing such diverse topics as college life, vocations, dating, love and marriage, personal grooming, Indian lore, fishing, camping techniques, cheating, religion, current events, and world affairs. Through these conversations campers can acquire information, broaden their interests and insights, and learn to better communicate with and understand others.

Discussion is also one of the best ways to clear up misunderstandings and solve problems, such as how to divide cabin duties and thus avoid shirkers and "workhorses," how to deal with campers who lie, steal, or spread malicious gossip, or to explain the reasons for certain camp rules, such as why all must wear shoes to and from the waterfront. When a wise counselor detects undercurrents of unrest that seem to be building up to a crisis, he or she gives the campers an opportunity to express their dissatisfaction and blow off steam. It is better to bring controversial matters out into the open and discuss what is bothering people before tensions build up and tempers reach the boiling point. A frank and open discussion often will be enough to solve the problem, for increased goodwill and mutual understanding will result once perfectly well-meaning people learn how their thoughtless actions have been irritating others or find that their suspicions and distrust were based largely on imagination, idle rumor, or gossip, or a chance act or statement that was misinterpreted.

Discussion is the best and most democratic way to plan a group project such as an overnight hike, a three-day canoe trip, a cabin name and slogan, a camp safety week, a stunt for stunt night, or ways of beautifying unit grounds.

Campers often have problems or interests that they hesitate to discuss privately with anyone except a buddy or a few close peers. Questions of general morality, personal health problems, standards of conduct for self or group, relationships with the opposite sex, camp rules or customs, the use of tobacco, alcohol and drugs, or other campers who disturb or puzzle them often fall into this category. Campers may feel somewhat ashamed of their interests or unsure of how adults or peers will react, so they will need assurance that you recognize their concerns as being perfectly normal and common. When these topics are brought up before the group, campers are often relieved to find that others share their interests and gladly enter into the discussion. The more relevant discussions are to the real problems and interests of campers, the more valuable they become.

The Role of the Counselor in Group Discussion

If you can gain enough of the group's confidence to be freely admitted into their discussions, you can give them the benefit of the wider knowledge and more mature viewpoint and way of thinking your greater age and experience should provide. It also will draw them closer to you when they find you so human and understanding. There is nothing to be gained from burying your head in the sand and refusing to admit that your campers are curious about sex, drugs, and other moral and ethical questions, for whether or not these subjects are brought out into the open, your campers will discuss them. With this in mind, make sure that your influence is for the good, and instruct, inform, and discuss as seems desirable.

Try to keep your campers from overstressing or going overboard in any one area, for there are too many exciting things to do and talk about in this world to concentrate exclusively on only a few. There is a trend in our society toward overemphasizing sex and certain other topics; with the aid of people like you, camping can help to offset this by recognizing the importance of these matters, but at the same time, showing campers how much they will miss if they allow their interests to become so limited. Are you mature enough to maintain for yourself and pass on to others a balanced set of values?

Preparing for a Planned or Semiformal Group Discussion

The how, when, where, and what of a planned discussion are important considerations. A group of 6 to 8 individuals (never more than 15) works best, for it permits a small, intimate grouping in which each can clearly hear and be heard, (a particularly important consideration in the out-of-door setting so common in camp). It also promotes a friendly climate in which each feels free to speak frankly, and even the timid can enter in without fear or embarrassment, and it encourages a tendency to think in terms of "We" instead of "I."

Either a counselor or a capable camper may serve as leader or chairperson. When serving in this capacity, it is your task to see that everything is in readiness; this includes setting a suitable time and place, notifying participants, and taking care of such details as lighting and seating. If participants are not already aware of what is on the agenda, you may want to inform them of it ahead of time so that they can come with well-thought-out ideas instead of talking off the top of their heads and saying things they don't mean or may later regret. You, as leader, may also want to prepare yourself by securing pertinent information and planning in some detail how to conduct the meeting. For instance, you may want to plan your opening remarks and outline the logical steps to follow in progressing to a meaningful conclusion in order to avoid having the discussion lag or become bogged down in digressions.

Conducting Group Discussions

It is usually best for everyone to sit in a circle so that each can see everyone else; you can join the circle yourself if the group is small and informal. It often creates a good atmosphere and makes people more willing to participate if you invite them to bring along a piece of handiwork, such as whittling or some arts and crafts project. If members are new to each other, have them introduce themselves and also have them supply a bit of pertinent information about themselves. (A variation might be to pair them off to ex-

(National Music Camp, Interlochen, Mich.)

change information, each then introducing the other.)

A good first step is to help them to define or arrive at a clear understanding of the exact topic or problem to be discussed and what should be accomplished. This starts everyone off on common ground and curbs any tendency to flounder about or bring in irrelevancies. As things progress, it helps to have someone record in large, legible characters such things as data presented, summarizations of decisions made and lists of duties and personnel. This may be done on a blackboard or with a crayon or broad felt pen on a large artist's pad or sheet of butcher's paper arranged easel-style. Someone may also be designated as secretary to keep a permanent record of proceedings. If several topics are up for discussion, you may want to ask the group to arrange them in the order of their importance, putting near the end those which could possibly be postponed until a later meeting. However, if discussion of topics cannot be postponed, draw up a schedule and allot the necessary time to each topic and make sure the schedule is followed.

You are now ready to introduce the first topic. Once the discussion has gotten started you should retire into the background, for the discussion should largely be between group members, not between you and the group. Your main function is to keep the discussion going in an orderly fashion, summarizing main points as they develop and steering the group members on to the next step as rapidly as is feasible in order to reach a satisfying conclusion. Though it is occasionally wise to permit some digression from the subject, you must use good judgment as to just how much and how far this should go before you tactfully but forcefully bring them back on course again. Keep a sharp eye out for signs of unrest or disinterest, for young children, in particular, have short interest spans, and, even more than their elders, grow impatient with purposeless monologues or repetitions by the long-winded who seem to crop up in every group.

One of the best ways to launch a subject, bring a wandering group back on course, or move them on to another topic is to ask a question. Express it as briefly as possible, choosing your words carefully to clearly bring out your meaning. Ask questions that will require a thoughtful answer rather than a simple "yes" or "no." For instance, you might begin by asking, "Since our meeting is to decide what to do Wednesday night, who has a suggestion to make?" (List the suggestions on the blackboard and encourage discussion until they finally agree on two or three.) Then, if the choice lies between several items like going on an overnight stargazing trip or working on their outdoor cooking site, you can ask for persons to speak for or against each idea. After discussion, call for a final vote. Once they decide on a plan, ask what preparations will have to be made for it; they will have to cover such things as the program, personal and group equipment and supplies needed, and work committees and their duties. Record these on the blackboard and then work out the details involved in each.

Before concluding a meeting, summarize what you have accomplished in some way, such as by asking campers to state the most important things they gained from the discussion or by briefly restating important decisions reached or responsibilities assumed by individuals or the group, and when, where, and how they are to be carried out. Keep notes for yourself, and in order to ascertain what progress is being made, follow up at a later meeting or ask individuals to report on the progress being made.

Additional Hints for the Leader

If your group lacks experience or has drifted into bad discussion habits, plan an early meeting to consider with them how to prepare and carry on a good discussion. This may call for a review of important rules of order and some of the courtesies and techniques of participation; for instance, each person should respect the rights of the one who has the floor and should listen intently and with an open mind to what is being said. Conversely, someone should never interrupt rudely or be so involved in his or her own point of view that he or she does not listen to the good points others make. Speakers should be brief and to the point and should avoid wasting time by restating points already made. After the group has reached a decision, each should accept it gracefully and wholeheartedly join in helping to carry it out.

With younger campers you will need to take quite a bit of the decision-making responsibility yourself, but you can and should let older campers gradually do more, since they are increasingly resentful of being dominated by their elders and are eager to demonstrate their own growing abilities to decide things for themselves and carry them out. Encourage them in this, even though they may make mistakes.

This is a good time for you to demonstrate your understanding of the true meaning of democratic leadership. Your campers often will surprise you with their good judgment and ingenuity when challenged and will enter into projects they have planned with enthusiasm and determination, for it will become a matter of individual as well as group pride to them. This "hands off" policy is hard for most of us to maintain, for we have a tendency to be impatient and to want to boost our own egos by stepping in to suggest what should be done and how and by whom. Yet our role should be one of standing by to prevent really serious mistakes, instructing and assisting as needed, and exerting a restraining hand only when necessary.

Introduce older campers to the committee system, in which committee members do certain parts of the job or perform preliminary work and then report back to the entire group. Ordinarily, the group should choose its own leaders and committee members, for they often know their peers much better than you, and when impressed with the importance of selecting people who will be responsible and capable will usually choose wisely and will follow those chosen more willingly.

Strike a happy medium between letting a discussion drag and rushing through it; undue haste and demonstrations of impatience on your part will make some hesitant to speak and cause others to feel hurried. Stay in the background, yet maintain control by such methods as tactfully discouraging timewasters and monopolizers and encouraging the quieter campers to participate. Give all campers the feeling that you *want* to hear what they have to say; then listen respectfully and intently and thank them when they finish. Don't assume the role of judge or critic, and avoid taking advantage of your position by belittling, using sarcasm, or making light of any idea expressed in sincerity. Bear in mind that your gestures and facial expressions convey impressions just as much as your words. If necessary, protect the members of the group from each other by immediately squelching rudeness, bickering, or derogatory remarks made by anyone to or about another's ideas. Set an example by showing respect for each individual and your attitude of courtesy and fairness to all will help to set the tone for the group.

Like any good referee, a discussion leader controls the situation while staying in the background. You are entitled to express your opinions like anyone else, but never take advantage of your position by forcing your ideas on the group or overruling majority opinion unless camp safety or policy demands it.

Of Course There Will Be Problems

As in every other camp activity, you will encounter problems in a group discussion. There will always be one or more who talk too much, apparently enamored with the sound of their own voices. Although they sometimes have good ideas, they often bury them in verbiage, merely repeat what others have said or just chatter on with words that apparently come from the mouth without benefit of having passed through the brain. Group members should refrain from garrulousness for, as George Eliot said, "Blessed is the man who, having nothing to say, abstains from giving in words evidence of the fact." For those who don't abstain, we would like to recommend the "South African treatment," which limits a speaker to what can be said while standing on one foot, with his or her speech automatically ending the instant the other foot touches the ground. Other ways to correct such tendencies are to discuss the importance of equal sharing of speaking time during one of your general sessions or to assign someone some special task, such as acting as blackboard recorder, to keep him or her occupied and feeling important. You may occasionally have to be even more direct, asking someone to keep a record of each person who speaks and the amount of time consumed, or possibly discussing the problem personally with the individual.

The opposite of the excessively talkative camper is the retiring type who speaks too little and listens without contributing. You must ask yourself why this person doesn't enter into the discussion, since you know that one of the normal fundamental needs is to belong and fit in with the group and establish oneself as an individual. Perhaps this individual may lack interest or fear making a mistake, being laughed at, or incurring the ill will of others; maybe the answer lies in your own leadership methods, which may inadvertently cause embarrassment or hurt feelings. Work hard to gain this person's participation and then work even harder to maintain it.

There usually will be at least one unpopular camper who is the butt of camp jokes, whose opinions are always scoffed at, and who isn't even permitted to finish a sentence. Unless you hasten to change matters and keep others from throwing cold water on his or her efforts, this person will soon stop trying to fit in and contribute.

Every group is likely to contain biased, opinionated persons or those who feel they know all there is to know. These people look upon a discussion as merely a sounding board for displaying their own wisdom before the admiring multitudes of the ignorant. Such are the intolerant campers or counselors who "only listen when they themselves speak" and furiously attack any person who dares to differ. They should be reminded of the Chinese saying that getting angry is a sign that one has run out of arguments.

Other Types of Discussions

THE CIRCULAR RESPONSE OR CIRCULAR DISCUSSION METHOD. In an effort to overcome some of the limitations of the usual discussion method, Hillsdale College has promoted the Circular Response or Circular Discussion Method.* It is based on a technique originated by Dr. Eduard C. Lindeman of the New York School of Social Work, and consists of arranging the group in the usual circle and choosing someone at random to start the discussion. Then, proceeding clockwise around the circle, all persons are given a specified amount of time, for instance, one minute, to express themselves. No one may talk out of turn or speak again until the discussion goes around the circle. Someone acts as timekeeper (a good job for one inclined to talk too much) and signals when the time is up, and, as usual, one person is assigned to record on the blackboard and another to take permanent notes. Continue around the circle as many times as seems profitable and then summarize the discussion as usual.

When a person's turn comes, he or she may use the allotted time to (1) add new thoughts or opinions; (2) comment on previous remarks; (3) add to or elaborate upon previous remarks; (4) "pass" with the understanding that another chance will be provided when the discussion returns to that person again; or (5) ask that the person's time be devoted to a period of silence to give others time to summarize their thoughts.

Before the first go-around, give all participants from one to three minutes to think about the subject and decide what they want to say, then devote an additional minute to let them condense it into brief or "telegram" form. They may then, of course, use their allotted time to elaborate as they wish.

The Hillside bulletin suggests that, even though the group is already familiar with the method, it is a good idea to go over the ground rules briefly before each session.

BRAINSTORMING. *Brainstorming* is a method often used successfully to solve a problem or plan an activity. It is based on the belief that certain problems can best be solved by allowing the freest exchange of ideas possible. It usually works best with groups of from 6 to 10, with all persons being encouraged to share their thoughts on the subject at hand. Nothing is rejected as being too extreme, for although the suggestion may have little value in itself, it may well stimulate someone else to come up with something of a more practical nature. Write down all ideas as given, and then go back and select for further exploration those that seem most promising.

Advantages of the Group Discussion Method

Although the discussion method is slow and sometimes inefficient, it has the advantage of being democratic because it gives everyone a chance to express thoughts and feelings as well as hear those of others and it minimizes the danger of letting the outspoken or more dynamic members exert undue influence. It also gives them an opportunity to ask questions and obtain

*Described in a four-page bulletin, *For Those Who Must Lead*, "The Hillsdale College Leadership Letter," Volume I, No. II, April, 1963, Hillsdale, Michigan.

more information about unclear points. The very act of participating gets people involved, keeps them aware of exactly what is going on and why, and makes them more willing to accept the decisions that result. This is particularly important with older campers who are becoming increasingly unwilling to be dictated to. Increased understanding and appreciation will result as campers learn to respect the opinions of others, even though not necessarily endorsing them, hopefully in the same spirit as Voltaire, who said, "I disapprove of what you say, but I will defend to the death your right to say it." Through discussion, you will often find that your campers have more insight and wisdom than you imagined, and sharing thoughts and ideas will help both you and your campers to gain a better understanding of each other.

ADDITIONAL READINGS

(For an explanation of abbreviations and abbreviated forms, see p. 13.)

Beal, George M., et al.: *Leadership and Dynamic Group Action.* Iowa State U., 1962, paper.

Cushing, Luther S.: *Modern Rules of Order.* Fawcett, 1972, paper.

Detweiler, Herbert J.: *How to Stand Up for What You Believe.* Ass'n Press, 1966, paper.

Edginton, Christopher, David M. Compton and Carol J. Hanson: *Recreation and Leisure Programming.* Saunders College Publishing, 1980, pp. 58–74.

Gordon, Thomas: *Leadership Effectiveness Training.* Wyden Books, 1977, 278 pp.

Herbert, W.L., and F.V. Jarvis: *Dealing with Delinquents.* Emerson, 1961, 207 pp.

Hollander, Edwin P.: *Leadership Dynamics.* The Free Press, 1978, 212 pp.

Klein, Alan F.: *Effective Groupwork.* Galloway, 384 pp.

Knowles, Malcolm and Hulda: *Introduction to Group Dynamics.* Galloway, rev., 96 pp.

Ledlie and Holbein: *Camp Counselor's Manual.*

Lifton, Walter M.: *Working With Groups.* Wiley, 2nd ed., 1966, 292 pp.

Loeb, Robert H., Jr.: *He-Manners.* Ass'n Press, rev., 1970.

Loeb, Robert H., Jr.: *She-Manners.* Ass'n Press, rev., 1970.

Loughmiller, Campbell: *Wilderness Road.* Hogg Foundation for Mental Health, (Order from ACA), 1965, 139 pp., paper.

Nolan, W. I.: *A Guide to Parliamentary Practice.* (Order from NRPA) 110 pp.

Reichert, Richard: *Self-Awareness Through Group Dynamics.* Pflaum/Standard, 38 West Fifth Street, Dayton, Ohio, 1970, 120 pp.

Rodney and Ford: *Camp Administration,* ch. 6.

Shivers, Jay S.: *Recreation Leadership.* Princeton Books, 1980, 268 pp.

Simon, Sidney B., et al.: *Values Clarification.* Hart Publishing Company, Inc., New York, New York, 1972, 379 pp.

Strean: *New Approaches in Child Guidance.*

Todd: *Camping for Christian Youth,* pp. 137–140.

Youth Forums (No. 3013). Boy Scouts, 1971, 32 pp., paper.

Van Krevelen: *Children in Groups: Psychology and the Summer Camp,* ch. 8.

von Hilsheimer, Rev. George: *How to Live with Your Special Child—Handbook for Behavior Change.* Acropolis, 1970, 272 pp.

Magazine Articles

CAMPING MAGAZINE:

Haskell, Helen L.: "Factors to Consider in Stimulating and Motivating Campers." Mar., 1970, p.12.

Hunter, D. Bruce: "Don't Use Food as Punishment." Nov./Dec., 1969, p. 18.

Rawson, Harve E.: "Research Attests to Behavior Change in Programs Geared to Specialized Camping." May, 1973, p. 16.

Smith, DeWitt: "How Counselors Use Authority." Apr., 1972, p. 12.

Wilson, Don: "Both Schools and Camps Can Offer a Place to Learn." Jan., 1973, pp. 11–13.

eight
The Counselor's Role in Guidance

It is said that man will work 8 hours a day for pay, 10 hours a day for a boss, but 24 hours a day for a cause.

—AUTHOR UNKNOWN

THE COUNSELOR'S ROLE IN GUIDANCE

The daily informal contacts of camp life give you an unlimited opportunity to study objectively all of your campers in a variety of situations, and by seeing them as whole persons and evaluating their individual strengths and weaknesses, you can gain a better understanding of them and why they are the way they are. After you have done this, you may hope to find ways to guide them in developing their potential and becoming better persons through their contacts with you and the camp, but be careful not to attempt the impossible or overestimate your capabilities in this area. When dealing with personalities, it is especially important to remember that "a little learning is a dangerous thing," and if you do not use sound judgment and lack adequate training and experience in the field of guidance, you can do much harm through misguided attempts to help a youngster during these very important formative years. In order to interpret campers' behavior, you must have an understanding of not only the normal processes of growth and development, but also the specific background conditions that have contributed to make them the sort of people they are. Under favorable conditions, camp offers a fine setting for giving positive guidance and helping boys or girls to develop and grow.

Self-Concepts

All campers come to camp with pre-formed opinions of themselves as persons, which are largely dependent upon the way they have been accepted by others in the past. If parents, teachers, or peers regard them as sloppy, lazy, or as troublemakers, they usually will consider this to be a true characterization and probably will expect their new associates to feel the same way about them. Their self-concept probably is so ingrained that they will try to live up to their reputation. If, on the other hand, children have been praised and are considered to be good children who are courteous, pleasant, and cooperative, they probably will behave that way at camp.

As discussed in Chapter 6, when campers demonstrate unacceptable traits, punishing, nagging, or bribing them will do little good and may only make them worse. These children may have become so accustomed to being blamed and scolded that they almost certainly will pay no attention to you anyway. A better approach is to try to discern how these children feel about themselves and what their true self-concepts are; you will then be in a position to try to alter their behavior by giving them new and different self-concepts. Remember that beneath a facade of indifference there is probably a longing to be admired and accepted as a respected member of the group. Therefore, try to reward others with a sincere smile and some token of approval each time they do something commendable. When occasions for positive reenforcement do not occur naturally, you may have to purposely create opportunities for individuals to do something praiseworthy. Nothing succeeds like success, and each time approval is won, children will be encouraged to try to win it again. Eventually, such children may begin to think of themselves as "good" rather than "bad," and, hopefully, this new self-concept will carry over into their life after they leave camp.

Changing Habit Patterns

In Chapter 6 we discussed the law of exercise, which states that we learn by practice since repetition develops habits. Habits are action patterns that have been repeated so many times that we perform them automatically, finding it easiest to drift along in customary ways that require little conscious thought. Let's face it, most of us are somewhat lazy and prefer to follow the line of least resistance. This tendency to become set in our ways starts at an early age, and even young campers are likely to prefer to maintain the status quo unless something important or even catastrophic happens to jar their lethargy and make them really want to change. Altering a pattern of life in even minor ways makes us uncomfortable and requires the expenditure of mental, emotional, and perhaps even physical effort. Also, our egos cause us to resist change, because we hate to admit to any imperfection in ourselves. We also hesitate to change because the well-worn path provides security, whereas a venture into the unknown produces fear.

You must bear these things in mind when trying to influence others to change and must fortify yourself with large quantities of patience, insight, empathy, and understanding and be prepared for occasional backsliding and delays. Don't expect miracles overnight, for even when people sincerely want to change, they are sure to suffer periods of discouragement and impatience that tempt them to give up. This is when they need you to step in with encouragement and a pat on the back, reminding them of the progress they have already made (even though you may need to search hard to find it). Point out that their feelings are common to all who try to change their habits, and it may help to tell them of the setbacks and frustrations you and others experienced on the way to eventual success.

Preparation for the Good Life

One of your basic aims in guidance is to help all campers to respect themselves. As we noted previously, children at camp can develop such traits as self-confidence, leadership skills, and followership ability, and can learn the techniques of group living and of cultivating and keeping new friends. They can also find acceptable ways to satisfy their fundamental needs or wishes by participation and achievement in as many aspects of camp life as possible. Hopefully, no matter what specific activities children engage in, their camping experience will teach them skills and ways of living that will provide immediate satisfaction and lay the groundwork for a well-balanced adult life.

In camp, children occupy the center of the stage, where they are fairly free to determine the role they will play. They can establish their own goals and then provide the momentum and drive to achieve them, setting their own course and deciding on the speed at which they will pursue it. This encourages the development of the self-reliance, personal adjustment, good mental health, and emotional maturity that any person involved in guidance or counseling strives for. You, the counselor, play an important role in this development as you apply a push in one direction or a restraining hand in another, as the occasion demands. You must encourage children to be as independent and self-reliant as they can, while you remain more or less in the background, ready to discreetly give them assurance, advice, and encouragement. Doing your job well requires tact and skill in knowing when and how to assist, admonish, or help, and how to do it so unobtrusively that campers are scarcely aware of your participation.

SUGGESTIONS FOR OBSERVING GROUP BEHAVIOR

Noting Individual Differences

As you observe your group in their daily activities, you will note marked differences in individual reactions to the group and in the amount of interest and enthusiasm shown toward participation in group activities. You will also detect similar differences in group response to various individuals. At home, children are usually accepted and loved just as they are, but at camp, their welcome will most likely depend on what they can contribute and the general compatibility of their personalities with others. A few lucky, outgoing newcomers are greeted with open arms and quickly assimilated, for they have customarily been well accepted in the past and so have acquired enough self-confidence to approach a new group with friendly self-assurance and an easy, relaxed manner. These fortunate individuals seemingly never know a stranger, and so do not understand the pangs of loneliness and rejection experienced by others. The large majority, however, do not stand out in any particular way, remaining more or less on the borderline while the group sizes them up and eventually decides what group status to accord them. There are usually several unfortunate souls who will remain on the fringe for a long time before being accepted, and then only with certain reservations, and a few others will be permanently branded as unacceptable. It often seems that, no matter how much time a child spends with the group or the amount of effort he or she exerts to try to fit in, the ultimate outcome is determined by some more or less intangible factor that is very difficult for either the child or an observer to pinpoint.

Interpreting These Differences

Campers' reactions to their peers can often reveal much about how they feel about themselves, especially to someone with the training and insight to interpret the message correctly. If

(Willamette Council of Camp Fire, Salem, Oreg.)

unsure of themselves and afraid of being ignored, campers may react in various ways. They may try to disguise their discomfort by adopting an indifferent attitude or by demanding the spotlight and showing off. They may assume an air of bravado and brag about themselves so much that they seem insufferably aggressive and conceited. Another tactic children employ is to retire into the background, trying to be as inconspicuous as possible and using every excuse imaginable to avoid the painful experience of making contact with others. They may be arrogant and quickly take offense when none was intended, or may become extremely sensitive and show signs of hurt feelings. They may adopt an apologetic manner and constantly belittle themselves, or may attempt to get attention by telling tales of woe to anyone who will listen. Most of these reactions tend to repel others, and this rejection only intensifies the feelings of inadequacy and self-doubt.

Insecure youngsters sometimes try to win acceptance and approval by being subservient and willing to serve as everybody's "doormat," eagerly running errands or performing little services for them. In so doing, they apparently abandon all efforts to establish their own identity and win approval and respect by their own accomplishments; instead, they are willing to accept any small signs of appreciation and attention they can get, no matter the cost.

Youngsters who react in any of these ways may do so because of a lack of previous experience in informal situations with a peer group or because they are trying to protect themselves from a repetition of painful experiences in the past. They may be trying too hard to cope with a situation they don't understand or lack the skill to control, causing others to shy away from them. No matter whether youngsters react with aggression and assertiveness or by surrender and withdrawal, you can be sure that they feel frustrated, unhappy, and lonely, and perhaps may even want to give up and go home because of their innate desire to belong and be accepted. When you encounter children like this, hurry to the rescue, for they desperately need someone to help them find a way out of their misery. If they give up and run away now, it will only deepen their sense of inadequacy and make it even harder for them to gain acceptance in the future, if they can summon up the courage to try again.

Such individuals may have certain personality traits or habits that others dislike, such as selfishness, bossiness, or personal uncleanliness. The possible reasons for these problems are legion, and it is indeed a challenge to discover what the problems are and what can be done to help troubled campers overcome them. Stay constantly on the alert to discover what forces are really at work, since an individual's outward behavior is often merely a camouflage to conceal the true underlying feelings and problems. What appears on the surface often bears surprisingly little resemblance to the turmoil boiling underneath.

COUNSELING WITH YOUR CAMPERS

Opportunities for the Counselor

Every association you have with campers is a potential counseling situation, for everything you do, every word, action, gesture, or facial expression sets a pattern or expresses an attitude that may influence them far more than you suspect. Each contact with your group or its individuals gives you an opportunity to know them better and perhaps influence them to some degree, and these contacts serve as important learning and growing situations for campers. In our increasingly complex world each person is forced to make choices and decisions to an extent never dreamed of by past generations, and this applies even to youngsters of camp age. A sensible and well-balanced camp counselor can do a great deal to give campers the knowledge and judgment they need to make the right choices.

Getting Acquainted

The foundation of your relationship with your campers must rest upon a real concern for each and every individual and an understanding of and readiness to accept them as they are. You should constantly seek to know them better, exploring their personalities, their relationships with others, and their problems and possibly helping them to realize and examine their true feelings and ideas. With continued contact, you should come to recognize them as unique individuals who differ from every other human being and whose individual patterns of thinking and feeling deserve your respect and acceptance.

Individual Discussions

Individual counseling or guidance is an integral part of your job, for in addition to exerting influence through group associations, you also will have many personal encounters with campers. These will occur as you find occasion to seek out individuals or are sought out by them for a private chat or discussion. These informal conversations will provide some of your best opportunities to influence others. Since there is already a congenial feeling between you and the other person, both of you are in a proper frame of mind to listen eagerly to what the other has to say. Such a favorable climate is hard to achieve in more formal interviews or in appointments scheduled specifically for counseling, since a formal situation may make a camper cautious and wary of free expression and hence less receptive to your comments or advice.

When the two of you are together, the child may often bring up topics that seem trivial to you but may be life and death matters to the youngster. In order to establish good rapport, it is essential that you give that person your undivided attention and avoid interruptions if at all possible. The camper should be put at ease and made to feel that you want to hear everything that is said.

Through listening, counselors can play an important role in helping campers understand their own feelings and be more in touch with themselves. Even as adults we occasionally have need for someone with whom we can talk out our problems or lean on in times of confusion or anxiety. Talking with a good listener can be helpful in encouraging open, honest, and free expression and in gaining understanding, insight, and meaning in our lives.

Those who are skillful in listening and responding help to facilitate this therapeutic process. For instance, a counselor can encourage campers to speak openly and say those things that are important to them and, in so doing, can help them gain better insight into themselves. On the other hand, a counselor's responses can hinder or retard a camper's self-understanding, especially if the response is judgmental, too full of advice, or of such a nature that it puts the camper in the position of listener. Therefore, when placed in the role of counselor, try to commend, praise, reassure, and encourage the person who is speaking. When appropriate, it may also be helpful to repeat or clarify what you have heard to show that you understand and want to help the person gain insight into his or her real problem and discover its solution.

A sense of closeness encourages campers to chat with you informally, and they sometimes pour out their innermost thoughts and emotions. If this occurs, do not become irritated or impatient with them but offer encouragement and treasure these confidences, since these individuals need a sympathetic, and understanding person with whom they can talk freely. People who trust no one and thus lack such a confidant tend to bottle up their thoughts and emotions until tension builds to such a degree that it may eventually explode in an uncontrolled outburst. By serving as their safety valve, you gain an unparalleled opportunity to learn more about the campers as they reveal a side of themselves that they may never have fully disclosed to anyone before. Learn to listen carefully, and be observant as you listen, for a camper's facial expressions, mannerisms, and gestures may tell you even more than his or her words do, if you have the sensitivity and wisdom to interpret them properly. Body movements, facial expressions, and any other indications of a camper's underlying emotions will often help you to discern what they fail to find words to express or perhaps are unconsciously trying to hide, sometimes even from themselves. Even a moment's lapse of attention on your part may cause you to miss an important key to understanding them and what they are trying to tell you.

Develop the ability to sense when to be quiet and let the other person talk and when to enter into the conversation yourself. Good listeners are rare, and thus are deeply appreciated, and by developing this trait you will acquire a skill that will serve you and be of inestimable value all your life. In talking about themselves campers may be better able to organize their thinking or see things more objectively. Your main function is to help them think things through and eventually work out possible ways to handle whatever is bothering them.

Offer your own opinions and insights sparingly and refrain from either approving or disapproving of what is being said until you are

(Camp Kooch-I-Ching, International Falls, Minn.)

sure you have a fairly complete picture of the entire situation. Try to avoid the common mistake of telling anyone exactly what to do, since this will only delay the process of learning to face up to problems and arrive at personal conclusions.

Ordinarily, you can and should reassure your campers that whatever they tell you is strictly confidential. However, there may come a time when a camper seems to be on the verge of divulging information that your position requires you to reveal to a higher camp authority. Fairness requires that you warn the person of your responsibility so that he or she will not continue unless willing to take this risk.

See It from the Camper's Viewpoint

When upset, perplexed, or worried youngsters come to you, or when you, realizing their needs, make the overtures, try first of all to get a picture of the problem or situation as they see it. This is not at all simple, for it is very easy to falsely assume that we start on common ground with others and that their view of problems are identical with our own. On the contrary, it is much more likely that each person will have a different view that is determined by such factors as past and present experiences, physical health, mood of the moment, personality, general attitudes toward life, and even one's own self-concept.

An important point to remember is that each of us has a tendency to see what we are looking for or want to see in a situation. When we meet a new camper for the first time and note how much his or her looks or mannerisms resemble those of another person whom we greatly dislike, we are apt to form an immediate dislike of the new person. If we ever fully come to accept and like him or her, it will be only after a long and consistently favorable association. If a camper is thrown and painfully injured while riding a horse, he or she is likely to invent a dozen excuses for never attempting to ride again. If a youngster was consistently misused and mistreated at home, he or she will most likely trust no one and rebuff every effort you make to be kind and helpful. If a student's school course in nature study was presented in a bookish, boring fashion, the nature counselor will find it hard to stir up even a flicker of enthusiasm in him or her; in fact, youngsters like this may be so preoccupied with thoughts of how much they dislike nature study that they will be completely deaf and blind to the fascinating things the nature counselor is doing and saying. When two people are confronted with an identical situation, they may each interpret it so differently that, if you could read their minds, you would not even recognize it as the same situation at all. This is why it is so important for you to try to see a problem through the eyes of the campers, for you cannot otherwise hope to understand their reactions or be of any real help to them.

Changing a Camper's Viewpoint

You may find that you will need to help campers to look at situations from a different perspective. For instance, if a young boy or girl comes to you incensed because the swimming counselor won't allow him or her to practice diving off the dock after dark, how can you help that person to see the situation through the swimming counselor's eyes? After all, the swimming counselor isn't just trying to assert authority and take delight in spoiling the campers' fun—indeed, he or she is devoted to youngsters and wants them to have all the *safe* fun they possibly can—but undue risks and hazardous activities must be curtailed. When campers realize that the counselor is concerned only for their safety, they will see that the staff member is acting as a conscientious swimming counselor.

In trying to broaden campers' viewpoints, it may help to encourage them to consider various aspects of a problem or situation, such as why it happened, the motives or thinking of the others involved, and any additional factors that have been influential in some way. They may want to consider alternative solutions to the dilemma and the probable consequences of each; this may often cause them to conclude that things actually happened for the best after all. By teaching campers to examine a problem from every possible angle (including others' viewpoints), you will help them to avoid hasty decisions and to choose a solution that will prove most satisfactory in the long run. This is the thinking process practiced by those who act with maturity and good judgment.

Be Aware of Your Limitations

Again, let us emphasize the importance of remaining humble and realistic about your own abilities to completely understand situations and guide people, for this is an area filled with potential danger, and you must exercise extreme caution. You cannot and must not put yourself on a par with a professional guidance counselor who has studied extensively in such fields of counseling as mental health, group behavior, and psychology.

In these chapters, we have merely tried to present some common-sense procedures to use when facing everyday situations. The aim has been to help you to effectively solve those problems that you are able to handle and to recognize those that are beyond your capabilities. Confine your efforts to the commonplace happenings and problems of normal camp life and to those occasions when youngsters mainly want guidance and advice or someone to listen to them as they unburden themselves of tensions and pressures that have build up inside.

In your close daily contacts with campers you may be the first to note individual behavior problems or symptoms that seem to point to a possible need for referral to the proper person. The following are examples of such indications:

- Confusion as to one's identity or extreme forgetfulness about common happenings and facts.
- Extreme muscle tremors and spasms, especially facial tics (twitches).
- Frequent absent-mindedness or disorientation to time and place.
- Uncontrolled or unusual homosexual or heterosexual practices or interests.
- Continued refusal to eat or being extremely "picky" about one's eating.
- Persistent *enuresis* (bed-wetting).

Do not be an alarmist or overemphasize the normal quirks that we all have, but if convinced that there is real need for concern, go immediately to the proper authority, such as your unit leader, head counselor or camp director. Under no circumstances should you discuss the situation freely with other campers or unqualified staff members; this could be quite harmful to the camper or could seriously hamper the efforts of someone in an official capacity who later tries to deal with the situation.

CASE STUDIES IN CAMP

Some camps use the case study method to help campers who have problems. A case study provides a method of studying a child or group of children to bring about a better understanding of them and eventually help them to make a better adjustment to camp and to society in general. It consists of gathering available data about a specific boy or girl, then assembling, organizing, and studying it to discover the nature and causes of whatever difficulty the camper has, and eventually deciding how best to help him or her to overcome it. The material gathered should present as complete and objective a picture as possible, but of course, the data alone will not provide an interpretation or pinpoint the problem facing the camper at the moment. Keen insight, knowledge, and intelligence are needed to assemble the material properly and then interpret it. Case studies should therefore not be undertaken except under professional supervision, and we should bear in mind that *treatment* is not usually the basic purpose in a camp situation. Rather, the study can, under certain circumstances, indicate a need for referral, or it can help to solve an immediate problem or provide constructive assistance in promoting the growth and adjustment of a camper or group of campers.

Imaginary case studies are often used with prospective counselors during precamp and inservice training sessions in order to make counselors aware of the importance of their role in leadership and to orient them to problems they may meet and various possible approaches toward solving them. Such studies usually prove quite helpful and interesting, as counselors examine the situation and present what they consider the best way to handle it and then participate in a general discussion and evaluation of the various viewpoints presented.

When properly conducted, case studies can broaden and deepen our understanding of individuals and their underlying motivations and can provide us with ways to analyze and deal with problems. However, a word of caution is necessary for everyone involved. Although the use of case studies in camp seems exciting and challenging, no individual or group should undertake it without the approval of the camp director and the assistance of adequately trained personnel who are capable of supervising it. Otherwise, much harm may result and both the counselor and the camp may become involved in unpleasant situations and possibly even legal difficulties.

ADDITIONAL READINGS

(For an explanation of abbreviations and abbreviated forms, see p. 13.)

Adams, Jay E.: *Competent to Counsel.* Baker, 1973, 287 pp.

Barksdale, L. S.: *Building Self-Esteem.* The Barksdale Foundation, Idyllwild, Cal., 1972.

Blanchard, Howard L., and Laurence S. Flaum: *Guidance: A Longitudinal Approach.* Burgess, 1969, 338 pp., paper.

Bloom, et al.: *Camper Guidance—A Basic Handbook for Counselors,* pp. 7–8, 19–23.

Budd, William C., Ph.D.: *Behavior Modification: The Scientific Way to Self Control.* Galloway, 96 pp.

Forrer, Dr. Gordon R.: *Psychiatric Self Help.* Galloway, 71 pp.

Kemp, C. Gratton: *Perspective on the Group Process, A Foundation for Counseling With Groups.* Houghton Mifflin, 2nd ed., 1970, 388 pp.

MacKay: *Creative Counseling for Christian Camps,* ch. 4.

O'Banion, Terry, and April O'Connell: *The Shared Journey.* Prentice-Hall, 1970, pp. 3–184.

Otto, Herbert: *Group Methods Designed to Actualize Human Potential.* Stone-Brandel Center, Chicago, Ill., 2nd ed., 1967.

Shea, Thomas M.: *Camping for Special Children.* Mosby, 1977, 244 pp.

Shivers: *Camping,* ch. 8.

Strean: *New Approaches in Child Guidance.*

Van Krevelen: *Children in Groups: Psychology and the Summer Camp,* ch. 3.

Vinton, Dennis A., and Elizabeth M. Farley: *Camp Staff Training Series, Module 5, Dealing With Camper Behavior.* Available from ACA, 1979, 131 pp.

Magazine Articles

CAMPING MAGAZINE:

Bavley, Fred: "Camp Can Change Campers' Attitudes." Sept., 1972, p. 18.

Bower, Robert and Mary: "Group Experience: The Essence of Camping." Insert in Jan., 1980, p. 21.

Campbell, Barry: "Focus on the Camper." Sept./Oct., 1973, p. 13.

Chenery, Mary Faeth: "Committing Yourself to the Campers." May, 1978, p. 18.

Rabban, Dr. Meyer: "What Camps Can Do to Meet Individual Camper Needs and Still Maintain Group Effectiveness." Mar., 1973, p. 8.

"Research Shows Campers Improve Self-Concept." Nov., 1972, p. 12.

Van Krevelen, Alice, Ph.D.: "Stop, Look and Listen if You Want to Be Heard." Mar., 1969, p. 17.

Webb, Keneth B.: "Camps Can Set New Life Style." Jan., 1976, p. 10.

People are Highly Individualistic

As you note the many similarities among people whom you know well, you are at the same time struck by the even more numerous ways in which they differ. First, they differ physically in such aspects as height, weight, musculature, hair coloring and texture, bone structure, complexion, facial features, and expressions. They also vary in body carriage, speed and way of moving, voice tone and pitch, favorite expressions and word choice, and even ways of laughing, so that you can recognize each individual when seen at a distance or heard talking in the next room. If someone recounts Jack's remarks or actions to you, your immediate reaction is likely to be "that is (or isn't) just like Jack," for you have come to identify him with certain characteristic attitudes, emotional reactions, wishes, ways of thinking, likes and dislikes, abilities, and ideals that make up his particular personality. Human traits are so numerous, and each exists in such varying degrees, that the countless possible permutations and combinations rule out any chance of finding exactly the same combination in any two individuals; this is why each of your friends and loved ones occupies a special niche in your heart that no one else could ever fill.

At the same time these differences add variety to your associations with others, they also increase the difficulty of always understanding different individuals and of establishing a mutually satisfactory relationship with them. Though modern study and research in human behavior have made tremendous strides, providing us with generalities and probabilities that *usually* hold true, each person still remains a unique entity that can always prove the exception to the rule. Even those who have studied extensively in this area confess their inability to classify people with assurance or fully explain what they are, how they got that way, what they will do in certain situations, or how they will respond to a certain type of treatment. Therefore, it certainly behooves those of us with relatively meager training and experience to refrain from setting ourselves up as experts and attempting to diagnose and prescribe in complex cases. Fortunately, most youngsters in camp seldom present serious problems since they are perfectly normal, healthy individuals with many good and

nine
Some Problems You May Meet

He drew a circle that shut me out—
Heretic, rebel, a thing to flout.
But Love and I had the wit to win,
We drew a circle that took him in.*

—Edwin Markham

Rudeness is a weak man's imitation of strength.

—*Newsweek*

*Reproduced by permission of Virgil Markham.

few bad qualities. Therefore, if you have some training that is supplemented with large doses of common sense there should be little difficulty in coping with most of the problems you will meet. However, at the risk of undue repetition, let us again caution you to adopt a policy of "hands off" and referral to the proper person when you note signs of serious trouble, for bungling attempts to help, no matter how well meant, can do irreparable harm during these important formative years in a youngster's life. It is far beyond our ability or purpose in this discussion to give more than general and nontechnical information designed to help you to better understand and meet common problems and situations.

Who or What is Normal?

Society has set up types of behavior that it considers normal or acceptable for given situations. These are not always the same, however, for they change with the passage of time, and each individual stratum of society or community has its own mores, or customs, so that what one considers as good or normal may be deemed just the opposite by another.

(Willamette Council of Camp Fire, Salem, Oreg.)

When our conduct follows pretty much along the accepted lines in a particular situation, we receive the stamp of approval and are called "normal." It seems that conformity or doing what our particular environment expects is the acid test, and if we stray very far from the norm we will be classified as exceptional, a genius, antisocial, an underachiever, a failure, a misfit, or whatever other terms happen to be in vogue at that particular time and place. If a youngster's behavior bothers others they will be likely to dub the person as a "problem child."

Such terms as good mental health and normal behavior are much bandied about today. Most people have a general understanding of what they mean, but would probably be at a loss if asked to give an exact definition of them. Although measurable human traits vary in degree, if you rated a group of people by means of these traits by plotting them on a "normal curve," the majority of people would be clustered about a center or norm, and the relatively few found outside this area on either side would be classed as abnormal or deviant. Obviously, the exact point at which the abnormal begins would not be universally agreed upon, since its location is a matter of opinion, and hence would differ with each individual.

Good Mental Health

People with good mental health adjust well to others and find ways to solve their problems and meet needs that are mutually acceptable to both them and society. This places them in a happy state of mind called *euphoria,* in which they are at peace and on good terms with themselves and others. This state is hard to steadfastly maintain, however, since the world is made up of individuals, each intent on satisfying his or her own particular wishes and needs; this makes conflicts and disappointments inevitable. Studies have also revealed that our moods vary for seemingly unexplainable reasons, carrying us cyclically from a phase of depression to one of exhilaration in which we float blissfully along.

People with emotional maturity and good mental health have learned to adjust their own wishes to those of their associates and are willing to give as well as receive, taking their disappointments and changing moods in stride without being unduly upset or reacting in extreme ways. We must be realistic, however, and admit that even the most exemplary person cannot always have the wisdom and fortitude to exercise perfect control and to act as others would like. As we have seen, our associates do not always agree on what they want or expect from us, and consequently each of us probably becomes, at some time or another, a "problem child" to someone else.

We Want What We Want When We Want It

Newborn babies are entirely selfish and think only of themselves. They cry when they want something and are encouraged to continue the practice when it proves successful. Fortunately, as children grow older, those around them are usually wise enough to realize that youngsters' desires must occasionally be denied, they must be taught to consider others, and, they must be willing sometimes to yield their needs and wishes, since society has effective and often painful ways of expressing its disapproval of those who remain self-centered and insist on always having their own way. Occasionally, however, we find a few people who have always managed to force others to give in to their wishes by crying, throwing temper tantrums, wheedling, cajoling, bargaining, blackmailing, begging, bullying, threatening, or making things generally disagreeable in order to get what they want. Parents often give in to their children out of a desire to keep peace or in a misguided attempt to show their love for their child, but whatever their motivation, they have effectively taught their child that these tactics can be used to get what they want.

When such children come to camp, they usually will continue to use these tactics to obtain material possessions, attain status, gain recognition or attention, or acquire anything else they want. Their methods may be so ingrained that they are scarcely aware of them and may be greatly astonished when their new camp associates ignore them when they exhibit these extremely immature traits.

Although you find such conduct unappealing and annoying, remember that these children are immature and have problems that are largely the creation of others. You will need to help these children understand and overcome this problem by learning to respect the rights and wishes of others or they will be resented and ostracized, making their lives even more miserable.

A Counselor Must Develop Insight

Children have wishes and needs they wish to satisfy immediately, but often they can find no easy and direct way of doing so. In desperation, some children may take action that is so counterproductive and so seemingly unrelated to their desires that neither they nor anyone else can understand exactly what they are trying to accomplish. For instance, a bully or braggart may be unconsciously demonstrating a need for status and attention. A counselor's natural reaction to this type of behavior might be to belittle or scold the camper in an attempt to take care of the problem as well as discourage others from engaging in similar conduct and thereby establish the counselor as a forceful leader who can maintain control in any situation.

If we look at the problem more rationally, however, it is obvious that such actions would only treat the symptom, not the underlying cause. Although the behavior might change temporarily, the net result would only be to intensify the situation and cause the camper to have deep and painful doubts about his or her worth as an individual. Unless you can find some healthy way to bolster this person's ego, his or her misgivings will continue to fester and grow, eventually breaking out again in a new direction. It is worth repeating here that misbehavior quite often is merely an outward sign of underlying dissatisfaction, which is rarely overcome by direct treatment of the behavior. Repressing one type of undesirable behavior will only cause different and often more severe problems. You must probe behind the symptoms until you can find the underlying cause and try to remedy it since only then will the symptoms subside. Treating only the symptoms is like carelessly brushing a mosquito away from your face; it will soon be back, hungrier than ever and bringing all its cousins with it.

Campers seldom understand why they misbehave or create problems. Although they may be aware of vague feelings of unrest and unhappiness, self-diagnosis is notoriously fallible, since behavioral difficulties have a cause that is as real and deep-rooted as physical problems that cause pain. Everything a person does is for the purpose of meeting a need, and when an individual's conduct is objectionable, we must have the wisdom to analyze the problems and help find acceptable ways to solve them.

This will present a real challenge, for emotional pains are even harder to diagnose and eliminate than physical ones. (Incidentally, as you become more adept at observing and understanding others, you will be better able to understand and solve your own problems.)

So-called "problem" campers are usually the products of problem environments or associates, and many arrive in camp with cases already full-blown. Conscientious but overdoting parents can spoil children so that they expect the same undue attention in camp or anywhere else. A child accustomed to living in a household of adults who center all their attention and affection on him or her is often at a loss when placed with others of the same age. We may also find a counterpart in children who are suffering from lack of love, who may be jealous of the family's esteem for a brother or sister, or who feel that they were sent to camp just to get rid of them while the parents enjoy a trip or vacation. Such children will understandably demonstrate an abnormal craving for the love denied them elsewhere. Their difficulties sometimes arise for the first time in camp, or if already present, get worse when they are subjected to unwise camp procedures that fail to recognize and meet the real issue. Camps sometimes carry on a rigid, strenuous program, and require each camper to participate in every part of it. Some individuals react badly to such a regimen, becoming sensitive, irritable, quarrelsome, or rebellious as their feelings of resentment and frustration build up. The child misbehaves as a reaction, causing discipline problems for the counselors, the entire unit, or even the whole camp.

Emotionally stable persons can usually face their problems and disappointments honestly and work out satisfactory solutions. The emotionally unstable meet them by (1) evasion or withdrawing, or (2) through aggression or fighting back. The strategy and cunning exhibited by the subconscious mind in an attempt to cover up the real trouble makes it hard to get at the source and help the person in a realistic way.

Even after the true cause is determined, there is no such thing as a never-failing remedy or magic recipe, for each situation is complex and individual in itself. Consequently, an unskilled counselor is likely to be mistreating instead of treating the camper.

THE CAMPER WHO WITHDRAWS OR EVADES

The need to help campers who are timid, apologetic and retiring often is unrecognized, for they cause little disturbance and are overshadowed by those who are aggressive and create problems that demand the counselor's attention; this is an example of the old saying that "It's the axle that squeaks the most that gets the grease." However, those trained in psychology realize that a child's failure to demand attention and his or her apparent happiness in pursuing a solitary way often indicate development of a serious problem. In contrast, aggressive people are so obnoxious that they cannot be ignored, but wise leadership will likely provide them with the help they need to understand their problems and start overcoming them while still in the early stages.

The evading camper, like the aggressive camper, usually has inner feelings of dissatisfaction, insecurity, or inadequacy, with behavior that may take one of many forms. Instead of facing their problems, they retreat into a little world all their own and may adopt any of several automatic, unconscious mechanisms to protect themselves from hurt and rebuff. Some of these mechanisms are described in the following paragraphs.

Daydreaming consists of retreating into a fantasy world to temporarily escape the stresses of everyday life. When kept under control, daydreaming affords pleasant relaxation and is often beneficial, for great doers are usually great dreamers whose dreams stimulate them to action. However, when dreaming becomes an end in itself and provides complete satisfaction, it is a waste of time, for no one can keep warm and well fed in an air castle.

Wishful thinkers persist in believing what they want to believe despite all the evidence to the contrary; they escape facing unpleasant facts by simply ignoring them. *Sweet lemons* or *pollyannas* likewise close their eyes to all unpleasantness and difficulty by simply refusing to worry about anything, expressing confidence that everything is predestined to turn out for the best. If any calamity befalls, they shrug it off by saying, "It might have been worse" or "It is God's will." This frees them from guilt feelings or responsibility for neglected work or failure to recognize and correct their own faults. Though often happy and carefree themselves, their unwillingness to do their share leaves others with a disproportionate amount of work to do and responsibility to assume.

Sorry-for-themselves retreat into a self-centered sanctum where they can dwell moodily upon how misunderstood and mistreated they are, until they often become literally obsessed with the idea. They may even go so far as to picture themselves as cold and silent in death, while those who have wronged them stand by in sorrow and contrition, or they may even morbidly play with the idea of suicide. Some want to run home to mother to have their aches and bruises kissed away when faced with the cold fact that others expect them to stand up to life instead of demanding childhood favors and pampering. Others develop a convenient *illness* to avoid unpleasant tasks, while still others become *self-worshippers* to compensate for their lack of status in the eyes of others. Some youngsters who have failed to secure affection and recognition from those of their own age become abnormally attached to an adult who has been kind or at least tolerant of them. They claim to be completely bored with those of their own age group.

Others crowd out the unhappiness caused by inability to fit in with their peers by becoming *loners* and turning to strictly solitary pursuits such as reading, drawing, or boating. Thus they eliminate the necessity of having to tailor themselves to group standards.

Those who have had their suggestions and remarks jeered at or ignored may avoid further hurt by degenerating into *yes-men* who need show no initiative and can retire into the background and avoid calling attention to themselves.

Rationalizers try to avoid blame from either their own consciences or the accusations of others by thinking up plausible excuses to make everything they do seem right and reasonable. A favorite form is *alibiing* or *projecting* the blame

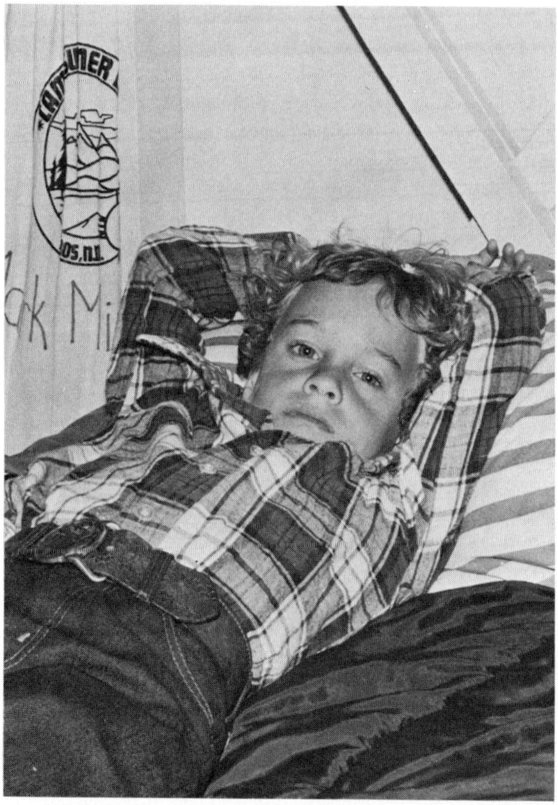

(Camp Summer Life, Odessa, Tex.)

(*passing the buck*) for what happens to other people or things. These are the campers who claim that they were late to breakfast because their counselor failed to rouse them, that their team lost because the umpire was partial, or that they lost the tennis match because of their inferior rackets. They are afraid to face facts and admit that they, like all humans, have faults and weaknesses. Another form of rationalization is found in the *sour grapes attitude* of the fox who couldn't reach the grapes and so pretended they were so sour that he didn't want them anyway. Thus the uncultured person calls those who like good music or literature "highbrow" and the nonathletic student speaks of "brainless wonders"; the poor student sneeringly refers to good students as "greasy grinds," and those with ambition and initiative are "eager beavers" to the lazy.

Self-repudiators are people whose feelings of insecurity about some trait make them fish for compliments by running themselves down with such remarks as "Oh, I'm terribly dumb" or "I'm awfully plainlooking." They, of course, are hoping that you will heartily reassure them that just the opposite is true.

Some, failing to achieve success in a desired field, *compensate* by redirecting their efforts into another. Thus the girl who is not blessed with physical beauty may work extra hard to become an outstanding student, a corporate executive, or a professional tennis player. The boy without the coordination and physical stamina to gain athletic prowess may become a skilled violinist, a great scientist, or a famous writer. Obviously, *substitution* or *compensation* at its best can be a great force for good, and a study of the lives of some of our foremost citizens shows that disappointments or feelings of inferiority in some area have spurred them on to achieve great distinction in another. But when such feelings distort the personality and cause the person to retire from human companionship or strive to be the biggest troublemaker, liar, gang leader or hoodlum, it is an equally potent force for evil.

THE CAMPER WHO RESPONDS WITH AGRESSION

Instead of trying to retire into obscurity, those with unmet needs sometimes try desperately to draw attention to themselves. The *braggart*, the *bully*, the *smarty*, and the *tough guy* who swagger about in an attitude of pretended fearlessness and assurance are examples; they are, in reality, covering up a feeling of insecurity because of their failure to attract attention and gain status by legitimate means. Bullies usually attack those younger or weaker than themselves or those who won't retaliate. Boasting campers are trying to convince themselves or others that they are actually the great people they inwardly fear they aren't; instead, such attitudes repel others and cause them to ridicule, dislike, ignore, or shun the aggressor, which only intensifies the problem.

Youngsters who *smoke* or *drink* to excess or who *swear* and use *foul language* may be indulging in a misguided effort to relieve their pent-up emotions and gain status and recognition. *Bossy, domineering* people exercise power in the only way they know how—by making themselves so unpleasant that others would rather give in than resist.

Physically or emotionally handicapped children sometimes take out their frustrations by being arrogant or antagonistic, or resorting to acts of cruelty or vindictiveness.

The *boisterous*, the *show-offs*, and the girls or boys who go to *extremes in dress* would actually prefer to find their niches by other means if they knew how. The antics of the *mimic*, the *cut-up*, and the *practical joker* have at one time brought the attention desired, but so far unattained in other ways, and so have been adopted as standard conduct.

Constant talkers who monopolize the conversation subconsciously envy their quiet, more socially acceptable companions who can feel secure of their place without constantly needing to occupy the limelight. People *who eat the fastest, most,* or *least* and those with numerous *food dislikes* or *idiosyncrasies* are often in the same category with those who bask in the "individuality" of *poor health*, or *unusual ailment*, or an *artistic temperament*.

People who cry at the drop of a hat or become *hysterical* and throw a *temper tantrum* have probably found these methods effective in getting their own way in the past and so continue the practice.

Quarrelsome, stubborn, or *rebellious* people are so unsure of themselves that they use loud words and violent action to drown out their own misgivings and discourage others from questioning them.

Intolerant people who "know all the answers" are, in spite of their dogmatic statements, really distrustful of their own beliefs and are loath to listen to others lest they show up their inferior reasoning. *Overcritical* people call attention to little flaws in others in hope that this will make them seem superior by comparison.

Campers who form little *cliques* of two or more are seeking comfort from each other for their inability to make a place for themselves in the larger group. Forcibly breaking up the alliance may cause acute misery as the disapproval forces their egos down still further; a better solution is to lead them gradually into general group participation so that they will no longer need the consolation of their little band. Some resort to *regression*, or reverting to behavior of an earlier period, such as baby talk or complete dependence, hoping to be sheltered and excused for childish behavior and shortcomings as they were at that age.

Other annoying ways of trying to draw attention are noisiness, getting in the way, asking innumerable questions, refusing to eat, deliberately running away, or constantly complaining of injuries and ailments. Although normal children and even adults sometimes use attention-getting devices, immature methods and excessive use should gradually disappear as youngsters grow older and eventually acquire more mature and satisfactory ways to meet their needs. *Thumbsucking, nailbiting* and facial *tics* are all nervous symptoms that act as "tension-reducers" and usually result from failure, frustration, or harsh disciplinary measures.

HOMESICK CAMPERS

Many campers feel a sense of loneliness and homesickness upon first coming to camp, but fortunately most of them adjust well and are soon having a fine time and joining enthusiastically in camp activities. However, some campers will remain teary-eyed and aloof, resisting any efforts to become part of the group and insisting that they want to go home. Before you can help them, you will need to try to determine just what is the root of their problem.

Children who have never been away from home before may be overwhelmed by the strange faces and unfamiliar surroundings. They may have had little experience in associating with others of their own age outside of school and may be so painfully shy that it is hard for them to seek out or even accept friendships, and having to wash and dress before others may be excruciatingly embarrassing. They may feel a vague uneasiness at the quiet strangeness of the woods, particularly at night when their ears magnify the unaccustomed rustlings of animal life a hundredfold.

This situation sometimes results from an overly dependent parent-child relationship, which may be of a mutual or one-sided nature. Parents, without realizing it, have sometimes come to depend upon the child to satisfy their own need to feel loved and important and therefore do everything they can to encourage his or her dependency. They may actually enjoy having their child express unhappiness at being away and long to have him or her clamor to come back to them. Their letters may dwell upon how everyone, including pals and pets, misses the child and how much fun they are having doing the things the youngster used to enjoy, and they show their love and concern by frequent letters, telephone calls, and boxes of goodies. It is for these reasons that camps often counsel parents on the type of letter to write and ask them not to send packages or call (except in an emergency) or visit the camper until after the first two weeks of a long-term camp session; by that time the camper will most likely be smiling and enthusiastic about what he or she is doing.

An opposite problem involves campers who feel that their parents do not love them and have sent them to camp so that the parents can go on a trip or enjoy an uninhibited social life without them. This feeling of rejection often leads children to believe that no one at camp will want them either.

Another type of trouble comes with campers who have learned to manipulate their parents by screaming, coaxing, flattering, cajoling, or throwing temper tantrums. When they find that these methods do not work at camp, it seems only natural that they will find fault with the camp and everyone connected with it and will want to return home where they know how to get their own way.

Spells of homesickness normally reach their peak about the third or fourth day of camp and are strongest at mealtime, in the evening around bedtime, or on Sundays. Note that these are relatively inactive times when campers have a good deal of time to think about themselves. Homesickness has its basis in fear, such as fear of strangers, of unfamiliar surroundings, or of not being accepted, and it is best forestalled by the methods suggested earlier to make campers feel welcome and at home. It may enlighten you and help campers by "talking it out." Assure them that such feelings are perfectly natural and are experienced by nearly everyone when they first stay away from home. It may also help to let homesick campers spend some time with an adult to whom they seem naturally attracted; this may, to some degree, provide a substitute for their missing parents. It also helps to keep campers busy in cabin- or unit-planned activities or ask them to do something at which they excel, such as drawing pictures for the camp paper, helping with an outdoor fireplace, or decorating the tables in the dining room, to give them a feeling of being important and needed.

You simply can't ignore homesick campers,

for their misery is very real and will probably only get worse if positive steps are not taken. Homesickness sometimes manifests itself as real or imaginary physical ailments, such as a stomachache or earache. If the nurse is sympathetic and gives the attention needed, the camper may seek excuses to go to the infirmary; a little of this is enough, and then some other satisfying substitutes need to be found.

Sometimes it helps to challenge a youngster's pride. Convince him or her to stick it out for a certain number of days with the promise that he or she may go home after this time if the desire to do so is still strong. You should realize that you are fighting for more than just retaining campers on the camp roster; in reality you are contributing to the youngsters' welfare by speeding them on their way to emotional maturity and gradual emancipation from overly restrictive home ties.

Sometimes the best efforts fail, however, and if it seems that the camper is being helped very little, the director may want to consider letting him or her go home, since homesickness is sometimes contagious and may spread to others who would adjust nicely if not exposed to it.

ENURESIS

Nearly all children are said to suffer from *enuresis* (bed-wetting) at some stage in their growth, and since there may be a physical cause, those experiencing repeated occurrences should be referred to the camp doctor or nurse. Many cases, however, are simply manifestations of a child's inability to satisfy his or her emotional needs, resulting in anxiety and worry to which they respond by reverting to regressive behavior. Failure to get enough sleep or relax properly may be contributing causes, and the child with enuresis may have other symptoms of anxiety or emotional unrest, such as nervousness, hyperactivity, defiant behavior, excessive daydreaming, exaggerating, lying, or stealing. An excessive state of anxiety may cause a child to be tense and poorly coordinated and consequently accident-prone.

If the health staff finds no physical cause and gives you the go-ahead, first set out to determine what is worrying or bothering the youngster and eliminate it if possible. Above all, do not add to an already wounded ego by shaming the child. Instead, be especially friendly and understanding, assuring the child that the trouble is not at all unique and that with his or her cooperation you feel sure that the difficulty can be overcome. In the meantime, use such precautionary measures as providing the camper with rubber sheets, limiting fluid intake after 5 o'clock, seeing that there is a visit to the latrine just before retiring and again three or four hours later until a dry bed becomes habitual. Also see that the child has a flashlight and companionship on night trips to the latrine.

SEX PROBLEMS

Role of Camp

Since camps are interested in educating the whole child and meeting his or her physical, mental, emotional, and social needs, you may be called upon to aid with some phase of sex education. Although all children have a normal and growing interest in sex, present-day social pressures and practices sometimes push them into an exaggerated or premature interest in sex and dating. (Bear in mind in this respect that girls mature approximately two years ahead of boys.) Unless children can receive the information they seek from some legitimate source, such as the home or school, they will seek it elsewhere, which unfortunately often turns out to be some equally uninformed or misinformed associate. Only a very naive or poorly informed person remains unaware of the presence of such interests and questions in every individual or group of young people, and instead of ignoring them in the hope that the questions will go away, it is usually better to recognize and face them openly.

Ways of Handling

Group discussions sometimes are helpful, since they give campers a chance to ask questions and learn that their own anxieties and problems are common to others. When sponsored by qualified, wise leaders, these discussions provide a means to substitute sound information for half-truths and misinformation so commonly available. Unless someone in authority asks you to, do not voluntarily launch out on a planned program in this area unless you detect a real desire or need for it, and then only after you have carefully examined your own qualifications for the task. Is your information sound and sufficiently broad to handle such an assignment, and are your attitudes healthy and your sense of values well balanced?

Always take a positive attitude toward sexual matters and do not be unduly alarmed at sexually oriented attitudes, language or behavior of your campers, for some of this is common. Similarly, do not become unduly suspicious or let your imagination run away with you, but if you are convinced that there is a real and serious problem that you cannot handle, seek the help of someone who is more qualified.

STRONG FRIENDSHIPS, HERO WORSHIP AND CRUSHES

Friendships

For reasons often not quite clear to us, we are strongly attracted to some people and just as strongly repelled by others, although the truly well-integrated person finds it possible to carry on pleasant relationships with almost everyone. Nonetheless, all of us are privileged to find a few people with whom we are always attuned and with whom doing almost anything is fun. Such mutual friendships afford one of life's most satisfying experiences and usually have quite positive benefits, except when they are allowed to absorb one or both of the participants to the point where they have neither the time nor the desire to carry on normal associations with other individuals or groups.

Changing Sex Preferences

As previously discussed, it is quite normal at certain stages in development for children to prefer associating with those of their own sex. This gradually changes into an acceptance of and then a preference for those of the opposite sex and finally focuses on a particular individual or a succession of them, eventually culminating in love and perhaps marriage. Although these developments ordinarily take place at approximately the same age in most youngsters, they may be premature or late in a few. This should not be a cause for alarm unless the fixation becomes unduly pronounced at one of the earlier stages. This is most likely to occur at the stage of preference for one's own sex and in extreme cases may involve a strong sexual attraction, sometimes accompanied by abnormal sexual practices.

Hero Worship and Crushes

It is also normal for youngsters to select someone who represents the embodiment of their highest ideals and aspirations and whom they idealize, cherish, and respect as a model or hero. This may prove of inestimable value if the model chosen is a worthy one, for it provides the child with a powerful stimulus to try to emulate this person in every detail.

The time at which hero worship is most pronounced often coincides roughly with the period of preference for one's own sex, and consequently the person chosen is often a particular pal, a member of a close knit group, or someone of the same sex who is older. In camp, it may well be a counselor or other member of the staff. If you become the object of your campers' admiration and respect, take pride in the compliment and recognize that it presents one of your greatest opportunities to steer youngsters along the right path as they develop to their full potential.

Occasionally a few youngsters prefer companions of their own sex for an unduly long period, sometimes even well into adulthood, and the feeling may become so emotional and intense as to almost exclude normal relations with other individuals or the group. This is usually termed a *crush.* It is more likely to occur in those who have not received the warmth and affection they need from their family and friends, and so they try to satisfy their emotional hunger by an abnormally close relationship with someone else. The feelings may or may not be mutual, and when extreme, the relationship may prove detrimental to one or both parties.

As a counselor, you should be aware of the possibility of becoming the object of such adoration and, if it does occur, take timely steps to prevent it from progressing to undesirable stages. Extend your customary warmth and cordiality to the camper, but avoid any show of favoritism or partiality. In time, with persistence and understanding, your relationship will revert to a perfectly healthy and worthwhile counselor-camper relationship.

Immature counselors, or those with unmet emotional needs, occasionally encourage this sort of attention for their own gratification. Such a relationship has a bad effect upon both the camper and counselor, for others may shun and criticize them, and the relationship brings neither complete nor lasting satisfaction to either. If the individuals are of different ages, as in a counselor-camper relationship, it is most unfair to the younger person, for the older individual is selfishly satisfying his or her own needs and wishes by taking advantage of someone less experienced.

Beware of the all-too-common error of mistaking a strong, wholesome friendship for a crush or homosexual attraction. Such misinterpretations are extremely unfortunate and produce serious complications that may prove damaging to both the personalities and reputations of the persons involved. Most so-called crushes are simply examples of hero worship, of the universal wish for mutual love and admiration, or of the strong, wholesome friendships that add so much pleasure to life.

As previously mentioned, it is humanly impossible to avoid being more attracted to some youngsters than to others, but counselors should keep such preferences to themselves, staying outwardly objective and impartial at all times. Remember that children who are unattractive to you probably affect others in the same way, and consequently they, most of all, are likely to be lonesome and in greatest need of your affection and attention.

ADMONITIONS FOR THE COUNSELOR

1. Learn all you can about campers who concern you, but do not take their previous records too seriously, for a change in environment often produces a change in behavior. Children who have been labeled as "bad" at home may completely change their conduct when exposed to the new personalities, influences and activities of camp.

2. Remember the ways in which to help campers satisfy their fundamental needs and attain a feeling of security in their group. Vary the program so that each child's interests and abilities can be recognized, rewarded, reinforced, and satisfied in some part of it.

3. Recall that misbehavior is usually a bid for attention, an expression of insecurity, or the result of feeling unloved and unwanted. Public reprimand or punishment ordinarily only aggravates the situation.

4. Inconspicuously try to draw aggressive or retiring campers into activities that afford them a feeling of success and achievement. Their distress and problems often disappear if they are provided with socially approved ways to satisfy their needs and wishes.

5. Make a particular effort to get close to campers who seem to be creating a problem for themselves or others. This may be tedious, for those who most need help are often too timid or proud to ask for or even accept it.

6. Cultivate the ability to be a good listener, especially for the problem camper who probably has a critical need for a trustworthy older person in whom to confide.

7. Seldom give advice; instead discretely question the camper and offer suggestions that enable him or her to work out a personal solution.

8. Do not heap blame on a camper for his or her misdeeds. Occasionally it may be necessary to strongly reprimand or punish campers who persistently refuse to recognize and accept their share of the responsibility for difficulties, but use these methods only when all others fail.

ADDITIONAL READINGS

(For an explanation of abbreviations and abbreviated forms, see p. 13.)

Adams, Jay E.: *Competent to Counsel.* Baker, 1973, 287 pp.
Adams, Jay E.: *What to Do About Worry.* Baker.
Amos, W. E., and J. D. Grambs (eds.): *Counseling the Disadvantaged Youth.* Prentice-Hall, 1968.
Barksdale, L. S.: *Building Self-Esteem.* The Barksdale Foundation, Idyllwild, Cal., 1972.
Blanchard, Howard L., and Laurence S. Flaum: *Guidance: A Longitudinal Approach.* Burgess, 1969, 338 pp., paper.
Brussel, James A., M.D., and Theodore Irwin: *Understanding and Overcoming Depression.* Hawthorn, 1973, 244 pp.
Budd, William C., Ph.D.: *Behavior Modification: The Scientific Way to Self Control.* Galloway, 96 pp.
Corbin: *Recreation Leadership,* ch. 10.
Drug Abuse: Escape to Nowhere. AAHPERD, rev., 1970, 104 pp.
Facts Aren't Enough, AAHPERD, 1973, 71 pp., paper.
Forrer, Dr. Gordon R.: *Psychiatric Self Help.* Galloway, 71 pp.

Kizziar, Janet W. and Judy W. Hagedorn: *Search For Acceptance: The Adolescent and Self-Esteem.* Nelson-Hall, available from ACA, 1979, 147 pp.

Ledlie and Holbein: *Camp Counselor's Manual,* ch. 16.

Loughmiller, Campbell: *Kids In Trouble: An Adventure In Education.* Wildwood Books, available from ACA, 1979, 94 pp., paper.

Menacker, Julius: *Urban Poor Students and Guidance.* Guidance Monograph Series, Houghton Mifflin, 1971, 84 pp.

Rubin, Isadore, and Lester A. Kirkendall: *Sex in the Childhood Years.* Ass'n Press, 1970, 190 pp.

Shea: *Camping for Special Children,* chs. 4 and 9.

Shivers: *Camping,* pp. 149–164.

Strean: *New Approaches in Child Guidance.*

Todd: *Camping for Cristian Youth,* pp. 137–140.

Van Krevelen: *Children in Groups: Psychology and the Summer Camp,* chs. 4, 5.

Vinton, Dennis A. and Elizabeth M. Farley: *Camp Staff Training Series, Module 5, Dealing With Camper Behavior,* 131 pp.

Magazine Articles

CAMPING MAGAZINE:

Bentley, Bradford M.: "How Tape Recorder Cured Acute Homesickness," Mar., 1965, p. 15.

Colton, Raymond H.: "To Aid a Problem Child, Use His Background Traits." June, 1965, p. 17.

Hill, Robert N.: "Discipline Must Have a Direct Relationship to Action . . ." June, 1963, p. 17.

Huck, Susan C., and Philip A. Denomme: "Checkpoints for Fighting the Drug Menace in Camp." Sept./Oct., 1970, p. 19.

Lainoff, Harold M.: "Help Homesick Campers With Understanding Guidance." May, 1965, p. 26.

Ohlson, Elaine, R.N.: "Handling 'S.S.' in Camp." May, 1969, p. 16. (Homesickness)

Palter, Elsie, Ph.D.: "When Stealing Occurs in Camp." May, 1972, p. 16.

Rotman, Charles B.: "The Problem Camper—To Tolerate, Treat or Terminate." Sept./Oct., 1973, p. 16.

Schlesinger, Mike: "Pot, Pills and People." Mar., 1970, p. 10.

Sohn, David and Sheila: "Drug Abuse—How to Stop It Before It Becomes a Problem." Apr., 1972, p. 18.

Spiegel, Jerry and Eleanor: "Start Treatment for Homesickness Before Child Comes to Camp." June, 1964, p. 20.

Tabeling, Elizabeth Joye: "Homesick—A Word to Avoid." Apr., 1966, p. 24.

PARENTS GUIDE TO ACCREDITED CAMPS, 1980, ACA:

Cleaver, Nancy and Richard Fransham: "Tune In—Learn Child's Feelings About Camp." p. 15.

three
Camp Activities

ten

Planning the Program

Planning is forethought. It pervades the realms of all human action. Whether a man plans a business, a career, a house, or a fishing trip, he is looking into the future in order to arrange his affairs so that they will work out to the best advantage. Applied to our everyday world, planning is nothing but common sense.

—C. EARL MORROW*

Counselors who sit on bottoms never get to top.

Everything has been thought of before, but the difficulty is to think of it again.

—JOHANN WOLFGANG VON GOETHE

*From *Planning Your Community*. Reproduced by permission of Regional Plan Association, Inc.

PROGRAM GOALS AND OBJECTIVES

Before designing a camp program or preparing the activities or events in it, you must have specific goals and objectives in mind. The modern camp's activities and programs are expected to demonstrate direction, meaning and purpose, especially now when our society demands that its institutions be accountable for performing adequately and furnishing evidence that positive results are occurring. Obviously, goals and objectives provide the necessary focus and direction of our efforts as well as those of the campers.

Properly developed objectives will enable you to furnish evidence that positive changes in the campers have taken place. When campers can perform those activities they have set out to accomplish you can be assured of the success of your program and leadership. In other words, by establishing objectives for our program we are furnishing steppingstones that lead us directly toward a concrete and meaningful accomplishment. Parents and sponsoring agencies also are able to more adequately judge the potential values and outcomes of the camp's activities for those individuals they have entrusted to the camp staff. Finally, objectives are beneficial in that they provide a measure for the effectiveness of our leadership, based upon how well campers have progressed toward meeting the objectives.

Goals are broad, general statements regarding the expected effect of the camp experience on the participants; however, these statements tend to be generalized and limited in meaning. Examples of the goals common to many camps are (1) developing the whole child, (2) aiding in character development, (3) developing leadership, (4) teaching good citizenship, (5) promoting good health and physical fitness, (6) developing appreciation of nature, and (7) encouraging independence and the ability to think for oneself. These are all goals worthy of camping, but they are stated broadly and are somewhat useless in developing specific programs and activities that can lead campers toward their achievement. Such broad statements are inadequate because they do not specify exactly what campers are to do or accomplish by the end of the camp experience. Therefore, goals

(Camp Mishawaka, Grand Rapids, Minn.)

should be developed as starting points, followed by more refined functional statements or *objectives.*

Objectives are relatively specific statements of changes or learning expected to occur, expressed frequently, but not always, in terms of the camper. In other words, an objective often is best expressed from the camper's point of view and includes a description of the behaviors expected to occur as a result of a learning experience.

In recent years the use of *behavioral* objectives has become common practice among educational and recreational institutions, including organized camps. With respect to camps, the clearest definition of behavioral objectives was made by Vinton and Farley:

> Behavioral objectives are the foundation of the camp instructional program. They define specific behaviors based on the goals and philosophy of your camp. When clearly stated, they help the camp counselor select activities and materials, communicate what is to be learned and evaluate whether or not learning has taken place.*

A properly expressed behavioral objective has three or four main features, although the fourth is not always present: (1) It is expressed from the participant's point of view, (2) it is specific, (3) it contains a behavioral description, and (4) it contains a description of the specific conditions, if any, under which campers will demonstrate the desired behavior.** Let us discuss these features in more detail.

1. *The objective is expressed from the participant's point of view.* It is not difficult to express objectives from the camper's viewpoint, although many counselors and staff members fail to do so and thereby place the emphasis in the wrong place. It is the campers who must learn or perform the appropriate tasks—not the counselor. Therefore, it is best to use expressions such as "the camper will," "the youngster is to," "the participants are to be able to," and so forth. On the other hand, avoid statements that emphasize the counselor's or leader's behavior, such as "to motivate the campers so they will," "to point out to the group," "to show the campers the impor-

*Vinton, Dennis A., and Elizabeth M. Farley: *Camp Staff Training Series, Module 3, Camp Program Planning and Leadership.* Washington, D.C., A joint publication of Project REACH, University of Kentucky; ACA; and Hawkins and Associates, Inc., 1979, p. 53.

**Burns, Richard W.: *New Approaches to Behavioral Objectives.* Dubuque, Iowa, Wm. C. Brown Company Publishers, 1972, p. 11.

(Camp Kingsmont, West Stockbridge, Mass.)

tance of," or "to demonstrate to the campers." These expressions emphasize what the counselor is doing rather than what the camper should be doing and obviously create a problem, since it is possible to have a number of counselor or leader behaviors that produce no change in camper behavior.

2. *The objective is specific.* We must avoid using vague expressions that can be interpreted in many ways since they do not communicate exactly what performance is expected or what is to be learned by the completion of the activity. Ambiguous objectives do not aid the counselor or leader in deciding on the proper methods to use nor do they provide criteria by which to determine whether the camper has achieved the desired outcome.

Let us look at several camper objectives that are not specific, and consequently of little value to either the counselor or the campers.

EXAMPLE 1. The campers are to gain an understanding of the natural habitat of several small wild animals.

Think about this objective. What is meant by "understanding?" What are campers to learn about the natural habitat? What small wild animals are we talking about?

EXAMPLE 2. The camper is to become acquainted with good health habits.

What is meant by the term "acquainted with?" What specific health habits do we mean? It is obvious that these objectives communicate very little to anyone. They are too broad and too vague as a basis for effective planning or for determining if a camper has successfully accomplished the objective.

3. *The objective contains a behavioral description.* Examples of the behavior a camper might be expected to demonstrate may be described through such terms as recite, demonstrate, write, assemble, define, repeat, do, complete, locate, identify, name, and so on. Such terms define exactly what behaviors are expected of the camper.

4. *The objective contains a description of the specific conditions, if any, by which campers demonstrate their behavior.* In other words, we must establish conditions such as when, where, and how the behavior will be completed (i.e., complete the activity within ten minutes; from memory; without the use of a book; with no more than two errors; with 100 percent accuracy; using one match; and so on).

By now you should recognize a correctly expressed objective; several examples of objectives containing appropriate behavioral descriptions follow. Note that they are expressed from the participant's point of view, they are specific, and they describe the behavior the camper will demonstrate. Some of the objectives also describe specific conditions for performance of an activity.

EXAMPLE 1. By the third week of camp, participants in the nature study program will be able to identify trees in the camp area as being maple, oak, pine or elm. They should be able to correctly identify 85 percent of the examples.

EXAMPLE 2. Using the map and compass provided, each camper is to determine the compass bearing from point A to point B within two degrees of accuracy.

EXAMPLE 3. Campers are to gain skill in accurately using maps and compass while on overnight excursions away from the main camp site so that they can plan and execute a proper cross-country route in the backcountry.

EXAMPLE 4. Campers are to name the parts of a flower by labeling an outline diagram of a typical flower.

EXAMPLE 5. Campers are to match any ten leaves with the proper tree name by the end of the camp experience.

EXAMPLE 6. By the end of the second day of camp, the campers are to know three poisonous plants common to the area so that they can identify them by type and point them out to the rest of the group.

EXAMPLE 7. Campers are to develop skill in building a fire. They will be able to collect and assemble the proper wood, construct and light a campfire using one match and, using a pot of water provided, bring the water to a boil within 20 minutes.

EXAMPLE 8. Prior to setting out on a three-day hike, campers will demonstrate knowledge of appropriate clothing to take along by gathering the correct items and packing them in a backpack.

EXAMPLE 9. At least four different times throughout the hiking experience, campers will demonstrate positive actions that reveal an understanding of the importance of conservation, wise use of natural resources and human dependence on the land.

Categories of Objectives

In developing statements of desired outcomes we must consider that most written objectives fall into one of three different categories, or domains, that generally relate to action, thinking, and feeling. These categories are the (1) psychomotor domain, (2) cognitive domain, and (3) affective domain.

The *psychomotor domain* includes those objectives that deal with body movement, such as muscular skill, manipulation or movement of materials or objects, or actions that include neuromuscular coordination. For instance, in a physical activity such as swimming or running we can determine how long it takes to travel a specified distance or how smoothly the task is performed. We also can determine how far or how accurately a ball is thrown or how easily a serve in tennis is performed. Similarly, we can measure the level of ability or performance in painting a picture or completing a crafts project. All of these are examples of performance of physical tasks.

Cognitive domain objectives include factual knowledge, understanding, processes and structures. These objectives emphasize remembering, reproducing a response that has been learned, or solving intellectual tasks and problems. In terms of measuring outcomes, it is fairly easy to determine how well an individual meets objectives that require understanding facts, processes, or strategies. Such objectives commonly form the content of school subjects that require knowledge of names, dates, places, and facts. Although such information is important, we should keep in mind that, in the camping program facts are not the sole end of learning and, consequently, objectives in the cognitive domain should be used sparingly.

Affective domain objectives deal with emotions and feelings, including attitudes, interests, and the degree of appreciation an individual has for what goes on around him or her. Attitudes might include one's opinion and reaction to an idea, another person, or to the opinions of others. A person also may have feelings and appreciation for the aesthetic value of objects or events, such as the beauty in the sunset, drops of dew on a leaf, the graceful flight of a bird, the music of the wind blowing through tall grass, or the sound of rain in the forest.

Of the three domains, objectives in the affective domain are the most difficult to express in behavioral terms. It is sometimes even harder to determine when the objective has been achieved since most of what we feel is an internal experience that may not be expressed openly. In attempting to measure affective objectives we usually must seek an indication that the desired internal behavior has been achieved through external behavior that is associated with it. The obvious difficulty here is that different people react in different ways to the same inner feelings. A smile on one person may be an external expression of pleasure, while on another it may mask dislike or rejection. Nonetheless, it should be stressed that many of the values and outcomes of a camping experience fall into the affective domain and therefore we should do the best we can to develop these objectives and measure their outcomes.

WHY PROGRAMS DIFFER

It is very hard to summarize programs, for there are as many different sorts as there are camps. This is not difficult to understand when we realize how many variable factors enter into determining them. The following are prominent among them.

Goals of the Camp or Sponsoring Organization

Naturally, the activities chosen for the program will be those that best help meet the goals and objectives of the particular camp. We would expect a church camp to lean heavily toward activities of a spiritual nature, a school camp to em-

(Camp Kingsmont, West Stockbridge, Mass.)

phasize the acquiring of information, and an agency camp to work toward its stated goals. Special camps, such as those featuring dance, music, or activities for the physically handicapped, obviously will have programs that concentrate mainly on their particular specialty.

Philosophy and Abilities of the Camp Director and Program Director

A camp program sometimes reflects the particular interests or abilities of the camp or program director. For instance, a person with a love of music will emphasize related activities, and a person who likes rather sedentary activities will not be likely to promote a strong campcraft and trips program. Superior leaders, however, try not to overemphasize their hobbies and interests, preferring to offer a well-rounded, versatile program that is built around the particular needs and interests of the campers.

Abilities of the Staff and Resource Personnel

Some camps hire a large number of specialists, whereas others hire mostly general counselors who bring with them a wide variety of more modest skills and interests. Specialists, of course, may provide better instruction in their fields, but when there are too many of them or if their interests are too limited, each may concentrate on promoting his or her own activity instead of cooperating as a team member to foster a well-balanced program. This is the exception rather than the rule, however. Broad-minded specialists not only do their own jobs well, but also promote the activities of others. A counselor who is good at tying knots will soon have others joining in and one who sings a song will be surrounded by happy campers similarly engaged. One who takes time on a hike to investigate some unusual plant life will be instilling an interest in nature in his or her followers.

Nature of the Camp Site

The nature of the camp site will be influential in determining the program. A camp located near a mountain would be foolish not to take advantage of the opportunity for mountain climbing. No one, obviously, will be weaving honeysuckle baskets if it doesn't grow in the camp environment. A remote unit in a decentralized camp can build its own council ring and outdoor kitchen right in its own backyard, whereas a unit in the middle of a centralized camp will need to venture into the wildwood in search of a private nook.

Equipment and Facilities

A camp with an elaborate outlay of backpacking equipment is in a position to sponsor a vigorous trips program. Although, in the minds of some, swimming and boating are almost synonymous with camp, there are camps without such facilities that have quite successfully built a program around other worthwhile activities too often neglected in camps where Neptune holds sway. Imagination and a positive approach can turn a lack of equipment into a challenge to campers to master the use of tools to make their own equipment from kits or raw materials or to substitute activities with less elaborate requirements.

Location and Terrain

When interesting historical sites abound in the vicinity, a camp should capitalize on this and plan to study and visit them. Paul Bunyan country will call for storytelling and special events built around this favorite character. A seaside camp may plan visits to fish-processing plants and fishing vessels. In one camp with a fairly steep hillside, enthusiasm over skiing and tobogganing on pine needles reigned, spurred on

(Camp Mary White, Zia Girl Scout Council, Mayhill, N. Mex.)

(Camp Kingsmont, West Stockbridge, Mass.)

by a local neighbor who had enjoyed these activities as a boy. In another, there was a meandering, babbling brook where campers loved to wade and search out the secrets of the animal and plant life within and around it.

Where Fires Are Not Permitted

Camp sites in areas where wood fires are not permitted will have to find substitute methods of cooking and conducting traditional campfire programs. Many are doing this successfully, and youngsters who have never seen a real campfire may scarcely notice the difference.

Climate

Camps in hot areas wisely plan campfire programs without benefit of fire and schedule an extra long siesta and quiet activities for the hottest part of the day. Camps with cool mornings and evenings will, on the contrary, lean toward vigorous activities, with swimming scheduled toward the middle of the day.

The Campers

The ages, previous experiences, skills, financial status, and social backgrounds of the campers are very influential in determining program. A camper who has seen his or her grandparents do a lively Lithuanian dance can teach it to the others, while another may contribute a German folk song, and still another demonstrate the art of pottery making, learned from a relative. Children from rural areas may be far ahead of their city cousins in nature lore, but may lag far behind in executing fancy dives and swimming strokes.

Length of the Camping Period

Campers who come for only a week or two will need fairly simple projects that they can complete in a short time; others in short-term agency camps may attempt more advanced projects, since they are putting into practice skills and knowledge already acquired under the sponsoring organization in the city. In short-term camps, planning the program involves deciding on the number and types of activities that can be accomplished in the time available.

Eight-week camps can approach a program in a more leisurely fashion and formulate more complicated plans that build up to a climax at the end of the season. One group of campers built a log cabin to shelter their arts and crafts equipment (with the help of some older men on the heavy, technical work); another group undertook to clear a vista and path through the underbrush down to the lake.

Ratio of Counselors to Campers

A high ratio of counselors to campers permits a more or less ideal situation in which campers can be divided into small groups with each person receiving more personal attention.

CHANGING PROGRAM EMPHASES

Early camps tended to keep the participants busy every moment of the day. Almost every instant was planned, and campers were registered in a number of activities. If the camper disliked the activity, it was just too bad, for the schedule and rules were rigid and permitted no deviation. Activities were scheduled like school classes, with attendance carefully checked each day, and motivation was supplied by achievement charts, testing programs, intense competition between individuals and groups, and elaborate systems of awards. In some cases, regimentation and scheduling were carried to a degree that almost obliterated the two things the camper most wanted—to have fun and to make new friends.

As with most trends, this period of regimentation was followed by a movement in the opposite direction; this was toward permissiveness, and when carried to extremes, the camp scheduled no activities at all, leaving campers free to do whatever they chose the entire day. This practice was apparently based on the assumption that the best way to teach children to make choices and to govern themselves was to loosen the reins and let them learn by the trial-and-error method. Unfortunately, programs planned exclusively by campers, or unplanned programs that "just grow," often lack continuity and are likely to degenerate into mere busy work and eventual boredom. The best results come from a tempering of the impetuosity and daring of youth with the sobering influence of experience and greater maturity, as occurs when campers and counselors plan the program cooperatively.

THE NEW CONCEPTION OF PROGRAM

The essence of "program" was once considered to be only the so-called activity periods, such as archery, swimming, storytelling, woodcraft, and dramatics, which children attended without question. This type of activity planning is termed a *structured program.* We now realize that program is much more, for a child's development certainly does not begin with arts and crafts at 8:30, stop for lunch at 11:30 and continue again at 2:30 with nature study, to then cease entirely after the 4:30 horseback-riding period. In reality, program is everything that happens to the camper throughout the day, for each single incident, no matter how trivial, is a potential influence for good or bad. Can we argue convincingly that archery, weaving, campcraft, or canoeing will be of more ultimate worth to someone than forming habits of orderliness, cooperativeness, punctuality, or friendliness? We can be sure that campers are constantly learning something from every experience that takes place.

HOW A CAMP PROGRAM IS PLANNED

The trend in program development is to let campers and staff cooperatively plan their own activities in what is known as an *unstructured*

(Camp Mishawaka, Grand Rapids, Minn.)

program. This allows enough flexibility to permit altering it as seems fit as the days pass and needs and wishes change. This flexible program satisfies youth's craving for variety and the need to be up and doing, yet it is by no means haphazard and unplanned, for it indeed requires superior planning to avoid conflicts over facilities, equipment, and the services of the specialists on the staff.

Certain hours, as for rising, going to bed, eating, resting, and swimming, that affect the whole camp must be scheduled or arranged in order to prevent groups from interfering with each other. Beyond that, individuals and groups are left pretty much on their own to choose from the possible activities offered by the camp, according to what seems exciting and worth while to them.

The program for the entire camp is usually coordinated by one person, either the program director, assistant camp director, or head counselor. Occasionally, particularly in small camps, the director serves in this capacity, but he or she more commonly acts as an advisor to someone else who has been delegated this particular responsibility.

In long-term private camps, each camper may be allowed to decide upon his or her own activities irrespective of what others in the unit are doing, and various methods for implementing this may be used. One is to have the program director announce at the end of a meal, such as breakfast, what activities are available for the morning; campers then indicate by a show of hands those in which they wish to participate. Duplicate lists are made up, one for the staff member in charge of each activity and the other for the camp office, where the location of each camper and counselor must always be known. It makes for better instruction when participants are classified according to degree of skill, such as sailing for beginners or advanced horsemanship for those who have passed their preliminary tests. Another method of programming offers still more freedom of choice. Here, the program director simply opens the field for suggestions, and when someone requests an activity such as fishing, the program director asks how many would like to join in.

This freedom of choice is usually more prevalent in long-term camps. Advocates claim as advantages that it focuses on the individual rather than the activity, widens a camper's circle of friends, allows campers to do what interests them, and prevents the possible animosities that may occur when the same individuals eat, sleep, and do everything else together over a long period of time.

Short-term camps usually find unit programming more useful, feeling that each camper will become better acquainted and feel more at ease if he or she spends time with only a small group of peers. In this small "family" the individual can gain recognition and have a better opportunity to voice opinions.

Under either plan of programming, it is customary to hold several all-camp events during the period, their number and character varying with the particular camp. Most camps sponsor some sort of *camp council*, which consists of counselor and camper representatives from each unit who meet with the program director to plan such all-camp events. Care must be exercised to see that the group is not dominated by older people, lest youngsters hesitate to speak up in front of them.

As wide a variety of activities as the camp facilities and talents of the staff permit should be offered to give all children a chance to determine their interests and abilities in several fields. One of the finest things a camp can do is to introduce youngsters to a variety of hobbies that may become lasting sources of joy or even financially profitable vocations or avocations.

HOW A PROGRAM DEVELOPS

When staff and campers join democratically in program planning, counselors act as consultants and advisors, not dictators, and must be able to guide and control the situation so that wise choices are made without forcing their ideas on the group.

Your ability to see opportunities, to select or reject, encourage or discourage, suggest, counsel, and use skill in changing directions will largely determine what all of you will receive as your summer's rewards. Younger campers need many ideas and suggestions, particularly during their first few days in camp, for many of them have unknowingly been so dependent on their parents and on radio, movies, and television for entertainment that they are almost at a complete

(Camp Mishawaka, Grand Rapids, Minn.)

loss when called upon to make decisions on how to spend their time. Even older campers will often not be able to suggest what they *really* want to do. They are inclined to choose what they have already done, even if they have become somewhat bored with it, because they have too little experience or imagination to see other possibilities. This represents an opportunity for you as their counselor to tactfully broaden their interests and point out new vistas by throwing out a hint or merely picking up and encouraging one of their own ideas. Suggestions from others will follow, and even when one is not accepted in its entirety, it may stimulate others until one idea finally "catches fire" and the group is off to an exciting experience. It is often possible to turn an impractical or unacceptable suggestion into a more suitable variation.

It is useful to begin by making a big calendar, entering on it the fixed dates for the season, such as all-camp activities and other special events. Within this framework, you then can plan your own particular unit activities, adjusting them and adding details as the season advances.

When youngsters feel at ease and free to express themselves, proposals literally fly back and forth, and it then becomes your job to help them to separate the wheat from the chaff and settle on those things that really hold priority with them. Encouraging them to look ahead and evaluate as they go along, forseeing obstacles and planning how to overcome them can give them valuable experience. You may, on rare occasions, have to come out with a flat "no" if what they are proposing is against camp policy or actually dangerous, but at other times you may want to let them go ahead and learn by experience, if the consequences will not be too serious.

Above all, get them involved in all your planning, for forcing preconceived ideas on

(Camp Mishawaka, Grand Rapids, Minn.)

them from higher up just won't work—it brings only half-hearted compliance and may even cause downright rebellion. When the plan is really theirs, they become so excited they can scarcely contain themselves, and your worries about discipline problems, program, and problem campers will largely disappear.

The Indigenous Program

Most camps now favor what is known as an *indigenous program*. This is one that is strictly personal to the camp and is based upon materials found in or near it. In arts and crafts, native woods are used for whittling, native vegetation for dyeing, and local grasses and reeds for weaving. Nature specimens are the flowers, trees and insects found on the camp grounds. (These projects are done, of course, only in accordance with good conservation practices.) The folk songs and ballads of the region find a place in singing, and the dances are those of the early settlers. Stories, dramatics, pageants, and original songs are based upon local folklore and legends, and information is obtained from local residents and the clippings, files, and other resources of the local librarian. It is evident that no two indigenous programs are ever quite the same, since no two communities offer identical natural resources and historical backgrounds.

The Test of a Good Program Activity

Teach campers to evaluate their program by asking themselves such questions as: What went well and what didn't? What did we learn from the experience and how can we use it in planning for the future?

Activities that bear up well under the following tests are likely to be good ones that make a real contribution to the objectives of camping:

1. Is the activity in accord with the idea of simple outdoor living? Does it further understanding and love of the out-of-doors and is it in line with good conservation and ecological practices?
2. Does it develop the ability to live harmoniously with others, respecting their individual personalities and potentialities?
3. Are campers sometimes given the chance to do individual projects or activities of their own, or is everything *always* decided by the vote of the majority?
4. Does it answer youth's longing for fun and adventure? Do campers *want* to do it or are they merely acceding to the wishes of some adults? Is it interesting in itself without outside motivation such as awards or special privileges?
5. Does it challenge campers' initiative, resourcefulness, and creative expression, or is it merely a cut-and-dried process in which they follow instructions to cut along the dotted line, then join part A to part B?
6. Does it broaden interests and appreciations and help youngsters to see with Robert Louis Stevenson that:

> The world is so full of a number of things.
> I'm sure we should all be as happy as kings.

7. Is it free from actual physical danger? Does it contribute to the greater health and vitality of the campers?
8. Could they do it just as well or better in their own home communities? (This is one of the most important tests and largely rules out the "city" type of arts and crafts and such organized sports as basketball and baseball.)
9. Does it have carry-over value for use at home or in later life?
10. Does it fulfill fundamental wishes and contribute to the camper's overall mental health?
11. Is it truly a group project to which each camper can feel he or she has made a real contribution, or do a few of the more aggressive and talented usurp all the positions of importance and claim an undue amount of credit?
12. Is some recognition given to those who make great efforts or develop better-than-average skills? (Keep this in balance, however, remembering that it can be easily overdone, for "every time there is a winner you also pick several losers.")

POSSIBLE PROJECTS

Construction Work

Among possible projects are making a:

Rustic entrance for unit, cabin, or camp
Totem pole
Outdoor kitchen
Outdoor theater

Campfire circle
Log cabin
Nature exhibit
Rock garden
Campcraft exhibit
Rustic bulletin board
Nature aquarium
Green cathedral—outdoor chapel
Improvised camping equipment (either from kits or raw materials)
Repair of boats, riding tack, tennis courts, trailways, etc.
Weathervane, weather flags, and instruments for forecasting the weather
Outpost camp
Council ring
Clearing a path
Sundial
Bridge across the creek
Tepee or Adirondack shack
Soil erosion control
Pottery kiln
Nature trail
Fernery
Cleaning up the campsite
Terrariums
Ropes courses

Evening Activities

Program of customs, costumes, and dances of other cultures
Potpourri
Informal dramatics
Folk, square, or round dancing
Parties—hard times, pioneer, gypsy, plantation, masquerade, etc.
Old-fashioned singing school
Spelling matches
Progressive games
Village night (invite the camp neighbors in)
Barn dance
Amateur night
Hay ride
Camp banquet
Moonlight hike
Star study
Lantern party
Poetry, stories, good music
Shadow plays
Torchlight or candlelight parade while singing
Quiz show
Discussion groups
Liar's contest (see who can tell the biggest whopper)
Come-as-you-are party

In many camps an occasional evening campfire program is a tradition dear to the hearts of the campers. Make it varied enough so that it goes beyond mere routine and becomes one of the most meaningful events of the summer. It is more romantic and inspiring when conducted in some secluded, special place of beauty reserved for such events, and many camps have worked out elaborate fire-lighting ceremonies for such occasions. Physical comfort warrants attention too, for no one can sit in rapt attention during a fierce bombardment by voracious mosquitoes. Evening programs should taper off to a quiet, sleep-inducing conclusion and should end on time even though it means omitting some part. Symbols, no matter how simple, mean much to campers and serve to stimulate their imaginations and loyalties. Hammett and Musselman* suggested having a "Town Crier" summon campers to a program instead of letting them saunter in, and crowning a winner with a wreath of "laurel leaves" instead of just announcing that he or she won an event.

Special Days

Woodcrafter's day—hold demonstrations or contests in such skills as building fires, using knife and axe, and erecting a tent.
County or state fair conducted at camp
Camp birthday
Mardi Gras
Gypsy day
Dude ranch rodeo
Circus day
Holiday of a foreign country (costumes, food, dances, games, songs and so on)
Staff day (when campers and staff interchange roles)
Western barbecue day
Regatta day
Water pageant
Local history day
Birthday of a famous person
Clean-up, paint-up day

---

*Hammett, Catherine T., and Virginia Musselman: *The Day Camp Program Book.* Ass'n Press, 1963.

Storybook day (theme of Robin Hood, Paul Bunyan, Robinson Crusoe or other story carried out through the day)
Village day (when neighbors from the village visit)
Gift day (when campers or groups present gifts, perhaps self-made, to the camp)
International day
Pioneer day
Guest day for another unit or camp
Free choice day

Rainy-Day Activities

Bad weather always looks much worse through a window.

—JOHN KIERAN, *Footnotes on Nature,* Doubleday.

Rainy days will often present a problem to the unimaginative counselor, and a steady downpour of several days duration is enough to tax the ingenuity and resourcefulness of even the doughtiest leader and reduce his or her spirits to a state of drippy dilapidation. Nevertheless, it is essential to keep campers busy and happy, for spells of homesickness are especially likely to sail in with the storm clouds. The counselor must turn such an occasion into a satisfying and enjoyable experience. Wise leaders will keep the threat of rain ever in the back of their minds so that they are ready for those inevitable rainy days. Here are some activity possibilities:

Plan a carnival or puppet show
Take a slicker hike in the rain; note the rainy day activities of wildlife
Compose a cabin or unit yell, song, symbol, slogan, or the like
Learn new songs and sing the old
Work on scrapbooks or snapshot albums
Make candy or popcorn or serve "tea"
Play charades and other indoor games
Plan an open house with simple refreshments for another cabin or unit
Plan stunts for the next all-camp program
Hold discussions
Read or tell stories
Write letters
Listen to recorded music
Plan a future trip, a nature trail, or outpost camp
Toast marshmallows
Hold a contest to determine the Biggest Liar
Compose a cabin or unit newspaper to be read at supper
Organize a harmonica, comb, kitchen, or kazoo band or other musical group
Have folk or square dances and singing games
Plan a banquet (with candles or some little extra item of food and a program)
Organize Fireside Clubs with small groups gathered in front of available fireplaces to pursue special interests
Arrange a hobby show or other exhibit
Plan a stunt night (keep it on a high level)
Make posters for the bulletin board
Make puppets or work on a play
Practice campcraft skills such as knots, tin-can-craft, and so forth
Make a model campsite or one of the entire camp layout
Do plaster casts or nature crafts
Carve or paint soap objects
Do string art or bead work
Work on arts and crafts, plan an exhibit
Whittle or carve objects
Mend clothing and get the cabin in apple-pie order
Work on costume box in readiness for the next play
Hold a spelling bee or quiz program
Read or write camp poetry
Make up indoor games and play them
Write a dramatic production and prepare to produce it
Make improvised camping equipment such as trench candles and waterproof matches
Study weather, make weather flags and other weather instruments
Study clouds as they change and move about with the storms
Play active games to relieve tension and get exercise
Mark tools and put them in good repair—sharpen knives, axes, etc.
Work on riding tack, archery tackle, and so on
Get extra sleep or rest
Fish, boat or swim in the rain (if no lightning)
Beautify living quarters by block printing curtains, using natural dyes for materials or adding other decorations
Practice Red Cross first aid techniques

(Camp Manito-Wish, Y.M.C.A., Boulder Junction, Wis.)

- Have a talent show
- Play indoor nature games or prepare for your next nature hike
- Study rules or techniques of such activities as tennis and horseback riding

You will find other suggestions for programs throughout various chapters of this book as well as in the sources listed at the ends of several chapters.

The Birthright of Children*

All children should know the joy of playing in healthful mud, of paddling in clean water, of hearing birds sing praises to God for the new day. They should have the vision of pure skies enriched at dawn and sunset with unspeakable glory; of dew-drenched mornings flashing with priceless gems; of the vast night sky all throbbing and panting with stars.

They should live with the flowers and butterflies, with the wild things that have made possible the world of fables.

They should experience the thrill of going barefoot, of being out in the rain; of riding a white birch, of sliding down pine boughs, of climbing ledges and tall trees, of diving headfirst into a transparent pool.

They ought to know the smell of wet earth, of new mown hay, of sweet fern, mint, and fir; of the breath of cattle and of fog blown inland from the sea.

They should hear the answer the trees make to the rain and the wind; the sound of rippling and falling water; the muffled roar of the sea in storm.

They should have the chance to catch fish, to ride on a load of hay, to camp out, to cook over an open fire, tramp through a new country, and sleep under the open sky.

They should have the fun of driving a horse, paddling a canoe, sailing a boat. . . .

One cannot appreciate and enjoy to the full extent of nature, books, novels, histories, poems, pictures, or even musical compositions, who has not in his youth enjoyed the blessed contact with the world of nature.

—Henry Turner Bailey

*From Proceedings for 1946 of the National Education Association of the United States; reproduced by permission.

ADDITIONAL READINGS

(For an explanation of abbreviations and abbreviated forms, see p. 13.)

Archery

Archery (No. 3381). Boy Scouts, 1964, 36 pp., paper.
Archery—A Planning Guide and Individual Instruction. AAHPER, 1972, 64 pp.
Burke, Edmund: *Archery Handbook.* Arco, rev., 1964, 142 pp.
Campbell, Donald W.: *Archery.* Prentice-Hall, 1971, 76 pp.
Forbes, Thomas A.: *New Guide to Better Archery.* Collier, 1967, 352 pp.
Gillelan, G. Howard: *Complete Book of the Bow and Arrow.* Stackpole, 1971, 326 pp.
Gillelan, G. Howard: *Modern ABC's of Bow and Arrow.* Stackpole, 1969, 192 pp.
Klann, Margaret L.: *Target Archery.* Addison-Wesley Publishing Co., Inc., Reading, Mass. 01867, 1970, 162 pp.
Kujoth: *The Recreation Program Guide,* pp. 38–43.
Lewis, Jack (ed.): *Archer's Digest.* Digest Books, 1971, 320 pp., paper.
McKinney, Wayne C.: *Archery.* Brown, 1971, paper.
Niemeyer, Roy K.: *Beginning Archery.* Wadsworth, rev., 1968, paper.
Outdoor Tips, pp. 172–177.
Pszczola, Lorraine: *Archery.* Saunders, 1971.
Selected Archery Articles. AAHPER, 1971.
Shivers: *Camping,* pp. 302–310.
Sigler, Howard T.: *Pocket Guide to Archery.* Stackpole, 1967, 96 pp.

MAGAZINE ARTICLES

Camping Magazine:
Miller, Myrtle K. and Edward B.: "Arrows, Bows, Targets—Does your Camp Have Them?" June 1979, p. 18.
Wadsworth, Bill: "Add Action to Your Archery Program." Feb., 1969, p. 14.

Fishing

Bale: *What on Earth,* pp. 57–88.
Bates, Joseph D., Jr.: *Streamer Fly Tying and Fishing.* Stackpole, 1966, 368 pp.
Bauer, Erwin A. (ed.): *Fisherman's Digest.* Digest Books, 8th ed., 1971, 320 pp.
Cardwell: *America's Camping Book,* ch. 26.
Crowe, John: *Modern ABC's of Fresh Water Fishing.* Stackpole, paper.
Decker, Maurice H.: *How to "Take" Fresh Water Fish in Lake, Pond and Stream.* Sentinel, 1958, 127 pp., paper.
Evanoff, Vlad: *A Complete Guide to Fishing.* Crowell, 1961, 206 pp.
Evanoff, Vlad: *1001 Fishing Tips and Tricks.* Harper & Row, 1968, 247 pp.
Evanoff, Vlad: *Another 1001 Fishing Tips and Tricks.* Order from NRPA, 206 pp.
Fichter, George S., and Phil Francis: *Guide to Fresh and Salt Water Fishing.* Golden, 1965, 160 pp., paper.
Fieldbook for Boys and Men, pp. 320, 420–435.
Goldberg, Howard: *The Angler's Book on Fly-Tying and Fishing.* Scribner's, 1973, 192 pp.
Kenealy, James P.: *Better Fishing for Boys.* Dodd, Mead, 1968, 64 pp.
Knight, John Alden and Richard Alden: *The Complete Book of Fly Casting.* Putnam, 1964, 129 pp.
Lafontain, Gary: *Challenges of the Trout.* Mountain Press Publishing Company, 1976, 243 pp.
Langer: *The Joy of Camping,* pp. 278–286.
Learn and Tallman: *Backpacker's Digest,* ch. 13.
McClane, A. J.: *The "Field and Stream" International Fishing Guide.* Scribner's, 1973, 224 pp.
McNally, Tom: *Fishermen's Bible.* Follett, 1970, 322 pp., paper.
Migdalski, Edward C.: *Angler's Guide to the Fresh Water Sport Fishes of North America.* Ronald, 1962, 431 pp.
Moore, E.: *Fresh-Water Fishing.* Macmillan, 1965, paper.
Ormond: *Outdoorsman's Handbook,* part 2.
Outdoor Tips, pp. 76–112.
Ovington, Ray: *Introduction to Bait Fishing.* Stackpole, 1971, 192 pp.
Parsons, P. Allen: *Complete Book of Fresh Water Fishing.* Harper & Row, 1963, 322 pp.
Power, John, and Jeremy Brown: *The Fisherman's Handbook.* Scribner's, 1972, 192 pp.
Shaw, Helen: *Fly-Tying: Materials, Tools, Technique.* Ronald, 1963, 281 pp.
Shivers: *Camping,* pp. 356–361.
Slaymaker, S. R. II: *Simplified Fly Fishing.* Harper & Row, 1969.
Tacklebox Library. Harper & Row, 1971 (five volumes, slipcased).
Wood: *Pleasure Packing,* ch. 13.

MAGAZINE ARTICLES

Boys' Life contains many articles about fishing.
Camping Magazine:
Metcalf, Harlan G.: "Approaches to Nature Recreation and Interpretation." June, 1968, p. 15.

Games and Other Activities

Berger: *Program Activities for Camps.*
Buskin, David: *Outdoor Games.* Lion Press, 1966, 64 pp.
Corbin: *Recreation Leadership.*
Donnelly, Richard H., William G. Helms, and Elmer D. Mitchell: *Active Games and Contests.* Ronald, 2nd ed., 1959, 672 pp.
Eisenberg, Helen and Larry: *The New Pleasure Chest.* Abingdon, 1972, 160 pp., paper.
Eisenberg: *Omnibus of Fun.*
Fowler, H. Waller, Jr.: *Kites—A Practical Guide to Kite Making and Flying.* Ronald, 1965, 95 pp.
Garrison: *Outdoor Education,* ch. XIII.
Harbin: *The Fun Encyclopedia.*
Harris, Jane A.: *File O'Fun, Card File for Recreation.* Burgess, 2nd ed., 1970.
Hartley, Ruth E., and Robert M. Goldenson: *The Complete Book of Children's Play.* Apollo, 2nd ed., 1970, paper.
Harty: *Science for Camp and Counselor.*
Hunt, Sarah E.: *Games and Sports the World Around.* Ronald, 3rd ed., 271 pp.
Kohl, Marguerite, and Frederica Young: *Games For Children.* Cornerstone, 1968, 184 pp., paper.
Kohl, Marguerite, and Frederica Young: *Games For Grown-ups.* Cornerstone, 1951, 176 pp., paper.

Kraus: *Recreation Leader's Handbook.*
Macfarlan, Allan A.: *Boy's Book of Rainy-Day Doings.* Stackpole, 1969, 160 pp.
Mason, Bernard S., and Elmer D. Mitchell: *Party Games.* Barnes and Noble, 1946, 193 pp., paper.
Mulac: *Fun and Games.*
Mulac, Margaret E.: *The Game Book.* Harper & Row, 1946, 385 pp.
Pelton, Barry C.: *Badminton.* Prentice-Hall, 1971, 82 pp.
Permin, Ib: *Hokus Pokus.* Sterling, 1969, 120 pp. (magic tricks).
Reeves, Robert: *Make It Yourself Games Book.* Emerson, 1964, 108 pp.
Richart, Genevieve: *The Master Game and Party Book.* Order from NRPA, 253 pp.
Smith, Robert G.: *The Boys' Entertainment Book.* Denison, 1957, 367 pp.
van der Smissen, Betty, and Helen Knierim: *Fitness and Fun Through Recreational Sports and Games.* Burgess, 1968, 122 pp.
Vinton, Iris: *The Folkways Omnibus of Children's Games.* Stackpole, 1970, 320 pp.
Wackerbarth, Marjorie, and Lillian S. Graham: *Games For All Ages and How to Use Them.* Denison, 1959, 122 pp.

Horses and Riding

Anderson, C. W.: *Complete Book of Horses and Horsemanship.* Macmillan, 1963, 192 pp., paper.
Ball, Charles E.: *Saddle Up!* Lippincott, 1970, 224 pp.
Corbin, Don E.: *Get A Horse.* Order from ACA, 1966, 48 pp., paper.
Disston, Harry: *Know About Horses.* Devin-Adair, 1961, 216 pp.
Ensminger, M. E.: *Horses and Horsemanship.* Interstate, 1969, 583 pp.
Froud, Lt. Col. "Bill": *Better Riding.* Scribner's, 1973, 96 pp.
Haley, Neale: *How to Have Fun With a Horse.* Arco, 1973, 119 pp.
Johnson, Patricia H.: *Horse Talk.* Funk and Wagnalls, 130 pp.
McTaggart, Lt. Col. M. F.: *The Art of Riding.* Arco, 1963, 128 pp., paper.
Mellin, Jeanne: *Ride a Horse.* Sterling, 1970, 128 pp.
Molesworth, Roger: *Knowing Horses.* Arco, 1962, 215 pp.
Nissen, Jasper: *The Young Horseman's Guide.* Barnes, 1965.
Price, Steven D.: *Teaching Riding at Summer Camps.* Greene, 1971, paper.
Selected Riding Articles. AAHPER, 1969.
Shivers: *Camping,* pp. 318–322.
Sports Illustrated Book of Horseback Riding. Lippincott, 1971, paper.
Wright, Gordon: *Learning to Ride, Hunt and Show.* Doubleday.

MAGAZINE ARTICLES

Camping Magazine:
Bennett, Betty M.: "Horsemanship Standards—Yes." June 1978, p. 17.
Hirn, Doris D.: "Your Riding Program—Do You Work and Plan to Keep It as Safe as Your Waterfront?" May, 1969, p. 31.
Loew, Franklin M.: "Planning and Managing Camp Riding Programs." May, 1964, p. 21.
Shepard, Alexander L., and Alan M. Beck: "The Role of Riding in Camp." Apr., 1966, p. 23.
Shires, Thomas E.: "50 Checks for Safe Riding Program." June, 1961, p. 14.

Indians

(See also the bibliography in the chapter on "Arts and Crafts.")

Baity, Elizabeth Chesley: *Americans Before Columbus.* Viking, 1961, 224 pp.
Berger: *Program Activities for Camp.*
Cody, Iron Eyes: *Indian Talk—Hand Signals of the American Indians.* Naturegraph, 1970, 112 pp., paper.
Collier, John: *Indians of the Americas.* Norton, 1947.
Curtis, Natalie (recorder and ed.): *The Indian's Book.* Dover, 1969, 548 pp., paper.
Dorian, Edith: *Hokahey! American Indians Then and Now.* McGraw-Hill, 1957, 112 pp.
Driver, Harold E.: *Indians of North America.* U. of Chicago, 2nd ed., 1969, 668 pp., paper.
Giplin, Laura: *The Enduring Navaho.* U. of Texas, 1968, 264 pp.
Grant, Bruce: *American Indians, Yesterday and Today.* Dutton, 1960.
Hofsinde, Robert: *The Indian and the Buffalo.* Morrow, 1961, 96 pp.
Hofsinde, Robert: *Indian Fishing and Camping.* Morrow, 1963.
Hofsinde, Robert: *Indian Hunting.* Morrow. 1962.
Hofsinde, Robert: *The Indian and His Horse.* Morrow, 1960.
Hofsinde, Robert: *Indian Picture Writing.* Morrow, 1959, 96 pp.
Hofsinde, Robert: *The Indian's Secret World.* Morrow, 1955, 94 pp.
Hofsinde, Robert: *Indian Sign Language.* Morrow, 1956.
Hunt: *The Golden Book of Indian Crafts and Lore.*
Indian Lore (no. 3358). Boy Scouts, 1959, 96 pp., paper.
Kujoth: *The Recreation Program Guide,* pp. 165–179.
La Farge, Oliver: *The American Indian.* Golden, 1960, 216 pp.
Laubin, Reginald and Gladys: *The Indian Tipi.* U. of Oklahoma, 1971, 208 pp.
Macfarlan, Allan A.: *Boy's Book of Indian Skills.* Stackpole, 1968, 160 pp.
Mason: *The Book of Indian Crafts and Costumes.*
Mason, Bernard S.: *Dances and Stories of the American Indian.* Ronald, 1944, 269 pp.
Rachlis, Eugene: *Indians of the Plains.* American Heritage, 1960, 152 pp.
Raphael, Ralph B.: *The Book of American Indians.* Arco, 1959, 144 pp.
Rosenfelt, Willard E.: *The Last Buffalo.* Denison.
Squires, John L., and Robert E. McLean: *American Indian Dances—Steps, Rhythms, Costumes and Interpretation.* Ronald, 1963, 132 pp.
Stember, Sol: *Heroes of the American Indian.* Fleet, 1971, 124 pp.
Sun Bear: *At Home in the Wilderness.* Naturegraph, 90 pp., paper.
Tomkins, William: *Indian Sign Language.* Dover, 1969, 180 pp., paper.
van der Smissen, Betty, and Oswald H. Goering: *A Leader's Guide to Nature-Oriented Activities,* pp. 193–196.
White, Anne Terry, and William Brandon: *The American Indian.* Random, 1963, 200 pp.

MAGAZINE ARTICLES

Camping Magazine:
Congdon, LeRoy: "Indian Tepee Accents Program Activities." Feb., 1963, p. 14.
Red Dawn (Stephen S. Jones, Jr.): "Emphasize Indian Lore in a Program for Girls." June, 1965, p. 15.
Wagener, Lloyd: "Indian Ceremonials Spark Entire Camp Program." Feb., 1965, p. 52.

Miscellaneous

Berger: *Program Activities for Camps.*
Brannan, Steve A. (ed.): *Project Explore—Expanded Programs and Learning in Outdoor Recreation and Education.* Hawkins and Associates, 1979, 460 cards plus manual, 138 pp.
Burns, Richard W.: *New Approaches to Behavioral Objectives.* Wm. C. Brown Company, 1972, 118 pp.
Duran, Dorothy B. and Clement A.: *The New Encyclopedia of Successful Program Ideas.* Ass'n Press, 1967, 511 pp.
Edinton, Christopher R., David M. Compton and Carole J. Hanson: *Recreation and Leisure Programming.* Saunders College Publishing, 1980, 419 pp.
Eisenberg: *Omnibus of Fun,* ch. 9.
Farrell, Patricia, and Herberta M. Lundegren: *The Process of Recreation Programming.* John Wiley and Sons, 1978, 313 pp.
Ford, Phyllis M.: *Principles and Practices of Outdoor/Environmental Education.* John Wiley and Sons, 1981, 348 pp.
Kujoth: *The Recreation Program Guide,* pp. 353–367.
MacKay: *Creative Counseling For Christian Camps,* ch. 7.
Rodney and Ford: *Camp Administration,* ch. 9.
Shivers: *Camping,* chs. 9, 10, 13, 15, 16.
Smith et al.: *Outdoor Education,* chs. 5, 6.
Thurston, LaRue A.: *Good Times Around the Campfire.* Ass'n Press, 1967, 128 pp., paper.
Todd: *Camping for Christian Youth,* chs. 16, 17, 18.
van der Smissen, Betty, and Oswald H. Goering: *A Leader's Guide to Nature-Oriented Activities.* Iowa State University Press, 3rd ed., 1977, 253 pp.
Vinton, Dennis A., and Elizabeth M. Farley: *Camp Staff Training Series, Module 3, Camp Program Planning and Leadership.* A joint publication of Project REACH, University of Kentucky; ACA; and Hawkins and Associates, Inc., 1979, 142 pp.
Wilkinson, Robert E.: *Camps: Their Planning and Management.* C. V. Mosby Company, 1981, chs. 1, 3, 6, and 11.

MAGAZINE ARTICLES

Camping Magazine:
Harrison, Gerard A.: "Camping Needs Revival of the Fundamental Ethic." June, 1970, p. 9.
Silva, Bernard J., and Brent Jackson: "Camping's Third Dimension." Jan., 1969, p. 12.

Photography

Cardwell: *America's Camping Book,* ch. 24.
Feininger, Andreas: *The Complete Photographer.* Prentice-Hall, 1965, 400 pp.
Ferguson, Robert: *How to Make Movies.* Viking, 1972, 88 pp., paper.
Gillelan, G. Howard: *The Young Sportsman's Guide to Photography.* Nelson, 1964, 96 pp.
Hattersley, Ralph: *Discover Your Self Through Photography: A Creative Workbook for Amateur and Professional.* Ass'n Press, 1970.
How to Make Good Pictures. By the editors of Eastman Kodak Co., Amphoto, New York, New York 10010, 1972, 192 pp., paper.
Johson, James R.: *Photography for Young People.* McKay.
Kinsey, Anthony: *How to Make Animated Movies.* Viking, 1970, 95 pp.
Kujoth: *The Recreation Program Guide,* pp. 75–83 and 299–302.
Langer: *The Joy of Camping,* pp. 292–299.
Learn and Tallman: *Backpacker's Digest,* ch. 12.
Maye, Patricia (ed.): *Fieldbook of Nature Photography.* Scribner's, 1973, 256 pp., paper.
Ormond: *Outdoorsman's Handbook,* Part 6.
Parsons, Christopher: *Making Wildlife Movies (A Beginner's Guide).* Stackpole, 1971, 223 pp.
Photography (No. 3334). Boy Scouts, 1960, 96 pp., paper.
Photography. Golden, paper.
Webb: *Light From A Thousand Campfires:* Haskell, Douglas: "The Camper With a Camera," p. 290.
Zarchy, Harry: *Photography.* Order from Galloway, 48 pp.

MAGAZINE ARTICLES

Backpacker:
Mensinger, Bruce: "You and Your Gear—Camera Care." *Backpacker-5,* Spring, 1974, p. 18.
Porter, Eliot: "Reflections In Nature." *Backpacker-2,* Summer, 1973, p. 52.
Smiley, Ruth: "Seashore Photography." *Backpacker-1,* Spring, 1973, p. 32.

Boys' Life:
Pryce, Dick: "Stalking With a Camera." Nov., 1970, p. 66.
Wagner, Glenn: "Take Better Camp Pictures." July, 1973, p. 32.
Wagner, Glenn: "Explore the Universe with Sky Photography." May, 1970, p. 56.

Camping Journal:
Grant, Ken: "Cameras." Sept., 1972, p. 30.
Grant, Ken: "Care for the Camping Camera." Oct., 1972, p. 29.
Grant, Ken: "Your Guide to Better Outdoor Pictures." Sept., 1970, p. 31.
Haddon, E. P.: "Tips on Taking Trophy Photos." Sept., 1971, p. 24.
Ormond, Clyde: "On the Trail." Sept., 1970, p. 10. (Best type of cameras for outdoor trips)
Park, Ed: "Improve Your Scenic Photos." Sept., 1973, p. 19.

Camping Magazine:
"Campers Get Better Pictures When Basic Rules are Set." June, 1965, p. 17.
Czura, Pete: "Camper's Camera Afield." Apr., 1967, p. 42.

Riflery and Target Shooting

Chapel, Charles E.: *The Boy's Book of Rifles.* Coward-McCann, 274 pp.

Kujoth: *The Recreation Program Guide*, pp. 321–326.
O'Conner, Jack: *The Rifle Book*. Knopf, 4th ed., 1964, 332 pp.
O'Conner, Jack, et al.: *Complete Book of Shooting*. Popular Science, 1965.
Rifle and Shotgun Shooting (No. 3311). Boy Scouts, 1967, 96 pp., paper.
Shivers: *Camping*, pp. 310–314.
Stebbins, Henry: *Teaching Kids to Shoot*. Stackpole, 1966, 96 pp.

MAGAZINE ARTICLES

Camping Magazine:
"How to Construct a Camp Rifle Range." Sept./Oct., 1963, p. 20.
"Riflery Programs." June, 1966, p. 20.
Stolz, Alan J.: "Camp Rifle Program Offers Skills, Safety and Fun." May, 1965, p. 24.

Tennis

Hopman, Harry: *Better Tennis for Boys and Girls*. Dodd, Mead, 1972, 95 pp.
Ideas for Tennis Instruction. AAHPER, 50 pp.
Jaeger, Eloise, and Harry "Cap" Leighton: *Teaching of Tennis for School and Recreational Programs*. Burgess, 2nd ed., 1963, 142 pp., spiral.
King, Billie Jean, and Kimi Chapin: *Tennis to Win*. Harper & Row, 1970, 157 pp.
Mason, R. Elaine: *Tennis*. Allyn and Bacon, 1973, 96 pp., paper.
Metzler, Paul: *Advanced Tennis*. Collier, rev., 1972, 192 pp., paper.
Murphy, Bill, and Chet Murphy: *Tennis for Beginners*. Ronald, 1958, 116 pp.
Scharff, Robert: *Quick and Easy Guide to Tennis*. Collier, 1972, 94 pp.
Tennis Group Instruction. AAHPER, rev., 1972, 64 pp.

eleven

Spiritual Life, Ceremonies and Special Events

SPIRITUAL ASPECTS OF CAMPING

One of the most significant outcomes of a camp experience is the development of spiritual feelings and values. The term "spiritual," as used here, does not have an exclusively religious meaning, although camp is an ideal place for youngsters to acquire religious values. Rather, the term connotes a keen appreciation of nature as well as a sense of kinship with one's fellow beings and an orderly universe. In the outdoors we have an opportunity to view forces at work over which humans have no control and, immersed in great natural beauty, we gain perspective, humility, understanding, and respect for the natural environment.

Spiritual experiences do not always occur at formally arranged times or in specially designated places. Instead, we might think of these experiences as being those times when our thoughts and senses rise to unusual heights of perception as we contemplate our wonderful universe. Sometimes we may simply experience a deep appreciation of the goodness of a companion or the unselfishness of a stranger. Occasions for sharing our deeper and more serious thoughts with others sometimes come unexpectedly, sometimes while sharing a brief time off with a fellow counselor, while looking out over the countryside from a vantage spot high on a hill, or when a small camper slips a hand trustingly into yours and confides some private thought. Other experiences may come in quiet periods of meditation while you enjoy the beauty of a sky full of stars or the call of a lone whippoorwill in the distance. "Although camps have different practices in regard to the spiritual life of campers, they almost without exception feel deeply their obligation along this line and have as an important aim the furthering of spiritual growth through an appreciation of the higher values of life."* There is much that we can do to heighten the spiritual aspects of our lives through camp programs, including worship services, special ceremonies or events, and similar programs.

**Camp Leadership Courses for Colleges and Universities,* ACA, p. 9, IIB.

WORSHIP SERVICES AND DEVOTION

Many camps have daily or weekly all-camp periods of devotion, supplemented by various cabin or unit endeavors to highlight a deeper sense of spiritual values as expressed in all phases of daily living.

Such supplementary experiences ordinarily consist of some combination of the following: (1) grace before meals (oral, spoken in unison, sung, silence during an appropriate musical selection, or a period of silent prayer); (2) outdoor vespers or inspirational programs of some sort; (3) sunrise services or morning watch; (4) cabin devotions or meditations just before taps; (5) attendance at religious services in a neighboring church of the individual's choice or at services conducted by visiting clergymen or camp personnel on the campsite in an indoor or outdoor chapel; (6) group discussions on religion, morals, and ethics; (7) singing of hymns and other appropriate songs.

Interdenominational Camps

Interdenominational camps often make it a point to include both counselors and campers of different faiths in the camp community. This provides an opportunity for living together in broad-minded acceptance of those of different faiths, as well as of those who profess no particular faith; in other words, with respect for the right of each person to worship as he or she pleases. If you accept a position in such a camp, be sure you can wholeheartedly support this attitude without trying to indoctrinate or unduly influence anyone else. Rather, your efforts should be directed toward helping all campers become the best possible members of their own particular faith. Care should be taken not to force any child, either through rules or group pressure, to attend any particular religious services.

In various ways, many camps now actively try to foster this spirit of understanding and brotherhood. Camp directors sometimes invite local priests, rabbis and ministers to take part in

(Cheley Colorado Camps, Estes Park, Colo.)

joint discussions of their faiths, with counselors' and campers' comments and questions encouraged. Many worthwhile pamphlets and other materials of aid in furthering such interaction within the camp family are available at nominal cost from the National Conference of Christians and Jews, Inc., 43 West 57th Street, New York, New York 10019.

Encourage your campers to observe such practices as they are accustomed to, such as a moment of silent grace before meals or an individual prayer before retiring.

Your personal conduct, including consistent observance of kindliness, tolerance, fairness to and respect for every individual in camp, will best express your own spiritual convictions and their influence on your relationships with others.

In a large camp, it is customary to arrange separate services for the three major religious groups, Catholic, Jewish and Protestant.

CATHOLIC. Catholic children usually attend Mass on Sundays and Holy Days. (The only Holy Day falling within the usual camp season of June to September is the Feast of the Assumption of the Blessed Virgin Mary on August 15.) A priest should be summoned in case of serious accident to a Catholic camper.

Camps usually take their Catholic campers and staff to the nearest Catholic church for Mass, but arrangements are sometimes made to celebrate it at the camp if a priest is available and the bishop of the diocese approves. Arrangements should be made for Catholics to go to confession and receive Holy Communion at least once a month. Catholics may attend non-Catholic services with the approval of the local Catholic Diocese.

JEWISH. Those of the Jewish faith observe Saturday, the seventh day of the week, as Sabbath, the day of rest. The Jewish Sabbath begins 20 minutes before sunset on Friday evening and ends about 30 minutes after sunset on Saturday. Sabbath candles should be lit at or before the beginning of the Sabbath, and the service usually follows immediately. Campers and staff may attend a nearby synagogue, or the services may be conducted by a counselor or other lay leader who understands the spirit and mode of Jewish worship.

Campers of the Jewish faith who come from homes that follow traditional observances will want to adhere to the Jewish dietary laws. No pork in any form should be served; if meat or fowl is on the camp menu, there should be an alternate menu of vegetables, salads, eggs or fish (not shellfish) for those who wish it.

The Jewish Holy Day *Tishoh B'ab* usually falls during the camp season; the date varies each year. Those from homes where there is strict traditional observance will wish to observe it as a fast day and will refrain from swimming and festive activities.

PROTESTANT. There are three ways of providing Sunday worship services for Protestant campers: (1) taking them to a nearby Protestant church that meets with the approval of their parents; (2) inviting local ministers of various denominations to conduct services at camp; or (3) having a worship service conducted by a lay person or by staff and campers.

Few Protestant denominations observe dietary restrictions, although some abstain from eating meat on Fridays. There are no Protestant Holy Days during the camp season.

Special Camp Services

Some camps hold inspirational services during the week, which may or may not substitute for the regular weekly worship service. The most appropriate place for these services is in some special "Retreat," "Wilderness Cathedral," or "Woodland Chapel" in the out-of-doors. A site on a hilltop with a commanding view of the valley below, a natural amphitheater beside a gently flowing stream, or a sequestered nook surrounded by the majestic trees of the forest are often most appropriate.

Programs planned jointly by campers and staff are usually most meaningful. The service can be built around some central theme of general interest, such as friendship, going the extra mile, what harmonious camp living means, tolerance, patriotism and love of country, beauty, the wonders of nature, the high ideals and motives of the organization sponsoring the camp, humility, walking in the other fellow's shoes, personalities who achieved greatly in spite of difficulties, or the application of the Golden Rule to camp life. There are so many references to nature and matters of conduct in the Bible that there is little difficulty in selecting passages appropriate to your chosen theme.

Attune the language and nature of the service to those attending it. Adopt an informal spirit of sincerity, dignity, and reverence but avoid sanctimoniousness or undue piousness. Unless there is an outside speaker, let some staff member or camper give a short talk, bringing out the main thought of the service; a short story or anecdote usually promotes interest and understanding.

Set the stage for the proper mood as the audience enters the area. Appropriate music helps, and having campers meet at a distance and file silently down to their seats is also effective.

Encourage all participants to use their creative abilities to furnish poetry, prose, songs and art for the occasion. Music should play an important part, with individuals and groups furnishing vocal and instrumental numbers. Antiphonal singing, dramatization of Bible stories, special prayers and choral readings also furnish variation. There are many spiritual and religious hymns that fit the outdoor setting.

To avoid the midday heat in summer, you may prefer to hold the service in the early morning or evening. A blazing campfire will provide light for a night meditation, which also lends itself nicely to an impressive candlelighting service. Counselors and older campers can be stationed along the path with flashlights, lanterns, or lighted candles to show the way.

Plan the service to last only 30 to 45 minutes, for youngsters tend to get restless and their attention wanders if they have to sit still much longer than that.

Here is a suggested order of service:

Procession—audience
Choir enters singing, approaching through the woods from a nearby meeting place
Scripture reading or opening remarks
Prayer
Hymn
Poem, choral reading, or special number
Musical selection by choir, soloist, or special group
Thought for the day (sermonette)
Hymn
Prayer or closing remarks
Recessional—program participants, choir, then the audience

Sunday in Camp

Sunday is the golden clasp that binds together the volume of the week.

—Longfellow

For those who observe Sunday as their special day of worship, the regular daily program is relaxed and campers are given much free time to engage in quiet, restful activities, although tennis courts, boats, waterfront and other facilities are available to those who want to use them. Breakfast is ordinarily served a little later than usual and some extra touch may be added, such as eating in a special place or being served cafeteria style. It is a day for spending time together as a cabin group, listening to music, singing, holding discussions, telling stories, or writing letters. It might be designated as Visitors' Day, with the camp playing host to parents and friends. A cold supper or cookout for small groups is customary to give the kitchen staff extra time off; this also provides an opportunity for small groups to take their meals to a secluded spot of beauty.

Sunday can and should be the most cherished day in the week. In planning for it, we must remember to look at it through the eyes of youth, for, if we fill it with taboos, stuffy pursuits, unnatural quiet and lengthy talks, we will build up rebelliousness, distaste, and even antireligious attitudes. Campers should know it as a change-of-pace day to renew strength of mind and spirit for the coming week.

God of the open air, we kneel reverently in this temple not made with hands. The tall pines lift our thoughts above us to the Source of all this beauty. The singing of the feather-throated choir puts a melody in our hearts, a song of joy and praise and trust. All the discordant notes of the world are muted; all the problems of life are forgotten. We are filled with an inner peace and know that here we have found Thee. As we leave this hallowed spot, may the reality of Thy presence go with us to give us courage and strength for our daily tasks. Amen.

—Dorothy Wells Pease.
From *Meditations Under the Sky.*
Abingdon, 1957.
Permission by Abingdon Press.

We Thank Thee

For flowers that bloom about our feet;
For tender grass so fresh and sweet;
For song of bird and hum of bee;
For all things fair we hear and see,
Father in Heaven, we thank Thee!

—Ralph Waldo Emerson

SPECIAL EVENTS

Special events are often planned for the beginning or end of each week of camp and usually involve the entire camp community. A wide variety of themes and ideas can be used, including the programs described below.

The Camp Banquet

Camp banquets can be festive dress-up occasions, with special menus and a candlelighting service: the director lights the candles of the staff and unit heads, who in turn pass the light on to the campers. A unit or committee plans a program of songs, poems, short talks, skits, or other activities around a central theme. There may also be inspirational talks, the presentation of awards and certificates, and the reading of selected poems, plays, and stories written by campers (Fig. 11-1).

Dedication Ceremony

A dedication ceremony may be arranged to recognize some new camp acquisition, especially a project campers have completed, such as a newly laid trail, a site for an outdoor chapel selected and furnished by them, or a new outpost camp. Plan a serious and impressive but brief program with appropriate songs and a special speech of dedication, with sincere praise for those who donated their time and efforts to create something of benefit both to present and future campers.

Fourth of July (Independence Day)

Hold a special flag ceremony and stress the day's history and traditions, as well as our reasons for celebrating it. Serve special food, with table decorations in a patriotic motif of red, white, and blue. More elaborate outdoor games or a parade might be planned (Figures 11-2 and 11-3).

Birthday Party

Campers appreciate having some notice taken of their birthdays. A monthly party for those having birthdays within the month with a special "unbirthday party" for the rest handles

Figure 11–1 A camp banquet for a special occasion. (Camp Kingsmont, West Stockbridge, Mass.)

Figure 11-2 A special event. (Camp Kingsmont, West Stockbridge, Mass.)

Figure 11-3 A parade is a great way to celebrate a special day (Camp Kingsmont, West Stockbridge, Mass.)

the situation nicely. Seat the celebrants together and serve them a special lighted birthday cake, with cake and ice cream for everyone. Use favors, sing a birthday song, and hold a brief program. Some camps also set aside a special day to celebrate the camp's birthday.

Closing Campfire

The last campfire should be a memorable event, starting with a processional to the fire, which may be lighted by one of the special methods discussed later on in the chapter. Plan to start off in a light mood, gradually progressing to one more serious and impressive. End on a note of beauty and sentiment, but avoid the type of overindulgence that causes weeping and wailing and badly upset emotions. If the philos-

Figure 11-4 Flag-raising ceremony. (Camp Summer Life, Taos, N. Mex.)

ophy of your camp sanctions awarding honors, badges, and certificates, this is a good time to present them.

MacKay* suggests putting the blue of the lake, the green of the forest, the violet of the distant mountain, and the red of the sunset into the fire to save for next summer. Symbolize them by casting in, one at a time, a paper cupful of each of the appropriate chemicals to produce these colors. (This is discussed in detail later on in this chapter.) Camps sometimes make a ceremony of saving some of the partially burned wood and ashes from this last campfire to use when lighting the first campfire of the next season.

If your program is held near water, a nice closing event consists of having each unit bring a "boat" fashioned from a piece of cardboard or other material that will disintegrate quickly; it can be tastefully decorated with pretty leaves and flowers. After a brief ceremony, each unit affixes a small lighted candle to their boat, and as it is set afloat, each camper makes a wish and watches it disappear into the distance. All then form a *friendship circle* (cross hands to clasp the hand of the person on either side) and sing *Taps* or a goodnight song or repeat a prayer or quotation in unison, perhaps ending with your own special camp or unit hand squeeze. They then file silently away to their cabins, just in time to get ready for bed. At some time early in the season, you may well spend a little time with your campers in thinking about the meaning of the words to *Taps* and why they serve so effectively as a closing prayer just before going off to sleep.

*MacKay: *Creative Counseling for Christian Camps,* p. 84.

FLAG CEREMONIES

A flag raising ceremony usually starts off the camp day, taking place even before breakfast; in many camps there is also a flag lowering exercise (Fig. 11-4). Such occasions offer a chance for campers to learn proper demeanor around the flag as well as how to handle and care for it. They also provide an opportunity both to learn about the history of the flag and its importance as a symbol of our way of life and the principles under which our nation functions and to develop patriotism and a sense of gratitude for the privilege of living in our wonderful country, for, as President John F. Kennedy so aptly said, our attitude should be "Ask not what your country can do for you. Ask rather what you can do for your country."

Concerning the Flag

Our flag has a field of blue, studded with 50 stars that represent the 50 states of the Union. There are also 7 red and 6 white stripes, arranged with red stripes at both the top and bottom; these represent the 13 original colonies. The blue of the flag stands for Justice, the red for Courage, and the white for Purity. The blue starred section is called the *Union* or *canton;* the stick to which the flag is attached is called the *staff* and the cord which attaches it is the *halyard.*

The complete rules and customs for the care and display of the flag are contained in a Flag Code, which is readily available from many sources. We will touch on only a few of the main points here.

1. The flag may be flown on any day when the weather is satisfactory, especially on holidays and historic occasions. It should never be left out in rain, sleet, or snow.

2. The flag may be raised at any time after sunrise and should be taken down before sunset.

3. It should be handled and displayed with the greatest respect at all times and should never be placed where it will be soiled or allowed to touch anything below it, such as the ground or water.

4. The flag should always be displayed aloft and free and should be maintained in good condition, mended when torn and cleaned when dirty.

5. Flying the flag at half-mast signifies a period of mourning. First raise it to the peak, then lower it to a position halfway down the pole. Later, when lowering it, again raise it to the top, then bring it down.

6. When the flag is approaching, a boy stands bareheaded and at attention, with his eyes on the flag. He gives a military salute if in uniform; if not, he places the palm of his right hand, holding his hat or cap if he has one, over his heart until it has passed by. A girl stands at attention with her right palm over her heart. Although it seldom creates a problem in the average camp, you must bear in mind that recent court decisions have forbidden forcing anyone to salute the flag.

Camp Flag Ceremonies

Some camps use only the briefest of ceremonies for flag raising and lowering, while others sponsor more or less elaborate services in an attempt to educate as well as inspire. At least two persons are needed to handle and raise a flag properly, but most camps use a Color Guard of at least five, one of whom acts as Color Bearer to carry the flag. These positions of honor are usually rotated among campers on a day-to-day or week-to-week basis. The Color Guard dresses in a distinguishing uniform, such as wearing red or blue sashes around their waists. A group should practice until they can perform their duties with snap and precision. In a flag raising ceremony the flag is raised at the beginning of the program; in lowering, it remains aloft until everything else has taken place.

A suggested program for flag raising and lowering ceremonies follows:

1. Color Guard enters the area, followed by those participating in the program, and finally by the campers, who form a horseshoe about the flagpole. Campers and Guard maintain complete silence during the program.

2. Color Guard unfolds the flag and the Color Bearer attaches it to the halyard and raises it *briskly* to the top of the pole as all others stand at attention, saluting it and keeping their eyes on it.

3. Maintaining the salute, all repeat the Pledge of Allegiance:

I pledge allegiance to the Flag of the United States of America and to the Republic for which it stands, one Nation under God, indivisible, with liberty and justice for all.

4. If desired, have a short talk, read a poem or sing a patriotic song.

5. Everyone salutes during the flag lowering ceremony. The Color Guard advances to the flag and the Color Bearer lowers it *slowly* and *ceremoniously* into the hands of the rest of the Color Guard, who fold it lengthwise, first into halves, then into fourths. The two Guards at the end away from the stars then begin to fold it into triangles, starting with a triangular fold across the end and continuing with triangular folds back and forth until it is completely folded into one triangle with stars on both sides. They then hand it to the Color Bearer to carry.

6. Color Guard leaves the area, followed by the other participants in the program, and finally the campers, who drop their salute and fall into line.

EVENING OUTDOOR PROGRAMS

Although, in the interest of ecology, many camps have ruled out the traditional campfire of wood, most still hold at least one outdoor program for the entire group each week, with additional programs for smaller groups in between, that use some type of simulated campfire. When well planned, such programs are quite impressive and tend to be remembered by campers long after camp days are over, influencing their attitudes and characters more than almost any other event of the summer. These programs usually are held in an area reserved especially for this purpose. There is a certain magic about sitting closely with friends in a muted light that shuts out the surrounding fringe of darkness and night sounds and makes even the most timid feel, "I belong." Most camps have developed certain traditions and customary ways of doing things that returning campers have come to love and eagerly look forward to each new season; traditional campfire programs fall into this category. Although certain phases are repeated year after year, each year some different touches should be added, for youngsters tend to become bored when they know exactly what will happen next. Like any program, superior evening outdoor programs don't just happen. They result from careful planning, down to the last detail.

Site for the Program

The site for the program should be secluded and free from outside distractions, but not too far from the main camp in case of a sudden downpour or if props have to be carried. This also prevents campers from traveling long distances over rough trails at night. However, try to avoid a seating arrangement that brings camp buildings into view, for this makes it hard to produce the mood of getting away from everyday surroundings. A position on high ground with adequate mosquito control helps campers to concentrate. If a wood fire is used, there should be some sort of windbreak to help control it and to create a vacuum to draw the smoke away from participants.

The site itself should be from 24 to 50 feet in diameter, depending on the number to be accommodated. Keep it as compact as possible, with seats arranged in tiers if necessary and with taller people in the back so that all can see and hear well. A good arrangement calls for seating in horseshoe form with the entrance and exit at the open end, the source of light inside, and the stage toward the rounded end where the audience sits. The program director or master of ceremonies occupies a seat of honor near the closed end of the area. Campers may simply sit on the ground on ponchos, blankets, sit-upons, planks laid across short lengths of logs, or wooden benches.

There are several successful alternative methods of providing light if your conscience or the law prohibits building a traditional campfire of wood. One method consists of the familiar device of using crepe paper in shades of orange, yellow, or red to camouflage such sources of light as camp lanterns, flashlights, or electric light bulbs. Plumber's or church candles placed upon flat stones produce a surprisingly cozy and pleasant atmosphere, although you may need to place some sort of fireproof windscreen about them if there is enough breeze to blow them out. Even the direct light from flashlights, electric lights, or camp lanterns may be used, although it is usually more effective to at least partially conceal them.

Wood Campfires

If you decide to build a wood campfire, prepare a safe fire site as usual and place fire tools and a pail of water or sand nearby, but where they won't be tripped over and spilled. There should also be a blanket or other heavy material at hand in case someone's clothing should catch fire.

If for some reason you can't build the fire on the ground at your program site, insulate a wheelbarrow or use a big metal drum as a fire pan by placing an inch or two of sand or gravel in it and build the fire on top. You can also build it out on a raft, covering it with dirt and anchor-

(Willamette Council of Camp Fire, Salem, Oreg.)

ing it close to shore or placing it out in the water with the participants coming out to it in canoes.

Since a large part of the effectiveness of your program depends on the success of your fire, pay strict attention to every detail in constructing it so that it will go off at the touch of a match and burn briskly with a minimum of smoke. Lay it well ahead of time and arrange it to feed itself without undue attention and refueling, but keep a reserve supply of wood handy in case of need. Keep the fire small to conserve fuel, to make it less hazardous, and to keep from roasting everyone with excess heat.

Campers usually regard it as an honor to be selected for the fire committee, which is headed by a Chief Fire Keeper under counselor supervision. They select the wood, tend the fire, put it out after the program, and clean up the debris around the site.

A log cabin fire, as discussed in Chapter 26, is usually best since it is long-lasting and less dangerous than many other types of fires. Build it as usual, using medium-sized sticks and filling the spaces in between with plenty of kindling and small-sized split wood. At the fifth or sixth layer of large sticks, lay a platform of small sticks across them and build a small teepee fire on it; continue with a few additional layers of large sticks. When you light the teepee fire, it immediately bursts into flame to ignite the surrounding structure, which soon burns down to embers, setting fire to the loose structure below. For an especially spectacular effect, soak the materials with a little kerosene well ahead of time. NEVER apply kerosene to a fire that has already been lighted.

LIGHTING THE FIRE

The actual lighting of the fire usually occurs after the campers have assembled and there has been some special opening ceremony. Someone may simply step up with a torch to light the fire, or it may be done by a costumed runner, a person on horseback, a delegation coming across the lake in a canoe, or four persons with lighted candles approaching from the four quadrants of the compass.

"Magic methods," which seemingly create fire without the aid of human hands, provide even more spectacular ways to light the fire. When choosing one of them, use only responsible people and test the method several times to make sure it works satisfactorily and isn't unduly hazardous. Even then, it is always best to provide an alternate method, since the whole program will get off to a bad start if the fire lighting is delayed.

FIRE FROM THE SKY. Using this method, someone releases a "ball of fire," that slides down a wire suspended from a tree to the bottom of a kerosene-soaked fire lay and sets it instantly ablaze. Make the "ball" by soaking a bag of sawdust, loosely wrapped gauze, or part of an old burlap bag wrapped around a stone in kerosene. Make the wire taut and keep the ball on course by fastening it to an old spool or loop of wire threaded on the wire. The person stationed in the tree holds onto the ball by an attached handle of wire until ready to release it. Alter the weight of the "ball" and the angle of the wire until the descent takes place with just the right amount of speed and without endangering anything or anybody.

SPONTANEOUS COMBUSTION. Fasten a piece of black fishline or wire to the bottom of a buddy burner or can with its top and one side cut out and a plumber's candle fastened in the bottom. Place the burner or can opposite a hole in the fire lay big enough to admit it and on the side away from the campers. Extend the wire through and under the kerosene-treated fire so that you can inconspicuously draw the can or burner into it when ready.

COLOR IN YOUR CAMPFIRE

Although you can use the chemically treated chips and logs produced commercially to give color in an indoor fireplace, it is usually less expensive and more challenging to make your own, using chemicals you can purchase at a drug store. Only adults should attempt this and they should work carefully and protect their hands with rubber gloves. Do not mix the chemicals together. Use them only in a crockery or wooden container, since most of them are corrosive to metal. The usual proportion calls for a half pound of chemical to a half gallon of water.

You may use pine cones, bits of wood, sawdust in a bag, or slick magazine pages, rolled tightly into one-inch "logs" and tied at both ends. Place them in a mesh or coarsely knit bag and submerge them in the solution, weighing them down with stones to keep them in place. Leave them at least a day or two to insure thorough saturation, then lift them out and suspend them over the container to drip briefly before placing them on thick newspapers and leaving them for three or four days to dry out thoroughly. Here are some colors and the chemicals that will produce them:

blue	copper sulfate
yellow	common salt
red	strontium
purple	lithium chloride
vivid green	borax
apple green	barium nitrate
orange	calcium chloride
lavender	potassium chloride
emerald green	copper nitrate

Entering the Campfire Area

A flashlight parade down a winding trail provides an impressive entrance to the campfire area. Each unit may assemble separately, uniting at the trail entrance on a signal that all is ready. They may sing an appropriate song or approach silently to the rhythm of a tom-tom and file into their assigned seats in the area.

Unit counselors should then collect flashlights or campers should place theirs at rest beside them to avoid the distraction of having lights flashed off and on during the program.

The Program

The Council Chief, who functions as master of ceremonies, wearing a special costume and operating from the seat of honor, is responsible for the tenor of the whole affair. He or she must be thoroughly acquainted with everything that is to take place and must keep things moving, coordinating the program to run like a well-oiled piece of machinery. The leader needs showmanship, tact, a well-developed sense of humor and a ready wit, together with an ability to adapt or cover up when things do not go just as anticipated. All proposed numbers and activities should be previously reviewed to screen out any that are ineffective, cheap, crude, in poor taste, or likely to embarrass or hurt someone.

The Council Chief uses hand signals to quiet and control the audience and insists that everyone display good manners and courtesy at all times, especially toward the performers. He or she holds up a hand to signal for attention and doesn't start talking until everyone is quiet. In the long run, a leader gains much more respect and genuine affection when he or she insists on courtesy and decorum and refuses to accept bad behavior.

As always, let the campers accept a major role in planning and carrying out the program, for it should indeed be entertainment *by* them, not *for* them. Plan it to last not longer than an hour or an hour and a half and stop on time, even if you have to cut out something, for attention spans are short and bedtime and adequate sleep are necessary. A good master of ceremonies can perform wonders in speeding things up or slowing them down to finish in the allotted time.

Make variety the keynote and provide for active audience participation to relieve the tedium and cramped muscles resulting from an excess of sitting still.

After lighting the fire, follow with lively, fun things and gradually taper off into more serious and quieter activities. End on a restful, quiet note, such as singing lullabies and other peaceful songs, reading poetry, or having discussions and storytelling. This puts campers in a mood for sleep and greatly simplifies counselors' problems in getting them quietly into bed.

Choose your main events from such activities as the following:

Singing
Games, contests
Challenges by individuals or group representatives
Short plays
Shadow plays
Quizzes, short riddles
Amateur or talent nights
Pantomimes
Tall stories—see who can tell the biggest whopper
Stunts, skits
Indian dances and activities
Short talks—humorous or serious
Announcements
Reading of the camp paper by the editor
Honors and awards
Musical numbers
Storytelling
Special theme such as Indians, pioneers, and so on

Always anticipate that old bugaboo, rain, and plan how to adjust to it when it comes. You can often transfer much of the program indoors, turn off the lights, and build a fire in the fireplace or construct a mock campfire with logs, colored light bulbs, and red or orange crepe paper.

ADDITIONAL READINGS

(For an explanation of abbreviations and abbreviated forms, see page 13.)

Barnes, Johnnie: *The Royal Rangers Leader's Manual.* Gospel Publishing House, Springfield, Mo. 65802, 1962, 122 pp., pp. 91–122.
Berger: *Program Activities for Camp,* ch. 9.
Bogardus, LaDonna: *Outdoor Living.* Abington, 1971, Leader's Guide, packet 1.
Camping Is Education, pp. 17–21.
Edgar, Mary S.: *Under Open Skies.* Clarke, Irvin, 1955
Ensign: *Camping Together As Christians.*
Kelsey, Alice Geer: *Seven-Minute Stories For Church and Home.* Abingdon, 1958, 128 pp.
Klein, Ernst E.: *God Speaks—To Me!* Judson, 1960, 135 pp., paper. (Counselor's Guide)
MacInnes, Gordon A.: *A Guide to Worship in Camp and Conference.* Westminster, 1965, 96 pp., paper.
MacKay: *Creative Counseling For Christian Camps,* ch. 5.
Messinger, C. F.: *Church Camping For Junior Highs.* Westminster, 1965, 96 pp., paper.
Messinger, C. F., J. E. Simpson, and G. F. Ulrich: *Seeking Meaning With Junior Highs in Camp.* Westminster, 1966, paper.
Pease, Dorothy Wells: *Inspiration Under the Sky.* Abingdon, 1963.
Schiechen, Samuel J.: *Wonder in God's Wilderness.* Augsburg.
Schroeder, Ruth: *Youth Programs on Nature Themes.* Abingdon, 1959, 192 pp.
Springer, James C.: *Boys, Girls and God.* Vantage, 1971, 82 pp.
Todd: *Camping For Christian Youth.*
Webb: *Light From A Thousand Campfires:* Baker, Edna Dean: "Religion in Camp." p. 251. Hazzard, Lowell B.: "Spiritual Values in Camping." p. 45. Rogers, Mrs. Dwight: "A Prayer for Camp Directors." p. 19.

MAGAZINE ARTICLES

Camping Magazine:
Brown, Stewart A.: "Youth Speaks a New Language at Camp Worship Services." Mar., 1969, p. 46.
Bullock, George: "Encourage Spiritual Awareness." Jan., 1962, p. 38.
Dunbar, David: "Creating Spiritual Awareness in Youth." Dec., 1960, p. 7.
Eells, Eleanor P.: "Church Camping Has Colorful Past." Jan., 1980, p. 7.
Jones, John H.: "Status of Church Camping." March, 1980, p. 13.
McLarty, Emmett K., Jr.: "Spiritual Values in Camping." Part I, Sept./Oct., 1967, p. 14; Part II, Jan., 1968, p. 18.

Mellinger, Marie B.: "Religion in Nonsectarian Camps." Jan., 1967, p. 22.
Schoonover, Barbara: "And God Created. . . ." Feb., 1962, p. 72.
Stith, Marjorie: "Spiritual Growth by Camping." March, 1979, p. 29.
van der Smissen, Betty: "Camping—The Outdoor Ministry of the Church." Jan., 1964, p. 14.
van der Smissen, Betty: "Nature's Proclamation." Nov./Dec., 1963, p. 32.

Special Events, Campfire and Council Ring Programs

Berger: *Program Activities For Camps.*
Nagel, Myra: *My Keys To Creative Ceremonies.* ACA, 1975, 80 pp.
Shivers, Jay S.: *Camping: Administration, Counseling, Programming.* Meredith Corporation, 1971, ch. 16.
Thurston, LaRue A.: *Good Times Around the Campfire.* Association Press, 1967, 128 pp.
Van Matre, Steve: *Sunship Earth.* ACA, 1979, ch. 12.
van der Smissen and Goering: *A Leader's Guide to Nature-Oriented Activities,* pp. 179–187.
Webb: *Light From A Thousand Campfires:* Buchanan, Bruce R.: "Campfire Programs." p. 248.

MAGAZINE ARTICLES

Camping Magazine:
Macfarlan, Allan A.: "Campfires Can be Memorable—With Wise Guidance and Planning." Nov./Dec., 1963, p. 28.
Nash, Harold W.: "How Campers Share Fun, Responsibility of Planning Campfires." Feb., 1961, p. 14.
"Philosophy for Fire Lighting." May, 1962, p. 3.
Schmidt, Ernest F., and W. Chester Frisbie: " 'Sure-Fire' Methods for Starting Campfires." Mar., 1962, p. 18.

twelve

Music, Rhythm, and Drama Activities

It is probable that from our earliest existence some form of rhythm has played an important part in our life. Nearly all studies of primitive peoples show that each had its chants and ceremonial dances to use in times of deep emotion. Some expressed joy, as after a successful hunt or encounter with the enemy, while others lamented a misfortune such as the death of a loved one. Still others were used to entreat their gods to supply the people's wants, such as rain, a bountiful food supply, or the speedy recovery of an ill or injured person. Throughout history, workers have sung to relieve the tedium of their long hours of labor, and armies have had songs as well as bands and drum and bugle corps to lessen marching fatigue and to raise their morale and patriotism to the highest possible pitch. Humans are, and always have been, lovers of rhythm of all types, and campers are no exception to the rule.

SINGING IN THE CAMP PROGRAM

It is the most natural thing in the world for happy campers to sing at any time and place they happen to be; conversely, campers who sing can scarcely avoid being happy. Song should burst forth as spontaneously as mushrooms after a rain, for the miles fly by while hiking, dishes seem almost to dry themselves, and even mediocre paddlers swing into a space-covering rhythm when there's a song in the air. Good music is a great leavening agent; few fail to succumb to a catchy tune, a strong rhythm, or the sheer beauty of a lovely melody. No camper or counselor should return home without a new and complete repertoire of good songs. In addition to free moments or rest periods, there are a number of other occasions in which music can enhance life in camp each day, including the beginning and ending of the day, at mealtime and in campfire programs, during spiritual occasions, for talent shows or special musical concerts, or while on outdoor hikes.

Types of Songs

Most songs can be divided roughly into three types, each having a definite place in the camp program.

FOLK SONGS. *Folk songs,* such as "Weggis Song" and "Walking at Night," cannot be traced to any one composer; rather, they originated at some time in the past and were passed down orally from generation to generation, no doubt with some modification along the way. These old folk songs seem to have come straight from the emotions and everyday experiences of those who sang them, and they now serve as lasting tributes to them. Fortunately for us, we are now experiencing a revival of interest in these songs, and are finding many of great value. However, we must bear in mind that many so-called folk songs are actually of recent origin and by a known composer and so are not true folk songs at all. This is not meant to belittle them, for some are quite excellent and well worth singing.

Many of the old true folk songs have now been written down. *Ballads,* such as the "Deaf Woman's Courtship,"* tell a story that campers may enjoy acting out as they sing. *Sea chanteys,* such as "Down the River," originated as sailors sang while they worked on the vast and lonely seas. There is a story behind all folk songs, be they singing games, spirituals, plantation songs, cowboy songs, or mountain ballads. Although it is sometimes difficult to trace their origins, the search is well worth the effort, for such knowledge makes them much more meaningful and enjoyable for both singers and listeners.

> Folk songs are not made; they grow. They fall out of the air; they fly over land like gossamer, now here, now there; and are sung in a thousand places at the same time. Our own actions and our life we find in these songs. It is as if we all had helped make them.
>
> —THEODOR STORM, (1917–1888) *Immensee.*

ROUNDS OR CANONS. *Rounds* or *canons* are sung with the group divided into two or more sections, each singing the same melody but starting at different times. "Harmony Greeting" and "Dona Nobis Pacem" are familiar camp songs of this type.

ART SONGS. *Art songs,* such as Bach's "Now Let Every Tongue Adore Thee" and Sibelius' "Song of Peace" ("Finlandia"), were composed by the masters and merit a special place in

(Camp Kingsmont, West Stockbridge, Mass.)

the camp program. Their sheer beauty makes them a pleasure to sing as well as a help in developing a taste for good music. A few of these art songs are based on old folk songs.

Songs for Every Occasion

There are songs appropriate for almost any time or place. They serve well as "ice breakers" to thaw out a group of new acquaintances. Singing in front of a blazing fire in an indoor fireplace banishes gloom on a cold, rainy day. Singing in close harmony develops a spirit of camaraderie and togetherness as voices blend to produce the total effect.

Well-chosen songs will put a group into a receptive mood for almost any activity, be it a serious campfire program, a discussion group, or an evening of pure fun and frolic. There are appropriate songs to welcome newcomers, to express regret at someone's leaving, or even to quiet hunger pangs while waiting in front of the dining room for the signal to enter. Music relieves tension and jangled nerves, and singing during a rest break on the trail helps to reduce fatigue. Singing a pretty lullaby or listening to soft, soothing music on a record player calms restless, boisterous campers and induces an appropriate mood for a siesta or quiet after taps. Music furnishes a background for writing letters, reading, readying equipment, or working on an arts and crafts project. There are appropriate songs to help with rowing, canoeing, horseback riding, hiking, or almost anything else on the agenda. Songs help to maintain campers'

*This, as well as other songs mentioned here, can be found in *Sing,* available from the American Camping Association.

spirits when a temporary blackout or a balky campfire disrupts activities or when an outbreak of homesickness threatens.

Music combines well with many other camp activities. Learning native songs and dances helps campers to understand the culture and ways of life of another people. No vesper or other worship service is complete without including some beautiful hymns. Arts and crafts combine with music when campers design costumes and stage sets for operettas and musical skits, or construct such simple musical instruments as shepherd's pipes, tom-toms, bongo drums, or rattles.

Who Should Lead Singing?

Although camps usually designate one or more staff members as official song leaders, this should in no way discourage others from participating at appropriate times and places; those who try it usually find it a very rewarding experience. Almost everyone has a sense of rhythm; if you doubt it, just watch a group listening to a catchy rhythm and note how many unconsciously sway their heads or bodies or tap their feet. After a little instruction and some practice, almost anyone with a good sense of rhythm can do a creditable job of song leading. Formal musical training undoubtedly helps if you do not let it curb your spontaneity or make you too insistent upon a "concert performance." Although perfection is a worthy objective in many endeavors, the main aim in camp singing should be providing enjoyment and satisfaction. Maintaining reasonably high standards of performance for really worthwhile songs is a major stepping stone toward achieving this goal. Of course it helps when a leader can sing well and has a strong voice to set the pace and keep the group together and on pitch, but many excellent leaders have quite ordinary voices and some don't even sing at all, merely mouthing the words as they lead. In fact, a superior singer can actually inhibit youngsters by making them hesitant to join in with their own, more average voices.

Using Songbooks

There are now many good song collections on the market, including some inexpensive paperbacks, with songs selected especially for their appropriateness to the camp setting and their appeal to those of camp age. Campers and leaders sometimes compile and mimeograph copies of their own favorites for use in camp and as souvenirs to take home so campers can refresh their memories as time dims the once familiar words and tunes.

If you have no songbook, but want to place the words and music before the singers, print large characters on a blackboard or a large piece of wrapping paper that can be rolled up to store. At night or in a darkened room you can use an opaque projector to show the words and music on a screen, a white wall, or a taut bed sheet.

Some song leaders prefer not to use songbooks, especially when teaching a new song; they prefer to maintain eye contact to allow the singers to concentrate more on their hand signals as well as on the melody and meaning of the words. This type of teaching is called *rote* teaching.

(Camp Kingsmont, West Stockbridge, Mass.)

Planning for a Song Session

As previously mentioned, singing may just spring forth spontaneously at any time and place; at other times, you may want to plan a special song fest or use singing as a part of another program. Plan to have the singing last no longer than ten to fifteen minutes, for it is better to stop while everyone is still enthusiastic and wanting more.

As with any successful program, a good singing session doesn't just happen. It comes about because a leader has planned and prepared it carefully so that the presentation seems almost spontaneous. Such preparation brings confidence and an ability to be relaxed and informal.

It is helpful to find out all you can about the background of each song. Of what nationality were the people who sang it and what were their occupations and general mode of living? When did it originate and on what occasions did they sing it? What interesting facts can you tell about the composer's life? Little anecdotes about the composer or the song add great interest. When you can convey to your group the mood of the people who sang the song, they will enjoy it more and sing it with more meaning and spirit.

When you encounter a group that lacks good taste in music or has poor singing habits, improving these may tax your patience and ingenuity to the utmost. It may sometimes even be best to let them sing some of their chosen songs while you try to bring about gradual improvements, for as in any type of teaching, we must start where the learners are.

You may want to start a program with rollicking fun or action songs, gradually passing on to those more serious and thoughtful, and perhaps finally ending with a hymn, a patriotic song, or your own special camp song.

Introducing New Songs

Before introducing a new song, practice and know it thoroughly. For your first presentations, choose songs with lively tunes, short verses, and oft-repeated choruses. It is often best to teach the chorus first so that the group has something familiar to return to after each new verse. It sometimes helps to teach the song first to a small group, such as a cabin group, which then can serve as a leader for the rest.

When leading, sing the song through once to show its general tempo and character. Then go back and sing the first phrase, asking campers to sing it after you, and then go on to the next. When you have finished this, go back and sing the whole verse and go on to the now-familiar chorus. Repeat the song several times within the next few days until it takes its place as an old familiar friend. When you notice a mistake in timing, phrasing, words, or pitch, correct it immediately before it has had time to become a hard-to-break habit.

Techniques of Song Leading

Although small groups sometimes sing without a leader, both quality and enjoyment increase when there is one, especially when learning a new song or when the group is large.

Leading camp singing isn't nearly as difficult as it may seem, for only simple movements and techniques are needed. Enthusiasm should show through in your facial expression, the sparkle in your eyes, and your whole general attitude. Establishing good rapport with the singers is all-important, so smile often and remain pleasant. Think of the group singers as individuals, each important in him or herself; this attitude quickly communicates itself to campers and enlists their cooperation.

Arrange the group about you in a close semicircle to give a feeling of unity, and place yourself where all can see and hear you clearly. Try to sense the group's mood and adapt your approach to it. Choose a key suitable for the average voice, remembering that children's voices are usually higher than those of adults. The use of a voice cue, pitch pipe, or tonette can help to set the pitch.

Don't try to be too fancy or to emulate the complicated movements of a symphony orchestra conductor. Some very successful leaders simply beat out the rhythm with a simple up-and-down or side-to-side movement. However, it isn't at all difficult to master some more meaningful gestures, such as those illustrated in Figure 12–1. Keep the rhythm with your right hand, using a vigorous downbeat to emphasize the first beat of each measure and ending it with an upbeat. Keep your right arm swinging like a

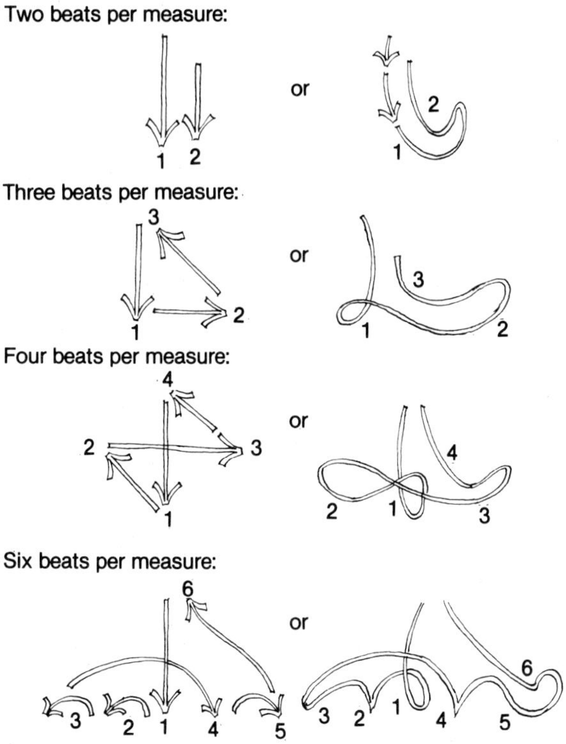

Figure 12–1 Right arm movements for leading singing.

pendulum and vary the vigor of your movements to indicate the desired mood or volume—strong for spirited, bold singing, less marked for soft, smooth passages. Stop your hand in a fixed position when you want a note held, and cross your hands briskly in front of your body at the end of the song so that all will stop together. Have definite signals for starting and stopping and insist on their being observed, for this adds interest and zest to a singing session and fosters pride in doing it well.

Regulate volume with your left hand, raising it palm up for an increase and lowering it palm down or placing your finger tips on your lips for a decrease. Beckon or point to a group when you want them to come in, as in a round, or when you want them to sing with more volume. Keep both hands high where everyone can see them clearly. Be sure to explain your hand signals to the group before starting.

Strive for clear enunciation, bringing out each word clearly so that listeners have no difficulty in understanding them. Aim for good tonal effect with no voices dominating, but all blending in a pleasing manner; tone down those who sing off key or too loudly, but be sure to compliment the group when they sing well, and encourage them to try for a still better performance.

Plan for Variety

Promote friendly, informal competition between groups occasionally, basing it upon superior harmony, depth of feeling, and best interpretation of the song, never on loudness and just plain noise. If they tend to sing too loudly and with little feeling for the song, have them sing it progressively more softly, dying away into a final pianissimo.

Since most songs tell a story, use modulation of tempo and volume to interpret and convey the meaning and to add variety to the program. Never let singing degenerate into a monotonous singsong with each number sounding very much like the others. A pace which is too rapid is preferable to one that drags.

Encourage good part singing, occasionally assigning solo parts to those able to carry them while the rest remain silent, whistle, hum, or "tra-la" in harmony.

Encourage campers who are especially interested to try their hand at leading, or ask them to help you to plan a song session. Always prepare more songs than can possibly be used so that you never run short and can do some juggling if things fail to go just as expected. It is also good to sometimes allow time in the program for special requests.

Although the aim of camp singing is enjoyment and the satisfaction that comes from doing it well and tastefully, you need not confine your repertoire to staid, serious numbers. There is a definite place for songs sung just for the fun of it and there are many light-hearted, nonsensical ditties and action songs that are dear to the hearts of live-wire youngsters. Include all types: slow, fast, happy, sad, plaintive, rollicking, thoughtful, sentimental, and just plain lovely. Sing songs such as "Alouette" (a gay Canadian voyageur song) and "Tongo" in which the leader sings a line or two, followed by a group response.

Rounds have been with us for a long time (it is claimed that "Three Blind Mice" appeared

(National Music Camp, Interlochen, Mich.)

in print as early as 1609), and they are usually camper favorites, possibly because they offer a mild form of group competition. When learning a new one, have everyone sing the melody together until it is familiar, then divide them into groups, perhaps appointing a leader for each. Each group then sings the song through a given number of times, usually as many as there are groups.

Descants, as for "Rio Grande," are high-pitched harmonies that accompany the regular melody. Campers may want to try their hand at improvising some for appropriate favorite numbers. *Contra-singing* consists of simultaneously singing two songs whose melodies blend. In *antiphonal singing,* an "echo" group sings from some distant point, as high on a nearby hill or across the lake or out in canoes (music carries particularly well across the water.)

Individuals may want to form duets, trios, or barbershop quartets, singing just for their own amusement or preparing selections for some special occasion. A choir group adds materially to a vesper or Sunday service, especially when they come singing through the woods on their way to the outdoor chapel or cathedral. A group may sometimes receive special permission to be out after taps to serenade another group or to wake them just before the morning rising signal.

It is often preferable to sing *a capella* (without instruments) so that singers learn to rely on themselves to carry the tune and keep the rhythm. For variation, use simple instruments such as a guitar, handmade shepherd's pipe, harmonica, or accordion to accompany the singing or for a solo part. An Indian tom-tom is effective in opening an Indian song or fading away at its close.

Some camps hold special music appreciation hours for those who want to listen to recorded music. Let camper committees help to plan them, and invite interested parties to submit requests. Plan an occasional program around a central theme, such as the celebration of some composer's birthday that falls during the camp season.

Unfortunately, campers sometimes become so infatuated with a song that they sing it until it is threadbare and almost unbearable to everyone else. Before condemning them too much for this, examine your program; perhaps there has been a failure to supply enough attractive new songs to alternate with the old. Some camps have successfully solved this problem by gathering everyone for a mock burial service to sing the offending number for the last time, then lay it away in a final resting place and decorate the grave with a bouquet of dandelions.

Encourage groups or units to compose original tunes to accompany favorite poems. This is more challenging and requires more originality than simply borrowing or adapting someone else's tune. Original songs can be made quite personal and can introduce funny little happenings and secret private jokes known only to the composers. You may find it fun to compose songs yourself, perhaps making up appropriate words to go with a favorite tune or one of your own creation.

SINGING GAMES AND DANCES

Old-time singing games and dances are very popular with campers. Many of them are quite vigorous and help campers let off steam, especially after they have been cooped up inside for some time because of bad weather; round, square, longways, and folk dances are in this category, along with party games.

As was originally done, the accompaniment can be provided by singing or by simple instruments such as fiddles, guitars, or accordions. You may find adequate callers on your own camp staff or in a nearby community, or you can use records that are available both with and without calls.

(Camp Kingsmont, West Stockbridge, Mass.)

A good way to begin a program is with a few "mixers" or "ice breakers," simple steps and figures. This gets everybody out on the floor and builds confidence as they gradually progress to something more complicated. There may also be a demand for modern dance forms that are currently in vogue.

An *International Night* featuring the native costumes and dances of one or more foreign countries is well received and helps participants to understand people of other cultures. This may be an all-camp project, one sponsored by one or two units, or each unit or cabin may be responsible for preparing one number and teaching it to the others.

RHYTHMICAL INSTRUMENTS

Musical Instruments

Many camps encourage campers to bring their own instruments so they can play in combos and other special groups, or perhaps even in an all-camp orchestra or band. Rhythm bands are also popular; most of the instruments are easy to play and are available for rent or purchase at most music stores, together with music and directions for organizing a band.

Make Your Own Percussion Instruments

Some *percussion instruments* (those for keeping time but not for playing a tune) are easily made and are enjoyable both to make and to use.

For a *drum* (Figure 12–2) use a round container such as a No. 10 tin can, an oatmeal box, a round wooden box, the bottom of a plastic bleach bottle, or even a round wooden bowl with the bottom sawed off. Construct drumheads from pieces of inner tube, rawhide, heavy plastic, oilcloth, an animal skin, or some heavy material such as sailcloth or unbleached muslin that has been stiffened by applying a coat of shellac. Draw a drumhead very tightly over each end of the drum, and use strips of leather, inner tube or strong cord to lace them together as shown, or use a rubber band, thumbtacks, or large-headed tacks to anchor each head separately. To tighten them still more, paint them with shellac after they are in place and let dry;

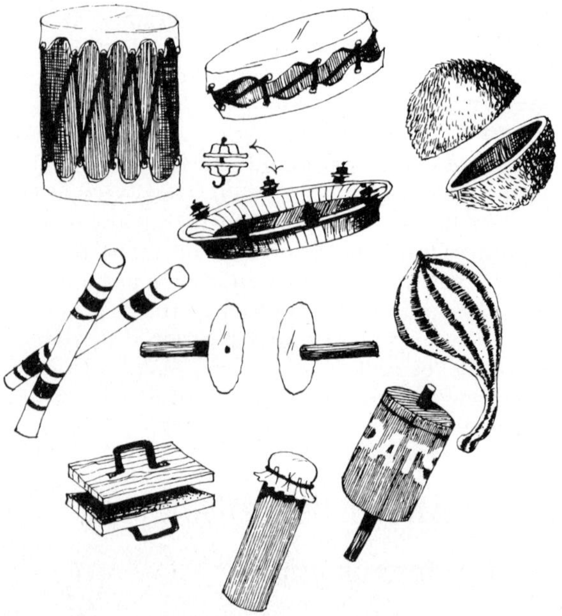

Figure 12–2 Percussion instruments you can make.

keep working with them until they have a satisfactory resonance. Make a *tom-tom* from a narrower container with a drumhead over only one end ot it.

The name "drumstick" for the leg bone of a chicken probably comes from the practice of some Indian tribes of beating their drums or tom-toms with the leg bone of a wild fowl. Certain African tribes beat the drums with their fingers, palms, or fists. You can make a suitable drumstick from a piece of wood, experimenting with different varieties until you find one that produces the sound you want. A spool glued to a stick or a piece of cloth tied tightly around the mop end of a small dishmop are also satisfactory. The drumsticks and the sides and heads of the drum can be painted using bright poster paint or a similar medium. With a tin can drum, campers can glue a piece of brown paper around it to serve as a base for other colors. In making nearly all percussion instruments, the materials used and the manner of finishing them will affect their tonal qualities.

Make *rhythm sticks* (Figure 12–2) to beat together by whittling them from round sticks and sandpapering them smooth, then shellacking and painting them.

To make *sand blocks* (Figure 12–2) glue or tack heavy pieces of sandpaper to the bottoms of wooden blocks and attach handles of leather, webbing, or wood to hold as you "swish" them together as a rhythmical accompaniment.

Shakers and *rattles* (Figure 12–2) can be made from a hollow object, such as a gourd, tin can, cardboard cylinder, or wooden box, partially filling it with pebbles, beans, hard seeds, bottle caps, or small nuts. Make a handle by glueing a stick firmly in place through holes made in the ends. Try varying either the container or the materials inside to get different sound effects. Cover the instrument with paper and decorate as desired.

Use a large nail or other metallic object to tap a resonant piece of metal such as a horseshoe for use as a *triangle*. A *kazoo* (Figure 12–2) can be made by using a rubber band to fasten a piece of waxed paper tightly over one end of a mailing tube. Hum through the open end of the tube.

Marimbas, cigar box violins, shepherd's pipes, and banjos are a little more difficult to make. You will find instructions for making them in some of the sources listed at the end of the chapter.

> Music washes away from the soul the dust of everyday life.
>
> —Auerbach

> Music . . . gives tone to the Universe, wings to the mind, flight to the imagination, a charm to sadness and gayety and life to everything.
>
> —Plato

DRAMA ACTIVITIES

> Of all people, children are the most imaginative.
>
> —Macaulay, *Essays on Mitford's Greece.*

Children are born imitators, aping almost anything and everything. To them, such imitation isn't really acting at all; they throw themselves so wholeheartedly into their roles that they *become* what they portray. This has the advantage of freeing them from the selfconsciousness and fear of ridicule that assail many of their elders. A child can transform almost instantaneously from one character to another without losing a sense of reality.

Figure 12-3 Everyone is an actor.

Dramatics in Camp

Formal plays and dramatic extravaganzas with elaborate scenery and costumes are generally too involved for the camp program. In fact, such productions tend to violate at least two criteria of good camping: (1) they could be done just as well if not better at home, and (2) they usurp a disproportionate amount of time from activities more indigenous to the outdoor camp environment. Such formalized dramatics should be left to those camps that specialize in that field. However, there are several types of informal dramatics that do fit in with the spirit of general camping and provide children with an outlet for their natural instincts to pretend and imitate.

SOURCES OF PLAYS. Only short, informal productions are recommended. You can cut long plays or use some of the one- or two-act plays and skits available for campers that can be worked up quickly so that they become *one of many*, not *the* activity of the summer. If you don't want to take the time to learn parts, use an offstage narrator or let the players familiarize themselves with their lines and act them out as they read them.

Most thoroughly enjoyed, however, are the homespun variety of plays concocted by staff and campers. Use either the whole group or a committee for planning, and as soon as the general theme has been decided upon, ideas and suggestions will probably come so fast that the chore will be to sort them out and weave them into a reasonable production.

Since children love all kinds of animals, you may want to work several into the script, giving them anything from walk-on parts to starring roles. Incidentally, shy children often lose their timidity when concealed behind a mask or walking about on all fours under the "fur" of some animal. Don't be afraid to exaggerate, both as to action and plausibility. Build up to a climax, ending on a happy note with all the "good" characters living in eternal bliss while the "bad" ones grovel in the discomfort of their just punishment. Incorporate appropriate dances and songs if you wish, letting the audience join in on

(Camp Summer Life, Odessa, Tex.)

any chorus that is familiar. After all, the main purpose of drama is enjoyment and the true measure of the results is what happens to the participants. This, of course, rules out anything hinting of poor taste.

Ideas for plays can come from many sources, such as nursery or Mother Goose rhymes, or well-liked stories such as those of Winnie the Pooh or Uncle Remus. Other possibilities are historical or current events, Bible stories, or the local history of the community or camp.

Play each character to the hilt, with a hero who is the wisest, most charming and honest person imaginable, in contrast to a villain who is the most underhanded, despicable creature that ever drew a breath. Virtue of every sort must be lavishly rewarded and evil as unfailingly punished.

Make the action brisk and colorful and end each act with a semiclimactic bit of humor, excitement, or grandeur while the audience hisses the villain, applauds the hero, or collapses in laughter. Such audience reactions are fine in moderation but shouldn't be allowed to get out of hand.

With somewhat serious plays, mimeograph enough copies of the script to give one to every participant from actors to those responsible for sound effects, lighting, and properties.

STAGE, SETS, AND PROPERTIES. Some camps provide a well-appointed stage with such conveniences as dressing rooms, backdrops, scenery, and curtains. These, however, are not at all necessary with such informal productions as we are discussing. For indoor staging, use a corner of the room with the chairs arranged diagonally across it, or place the audience in a circle around the actors to create a theater-in-the-round. However, an outdoor setting is more in keeping with the camp ideal. Look for a natural amphitheatre with the stage below and a gentle slope for seating the audience, or seat them on level ground with the stage located above on a flattened elevation. Since children's voices do not carry well, place the audience close to the action, and avoid locating the stage in front of a body of water, for it will absorb sound and make hearing difficult.

You are fortunate if your outdoor setting has a natural backdrop of trees and shrubbery to serve as a screen for behind-scenes activity and actors awaiting their cues. If you have no foliage, you may want to plant or transplant some to provide a screen in the future. Scenery is not at all indispensable, but, if used, can be extremely simple, for the youngsters' imaginations will supply details. Indeed, they may find it hilariously funny when you use only token props, such as packing boxes for buildings and cardboard silhouettes for mountains, birds, or the sun, labeling them if necessary. A little resourcefulness does wonders as an inverted tablespoon serves for a telephone, a large towel or blanket for a rug, and a cardboard, crescent-shaped moon dangles from a fishing pole held by someone standing on a ladder behind the scenes. Colored sheets, tent halves, tarps, or blankets can be fastened over ropes or wires to serve as curtains. Lanterns, strong flashlights, or spotlights furnish adequate stage lighting, and Figure 14-14 shows how to make footlights by inserting candles in tin can holders.

COSTUMING. Here again, odds and ends will do and the children's imaginations will fill in all necessary details. Many camps have a costume box in which to accumulate discarded apparel for use when the need arises. Campers' personal gear will provide such possibilities as berets, camp hats, rain hats, raincoats and boots, pajamas, bathrobes, washcloths, towels, bandanas, hiking boots, bed sheets, blankets, and pillow slips. Burlap bags, old curtains, draperies, dish towels, and bits of remnants also can be pressed into use. Crepe paper comes in a large variety of shades and is helpful for costume-making and other purposes.

Paper bags just large enough to fit over the head make good animal or human masks when ears and noses are pasted on and holes are cut for eyes and mouth. You can improvise beards and false wigs from pipe stem cleaners, frayed rope, shrubbery, or an old mop head, and feathers, grasses, or branches make good hat decorations. You can fashion buckles from cardboard, pieces of wood, or tin cans; bits of metal, shells, nuts, or seeds produce attractive jewelry. A painted piece of metal or wood will serve as a shield, or one can be fashioned from the lid of a large cooking pot or an old wash boiler.

SOUND EFFECTS. Use recorded music before the show, between acts, or to set moods during the action.

Here are a few suggestions for sound effects:

Hoof beats—clap soft drink cups or wooden

(Camp Mishawaka, Grand Rapids, Minn.)

blocks on wood, varying the intensity to indicate whether the horse is approaching or disappearing.

Dog barking, cock crowing, cow mooing—use human voices.

Thunder—shake a piece of sheet metal with one edge resting on the floor.

You get the idea; now use your ingenuity to invent what you need.

EVERYONE HAS A PART. Some children may not have parts in the play, either because they don't want them or because there aren't enough to go around. Nevertheless, there are many non-acting chores to keep everyone occupied. The following are suggested:

- Director
- Prompter
- Properties
- Programs
- Sets
- Costumes
- Lighting and sound effects
- Seating
- Ushers
- Superintendent of Clean Up (give a fancy title to compensate for undertaking this unpleasant task).
- Publicity (issue invitations and publicity and write a story for the camp newspaper).

AN AUDIENCE IS NOT ALWAYS NECESSARY. Productions need not always be for an audience. Some of the most successful and enjoyable dramatic activities are those that arise spontaneously simply to pass the time on a rainy day or programless night. However, the initial effort often proves so successful that it stimulates the group to put a little more work into the production and to stage it on some special occasion such as a council fire or visitors' day.

CAMP SPOOFS AND TAKE-OFFS. Most popular of all are the productions built around camp personalities and local happenings, as when campers lampoon their terrible, tyrannical counselors or the staff depicts the campers as seen through counselors' eyes. Campers can usually see the funny side of their own experiences when viewed in retrospect—that long, long trip when the rain came pattering down every day and night or their gruesome first experience at cooking out-of-doors.

Activities Related to Dramatics

Several activities, although not really dramatics, are related in that they contain some elements of make-believe and dramatizing.

READING PLAYS. Play reading may serve as a satisfying substitute for those who like

(Camp Kingsmont, West Stockbridge, Mass.)

plays but don't want to go into them extensively enough to memorize lines and actions.

STUNT NIGHT. Stunt night is a traditional fun night when campers and staff display their talents in almost any area, such as roping a "bronco," demonstrating feats of magic, putting on a skit or play, or performing on a musical instrument. Let a counselor or responsible camper act as master of ceremonies and hold a preview of the numbers to see that they are suitable.

PANTOMINE WITH READING. Actors take parts as someone reads a ballad, story, poem, folk song, or original skit. In one version, each person takes a part, such as a horse, crow, or freight train, and whenever that character is mentioned, he or she makes the appropriate noise (the horse "neighs," the crow "caws," etc.)

(Camp Namanu, Sandy, Oreg.; courtesy of ACA)

CHARADES. Charades is an old game in which one team or individual selects a word such as "dandie-lyin" or "eye-doll-a-tree" and pantomimes the syllables while the others try to guess the word. You may wish to substitute such categories as Mother Goose rhymes, book titles, folk songs, story book characters, advertising slogans, famous people of today or yesterday, or different professions.

In one variation a team chooses a word that it whispers to the first member of the other team who must then act it out for his or her team to guess. Measure the time it takes and then give the other team its turn. Continue, alternating teams until each player has had a chance to act out a word. Time each player and add the total time consumed by each team in successfully guessing the other's words. The team with the least total time wins.

NEW ORLEANS. This variation is an old childhood favorite. Each team has a base line that it must stay behind while the other team takes a turn at coming close and acting out a chosen occupation, such as pushing a lawn mower, chopping wood, or rowing a boat. The team behind the line tries to guess the occupation and, as soon as successful, tries to tag as many of the acting team as possible before they can scurry back to safety behind their own baseline. Any member tagged must transfer to the other team, which then takes its turn at acting.

PAPER-BAG DRAMATICS. Each group receives a bag of simple properties that they must use in presenting a skit for the other group.

SEALED ORDERS. A number of humorous or serious situations are written on slips of paper and placed in a hat; each individual or group draws a slip and must then act out the situation while the others attempt to guess what it is. Suggested situations: timid old lady caught in the middle of a busy street with the traffic light changing; Uncle Neddie coming home late and trying to sneak up to his room without being heard; the little camper who is afraid to get into the pool for his first swimming lesson. Categories such as those mentioned previously in regard to charades may also be used, or each group may be given a list of characters to work into a skit.

BURLESQUES. These are take-offs on camp life (or any other desired topic). Subjects might be the camp unit's first overnight trip; cabin cleanup; a camper's version of a camp staff meeting or visiting day at camp. Again, beware of hurt feelings.

ALBUM OF FAMILIAR PICTURES. Arrange a "curtain" of blankets and turn off the lights. Have the group behind the curtain pose in a stiff picture (like those in grandmother's album), such as a ladies' bridge club or a bird's-eye view of the camp dining room. Draw open the curtain, turn on the lights, and see what you have. Exaggerate and make it fun.

SHADOW PLAYS. Stretch a sheet (preferably wet) tightly to serve as a transparent curtain with the stage directly behind it and bright lights (auto lights, flashlights, or spotlights) set far enough back to make the actors stand out in silhouette. Turn off all other lights and keep the actors close to the curtain so that their silhouettes will be sharp and clear. Act out a skit, story, ballad, or burlesque. You need use only suggestions of costumes and can cut one-dimensional settings and props from cardboard or old packing boxes and glue them together. Describe the situation briefly or read a whole script as you act it out. Accompany it with mood music, if you wish.

MARIONETTE AND PUPPET SHOWS. Puppets are designed to slip over your hand so that they can be manipulated with your fingers; marionettes are more elaborate, and are manipulated by using from 1 to 15 strings that are attached to control sticks held by the operator. These little characters can be fashioned quickly from sacks, bags, boxes, socks, or other materials (Figure 12–4, 12–5 and 12–6). It is also fun for campers to make "nature puppets" (Figure 12–6) by using materials found in the wilds, such as seaweed for hair, shells for mouths, driftwood for noses, and the like. Unforgettable stories and tales can be told around the campfire with these creatures made of natural materials.

Figure 12–4 Bag and box puppets.

The more elaborate shows involve various skills and interests; someone must design and dress the marionettes or puppets, while others are needed to operate them, make stage sets and

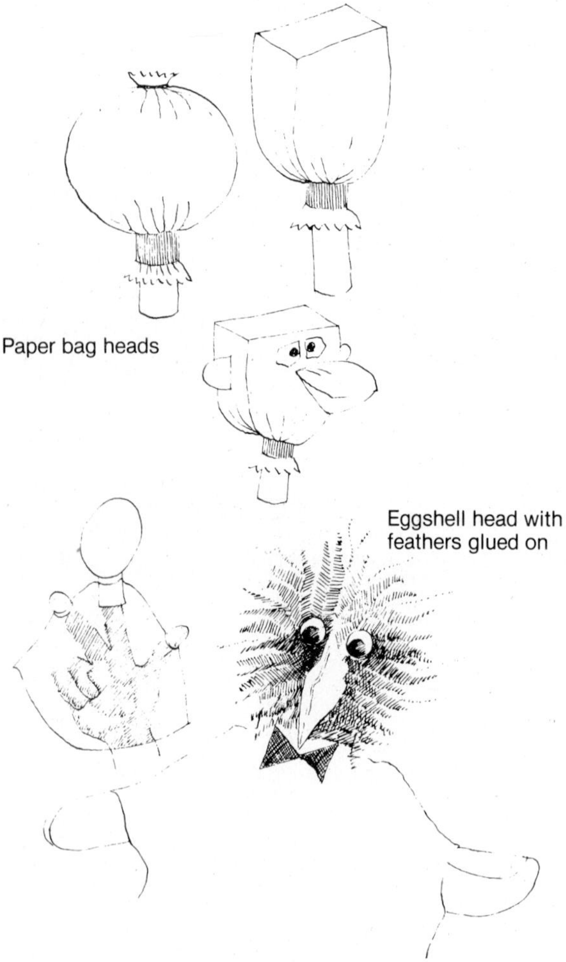

Figure 12-5 Finger puppets.

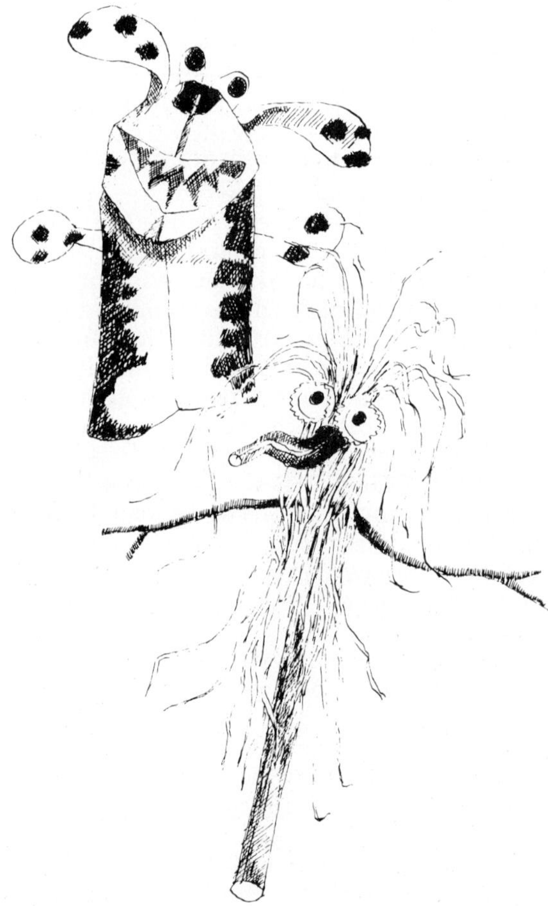

Figure 12-6 Nature puppets.

props, arrange the lighting, write or arrange the script, read the script or story as it is acted out, and furnish musical accompaniment if it is wanted. Children greatly enjoy these shows, and it is well worth the effort to try at least some of the more simple ones.

ADDITIONAL READINGS

(For an explanation of abbreviations and abbreviated forms, see page 13.)

Music and Rhythm

LEADERSHIP AND GENERAL

Batcheller, John, and Sally Monsour: *Music in Recreation and Leisure.* Brown, 1972, 135 pp., paper.

Corbin: *Recreation Leadership,* ch. 19.

Etkin, Ruth: *The Rhythm Band Book.* Sterling Publishing, 1978, 96 pp.

Hoffelt, Robert O.: *How To Lead Informal Singing.* Abingdon, 1963, 111 pp., paper.

John, Robert W., and Charles H. Douglas: *Playing Social and Recreational Instruments.* Prentice-Hall, 1972, 112 pp., paper.

Kraus, Richard, Gay Carpenter, and Barbara J. Bates: *Recreation Leadership and Supervision,* Saunders, 2nd ed., 1981, pp. 102–108.

Kujoth: *The Recreation Program Guide,* pp. 225–237.

Shivers, Jay S.: *Camping: Administration, Counseling, Programming.* Meredith, 1971, pp. 396–414.

Tobitt, Janet E. (Revised by Phyllis Ford and Kathleen Mote): *A Counselor's Guide to Camp Singing.* ACA, 1971, 44 pp., paper.

Webb: *Light From A Thousand Campfires:* Wagner, Doris: "Let There Be Good Music," p. 296.

MAGAZINE ARTICLES

Camping Magazine:

Badeaux, Ed: "Folk Songs in Camp." June, 1966, p. 12.

Brobston, Stanley Heard: "Good Music—An Enriching Addition to Your Camp Program." Mar., 1971, p. 18.

Nissman, Blossom: "Singing Gives a Camp Spirit." June, 1967, p. 14.

Roberts, Bette A.: "Bring More Singing Into Your Camp." Feb., 1972, p. 22.

Short, Alison: "A Singing Camp is a Happy Camp." June, 1970, p. 11.

SONG COLLECTIONS

Burl Ives Song Book. Ballantine, 1953, 276 pp., paper.

Chase, Richard: *Old Songs and Singing Games.* Dover, 1972, 49 pp.

Felton, Harold W.: *Cowboy Jamboree* (Western Songs and Lore). Knopf, 1951.

Girl Scouts of USA: *Sing Together: A Girl Scout Songbook.* Girl Scouts of USA, 3rd. ed., 1973.

Glazer, Tom: *Treasury of Folk Songs For the Family.* Grosset & Dunlap, 253 pp.

Handy Songs, Coop. Rec. Service.

Hill, Cherie: *Joy in Music with Special People.* ACA, 1978, 48 pp., paper.

Let's Sing Together. Westminster, 1965, 96 pp., paper.

More Burl Ives Songs. Ballantine, 1966, 224 pp., paper.

Nye, Robert, Neva Aubin Vernice, and George Kyme: *Singing With Children.* Wadsworth, 1962, 264 pp.

101 Plus 5 Folk Songs for Camp. Oak, 1966, 152 pp.

Scout Songbook (No. 3224). Boy Scouts, 1972, 128 pp., paper.

Sing. ACA, 1978, 95 pp.

Tent and Trail Songs. Coop. Rec. Service, 1966, 80 pp., paper.

Tobitt, Janet E. (Compiler): *The Ditty Bag* (No. 23-4606). Girl Scouts.

MAKING YOUR OWN INSTRUMENTS

Kettlekamp, Larry: *Drums, Rattles, and Bells.* Morrow, 1960, 47 pp. (ages 8–12)

Mandell, Muriel, andRobert E. Wood: *Make Your Own Musical Instruments.* Sterling, rev., 1959, 128 pp.

Mason, Bernard: *Drums, Tom-Toms and Rattles.* Dover, 1974, 208 pp.

MAGAZINE ARTICLES

Boys' Life:

Cohen, Saul M.: "An Electric Organ." Apr., 1964, p. 36.

"Instruments for the Music of South America." Dec., 1960.

Waltner, Willard and Elma: "Horn Bugle." May, 1964.

Wheeler, Alan: "Pioneer Musical Instruments." Oct., 1970, p. 67.

RHYTHMIC ACTIVITIES

Burchenal, Elizabeth: *Folk Dances and Singing Games.* Order from NRPA.

Davis, Buleah, and Fran Riel: *Happy Dancing.* Burgess, 1966, 45 pp.

Flood, Jessie B., and Cornelia F. Putney: *Square Dance, U.S.A.* Brown, 120 pp.

Gilbert, Cecile: *International Folk Dance At a Glance.* Burgess, 1969, 171 pp., paper.

Handy Folk Dance Book. Coop. Rec. Service.

Handy Square Dance Book. Coop. Rec. Service.

Harris, Jane, Anne Pittman, and Marlys S. Waller: *Dance A While.* Burgess, 4th ed., 1968, 386 pp., paper.

Jensen, Clayne R. and Mary B.: *Beginning Square Dance.* Wadsworth, 1966, paper.

Jensen, Mary B. and Clayne R.: *Beginning Folk Dancing.* Wadsworth, paper.

Kirkell, M., and I. Schaffnet: *Partners All, Places All: Forty-Four Enjoyable Square and Folk Dances for Everyone,* Dutton.

Kraus, Richard G.: *Folk Dancing.* Macmillan, 1962, 221 pp.

Lunt, Lois: *Mix 'Em and Match 'Em.* Denison, 109 pp.

Mulak: *Fun and Games,* chs. 12, 15, 16.

Tobitt, Janet E. (Compiler): *Promenade All* (#23-4697). Girl Scouts, paper.

Vick, Marie, and Rosann McLaughton Cox: *A Collection of Dances for Children. Burgess, 1970. (Card File)*

MAGAZINE ARTICLES

Camping Magazine:

Pasvolsky, Richard L.: "Square Dancing at Camp." Jan., 1966, p. 15.

Drama Activities

MARIONETTES AND PUPPETS

Ackley, Edith Flack: *Marionettes: Easy to Make! Fun To Use!* Lippincott, 1939, 118 pp.

Adair, Margaret W.: *Do-It-In-A-Day Puppets for Beginners.* Day, 1964, 89 pp.

Alkema, Chester Jay: *Puppet-Making.* Sterling, 48 pp.

Cummings, Richard: *101 Hand Puppets: A Guide for Puppeteers of All Ages.* McKay, 1962, 147 pp.

French, Susan: *Presenting Marionettes.* Van Nostrand, 1964, 112 pp.

Goaman, Muriel: *Judy and Andrew's Puppet Book.* Plays, 48 pp.

Hopper, Grizella H.: *Puppet Making Through the Grades.* Davis Mass, 64 pp.

Howard, Vernon: *Puppet and Pantomine Plays.* Sterling, 108 pp.

Kampmann, Lothar, *Creating With Puppets.* Van Nostrand, 1972, 76 pp.

Kujoth: *The Recreation Program Guide,* pp. 306–309.

Lewis, Shari: *Making Easy Puppets.* Dutton, 1967, 86 pp.

Mulholland, John: *Practical Puppetry.* Arco, 1962.

Renfro, Nancy: *Puppets For Play Production.* Funk and Wagnalls, 1969, 129 pp.

Richter, Dorothy: *Fell's Guide to Hand Puppets: How To Make and Use Them.* Fell, 1970, 202 pp.

Shivers, Jay S.: *Camping: Administration, Counseling, Programming.* Appleton-Century-Crofts, 1971, pp. 396–408.

Slade, Richard: *You Can Make a String Puppet.* Plays, 1957, 46 pp.

Stahl, Leroy, and Effa E. Preston: *The Master Puppet Book.* Denison, 390 pp.

Worrell, Estele Ansley: *Be A Puppeteer.* McGraw-Hill, 1969, 96 pp.

PLAY PRODUCTION

Alberts, David: *Pantomine: Elements and Exercises.* U. of Kansas, 1971, 69 pp.
Alkema, Chester Jay: *Masks.* Sterling, 1971, 48 pp.
Alkema, Chester Jay: *Monster Masks.* Sterling, 1973, 48 pp.
Ball, Edith L. and Robert E. Cipriano: *Leisure Services Preparation.* Prentice-Hall, Inc., 1978, pp. 91–96.
Berger: *Program Activities for Camps.*
Brown, Andrew: *Drama.* Arco, 1962, 160 pp., paper.
Carson, Bernice Wells: *Play A Part.* Abingdon, 1970, 240 pp.
Convention Highlights: Kovner, Albert: "Techniques in Creative Dramatics." p. 82.
Corbin: *Recreation Leadership,* ch. 16.
Crosscup, Richard: *Children and Dramatics.* Scribner's, 1966.
Franklin, Miriam A.: *Rehearsal.* Prentice-Hall, 5th ed., 1972, 288 pp., paper.
Goodridge, Janet: *Creative Drama and Improvised Movement for Children.* Plays, 1970, 158 pp.
Hacker, Fred, and Prescott Eames: *How to Put on An Amateur Circus.* Order from NRPA, 112 pp.
Kujoth: *The Recreation Program Guide,* pp. 84–105.
Lounsbury, Warren C.: *Theatre Backstage From A to Z.* U. of Washington, 1967, 172 pp., paper.
McGee, Cecil: *Drama For Fun.* Broadman, 1969, 175 pp.
Olfson, Lewy: *You Can Act!* Sterling, 128 pp.
Purdy, Susan: *Costumes For You To Make.* Lippincott, 1971, 121 pp.
Stahl, LeRoy: *Simplified Stagecraft Manual.* Order from NRPA, 218 pp.
Theater (no. 3328). Boy Scouts, 1968, 88 pp., paper.
Webb: *Light From A Thousand Campfires:*
Booth, Judy: "Camp Dramatics—A Performance for Stars—Or a Creative Experience for All?" pp. 292–295.
Winslow, Barbara Brown: *Spotlight on Drama.* ACA, 1979, 22 pp. paper.

MAGAZINE ARTICLES

Boys' Life:
"Arms and Armor." Feb., 1973, p. 50.
"Big Top Makeup." Mar., 1970, p. 44.
"Costumes." Sept., 1972, p. 57.
Stenzel, Al: "Masks From Paper Bags." Dec., 1969, p. 63.

Camping Magazine:
Gudgel, Jeanette A.: "How To Use Drama Effectively." Sept./Oct., 1968, p. 16.
Jackson, Marni: "Drama In Camp." Nov./Dec., 1967, p. 20.
Kase, Judith B.: "Informal Theatre: An Any Place, Any Time, Anybody Camp Activity." Mar., 1970, p. 16.
Telleen, Robert: "Informal Dramatics Can Provide the Means." May, 1971, p. 12.

PLAYS

Ames, Marilyn, and Jane MacDonald: *Easy Skits For Youngsters.* Order from NRPA, 48 pp., paper.
Haney, Germaine: *Five-Minute Plays For Children.* Order from NRPA, 45 pp.
Kamerman, Sylvia E.: *Dramatized Folk Tales of the World.* Plays. 1971, 575 pp.
Murray, John: *One-Act Plays for Young Actors.* Order from NRPA, 336 pp.
Siks, Geraldine Brain: *Children's Literature For Dramatization—An Anthology.* Harper & Row, 1964, 332 pp.
Thane, Adele: *Plays From Famous Stories and Fairy Tales.* Plays, 1967, 463 pp.

STUNTS AND SKITS

Brings, Lawrence M.: *The Master Stunt Book.* Denison, 470 pp.
Brings, Lawrence M.: *Rehearsal-Less Skits and Plays.* Denison, 318 pp.
Carlson, Bernice Wells: *Do It Yourself!* Abingdon, 1952, paper.
Chalmers, Van, and LeRoy Stahl: *Laugh Hits.* Denison, 250 pp.
Deason, Myrna Reeves, et al.: *The Modern Skit and Stunt Book.* Denison, 314 pp.
Eisenberg, Larry and Helen: *Fun With Skits and Stunts.* Ass'n Press, 1953, 254 pp.
Eisenberg, Larry and Helen: *The Handbook of Skits and Stunts.* Ass'n Press, 1953, 254 pp.
Howard, Vernon: *Pantomimes, Charades and Skits.* Sterling, 124 pp.
Mulak: *Fun And Games,* ch. 9.
Preston, Effa E.: *Fun With Stunts.* Denison, 351 pp.

THE WONDERFUL WORLD OF LITERATURE

Far too many people of all ages have never learned to appreciate the delights of good literature. It is not only a depository of all the accumulated wisdom of mankind, but it also serves to transport the reader into a fantasy world of entertainment, excitement or sheer beauty that allows a temporary escape from the cares and worries of the work-a-day world. A well-stocked camp library, judiciously used, may well be the launching pad to start campers on a lifetime of enjoyment as they come to know literature as a source of knowledge, adventure, and fun instead of merely an irksome chore to complete for a required school assignment. Discriminative reading is a habit that may well prove contagious when a few demonstrate their enjoyment of it. The wise reader keeps a notebook and pencil handy for jotting down particularly meaningful passages or bits of information to preserve for future use.

Literature fits in harmoniously with many phases of the camp program, and some camps even schedule reading as one of the choices available during an activity period, especially on bad-weather days. Of course, no one should be encouraged to become a bookworm to the exclusion of the many unique outdoor opportunities camp offers, but reading provides a wonderful way to enjoy oneself in front of a blazing fireplace on a chilly, gloomy day or in a group that gathers for story telling, reading aloud, or simply curling up individually, each with a favorite book. There are literary selections that can add immeasurably to an evening program or a vesper or spiritual service or can even constitute a whole program in itself when selected and arranged by a group or committee with each person contributing a selection or an original piece of writing. Banquets and ceremonial occasions are scarcely complete without some form of literature. A brief, appropriate "Thought for the Day" may be posted on the bulletin board or read at a set time, such as before or after the morning or evening meal, at the beginning of rest hour, or in a cabin gathering just before taps.

thirteen
Literature in Camp

Books are the treasured wealth of the world, the fit inheritance of generations and nations.

—HENRY DAVID THOREAU

A man learns only by two things: One is reading and the other is association with smarter people.

—WILL ROGERS

THE CAMP LIBRARY

Among its many and varied possessions, a camp should have a good collection of books available to both campers and staff members. First, there should be books for pure enjoyment, about Indians, animals, legends, folk tales, travel, biography, science, or almost anything else that interests people. These books are for leisure reading, alone or to a group, during rest hour, under a shady tree by the brook, on rainy days, in the evening while the corn's popping and there's a campfire blazing merrily, or for tucking in with other duffle for use at odd moments on a trip.

There also should be an ample supply of what might be called "how-to-do-it books." To these a counselor can turn for general enlightenment or to consult a group of experts on any problem, be it constructing a bridge across the brook, identifying raccoon tracks, making a tent or wigwam, portaging a canoe, or braiding a lanyard. A camper can turn to these also to find a recipe for ring-tum-diddy or to learn about sailing, waterproofing a tent, or making plaster casts.

Camp books should have a permanent location, along with a card file listing what is available. When the collection is well-chosen and functional, however, the books won't remain on the shelf long enough to need dusting, but will become part of a true "traveling library" that is available right on the job, when and where needed. As in any public or school library, each book should have a book pocket and a card to be signed when the borrower takes the book out. In this way, no book will be lost for the camp season because someone carelessly left it at the swimming area or tossed it into the bottom of a closet on the second day of camp. Usually one counselor, perhaps with camper help, assumes responsibility for the library.

Camps use various methods to build up their libraries, usually starting by purchasing a basic selection covering the major areas of camping and outdoor life. It is often possible to borrow others for a whole or part of the summer from the local, county, or state library. Some camps suggest in an early precamp letter to campers and counselors that each bring along a favorite book or two to read or exchange with others during the summer; they often leave the books behind when they go home. Parents may also be urged to bring or send books. You may want to recognize a donor by placing a book plate with his or her name on it in each book given. An appeal through the local press or radio may bring in worthwhile contributions. You must use discretion, however, in determining which books to make a permanent part of your camp library, for it is better to have only a few really worthwhile volumes than whole shelves of unopened books and odds and ends from other peoples' attics.

STORYTELLING

> You cannot tell a good story unless you tell it before a fire. You cannot have a complete fire unless you have a good storyteller along.
>
> —G. Stanley Hall

An Ancient Heritage

The art of storytelling is probably almost as old as man, for history reveals that from the advent of speech, primitive peoples loved to cluster about one of their most esteemed and beloved members, the storyteller. From about 800 B.C., when the blind bard Homer was recounting the Iliad and Odyssey, down through the minnesingers, troubadours, and traveling minstrels, men have loved to gather to listen again to the oft-repeated tales of courage and adventure that doubtless lost nothing in the telling under the golden tongue of the skilled narrator. The American Indians also made much of storytelling, their legends serving to entertain, pass on traditions and instruct the younger members of the tribe in geography, history, and biography. What golden spells they must have woven with their tales of bravery and daring!

To this day, everyone from the toddler to the aged loves a well-told tale. Though television, radio, movies and comic books may have somewhat lessened the interest and ability of both "teller" and "listener" in the home and in other gathering places, this is not the case in the summer camp, where "Tell us a story" is just as frequent and fervent a plea as ever. True, you may need to encourage some campers to participate the first few times since it may be an entirely new experience for them, but a few ses-

Figure 13-1 Storytelling is fun for everyone. (Camp Kingsmont, West Stockbridge, Mass.)

sions usually will convert them into avid listeners.

No counselor should fail to have a few good stories for that inevitable moment when nothing else quite fills the bill. Almost anyone can learn to be a "good" storyteller, even though not all of us may become unsurpassed spinners of yarns (Fig. 13-1).

The Why

There are numerous reasons for telling stories; here are four of the most important:

ENJOYMENT. Hearing a *good* story is fun and that is important enough in itself to warrant its inclusion. It is hard to think of anything we can do that could bring boys and girls more lasting happiness than implanting in them an enjoyment of good literature. So much worthwhile writing exists that we could never read all of it if we devoted a lifetime to the task.

RELIVING GREAT MOMENTS. Who among us does not thrill to the adventures of the pioneers and the doings of such heroes as Paul Bunyan, Robin Hood, Johnny Appleseed, John Henry, or Robinson Crusoe? Campers also become much more interested in and appreciative of their camp community after learning of the customs and daily lives of the Indians and early settlers who once lived there, of famous battles that took place nearby, or the founding of the towns and cities of the area. You usually can gather such information from local historical associations or the clipping files and catalogued books of the local library.

GAINING NEW FRIENDS. Though we were not privileged to know Juliette Low, John Muir, Lord Baden-Powell, or Abraham Lincoln in person, we can form an intimate acquaintance with them through the storyteller. What child can fail to develop a kinder feeling toward animals as he or she sees them through the eyes of Albert Payson Terhune, Ernest Thompson Seton or Uncle Remus?

MORAL AND CHARACTER VALUES. Since youth is the age of hero worship, there is no better way to teach that "virtue has its own reward" and "crime does not pay" than through the stories of the great and good of all ages. Fortunately, this can come about in a perfectly painless way if we avoid sticky sentimentality and over-moralizing that may create resentment and rebellion instead of the good qualities we want to develop.

The When and Where

Almost any time can be story time, but there are occasions that literally seem to beg for a story. A campfire, a lovely hilltop at sunset, or a peaceful dell are "naturals" and a circle of listeners, rolled in their blankets under a starlit sky, forms a perfect setting for studying the stars and retelling the same star myths heard by Indian, Greek, and Roman boys and girls many centuries ago. A rainy day seems less dreary when there's an open fireplace and an exciting tale. Camp disappointments and minor tragedies fade under the spell of a Kipling adventure and dishwashing and other chores seem almost to do themselves when there's a good yarn in the spinning. A well-chosen story often will keep restless youngsters relaxed during the rest hour or put them in a mood for going to sleep quickly at night. Here, also, a counselor may find a good way to resolve unsocial attitudes or problems detected in his or her cabin. Storytelling also provides pleasant entertainment for restless infirmary inhabitants.

The Who

Though everyone likes to hear stories, not everyone likes the same story, for the teenager is bored beyond words with the adventures of Billie Goat Gruff or Jimmie the Jumping Frog; consequently, it is best to have listeners of approximately the same age. If there are age differences, select a story appropriate for the older ones in the group so that they do not feel you are being condescending toward them.

All should understand from the very start that there is to be no disturbance of any sort until the story is finished; therefore, request campers to save any questions and comments until the story is finished. Encourage those who don't like stories to sample them a few times. Then be sure to choose appropriate ones and tell them well; it's a good bet that few will fail to come back for more.

The What

There are a few sure-fire stories that appeal to almost everyone but, in general, the group dictates the story and what would be adored by one assemblage may fall perfectly flat with another. You must learn to size up your group and pick your story for *them.* Suit it to their general age, background, and personalities.

Boys and girls ordinarily like the same stories until they are about ten, when boys usually begin to disdain "kid" or "sissy stuff." Tales of Indians, cowboys, pioneers, pirates, airplanes, sports, and science now appeal to them. In general, girls are not quite so exclusive and still enjoy many of the stories they previously liked as well as some of those now chosen by boys. Small children, of ages six to ten, like stories containing alliteration and nonsensical jingles as well as those about animals and people. They are particularly fond of the ludicrous and illogical, such as "Corabelle Cow Who Goes Shopping on Roller Skates" or "Dulcimer Duck Who Carries a Pink Silk Umbrella and Wears Green Spats When She Goes to the Beach." They revel in fantasy and make-believe and so are particularly fond of folk tales, fairy tales and such. They especially like to hear stories a counselor has made up out of his or her imagination and that involve the antics of such characters as Wooly, the caterpillar, Honey, the bear or Porky, the porcupine.

Older children, 10 to 14, demand something that challenges their developing judgments a bit more. They prefer to draw their own morals and conclusions from well-constructed but more subtle plots. Stories of Indians, animals, and legendary heroes still interest them.

Still older campers are even more discriminating and present a real challenge to the storyteller, for their tastes are now approaching, but not yet quite ready for, adult literature. Youngsters of all ages have a good sense of humor, though what strikes them as funny may seem silly or flat to adults and vice versa.

For the novice at choosing stories, many lists are available that classify stories according to type and age appeal; you will find some in the sources given at the end of the chapter. Another safe way to pick a story is to recall your own childhood favorites or note stories that would be good for telling as you read for your own pleasure.

You may tell several very brief stories at one sitting, particularly if they vary in style and subject matter, but a single long story may be enough, since the story period should never exceed 20 to 30 minutes for small children and 45 to 60 minutes for older ones. An expert can successfully condense a book or long story. However, it is sometimes better to divide it into parts to tell in successive sittings like a serial, ending each at a natural break that temporarily satisfies the listeners yet leaves them curious about what will happen next. Recall how Scheherazade prolonged her life 1001 nights as she kept her fickle husband, Sultan Schariar, entranced and anxious to find out what would happen next as she purposely abandoned her story each night at some extremely exciting spot. That is really storytelling! Books containing long stories are often more successfully read than told. To read a story effectively, however, familiarize yourself with it in advance so it can be read with real expression, using appropriate gestures, and frequently glancing up at your listeners.

Not every story that makes good reading is equally good for telling. Rapidly moving action stories without long descriptions of people or situations are usually best. Despite popular opinion to the contrary, children enjoy well-chosen poetry, particularly that which has been written especially for them. In keeping with the spirit of camping, it is well to choose from the vast quantity of material pertaining to the out-of-doors, animals, tales of high adventure and our natural heritage and the people responsible for preserving it. Stories involving such positive attributes as love, beauty, wholesomeness, honesty, and altruism are especially appropriate.

The inevitable cry, "Tell us a ghost story," sometimes poses a problem, for there are bound to be some campers who find them seriously upsetting. However, there are *some good* ghost and mystery stories that may be used to quench the thirst for the mysterious and supernatural. The best procedure to use with those who clamor for nothing else may be to gradually wean them away by a persistent diet of carefully chosen selections with only an occasional *good* ghost story interspersed. You should, of course, never tell scary or exceedingly exciting stories just before bedtime. Omit off-color stories and those that are in poor taste, such as those that tend to belittle or degrade occupations, races, or creeds.

The How

After you have selected your story, read it carefully for general plot and action and decide upon the best method of presentation. Then read it again several times until it is almost memorized, for there is much more danger of failing through not knowing your story well than of going stale through knowing it too well. Nothing is so disconcerting to listeners as a faltering "er" interjected to give you time to recall what comes next or an "Oh, I forgot to tell you," as you go back to insert something you should have told five minutes before. Practice telling the story to yourself until you are positive of every character and bit of action.

When the fateful moment arrives, gather your group and seat yourself where all can see and hear you clearly; a semicircle is usually best. Place yourself in the firelight or suspend a lantern on a post or tree so that all can clearly see your facial expressions and gestures. Many people lip read without realizing it and so find it difficult to understand when they cannot see your face.

If the setting is around an open fire, use hardwood and build it sufficiently early to let it die down to coals. Appoint one person to inconspicuously take charge of it and keep it going steadily, for a spluttery, smoky fire or one throwing out alarming sparks provides too much competition for any storyteller.

If your listeners are excited or full of pent-up energy, try playing a quiet game or two to put them in an attentive frame of mind. Arouse interest by pausing a moment before you begin and choose a first sentence that compels immediate attention and curiosity as to what will follow.

Since your voice is the center of attention, make it pleasant, enunciate clearly, and avoid mumbling. Keep your tone low to demand close attention yet loud enough to be audible to those on the outskirts; check by asking if campers can hear you. Talking too loudly is irritating and tends to encourage listeners to be restless or to create disturbances.

Vary your tone and rate of speed, for a sing-song manner is monotonous and tends to lull listeners to sleep. Get excited when the story calls for it, and talk in a tired or dispirited tone if that best expresses the mood of the action or character of the story. Appreciate the value of a pause in arousing anticipation. Elicit active participation from your listeners by asking them to guess what will happen next or what they would do in this situation.

Pick a story you thoroughly enjoy and let yourself get involved in it until you actually feel you are a part of it. Your enthusiasm, facial expressions, and gestures then come naturally and make it much more enjoyable for your listeners. Change your voice or turn your head to indicate a change in characters and pause subtly for effect or change your timing to suit the action of the story. Mimicry and dialect, where indicated, add much if you can do them without sounding stilted or forced. Keep your story moving, for a dragging pace kills interest. Avoid over-dramatizing and such mannerisms as dandling something in your hands or slicking down your hair, for they divert attention from the story. You may also want to substitute names of campers for those of the characters in the story to make it seem more real to them.

Look at your listeners and talk to *them* instead of mumbling down your shirt collar. Watch their faces for reactions, making a mental note for future use of those techniques that are most effective. If one or two of your audience seem inattentive, look and talk directly to them to bring them back into the fold. Quell disturbers with a sharp glance.

A good storyteller paints a vivid mental picture of what is happening in the story and of the locality and surroundings in which the action takes place. You must deal, therefore, in what is already familiar to your listeners or must take time to familiarize them with what you are talking about. If a listener is to actually "feel" the story and enjoy it to the utmost, he or she must be drawn into the action by visualizing each character and the environment in which the action occurs. Realism can be enhanced by dressing in costume, using simple props, or having someone cued to blow a bugle, give an Indian war whoop, or beat a tom-tom at the appropriate time. Where locations and lay-outs are important, draw a map in the dirt, use a crayon on a large piece of wrapping paper, or use cut-outs from construction paper on a flannel board to show the locations of the homes of the characters and other scenes.

If your story has a moral, do not overstress it; ask your listeners to point it out or let them draw their own conclusions. When you reach the climax, end the story quickly. If they ask if the story is true answer them honestly. Pause for a moment before dismissing the group or end with an appropriate "Thought for the Day" selected by you or your campers.

Encourage your campers to read for themselves by telling or reading well-chosen excerpts from a book and suggesting that it is available for those who want to read more of it. It is often enjoyable to read or tell a long story to a small group, setting aside a certain time for it each day. Each member of the group can take a turn at telling or reading it, and the group may also want to act the story out. It is good fun, too, for the group to write a story or play. Another too-seldom appreciated activity is the reading of a play by a group, with each member reading a part and perhaps following the stage directions for it.

There is no secret formula for telling stories; each good storyteller develops his or her own techniques. Observe skilled performers and practice whenever possible, for you learn from each experience. You will find that the technique of telling stories is like a piece of good leather: it improves with use.

CHORAL READING

This activity was popular in the past and is well worth reviving. It consists of reciting in unison poetry, Bible quotations, stories, or other types of literature. Group the voices according to pitch and volume and arrange the performers in a semicircle around the leader, who gives inconspicuous signals for starting, stopping, emphasis, pauses, and such. Participants should know the selection well enough to be able to pay close attention to the leader. Add variety by assigning solo parts or by having groups recite alternately, as in antiphonal singing. Poems that the group enjoys and that swing along with marked rhythm and are full of repetition are most effective. Choral reading is particularly good for devotions or a campfire program.

CREATIVE WRITING

Writing Creatively

> I would rather be the author of one original thought than conqueror of a hundred battles.
>
> —W. B. CLULOW

To be creative you must take some old material and fashion it, through your own imagination and personality, into an entirely new and unique product. If you would foster creative

(Star Lake Camp, Bloomingdale, N.J.)

work in others, you must use a cautious and sensitive touch, for dictatorial methods and too many unwanted suggestions soon crush the spark of originality. Your role as a counselor is one of encouraging, giving aid where needed and, in general, setting the yeast that in the hands of the camper, will foam and bubble over into a true creative product. Hammett and Musselman* emphasize that writing is simply putting words together to show how you think and feel and that there are just three steps to it: (1) see it, (2) feel it, (3) write it down. Instead of talking, you are writing, so put it down just as if you were saying it.

Campers often are inclined to dismiss with a shrug the suggestion that they compose a poem or do a piece of creative writing, for some of them have been discouraged by insistence in school upon such mechanical details as neatness, legibility, exact diction, spelling, and punctuation. Though these things are admittedly important, original thought and self-expression are the paramount objectives in creative work. Do not expect youngsters to attain adult standards, but, as always, they should do their best.

Encourage campers to jot down their thoughts, for their own benefit if not for sharing with others, and give them recognition by posting especially good achievements on the bulletin board, reading them at the campfire, or publishing them in the camp newspaper. Encourage everyone to write poems, plays, pageants, diaries, letters, and accounts of things seen and done, and to illustrate them with simple line drawings.

The Camp Newspaper

It is advantageous to have a camp newspaper, for it serves to encourage and recognize creative writing, keeps campers and staff as well as parents and friends informed of doings of the whole camp, fosters good camp morale, and serves as a souvenir to recall many pleasant memories of the summer.

Camp papers vary greatly in frequency of publication. Some camps put out a page or two every day, while others go to the opposite extreme and publish only one or two papers during the entire summer, with an occasional "extra" to celebrate some special camp event. A few camps print their papers but most mimeograph them and this process gives satisfaction to many campers, since many different talents are needed to write and edit copy, make up the dummy, do the artwork, type, cut stencils, run off the pages, and assemble and staple them. Colored inks and paper add variety and allow artistic expression. Some camps type only one copy that is read at a campfire or other gathering, but most supply each camper with his or her own copy.

The staff usually is assisted by an interested counselor with an appointed or elected camper editor-in-chief. Other staff writers act as reporters for units or activities such as waterfront, riding, riflery, campcraft, and arts and crafts. Encourage those not officially on the staff to submit contributions.

Prepare and cut the stencils for materials that do not need to be current and run them off ahead of time to minimize inaccuracies, sloppy

*Hammett and Musselman: *The Camp Program Book*, Ass'n Press, 1951.

(Camp Manito-Wish, Y.M.C.A., Boulder Junction, Wis.)

appearance, and last-minute rush. Hold a staff meeting soon after the issue appears to make a critical evaluation and plan for the next issue. Follow up by posting written assignments for future issues and carry on the project in a businesslike fashion appropriate to a juvenile newspaper office. Include poems, jokes, news flashes, honor achievements, stories, editorials, special features, puzzles, interviews, gossip columns, or other items as you and the campers wish. Since everyone likes to be recognized in print, make a point to include each camper's name frequently in some connection. Use "by-lines" for those who write good articles; this stimulates future contributions and gives recognition where it is due.

The staff should be representative of the whole camp instead of letting it fall under the control of a little clique. Wholesome, kindly humor adds immeasurably, but anything that might hurt or serves as a personal attack is strictly taboo. Although working on the camp paper is a very worthwhile activity, again, do not encourage campers to become so engrossed in it that they fail to take advantage of the wonderful opportunity for outdoor living available only in camp.

The Camp Log

The Camp Log is a sort of camp annual put out at the end of summer. You may mimeograph or otherwise reproduce it, or it may be in the form of a scrapbook, compiled by a central staff or by each individual on his or her own. In it go photographs, programs, invitations, pressed flowers or leaves, place cards, a few pages for autographed messages, poems read at special events, or almost anything else one wants to take home to show friends and relatives and to look over in future years. The cover may range from a simple mimeographed sheet to a leather or wooden portfolio form that was constructed and decorated in the arts and crafts shop.

ADDITIONAL READINGS

(For an explanation of abbreviations and abbreviated forms, see page 13.)

Choral Reading

Breeding, Mrs. Lonnie H.: *Let's Play a Story.* Order from NRPA, 133 pp.

Brown, Helen A., and Harry J. Heltman (eds.): *Choral Readings for Teenage Worship and Inspiration.* Westminster, 1959.

Brown-Azarowicz, Marjorie: *A Handbook of Creative Choral Speaking.* Burgess, 1970.

Enfield, Gertrude: *Verse Choir Technique.* Drama Bookshop.

Gullan, Marjorie: *Speech Choir.* Harper & Row, 1937.

Lists of Books Recommended for Children

American Library *Booklist.*

Good and Inexpensive Books for Children. Childhood Education International, 3615 Wisconsin Ave., N.W., Washington, D.C. 20016.

Library Journal.

Reader's Choice Catalogue. Scholastic Book Service.
Reading (No. 3393). Boy Scouts, 1965, 32 pp., paper.
Recommended Paperbacks. Horn Books, Inc., 585 Boylston Street, Boston, Mass. 02116.
School Library Journal.

Materials for Reading or Telling

Arbuthnot, May H. (compiler): *The Arbuthnot Anthology of Children's Literature.* Scott Foresman, 1961.
Berg, Jean Horton: *Mr. Koonan's Bargain.* Nautilus, 1971, 48 pp., (ages 6–10)
Botkin, B. A.: *A Treasury of New England Folklore.* Crown, 1965.
Carrighar, Sally: *One Day on Beetle Rock.* Knopf, 1944, 196 pp.
Carrighar, Sally: *One Day at Teton Marsh.* Ballantine, 220 pp., paper.
Cathon, Laura, and Thusnelda Schmidt (compilers): *Perhaps and Perchance Tales of Nature.* Abingdon, 1962, 260 pp.
Chase, Richard: *American Folk Tales.* Dover, 1971, paper.
Chase, Richard: *Grandfather Tales.* Houghton Mifflin, 1948.
Chase, Richard: *The Jack Tales.* Houghton Mifflin, 1943.
Child, George G.: *Child's Book of Folk Lore.* Dial.
De Angeli, Marguerite: *Bright April.* Doubleday, 1946.
De La Mare, Walter: *Animal Stories.* Scribner's, 1940, 420 pp.
Dorson, Richard M.: *Buying the Wind.* U. of Chicago, 1964, 573 pp.
Feurlicht, Roberta Strauss: *The Legends of Paul Bunyan.* Macmillian, 1966.
Foster, Laura Louise: *Keer-Las, The Life Story of a Young Wood Duck.* Naturegraph, 1965, 80 pp., paper.
Gagliardo, Ruth: *Let's Read Aloud.* Lippincott, 1962, 256 pp.
George, Jean: *My Side of the Mountain.* Scholastic Book Service, 1959, 208 pp., paper.
Grahame, Kenneth: *The Wind in the Willows.* Scribner's, 1953, Dell, paper.
Gruenberg, Sidonie M. (ed.): *Favorite Stories Old and New.* Doubleday, rev.
Harris, Joel Chandler: *Uncle Remus: His Songs and His Sayings.* Grosset & Dunlap.
Hazeltine, Alice I.: *Hero Tales From Many Lands.* Abingdon, 1961.
Hollowell, Lillian (ed.): *A Book of Children's Literature.* Holt, Rinehart, 1966.
Johnson, Edna, Carie Scott, and Evelyn R. Sickels: *Anthology of Children's Literature.* Houghton Mifflin, 1970.
Kane, Henry B.: *The Tale of a Meadow.* Knopf, 1959, 110 pp.
Kane, Henry B.: *The Tale of a Pond.* Knopf, 1960, 110 pp.
Kane, Henry B.: *The Tale of a Wood.* Knopf, 1962, 120 pp.
Kipling, Rudyard: *The Jungle Books.* Doubleday, 1964, Signet, paper.
Kipling, Rudyard: *Just So Stories.* Doubleday, 1952.
Lang, Andrew (ed.): *The Red Book of Animal Stories.* Tuttle, 1972, paper.
Leach, Marie: *The Rainbow Book of American Folk Tales and Legends.* World, 1958, 319 pp.
Maxwell, Gavin: *A Ring of Bright Water.* Dutton, 1961. (grades 8–9)
Morrow, Betty: *See Up the Mountain.* Harper & Row, 1958, 47 pp., (ages 8–10)
Murphy, Robert: *The Pond.* Dutton, 1964, Avon, paper.
North, Sterling: *Rascal.* Dutton, 1963, 189 pp.
O'Dell, Scott: *Island of the Blue Dolphins.* Houghton Mifflin, 1960, 184 pp., paper.
Olson, Sigurd F.: *Runes of the North.* Knopf, 1963, 255 pp.
Olson, Sigurd F.: *The Singing Wilderness.* Knopf, 1956, 245 pp.
Parnall, Peter: *The Great Fish.* Doubleday, 1973.
Parnall, Peter: *The Mountain.* Doubleday, 1971.
Rawlings, Marjorie Kinnan: *The Yearling.* Scribner's, 1939, paper.
Reynolds, Barbara Leonard: *Pepper.* Scribner's, 1952.
Rush, William Marshall: *Duff: The Story of a Bear.* McKay, 1950, 149 pp. (ages 11–14)
Salten, Felix: *Bambi.* Grosset & Dunlap, 1929, 293 pp., paper.
Seredy, Kate: *The White Stag.* Viking, 1937.
Seton, Ernest Thompson: *The Biography of a Grizzly.* Grosset & Dunlap, 1958, 167 pp.
Seton, Ernest Thompson: *Two Little Savages.* Dover, 1903, 206 pp., paper.
Seton, Ernest Thompson: *Wild Animals I Have Known.* Scribner's.
Shephard, Esther: *Paul Bunyan.* Harcourt, 1941.
Simley, Anne: *Folk Tales To Tell or Read Aloud.* Burgess, 1963, Vol. II, 112 pp.
Smith, Helen R. (ed.): *Laughing Matter.* Scribner's, 1949, 166 pp.
Stanger, Margaret A.: *That Quail, Robert.* Fawcett, 1966, paper.
Viereck, Phillip: *The Summer I Was Lost.* Day, 1965.
Wadsworth, Wallace: *Paul Bunyan and His Great Blue Ox.* Doubleday, 1964. (ages up to 12)
Ward, Jane Shaw: *Tajar Tales.* Order from ACA, rev. 1967, 36 pp., paper.
White, E. B.: *Charlotte's Web.* Dell, 1952, 184 pp., paper.

Miscellaneous

Kujoth: *The Recreation Program Guide,* pp. 188–197. (Journalism)
Walter, Nina Willis: *Let Them Write Poetry.* Holt, Rinehart, 1962, 179 pp., paper.

Poetry

Arbuthnot, May Hill: *Time for Poetry.* Scott Foresman, rev., 1965, 228 pp.
Edgar, Mary S.: *Once There Was a Camper.* Welch, 222 Evans Ave., Toronto 18, Ontario, 1970, 48 pp., paper.
Fisher, Aileen: *In the Middle of the Night.* Crowell, 1965, 40 pp.
Frost, Frances: *The Little Naturalist.* McGraw-Hill, 1959, 47 pp.
Frost, Robert: *You Come Too.* Holt, Rinehart, 1959, 94 pp.
Gregory, Horace, and Marya Zaturenska: *The Crystal Cabinet.* Holt, Rinehart, 1962, 225 pp.
Hughes, Rosalind: *Let's Enjoy Poetry.* Houghton Mifflin, 1958, 278 pp. (ages 7–9)
McDonald, Gerald D.: *A Way of Knowing: A Collection of Poems for Boys.* Crowell, 1959, 288 pp. (ages 12 and up)
Ward, Herman M. (ed.): *Poems for Pleasure.* Hill and Wang, 1963, 137 pp., paper.

Storytelling

Anderson, Paul S.: *Storytelling With a Flannel Board. (Books One and Two.)* Order from NRPA, 260 pp.
Corbin: *Recreation Leadership,* ch. 21. (Contains lists of materials to use.)
Cundiff, Ruby Ethel, and Barbara Webb: *Story Telling For You.* Kent State U. Press, 1957, 103 pp.

Dorson, Richard M.: *American Folklore.* U. of Chicago, 1959, paper.

Goodreds, V. S.: *Good Stories and How To Tell Them.* Order from NRPA, 281 pp.

Kujoth: *The Recreation Program Guide,* pp. 374–380.

Sawyer, Ruth: *The Way of the Storyteller.* Viking, rev., 1962, paper.

Shedlock, M. L.: *The Art of the Story-Teller.* Dover, 1951, 320 pp., paper.

Smith, Helen Reagan: *Basic Story Technique.* U. of Oklahoma, 1967, 253 pp.

Tooze, Ruth: *Story Telling.* Prentice-Hall, 1959, 268 pp.

Webb: *Light From A Thousand Campfires:* Goellner, William A.: "Revive the Art of Storytelling," p. 300.

MAGAZINE ARTICLES

Camping Magazine:

Brown, Ruth: "What Would Camp Be Without Books," Jan., 1972, p. 16.

MacRae, Roderick: "Johnny and the Goblins," May, 1964, p. 11.

fourteen Arts and Crafts

THE CAMP PROGRAM

General Characteristics

Arts and crafts constitute an important segment of the overall camp program, for such activities make a unique contribution toward the accomplishment of major camp objectives. The arts and crafts program allows all campers to experience the personal satisfaction of handling materials and learning new skills that provide an outlet for self-expression. The camp program need not and should not duplicate the child's city crafts activities, which are often carried on in an elaborately equipped room under the direction of a highly trained specialist and are sometimes geared mainly to those of unusual talent and interest. Instead, it should include something for everyone, from the gifted to those who claim to be too inartistic to even draw a straight line. There are many possibilities, including such utilitarian activities as repairing or making camping equipment or recycling scrap lumber by building tables, chairs, shelves, and other comforts for the camp living quarters and decorating them according to each individual's particular taste and personality. There are a multitude of things to do, ranging from making souvenirs to activities carried on just because of the satisfaction creating something brings to the individual or group.

Good programs can be conducted without any special crafts center at all, but it is more common to have some sort of central area with at least one staff member especially trained and skilled in this field who acts as consultant or instructor. The center may be quite simple, with only a well-lighted room, comfortable chairs, tables, workbenches and improvised storage cabinets, bins and shelves, and a few simple tools and raw materials. Some camps, however, feature elaborate quarters with a relatively expensive and complete outlay of tools and raw materials.

Programs are conducted in a variety of ways. In a more formal programming setup, each living unit is scheduled to come to the crafts center at a designated time, or individuals may choose to come during a regular activity period or in their free time. In informal programming, living units may be supplied with basic materials and have the privilege of checking out special tools and materials to work with in their living units. The arts and crafts center is kept open for those who want to work there with the staff either being present to give help and advice or available on call whenever they are needed. This latter arrangement makes sense, since many activities, such as whittling a lapel pin or name tag or sandpapering and waxing a piece of driftwood, require painstaking, time-consuming work that can be done at odd moments in living quarters, during stops along the trail, or while attending story hour, taking part in a cabin discussion, or as the soup is simmering over the fire.

AN INDIGENOUS PROGRAM

Like all phases of camp program, arts and crafts should supplement rather than duplicate the camper's home or school activities by utilizing to the fullest the uniqueness of the camp setting and the raw materials and inspiration from nature available there. This pretty much rules out the use of kits or "pre-fab" crafts such as strip braiding or fitting part A into B in an already prepared model where youngsters merely follow someone else's ideas. Instead, they should use their own imaginations, creativeness, and self-expression to produce something with their own hands out of materials they have gathered and prepared.

Activities carried on with native materials, gathered and prepared on the camp site, constitute what is called an *indigenous* program, as distinguished from the type of program in which the materials are purchased from a supply house in a prepared or semiprepared state. Participants in an indigenous program may supplement their native findings with odds and ends of waste materials, such as bottle caps, old purses, boxes, and such, as well as inexpensive things readily available at neighborhood stores such as pipe cleaners, paste, glue, crayons, and cord. An indigenous program is in line with the do-it-yourself idea of modern camps and is the one usually practiced in most camps.

Advantages of an Indigenous Program

Nearly everyone agrees that one of the prime objectives of the summer camp should be to better acquaint campers with and make them more appreciative of nature, but past efforts in this direction have often been conducted in such bookish, uninteresting ways that the very name "nature study" or "nature program" has turned participants off to the idea. However, when

(Camp Mishawaka, Grand Rapids, Minn.)

campers become absorbed in searchng for materials to weave into a basket, plants or flowers to provide natural dyes for a grass mat, or wood suitable to cut and sand into a tie rack or a photograph album, they almost unconsciously learn a great deal about nature in a completely absorbing and enjoyable way.

Campers not only become sharp-eyed and alert in locating and recognizing native materials, but they also acquire skill in judging textures and qualities. This developes youngsters' creative abilities and helps them acquire manual skills as well as develop hand-eye coordination as they gather, prepare, and construct what they have pictured in their mind.

A broad arts and crafts program exposes campers to a whole panorama of possibilities for self-expression and encourages them to dabble in many activities, thereby learning where their true preferences lie. They are free to explore and experiment in order to expand their knowledge of nature and the arts. This not only provides present enjoyment and learning, but may even lead to a future vocation or a lifelong hobby. An additional advantage is that campers learn the relative unimportance of money in achieving true relaxation and entertainment, for indigenous materials are free to those who seek them out.

Many projects require patience to carry them through to completion, and this is certainly a desirable quality to cultivate. Campers also learn to make judgments and solve problems, for these are necessary when deciding what to use and how to use it.

As a general counselor, you will want to work with your campers in this area as in all other phases of their program. You, too, will enjoy the activity and will profit from it just as much as they.

Conducting the Program

In searching for the beautiful in color and design, there is no more promising source than nature. However, many of us have never learned to recognize these things when we see them. To help campers gain an eye for this, a good way to start is to take them on an observation tour. Proceed slowly and pause at likely spots to look about and point out interesting things such as pleasing contrasts and blendings of colors, graceful curves and shapes found in grasses, trees, or shrubs, the contours of hills, valleys, and water lines, the movements, formations, and coloring of clouds, and the speed and grace of animal, bird and insect movements. At times like this it is also important to take the opportunity to point out that all creatures have individual physical makeup, even down to their protective colorings, that fit them for a particular mode of life and natural habitat. With practice, the campers will develop a true awareness and sensitivity to their natural surroundings.

Campers should take along a sketch pad or notebook to jot down details they may want to recall. They should also be encouraged to be original in their work rather than copy from a neighbor or a book. However, don't minimize the importance of books and examples of all sorts, for they often point up possibilities, furnish inspiration, and enable the beginner to profit by the experience of others to save time and avoid disappointment and wasted materials. They can also help campers to learn such things as the essentials of design, the choice and use of tools, and the possibilities of various media in constructing and finishing products.

In presenting new information, a new technique, or the use of a new medium, such as papier mâché or tincancraft, it is best to demonstrate by using the actual materials as you explain what you are doing and why.

If campers tend to imitate rather than use a creative approach, put your point across tactfully by commenting favorably so others can hear when you find someone who is being original and creative and weight these qualities heavily when giving ratings or choosing items for display.

You will need to use a great deal of discretion in determining just how much help to give an individual and when and how to give it. Some prefer to be left pretty much alone and are frustrated and irritated when someone stands over them, giving unsought suggestions and advice. Others may lean on you too much, to the detriment of their own creativeness and originality.

The type of program we are advocating is indeed time consuming, and some campers may become so engrossed in a project that they are reluctant to lay it aside to participate in other phases of camp life. Indeed, why should they have to, if your camp program is flexible and truly geared to meet individual campers needs and preferences as long as this doesn't adversely affect others or interfere with general camp routines or policies?

CARRYING ON THE PROGRAM

Collecting Materials

Almost every camp site has a wealth of possible natural materials that can be used for arts and crafts, providing you are able to recognize them. Therefore, one of your first tasks may well be to make a general survey of the area to learn what it has to offer.

When you are ready to start out with your campers to collect materials, equip them with a good-sized bag to carry back the things they find. Let them gather anything that they feel may be useful as long as it does not violate the principles of good conservation. This obviously means that they must never needlessly destroy or damage any living thing, especially if it would deplete the supply so that not enough remains to quickly replenish it. Only a selfish, unthinking individual would take nature's creations when doing so could affect the ecology of the area or would deprive those following of their rightful heritage. To prevent this, campers sometimes plant and cultivate a continuing supply of useful natural materials such as honeysuckle and Virginia creeper for basket weaving and seeds or nuts for making jewelry, model animals, and such.

Here are examples of some native materials which may prove useful:

- Native clay
- Seashells
- Cattails
- Bones
- Bird feathers
- Dead animal skins and fur
- Fish scales
- Acorns
- Fungus
- Nuts
- Horns
- Corn husks
- Hickory and other nuts
- Moss
- Fallen birch or other bark
- Sand
- Gourds
- Growths of bamboo
- Ears of corn
- Weeds and grasses
- Seeds
- Discarded birds' eggshells
- Pine cones and needles
- Lichen
- Dried pods

Vary the types of locale you visit, because, be it deep woods, swampy territory, a meadow, the beach, or a river bank, each area offers unique natural materials.

Although we believe the program emphasis should be indigenous in nature, there are a number of materials that often can be used to supplement individual projects. Therefore, alert both staff and campers to watch for and save such commonly discarded things as:

- Straws
- Pocketbooks
- Chicken wishbones (fine for making bow-legged cowboys)
- Linoleum or rugs
- Corks
- Paper cups
- Oilcloth
- Bits of cardboard
- Old inner tubes
- Bags and sacks
- Milk bottle caps and cartons
- Discarded toothbrushes
- Corrugated cardboard
- Empty cereal boxes and other cartons
- Cellophane wrappings
- Egg cartons
- Sewing scraps
- Cans and can lids
- String
- Old boards
- Bottles, (glass or plastic)
- Discarded clothing
- Cord and rope
- Feathers
- Old drapes and sheets
- Old furniture
- Newspapers
- Coat hangers and odd bits of wire
- Mop and broom handles
- Buttons
- Magazines
- Spools
- Lollypop and ice cream sticks
- Coconut shells
- Bottle caps
- Old felt hats
- Toothpicks
- Aluminum foil
- Eggshells

Supplement the above with such readily available supplies as:

- Pins
- Pipe cleaners
- Inks
- Shellac
- Enamels
- Needles
- Wallpaper samples
- Unshelled peanuts
- Wax crayons
- Construction paper
- Marking pens
- Cellophane tape
- Compass
- Brayer
- Craft foam (Styrofoam, etc.)
- Stapler and staples
- Rubber bands
- Oil paints
- Gumdrops
- Popcorn
- Thread
- Colored thumbtacks
- Poster paints
- Ribbon
- Dowel sticks
- Paper clips

Brushes
Various types of paper
Paste and glue
Rubber cement
Colored toothpicks

Trips to nearby factories often will yield waste scraps of leather, suede, cotton and other cloth, plastic, linoleum, metal, rubber, and wood. Stores, salesmen, or factories sometimes will donate outdated samples or sample books.

Let individuals use what they have gathered or put everything together for common use, sorting it into piles of related items and placing them on shelves or in boxes and bins where all can see what is available.

What To Make

Although we can discuss only a very few of the possibilities in this chapter, you will find other suggestions for projects in other chapters.

The following list of projects may prove helpful:

Wall plaques
Doorstops
Tie racks
Lapel pins
Coin purses
Toys
Vases
Lamps
Bookends
Trinket boxes
Knot boards
Fishing equipment
Table decorations
Winter bouquets
Plant boxes
Camping furniture and equipment
Nature displays and trails
Musical and rhythm instruments
Potholders and hot plate pads
Costumed dolls
Coasters
Wooden buttons
Games
Mobiles
Bookmarks
Candle holders
Greeting cards and stationery
Wooden buckles
Party favors and place cards
Indian costumes, rattles, tom-toms
Outdoor campsites and other structures
Model campsites
Birdhouses and feeders
Candles
Bookbinding
Relief maps
Letter trays
Yarn animals and dolls
Belts
Mosaics
Wastebaskets
Picture frames
Soap sculpture
Rustic signs
Scrapbooks and memory books
Katchina dolls
Photography (develop own films and prints)
Paperweights
Napkin rings
Murals
Baskets
Masks
Totem poles
Bows and arrows
Whistles
Hiking sticks
Marionettes and puppets
Jewelry
Kites

BASKETRY

Basketry is an ancient art common to nearly every country, and its true origin is lost in antiquity. In the United States, we can use such native materials as willow branches (cut in the spring when the sap in running), cattail leaves from low damp places, flags, rushes, straw, wire grass, sweet grass, sedge, broom wheat, rye, and corn husks. Honeysuckle and Virginia creeper vines, when peeled and allowed to dry for two years, work up fast and make an even coil. Using wood splints from hickory, ash, oak, and maple trees requires more experienced hands than those of the average camper.

PIXIES AND OTHER THINGS

The dictionary defines a "pixie" as an elf or fairy, but campers often apply the term to all sorts of two- and four-legged creatures that their hands and imaginations create from the materials they have. Figure 14–1 shows some of the things that can be made.

A hike in season will disclose such nuts as acorns, hazelnuts, walnuts, and buckeyes, which can be used for making lapel pins, buttons, bracelets, and tops. To make a lapel pin, use either a half or a whole acorn or other nut and paint on a face, remembering to place the eyes halfway between the top and bottom and the mouth halfway between the chin and eyes. Use epoxy or glue to attach a safety pin on the back and add such details as hair, earrings, and hats. Make a bug or other creatures by painting half a walnut or other shell and gluing on antennae of vines or pipe cleaners. Place a marble on the bottom to make it movable. With a few additions, the shell can become a mouse or a turtle (Fig. 14–1). You can make a sailboat (Fig. 14–1) from a half shell of a walnut or a pecan. Make the sail from construction paper and run a toothpick mast through it.

You can convert coconut shells into many

Figure 14–1 Some pixies you can make.

things. Figure 14–2 shows a wind chime made from a half shell.

Pine cones are beautiful in themselves and come in many sizes and forms that make them quite versatile. Large ones make lovely wall or Christmas tree ornaments when you paint the tips and attach a string between the scales or into a small screw eye inserted at the top to hang them. Big cones also can be converted into candlestick holders by slicing off the bottom to provide a flat base and inserting a candle in the top.

Cones also serve as a base or body for all sorts of animals, and the possibilities are limited only by your imagination. A woodpecker can be made from a cone by adding a maple seed or acorn head and a maple seed or feather tail. Glue on twig or matchstick legs and whittle a beak from a match, toothpick, or bit of wood. Glue the woodpecker in position on a "hollow tree" and mount it on a base. You can also perch birds by gluing on pipe cleaner feet and legs and gluing them to the limb of a branch "tree" or you can make them stand upright by embedding their feet in a large chunk of clay and letting it dry.

Figure 14–1 shows a turkey and other birds made with large cones for their bodies. Glue on discarded bird feathers or leaves for wings and tail and paint on the eyes or glue on seeds to represent them.

Make a fish by painting the large end of a pine cone a light color, adding eyes and a maple wing tail, and mounting it on a slab of wood or a flat stone. Use it as a decoration or paperweight.

Make the bird feeder shown in Figure 14–2 by inserting a mixture of honey, peanut butter, suet and bird seed into pine cones and hanging them on a tree or other convenient place not too near people.

An armadillo can be made with a small chestnut burr head, a pine cone body and twig tail and feet.

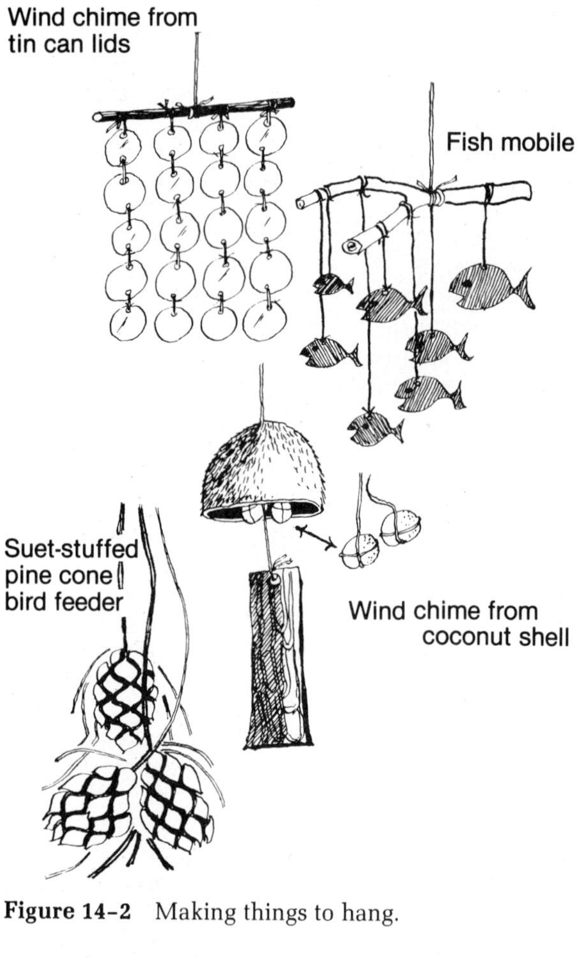

Figure 14–2 Making things to hang.

(Columbine Girl Scout Council, Inc., Pueblo, Colo.)

Shells, bits of sponge, coral, dried seaweed, sharks' teeth, or fish fins, when combined with pipe cleaners and liquid glue, can be made into many beautiful and useful objects, such as earrings, pins, brooches, hairpins, and decorations for such things as boxes and place cards. You can create animals and dolls by using various kinds and sizes of shells for heads, bodies, and legs.

You can produce artistic pictures by gluing seeds of assorted sizes and colors onto a suitable background. If you can't find seeds of the color you want, you can, of course, dye or paint them.

Milkweed pods are also versatile. To convert them into birds, select partly open, dried pods that resemble bird bodies, then insert a toothpick bill and black seed eyes and make legs and feet from pipe cleaners. Paint the pods in gay bird colors.

You can often find lichen or fungus in attractive natural colors or you can paint them any color you want. They make very attractive centerpieces, paperweights or wall plaques.

THINGS TO HANG

Mobiles and wind chimes are fascinating creations made by suspending a number of objects from a solid support so that even a slight breeze keeps them in constant motion (Fig. 14–2). Use very light objects and hang the creation fairly high to take full advantage of air currents. Tie or glue a heavy dark thread or light thin wire to the object to suspend it from the support. Use varied shapes and colors to add interest. For mobiles you may use objects related to a central theme or motif such as Indian or pioneer life, trees, flowers, animals, storybook heroes, or geometric forms. Another possibility is to feature various nature specimens, such as berries, pine cones, leaves, dried flowers, pods, or seeds. You may also cut out interesting folded paper designs or construct three-dimensional objects, such as an Indian tepee or tom-tom. You also can use such items as paper cups or plates, papier-mâché figures, bits of bright cloth or plastic, beads, feathers, buttons, pipe cleaner figures, thin bits of metal, shapes whittled from light wood such as balsa, cardboard, bits of ribbon, or designs cut from wallpaper. The mobile will not work well unless everything is exactly balanced, so begin by suspending and balancing the framework and then add objects to maintain an exact balance. Avoid monotony by balancing several small objects with a heavy one. Try to select light objects that will appear to dance or float gently in the air.

DRIFTWOOD

Along a seashore you can frequently find pieces of driftwood that are interesting in themselves. The constant erosion by salt water may have eaten away the bark and soft spots in the wood and the soaking has preserved the wood and given it an attractive silver-gray color, while constant buffetings by tides have rounded off rough corners and protrusions. Similar pieces of wood also can be found near inland lakes or rivers as well as in deserts, open fields, or forests where constant exposure to sun and changing weather conditions produce similar effects. Driftwood pieces exist in all imaginable shapes and sizes and offer you a challenge to determine

Figure 14–3 Things to make from native materials.

how best to capitalize on their particular "personalities."

Possible Uses For Driftwood

What does your piece of wood look like? Would it make a good tree if you stood it on end and added bits of felt, gum drops, or moss for foliage? Does it resemble the body of a fish, animal, or bird, so that by adding small pieces for a tail, feet, legs, ears, and so forth you can make it into a good caricature? Could you convert it into a sign for your camp or cottage by flattening it on one side and incising letters with a wood burner and painting them in a contrasting color or by whittling letters from other wood and gluing them on? Figure 14–3 shows this, plus other attractive decorations such as a pot, planter, stool, lamp base, candle holder, book binder, and picture frame.

Preparing Driftwood

Select only firm, solid pieces without dry rot, and if they are water soaked, set them aside for three to six months to dry out thoroughly. When you have decided what you want to make from a piece, saw off unwanted parts or projections and use sandpaper to round off the sawed ends to make them blend in with the rest of the piece. The best way to attach a small piece is to drill a small hole in both it and the main piece and glue a small stick or dowel of appropriate size into the holes.

Use a wire or very stiff brush to remove all loose particles. There are several methods of finishing the piece and you may want to experiment with them on waste portions. Some woods, particularly hard woods, have a naturally beautiful grain that you may want to make the most of; if so, use rough sandpaper to get down to the grain and finish off with fine sandpaper to produce a satin smooth finish. If you prefer to keep the natural gray finish, use very fine sandpaper to sand it lightly, for the gray layer is thin and easily destroyed. Conceal sawed-off places with a matching shade of gray.

Apply a coat of white shellac first to keep later treatments from sinking into the wood and eventually darkening it. To produce a pleasing rich, deep luster, rub in successive coatings of linseed oil, protecting them with a coat or two of wax rubbed in well.

Another possibility is to apply a thin coat of paint in one or more pastel shades, blending them into each other to give a light tinted effect. A pleasing finish results if you apply a light coat of white to the main parts, then add touches of black to recessed areas and use your fingers to blend them in while still wet. Add metallic touches by placing a small amount of metallic powder on a piece of paper and blend it in sparingly with your finger while the black and white are still wet. Rubbed-in oil paint also gives a pleasing tint. Apply metallic finishes of gold, copper, bronze, or aluminum from a spray can.

Protect these finishes with a coat or two of good quality, hard-drying varnish or shellac, topped off with a coat or two of wax rubbed in well. Use outdoor paint or varnish if the object will be exposed to the weather.

WOOD CARVING

General Procedures

Although advanced whittlers often use such specialized tools as crooked knives, chisels, gouges, special wood-carving knives, jigsaws, coping saws, and eggbeater drills, it is surprising

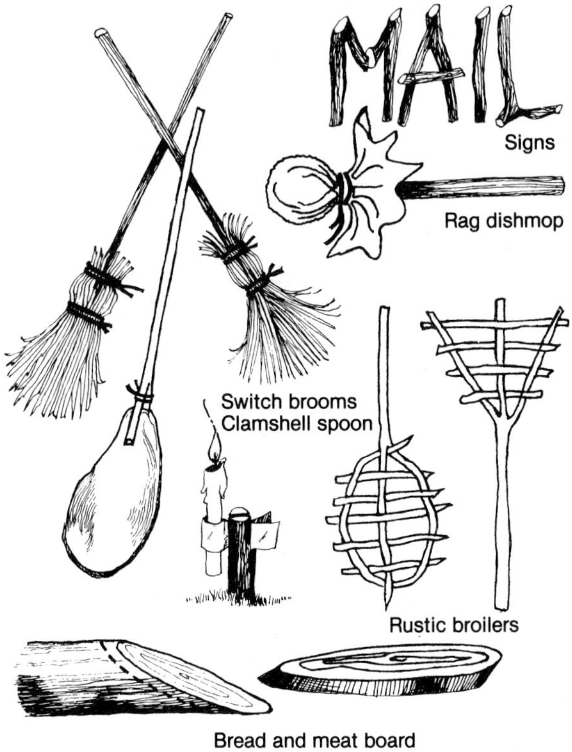

Figure 14-4 More things to make from native materials.

what you can do with an ordinary pocketknife. There are many simple items that can be made if you have patience and an average amount of skill (Fig. 14-4).

Many kinds of wood are suitable for carving, but some are better than others. White pine, oak, white ash, white or yellow poplar, red cedar, basswood, butternut, maple and holly are all recommended, and prunings from such fruit trees as cherry and apple are also good. Choose a well-seasoned piece that has dried for at least a year. If you look carefully, you should be able to find suitable pieces in any wooded area, in the scrap lumber around a building site, or in the odds and ends that carpenters and cabinetmakers collect. Especially fine pieces can be obtained from a lumberyard or hobby shop.

Wood for whittling should be straight-grained, fine-textured, and soft enough to cut well, yet with enough "body" to hold together. It should be free from knots and should split straight and smooth ahead of your knife, but not farther than you want it to. Avoid brittle woods and those that will not hold together after large sections have been cut away. Porous woods are usually too coarse-grained for good whittling.

If the piece is much larger than you need, rough-shape it to size with an axe or saw. Use your knife slowly and patiently, for it is very discouraging to make a careless or hasty miscut that completely ruins the result of many laborious hours. For specific information on using the knife, see Chapter 23.

Things to Make

Campers and staff members often wear name tags during the first few days of a camp session to help everyone to connect names with faces. The "woodsy" way to make them is to use a small twig or scrap of wood about 2 to 2½ inches long and as big around as your index finger. Use your knife to flatten the wood on one side and then sandpaper it smooth. Print your name or nickname on it with India ink, burn it in with a wood-burning pen, or carve away around it to make it stand out in relief. You also can paint or stain the letters to make them stand out. Gouge out a small groove above center on the back and use tape, plastic wood, or epoxy or household cement to anchor a safety pin in it. Apply a thin coat of wax to the whole pin or rub it well with clean hands until the oil from your skin permeates it; you will find that rubbing your fingers over your nose gives you an especially generous supply of body oil.

Make pins, buttons, or belt buckles (Fig. 14-5) by using a small saw to cut off thin, cross-section slices from a piece of hard wood that has an interesting grain. Shape them as you wish with

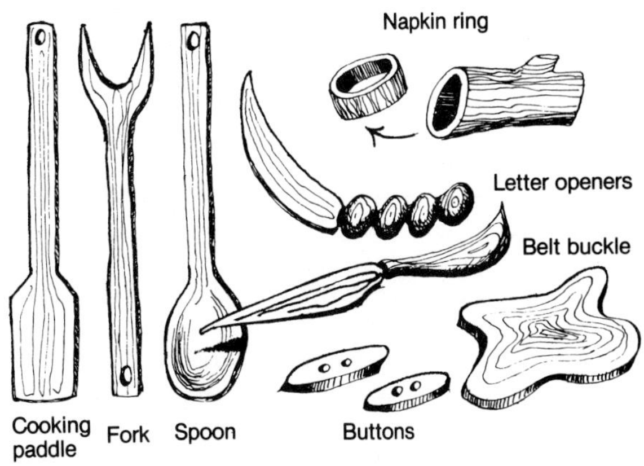

Figure 14-5 Whittling.

your knife and use a small drill to make holes in them or drive a nail through them. Finish them as described later in this chapter.

A hiking staff is handy to have when traveling over rough or hilly country. Choose a fairly straight, sturdy stick about chest high and an inch or more in diameter. Carve your initials with bark carving (described later in this chapter) and work out special designs to give it personality and make it uniquely your own.

Many other whittling projects are described elsewhere in this book, and it is even more fun to be original and think up your own.

To get your campers whittling, start some project of your own and casually pursue it at odd moments as during rest hour or while listening to someone read aloud or tell a story. They'll soon get the fever and you'll all be having fun together while producing useful gadgets for camp life or souvenirs to take home.

Carving Totem Poles

Indian totem poles (Fig. 14–6) are fun to make and can vary from large ones to miniatures only a few inches to a foot or two in height. Carefully lay out the design (including the colors) on paper and then transfer it to your piece of wood. Rough-shape it with large tools and then use your knife to cut it to shape. To impart a true Indian flavor, avoid intricate detail and don't strive for perfection, for Indian totems were merely rough outlines with the refinements left to the imagination. Glue on such protruding parts as tails and beaks and use paint or enamel to bring out details or use native stains as the Indians did.

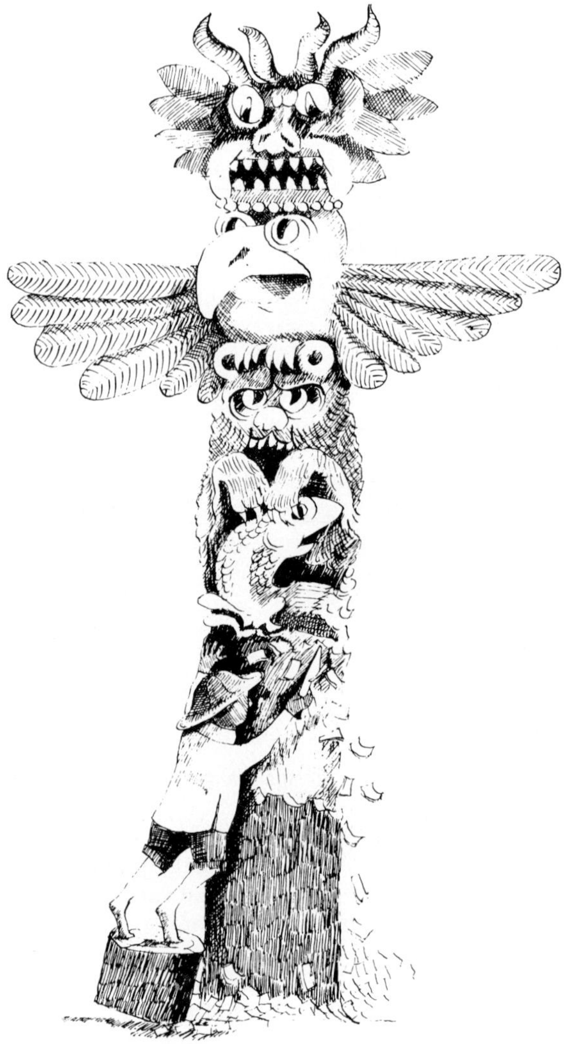

Figure 14–6 Carving a totem pole.

FINISHING WOODEN ARTICLES

There are many ways to finish a wooden article. Skillful, experienced whittlers can produce what they want with a minimum of sharp, decisive strokes and often leave their stroke marks showing. As a beginner, however, you may prefer to hide your more inaccurate and indefinite strokes by sanding the surface smooth. Use steel wool or progressively finer sandpaper if you want a velvety smooth surface. When sandpapering a round object, wrap the sandpaper around it to distribute the pressure evenly over a large area instead of gouging into the wood. Use a whisk broom to remove clinging bits of sand or steel wool that might get onto your skin or remain on the wood where they would interfere with your finishing process.

The modern trend is to retain the natural color of the wood, applying substances only to protect it from moisture and wear or to enhance and bring out the natural beauty of the grain. A soft, velvety glow is preferable to a high sheen.

Ways to Apply a Design

1. Burn the design in with a wood-burning set.

2. Incise the design by cutting it out with a knife or special carving tools, or cut away around it to leave it standing out in relief.

3. Decorate the object with chip carving or inlays.

4. Carve the design out of other types of wood or other materials and glue it on.

5. Use the Indian method to smoke on a design. Rub the object well with grease and hold it over the fire until it becomes dark brown. Then, while it is still warm, burnish it vigorously with a cloth. Now gouge out your design so that it stands out in a pleasing white contrast. You can achieve a similar effect by cutting out the design in adhesive tape and applying it to the wood, then smoking the whole thing. (The tape acts as a mask, leaving the design standing out in the original wood color when you remove it.) To get a dark design on a light background, cut away the bark around the design and smoke the whole thing. When you remove the remaining bark, the design will stand out dark against a light background.

6. Use bark carving, which is best done in the summer or fall when the bark is less inclined to peel off. Cut the bark away around the design or cut the design into the bark (incise it) and apply a coat or two of clear varnish to help anchor the remaining bark to the wood.

Methods to Enrich and Protect Your Woodcarving

Here, too, there are many methods from which to choose, and you may want to experiment with several on pieces of scrap wood before making a final choice. Here are some possibilities:

1. Smooth on melted white candle wax or paraffin with a brush or apply a coat or two of good furniture polish with a cloth, using a circular motion to rub it in well. Allow each coat to dry thoroughly before putting on the next. For a tinge of color, melt colored candles or use wax crayons. These methods will protect the wood, preserve its beauty, and impart a sheen. To melt paraffin, cut it into fine slivers, put them in an old tin can, and place the can in a container of water boiling over a fire. Watch it carefully and take it off the heat as soon as it is melted. Handle it with extreme care for hot paraffin can cause severe and painful burns.

2. Rub in beeswax with the palm of your hand (your body heat causes it to go on properly). You can also mix the beeswax with turpentine or a bit of liquid furniture polish.

3. Use a coat or two of boiled linseed oil, followed by one or two coats of wax, rubbed in well. Athough oil will alter the color of the wood to some degree, it helps to preserve it and also imparts a slight polish.

4. Apply one or two coats of white shellac, mixed with an equal volume of alcohol. When using any type of shellac, varnish, lacquer, or paint, you will get better results if you apply several *thin* coats rather than one thick one. Let each coat dry thoroughly and sandpaper it smooth before you put on the next.

5. For a soft tint, soak crepe paper in water to produce a transparent dye or paint on a heavy coat of water color which will soak into the wood. Adopt the Indian method of using plant dyes for a natural touch.

6. For a dark shade to conceal unwanted blemishes or unattractive wood grains, use paints, enamels, varnishes, or lacquers. Many of these substances, as well as such thinners as turpentine, alcohol, and benzol commonly used with them, are both toxic and combustible, so use them only in a well-ventilated area where you will not inhale the fumes and cleanse your hands thoroughly before proceeding with other activities. Destroy any rags or papers you use for they are also highly flammable. Clean your brushes thoroughly and then wash them out in a good detergent and hang them up to dry. Never leave them standing on end as this will press the bristles out of shape.

7. Spray the wood with a thin coat of clear plastic to protect it. Apply it over a stain or other coloring or alone if you want to maintain a light color.

Occasionally rub down wooden objects with a good quality of oily furniture polish or boiled linseed or other type of oil. This helps to replace the natural oils that are lost as the wood gradually dries out.

COLLAGES

Collages are made by pasting or gluing a large assortment of materials to some sort of background to produce a picture or design. Since a large variety of textures, surfaces, and mate-

(Pacific Peaks Girl Scout Council, Olympia, Wash.)

rials are used, making collages provides valuable experience in recognizing and appreciating the individual qualities and characteristics of many media.

SAND PAINTING

Painting pictures with colored sand is an interesting activity that brings pleasing results. Builders' sand gives better results than regular beach sand, which is too fine. First design the picture (flowers, seascape, landscape, house, or whatever) on a piece of paper with water colors or wax crayons; then outline it roughly on a piece of thin board or heavy cardboard that will serve as a background. Mix vegetable or other dyes in water, placing the colors you want in available containers such as bottles, cans, cups, or shallow dishes. Estimate the amount of sand you will need for each color and place it in the proper container of dye, stirring or shaking it to see that each grain of sand is dyed. Remembr that wet sand is darker than it will be when dry so mix your colors accordingly. Spread out each batch of sand on newspapers to dry. Cut off enough lengths of string to cover the outlines of the areas of the picture and dip each in the appropriate dye bath and let dry. Use a small stick or paint brush to outline each area of the picture with glue and press a piece of string of the right color into it. Be sure to make all applications while the glue is still damp and let it dry thoroughly each time. Apply glue to one area and spread it uniformly with a bit of cardboard or a brush and sprinkle it thickly with the proper color of sand. Let dry and repeat until all areas of the picture are covered. If desired, you can add another layer of glue and sand to produce a deeper texture. Spray a coat of clear plastic or varnish over the picture to preserve it, then frame and hang it.

MAKING FLOUR PASTE

There are many ways to make your own paste. One method is to mix a half cup of flour (rye is preferable to wheat) with enough water to form a creamy mixture and then heat it over a low flame for about five minutes, stirring it constantly to prevent lumping. If you want to preserve it for future use, add a few drops of glycerine, oil of wintergreen, or alum.

PAPIER-MÂCHÉ

Papier-mâché is a very inexpensive and versatile medium for constructing useful and decorative objects. You will need only paper (newspapers, tissues, or paper toweling), fine wire or string, and some sort of paste or glue, such as ordinary school paste, flour paste, or wallpaper paste, mixed as directed on the package.

Strip Method

This is a simple method that consists of wrapping layers of damp paper strips around a frame and applying some adhesive substance to hold them together.

To make a plate, bowl, tray, or similar object, choose some form such as a bowl, bottle, can, or half of an orange or apple that is the appropriate size and shape. Tear, rather than cut, narrow strips of paper an inch or less in width on the bias and soak them in water until they are pliable but not too weak to handle; this may take up to 24 hours or more. Cover the outside of the form with a light coating of petroleum jelly or grease to keep the finished product from sticking to it. If you want added strength and body, wrap a layer or two of cheesecloth over the form either before you begin or after you have applied the first two or three layers of paper. Wrap a layer of paper strips horizontally around the form, overlapping each slightly, and use a brush to cover it lightly with a coat of paste. Next apply a layer of paper strips vertically, overlapping them as before, and again cover them with paste. Continue with additional layers, applying them in alternate directions or crisscrossing the strips in each layer, until you have built up a shell at least ⅛ inch thick. Let the object dry thoroughly, allowing as much as two or three days if the weather is damp. Slip the product off the form, sand it smooth, and paint or otherwise finish it as you wish, adding a top layer or two of shellac to protect it and make it semi-waterproof. A coat of wax on top will give even more sheen and protection.

To make large papier-mâché figures, such as people or animals, rough shape the body from crumpled newspapers, chicken wire, or lengths of straight wire. Fasten on additional crumpled or rolled pieces for neck, arms, and legs. Bend and shape the frame or armature as you wish and wind string or fine wire around it to hold it in place. Tie on wads or rolls of paper or cloth for noses, ears, and tails. Then cover the armature with strips of paper narrow enough to follow the contours closely, alternating the directions and using paste as before. For a really smooth finish, allow each layer of paper to dry thoroughly, then sand it smooth before you apply the next. Paper toweling on the outside layer provides an excellent surface for painting. Add strands of yarn or twine to the wet papier-mâché to simulate fur or hair.

Pulp Method

Though slightly more complicated, the pulp method provides a medium of finer texture that will produce a smoother and more "finished" product. Tear newspapers into tiny, confetti-sized pieces and soak them in water overnight or as long as necessary to get a smooth, fine gray pulp or mâché. If you want to use white rather than gray mâché, scoop the pulp up in a sieve and run clear water through it until the ink is removed. Squeeze out excess water and knead in enough commercial or flour paste to produce a mixture that has the consistency of heavy cream and is sticky enough to adhere well yet not too sticky to handle. Add color to the mixture if you wish. For a still smoother medium, mix 2 cups of powdered modeling clay, 1 cup of calcimine (any color), and 2 cups of water and stir as you gradually add bits of toilet or cleansing tissue until you have the same heavy-cream consistency. Let it stand 24 hours before using it.

Apply the mixture to an armature or over a form such as a bowl, bottle, or piece of wood. If you want to model figurines or other objects as you would with clay, start with a large enough mass to complete the entire figure and pull out portions for the arms, legs and head. Etch in details with a sharp instrument such as a knife, and use a flat knife or spoon to smooth the surface. Use fur, rope, or yarn to add hair, manes, tails or eyebrows while the mâché is still damp. When the object is quite dry, sandpaper it smooth and decorate it with colored paper, poster paint, oil paint, or water colors; use crayons, India ink, or colored inks to draw in details. Add a coat of shellac for protection and a coat of wax on top to give a high gloss. Some raveled burlap will provide a shaggy coat for an animal, and construction paper, crepe paper, or pieces of fabric may be used for clothing for human figures. Construct hats from felt or cardboard and trim them with such things as wild bird feathers, small colored stones, beads, or sequins.

Other Papier-Mâché Projects

You can use papier-mâché to make many other attractive items, such as jewelry, table decorations, wall plaques, puppet heads, doll heads, favors for parties, or models of circuses, towns, or camps. Glue on sequins, beads, snips of metal, or glitter to add sparkle and shine. Papier-mâché relief maps are lovely and lighter than clay maps, and you can also insert pins or thumb tacks into them. When making masks, start with a layer of cheesecloth as a base.

(Gold Arrow Camp, Marina Del Rey, Calif.; courtesy of ACA)

CLAY MODELING

Clay that can be used for modeling exists in all parts of the world and may be colored white, yellow, green, gray, or even black or blue. You will probably be able to find a satisfactory type right on your own camp site. The bibliography at the end of the chapter lists sources that tell how to construct a potter's wheel and kiln at little cost.

Figurines, animals, pendants, plaques, tiles, and bowls are quickly made and bring out the creative imagination of even the most inhibited. As one child ungrammatically said, "I closed my eyes and seen an angel and made one like I seen it."*

MARBLEIZING PAPER

Even a novice can turn out lovely marbleized paper. Use any kind of paper that is not too absorbent. Pour kerosene, turpentine, or

*Cole, Natalie Robinson: *The Arts in the Classroom.* John Day Co., 1940, p. 39.

other oil into a large pan of water and add a little oil paint in one or several colors; since water and oil won't mix, both the oil and the oil paint will remain floating on top. Breathe on the mixture or stir it slightly to make it swirl, then marbleize the paper by laying it on top of the mixture. You can add further decoration with wax crayons after the paper is dry.

CHIP CARVING

Chip carving requires precision and patience, and therefore may not be suitable for younger campers. Most chip carving designs are based upon geometrical patterns that usually are laid out with the aid of a ruler and compass. The "chips" are triangular pieces of wood, removed with a slicing knife (a razor blade will do in an emergency). Slope the chips gradually rather than gouge them out. Basswood (linden) is best because it is soft and workable, is fine grained, and takes a nice finish, but pine or apple wood is also satisfactory.

Trace your design on an object such as a box, album, scrapbook, coaster, tray, letter knife, checker, belt buckle, costume pin, or carved button. Dye or stain the chips or use chips from different kinds of wood to bring out the design and glue them on. Finish as you would any other wooden object.

DYEING WITH NATURAL DYES

When tied and dyed, silk, chiffon or cheesecloth can be made into beautiful cabin curtains, bedspreads, scarves, costumes, and similar items. Natural dyes from berries, bark, or plant roots produce soft, attractive shades, though they are usually less brilliant than those obtained from commercial dyes.

You must first treat the material with some sort of mordant to increase the brillance of the dye and set it permanently. For cotton, linen, rayon, or other vegetable fibers, use ¼ ounce of plain washing soda combined with 1 ounce of alum and a gallon of water. For animal fibers, such as silk or wool, substitute ¼ ounce of cream of tartar for the soda. First wash and rinse the material thoroughly, squeeze out excess water, place it in the mordant, and bring it to a boil, letting it boil gently for an hour. Replace the water as it evaporates to maintain the right proportion. Then rinse the material thoroughly.

To prepare the dye bath, break, crush, or cut into small bits about 1 peck of plant materials for each pound of material to be dyed. Place them in a steel, copper, or enamel container and cover them with water (rain or soft water if at all possible) and let them soak overnight or until your dye is of the intensity you want. Run the dye through a strainer to remove solid materials and add hot water to produce enough lukewarm mixture to easily cover the material. Place the material in the dye and stir it around with a wooden paddle. Slowly bring the solution to a simmer (just below the boiling point) and add ½ cup of salt for cottons or ½ cup of vinegar for wools about five minutes after the simmering begins. Stir the material occasionally to assure even dyeing and continue to simmer for from a half hour to an hour or until the material is somewhat darker than you want it to be when dry. If water boils away, lift out the material and add boiling water to restore its consistency.

Rinse the material several times, starting with boiling water and gradually reducing the temperature each time until the rinse water is clear. Squeeze out excess moisture and dry in the shade. You can use the dye water several times but it will give a somewhat lighter shade after each use.

The following are indigenous sources of the principal colors:

Blue:

Blackberry—berries
Blue ash (boiled with copper sulphate)
Hazel—roots
Larkspur—flowers
Red maple—bark (boiled with copper sulphate)
Sunflower—seeds

Black or Dark Brown:

Alder—bark
Butternut—bark
Coffee bean—inside kernel
Hemlock—bark
Hickory—bark
Onion—skins (boil them)
Red oak—bark
Sumac—leaves, roots, or bark
Black walnut—hulls and shells

Purple:
Barberry—berries
Blueberry-berries
Cedar—tips of branches
Elderberry—berries
Maple—rotted wood
Pokeweed-berries
Purple flag—petals
Juniper (Red cedar)—rootlets
Sumac—berries
Wild cherry—roots

Gray:
Bayberry—leaves
Blackberry—young shoots
Butternut—hulls
Red maple—bark (use mordant of copperas)
Rhododendron—leaves
St. John's wort—flowers (pick in July)
Sumac—leaves (use mordant of copperas)
Willow—bark

Green:
Elderberry—leaves
Giant arbor vitae—twigs and leaves
Laurel—leaves
Plantain—roots and leaves
Spinach—leaves
Water scum (algae)—whole plant

Red:
Alder—inner bark
Amaranth—seeds
Beets—boiled with alum (red violet)
Bloodroot—root
Calliopsis—flowers
Cedar—inner bark
Dahlia—flowers
Dandelion—roots
Hemlock—bark
Lady's bedstraw—roots
Pokeberry—berries (boil with alum)
Raspberry—berries (dark red)
Red dogwood—inner bark
Red sumac—berries
Strawberry—berries
Sycamore—old, half-rotten roots

Yellow:
Alder—inner bark or leaves
Apple—bark
Balsam—flowers
Bayberry—leaves
Black oak—inner bark
Broomsedge—stalks and leaves
Coreopsis—flowers
Cottonwood—seed vessels or leaf buds
Dock—roots
Elderberry—leaves
Goldenrod—flowers
Holly—boiled with alum
Lady's bedstraw—flowering tops
Gray lichen (from oak and pine trees)—whole plant
Marigold—flowers
Peach—leaves
Pear—leaves (dull yellow)
Pignut hickory—inner bark
Privet—branch tips or clippings
Saffron—dried stigmas
Sassafras—bark
Shiny sumac—roots
Smartweed plant (use mordant of alum)
St. John's wort—flowers (pick in August)
Sumac—roots
Thistle—flowers
White mulberry—roots and leaves
Zinnia—flowers

Orange:
Lombardy poplar—leaves (use mordant of chrome)
Mountain ash—berries
Onion—papery brown skins (steep them)

Magenta:
Dandelion—tap root

Khaki:
Juniper (Red cedar)—berries

WEAVING

Weaving, which consists of lacing one set of threads or strips of material in and out of another to form a solid material, is a very old craft, long used for both utilitarian and decorative purposes. The colonists brought weaving with them to America, although the Indians had developed their own weaving techniques long before. Weaving is quite popular in many camps, some of which have elaborate table or floor

(Gnaw Bone Camp, Nashville, Ind.)

looms and competent instructors to show campers how to use them. Some looms are simple to construct and with them you can make such things as mats, trays, belts, scarves, sit-upons, and book marks.

Commonly Used Terms

Loom—the frame that holds the raw materials.

Warp—the stationary threads, placed lengthwise on the loom to provide a base through which to weave the woof.

Weft or *woof*—the cross threads that are laced in and out of the warp.

Shuttle—an implement used to hold the woof while weaving it through the warp. It may be a needle with an eye through which the woof is threaded or a flat piece of plastic, wood, cardboard, (Fig. 14–7), or other material around which it is wound. Heavy materials, such as reeds, grasses, or large strips of cloth or plastic can be manipulated by hand instead of with a shuttle.

Beater—an instrument used to press the woof tightly up into place to keep the weaving tight and even. A round stick, an ordinary comb, or a coarse comb of plastic or whittled wood is commonly used.

Darning Stitch Weaving on a Wooden Loom

The loom shown at the top of Figure 14–8 can be used to weave such things as small doormats, sit-upons, place mats, or decorative wall mats. Use four sticks long enough to form a rectangle somewhat larger than your completed

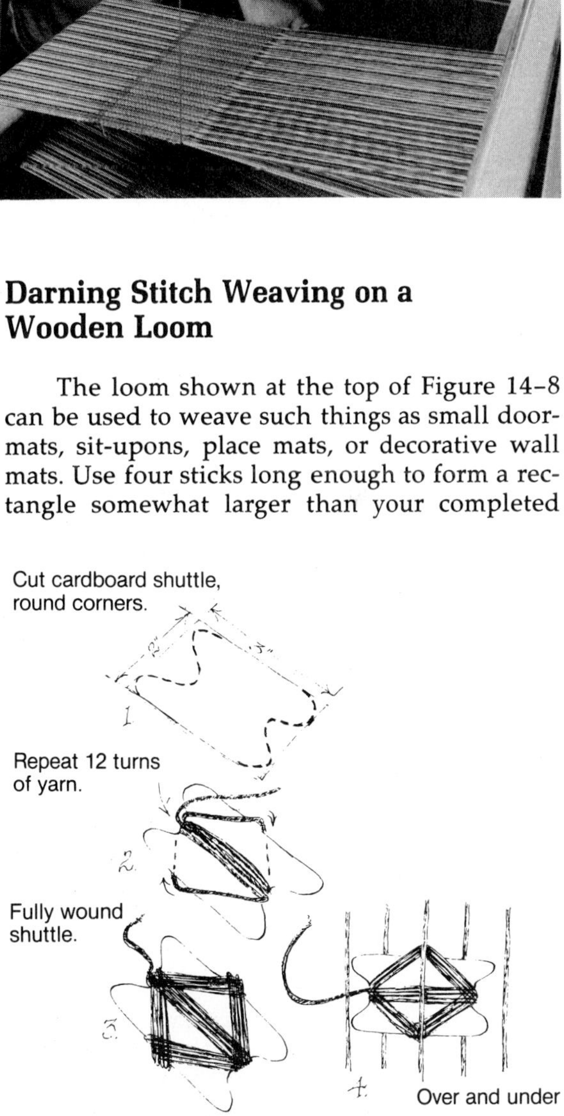

Figure 14–7 Weaving with a cardboard shuttle.

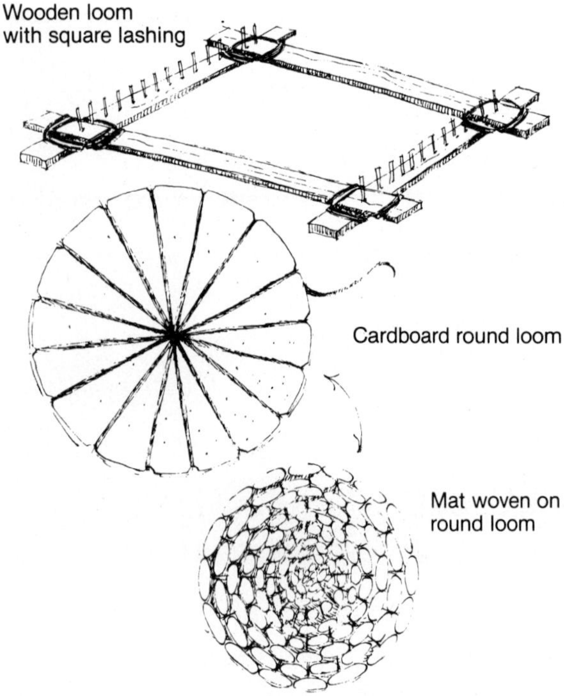

Figure 14–8 Round and rectangular looms.

mat is to be. Flatten each stick on two opposite sides, and use square lashing to join them together in a rectangle with the flattened sides of the sticks on the top and bottom. Drive in an even number of brads or nails about ⅛ to ¼ inch apart across the top and bottom sticks of the rectangle.

Use a clove hitch to anchor the end of the warp to the first nail on the bottom stick and then wind it back and forth between the nails on the top and bottom sticks to form the warp. Fasten the end to the last nail with another clove hitch. If you want to add extra strength or intensify the color effect of the warp, wind multiple thicknesses of the string between each set of nails before going on to the next. Now lace the woof alternately in and out of the warp, pressing it tightly up into place to keep it compact and even.

Use ribbon, strips of cloth, heavy string, rope, craft strip, or strips of leather for the warp, and use these or native materials such as broad-leaved grasses, long pine needles, sedges, rushes, twigs, corn husks, honeysuckle, or willow for the woof.

To prepare native materials, cut them as long as possible and hang them up to air dry thoroughly. When you are ready to use them, soak them in water until they are soft and pliable and then lay them on newspapers to remove excess moisture. Lace them singly or in uniform bundles in and out of the warp, placing the butt ends at alternate sides for a uniform appearance. Alternate each row so that the woof goes over the warp thread it previously went under, and continue until you have a mat as long as you want. You can use native or commercial dyes to dye the warp and woof and weave it in uniform colors or in stripes, checks or any other patterns desired.

Darning Stitch Weaving on a Cardboard Loom

Figure 14–9 shows a cardboard loom that is used to weave square or rectangular pieces. Use a piece of corrugated or other heavy cardboard to make a loom somewhat larger than you want your finished article to be. Cut notches ⅛ to ½ inches apart across both the top and bottom.

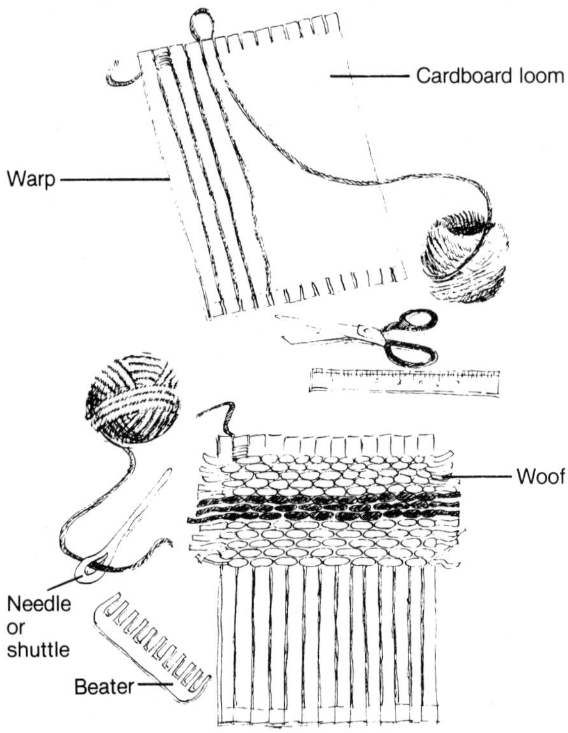

Figure 14–9 Cardboard loom.

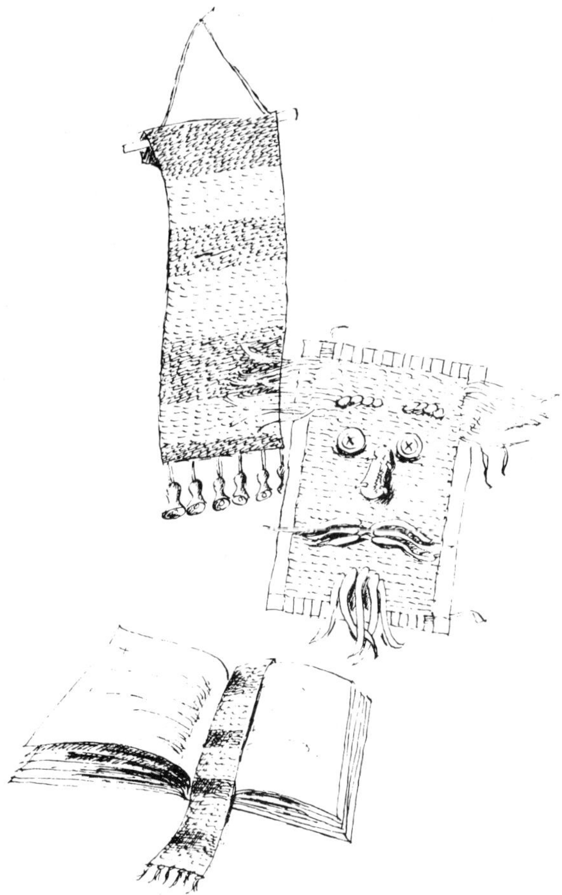

Figure 14-10 Weaving using buttons, bells and peanut shells.

Wind the warp lengthwise on the loom, crossing it over behind the cardboard projections at each end to reach the next notch. Use any thin material desired for the woof and fasten it to the warp at one side. Use a flat shuttle or your hand to lace it alternately under and over the warp, using a beater to press it tightly up into place as you proceed.

Either tie off each loose end or else make a turn around the warp at the end of the row and come back through the warp, passing under the thread you went over before, and fasten the end of the woof securely at the end of the last row. Remove the piece by slipping the loops in the warp off the projections in the cardboard. You can tie lengths of materials through the loops to add fringe. Work out a design by using various colors of warp and woof. When trying to work out a pattern, it is usually wise to first draw it to scale in color on paper.

To construct a cardboard loom for making a circular or oval mat, use a compass or trace around a bowl or other object of appropriate size and shape. Then cut it out and notch it. Lay down your warp as shown in the middle of Figure 14-8 and weave the woof in and out as before.

A Navajo Loom

With a Navajo loom you can weave mats, rugs, mattresses, or sit-upons out of broom grass (also called sedge grass or sage grass) or any other long grass that is fairly straight and does not have greatly enlarged joints. Wheat straw, cattails, or suitable reeds will also serve. Gather the grass when it is mature, cutting it close to the ground to get as much length as possible. Hang it up to dry and when it has dried, remove the leaves by giving them a sharp pull. Soak the dried grass in water to make it more flexible and easier to handle and lay it on newspapers to soak up excess moisture.

CONSTRUCTING THE LOOM

Construct the loom in the manner illustrated in Figure 14-11.

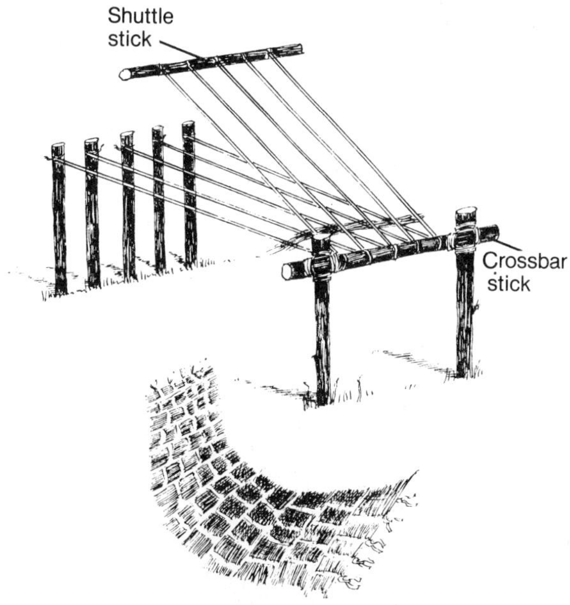

Figure 14-11 Navajo loom and finished mat.

1. The shuttle and crossbar sticks should be about 1 to 1½ inches thick and somewhat longer than the grass.

2. For the stakes (at the left of Figure 14–11), divide the length of your grass by 3 and drive that number of stakes, 16 inches long, into the ground, spacing them slightly less than 3 inches apart.

3. For the crossbar supports (at the right of Figure 14–11), make two 16-inch long stakes and drive them in opposite the two outside stakes described in step 2 and slightly farther from them than you want the length of your mat to be.

4. Use square lashing to attach the crossbar stick to the crossbar supports.

5. Using clove hitch knots, attach opposite ends of heavy string (carpet warp, twine, or light rope) to each of the stakes and to the crossbar.

6. Again using clove hitches, the same number of strings 6 inches longer than the first set should be attached at one end to the crossbar and to the shuttle stick at the other end. In weaving, the shuttle stick is manipulated up and down between the stakes, therefore the string must be long enough to allow the shuttle to fall well beyond the stakes when you lower it to the ground.

WEAVING WITH THE LOOM

Use single heavy reeds or divide fine materials such as grass into bundles. Raise the shuttle stick, push a bundle of grass tightly up between the two different sets of strings and lower the shuttle stick to bring its strings over the top of the bundle. Insert another bundle of grass between the two sets of strings, push it up tightly into place, and bring the shuttle stick up so its strings are under the bundle. The shuttle is now back in its original position and you are ready to repeat the process, inserting new bundles of grass as you lower and raise the shuttle to bind them securely in place.

Continue until you have a mat of the length desired. Untie all of the strings at one end of the mat and tie them together and repeat at the other end.

When weaving wide mats from long lengths of grass it is easier if two people help. These people station themselves on opposite sides of the loom to place the bundles in position and push them compactly into place; a third could assist by lowering and raising the shuttle.

VARIATION

Although many native materials come in quite attractive colors, other colors can be added by using native or commercial dyes. You can weave with single colors or work out interesting patterns by combining them into stripes or other designs. A touch of color also can be added by using colored strings (or dyeing your own), using multiple strands together to intensify the effect. This method produces attractive place mats when used with fine grasses.

The mat can be converted into a *carry-all* by folding it in half lengthwise and then sewing the sides together with heavy thread or cord. Braid together heavy rope, webbing, or fine cord to make handles.

Making a Mat Without a Loom

Figure 14–12 shows a circular or oval mat made from native materials without using a loom. Prepare bunches of long pine needles, long grass, or other materials, and weave them into a long rope or strand about the size of your finger, introducing new materials to replace the old as they run out. Hold them in place by means of buttonhole stitches as shown. Weave a mat with the strand as shown, fastening each row firmly to the previous one by means of frequent buttonhole stitches. Such mats can be used as rugs, hot dish mats, or decorations.

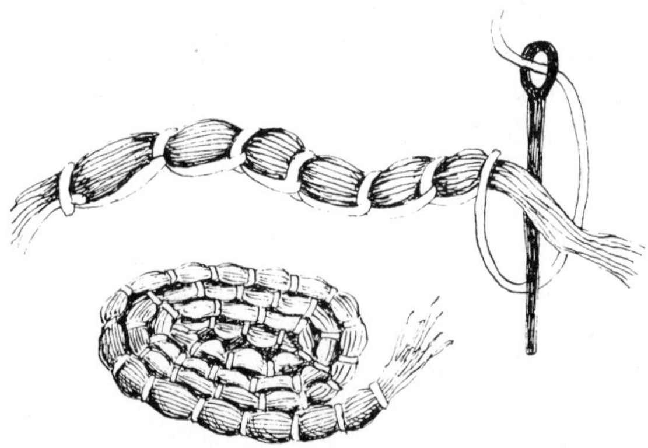

Figure 14–12 Pine needle mat using buttonhole stitch.

TINCANCRAFT

The Versatile Tin Can

A tin can is one of the most versatile objects in existence and you will be surprised to discover how easy it is to convert one or more into useful or decorative objects.

Tin cans are light and easy to work with and are easy to solder. Working with them also provides preliminary practice in using tools and patterns preparatory to working with such relatively expensive metals as copper, pewter, aluminum, brass, and silver. If you make a mistake, you can simply throw the can away and begin again with the loss of nothing more serious than a little time.

Materials Needed

It is possible to purchase sheet tin at a hardware store, but it is simple to get your own free by cutting and straightening out a tin can of suitable size. (Incidentally, tin cans are really misnamed for they consist of only about 2 percent tin, placed as a thin covering on both sides of a layer of steel.) Scrap wire for handles is free for the picking up around the house, camp, or in nearby scrap heaps.

The tools you need for making simple things are few and inexpensive and so common that most homes or camps already have them (Fig. 14–13). Tin snips, cotton gloves, pliers, hammer, hack saw, flat file, three-cornered file, and nails or nail sets are all that are really essential.

After you progress to more complicated or decorative items, you may want to add *duck bill tin snips* for cutting curved surfaces neatly and a *jeweler's saw* for cutting out intricate designs or orifices in metal, as when making letters of the alphabet. The thin blade of the jeweler's saw is removable so that you can insert it into the metal by making a hole just large enough to admit it, then reinserting the blade in the handle and fastening it in place with wing nuts. Point the teeth downward toward the handle and cut by pulling downward. Keep the blade straight up and down and work slowly and carefully, especially when turning corners or working in tight spots, for it is easy to break the thin blade.

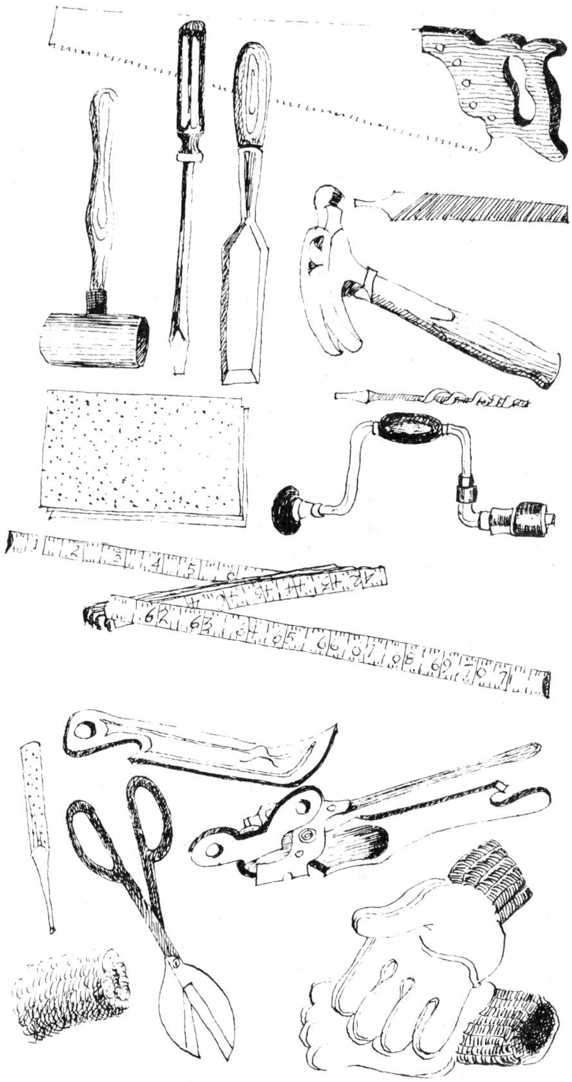

Figure 14–13 Wood and metal campcrafting tools.

Use a hammer and *cold chisel* to cut through metal that is too heavy to cut with tin snips. A screwdriver can be used for this but it won't do as neat a job. A *hard rubber* or *wooden mallet* or *ball peen hammer* will enable you to pound metal without scarring and denting it as the metal head on a regular hammer would. You will need *steel wool* if you want to polish the metal. A work board is a great convenience, and a ruler or tape measure attached to one side by means of wire nails will permit using it to measure as well as to lay off angles with a T-square and triangles.

You will need an *eggbeater drill* if you want to make small, neat holes.

For soldering, you will need a can of soldering paste, a tube of wire solder, and an alcohol lamp. Follow the directions that come with them. Use fine wire such as lightweight stovepipe wire to hold the parts together while you solder.

Preparing Tin Cans

Tin cans are available in almost any shape and size desired, varying from small tobacco tins to large oil cans. The standard sizes used for canning fruits and vegetables are as follows:

No. 1—large evaporated milk can
No. 2—most canned vegetables
No. 3—canned tomatoes
No. 5—twice the size of a no. 3 can
No. 10—gallon size, available from restaurants, school or camp dining rooms, etc.

Always wear cotton or canvas work gloves when working with metal; the sharp, jagged edges can easily cut you, or unaccustomed work with heavy tin snips and other tools may cause blisters.

Some cans are used just as they are or are merely cut down in height. When you want to convert a can into a flat sheet of metal, use an ordinary wall can opener to cut off both ends, then cut down on both sides of the side seam with your tin snips and remove it. Place the resulting circular piece of metal on your work board or a sturdy work table, hold one side with one hand and press it out flat with the other. Complete the flattening process by rolling over it with a stick or use the head of your hammer.

Working With Metal

When making something rather complicated, it is best to make a paper pattern, shaping and reshaping it until you are sure it is just right. If some sections are to be cut out for decorative purposes, it will help you to visualize the finished product if you color them dark on the pattern. Use a pencil to trace the pattern on the tin and cut along the marked line with your tin snips, resting the bottom of them against your work board or table as you cut. Take your time so that you won't injure yourself or do a jagged job of cutting.

There are several ways to make the cut edges more attractive and safer to handle. You can simply smooth them off with a file, but this leaves them still somewhat sharp and hazardous to handle. A better way is to turn the edge over with your pliers, then place the object over a post or the butt of a log and mash the edge flat with a regular or ball peen hammer or a mallet. If the surface is curved, you will need to cut out a series of small V-shaped pieces along the edge before turning it over. The best method of all is to make small cuts in the tin, each ⅛ to ¼ inch deep, then fit a piece of wire right at the base of the cuts and use your pliers to turn the edge over and tuck it in around the wire. Keep working at it until the edge is smooth and well rounded.

When you need to bend a piece of metal at a right angle, bend it over the edge of a work table or place it between two boards in a vise and flatten it over the tops of the boards.

Holes can be used for decoration, for inserting a wire handle, or for suspending the object from a nail. To make them, place the article over a tree stump or block of wood and use a hammer and nail set, ice pick, or other sharp object of appropriate size. As mentioned previously, you can make neater holes with a hand drill, resting the object on a soft piece of wood for the drill to enter after piercing the metal. When possible, flatten the other side of the holes you have punched out.

To convert a flat piece of metal into a cylinder, choose some round object such as a nail, an empty spool, a wooden dowel, or other item of the size you want, then place the piece of metal over it and use your hand or a narrow board to fit the metal around it.

Pieces of metal can be joined by riveting, nailing, soldering, or leaving tabs on one piece to insert into slits in the other and then bending the tabs over.

Adding Handles

As can be seen in Figure 14–14, there are a number of ways to add handles. A strip left on both sides of the seam can be bent around a wooden handle and fastened with nails and wire lashing or made detachable by fastening it with wing nuts (G). *H* shows a wire handle in-

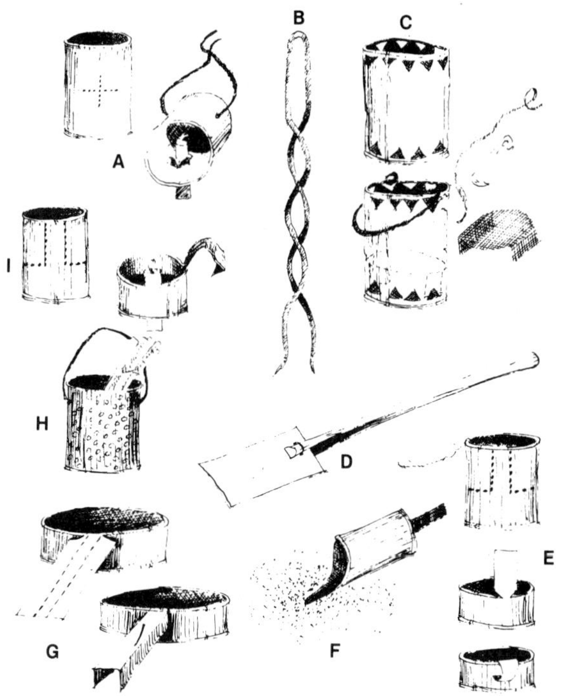

Figure 14–14 Tinwork.

serted through two holes in the tin can; and *E* shows how to make a simple handle for a cup.

Some Things to Make

Figure 14–14 shows a variety of useful things fashioned from wire or tin cans of appropriate size, including (*A*) a candle floodlight; (*B*) a fork made from a wire coat hanger; (C) a hobo stove; (*D*) a spatula; (*E*) a cup with handle; (*F*) a scoop for dry foodstuffs such as sugar or flour (use a screw to attach the handle); (*G*) a pan designed to be fitted with a wooden handle (strips left on both sides of the seam can be bent around a wooden handle and fastened with nails and wire lashing or wing nuts); (*H*) a perforated can with handle used for dipping silverware into hot, sterilizing water; and (*I*) a candle lantern (anchor the candle by cutting an "X" in the bottom of the tin can and bend the edges up until they fit snugly around the candle).

You can also make a complete set of nested cooking utensils by choosing tin cans of appropriate sizes. Be sure to equip them with detachable handles so that they will nest compactly. Kettles, stew pots, plates, and frying pans are best made from number 10 or gallon tin cans cut to appropriate depths. Cups are made from number 2 or number 2½ cans, while number 2½ or number 5 cans are about right for cereal bowls. (Before using tin-can cooking or eating utensils, heat them and scrub them thoroughly with hot water and a good scouring powder to remove the lacquer that is usually present on them.) Use only cans that have contained food, not paint or oil, for cooking utensils. Make a ditty bag of denim or other strong material with a drawstring at the top to carry your nested cooking outfit. Always be sure to dry out tin utensils thoroughly immediately after using them, for they rust very quickly. Use a plastic scouring pad rather than steel wool to clean them.

Reflector ovens can be propped up in front of the fire and will do a fine job of baking almost anything you want. The shelf or baking sheet is suspended in the middle so that the heat is reflected onto the surface from both above and below. Its easy to make one from a rectangular can cut diagonally across, with a shelf made from one side of the can. Perhaps you can devise a way to make the sides detachable so that you can pack it flat like commercially made reflector ovens. Make a ditty bag to carry it in.

OTHER ARTICLES

To make a useful and decorative set of kitchen canisters, select tin cans of the right size and enamel them (two coats for permanence) in any color scheme desired. Paint the name of the contents on the outside and add further decoration with your own free-hand painting or with decalcomania designs. You can buy glass or wooden knobs at the variety or hardware store or you can make your own wooden ones to fasten on with a screw.

To leave a bright metal finish, burnish the outside with steel wool. Another method of finishing consists of holding the object over the fire until it assumes a cloudy dullness, then quickly burnishing it with a brush and a good scouring powder.

ADDITIONAL READINGS

(For an explanation of abbreviations and abbreviated forms, see page 13.)

Basketry

Basketry (No. 3313). Boy Scouts, 1968, 32 pp., paper.
Christopher, Frederick J.: *Basketry*. Dover, 1952, 108 pp., paper.

Braiding and Knotting

Barnes, Charles, and David P. Blake: *Creative Macrame Projects*. Dover, 1972, 256 pp., paper.
Graumont, Raoul M., and Elmer Wenstrom: *Square Knot Handicraft Guide*. Random, 1971, paper.
Phillips, Mary Walker: *Step-by-Step Macramé*. Western, paper.
Shaw, George Russell: *Knots: Useful and Ornamental*. Collier, 1972, 194 pp., paper.
Strom, Nils, and Anders Enestrom: *Big-Knot Macramé*. Sterling, 48 pp.

Bookbinding

Bookbinding (No. 3378). Boy Scouts, 1969, 24 pp., paper.

Ceramics and Pottery

Andrews, Michael F.: *Sculpture and Ideas: For School and Camp Programs*. Prentice-Hall, 1965.
Hofsted, Jolyon: *Ceramics*. Golden.
Hyman, Richard: *Ceramics Handbook*. Arco, 1959, 144 pp.
Isenstein, Harald: *Creative Claywork*. Sterling, 96 pp.
Kampmann, Lothar: *Creating With Clay*. Van Nostrand, 1972, 77 pp.
Kujoth: *The Recreation Program Guide*, pp. 67–71.
Pottery (No. 3314). Boy Scouts, 1969, 64 pp., paper.
Priola, Joan B.: *Ceramics—and How to Decorate Them*. Sterling, 144 pp.
Rhodes, Daniel: *Clay and Glazes for the Potter*. Chilton, rev., 1973.
Supensky, Thomas G.: *Ceramic Art in the School Program*. Davis, 1968, 111 pp.

Carving and Whittling

Aller, Doris: *Sunset Wood Carving Book*. Lane, 1964, 95 pp.
Anderson, (H.S.) Andy: *How to Carve Characters in Wood*. U. of New Mexico, 77 pp.
Ball, A.: *Wood Carving For Fun and Profit*. Exposition.
Gottshall, Franklin: *Wood Carving and Whittling Made Easy*. Bruce, 1963, 128 pp.
Gross, Chaim: *The Technique of Wood Sculpture*. Arco, 1964, 136 pp.
Hoppe, H.: *Whittling and Woodcarving*. Sterling, 1969, 48 pp.
Hunt, W. Ben: *Ben Hunt's Big Book of Whittling*. Bruce, 1970, 182 pp.
Peterson, Harold A.: *American Knives*. Scribner's, 1958. (A history of knives)
Road, John: *Sculpture in Wood*. U. of Minn., 1950, paper.
Tangerman, E. J.: *Whittling and Woodcarving*. Dover, 1962, 293 pp., paper.
Waltner, Elma: *Carving Animal Caricatures*. Dover, 1972, paper. (Grades 7–12)
Woodcarving (No. 3315). Boy Scouts, 1966, 48 pp., paper.
Woodcraft Techniques and Projects (Sunset Editors). Lane.

Design

Ballinger, Louise Bowen, and Thomas F. Vroman: *Design: Sources and Resources*. Van Nostrand, 1965.
Guyler, Vivian Varney: *Design in Nature*. Davis, 1970, 124 pp.
Moseley, Spencer, et al.: *Crafts Design: An Illustrated Guide*. Wadsworth, 1962, 436 pp.
Wolchonok: *Design for Artists and Craftsmen*. Dover, 1953, 224 pp., paper.

Drawing and Painting

Art (No. 3320). Boy Scouts, 1968, 48 pp., paper.
Bogerad, Alan D.: *It's Fun to Draw*. Tudor, paper.
Brandt, Rex: *Watercolor Technique*. Van Nostrand, 1963, 160 pp.
Brooks, Leonard: *Oil Painting: Basic and New Techniques*. Van Nostrand, 1971, paper.
Gollwitzer, Gerhard: *Express Yourself in Drawing*. Sterling, 1960.
Guptill, A. L.: *Pencil Drawing: Step by Step*. Van Nostrand, 1959, 147 pp.
Hawkinson, John: *Collect, Print and Paint From Nature*. Whitman, 1963, 40 pp.
Hawkinson, John: *More to Collect and Paint From Nature*. Whitman, 1964, 40 pp.
Hawkinson, John: *Our Wonderful Wayside*. Whitman, 1966, 40 pp.
Hill, Adrian: *Beginner's Book of Oil Painting*. Emerson, 1959, 76 pp.
Hill, Adrian: *Beginner's Book of Watercolor Painting*. Emerson, 1959, 78 pp.
Kujoth: *The Recreation Program Guide*, pp. 106–113.
Williams, Guy R.: *Paint Now, Learn Later*. Emerson, 128 pp.

Driftwood

Ishimoto, Tatsuo: *The Art of Driftwood and Dried Arrangements*. Crown, 1951, 143 pp.
Thompson, Mary E., and Leonid Skvirsky: *The Driftwood Book*. Van Nostrand, 1966, 216 pp.

Indian Crafts

D'Amato, Janet and Alex: *Indian Crafts*. Lion, 1968, 65 pp.
Hofsinde, Robert: *Indian Games and Crafts*. Morrow, 1957, 127 pp.
Hunt, Ben, and J. F. "Buck" Burschears: *American Indian Beadwork*. Bruce, 1951, 64 pp., paper.
Hunt, Ben: *Ben Hunt's Big Indiancraft Book*. Bruce, 1969, 188 pp.
Hunt, Ben: *The Golden Book of Indian Crafts and Lore*. Golden, 1954, 112 pp.
Minor, May Nono: *The American Indian Craft Book*. Popular Library, 1972, 416 pp.
Norbeck, Oscar E.: *Indian Crafts for Campers*. Order from Galloway, rev., 1974, 260 pp.
Salomon, Julien H.: *Book of Indian Crafts and Indian Lore*. Harper & Row, 1928, 418 pp.
Seton, Julia M.: *American Indian Arts: A Way of Life*. Ronald, 1962, 246 pp.
Sides, Dorothy Smith: *Decorative Art of the Southwestern Indians*. Dover, rev., 1962, 101 pp., paper.

Turner, Alta R.: *Finger Weaving: Indian Braiding.* Sterling, 1973, 48 pp.

Whiteford, Andrew H.: *Indian Arts.* Golden, 160 pp., paper.

Leathercraft

Cherry, Raymond: *General Leathercraft.* McKnight, 4th ed., 1955, 144 pp., paper.

Ginnett, Elsie: *Make Your Own Rings: Working With Leather.* Sterling, 1974, 88 pp.

Grant, Bruce: *Leather Braiding.* Cornell Maritime, 1950.

Groneman, G.: *Leathercraft.* Bennett, 1963, 151 pp.

Kujoth: *The Recreation Program Guide,* pp. 211–224.

Leatherwork (No. 3310). Boy Scouts, 1970, 56 pp., paper.

Petersen, Grete: *Leathercrafting.* Sterling, 1973, 48 pp., paper.

Sunset Things to Make With Leather. Lane, paper.

Williams, Guy R.: *Working With Leather.* Emerson, 1967, 128 pp.

Metal Work and Jewelry Making (See Also Tincraft)

Clegg, Helen, and Mary Larom: *Jewelry Making for Fun and Profit.* McKay, 1951, 162 pp.

Ginnett, Elsie: *Make Your Own Rings and Other Things: Working With Silver.* Sterling, 1974, 88 pp.

Kramer, Karl and Nora: *Coppercraft and Silver Made at Home.* Chilton, 1959.

Maryon, H.: *Metalwork and Enameling.* Dover, 4th ed., 1971, 374 pp., paper.

Metalwork (No. 3312). Boy Scouts, 1969, 36 pp., paper.

Quick, Lelande: *Gemcraft—How to Cut and Polish Gemstones.* Chilton, 1959, 182 pp., paper.

Shoenfelt, Joseph F.: *Designing and Making Handwrought Jewelry.* McGraw-Hill, 1960, 170 pp., paper.

Untracht, Oppi: *Enameling on Metal.* Chilton, 1957, 191 pp., paper.

Zarchy,Harry: *Jewelry Making and Enameling.* Knopf, 1959, 120 pp.

Zechlin, Katharina: *Creative Enameling and Jewelry-Making.* Sterling, 1965, 100 pp.

Miscellaneous

Abell, Vivian: *Don't Throw It Away.* Meredith, 1974, 180 pp.

Alkema, Jay: *Alkema's Scrap Magic.* Sterling, 1976, 119 pp.

Bachert, Russell E., Jr.: *Outdoor Education Equipment.* Order from Galloway, 1974, 204 pp., paper.

Bale: *What On Earth.*

Benson, Kenneth R.: *Creative Crafts for Children.* Prentice-Hall, 1958, 106 pp.

Carlson, Bernice Wells: *Make It and Use It.* Abingdon, 1958, 160 pp.

Di Valentin, Maria and Louis, et al.: *Practical Encyclopedia of Crafts.* Sterling, 1973, 600 pp.

Facklam, Margery, and Patricia Phibbs: *Corn-Husk Crafts.* Sterling, 1973, 48 pp.

Family Book of Crafts. Sterling, 1973, 576 pp.

Frankel, Lillian and Godfrey: *Creating From Scrap.* Sterling, 128 pp.

Grimm, Gretchen: *Creative Adventures in Arts and Crafts.* Bruce, 1962, 96 pp.

Griswold, Lester and Kathleen: *The New Handicraft: Processes and Projects.* Burgess, 10th ed., 1969, 462 pp., paper.

Hellegers, Louisa B., and Anne E. Kallem (compilers): *The Family Book of Crafts.* Sterling, 1973, 608 pp.

Horn, George F.: *Posters: Designing, Making, Reproducing.* Davis, 1964, 96 pp.

Howie, Olive: *Handy Crafts from Scraps.* Denison, 1967, 77 pp.

Hunt, Ben: *The Golden Book of Crafts and Hobbies.* Golden, 1954, 112 pp.

Ickis, Marguerite, and Reba: *The Book of Arts and Crafts.* Dover, 1974, 276 pp.

Kampmann, Lothar: *Creating With Printed Materials.* Van Nostrand, 1969, 76 pp.

Kujoth: *The Recreation Program Guide,* pp. 44–58.

Liebers, Arthur: *Fifth Favorite Hobbies.* Hawthorn, 1968, 188 pp.

Lindbeck, John R., et al.: *Basic Crafts.* Bennett, 1969, 274 pp.

Mann: *Outdoor Education,* ch. 5.

Mattil, Edward L.: *Meaning in Crafts.* Prentice-Hall, 3rd ed., 1971, 201 pp.

Portchmouth, John: *Creative Crafts for Today.* Viking, 1970, 190 pp.

Reed, Carl, and Joseph Orze: *Art From Scrap.* Davis, 1960, 89 pp.

Reeves, Robert: *Make-It-Yourself Games Book.* Emerson, 1964, 108 pp.

Shivers, Jay S., and Clarence R. Calder: *Recreational Crafts.* McGraw-Hill, 1974, 440 pp.

Stevens, Harold: *Ways With Art: 50 Techniques for Teaching Children.* Van Nostrand, 1963, 224 pp.

Sunset Crafts for Children. Lane, 1968, 96 pp., paper.

Things to Make for Children. Lane, 1964, 96 pp.

Turner, G. Alan: *Creative Crafts for Everyone.* Order from Galloway, 263 pp.

Zarchy, Harry: *Here's Your Hobby.* Knopf, 1957, 337 pp.

Zechlin, Ruth: *Complete Book of Handicrafts.* Branford, 1968, 347 pp.

MAGAZINE ARTICLES

Camping Magazine:

Bale, Robert O.: "How Crafts Programs Can Serve Campers." May, 1962, p. 31.

Brandon, T. Edmund: "A Pioneer Theme Enhances Camp Arts and Crafts," Jan., 1975, p. 11.

Prentice, Charlotte Kramer: "Use Local Resources to Find Materials for Creative Crafts." Jan., 1973, p. 15.

Wrenn, Barbara: "Crafts At Camp." Mar., 1980, p. 34.

Mosaics

Argiro, Larry: *Mosaic Art Today.* Int'l Textbook, rev., 1968.

Timmons, Virginia Gayheart: *Designing and Making Mosaics.* Davis, 1971, 112 pp.

Unger, Hans: *Practical Mosaics.* Viking, 1965, 80 pp.

Nature Crafts

Alkema, Chester Jay: *Crafting With Nature's Materials.* Sterling, 1972, 48 pp.

Bale: *Creative Nature Crafts.* Burgess, 1959, 120 pp.

Bauzen, Peter and Suzanne: *Flower Pressing.* Sterling, 1976, 48 pp.

Benson, Kenneth R., and Carl E. Frankson: *Creative Nature Crafts.* Prentice-Hall, 1969, 97 pp.

Fiarotta, Phyllis: *Snips and Snails and Walnut Whales—Nature Crafts for Children.* Workman, 1975, 281 pp., paper.

Jaeger, Ellsworth: *Nature Crafts.* Macmillan, 1950, 128 pp.

Kujoth: *The Recreation Program Guide,* p. 66.

Linsley, Leslie: *Wildcrafts.* Doubleday, 1977, 192 pp.

Musselman, Virginia: *Learning About Nature Through Crafts.* Stackpole, 1969, 128 pp.

Nagle, Avery, and Joseph Leeming: *Fun With Naturecraft.* Lippincott, 1964, 80 pp.

Plummer, Beverly: *Earth Presents: How to Make Beautiful Gifts From Nature's Bounty.* Atheneum.

Stinson, Thelma: *Native 'N Creative.* Cokesbury, 1957, 29 pp., paper.

van der Smissen, Betty, and Oswald H. Goering: *A Leader's Guide to Nature-Oriented Activities.* Iowa State U., 1977 (3rd ed.), ch. 2.

MAGAZINE ARTICLES

Camping Magazine:

Hager, Gwen: "A Potpourri of Nature Crafts for Your Summer Use." May, 1972, p. 22.

Paper

Alkema, Chester Jay: *Creative Paper Crafts in Color.* Sterling, 1973, 168 pp.

Johnson, Pauline: *Creating With Paper.* U. of Wash., 1966, paper.

Johnston, Mary G.: *Paper Sculpture.* Davis, 1965, 82 pp.

Murray, William D., and Francis J. Rigney: *Paper Folding For Beginners.* Dover, 96 pp., paper.

Rottger, Ernst: *Creative Paper Design.* Van Nostrand, 1961, 96 pp.

Papier-Mâché

Anderson, Mildred: *Papier-Mâché and How to Use It.* Sterling, 96 pp.

Betts, Victoria Bedford: *Exploring Papier Mâché.* Davis, rev., 1966.

Johnson, Lillian: *Papier Mâché.* McKay, 1958, 88 pp.

Silk Screen

Biegeleisen, J. I., and Max A. Cohn: *Silk Screen Technique.* Dover, 1963, 187 pp., paper.

Eisenberg, James, and Francis J. Kafka: *Silk Screen Printing.* McKnight, rev., 1957, 55 pp.

Termini, Mari: *Silk Screening.* Prentice-Hall, 1978, 182 pp.

Special Techniques

Arnold, Susan Riser: *Eggshells to Objects.* Holt, Rinehart, 1979, 126 pp.

Belfer, Nancy: *Designing in Batik and Tie Dye.* Davis, 1972, 116 pp.

Conroy, Norma M.: *Making Shell Flowers.* Sterling, 1972, 48 pp.

Fletcher, Edward: *Pebble Collecting and Polishing.* Sterling, 1973, 96 pp.

Fressard, M. J.: *Creating With Burlap.* Sterling, 1970, 48 pp.

Goodman, Stuart and Leni: *Art from Shells.* Crown.

Janvier, Jacqueline: *Felt Crafting.* Sterling, 1970, 48 pp.

Krauss, Helen A.: *Shell Art.* Hearthside, 1965, 160 pp.

Kujoth: *The Recreation Program Guide,* pp. 426–430. (Woodworking)

LaCroix, Gretha: *Creating With Beads.* Sterling, 1969, 48 pp.

Leavitt, Jerome E.: *Carpentry for Children.* Sterling, 1970, 91 pp.

Lynch, John: *How to Make Collages.* Viking, 1961, 136 pp., paper.

Lynch, John: *How to Make Mobiles.* Viking, 1953, 96 pp.

McDowall, Pamela: *Pressed Flower Pictures: A Victorian Art Revived.* Scribner's, 1970, 78 pp.

Maile, Anne: *Tie and Dye.* Ballantine.

Marks, Mickey Klar: *Sand Sculpturing.* Dial, 1963, 40 pp.

Olson, David F.: *Stone Grinding and Polishing: Make Your Own Gems.* Sterling, 1974, 48 pp.

Priolo, Joan B.: *Ideas for Collage.* Sterling, 48 pp.

Saeger, Glen: *String Things You Can Make.* Sterling, 1973, 48 pp.

Schegger, T. M.: *Make Your Own Mobiles.* Sterling, 1977, 96 pp.

Van Rensselaer, Eleanor: *Decorating With Seed Mosaics, Chipped Glass and Plant Materials.* Van Nostrand, 1960, 214 pp.

Villasenor, David and Jean: *How to Do Permanent Sandpainting.* Order from ACA, 1972, 32 pp.

Williams, Guy R.: *Making Mobiles.* Emerson, 1969 94 pp.

Yates, Brock: *Plastic Foam for Arts and Crafts.* Order from Galloway, 128 pp.

Tincraft

Howard, Sylvia W.: *Tin-Can Crafting.* Sterling, 1960, 64 pp.

Jaeger: *Wildwood Wisdom.*

Mason: *The Junior Book of Camping and Woodcraft.*

Richardson, Nancy: *How to Stencil and Decorate Furniture and Tinware.* Ronald, 1956, 186 pp.

Skibness, Edward J.: *How to Use Tin Can Metal in Science Projects.* Denison, 1960, 120 pp.

Weaving

Lawless, Dorothy: *Rug Hooking and Braiding for Pleasure and Profit.* Crowell, rev., 1962, 286 pp.

Lewis, Roger: *Weaving.* Knopf, 1953, 44 pp.

Rainey, Sarita R.: *Weaving Without a Loom.* Sterling, 132 pp.

Tidball, H.: *The Weaver's Book.* Macmillan, 1961, 173 pp.

White, A. V.: *Weaving is Fun.* Dover, 1975, 154 pp., paper.

Znamieroski, Neil: *Weaving.* Golden.

Conservation Pledge

I GIVE MY
PLEDGE AS AN AMERICAN
TO SAVE AND FAITHFULLY TO
DEFEND FROM WASTE THE
NATURAL RESOURCES OF
MY COUNTRY — ITS SOIL
AND MINERALS, ITS
FORESTS, WATERS,
AND WILDLIFE

Figure 15-1 This pledge originated in a national competition conducted in 1946 by *Outdoor Life Magazine* and is reprinted through their courtesy.

NATURE COUNSELING

Learning about the out-of-doors is sometimes called nature study, ecology, conservation education, environmental education, or outdoor education. No matter what term is used, the ultimate objective should be to enable campers to think reasonably and with understanding about their environment—to see patterns of cause and effect and to relate these patterns to other aspects of their lives. No one can be taught environmental awareness; it must be experienced.

There is a tendency among new camp counselors to feel that teaching environmental activities is a complicated and scientific procedure they are ill prepared to handle. However, it is possible to develop pleasant, interesting, exciting, and worthwhile learning situations without being an expert on the subject. Outdoor education can occur by creating the proper climate for learning and need not depend upon a thorough understanding of facts and concepts.

Each counselor must, in a sense, be a nature counselor. This does not mean that you are expected to be an authority on nature lore but rather than you are interested in nature and willing to use whatever meager knowledge you may have, adding to it as you learn along with

fifteen

Nature and Ecology

The old log in the woods will never be a great tree again—things never go back—yet lying there—covered with moss—it is creating new life—which in turn will be great and beautiful. . . .

The fish eats the insect—the bird the fish—the mammal the bird—and—the insect the mammal—as each—in a universal rhythm is creating new life—for there is no life except life which comes from life. . . .

Waters flow where daisies grew—

Trees grow where swans once swam—

All things upon this earth are developing into new things—from what is here must come what is to be . . . there is no other material. . . . *

—Gwen Frostic

*Reprinted by permission of the author and publisher from Gwen Frostic "These Things Are Ours," 1960, Presscraft Papers, Benzonia, Mich., 49616.

the campers. You need not be ashamed to admit that you don't know all the answers; even specialists start out knowing absolutely nothing about their subject. Gradually, you will need to say, "I don't know, but let's find out," less and less often as you explore with the campers and consult the camp naturalist and source books.

Nature, like happiness, lurks in unexpected places, more often disclosing itself to those who are alert rather than to those who consciously seek it. A hike may end a hundred yards from the cabin when a fascinated group stays to watch a spider weave its web, or a trip to gather materials for arts and crafts may turn into a study of different woods and their uses. Who can say that these side excursions are less valuable than the original objectives?

The qualities you need most to develop a good program are curiosity, enthusiasm, and insight into the possibilities for integrating nature with other camp experiences. However, the most important quality is interest in and love of *human* nature. Don't let the program degenerate into a boring and tedious routine. Your attitude is important, so show enthusiasm and an eagerness to learn. Every undertaking should be done in a spirit of fun and adventure, although sometimes for a specific purpose such as catching minnows for bait, searching for wild strawberries or blueberries for a pie or cobbler, visiting an old lumber mill, or learning about the measures a neighboring farmer is taking to prevent erosion. A leisurely pace and a receptive attitude can turn an excursion into a perfect opportunity to answer youngsters' questions.

A trip offers a wonderful chance to acquire information about the world in which we live. What camper could fail to be interested in nontechnical information about different terrains and soils and their effect upon flora and fauna, about watersheds, rivers, drainage, currents, and water life, or about any of the other hundreds of natural subjects? When presented informally and enthusiastically, the study of ecology becomes one of the most interesting activities in camp. It should be conducted in the out-of-doors under the sun, skies, winds, and rain of nature's own laboratory whenever possible.

Such equipment as microscopes, pocket magnifying glasses, butterfly nets, binoculars, and attractive nature books can help stimulate youngsters' interests. Learning is enhanced when hands and imaginations are occupied in making equipment, arranging bulletin boards, mounting displays, and planning museums and nature trails.

CHANGING EMPHASES IN CAMP NATURE PROGRAM

A return to the simple life and its intimate contact with nature has always been a recognized purpose of camping, but the methods used have not always brought the appreciation and love of nature hoped for. Campers have victoriously displayed badges and ribbons won by learning the scientific names of 20 insects or mounting 20 flowers, and have returned to the city bearing such live pets as squirrels, turtles, grasshoppers, snakes, and even skunks to foist upon long-suffering parents or to let die of neglect and mistreatment. Only an occasional camper acquired enough interest in nature to make it a lifelong hobby, for, like human friends, plants and animals become truly cherished only after long and personal acquaintance. Learning a name or viewing a still, cold corpse impaled upon a mounting pin will never bring about such a result.

It may bolster one's ego to identify a giant dragonfly as *Epiaeschna heros,* but knowing its name is far less meaningful than knowing something about the creature. There is enchantment in watching it zoom and bank through the air, using its basketlike undercarriage of legs to scoop up flies, mosquitoes, and other insects, which it later crams into its capacious mouth. Its appetite is enormous, and it has been known to bolt down 42 flies and large quantities of its own tail, which is bent around and fed into its mouth. Its needle is only an elongated stomach, and its huge eyes have 30,000 facets, enabling it to see in all directions. These, along with its fierce expression, give it a truly sinister look, but it is helpful, not harmful, to man and does not merit its common names of devil's darning needle, horse killer, and snake feeder. Perhaps it is unfortunate that its long "darning needle" does not have its reputed power to sew up the lips of liars.

(ACA)

New Conceptions of Nature Programs

One frog in the pond is worth five in formaldehyde.*

As already indicated, a nature program should not be conducted in a bookish, school-like manner with formal methods and highly technical terms. Instead, it should have a niche in many camp activities and make use of teachable moments as they arise and capitalize on a youngster's curiosity and desire to know the how, why, where, when, and what of anything. When you can't answer a question, your response may well be, "I don't know, but let's see if we can find out."

A group should seldom be in too big a hurry to stop and watch the antics of a venturesome squirrel or listen to a noisy blue jay. Instead of acquiring knowledge in order to pass tests or to pose as a walking encyclopedia, campers learn through hands-on experiences using techniques of inquiry, discovery, problem solving, and personal observation. In so doing, they develop a genuine feeling for nature as it seeps in pleasantly and unconsciously through all of their senses, including sight, sound, smell, touch, and even taste to discover the natural world. Van Matre terms such a feeling for the environment

*van der Smissen, Betty, and Goering, Oswald H.: *A Leader's Guide to Nature-Oriented Activities.* Iowa State University Press, 1965, p. 8. By permission.

*acclimatization.** Specimens are not the smelly laboratory variety nor the foreign imports of zoo and circus but what the campers find as they venture forth to look at whatever lies beside the path, under rocks or old logs, in trees, or at the bottom of a creek or pond. How much more interesting nature's creatures are as we see them carrying on their normal activities in their natural habitats. With the aid of such inexpensive pieces of equipment as a homemade butterfly or dip net and a little pocket microscope, the field of exploration is unlimited.

A night of restless slumber under a quaking aspen creates a real interest in noting how the flat, wide stem is set "on edge" against the broad leaf so that the least breeze keeps it stirring to produce the very disturbing rainlike patter of the previous night. Like opportunity, nature experiences often knock but once, and each should be seized upon when it appears. We cannot schedule happenings for a definite time and place, for Mother Earth's children are too busy carrying on their daily activities to be amenable to man-made schedules. Let us not emulate the poor misguided nature counselor who said, "Now, children, come away from that porpoise washed up there on the beach! Remember, we're studying birds today, and we won't get around to porpoises until two weeks from Tuesday."

A child's feeling of confidence and security in the out-of-doors increases as he or she becomes familiar with it and learns that most wild creatures are timid and that they will not harm anyone unless surprised, teased, cornered, or frightened. A healthy respect and love for all living things should always be maintained and they should never be killed for the fun of it or because of our intrusion on their territory.

In the camp program, information secured through firsthand observation is usually better than learning from books. Yet, a well-selected supply of nature books serves as a useful tool in a good camp program. First should come an assortment of handbooks on all topics, each small and light enough to be slipped into a pocket or knapsack and used for identification on the trail. When divided among the members of a group, they do not prove a burden to anyone. Back in camp, all sorts of pamphlets and larger resource books should be available. They should be well illustrated, preferably in color, and complete enough to give full information as well as interesting anecdotes about what has been seen. Bulletin boards, pictures, slides, film strips, photographs, and movies are valuable supplements.

*Van Matre, Steve: *Acclimatization.* ACA, 1972, p. 10.

Ecological and Conservation Approaches

The dictionary defines *ecology* as "that branch of zoology which deals with the relationship of living things to their environment and to each other." This, of course, includes humans. In the camp setting there is much that we can observe about ecological relationships when we start with the principle that every living organism is related to other organisms (plants and animals) and the basic substances (sunlight, air, water, and soil) in its environment. This concept proves fascinating as one notes how the individual members of a nature community interact to further the welfare of the whole just as is done by the members of a human community. Information about this subject is available from many sources such as Storer: *The Web of Life,* which is listed in the bibliography at the end of this chapter.

We all know more than we think we do about living organisms, so we can recognize their role in ecology by asking some questions about interrelationships. In order to better understand the use of the inquiry technique as a learning tool for campers, consider this example using the beaver. Such questions may be asked as what is the beaver's role in nature? Where is the beaver's home? What organisms and substances in its environment does the beaver depend upon for survival? How does it use these organisms and substances? How does the beaver affect other organisms and substances? What organisms and substances in this environment depend upon the beaver? How do these organisms and substances use it? How do other organisms and substances affect the beaver? Where does the beaver fit into the food cycle in its environment? How does the beaver reproduce? (Sexually or asexually?) How may the beaver be affected by climatic conditions? What adaptations has the beaver developed to suit itself to this environment?

(Evergreen Section of ACA)

By now you should begin to see that a variety of interrelationships that occur in nature can be revealed if you ask general questions about the plants and animals with which you are familiar. Even very young children are capable of perceiving meaningful answers to similar problems. Life histories also are interesting and useful in learning about the environment. How does an oak tree start? What determines where trees will grow? Where and how does a young sapling get the food to nourish itself? What are its enemies, and how do they harm it? What defense does it have against them? Do other members of the bird or animal world help? For what does it furnish food and shelter? Of what use are oak trees to us?

Ultimately, all living things are dependent upon plants, for every animal, including man, either dines directly upon some form of plant life or upon some other animal that in the final analysis, does so. Each is simultaneously engaged in a struggle to secure its own food and to avoid becoming the food of another. Each has its own means of securing food, some of them unique and interesting. The opposite leaves of the teasel are joined into a small cup at the stem, that catches water to drown minute ants for its banquet dish. The rare Venus' flytrap has a hair-trigger mechanism that causes the sharp teeth along the edges of its leaves to interlock instantly and trap any insect unlucky enough to merely brush against them.

Everything has a way of protecting itself. Deer can outrun most of their enemies, and cats climb trees to evade dogs. Porcupines pursue their leisurely way, secure in the knowledge that their barbed quills will deter most attackers. Nature has given skunks the power to exact a fiendish revenge on whatever frightens or attacks them. The chameleon changes color, the rabbit "freezes," the rosebush has thorns, and the thistle has prickles to help protect it against its enemies. Camouflage also provides an effective means of protection.

Nature provides each variety of life in abundance, so that, though some may become food or succumb to disease, wind, flood, or unfavorable climatic conditions, there always will be enough left to carry on the species. The female frog lays 20,000 eggs, but only 200 develop into adult frogs, while the other 19,800 lose their lives by accident or become food for fish and water insects. Nature, if left to her own devices, usually will keep all species in balance so that they neither die out nor become so numerous as to overrun the earth, and every single form of life has its own role in maintaining this equilibrium, which is called the *balance of nature.*

Enough birdlings are created to spare a few for the snake, just as enough lettuce and green beans grow to supply our needs. We must erase from our minds once and for all the idea that certain forms of life are more worthy than others, for our previous efforts to kill out what we

(Evergreen Section of ACA)

considered to be unworthy species sometimes backfired in a most unfortunate way. A concentrated drive to eradicate "chicken-killing" hawks, for instance, may bring about a huge oversupply of rats, mice, snakes, and frogs, which really constitute over 90 percent of the hawks' diet in contrast to the occasional chicken that they might eat.

Almost everything we do affects plant or animal life in some way. Picking berries in the fall cuts down on the supply of winter food for some bird or animal as well as the number of seeds that might sprout and grow into new plants. Squirrels lose out when we gather nuts. Draining a swamp to provide more farm land kills thousands of plants and animals that cannot survive without a wet environment. Spraying trees kills the insects and grubs that provide food for certain birds, and it may leave residues harmful to bird and animal life, including people. Killing squirrels will eventually mean fewer trees, for dead squirrels cannot bury nuts to sprout and grow into future forests.

Trappers, in their greediness to sell beaver pelts, thinned out these little animals until no more beaver dams were built in certain areas. When hard rains came, water rushed down the open streams, causing floods that destroyed both property and life; between rains, the creek beds dried out so that water life could not survive, and land animals went thirsty.

Humans have used the rivers as garbage tanks and open sewers and as drains for the various chemicals and waste products of manufacturing; as a result, they are no longer fit for swimming, and even plant and fish life often cannot survive in them.

Humans have cut down the trees and shrubs and cleared the fence rows that used to provide food and shelter for animals and birds. People have shot and trapped so many animals for food, furs, or sport that some, such as the buffalo and grizzly bear, are scarce, and others, including the great auk and passenger pigeon, are extinct.

> *Conservation* is the appreciation, understanding, and wise use of natural resources for the greatest good for the most people for the longest time.*

Forest preserves, mandatory hunting and fishing licenses, open and closed seasons, bag limits, and the nurturing and "planting" of young birds, fish, animals, and trees are feeble strides toward preservation of what little remains of our once great heritage, but the understanding and loyal support of millions are necessary to make our efforts effective. Camp provides an ideal climate for instilling in young people an appreciation of ecology and a deep love and appreciation for all nature's wildlife. These campers will go home to cooperate in an all-out effort to protect what we have left of our natural environment for future generations. After all, they are the voters of tomorrow and will determine the policies of the future.

One of man's most myopic perspectives has been in regard to conservation of the soil, upon which all plant and animal life depends. Topsoil, a mixture of minerals and the decaying remnants of animals and plants, is admirably suited for plant growth. It lies above the nonfertile subsoil and varies from a depth of a few inches on hilltops to several feet in the valleys.

**You and Conservation*, ACA.

When our ancestors came to America, they were delighted with the rich topsoil produced by many years of undisturbed natural processes. They hastened to clear the land to plant crops, but after several years of repeatedly planting the same crop with no efforts made to replenish what was taken from the soil, the land became less and less productive. This concerned them little, however, for so much new land was available that they simply moved on to repeat the process in a new spot. Progressive farmers now plant crops in rotation so that one crop can partially restore what the other depleted, and they judiciously apply fertilizers and other top dressings to keep their topsoil in good condition.

Vegetation keeps soil porous and loose, enabling it to absorb and hold large quantities of water, which is gradually absorbed by the plants and returned to the air by evaporation. Without plant growth, rains quickly run off down sloping surfaces, forming ever-enlarging gullies and carrying away large quantities of topsoil. When the farmer plows straight up and down the hillsides, wastage increases. To avoid this problem, the careful farmer uses contour plowing. However, every year 25,000,000 cubic feet of our richest topsoil is washed away and eternally lost for cultivation. This is not a cheering picture, when we stop to think that from 500 to 1,000 years are required to create a depth of one inch of fertile topsoil. Rapidly draining slopes cause swollen streams and eventually floods, which carry away still more topsoil and destroy the plant and animal life along the banks.

Topsoil in dry areas, without roots of vegetation to hold it in place, blows away as dust, leaving behind whole areas of infertile and desolate dust bowls. Some ill-informed farmers still burn off their land each year in a misguided attempt to kill off weeds and get the ground "ready" for spring crops, but this practice actually does irreparable damage to their precious topsoil.

Testing of the soil and supplying needed chemicals, rotation of crops, planting of cover crops to hold moisture and prevent erosion, and use of terraced and contour plowing on hillside areas are valuable steps in soil conservation.

True conservation is based upon an appreciation of the value of each living thing in maintaining the balance of the whole. It tells us that it is prudent to use the surplus that nature lavishly supplies but that we must always carefully leave enough of everything to insure its continuance for our own future use and that of coming generations. We may liken this to an investment at the bank, where the interest always continues to accumulate as long as we leave the principal intact. When we, in our infinite shortsightedness, set ourselves up to decide which varieties of life are worthy to continue, we are likely to upset nature's nicely poised balance in ways difficult to foresee. It is much wiser to take the attitude that any wanton destruction of wild life is extremely undesirable.

Conservation Begins at Home

One of the best ways to familiarize campers with nature and good conservation practices is to involve them in projects of their own choosing to improve the camp or a nearby area. This helps to develop in them a sense of proprietorship about the land so that each feels a glow of accomplishment when he or she has helped to do something to improve it. Be sure to discuss any plans with your camp director before going ahead. It is also wise to confer with such experts as the camp caretaker, county agent, conservation officer, park superintendent, or forester, since ill-advised efforts by amateurs sometimes do more harm than good. Here are some possible ideas for conservation projects:

1. Take your group on a tour of the camp, noting spots that show the results of violations of good conservation practices. Make a list of what needs to be done and arrange it in the order of priority. Let each group decide which, if any,it would like to undertake. Involve your campers in all proceedings; remember, do *with*, not *for*, them; their eager minds and willing hands are capable of great accomplishments.

2. Make a bird and animal sanctuary and seek ways to further their welfare and safety. Provide a source of fresh water and plant shade, fruit, or nut trees, berry bushes, sunflower seed, commercial bird seed, sweet corn, beans and other vegetables, small grain, and so forth. Make brush piles and plant shrubbery and other forms of cover along fencerows, camp roads, and wagon trails.

3. Make and erect birdhouses; you may get occupants this summer, or at least they will be ready for next year's nesting. Short bits of string

and cord are appreciated at nesting time. Suspend a hummingbird feeder (they can be purchased commercially) and fill it with a 50-50 solution of sugar and water with a bit of food coloring added; you'll enjoy their grace and beauty while feeding. Attract birds and other creatures that eat mosquitoes; this is preferable to using poisonous sprays, which kill helpful insects.

4. Make a bird center near camp and where there is ample foliage to provide hiding places. Keep bird baths and food handy. Construct a bird blind to hide behind to give you a better look at birds. If the light is right, take photographs. Groups can adopt a bird family as their own to watch through the summer.

5. Help forest development by thinning out places where trees are too thick for any to grow well. Weed out those that are less desirable or are crooked or diseased. Prune off dead or diseased limbs, painting over the wounds (green or black blend in nicely) to prevent sap from bleeding and to keep diseases and insects out. Clear out any brush or vines that are choking young trees. Remember that it is sometimes wise to let dead trees stand. They furnish homes and nests for certain birds and animals and will eventually rot away, returning their substance to enrich the soil as nature intended.

6. Promote a Conservation, Anti-Litter, Earth, or Ecology Day with appropriate posters, films, slides, filmstrips, pamphlets, and books, and bring in outside resource personnel. Plan special projects to carry out.

7. Hold a scavenger hunt, awarding varying points for bringing in such unwanted debris as pieces of glass, bottles, bits of loose paper (we hope, not left by camp personnel, who should always use waste cans and keep their camp ground so neat that periodic clean-up crusades are unnecessary). Make a wire enclosure to display the haul, and recycle when possible.

8. Volunteer for community service in cleaning up adjoining roads, a public beach, or park, always, of course, under the direction of those in charge.

9. Clean up the banks of a lake or other body of water and improve living conditions for its surrounding wildlife. If erosion is taking place, it is carrying away topsoil, which makes the water muddy, unpleasant, and uninhabitable for fish and other water life. Take steps to stop the erosion by filling in gullies, planting brush and other cover along the shore, and building conversion dams and canals to distribute the water over the area.

10. If trails begin to show signs of wearing through or becoming impacted, repair them as described above. Trails that go up steep slopes should have switchbacks or zigzags to prevent erosion. To prevent unthinking individuals from cutting corners or walking outside the designated track, post signs such as "Stop! Your feet are killing me." Better yet, make "Stay on the Path" your camp motto to avoid careless destruction of outside tender vegetation. Campers may also want to outline main paths with small rocks.

11. Let each child or unit plant its own bed of tree "seeds," such as acorns, nuts, maple wings, or fruit pits, watering and caring for it and watching the tiny treelets sprout and grow. In future summers, other campers can transplant seedlings to permanent homes.

12. Small trees and shrubs, if taken with plenty of dirt, can be transplanted at almost any season of the year. Water them well weekly until the roots have had time to become well established. Spare trees can sometimes be found where not needed on the campsite; they may be purchased from nurseries; or they are often available free or at nominal cost from state and federal nurseries. Plan your own Arbor Day as an annual event, with an appropriate dedication ceremony. Each child can mark the planting by use of a stake with his or her name on it. Campers will be proud to watch their trees grow, especially if they come back in succeeding summers.

13. Stress good principles of conservation, such as cutting no living trees unless absolutely necessary (the same toasting sticks and lug poles will serve repeatedly) and choosing wisely when you cut. If you build wood fires, prepare safe fire sites and put out fires completely. Seriously consider using stoves instead of wood fires. Choose materials for arts and crafts judiciously, and use sparingly. Avoid ditching tents. Replace all sod removed and leave a trip campsite in better condition than you found it.

14. Plant or transplant materials for future use in arts and crafts projects (grow your own).

15. Organize camp and unit Fire Brigades, using older campers especially. Ask your local conservation agent or other official to help you

set it up and to pick out those areas in camp that are especially hazardous. Set up fire stations in strategic locations that are equipped with axes, shovels, stirrup pumps, buckets, and fire brooms. See that staff and campers know where fire stations are and how to use them. See that everyone in camp knows exactly what to do in case of fire. Hold frequent fire drills at unexpected times and when campers are in various locations.

16. At appropriate times discuss what conservation progress is being made on a local, state, and national level. What still needs to be done? What regulatory laws exist, and how do they help? Who is harmed when regulations are not followed? How are conservation efforts financed? How can each camper contribute in camp and in his or her own home community?

17. Improve pond and stream habitats and then restock your fishing area. Ask for help and advice from your state hatchery or other sources. Don't take fish you won't use, and return little ones to the water unharmed.

18. Study the helpful roles played by commonly despised creatures such as bats, ants, skunks, worms, spiders, snakes, bees, wasps and the like. Since all of them play an important role in nature's master plan, coming to understand them will help to develop a tolerant attitude toward them.

19. Discuss the harm done by indiscriminate weed spraying (killing off *all* growth, and so on). Sprays that kill flies and mosquitoes also kill off other insects. Use good practices in camp.

20. Collect in a glass jar water from a spot where erosion is taking place. Let it sit for 24 hours, and note the good topsoil that it carried.

21. Take a wildlife census of the camp with groups or individuals designated to watch for certain varieties, such as birds, insects, butterflies, animals, and snakes. Post colored pictures to help in identification. Keep a scrapbook or use a file card for each type seen, noting name, date, place spotted, occupation when seen, and the name of the spotter. Detailed information and photographs or colored pictures can be added.

22. Make a compost pile at some distance from the main camp, placing on it grass cuttings, excess leaves, vegetable parings, and the like. Place some lime between each layer to hasten disintegration, and add fertilizer if you wish. Keep it damp, and stir it up occasionally. This provides excellent humus to mix with soil in the camp garden or other area where you want luxuriant growth to occur. A border of trees and shrubbery planted around your compost pile will make it less conspicuous.

23. Have your group determine in what ways the camp and campers use natural re-

(Edwards Y.M.C.A., East Troy, Wis.; courtesy of ACA)

sources unnecessarily (gasoline, water, paper, electricity, etc.)? What can they as individuals and as a group do to stop this waste?

24. Consider the environmental effect of some camp activities such as campfire rings, cookouts, games and sports, trips, fishing, arts and crafts, and hiking. Do you need to change any procedures?

25. Set up and operate a camp weather station.

SENSORY AWARENESS ACTIVITIES

Having campers refine the use of their five basic senses (taste, smell, touch, sight and sound) to the greatest extent possible can help them develop a greater appreciation and understanding of nature and become more aware of their physical environment. Native American Indians developed their senses to a degree seldom seen today, for their livelihood and even their lives depended upon it. They were instantly aware of anything unusual in their surroundings—a new smell, a new sound, a broken twig, crushed blades of grass, animal droppings, or a track or claw mark in mud or soft ground. It is only through a long period of training and experience that we can hope to emulate them, although there are a number of activities and experiences that can be done in a camp setting that furnish shortcuts to improving sensory awareness.

SIGHT. Although we may pass a vision test with a 20/20 rating, we might be perfectly oblivious to many things we should see in the out-of-doors. To illustrate just what is possible, have your campers stand or sit quietly in the woods in order to concentrate upon the trees around them. How do they vary in size, shape, limb arrangement, and leaf structure? How many can they identify? Do any show signs of disease or pests? Are there birds' nests or signs of animal homes? You might also have the campers lie on their backs looking up with their feet pressed against the base of a tree as spokes in a wheel (perhaps they could pretend to be limbs or roots of the tree). From this location they can gain yet a new and different perspective of the natural world.

Next, to help campers understand the importance of all components in the environment and the interrelationships that exist, you might have them look closely at the miniature world of a fallen tree. If we look very closely, we will see that it is a tiny community in itself since everything living has a home. What can be seen living here? What do each of those things give to their community?

An interesting variation of this activity involves having each camper use a string, four metres long, to form a circle on the ground. Have each person observe the enclosed area carefully and make a list of everything seen in a given time (pebbles, insects, vegetation, movement, soil texture, a feather, leaf, and so forth). Try the same project in different types of terrain. This fact-gathering activity can provide excellent training in both observation and recording information. It also can provide you with the opportunity to focus the groups' attention on one portion of the environment at a time and in a challenging fashion.

Go slowly along the trail and have campers look for signs of other inhabitants. Carefully turn over a rock to show what is underneath it; be sure to replace it in order to avoid disturbing the natural environment.

Other activities for consideration can be found under *Nature Games* in the last section of this chapter.

SMELL. In order to improve your campers awareness of smell, have them take a deep breath; what odors can they detect? How does the smell of a swamp, bog, or pine forest differ from that of the city? Why? As your group walks along a trail, have them note any change in odors and try to find out what causes them. Many animals have a much keener sense of smell than we do and thus detect our presence long before we are even in their sight. For this reason, you will need to keep an animal downwind when trying to approach it.

Select some familiar substances such as moss, a wild onion and a crushed mint leaf and pass them along in front of a blindfolded person to see how many he or she can identify. Does smell have anything to do with the fact that food is tasteless to someone with a bad cold?

TASTE. Beware of indiscriminately tasting things with which you are unfamiliar, but have campers try out such items as a leaf of wintergreen, an Indian turnip, and other substances that you know to be harmless.

TOUCH. Encourage campers to feel the texture of a great many things and note the differences. Try this with a circle of blindfolded persons to see how many "mystery objects" collected from outdoors each can identify. With the loss of sight one becomes more aware of the sense of touch.

Blindfold the members of your group and direct them to put their left hand on the shoulder of the person in front of them. Follow a trail around the area, stopping to touch any objects within reach. Ask individuals to express three different words about what they feel. (Note: This same activity can be repeated with smelling, listening, and tasting.)

HEARING. In order to help campers become more aware of the sounds around them, have them sit down, close their eyes, and really listen. They should make a mental note of everything they hear in a period of five minutes and then have them compare their perceptions with one another. How many noises or sounds can they identify? Can they locate the source?

This type of activity can be performed at various times of the day and night in order to bring into focus the changes in frequency, pitch, and intensity of sounds in the natural environment. Campers might notice a calmness near twilight or dawn or the variety of sounds from different forms of wildlife that communicate during the day in comparison to the evening. Many birds and animals can communicate with each other to convey feelings, such as contentment, anger, and fear and to give mating calls or warnings of danger. Have your group try to learn some of these.

TRACKING, STALKING, AND VIEWING WILDLIFE

Patience and the ability to glide silently along a path or remain still for long periods of time are essential for meaningful nature viewing. When tracking, stalking, or viewing wildlife it is usually best to keep the group small (three to eight) and travel slowly and quietly. The leader should work out signals such as a finger on the lips for "freeze where you are" or a beckoning hand for "come closer." Individuals should stay at least a yard apart on the trail and move slowly. The best time depends somewhat upon the weather and other factors, but in general most birds and animals tend to be most active and out searching for food during the early morning hours and just before dusk, preferring to seek shade and a secluded spot to rest during the hot part of the day.

A quiet wait near a body of water is often rewarded, since nearly every creature seeks water at customary times once or twice a day. As your group approaches a vantage point, you can be sure that almost every living thing is aware of your coming, since their senses are so superior to ours. Have the campers make themselves comfortable, lying down or sitting on a convenient stump or rock. You may even want to construct a natural-looking blind, tree house, or observation tower, complete with mosquito netting, for closer watching and better photography. Be prepared to wait at least 15 to 30 minutes to give wildlife time to resume activity.

Night Trips

Night trips furnish an interesting variation, since the viewer will find an entirely different type of life out hunting for its supper. A revealing way to start out is simply to sit quietly outside your cabin door. Then you can progress to careful trips along the trail, made less conspicuous by wearing dark clothing and streaking your face with charcoal (it is easy to wash off). Move quietly and smoothly, pausing now and then to listen, smell, and look. Ordinarily, you will not need a flashlight, for the stars give enough illumination even on a moonless night. However, few creatures will notice your flashlight if you cover the end of it with piece of lightweight red cloth, plastic, or crepe paper. Allow at least 45 minutes for your eyes to become accustomed to the darkness.

How to Track and Stalk

It is great fun to trail an animal through woods or fields and, if the trail is fresh, you may be able to creep up close to watch it. Your group will need to be skilled to follow tracks, so start out by studying tracks along a sandy beach or the edge of a river or lake where they are easy to

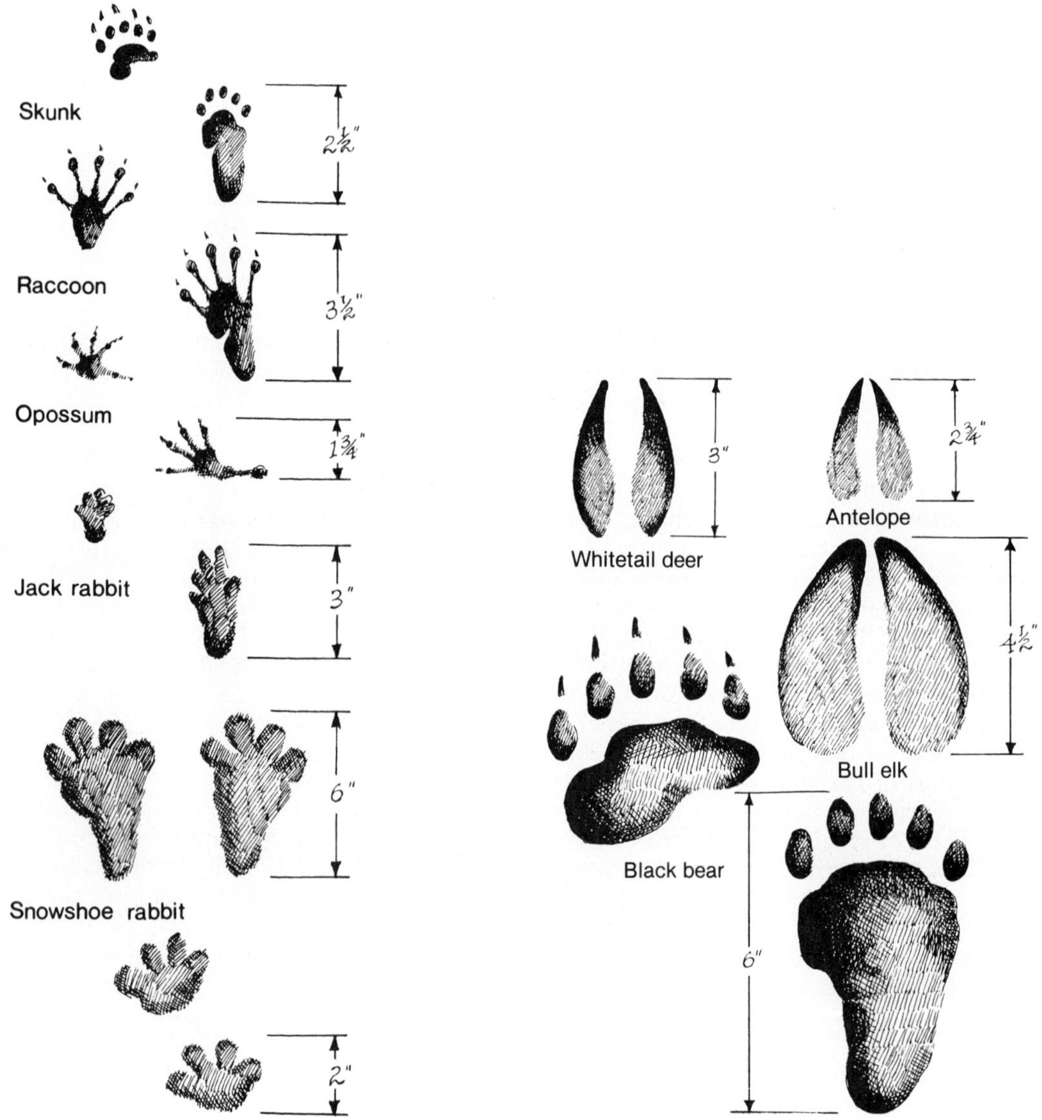

Figure 15–2 Animal tracks.

see. Learn to distinguish whether the animal was walking or running and try to estimate how fresh the tracks are; those newly made will have sharp edges and no debris will have yet blown into them. Campers can learn to identify tracks found in Figure 15–2, or from some of the good source books available.

Glance ahead for such traces as droppings, bits of hair left on bushes, signs of feeding, or places where branches were displaced or the undersides of leaves turned upward. This lets you follow more rapidly and provides a better chance of catching up with your quarry. If you lose the trail, mark the last spot of identification and investigate in ever widening spirals until you pick it up again.

Getting near an animal without letting it become aware of you is called *stalking*, and it requires a great deal of ingenuity and skill, for animals have very highly developed senses of smell and hearing (and sometimes sight) and will quickly flee at the smallest sign of an intruder. Avoid stepping on dry twigs that may snap like the crack of a rifle and be ready to "freeze" if the animal looks your way. When walking on grass you should step toe first, but step heel first on hard ground.

It often helps to have your group proceed with their backs to the sun so colors will show up more brightly. Your group may want to camouflage itself in order to blend in with the surrounding terrain. Avoid bright colors and belt buckles or other metal that might reflect light. Your faces can be concealed with masks of green branches. Since most animals have a keen sense of smell, approach them by moving into the wind, even though it may force you to make a full half-circle.

Conceal yourselves behind such natural hiding places as bushes, large rocks, and trees. Stay low to avoid being silhouetted against the sky; stoop down, go on all fours, or even wriggle along on your stomach if necessary. Quick movements draw attention so avoid them unless you are sure the animal is looking in another direction. Wild animals must maintain a constant watch for their natural enemies since their lives depend on it; hence, through instinct and practice they have developed an uncanny wariness and ability to detect the unusual. Your group will need infinite patience and skill to study wildlife intimately and for good close-up photographs, but it will be well worth the effort.

COLLECTING

Though making collections still has its place, it does not occupy the pinnacle it once did. One reason is that previous collectors, in their zeal to get "just one more specimen," all but annihilated some of our rarer species of flora. Before picking a flower or other specimen, apply good principles of conservation by being sure that there are ample quantities left to carry on the species.

Collections also sometimes become ends in themselves, with the collector heaving a satisfied sigh each time he or she has corralled another specimen, fastened it on paper, and labeled it with a polysyllabic title. The person may neither know nor care anything about Exhibit X beyond having a mere nodding acquaintance with its name. This sort of collecting becomes busy work, contributing nothing whatsoever toward furthering a real love of nature.

When properly regarded, collections of rocks, minerals, flowers, leaves, seeds, insects, shells, ferns, mosses, and the like add to a nature program. Usually collecting is best done as a group project rather than as an individual effort. Each mounting can be accompanied with the item's name, place found, and any data concerning its life or place in the balance of nature or its commercial value, if any.

Reproducing specimens by painting, sketching, or photographing them rather than collecting them is every bit as meaningful and more in accordance with good conservation practices, since it leaves the specimen intact.

> Take nothing but pictures; leave nothing but footprints.
>
> —Wilderness Society, *Off on the Right Foot*

Useful Plants

Samples of medicinal plants can be collected and labeled by their names and uses. It is also interesting to gather and supplement a meal with wild foods, but be sure to get expert help to avoid eating something harmful or poisonous and be sure the food sources are in proper abundance before taking them. Consult listings in the Additional Readings section on "Wild Foods" in Chapter 27 for help.

Pressing Plants

It is easy to make a press to prepare leaves, ferns, and flowers for mounting. A 10- by 12-inch press will meet ordinary needs and should be constructed so as to simultaneously dry and flatten specimens. Two pieces of board, approximately 10 by 12 inches and about ½ inch thick, are needed for the outside covers. Cut a dozen or more sheets of blotting paper (or newspaper) and half as many sheets of corrugated cardboard from packing boxes to fit, and complete the outfit with two web or leather straps.

Place each plant between sheets of blotting

(Willamette Council of Camp Fire, Salem, Oreg.)

paper and separate from the others by a sheet of corrugated paper. Place the covers on the top and bottom, draw the straps tight, and leave for several days while the plants dry and flatten. If desired, a weight can be placed on top of the press. Beware of picking rare specimens or large quantities of even the plentiful; a hundred campers make a serious inroad if each picks only one leaf.

Keeping Wild Things in Camp

A fernery or wild flower garden, an insect cage, an aquarium for water life, or a terrarium for things that live on land may be made if you know how to care for them properly.

Even though your state may be one of the few in which it is not illegal to keep wild animals in captivity, it is usually much wiser not to do so. Many of them die from fright and lack of proper food and care, and those successfully kept for some time lose their ability to fend for themselves when turned loose. Many wild parents such as deer, rabbits, and even birds will not accept their young if they detect human odor upon them. Often seemingly deserted babies have only been left temporarily while their parents go out searching for food. It is much better to leave them in the wilds as nature intended and watch them in their normal pursuits.

MAKING A NATURE TRAIL

Laying Out the Trail

Laying out a nature trail teaches much to those who do it and also provides an educational experience for other campers and incoming visitors. It may be the undertaking of a single unit, or the whole camp may cooperate on various phases of it. A trail about one-half to a mile long, arranged as a loop or figure-of-eight, takes about an hour to wander through and brings the traveler back to the starting point without having to retrace steps. Short side trails or spurs can be indicated to show interesting sights, such as an unusually large tree or a deserted bee's nest. Ideally, it should go through several varieties of terrain (woods, meadow, streams, marshland, ponds, and brushy areas) to show differences in flora and fauna.

A winding trail is more interesting than a straight one and it should be cleared just enough to permit passage single file in order to avoid destroying more wild growth than is necessary. Some advocate putting wood chips on camp paths because chips improve the footing and eventually disintegrate to enrich the soil. Lay flat stones or build a "corduroy road" of sticks across damp places and build rustic bridges across streams. Zigzag up and down slopes to avoid causing erosion.

Labeling

A nature trail provides opportunities for self-conducted tours using signs or labels instead of a human guide. Pick out the things you want to show along the way and ask for volunteers to look up information about them. Although each situation varies, 15 to 18 features are about the right number for a half-mile trail. A committee can select what is to be told and exactly how it is to be said. In general, brevity should be the keyword, for few will take the time to read long messages. If more information seems desirable, put the most pertinent first.

Relate your message in everyday language, and use bits of information with human interest quality, little poems, and touches of humor. Invite people to touch, taste, smell, or listen, as the characteristics of the specimen dictate. Point out relationships, telling why this environment is particularly appropriate for the subject. Ask a provocative question on one side of a card, which the reader must turn over to find the answer. Add a colored picture, arrows, or cues in puzzle form to help the hiker find what he or she is looking for. Strategically placed bulletin boards and a bench for campers to rest on are also worthwhile. Another project may be to prepare printed trail guides that contain a map and numbers that correspond to numbered stakes along the trail. The numbered keys on the map should include written information about the specific location identified. Copies of the guide can be given to each person starting out on the trail.

Changes will be in order as the summer progresses and new flowers or other seasonal changes appear. Let a maintenance committee take care of changes as well as insure that the trail is kept in good condition.

Never nail labels to trees. Instead, use numbered or labeled stakes or fasten signs to ropes or wire between trees. Tie ropes or wires loosely about the tree so that they won't cut into the bark. Temporary labels can be made to last through a summer by printing them with India ink on filing cards or pieces of poster board and painting both sides with two or three coats of clear shellac or varnish. For more permanent signs, use paint or enamel in contrasting colors on pieces of wood or metal, again protecting them with coats of clear shellac or varnish.

NATURE MUSEUMS

Camp museums may be located in the nature house, under a tree near camp, or along a nature trail. Use them to display such camper activities as a nature bulletin board, mounted specimens, indigenous arts and crafts projects, trail maps, writings about nature topics, papier-mâché relief maps, live pets, weather predictions and equipment, knot display boards, friction sets made from camp materials, mats and baskets woven of native materials, and articles fashioned from local clay.

The nature house should be supplied with guide books, displays, tools, storage facilities, and working space at tables. Campers should plan and maintain all exhibits themselves, keeping an eye out for new and different materials. Maintain a "What Is It?" shelf or corner for unidentified curios, placing the name of the person who first correctly identifies it in a place of honor on the bulletin board. Change the display frequently so that campers do not pass it by because "it's just the same old thing."

BIRDS*

Bird study is one of the most popular nature activities. The following projects for conducting such a study are suggested as suitable for camps.

Birdwalks—best in early morning or late evening, when the birds are most active. Learn to identify by nest, color, sound, and manner of flight.

Collect feathers. Collect old nests (no birds except hawks use them a second time) and dissect them to see what materials were used in their construction. Place modeled eggs painted the proper colors in whole nests and display them on branches arranged to resemble trees.

Contrast the bills and feet of birds to see how they are adapted to their diet and habits. Listen to the bird's song and watch its pattern of flight.

Make a bird scrapbook of pictures, stories, anecdotes, and poems.

Make plaster casts of tracks in mud or at the beach.

Construct a bird sanctuary somewhere near camp with protective cover and other items to attract birds and provide a bulletin board with identifying pictures. Construct bird houses and hang them in the area to increase the bird population from year to year. A nearby blind to hide behind helps watchers see more action.

*Write to the National Audubon Society, 1130 Fifth Avenue, New York, N.Y. 10028, for information about the Audubon Junior Clubs for Summer Camps.

PLANTS

Following below are useful camp projects that focus on plants.

Make a wild flower garden or fernery. (Ferns and wild flowers will grow only with soil and other conditions similar to those of their natural habitat.)

Draw or paint pictures of wild flowers, adding name, date, where found, and such information as native country, seeds and their dispersal, pollination, and uses (medicinal, dyes and so on). In mounting specimens, use small pieces of Scotch tape or dip the specimens in a mixture of glue and vinegar spread evenly on glass, and transfer them to heavy paper.

Study seeds and their dispersal by barbs, parachutes, wind, animals, and other means. Collect seeds and keep them for making a wild flower garden. Glue some specimens on mounting boards and label them.

Make a plant gall collection.

Study lichens, mosses, and ferns. Look at them through a microscope.

Identify nut-bearing bushes and trees. Learn when the nuts ripen and what animals eat them.

Study flower arrangement for indoor decoration.

Identify poison ivy, poison oak, and poison sumac.

Identify different types of mushrooms, particularly the morels, which are safe to eat. Do not trust other kinds, for even experts have difficulty in distinguishing the poisonous ones.

Which flowers open at different times of the day? Could you devise a flower clock?

TREES

Identify trees by contour, color, leaf, bark, flower, seed, and wood structure. Help campers learn all they can about them: what they are used for, how they burn, and so on.

Press and mount leaves, using methods suggested for flowers.

Photograph trees; make sketches or watercolors of them.

Learn how individual trees serve for shade, beauty, soil conservation, firewood, or commercial products. Do you realize that a single large tree in full leaf during summer furnishes moisture to the air and has the cooling effect of ten room-sized air conditioners operating 20 hours a day? They also serve as windbreaks, and they cushion noise, provide protection for birds and animals, and convert carbon dioxide to oxygen for us to breathe. Learn about their early uses by the Indians and pioneers. Identify the kinds found in camp furniture, walls, and so forth.

Study stumps to learn the life history of the tree, such as its age, injuries, insect damage, favorable and unfavorable seasons, and the like.

Learn the uses of different kinds of woods in fire-building (tinder, kindling, heat, light, fire dogs, and others). Which ones are best for whittling? Notice how the growth of a tree is affected by those surrounding it.

INSECTS

There are over 900,000 varieties of identified insects in the world. Learn the distinguishing characteristics of insects, spiders, bees, wasps, grasshoppers, bugs, beetles, flies, moths, butterflies, and others. Identify the various sorts and learn their habits, food, life cycles, and use or destructiveness. Watch them in their native habitat.

Make sketches of common varieties.

Prepare and mount specimens, adding pertinent information about them.

Raise families of butterflies, moths, ants, and other insects.

Lay a large piece of butcher's paper under a bush. Shake the bush gently and note what insects fall out of it.

Watch an ant colony at work.

Stay long enough to watch a spider weave its web. Take a photograph of it.

ROCKS AND MINERALS

Distinguish between minerals and rocks.

Visit a quarry, a fresh road cut, a dried-up stream bed, or a mine opening.

Gather specimens, using a geology hammer (an ordinary hammer will serve) to prepare uniform sizes (about 1½ by 2½ inches) for collections. Wash carefully and label. Keep the specimens in boxes with compartments of cardboard; mount small samples on a mounting board or in plaster of Paris. Enter dates, places, and interesting facts about each find.

Study the characteristics of rocks, determining which are best for use in fireplaces, as kettle supports, and so on.

FISH

Have campers make their own poles, baits (flies and lures), and lines. They can catch or dig their own live bait.

Learn to recognize the different species and learn their life histories.

Mount an especially good specimen.

Learn to clean fish and study their structures as you clean them.

ANIMALS

Take close-up photographs. Use a portrait attachment.

Make plaster casts of tracks.

Play stalking games.

Look for traces of animals, such as droppings, tracks, dens, burrows, bits of fur, and homes.

Find out which animals can see, hear, smell, or taste more acutely than humans.

(Evergreen Section of ACA)

Stalk animals with a camera (takes patience and skill). Lie or sit still and watch them. If you wait long enough, you may be able to discover where they live.

STARS

It is best to study stars on a clear evening when there is no moon to detract from their brightness.

Use the beam of a focusing flashlight to help point out stars.

Learn the folklore regarding the stars and constellations.

Paint diagrams of the heavens on dark blue or black paper with luminous paint so you can use them at night.

Take time exposures of stars with your camera.

Binoculars make the observation of stars more interesting. You will also need a simple telescope and a star map for the current month.

MAKING PRINTS

There are several methods of printing feathers, flowers, leaves, and ferns. Better results are obtained by first pressing the specimens flat. Prints can be used to decorate a memory book, place cards, invitations, stationery, handkerchiefs, or cabin curtains.

Ozalid Prints

These give beautiful results but are slightly more expensive than other prints and require some skill to make well. You will need a one-gallon wide-mouth container with a lid and enough gravel or small rocks to cover the bottom of the container. Pour in about a half cup of household ammonia and place the lid on the container. For each print you need a piece of Ozalid paper in a lightproof envelope and a piece of clear plastic wrap. Staying out of direct sun light, remove the Ozalid paper from the envelope and arrange the desired objects on the paper, covering them with the sheet of clear plastic wrap. Expose the paper to direct sunlight for 30 to 60 seconds or until the paper turns white. After removing the objects, place the paper into the container and replace the cover. Allow the paper to develop until the image appears. This should take about a minute. (Note: If the prints take too long to develop it may be necessary to shake up the gravel in the container to make more fumes.)

Crayon Prints

Place a leaf, vein side up, on a flat surface, cover it with a sheet of unlined paper, and, holding leaf and paper firmly in place, rub a soft crayon over the paper with parallel strokes until the edges and veins stand out clearly. Outline the edge with a firm black line and cut out the print and mount it, or use it for decorating menus or stationery.

Ink Pad Prints

Lay a leaf, vein side down, on an ink pad, cover with a layer of newspaper cut to fit the ink pad, and rub thoroughly. Transfer the leaf, inky side down, onto a piece of paper, cover it with a fresh newspaper, hold it firmly in place, and rub until the ink pad print appears clearly on the paper.

Printer's Ink Prints

Spread a small quantity of printer's ink of any desired color on a piece of glass and run a rubber photographic roller through it until it is thinly and evenly spread. Place the leaf, vein side up, on a newspaper and rub the inky roller over it, transferring a uniform coating of ink. Reverse the leaf, place it on a fresh sheet of paper, cover with newspaper, and, holding it firmly in place, rub over it with a clean roller until the transfer is completed.

Smoke Prints

Many consider smoke prints to be the most attractive of all. Candles (plumber's are best) and some grease such as lard or petroleum jelly are necessary. Spread a small quantity of grease evenly over one fourth of a sheet of newspaper and pass it through the candle flame (being careful not to let it get close enough to burn) until it is uniformly coated with carbon. Then lay it on a flat surface, place the leaf vein side down on it, cover with a clean piece of newspaper, and rub over the newspaper, holding the leaf firmly in place. Transfer the leaf, carbon side down, to a fresh sheet of paper, again cover with newspaper, and rub until the smoke print is transferred.

Spatter Prints

An old toothbrush and some India ink or diluted poster paint are necessary for this method of printing. Protect the work site by spreading newspapers about, and place the leaf on a plain sheet of paper. Pin the edges flat so that no paint can get under them, and slant the heads of the pins slightly toward the center of the leaf. Dip the toothbrush into the paint to get a thin but uniform coating ot it. Holding the brush at a 45-degree angle and about 2 inches from the paper, use a knife, nail file, or thin, flat stick, to scrape *toward you* across the toothbrush. Continue the process until a sufficiently heavy "spatter" has been deposited around the leaf. Do not remove the leaf until the paint is dry. You can also make spatter prints with a spray gun or with an aerosol can of paint.

PLASTER CASTS

Inexpensive plaster casts of flowers, animal tracks, leaves, and the like are simple to make and are quite attractive when used as paper weights, book ends, or wall plaques. They may be tinted in natural colors if desired. Plaster of Paris may be purchased at the hardware or drugstore and should be mixed in an old container such as a tin can, using a stick for stirring. (It is practically impossible to remove the plaster from anything with which it has come in contact.) Estimate the amount of plaster needed for the cast desired and place three fourths of that amount of water in the container. Pour in as much plaster of Paris as will sink to the bottom, then add a trifle more for good measure. Put in a pinch of salt to hasten setting and stir thoroughly. A good mixture has the consistency of pancake batter.

If an animal track is to be cast, dust it lightly with talcum powder and press a circular or rectangular collar of cardboard of the size desired for the finished cast into the earth around it. Pour in the plaster of Paris slowly and let it harden for about 30 minutes. Then lift the cast carefully, remove the cardboard collar, and scrub it well with water (Fig. 15-3). Plaques should have a screw eye or paper clip for hanging inserted in the edge before they are dry. Paint them in natural colors.

Figure 15-3 Track in plaster mold.

To make a positive cast (with the track in relief), powder the negative cast lightly, place a collar about it, and pour in more plaster of Paris. When dry, carefully separate the two casts.

To make casts of leaves, ferns, flowers, seeds, and so forth, pour the plaster of Paris into a mold, dampen the specimen, and place it on the plaster of Paris, brushing it with a paintbrush to make a tight contact over its entire surface. When about half dry, remove the leaf and let the plaster continue to harden.

Obviously, superfluous plaster of Paris should never be poured down the drain.

NATURE GAMES

Nature games are not only fun for the participants, but also can sharpen their observation skills. Following are activities that can acquaint youngsters with the outdoor environment. In addition to these, many other good activities can be found by referring to the materials listed under *Nature Games* in the Additional Readings at the end of this chapter.

STARVATION HIKE. Go out and cook a meal, using only things found growing in the woods. Be sure you *know* what is safe to use.

NATURE QUESTS. See who can bring in and identify a square-stemmed plant; a lady beetle; a piece of wood that is shaped like an animal; and so on. Be careful not to cause harm or destruction.

NATURE TREASURE OR SCAVENGER HUNT. Give each group, person, or pair a list of from 10 to 20 nature objects to bring in, such as leaves of certain trees, common flowers, certain kinds of rocks, discarded birds' nests, discarded feathers, and so forth. The first back with the correct and complete list wins. Some of the items should be easy to find, others hard. Be sure campers maintain good conservation practices; they should not tramp over or collect items that are not in such plentiful supply that a few will not be missed.

LEAF RELAY. Give each team a list of trees. The first one in line runs to get a leaf of the first tree on the list, returns, and gives the list to the second in line, who then reads the second kind of tree and runs to get a sample, and so on. The first group finished wins.

IDENTIFICATION. Have pictures of animals, trees, birds, insects, and the like pasted on cards. Flash them. The first person to identify the picture correctly receives the card.

TOUCH, TASTE, SMELL IDENTIFICATION. Blindfold players and pass around objects for them to identify, designating whether they are to do so by tasting, smelling, or feeling.

TREE IDENTIFICATION. Make a tour, stopping at various trees, so that each person can fill in the name of the tree on his or her numbered chart. When first learning, participants may take their tree identification books along and be given three or four minutes to identify the tree with the assistance of the book. Ferns, flowers, birds, sea shells, animals, or any other kind of wildlife desired may be identified in this game.

NATURE SOUNDS. Each participant listens for five minutes, listing all the nature sounds heard and identified. This is a particularly good game to play at night.

UPSIDE DOWN HIKE. Turn over rocks, decaying logs, and large sticks to see what is living underneath them. Be sure to restore them without harming any inhabitants living under them.

WHAT IS IT? Have a number of clues describing a nature object written on a card, with the least well known first. Read them one at a time until someone is finally able to guess the object and receives the card as a reward. A variation is to let campers take turns giving oral clues until a fellow camper is able to guess what he or she has in mind.

WHAT'S WRONG WITH THIS PICTURE? Announce that a certain nature object is to be described and that, although most of the characteristics given will be true, a few erroneous ones will be included. See how many can detect the incorrect ones.

Tracking and Stalking Games

TRAIL THE DEER. A leader, wearing shoes with a peculiar heel plate or arrangements of brads, starts out ahead while the others try to follow his or her trail. To make your tracks unique you can insert hob nails or upholstery nails into rubber heels, then remove them later without damage to your shoes.

DEER STALKING. One player, the "deer," finds a suitable environment that has some covering such as grass, bushes, or trees. The others scatter out about 100 yards away and each then tries to approach the "deer" without being seen. Anyone seen well enough to be identified is eliminated and the one nearest the "deer" at the end of a designated time wins and becomes the "deer" for the next game.

FREEZE. "It" is in front of the others, who are lined up about 100 feet away. "It" turns his or her back and counts to ten while they move toward the person as rapidly as possible. At the end of the count "it" shouts "freeze" and quickly turns around and calls out the name of any person seen making the slightest motion. That person must return to the starting line. The first person to touch "it" or cross the finish line wins and becomes the new "it."

TRAILING. The person chosen to be "it" walks carelessly through the woods, making no effort to conceal his or her footprints or avoid breaking branches. Ten minutes later, a small group or an individual tries to follow the trail and spot where "it" is hiding beside it. A variation is to have two persons walk in single file through the woods. At a given signal they reverse, and the one originally in the rear tries to lead the way back over the same trail. This person may be given a start of 25 points, with 2 points deducted each time he or she wanders off the trail and 1 each time he or she hesitates more than a minute in determining the correct course.

QUIET, PLEASE! The members of one group sit blindfolded with some designated object located about 6 feet in front of them. The idea is for the second group to creep stealthily in and steal the object without being detected. When members of the blindfolded group hear an opponent approaching and point directly at the person, he or she is eliminated. A variation is to have only one member blindfolded while the others are scattered in various directions and at different distances. They take turns whistling, rustling leaves, stamping a foot, and so forth. If he or she can judge the direction and point directly to the person, the two exchange places.

SLEEPING RABBIT. "It" sits with his or her eyes closed while the others gather around in a circle. The leader points to one player who tries to sneak up to "it" and touch him or her without being detected. If "it" hears the person and points directly to him or her, the person must return to the original starting place. Anyone able to come in and touch "it" without being detected becomes the new "it."

CAPTURE THE FLAG. The field is divided into two halves with a center line marked across it. Each team occupies its own half of the area and has its own flag erected 100 to 200 yards behind the center line. The object of the game is to enter your opponents' half of the field, capture their flag, and return to your own half without being tagged. Any person tagged in enemy territory is "caught" and must remain in prison, an area off at one side about 20 to 30 yards in back of the center line. To "catch" a player, it is necessary to hold the person long enough to pat him or her three times on the back. (If this proves too rough, rule that the opponent need only touch the person once.) A prisoner can be released by having a teammate touch the captured person while he or she is still in prison and both of them can then return home "free." Each team may choose players to act as color guards; they must stay outside of a circle drawn 25 steps around the flag unless they are pursuing an opponent who has entered it. Set a time limit, such as a half hour, and if neither team has captured the other's flag by then, the winner is the team with the most prisoners.

A variation is to widen the area and include trees, rocks, bushes, and natural hiding places which players may use to conceal themselves while approaching to capture the flag or release prisoners. The time may be extended to hours or even a half day without having the players lose interest. Choosing a good terrain is the secret of success in this game.

ADDITIONAL READINGS

(For an explanation of abbreviations and abbreviated forms, see page 13.)

Conducting the Program

Bale: *What on Earth*, pp. 91–156.

Boy Scout Handbook, pp. 274–316.

Brannan, Steve A. (ed.): *Project Explore—Expanded Programs and Learning in Outdoor Recreation and Education.* Hawkins and Associates, 1979, 460 cards plus manual, 138 pp.

Brown, Vinson: *The Amateur Naturalist's Handbook.*

Brown, Vinson: *How to Explore the Secret World of Nature.* Little, 1962, 174 pp.

Brown, Vinson: *Knowing the Outdoors in the Dark.* Stackpole, 1972, 192 pp., paper.

Brown, Vinson: *Reading the Woods.* Stackpole, 1969, 160 pp., paper.

Buck, Margaret Waring: *Small Pets From Woods and Fields.* Abingdon, 1960, 72 pp., paper.

Cardwell: *America's Camping Book*, ch. 23.

Corbin: *Recreation Leadership*, ch. 26.

Delucchi, Linda and Robert C. Knott: *How to Lead an OBIS Workshop.* Delta, 1979, 12 pp., paper.

Ecology Workshop Instructor's Guide (No. 4158). Boy Scouts, 1972, 72 pp.

Elman, Robert: *Discover the Outdoors.* Lion, 1969, 224 pp.

Fieldbook for Boys and Men, pp. 386–403, 414–419, 443–447, 456–463, 481–493.

Ford, Phyllis M.: *Principles and Practices of Outdoor/Environmental Education.* Wiley, 1981, 348 pp.

First Aid to Animals (No. 3318). Boy Scouts, 1963, 56 pp., paper.

Forestry Activities. Supt. of Documents, 31 pp., paper.

Hammerman and Hammerman: *Teaching in the Outdoors.*

Harty: *Science for Camp and Counselor.*

Headstrom, Richard: *Adventures With a Hand Lens.* Lippincott, 1962, 22 pp.

Hillcourt: *New Fieldbook of Nature Activities and Conservation.*

Hoke, John: *Terrariums.* Watts, 1972, 90 pp.

Hussong, Clara: *Nature Hikes.* Golden, rev., 1973, 48 pp.

Invite Birds to Your Home (No. 0100). Supt. of Documents, 1971, 16 pp., paper.

Kohn, Bernice: *The Beachcomber's Book.* Viking. 1970, 96 pp.

Langer: *The Joy of Camping*, pp. 271–277.

Mand: *Outdoor Education.*

Nature Hobbies and Activities (No. 26-094). Boy Scouts, paper.

Nickelsburg, Janet: *Field Trips—Ecology for Youth Leaders.* Burgess, 1966, 120 pp.
Schramm, Wilbur: *Classroom Out-of-Doors—Education Through Camping.* Sequoia, 1969, 192 pp., paper.
Shivers: *Camping,* ch. 10.
Shuttlesworth: *Exploring Nature With Your Child.*
Smith and others: *Outdoor Education,* ch. 4.
Snediger, Robert: *Our Small Native Animals: Their Habits and Care.* Dover, 1963, 248 pp., paper.
Swan, Malcolm D. (ed.): *Tips and Tricks in Outdoor Education.* Interstate, 1970, 184 pp., paper.
van der Smissen, Betty, and Oswald H. Goering: *A Leader's Guide to Nature-Oriented Activities.*
Van Matre, Steve: *Acclimatization—A Sensory and Conceptual Approach to Ecological Involvement.* ACA, 1972, 138 pp., paper.
Van Matre, Steve: *Acclimatizing—A Personal and Reflective Approach to a Natural Relationship.* ACA, 1974, 225 pp., paper.
Van Matre, Steve: *Sunship Earth.* ACA, 1979, 265 pp., paper.
Vinal: *Nature Recreation.*
You and Conservation—A Check List for Camp Counselors. ACA, rev., 1971, 12 pp., paper.
Zehnpfennig, Gladys: *Ecology for Young People.* Denison, 1972, 92 pp., paper.

MAGAZINE ARTICLES

Boy's Life:
"Save Trees By Trimming." Feb., 1973, p. 69.
Shaman, Diana: "Start a Rock Collection." Mar., 1972, p. 44.
Spencer, Billie: "Insect Collections." Apr., 1973, p. 7.
Taylor, John: "Anti-Litter Kit." Aug., 1972, p. 58.

Camping Journal:
Farmer, Charles G.: "Close to Nature." Aug., 1974, p. 33.

Camping Magazine:
Abraham, Eugene, and Ronald James Moglia: "Let's Study Our Environment in its Natural Setting." Jan., 1973, p. 14.
Bacon, E. M.: "Make Your Woodlands Work for You." Jan., 1971, p. 13.
Fenn, Roger C.: "Achieving Relevancy in Nature Programming." Apr., 1971, p. 24.
Fluckel, Robert W., and Charles A. Gregory: "Ecology Goes to Summer Camp—An Experimental Itinerate Approach to Environmental Education." Nov., 1972, p. 13.
Hammerman, William M.: "ACA Sets Up Criteria for Counselors to Teach Ecology at Camp." May, 1973, p. 14.
Katsanis, Andrew: "Good Conservation Pays." Apr., 1968, p. 28.
McMaster, Bob: "Standing Nature Study on Its Head." May, 1981, p. 12.
Mooney, Bill: "How to Meet the Challenge of a Limited Budget When Planning a Nature Program." Mar., 1973, p. 18.
Neely, Dan: "Tree Problems Need Early Diagnosis in Order to Save Our Wooded Camp Areas." Part I, May, 1973, p. 18; Part II, June, 1973, p. 16.
Olsen, Margaret E.: "How Campers Can Help Improve Your Camp's EQ." Mar., 1972, p. 9.
Seed, Allen H., Jr.: "Campers vs. Litter—Practical Ecology in Camp." June, 1971, p. 13.
Stahr, Elvis J.: "Camp—The Ideal Place for Teaching Environmental Urgencies." Mar., 1971, p. 20.
Stinson, Thelma: "FIRST to Stimulate Campers' Interest in Nature Find Out What Interests Them!" Sept./Oct., 1969, p. 16.
Stinson, Thelma: "More Ways to Build Nature Interest." Nov./Dec., 1969, p. 15.
Stinson, Thelma: "To Build Nature Interest Use What You Have!" Jan., 1970, p. 13.
Van Matre, Steve: "Acclimatization—A Vital Part of Your Camp Ecology Program." June, 1971, p. 8.
Wadsworth, William H.: "Camp Environment Checklist." June, 1971, p. 11.
Witt, Ted: "The Teachable Moment." Feb., 1978, p. 14.

National Wildlife:
Adams, Marjorie Valentine: "Have You Started Your Life List?" June/July, 1975, p. 14. (A discussion of the sport of "birding.")
Harrison, George H.: "How People Are Planting for Wildlife." Apr.,/May, 1975, p. 24.

Conservation and Ecology

Alexander, Taylor R., and George S. Fichter: *Ecology.* Golden, 1973, 160 pp., paper.
Allen, Durward L.: *Our Wildlife Legacy.* Funk & Wagnalls, 1962, paper.
Asimov, I.: *ABC's of Ecology.* Walker & Co., 720 Fifth Ave., New York, N.Y. 10019, 1972.
Bridge: *America's Backpacking Book,* ch. 26.
Caldwell, Lynton Keith: *Environment: A Challenge to Modern Society.* Natural History Press, 1970, 292 pp.
Callison, Charles H.: *America's Natural Resources.* Ronald, 1967, 220 pp.
Cardwell: *America's Camping Book,* ch. 52.
Conservation of Natural Resources. Boy Scouts, 1967, 80 pp., paper.
Conservation of the Campsite. ACA, 1960, 48 pp., paper.
Day, Albert: *Making a Living in Conservation.* Stackpole, 1971, 96 pp.
DeBell, Garrett (ed.): *The Environmental Handbook.* Ballantine, paper.
Environmental Science (No. 3363). Boy Scouts, 1972, 64 pp., paper.
Fieldbook for Boys and Men, chs. 20, 21.
Forestry (No. 3302). Boy Scouts, 1971, 84 pp., paper.
Frome, Michael: *Battle for the Wilderness.* Praeger, 1974, 246 pp.
Gabrielson, Ira N.: *Wildlife Conservation.* Macmillan, rev., 1965, 244 pp.
Gibbons, Euell: *Stalking the Good Life.* McKay, 1971, 248 pp.
Grossman, Shelly and Mary Louise: *The How and Why Wonder Book of Ecology.* Grossett & Dunlap, 48 pp.
Guggisberg, C. A. W.: *Man andWildlife.* Arco, 1970, 224 pp.
Helping Wildlife: Working with Nature. Wildlife Management Institute, 1977, 26 pp.
Hoke, J.: *Ecology.* Watts, 1971.
Jennings, Gary: *The Shrinking Outdoors.* Lippincott, 1972, 181 pp.
Klein, Stanley: *A World of Difference.* Doubleday, 1971, 63 pp.

Kolbas, Grace Holden: *Ecology: Cycle and Recycle.* Sterling, 1972, 168 pp.

Lapedes, Daniel N.: *Encyclopedia of Environmental Science.* McGraw-Hill, 1974, 754 pp.

Laycock, George: *America's Endangered Wildlife.* Grosset & Dunlap, 1970.

McHenry, Robert and Charles Van Doren (eds.): *A Documentary History of Conservation in America.* Praeger, 1972, 422 pp.

Mand: *Outdoor Education,* ch. XI.

Manning: *Backpacking One Step at a Time,* ch. 20.

Nickelsburg, Janet: *Ecology, Habitats, Niches, and Food Chains.* Lippincott, 1969.

Nobile, Phillip, and John Deedy (eds.): *The Complete Ecology Fact Book.* Doubleday, 1972, 472 pp.

Olsen, Jack: *Slaughter the Animals, Poison the Earth.* Simon & Schuster, 1971.

Olson, Sigurd F.: *Open Horizons.* Knopf, 1969, 230 pp.

Parnall, Peter: *The Mountain.* Doubleday, 1971, 32 pp., (A copiously illustrated account of what happened when a mountain was inundated by people after being made a National Park.)

Passmore, John: *Man's Responsibility for Nature: Ecological Problems and Western Transactions.* Scribner's, 1974, 213 pp.

Pearson, John: *The Sun's Birthday.* Doubleday, 1973, 111 pp., paper.

Reed, Keith: *Nature's Network: The Story of Ecology.* Natural History Press.

Riviere: *Backcountry Camping,* chs. 10, 14.

Schoenfeld, Clay: *Everybody's Ecology: A Field Guide to Pleasure in the Out-of-Doors.* Barnes, 1971, 316 pp.

Shepherd, Odell (ed.): *The Heart of Thoreau's Journals.* Dover, 1961, 228 pp., paper.

Simon, Noel, and Paul Geroudet: *Last Survivors.* World, 275 pp.

Soil and Water Conservation (no. 3291). Boy Scouts, 1968, 96 pp., paper.

Storer, John H.: *The Web of Life.* Devin-Adair, 1972, 128 pp., paper.

Turk, Amos, Jonathan Turk, and Janet T. Wittes: *Ecology, Pollution, Environment.* Saunders, 1972, 217 pp., paper.

Vogt, Bill: *How to Build A Better Outdoors.* David McKay, 1978, 149 pp.

Warner, Matt: *Your World—Your Survival.* Abelard, Ltd., 257 Park Ave., New York, N.Y. 10010, 1970, 128 pp.

MAGAZINE ARTICLES

Boys' Life:

Laycock, George: "Their Time Is Running Out." Nov., 1970, p. 8.

Backpacker:

"Directory of Leading Conservation Organizations." *Backpacker-6,* Summer, 1974, p. 64.

"The Need for Water Conservation." Nov., 1969, p. 58.

Camping Journal:

"Man's Best Friend, the Tree." Feb., 1971, p. 32.

Steindler, Gerry: "Wagon Tongue." Nov., 1968, p. 4.

Edible Wild Plants

See the bibliography in Chapter 27.

Identification

ANIMALS (SEE ALSO TRACKING AND STALKING)

Breland, Osmond P.: *Animal Life and Lore.* Harper & Row, 1972.

Burt, William H., and Grossenheider, Richard B.: *A Field Guide to the Mammals.* Houghton Mifflin, 2nd ed., 1964, 284 pp.

Caras, Roger: *North American Mammals.* Hawthorn, 1967.

Carrighar, Sally: *Wild Heritage.* Houghton Mifflin, 1965, 276 pp.

DuPuy, William Atherton: *Our Animal Friends and Foes.* Dover, 1969, 276 pp., paper.

Fieldbook for Boys and Men, pp. 405–407, 465–479.

Mammals (No. 3271). Boy Scouts, 1972, 48 pp., paper.

Musselman, Virginia: *Learning About Nature Through Pets.* Stackpole, 1971, 128 pp.

Ormond: *Complete Book of Outdoor Lore,* pp. 345–481.

Orr, Robert T.: *Mammals of North America.* Doubleday, 1971, 250 pp.

Rood, Ronald: *Animals Nobody Loves.* Green, 215 pp., Bantam, 1971, paper.

Rue, Leonard Lee, III: *Sportsman's Guide to Game Animals.* Harper & Row, 1968, 655 pp.

Shuttlesworth, Dorothy: *Animal Camouflage.* Doubleday, 1966, 63 pp.

Wallmo, Olof C. (ed.): *Mule and Blacktail Deer of North America.* Univ. of Nebraska, 1981, 629 pp.

Zim, Herbert S., and Dr. Donald F. Hoffmeister: *Mammals.* Golden, 1955, 160 pp., paper.

BIRDS

Adler, Helmut E.: *Bird Life for Young People.* Sterling, 1970, 155 pp.

Armstrong, Edward A.: *The Way Birds Live.* Dover, rev., 1968, 98 pp., paper.

Austin, Oliver L: *Families of Birds.* Golden, 1971, 200 pp., paper.

Austin, Oliver L.: *Water and Marsh Birds.* Golden, 1967, 224 pp.

Bellrose, Frank C.: *Ducks, Geese and Swans of North America.* Stackpole, 3rd ed., 1980, 544 pp.

Bird Study (No. 3282). Boy Scouts, 1967, 72 pp., paper.

Blachly, Lou, and Randolph Jenks: *Naming the Birds at a Glance.* Knopf, 1963.

Bosiger, E., and P. Faucher: *Birds That Fly in the Night.* Sterling, 1973, pp. 80–112.

Chapman, Frank M.: *The Warblers of North America.* Dover, 1968, 308 pp., paper.

Cruickshank, Alan: *A Pocket Guide to Birds.* Pocket Books, 1972, 216 pp., paper.

Davids, Richard: *How to Talk to Birds.* Knopf, 1972.

DuPuy, William Atherton: *Our Bird Friends and Foes.* Dover, 1969, 330 pp., paper.

Fieldbook for Boys and Men, pp. 449–463.

Peterson, Roger Tory: *A Field Guide to the Birds.* Houghton Mifflin, 1968, 290 pp., paper.

Peterson, Roger Tory: *A Field Guide to Western Birds.* Houghton Mifflin, 2nd ed., 1961, 366 pp., paper.

Rand, Austin L.: *Birds of North America.* Doubleday, 1971, 256 pp.

Robbins, Chandler S., Bertel Brunn, and Herbert S. Zim: *Birds of North America.* Golden, 1966, 340 pp., paper.
Schultz, Walter E.: *How to Attract, House and Feed Birds.* Collier, 1974, 196 pp., paper.
Stefferud, Alfred, and Arnold L. Nelson (eds.): *Birds In Our Lives.* Arco, 1970, 447 pp., paper.
Thomas, Arline: *Bird Ambulance.* Scribner's, 1972, 130 pp., paper. (Caring for injured birds.)
Zim, Herbert S., and Ira N. Gabrielson: *Birds.* Golden, 1956, 160 pp., paper.

MAGAZINE ARTICLES

Reader's Digest:
George, Jean: "The New Art of Bird 'Reading'," Mar., 1973, p. 136.

BUTTERFLIES AND MOTHS

Clarke, J. F. Gates: *Butterflies.* Golden, 1964, paper.
Dickens, Michael, and Eric Storey: *The World of Butterflies.* Macmillan, 1973, 127 pp.
Dickens, Michael, and Eric Storey: *The World of Moths.* Macmillan, 1974, 128 pp.
Ehrlich, Paul: *How to Know the Butterflies.* Brown, 1961, 262 pp., paper.
Hogner, Dorothy Childs: *Butterflies.* Crowell, 1962, 68 pp.
Hogner, Dorothy Childs: *Moths.* Crowell, 1964, 71 pp.
Klots, Alexander B.: *A Field Guide to the Butterflies.* Houghton Mifflin, 1951, 349 pp.
Werner, Alfred, and Bijok, Josef: *Butterflies and Moths.* Viking, rev., 1970.
Zim, Herbert S., and Robert Mitchell: *Butterflies and Moths.* Golden, 1964, 160 pp., paper.

FISH

Eddy, Samuel: *How to Know the Freshwater Fish.* Brown, 2nd ed., 1970, 253 pp., paper.
Fieldbook for Boys and Men, pp. 421–435.
Herald, Earl S.: *Fishes of North America.* Doubleday, 1972, 256 pp.
Walden, Howard T.: *Familiar Freshwater Fishes of America.* Harper & Row, 1964, 324 pp.
Zim, Herbert S., and Hurst H. Shoemaker: *Fishes.* Golden, 1956, 160 pp., paper.

FLOWERS AND OTHER PLANTS

Botany (No. 3379). Boy Scouts, 1964, 64 pp., paper.
Cobb, Boughton: *A Field Guide to the Ferns.* Houghton Mifflin, 1956, 281 pp., paper.
DuPuy, William Atherton: *Our Plant Friends and Foes.* Dover, 1969, 292 pp., paper.
Durand, Herbert: *Field Book of Common Ferns.* Putnam, rev., 1949, 219 pp.
Fieldbook for Boys and Men, pp. 335–341, 347–353, 360–371.
Hardin, James W., and Arena, Jay M., M.D.: *Human Poisoning From Native and Cultivated Plants.* Duke, 1973, 167 pp.
Harty: *Science for Camp and Counselor,* ch. 6.
Hausman, Ethel H.: *Beginners Guide to Wild Flowers,* Putnam, 1955, 384 pp.
Hylander, Clarence J.: *Flowers of Field and Forest.* Macmillan 1962, 231 pp.
Martin, Alexander C.: *Weeds.* Golden, 1973, 160 pp., paper.
Mathews, F. Schuyler: *Field Book of American Wild Flowers.* Putnam, 1966, 601 pp.
Peterson, Roger Tory, and Margaret McKenny: *A Field Guide to Wildflowers of North-Eastern and North-Central North America.* Houghton Mifflin, 1968, 448 pp., paper.
Selsam, Millicent E.: *Plants That Heal.* Morrow, 1959.
Shuttleworth, Floyd S., and Herbert S. Zim: *Non-Flowering Plants.* Golden, 1967, 160 pp., paper.
Taylor, K., and Hamblin, S. F.: *Handbook of Wild Flower Cultivation.* Macmillan, 1962, 307 pp.
Zim, Herbert S., and Alexander G. Martin: *Flowers and Plants.* Golden, 1950, 156 pp., paper.

INSECTS

Barker, Will: *Familiar Insects of America.* Harper & Row, 1960, 236 pp.
Borror, Donald J., and Richard E. White: *Field Guide to the Insects of American North of Mexico.* Houghton Mifflin, 1970, 404 pp., paper.
Clausen, Lucy W.: *Insect Fact and Folklore.* Macmillan, 1962, paper.
Fieldbook for Boys and Men, pp. 409–419.
Headstrom, Richard: *Adventures With Insects.* Lippincott, 1963, 221 pp.
Hylander, Clarence J.: *Insects On Parade.* Macmillan, 1967.
Insect Life (No. 3348). Boy Scouts, 1963, 64 pp., paper.
Klots, Alexander and Elsie: *Insects of North America.* Doubleday, 1971, 252 pp.
Parenti, Umberto: *Insects: World of Miniature Beauty.* Golden, 1972, 80 pp.
Snodgrass, Robert Evans: *Insects: Their Ways and Means of Living.* Dover, rev., 1967, 362 pp., paper.
Sterling, Dorothy: *Insects and the Homes They Build.* Doubleday, 1954, 125 pp.
Zim, Herbert S., and Clarence Cottam: *Insects.* Golden, 1951, 160 pp., paper.
Zim, Herbert S., and George S. Fichter: *Insect Pests.* Golden, 1966, 160 pp., paper.

MISCELLANEOUS AND GENERAL

Berman, Lucy: *Nature Thought of It First.* Grosset & Dunlap, 97 pp.
Borland, Hal (ed.): *Our Natural World.* Lippincott, 1969, 849 pp.
Brown, Vinson: *The Amateur Naturalist's Handbook.*
Collins, Henry H., Jr.: *Complete Field Guide to American Wildlife: East, Central & North.* Harper & Row, 1959.
Forest Service: *Developing the Self-Guiding Trail in the National Forests.* U.S. Dept. of Agriculture, Forest Service, Miscellaneous Publication 968, 18 pp.
Laun, H. Charles: *The Natural History Guide.* Alsace, rev., 1970, 530 pp., paper.
Martin, Alexander C., Herbert S. Zim, and Arnold L. Nelson: *American Wildlife and Plants.* Dover, 1961, 500 pp., paper.
Milne, Lorus and Margery: *Invertebrates of North America.* Doubleday, 1972, 252 pp.
Ormond: *The Complete Book of Outdoor Lore,* pp. 287–481.
Watts, May Theilgaard: *Reading the Landscape.* Macmillan, 1966, 230 pp.
White, Sara Jane: *A Terrarium in Your Home.* Sterling, 1976, 92 pp.

MUSHROOMS

Bigelow, Howard E.: *Mushroom Pocket Field Guide.* Macmillan, 1979, 116 pp.
Christensen, Clyde M.: *Common Edible Mushrooms.* U. of Minn., 1969, 124 pp., paper.
Kleijn, H.: *Mushrooms and Other Fungi.* Doubleday.
Krieger, Louis G. C.: *The Mushroom Handbook.* Dover, 1967, 560 pp.
Smith, Alexander H.: *The Mushroom Hunter's Field Guide.* U. of Mich., rev., 1963.

REPTILES AND AMPHIBIANS

Barker, Will: *Familiar Reptiles and Amphibians of America.* Harper & Row, 1964, 220 pp.
Cochran, Doris M., and Coleman J. Goin: *The New Fieldbook of Reptiles and Amphibians.* Putnam, 1970.
Conant, Roger: *A Field Guide to Reptiles and Amphibians.* Houghton Mifflin, 1958, 366 pp.
Fieldbook for Boys and Men, pp. 437–442.
Leviton, Alan: *Reptiles and Amphibians of North America.* Doubleday, 1972, 252 pp.
Morris, Percy A.: *Boy's Book of Turtles and Lizards.* Ronald, 1959, 229 pp.
Reptile Study (No. 3342). Boy Scouts, 1971, 64 pp., paper.
Schmidt, Karl P., and R. F. Inger: *Living Reptiles of the World.* Doubleday, 1957.
Villiard, Paul: *Reptiles As Pets.* Doubleday, 1969.
White, William, Jr.: *A Frog Is Born.* Sterling, 1972, 80 pp.
White, William, Jr.: *A Turtle Is Born.* Sterling, 1973.
Zim, Herbert S., and H. M. Smith: *Reptiles and Amphibians.* Golden, 1956, 160 pp., paper.

ROCKS, FOSSILS, MINERALS, ETC.

Collins, Henry Hill, Jr.: *The Wonders of Geology.* Putnam, 1962, 129 pp.
Fay, Gordon S.: *Rockhound's Manual.* Harper & Row, 1972, paper.
Fieldbook for Boys and Men, ch. 21, pp. 495–500.
Geology (No. 3284). Boy Scouts, 1953, 88 pp., paper.
Harty: *Science for Camp and Counselor,* ch. 5.
Pearl, Richard M.: *How to Know the Minerals and Rocks.* New American Library, 1965, paper.
Pough, Frederick H.: *A Field Guide to Rocks and Minerals.* Houghton Mifflin, 3rd ed., 1960, 349 pp.
Rhodes, Frank H. T.: *Geology.* Golden, 1971, 160 pp., paper.
Zim, Herbert S., Frank H. T. Rhodes, and Paul R. Shaffer: *Fossils, A Guide to Prehistoric Life.* Golden, 1962, 160 pp., paper.
Zim, Herbert S., and Paul R. Shaffer: *Rocks and Minerals.* Golden, 1957, 160 pp., paper

SHELLS

Abott, R. Tucker: *How to Know the American Marine Shells.* New Am. Libray, 1961, 222 pp., paper.
Abott, R. Tucker: *Seashells of North America.* Golden, 1968, 280 pp., paper.
Johnstone, Kathleen Yerger: *Collecting Seashells.* Grosset & Dunlap, 1970, 198 pp.
Melvin, A. Gordon: *Gems of World Oceans, How to Collect World Sea Shells.* Naturegraph, 1974, 96 pp., paper.
Murray, Sonia J.: *Shell Life and Shell Collecting.* Sterling, 96 pp.

SPELUNKING

Anderson, Jennifer: *Cave Exploring.* Association Press, 1974, 126 pp., paper.
Cardwell: *America's Camping Book,* ch. 28.
Harrison, D.: *World of American Caves.* Henry Regnery.
McClurg, David R.: *The Amateur's Guide to Caves and Caving.* Stackpole, 1973, 191 pp., paper.
Sterling, D.: *Story of Caves.* Doubleday, 1956.

SPIDERS

David, E.: *Spiders and How They Live.* Prentice-Hall, 1973.
Dupree, R.: *Spiders.* Follett.
Levi, Herbert W., and Lorna R.: *Spiders and Their Kin.* Golden, 1969, 160 pp., paper.
Shuttlesworth, D.: *Story of Spiders.* Doubleday, 1959.

STARS

Adler, Irving: *The Stars: Stepping Stones Into Space.* Day, 1956.
Astronomy (No. 3303). Boy Scouts, 1971, 80 pp., paper.
Fieldbook for Boys and Men, ch. 23, pp. 513–529.
Harty: *Science for Camp and Counselor,* ch. 4.
Jennings, Gary: *The Teenager's Realistic Guide to Astrology.* Association Press, 1971, 222 pp.
Joseph, Joseph M., and Sarah L. Lippincott: *Point to the Stars.* McGraw-Hill, rev., 1972.
Kals, W. S.: *How to Read the Night Sky: A New and Easy Way to Know the Stars, Planets and Constellations.* Doubleday, 1974, 155 pp.
Levitt, I. M., and Roy Marshall: *Star Maps For Beginners.* Simon & Schuster, 1969, 47 pp., paper.
Mayall, R. Newton, Margaret W. Mayall, and Jerome Wyckoff: *The Sky Observer Guide.* Golden, 1965, paper.
Mundt, Carlos: *Stars and Outer Space Made Easy.* Naturegraph, 1963, 80 pp., paper.
Rey, H. A.: *The Stars, A New Way to See Them.* Houghton Mifflin, 3rd ed., 1967.
Zim, Herbert S.: *Stars: A Guide to the Constellations.* Golden, rev., 1957, 160 pp., paper.

TREES, SHRUBS, ETC.

Brockman, C. Frank: *Trees of North America.* Golden, 1968, 280 pp., paper.
Fieldbook for Boys and Men, pp. 354–359, 372–385.
Grimm, William Carey: *Home Guide to Trees, Shrubs, and Wildflowers.* Stackpole, 1970, 320 pp.
Grimm, William Carey: *Home Guide to Trees, Shrubs, and Wildflowers.* Stackpole, 1970, 320 pp.
Hepting, George H.: *Diseases of Forest and Shade Trees of the United States.* Supt. of Documents, 1971, 658 pp.
Martin, Alexander, and Herbert S. Zim: *Trees.* Golden, 1956, 160 pp., paper.
Mathews, F. Schuyler: *Field Book of American Trees and Shrubs.* Putnam, 1915, 465 pp.
Ormond: *Complete Book of Outdoor Lore,* pp. 287–344.
Petrides, George A.: *A Field Guide to Trees and Shrubs.* Houghton Mifflin, 2nd ed., 1973, 431 pp., paper.
Platt, Rutherford: *A Pocket Guide to Trees.* Pocket Books, 1972, 256 pp., paper.

Symonds, George W. D.: *The Shrub Identification Book*, Morrow, 1963, paper.
Viertel, Arthur T.: *Trees, Shrubs and Vines.* Syracuse, 1970, paper.

WATER LIFE (SEE ALSO FISH)

Amos, W. H.: *The Life of the Seashore.* McGraw-Hill, 1966.
Bartsch, Paul: *Mollusks.* Dover, 1968, 112 pp., paper.
Buck, Margaret Waring: *Along the Seashore.* Abingdon, 1960, 72 pp., paper.
Buck, Margaret Waring: *In Ponds and Streams.* Abingdon, 1955, 72 pp., paper.
Goetz, Delia: *Swamps.* Morrow, 1961, 63 pp.
Golden Nature Guide to Pond Life. Golden, 1967, 160 pp., paper.
Hausman, Leon A.: *Beginner's Guide to Freshwater Life.* Putnam, 1950, 128 pp.
Hofmann, Melita: *Trip to a Pond.* Doubleday, 1966, 64 pp.
Klots, Elsie: *New Field Book of Freshwater Life.* Putnam, 1966, 398 pp.
Reid, George K.: *Pond Life.* Golden, 1967, 160 pp., paper.
Vogt, D., and H. Wermuth: *The Complete Aquarium.* Arco, 1963.
Zim, Herbert S., and Lester Ingle: *Seashores, A Guide to Animals and Plants Along the Beaches.* Golden, 1955, 160 pp., paper.

Learning to Observe

Bridge: *America's Backpacking Book*, ch. 24.
Brown, Vinson: *Reading the Woods.* Stackpole, 1969, 160 pp., paper.
Elliott, Charles: *The Outdoor Observer.* Dutton, 1969, 119 pp.
Gregg, James: *The Sportsman's Eye: How to Make Better Use of Your Eyes in the Outdoors.* Backpacker Books, 1971, 210 pp.
Van Matre, Steve: *Acclimatization.* ACA, 1972, 138 pp., paper.
Van Matre, Steve: *Acclimatizing.* ACA, 1974, 225 pp., paper.
Van Matre, Steve: *Sunship Earth.* ACA, 1979, 265 pp., paper.

Nature Crafts

See Chapter 14.

Nature Games

Cassell, Sylvia: *Nature Games and Activities.* Harper & Row, 1956, 91 pp.
Frankel, Lillian and Godfrey: *101 Best Nature Games and Projects.* Order from Galloway, 128 pp.
Hillcourt: *New Fieldbook of Nature Activities and Conservation.*
Musselman, Virginia W.: *Learning About Nature Through Games.* Stackpole, 1967, 128 pp.
OBIS Modules (Outdoor Biology Instructional Strategies), Delta Education, Inc. The following modules, developed by the Lawrence Hall of Science, University of California at Berkeley, through a grant from the National Science Foundation, are suitable for camp activities:
OBIS Backyard, 1979.
OBIS Bio-Crafts, 1980.
OBIS Child's Play, 1980.
OBIS Games and Simulations. 1980.
OBIS Pavement and Parks Module, 1980.
OBIS Adaptations, 1980.
OBIS Desert, 1980.
OBIS for Eight to Eleven Year Olds, 1980.
van der Smissen, Betty and Oswald H. Goering: *A Leader's Guide to Nature-Oriented Activities*, ch. III.
Vinal, Willam Gould: *Nature Recreation.* Dover, 1963, 2nd ed., 310 pp.

MAGAZINE ARTICLE

Boy's Life:
Wheeler, Alan: "Camping Games." June, 1971, p. 42.

Photography

See the bibliography in Chapter 10.

Tracking and Stalking

Fieldbook for Boys and Men, pp. 470–479.
Jaeger, Ellsworth: *Tracks and Trail Craft.* Macmillan, 1948, 381 pp.
Langer: *The Joy of Camping*, pp. 271–277.
Murie, Olaus J.: *A Field Guide to Animal Tracks.* Houghton Mifflin, 1954, 374 pp.
Ormond: *Complete Book of Outdoor Lore*, pp. 345–481.
Pocket Guide to Animal Tracks. Stackpole, 1958, 96 pp.
Seton, Ernest Thompson: *Animal Tracks and Hunter Signs.* Doubleday, 1958, 160 pp.

MAGAZINE ARTICLES

"Animal Tracks." May, 1967, p. 69.

sixteen
The Waterfront

I wish that I'd been born a fish
So I could swim whene'er I wish.
Then mother would not have to say
It is too cold for you today.
—*The Eavesdropper*

Water holds a certain fascination for almost everyone and camp aquatic activities rank high in popularity. All types of swimming and boating are enjoyable and nearly every other camp activity can be integrated at one time or another with the waterfront. For instance, a beautiful waterscape provides an almost perfect setting for a campfire or spiritual program, storytelling, sketching, discussions, painting, or photography. Singing is particularly beautiful when performed by a group on the opposite shore or out in boats, for the sound is especially resonant over water; rounds, antiphonal singing, and answer and response and echo songs are especially appropriate.

Near water, one can study an entirely different assortment of plants and animals. Water goggles are helpful in studying underwater life and some camps provide glass-bottomed boxes and boats for this purpose. Almost any type of boat, from a canoe to a raft, will furnish transportation to get away from the humdrum of familiar camp surroundings.

Children find fun things to do in bodies of water no larger than a small brook, for they can wade, study wildlife, search for pebbles, catch minnows with their hands, construct bridges and dams, and make and sail miniature boats. Beachcombing is a favorite activity in camps located near a seashore.

WATER SAFETY

The Problem

Literally thousands of deaths by drowning occur each year and many of them are needless, for had the victims used more common sense or had even a minimum of instruction in proper water skills and safety procedures, they might still be alive today.

Some Safety Precautions

Activities in or near water will continue to grow in popularity and most people at some time in their lives will venture into or near water. Consequently, it seems obvious that it is almost as important to give everyone instruction in correct swimming and boating techniques as it is to teach them to read. Although good swimmers occasionally drown, it is quite true that safety as well as pleasure increases in direct proportion to the skill and confidence of the participant. The following safety precautions will help to minimize hazards and prevent accidents:

1. Teach children to swim and feel confident in the water at the earliest age possible; approximately 29 percent of drownings occur in children under 15 years of age. Scaring children by telling them that "water is dangerous, so stay away from it" never works very well and certainly won't help to prevent the many deaths that result from accidentally falling into the water or from falling out of a boat or having it capsize. More important than learning to do fancy swimming strokes and dives is developing the ability to do one or two dependable strokes. Still more essential is developing the participants' sense of at-homeness in the water, so that they can relax and be secure in staying afloat for hours by treading water, doing a face or back float, or, best of all, using the technique of *drownproofing* or the *bobbing jellyfish float* with its accompanying travel stroke.

By far the greatest cause of tragedies is that people tend to panic in an emergency and become tense or struggle frantically so that they soon wear themselves out or dip below the surface, ingest water, and become even more frightened. A human body with air in the lungs simply can't sink. If you swim, you are probably aware of this because of the difficulty you encounter when trying to lower yourself to the bottom of a pool to pick up a coin.

Camps should join with the American Red Cross, youth organizations, schools, recreation and park departments, and other organizations that are endeavoring to teach everyone how to swim and observe proper safety precautions. One difficulty lies in the scarcity of people qualified to offer instruction in these areas. If you are interested, inquire about the aquatic, small craft, and first aid instructor schools conducted each year by the American Red Cross. The classes are offered at various locations and at minimal cost to the participants, who must be at least 17 years old and have good swimming ability. Most are held in early June, giving participants time to qualify for positions in summer aquatic programs such as those carried on in camps. The courses offer instruction in first aid, swimming, lifesaving, boating, canoeing and sailing. For

(Camp Mishawaka, Grand Rapids, Minn.)

further information, contact your local area office of the American Red Cross.

2. Parents and others responsible for children should never leave them unattended near water.

3. Those unskilled in handling boats should practice in safe water and receive instruction before taking them out.

4. Allow swimming only at patrolled beaches or swimming pools and never allow campers to go swimming without a companion. If your group consists of four or more swimmers, use a buddy system. This is important, even in the most informal groups.

5. Those without good swimming skills should not go out in water over their heads while depending on such artificial supports as water wings, inner tubes, plastic animals, swimming boards, or air mattresses. Many deaths result from slipping off them or having them slip out of the person's grasp.

6. Perfect your own lifesaving and water safety skills, not only to benefit yourself but also so you can help someone else in trouble.

7. Do not allow running or horseplay while in or near water.

PROGRAM TRENDS

Paralleling the increased public interest of the last few decades in all sorts of water activities, camps have shown a corresponding increase in their offerings. In addition to the usual forms of swimming, diving, lifesaving, and boating, there is increasing use of such accessories as flutter boards, water skis, swim fins, and surfboards. Some camps now include such activities as snorkeling and skin and scuba diving, although these usually are available only to older campers and counselors who are expert swimmers, and then only if truly competent supervision is available. Increased participation has placed more emphasis on such related events as water pageants and water carnivals, synchronized swimming, competition in swimming and diving (sometimes with other camps), tilting from boats and canoes, using war canoes, water polo, water basketball, and a large assortment of other water games and contests.

Rowboats are still as popular as ever and are sometimes used with outboard motors for lifesaving and water skiing and for transportation for fishing and camping trips. The ever-popular canoe is more than holding its own, and canoe trips lasting from one night to several weeks are now standard in many camps. Sailing, too, is showing a decided upswing in popularity, with such exciting events as sailing regattas on the agenda of many camps. Many camps, though possessing natural bodies of water, are turning to swimming pools for their aquatic program.

Waterfront activities are naturally popular and little motiviation is needed to enlist the wholehearted participation of campers. The aquatic program ordinarily consists of these divisions: (1) swimming (instructional and recreational); (2) diving; (3) lifesaving, water skiing, scuba diving, surfing; (4) boating (canoeing, sailing, kayaking, rowing, and the like); and (5) trips by water.

THE WATERFRONT STAFF

The Waterfront Supervisor

The waterfront supervisor is in charge of all waterfront activities, and, according to ACA standards,* should be at least 21 years old and should be currently certified as an American Red Cross water safety instructor, a YMCA instructor in swimming and lifesaving, or a Boy Scouts of America national aquatic instructor. If the small craft area is separate from the swimming area, it should be under the supervision of a currently certified American Red Cross small craft instructor, a water safety instructor or someone with equivalent training. The waterfront supervisor is responsible for assigning duties to his or her staff of assistants and for seeing that they are used to best advantage in carrying out a well-planned program that must also be coordinated with the entire camp program. All activities using the waterfront, such as boat trips or fishing, must be cleared by the supervisor.

The waterfront supervisor also sees that campers are tested and classified for a well-

*Camp Standards with Interpretations for the Accreditation of Organized Camps, 1980, p. 32.

(Camp Mishawaka, Grand Rapids, Minn.)

planned program of instruction. He or she trains and supervises the aquatics staff, which may include instructors in such waterfront activities as swimming, diving, lifesaving, scuba and skin diving, water skiing, canoeing, rowing, outboard boating, and sailing. He or she assigns duties, checks on their successful completion, and makes sure that all equipment is adequate in quantity and quality and that safety precautions are invariably observed. The supervisor also makes appropriate seasonal reports and recommendations for the following season.

Although these many duties usually exempt the waterfront supervisor from cabin responsibilities, he or she should be a trained camper and in sympathy with all phases of camp life so that he or she sees the waterfront in its proper relation to the total program. The supervisor has one of the most demanding jobs in camp and is at one time or another likely to be responsible for the safety of every person there. He or she must have presence of mind, sound judgment, and the ability to remain calm, even when faced with an emergency.

The supervisor also is responsible for staff use of the waterfront. Usually during precamp training he or she tests and classifies all staff members according to their swimming and boating abilities and sets up procedures and schedules for their instruction and use of equipment. He or she also acquaints them with swimming hazards and safety measures and the general rules and procedures for camper and staff use of the waterfront.

Waterfront Assistants

According to ACA standards, in addition to the waterfront supervisor, there should be a minimum of one person with at least a Red Cross advanced lifesaving, YMCA lifesaving, or Boy Scout lifeguard certificate on duty for each 25 campers in the water. These persons may be supplemented by others who hold Red Cross junior or senior life saver certificates or their equivalent. There must be a total of one responsible guard for every 10 persons in the water, although they are not required to have had lifesaving training. These members of the waterfront staff may or may not have cabin responsibilities, and their waterfront duties are determined by the waterfront supervisor in accordance with their abilities in swimming, diving, or boating. All waterfront personnel should be trained and interested in the whole camp program and should consider their activities as integral parts of it. All should cooperate willingly in helping out with the general camp program on rainy days and as their duties at the waterfront permit.

General Counselors' Duties at the Waterfront

A cabin counselor usually is expected to accompany his or her campers during their periods at the waterfront and may be asked to assist in any way needed. Also, those with appropriate skills may be asked to help out during the peak periods of the day. Waterfront rules must be obeyed immediately and without question and counselors should set a good example themselves as well as make sure that their campers follow the rules.

Counselors who wish to participate in waterfront activities will be asked to take classification tests, just as the campers do. Though it is sometimes possible for staff to receive instruction from waterfront personnel, they must bear in mind that this is a privilege that can be granted only when it does not interfere with their regular duties or those of the waterfront staff.

THE SWIMMING, DIVING, AND LIFESAVING PROGRAM

Early in the camp season, all campers are tested and classified as nonswimmers, beginners, intermediates, swimmers, or lifesavers. Two swimming periods (ordinarily 30 to 45 minutes in length) are scheduled during the day, one in the late morning for instruction, and the other in the late afternoon for recreation and informal practice of what was learned in the morning. In decentralized camps, campers usually go to the swimming area as a unit and separate according to classification upon arrival at the dock or pool, each going to his or her respective area for instruction.

WATER SAFETY TECHNIQUES

Vigilance at every single moment is necessary, for one accident during a summer can cause untold grief, seriously damage the reputation of the camp, and even do a great disservice to the whole field of organized camping. Three special safety techniques are in common use.

THE BUDDY SYSTEM. The buddy system provides each camper with a companion of similar ability. The two enter and leave the water together and stay near each other at all times; thus, it is impossible for one of them to disappear or get into difficulty without this immediately being known to the other. When the signal for "buddy call" is given (about every ten minutes), they quickly join hands and raise them in the air. Failure to stay close to and watch over a buddy means prompt banishment from the water for the rest of the day or even longer.

THE CHECK BOARD SYSTEM. As swimmers enter the water they turn over a tag bearing their names or an assigned number on the check board so that the red side is uppermost. As each leaves the swimming area, he or she turns it back to expose the white side again. A counselor should be stationed near the board to see that no one forgets. Some camps use pegs with the camper's name on them to insert into a peg board in a similar manner as in Figure 16-1.

Figure 16-1 The checkboard is a good safety device. (Camp Mishawaka, Grand Rapids, Minn.)

COLORED CAPS. Each swimmer wears a colored cap denoting his or her swimming ability so that waterfront staff immediately can spot campers out of their proper area or those engaging in activities too hazardous for their abilities. The following color system is suggested:

Nonswimmer—red (danger)
Beginner—yellow (caution)
Intermediate—green
Swimmer—blue
Lifesaver—white

HINTS FOR THE USE OF THE WATERFRONT

Waterfront counselors must keep their eyes and attention on swimmers at all times; chatting, reading, or basking in the sun are definitely out of place. When on duty, they never enter the water except to rescue a swimmer or when necessary for some particular phase of teaching. Docks are not lounging places; use them only as directed by the waterfront staff.

Sunburn is even more of a danger for waterfront staff than for others, since they must spend long hours exposed to the sun's rays; they should apply a good sunscreening lotion and wear long trousers and long sleeves, at least during a portion of the hours on duty. Campers should also take precautions. Recent studies indicate that constant exposure to the sun and heavy tanning can cause premature aging of the skin, permanently damage it, or may even predispose individuals to cancer.

As in all camp activities, informality and fun are of great importance, but waterfront rules must be rigidly enforced, for there is too much at stake for even minor breaches of the rules. Campers will respond readily if shown the importance of this requirement. Waterfront staff must be businesslike when on duty and see that every instruction is obeyed immediately.

Campers and counselors should never go swimming alone or at times when the waterfront staff is not on duty. They should never swim when overly tired and they should wait for at least an hour after eating before going in the water. On trips they should swim only in approved areas and when at least one lifeguard is on guard. Never allow diving into unknown waters that have not been thoroughly investigated for sufficient depth and hidden hazards. Visitors should use the waterfront only under the same regulations as staff and campers.

Campers enter the water only on signal and come out promptly on signal. You can lessen their natural resentment at mandatory orders by giving some preliminary warning such as "one more dive and out" instead of a "sudden death" blast of the whistle meaning "Come out *now.*"

Thunderstorms are a particularly serious menace to those near water. Everyone in swimming or out in boats must immediately head for shore.

A night swim of 5 to 20 minutes is sometimes permitted on hot evenings if there is enough lighting to make the entire area clearly visible and it is carried on under the careful arrangement and supervision of the waterfront staff. Powerful, focusing-beam flashlights and white swimming caps help to reduce hazards.

Distance swimming is allowed at the discretion of the waterfront staff and only if each swimmer is accompanied by his or her own rowboat, oarsman, and senior lifesaver.

Whereas swimming in moderation is one of the best forms of exercise known, too frequent or too long a period in the water is debilitating and lays the foundation for colds, sinus infections, and other ailments. Two half-hour periods a day, even less if the water is cold, are uually enough. Campers with open sores, skin infections, or colds should not go into the water, and those who develop blue lips or nails, a pale face, or shivering or whose teeth chatter must come out immediately.

Remember that overestimating one's own ability and taking chances are among the major causes of swimming catastrophes. Unexpected fatigue and muscle cramps can incapacitate even experienced swimmers.

BOATING

(See also the section on Trips by Watercraft in Chapter 17.)

The popularity of boating almost equals that of swimming. It not only gives pleasure in itself but also provides transportation to outlying regions for fishing or camping and a means of rescuing those in distress.

Contrary to popular opinion, properly constructed and maintained boats do not capsize when used with common sense and some degree of skill. Most catastrophes result from using boats in poor condition or from such misuses or indiscretions as improper loading or overloading, traveling in dangerous or rough water, fooling around, standing up, rocking the boat, or changing positions improperly. All small craft should be tested for seaworthiness and steadi-

(Luther Gulich Camps, South Casco, Me.; courtesy of *Camping Magazine*)

ness, and they should be used only by those persons who have passed appropriate tests (including actual practice in shallow, safe water) in recovering from capsizing and swamping.

The Federal Boating Safety Act of 1971 requires that *every* passenger in *any* boat on Federal waterways must have a U. S. Coast Guard approved life preserver (technically known as a personal flotation device or PFD), and most states have wisely passed similar legislation. New types of safety equipment now are available that are quite comfortable and in no way interfere with the wearer's activity. Children quickly become accustomed to them and regard wearing them as a normal part of small-craft boating.

Always keep the center of gravity low in a canoe; to this end, remove the seats and kneel on a light kneeling pad at the bottom. Some prefer to kneel on the paddle-side knee, resting their back against a thwart and stretching the other leg out in front, braced against a rib of the canoe. Sit on the floor or even lie flat in the canoe to further increase stability if you should inadvertently be caught in rough water.

Paddle vigorously to keep the canoe at an angle to the waves instead of letting it drift crosswise, which increases the danger of shipping water and swamping. If a paddle is lost, kneel and paddle with your hands. In an emergency, lash two canoes together broadside and exactly parallel by placing two poles across them. Step, sit, or kneel in the exact center of the canoe to keep your weight balanced. In two-person paddling, the bowman uses a straight stroke while the person in the stern, who is responsible for steering, paddles on the opposite side with a "J" stroke.

Change seats only in shallow water and keep your weight as low as possible and exactly in the center of the canoe, grasping a gunwale with each hand as you proceed. Move slowly and deliberately. Save your horseplay for land—there is no place for it in a canoe!

Of all small craft, rowboats are least likely to upset, canoes are the second safest, and sailboats are trickiest of all. Tipped boats, even if submerged, will not sink to the bottom; a capsized canoe can support several people and a rowboat up to a dozen. Therefore, if you are thrown out into the water, instead of striking out for shore, swim to the boat and hang on until help comes. (This is why endurance and the ability to tread water and float occupy such a prominent place in boating tests.)

Before venturing far from shore, boaters should learn to interpret weather signs, for it is imperative to head for the nearest land at the first signs of an approaching storm. Stay near shore on trips, even though it means traveling greater distances.

Neither visitors, counselors, nor campers should use boating equipment until they have passed appropriate tests and secured specific permission from the waterfront staff and given their exact departure time, destination, and expected time of return. Boating after dark is permissible only in an emergency or for an occasional moonlight cruise under the immediate supervision of the waterfront staff.

Those who do not swim well enough to qualify as boaters often find the waterfront a

(Pacific Peaks Girl Scout Council, Olympia, Wash.)

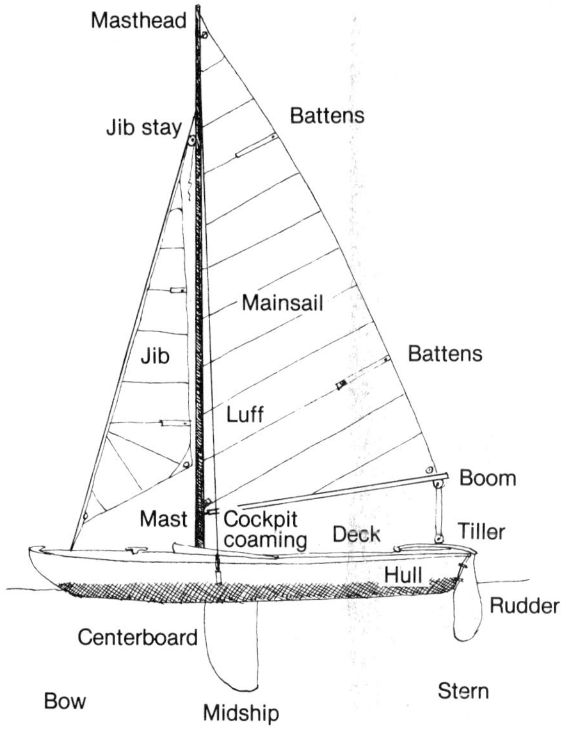

Figure 16-2 Sailboat nomenclature.

tantalizing but forbidden temptation. To appease them, camps sometimes permit an occasional excursion under careful surveillance of the waterfront staff and with one senior lifesaver and a life preserver for each nonswimmer.

Stow all waterfront equipment neatly away; never carelessly leave it lying about to be stumbled over or misused. Keep equipment in good repair and teach campers to respect it as they do fine tools, repairing any damage themselves or instantly reporting it to the proper person. Train campers thoroughly in the care of boats, and provide practice in launching them and taking them from the water, entering and disembarking, and so forth. Never drop or drag canoes over the ground when launching them or removing them from the water. Carry them when on land, and wade out into shallow water to launch them so they don't drag on the bottom. Real boaters are not satisfied to just splash about haphazardly but pride themselves on neat and exact manipulations performed with perfect timing and skill.

ADDITIONAL READINGS

(For an explanation of abbreviations and abbreviated forms, see page 13.)

Boating, Canoeing, etc.

Angier, Bradford, and Zack Taylor: *Introduction to Canoeing.* Stackpole, 1973, 191 pp., paper.
Berger: *Program Activities for Camps,* pp. 81–82.
Blandford, Percy W.: *Canoes and Canoeing.* Grosset & Dunlap, 1968. (Also contains plans for building)
Boats and Canoes (no. 26-038). Boy Scouts, paper.
Bohannan, John: *Your Guide to Boating: Power or Sail.* Barnes and Noble, 1965, 400 pp., paper.
Brosius, Jack and Dave LeRoy: *Building and Repairing Canoes and Kayaks.* Contemporary Books, Inc., 180 North Michigan Ave., Chicago, Ill. 60601, 1978, 134 pp., paper.
Canoeing. ARC, 1977, 452 pp.
Canoeing (No. 3308). Boy Scouts, 1968, 56 pp., paper.
Cardwell: *America's Camping Book,* chs. 45, 46.
Clark, Alice and Lincoln: *The ABC's of Small Boat Handling.* Doubleday, 1963, 225 pp., paper.
Corbin: *Recreation Leadership,* ch. 28.
Evans, Jay and Robert R. Anderson: *Kayaking.* Greene, 1975, 192 pp.
Fieldbook for Boys and Men, ch. 12.
Gabrielson et al.: *Aquatics Handbook,* chs. 16–19.
How to Repair Fiber Glass Boats. Ferro Corp. (C. M. Magarian), Fiber Glass Div., Fiber Glass Road, Nashville, Tenn. 37211, 1969, 38 pp.
Johnson, Joann M.: *Canoe Camping.* Brown, 1978, 77 pp., paper.
Kenealy, James P.: *Boating From Bow to Stern.* Hawthorn, 1966, 327 pp.
Kuhne, Cicil: *River Rafting.* World, 1979, 153 pp., paper.
Lane, Carl D.: *The New Boatman's Manual.* Norton, 1964, 643 pp.
Langer: *The Joy of Camping,* pp. 147–185.
McNair, Robert E.: *Basic River Canoeing.* ACA, 1969, 104 pp.
Merrill: *The Survival Handbook,* ch. 13 to p. 237.
Miracle and Decker: *Complete Book of Camping,* ch. 16.
Motorboating (No. 3294). Boy Scouts, 1962, 80 pp., paper.
Ormond: *Complete Book of Outdoor Lore,* ch. 3.
Rodney and Ford: *Camp Administration,* p. 233.
Ruck, Wolf: *Canoeing and Kayaking.* McGraw Hill, 1974, 95 pp.
Rowing (No. 3392). Boy Scouts, 1964, 44 pp., paper.
Sea Exploring Manual (No. 3229). Boy Scouts, 8th ed., 1974, 448 pp.
Scharff, Robert: *The Collier Quick and Easy Guide to Motor Boating.* Collier, 1963, 123 pp., paper.
Shivers: *Camping,* pp. 332–347.
Skinner, Rulon Dean: *Basic Canoeing Techniques.* Brigham Young, 1975, 174 pp.
Smith, Hervey G.: *The Small Boat Sailor's Bible.* Doubleday, 1964, 147 pp., paper.
Wells, George S.: *Happier Family Boating.* Stackpole, 1966, 96 pp.
Whitney, Peter Dwight: *White-Water Sport: Running Rapids in Kayak and Canoe.* Ronald, 1960, 120 pp.
Zarchy, Harry: *Let's Go Boating.* Knopf, 1962.

MAGAZINE ARTICLES

Camping Journal:
"Boats." Feb., 1973, p. 41.
McKeown, William T.: "Boat Camping." Sept., 1972, p. 15 (Life preservers).
Miller, Stephen: "So You Want to Own a Canoe." June, 1971, p. 32.
Camping Magazine:
Cooper, Richard E.: "Camp Water Safety Aided by Red Cross Courses." Mar., 1972, p. 42.
Walbridge, Charles C.: "White Water Canoeing." May, 1978, p. 8.
Journal of Health, Physical Education and Recreation:
Holtz, Doris D.: "Safe Boating." May, 1966, p. 38.
Reader's Digest:
Carper, Jean: "Boating Safety Is No Accident." May 1973, p. 57.
Wilderness Camping:
Harrison, David: "Wood and Canvas Lives." May/June, 1974, p. 33.
Lange, Richard H.: "The Beginning Kayak—Getting Started." Sept./Oct., 1973, p. 18.
Ruhl, James R.: "A Canoe in Your Future." May/June, 1973, p. 40.
Trevor, John B., Jr.: "Abenaki Canoe Lift." May/June, 1974, p. 55.
Walbridge, Charles: "Reading White Water." May/June, 1974, p. 36.

Sailing

Aymar, Gordon C.: *Start 'Em Sailing.* Ronald, 2nd ed., 1959, 128 pp.
Basic Sailing. ARC, 1966, 122 pp., paper.
Carter, Samuel, III: *How to Sail.* Sentinel, 1967, 127 pp., paper.
Colgate, Stephen: *Colgate's Basic Sailing Theory.* Van Norstrand, 1973, 128 pp.
D'Alpuget, Lou: *Successful Sailing.* Sterling, 80 pp.
DeFontaine, W. H.: *The Young Sportsman's Guide to Sailing.* Nelson, 1961, 96 pp.
Drummond, A. H., Jr.: *The Complete Beginner's Guide to Sailing.* Doubleday.
Farnham, Moulton H.: *Sailing for Beginners.* Macmillan, 1967, 272 pp.
Gabrielson et al.: *Aquatics Handbook.*
Henderson, Richard: *Hand, Reef and Steer: A Practical Handbook for Sailing.* Reilly & Lee, 95 pp.
Knights, Jack: *Sailing—Step By Step.* Arco, 1966, 160 pp., paper.
Marchaj, Czeslau: *Sailing Theory and Practice.* Dodd, Mead, 1964.
Mitchell, Leeds: *Introduction to Sailing.* Stackpole, 1971, 192 pp.
Pearson, Everett A.: *The Lure of Sailing.* Harper & Row, 1965, 328 pp.
Sailing. Golden, paper.
Small-Boat Sailing. Boy Scouts, 1972, 92 pp., paper.
Smith, Rufus G.: *Sailing Made Easy.* Dodd, Mead, 1964.
Sports Illustrated Book of Junior Sailing. Lippincott, 1964, 85 pp.

MAGAZINE ARTICLES

Camping Magazine:
Frederickson, Bruce E.: "Selecting Sailboats for Your Camp." Apr., 1970, p. 18.
Gidwitz, Betsy: "Plan a Safe Sailing Program." Apr., 1963, p. 23.
O'Day, George D.: "Basic Ingredients For Camp Sailing." Mar., 1962, p. 25.

Skin and Scuba Diving, Water Skiing, etc.

Allen, Barry: *Sports Illustrated Skin Diving and Snorkeling.* Lippincott, 1973, 96 pp., paper.
Anderson, Glen E.: *Water Skiing Skill.* Macmillan, 1968, 128 pp., paper.
Bergaust, E., and W. Eoss: *Skin Divers in Action.* Putnam.
Borgeson, Lillian, and Jack Speirs: *Skin and Scuba Diver.* Arco, 1962, 144 pp.
Clifford, William D., and Thomas C. Hardman: *Let's Go Water Skiing.* Hawthorn, 1969, 157 pp.
Counsilman, James and Barbara Drinkwater: *Beginning Skin and Scuba Diving.* Wadsworth, 1964, 52 pp., paper.
Dixon, Peter L.: *The Complete Book of Surfing.* Ballantine, rev., 1969, 220 pp., paper.
Floherty, J., and M. McGrady: *Skin Diving.* Lippincott.
Frey, Hank and Shaney: *Diver Below.* Collier, 1969, 182 pp. (Skin and scuba diving)
Gabrielson et al.: *Aquatics Handbook,* chs. 13, 14, 18.
Joseph, James: *Better Water Skiing for Boys.* Dodd, Mead, 1964.
Sand, G.: *Skin and Scuba Diving.* Hawthorn.
Scuba Diving, Golden, paper.
Shivers: *Camping,* pp. 347–351.
Sullivan, G.: *Teen-Age Guide to Skin and Scuba Diving,* Fell.
Tillman, Albert A.: *Skin and Scuba Diving.* Brown, 1966, 160 pp., paper.
Tinker, Gene and Barbara: *Let's Learn to Snorkel.* Walker & Co., 80 pp.
Water Skiing (No. 3357). Boy Scouts, 1969, 64 pp., paper.

MAGAZINE ARTICLES

Boy's Life:
"Water-Skiing Signals." July, 1972, p. 42.
Camping Magazine:
"Water Skiing Hand Signals." June, 1967, p. 13.
Journal of Health, Physical Education and Recreation:
Vickers, Betty Jane: "First Lessons in Synchronized Swimming." Apr., 1963, p. 32.

Swimming, Diving, Lifesaving

Armbruster, David A., Robert H. Allen, and Herbert S. Billingsley: *Swimming and Diving.* Mosby, 6th ed., 1974, 290 pp.
Barone, Marian: *Beginning Diving.* National Press, 1973, 90 pp.
Batterman, Charles: *Techniques of Springboard Diving.* MIT Press, 1968.
Berger: *Program Activities for Camps,* pp. 97–103.
Billingsley, Hobie: *Diving Illustrated.* Ronald, 1965, 245 pp.
Camp Standards with Interpretations for the Accreditation of Organized Camps. ACA, 1980, pp. 32–33.

Cardwell: *America's Camping Book*, chs. 29, 30.
Collis, Martin, and William Kirchhoff: *Swimming*. Allyn and Bacon, 1973, 120 pp., paper.
Corbin: *Recreation Leadership*, ch. 28.
Counsilman, James E.: *The Science of Swimming*. Prentice-Hall, 1968, 457 pp.
Fairbanks, Anne Ross: *Teaching Springboard Diving*. Prentice-Hall, 1963, 208 pp.
Ferinden, William: *Teaching Swimming*. Remediation Associates, Inc., Box 318, Linden, New Jersey 07036, 1970, 89 pp.
Gabrielson, M. Alexander (ed.): *Swimming Pools—A Guide to Their Planning, Design and Operation*. Hoffman Publications, 1972, 2nd ed., 266 pp.
Gabrielson et al.: *Aquatics Handbook*.
Howes, Gordon T. ("Mike") (ed.): *Lifeguard Training—Principles and Administration*. AAHPER, rev., 1974, 124 pp.
Kiphuth, Robert: *Basic Swimming*. Greenwood, 125 pp.
Lanoue, Fred: *Drownproofing, a New Technique for Water Safety*. Prentice-Hall, 1963, 112 pp.
Lifeguard Training: Principles and Administration. A Project of the Council for National Co-operation in Aquatics. Ass'n Press, 2nd ed., 1973, 223 pp.
Lifesaving (No. 3278). Boy Scouts, 1965, 56 pp., paper.
MacKenzie, Marlin M., and Betty Spears: *Beginning Swimming*. Wadsworth, 1965, 88 pp., paper.
McAllister, Evelyn D.: *Easy Steps to Safe Swimming*. Barnes, 4th ed., 1969, 128 pp.
Merrill: *All About Camping*, pp. 365–367.
Merrill: *The Survival Handbook*, pp. 237–242.
Midtlyng, Joanna: *Swimming*. Saunders, 1974, 130 pp.
Newman, Virginia Hunt: *Teaching Young Children to Swim and Dive*. Harcourt, 1969, 86 pp.
Nolte-Heuritsch, Ilse: *Aqua Rhythmics: Exercises for the Swimming Pool*. Sterling, 1978, 96 pp.
Rodney and Ford: *Camp Administration*, pp. 231–233.
Roy, Harcourt: *Beginner's Guide to Swimming and Water Safety*. Drake, 1972, 159 pp.
Ryan, Jack: *Learning to Swim Is Fun*. Ronald, 1960, 80 pp.
Scout Handbook, pp. 346–355.
Shivers: *Camping*, pp. 323–332, 351–356.
Silva, Charles E.: *Lifesaving and Water Safety Today*. Ass'n Press, 1965, 175 pp., paper.
Smith, Hope M.: *Water Games*. Ronald, 1962, 95 pp.
Spears, Betty: *Fundamentals of Synchronized Swimming*. Burgess, 3rd ed., 1966, 130 pp.
Sports Illustrated Book of Diving. Lppincott, 1961, 96 pp.
Sports Illustrated Book of Swimming. Lippincott, 1961, 96 pp.
Swimming and Water Safety. ARC, 1968, 142 pp., paper.
Swimming and Water Safety Courses (Instructor's Manual). ARC, 1968, 97 pp., paper.
Vickers, Betty J.: *Teaching Synchronized Swimming*. Prentice-Hall, 1965, 170 pp.
Vickers, Betty J., and William J. Vincent: *Swimming*. Brown, 2nd ed., 1971, 61 pp., paper.
Water Fun for Everyone. Ass'n Press, 1965, 191 pp.
Waterman, Frank: *Learn to Swim*. Funk & Wagnalls, 1968, 160 pp., paper.

MAGAZINE ARTICLES

Camping Journal:
Martenhoff, Jim: "Make Yourself Drownproof." July, 1968, p. 36.
Camping Magazine:
Beck, Albert W.: "A Refreshing Change in the ARC Swimming Program." Feb., 1970, p. 18.
Berlyle, Milton K.: "Planning Waterfront Facilities." Part I, Sept./Oct., 1965; Part II, Nov./Dec., 1965.
Bredamus, James C.: "Swimtime is When a Camp Director Needs a Friend." Apr., 1971, p. 23.
Buchanan, Ernest T., III: "The Reluctant Swimer." June, 1969, p. 14.
Cooper, Richard E.: "Camp Water Safety Aided by Red Cross Courses." Mar., 1972, p. 42.
Gidwitz, Betsy: "Waterfront Safety Check." Feb., 1963, p. 12.
Hainsfeld, Harold, and Irv Simone: "Teaching Aids for Water Sports." June, 1961, p. 12.
Lent, Arnold D.: "New Buddy Plan Aids Waterfront Safety." May, 1970, p. 14.
Price, Fern E.: "Water Pageants Build Creativity." Feb., 1968, p. 17.
Santoro, Joel T.: "Training of Waterfront Personnel." Apr., 1967, p. 19.

seventeen

Outdoor Adventure Programs

There is a wide variety of outdoor adventure programs, some of which are more suitable for organized camps than are others. Many activities are so specialized that entire books have been devoted to them, therefore this chapter will not attempt to cover them all. Rather, the purpose here is to familiarize the reader with some general considerations and ideas on those programs most suited for camp use. To really understand and master the required skills, however, you will need to consult other sources as well as gain personal experience under competent leadership. Some of the better sources for review are noted at the end of the chapter.

Everyone dislikes monotony, particularly youth. Teenagers especially crave excitement, new experiences, and a chance to test their maturity. All of us are aware of the increasing problems related to this age group, including crime, delinquency, and drug and alcohol abuse. One of the reasons for this lies in the failure of society to provide legitimate and socially approved ways for teenagers to satisfy their desire for thrills, excitement, and high adventure.

Many camps have reported that the proportion of young campers is increasing since older campers have lost their interest and fail to return. Obviously, this presents a clear message insofar as camp programming is concerned. To keep these youngsters eager to return, our programs must be innovative, varied, and progressive. Do we, as a camping profession, have enough imagination and willingness to change our traditional programs to meet this challenge?

Fortunately, in recent years many organized camps have expanded their programs to include new ones that serve youth through intensive, thrilling, and physically challenging high adventure outdoor pursuits. This shift toward adventure programming allows people to seek and enjoy stress through self-imposed obstacles and test their limitations in exciting and satisfying experiences. Adventure programs have been particularly effective in helping teenagers develop leadership ability, social skills and a sense of responsibility as well as gain appreciation for the strengths and weaknesses of themselves and others.

CHARACTERISTICS OF ADVENTURE PROGRAMS

One of the characteristics shared by almost all adventure programs is the role of the natural environment in posing challenges to the participants. Here we are talking about air currents, gravity, height, water, ice, snow, rocks, mountains, rivers, and caves. Although it is obvious that we usually need a natural outdoor setting to carry out the program, manmade structures may also be utilized.

What are some of the types of activities that are commonly associated with adventure programs? For most camps, trip camping (sometimes called pioneering, tripping or backpacking) provides the means for adventure. Tripping allows a group of individuals to travel from one site to another over an extended period of time. Travel might be by foot or by horseback, canoe, raft, kayak, sailboat, bicycle, or the like. There are other activities that can be included in adventure programs, such as mountaineering or rock climbing, skin or scuba diving, spelunking, orienteering, winter camping, and cross-country ski touring. Whatever the activity might be, adventure programming utilizes direct experiences and includes methods and settings that are generally unfamiliar and exciting to the participants.

Some camps may not have a geographic situation that allows them to carry out programs such as those just mentioned; however, as a segment of their regular camp activities, they might be able to include suitable adaptations that include activities such as initiative games and trust exercises, aerial ropes courses or wall climbing. These activities, which will be discussed in more detail later on, can be utilized alone as exciting events or they can serve as valuable introductions for other adventure programs.

VALUES OF ADVENTURE PROGRAMS

In addition to those values mentioned at the start of this chapter, there are others that might be gained by providing campers with opportunities for participation in various forms of adventure programs. One is the development of a good self-concept (including self-image, self-re-

(Alpine Trails Outings, Denver, Colo.)

spect, self-satisfaction, and self-realization) that can come about by successfully meeting new challenges and overcoming personal fears. For instance, Iida* reviewed some 60 studies on adventure-oriented programs and concluded that positive changes in self-esteem and self-confidence were gained by the participants.

Another value of adventure programs is that campers can improve their physical fitness from the sustained and strenuous activity. A moderate amount of psychological or physical stress also can help one to gain insight about oneself and others and encourages self-evaluation and reappraisal of one's relationships with others. Such stress also can develop one's determination and tenacity. Campers also learn to cooperate with others by identifying conflicts, making decisions, communicating, solving problems and sharing responsibilities under stress conditions. It should also be mentioned that through adventure programs campers can come to recognize the harmony and delicate balance of the natural world and can put this awareness into practice by showing respect for the environment by having minimum physical impact on it.

As anyone who has dealt extensively with youngsters knows, they never tire of hearing of the exploits of our pioneers in their struggle to conquer the wilderness and wrest a living from the soil by their strength and the use of crude tools and methods. Almost invariably, history pictures them as rugged individualists, brave, hardworking, ingenious, and persistent. In those times, a man established his position with his fellow men by those characteristics most needed for the circumstances—resourcefulness, physical prowess, bravery, and a willingness to work hard, and it mattered little if he had wealth and social background. These true values have persisted in our thinking through the years and we must recognize them to evaluate our present ideals and our great American heritage.

These same values are evident in a modern camp that promotes rugged living. The boy who was sought after by his peers at home because of his ample spending money and material possessions but who can't build a fire or keep up on the trail is soon scorned by his trail mates. He is judged solely on his own merits—his parents can't run interference for him now. Following a trail by foot or canoe and making camp in comparatively virgin country is hard work and the boy or girl with the stamina and know-how to do it successfully can be rightfully proud of his or her achievements.

Helping to plan and carry out a trip successfully results in a lot of growing up. Campers must learn to anticipate and plan ahead as they make check lists and use them for packing. They must work and cooperate closely with others, accepting responsibility and carrying their own duffel as well as a share of group supplies. The vigorous activity and ample quantities of good nutritious food, which they have helped to prepare, serve to promote exuberant good health and physical fitness.

What better way to instill a love of nature than to live intimately with it 24 hours a day? How better to instill a sense of the urgency for practicing good conservation than to live it day by day? Attitudes and practices acquired will probably last through a lifetime of family camping, boating, picnicking, or hunting and fishing.

When well-trained youngsters become an integral part of the planning of an exciting trip, they enjoy it to the utmost. Deep and lasting friendships form as a small group goes off into a little world of its own. Sharing inner thoughts, laughing together over amusing incidents, working and struggling together toward a common goal all develop a true knowledge of the meaning of "one for all and all for one." As in any intimate association, of course, occasional frictions and misunderstandings will arise. Some campers will surely at some time display selfishnes, thoughtlessness, or a tendency to rationalize and blame others for their failures and mishaps. However, they will most certainly be subjected to what is generally considered to be the most effective of reforming influences—the disapproval and lack of acceptance by peers.

While each person in the group learns to be self-reliant and independent, he or she must also learn to fit in as part of the group, which eventually develops the spirit of "we-ness' and cooperation so essential for living happily in today's society.

The important point is that a wide variety

*Iida, Minorv: "Adventure-Oriented Programs: A Review of Research" In van der Smissen, Betty (ed.): *Research, Camping and Environmental Education.* Penn State HPER Series No. 11, Pennsylvania State University, 1975, pp.218–241.

(Girl Scouts, U.S.A.)

of human needs can be satisfied through well-developed camp programs that contain elements of challenge and adventure. You, as a counselor, will never have a better opportunity to get intimately acquainted with your campers and exert a subtle influence on them in various ways.

CORE COMPONENTS

One of the people to first apply the adventure approach was Kurt Hahn, a German who recognized and used the concept of challenge as an important part of his educational philosophy and practice. As a result of his program's success, during the Second World War, he was asked to develop a plan to train British seamen so that they could cope better with high stress and overcome adverse situations at sea. This concept, which emphasizes physical and emotional development, became known as Outward Bound training. The idea was expanded upon later, with similar programs being made available to people of all ages throughout the English-speaking countries of the world. Currently, Outward Bound schools in 17 countries have incorporated to provide self-discovery programs that use challenges found primarily in a natural setting.

We can learn much from studying these programs. The core components include activities that are both intense and sustained, demanding the best from the participant. Intense aspects (often called stress components) might consist of activities that include challenging natural and manmade obstacles and various elements of uncertainty. Sustained aspects (endurance components) can include hiking long distances or taking on tasks that cannot be completed quickly. Typical of intense and sustained components are mountaineering expeditions, rock climbing, survival camping, initiative tests, and endurance training. These activities help people understand their potential and limitations and reveal to them that difficult and sometimes frightening situations can be overcome, regardless of personal limitations. Since cooperation is important to successfully complete many of the tasks, participants quickly learn that there is a need for dependency, trust and close interaction with others.

To develop a program with sound content, there must be a blend of physical and recreational activities that contain structured exercises

(Recreation Management Curriculum, University of Montana, Missoula, Mont.)

in leadership, self-discovery, group dynamics, and teamwork. Like most other programs in camp, the emphasis on small peer groups is important. Whatever the activity, its purpose is to allow each participant to experience success and a sense of accomplishment. To do so, the magnitude of the challenge should be matched to the skill of individual participants.

RISK VS. CHALLENGE

Obviously, some adventure programs might seem to have high levels of risk associated with them. Yet, if the programs are planned properly and good equipment is used under careful supervision and direction, they can be every bit as safe as other types of camp activities. Of course, leaders and supervisors always have the moral obligation to be reasonable and prudent in choosing the activities in which campers will engage. Participants can be challenged physically and psychologically without confronting a *real* risk, even though they may *perceive* the activity to be risky. In other words, one's fear or anxiety may well be irrational, since the danger or risk may be imagined rather than real.

The focus of adventure programs should be on the word "challenge"— challenge through stress and adventure, not challenge through risk. What must be understood by the program leader is that stressful, challenging activities need not necessarily be risky. After all, what may be truly exciting and challenging to an unskilled or inexperienced camper may actually be quite routine and unchallenging to the leader. In other words, elements of challenge or stress can be regulated to assure that the penalties for failure are not too high. The type of challenge can be adapted to all levels of skill and risk. To accomplish this, activities should be structured in a sequence of progressive difficulty, so that success is achieved by building upon previous successes. As skill is acquired, participants will be able to successfully meet more difficult tasks.

THE ROLE OF THE LEADER

In order to justify programs containing elements of challenge, adventure and stress, camps must be able to guarantee that the danger involved is at a reasonably low objective baseline level. It is the instructor or leader who must ensure that any danger is apparent rather than real and that the exposure to danger involves minimal personal risk while keeping the stress and excitement level high. The key here is the use of controlled or disciplined adventure that is based on the participant's level of skill and ability. A participant's involvement in any adventure program should be geared by the leader at a level commensurate with his or her competency and experience, just as it would be with any other camp activity.

The level of control, diversity of situations, and variety of resources used can be moderated by competent instruction. The leader's efforts should concentrate on providing the proper program content, activity sequencing, and safety measures. By doing these things the leader is taking positive steps to reduce the degree of hazard without removing or diminishing the excitement-producing elements. Therefore, as far as leadership and responsibility are concerned, a fine balance must be struck between challenge and risk.

In addition to a concern for reducing the potential for physical harm, the leader must also see to it that adventure programs are not psychologically harmful. Emotional trauma can result when a camper is forced into situations for which he or she has not been adequately prepared. No one should ever be forced to do anything that could possibly result in this sort of psychological injury.

By now it should be obvious that the key to the development of an adventure program is competent leadership. Potentially dangerous activities such as whitewater boating, caving, and mountaineering demand competent and responsible staff. Those who conduct the program must be thoroughly familiar with the equipment and skills needed as well as possess other strong leadership abilities including general knowledge of the outdoors, technical ability in the specific activity, actual experience in the activity, sound judgment and decision-making skills, and pragmatic realism about one's abilities and limitations.* Among these, the ability to make sound judgments is probably the leader's most important trait, since skill alone does not make a good leader.

(Camp Kooch-I-Ching, International Falls, Minn.)

LEADERSHIP TRAINING

The staff responsible for conducting adventure programs is different from other staff in the camp. The adveture staff needs to be more qualified in terms of safety and must have advanced training and experience in outdoor leadership. Certification in American Red Cross advanced life saving, advanced first aid, and basic canoeing also helps. The program director probably would want to have water safety instructor, first aid instructor and small craft instructor certification as well so that he or she could certify other staff during precamp training.

Camps are wise not to sponsor adventure activities unless they have enough experienced personnel and the necessary equipment to do it safely. Fortunately, the lack of qualified leaders is being somewhat overcome since interested persons now can acquire such training in a variety of ways. The American Camping Association is increasing its efforts to improve and expand counselor training, and some institutions of higher learning now also provide good leadership training courses. There also are several nationally recognized programs that warrant a closer look.

PROJECT ADVENTURE.** This is an Elementary and Secondary Education Act Title III program that began in Hamilton-Wenham Regional High School, Hamilton, Massachusetts in 1971. Since then, it has played an important role in providing adventure programs for the academic and physical education curriculums of public schools. The concept emerged from the

*Petzoldt, Paul: *The Wilderness Handbook.* Norton, 1974, pp. 146–147.

**Project Adventure, P.O. Box 157, Hamilton, Massachusetts 01936.

Figure 17-1 Adventure and challenge brings joy and self-satisfaction. (J. Meier)

Project's efforts to incorporate various aspects of Outward Bound with ongoing school activities in order to help students develop confidence and competence. The program uses initiative games, ropes course activities, and other outdoor skills designed to develop confidence and problem-solving skills. The Project also offers workshops and technical assistance to schools and other groups throughout the country.

OUTWARD BOUND.* Outward Bound, Inc., is an action-oriented program of self-discovery that uses challenges found in a natural setting. In the United States, six schools and the Dartmouth Outward Bound Center offer participants a vast choice of experiences. Depending on location, activities might include sailing, mountaineering, backpacking, skiing, canoeing, kayaking, or whitewater rafting. There are special seminars and training programs designed for teachers and instructors. Courses range from a week to three and one-half weeks in length.

NATIONAL OUTDOOR LEADERSHIP SCHOOL.** This school is a private, nonprofit educational institution dedicated to teaching people how to enjoy and conserve the outdoors. Leadership courses are conducted in a variety of geographic settings and range from 7 days to a full 16 weeks in length. The courses are compre-

*Outward Bound, Inc., 165 West Putnam Ave., Greenwich, Connecticut 06830.

**National Outdoor Leadeship School, P.O. Box AA, Lander, Wyoming 82520.

hensive and consist of intense outdoor experiences. Skills are oriented around wilderness expeditions, mountaineering, snow and ice climbing, ski touring, winter mountaineering, horsemanship, and whitewater and ocean canoeing. The school offers an outdoor leadership certification program for its students.

TRIP CAMPING

When there's a yellow sun on the hill
And a wind is light as a feather
And the clouds frisk gaily, as young clouds will,
Oh, then it is gypsy weather!
That's the weather to travel in,
With the sun and wind against your skin,
No matter how glad to rest you've been,
You must go when it's gypsy weather.

—MARY CAROLYN DAVIES, *Gypsy Weather.*

As mentioned earlier, many organized camps utilize a trip camping program as a means of providing adventure. Because it is such a popular activity, a detailed discussion is necessary to describe all its components.

Trip camping involves overnight travel away from the central resident camp. Travel may include hiking, bicycling, boating (canoeing, rafting, sailing or kayaking), or by any other appropriate form of transportation. Such an opportunity allows campers to put into practice what they have learned about finding their way with map and compass, using tools, cooking outdoors, pitching and lashing a tent, packing, and carrying equipment to make themselves safe and comfortable in a "home away from home."

No matter what mode of travel is used, trip safety and comfort require at least a minimum of special equipment and supplies. Camps must usually invest enough to supply such group necessities as tents and cooking equipment, and they, or the campers, must provide whatever personal gear is needed. However, elaborate outlays are unnecessary and good care and handling will lengthen the life of whatever equipment is on hand. Where finances are limited, campers can make many things for themselves using the methods described in this book as well as those included in some of the additional readings listed at the end of this chapter and Chapter 28.

Trip Progression

A trip can include a wide variety of experiences, but should progress from simple cookouts and overnights to longer outings that make full use of growing skills and knowledge. For quite young, inexperienced campers, the first excursion may be only a very simple lunch or supper cookout. Next may come an overnight, perhaps only a few feet from the cabin door, but it will involve making a bedroll, packing up a few belongings, getting the provisions for a simple meal or two and sleeping under the open sky or out in a tent. Nevertheless, the neophyte will be gaining experience as he or she helps to plan what supplies and equipment will be needed and uses a check list to see that nothing is left behind. Perhaps the group will enjoy pretending that they are part of a covered wagon train bound for California, which is so far from their cabin that they will just have to get along without anything they were careless enough to forget. See that this first overnight is really fun, for a successful experience whets a camper's appetite to return to main camp and start mastering the necessary skills for going on a still longer trip.

(YMCA Camp Widjiwagan, Ely, Minn.)

A good trip program will provide for progressively longer and more exciting outings with each succeeding summer, so that a returning camper always has something new and more challenging to look forward to. Note that extended trips are not recommended for those who are under the age of twelve or thirteen and who have not built up to them through a program of easy jaunts.

How and Where to Go

Some camps are fortunate enough to have several possibilities for trip camping within their own confines. Picking out a suitable route and destination and perhaps establishing there an *outpost* or *primitive camp* with a permanent Adirondack shack to provide shelter overnight can well become a camper project that will keep them happily engaged for days. It is best to have several alternate destinations that vary in distance and difficulty, and different groups may forage about, vying with each other in trying to find the one "perfect" spot with the most natural advantages.

When a camp has only limited acreage available or when older campers have pretty much explored their own grounds, you may find it advisable to look elsewhere for new places to go. There may be some farmer with suitable facilities who will agree to let you use them, perhaps upon payment of a modest fee. Most people enjoy having well-behaved youngsters around and will cooperate 100 per cent if you can assure them that you and your campers understand the meaning of good outdoor manners and will take every precaution to maintain the property as they found it.

It may be possible to travel by canoe, sailboat, rowboat, or even raft or kayak to a distant shore where sites are available for overnight stops. Bicycles are another means of covering distances in a surprisingly short time; stay off dangerous main highways and seek the always more interesting back roads. Campers, supplies, and bicycles may be transported to suitable take-off points in order to visit more distant areas and can be picked up again at the same spot after the trip. For places to go bicycle tripping, contact Bikecentennial, a service organization that promotes bicycle touring and provides books and maps. Its address is listed in Appendix C.

Some enterprising camps, such as Camp Wakeela,* have converted an old, unused farm wagon into a covered wagon, with an old tent to cover the wagon bed. A neighboring farmer supplied the "horse power" to pull the wagon, loaded with duffel, while the twelve- and thirteen-year-old campers took turns riding and walking, pioneer style. Other camps convey heavy equipment to outlying districts by pack animal, jeep, camp truck, or station wagon. Horseback trips are always popular.

Nearly every camp will find public areas with camping facilities somewhere nearby where arrangements can be made to take a group. Good possibilities lie in national, state, county, and local parks, forests, and wildlife refuges, where arrangements often can be made to camp and explore well-marked trails. It is best to avoid the more popular areas, especially during their peak seasons, for they offer little chance for privacy. Many areas have restrictions on cutting timber and burning wood, making it mandatory to cook over a camp stove, but this is really no handicap to skilled campers. Trail maps, guide books, and professional personnel usually are available to help. It may also be possible to affiliate with the AYH (American Youth Hostels) and make use of their maps and sleeping facilities, if any are located near you.

To meet the ever-increasing outdoor recreation needs of our population, and to provide access to, travel within, and enjoyment and appreciation of the outdoors, trails are being established by government agencies. Today the United States has about 135,000 miles of existing trails. In 1968, Congress adopted a significant law, the National Trails System Act, which established a system of scenic and recreational trails. At the outset, two scenic trails were designated—the Appalachian Trail and the Pacific Crest Trail. The Appalachian Trail is a 2,044-mile footpath leading from Mount Katahdin in Maine to Spring Mountain in Georgia that winds through the beautiful scenery of the Green and White Mountains, the Berkshires, Alleghenies, Catskills, Blue Ridge mountains and Smokies. The Pacific Crest Trail, of about 2,350 miles, leads from Canada to Mexico through the Cas-

*Segal, Harvey C.: "Westward Ho." *Recreation*, March, 1957, p. 82.

(Bikecentennial, Inc., Missoula, Mont.)

cades and Sierra Nevada and Sierra Madre Mountains. Though both of these trails contain rugged sections suitable only for seasoned trippers, other parts can be reached by automobile or public transportation and are quite suitable for young, inexperienced groups under good leadership. Both offer some campsites and permanent shelters at convenient stopping places.

During this same time, a number of other trails were identified for study as potential additions, and 40 more were cited as recreation trails to be administered by local, state, or federal agencies. Today more than 175 trails have been so designated across the nation. The reader can gain further information about suitable places for trip camping by writing to some of the addresses listed in Appendix C at the back of this book.

How Rugged Shall the Trip Be?

Always bear in mind that no trip is good camp practice or fun when it degenerates into an endurance contest or a race against time. Five to 10 miles a day may be enough for average hikers, or even less if the going is rough, while seasoned trippers might well go at least twice as far. Those going by canoe or other watercraft may cover 12 to 20 miles or more a day and cyclists may count on 20 to 50 miles. Allow plenty of opportunity for seeing, exploring, and just plain having fun, for it's not how far but how much that counts when evaluating a trip. On long excursions, it is wise to take it easy the first day while the group warms up. Later, allow for at least one "lazy" day out of five, with campers remaining at the same site to sleep late and do their laundry and mending, explore the country, play games, fish, sing, enjoy cheerful banter, or just relax as the mood dictates. Trippers should return alert and rested, not mentally and physically fagged out so that they have to spend an extra day or two recuperating.

Before taking a group over a proposed route, at least two counselors and perhaps some especially able campers should survey it. They may make a trail map, indicating good places to stop overnight, sources of water and firewood (if needed), scenic views and other points of interest, and so on. Plan to return by a different route if it seems feasible.

Who Should Go on Trips?

The best number for a trip group is six to ten campers with at least one counselor for each five campers, depending on their ages. No group no matter how small, should ever start out without at least two leaders, for in case of an emergency there must be one adult to stay with the group while the other goes to use the telephone or secure help. At least one of the counselors

(Cheley Colorado Camps, Estes Park, Colo.)

should be 21 years of age and must be a trained and experienced trip camper, having learned by practice as well as through training courses and extensive reading. At least one should have had training in first aid and preferably hold a current American Red Cross certificate.

Campers should be of aproximately the same age, strength, and experience, lest the young and inexperienced wear themselves out or be unjustly called "lazy" or "tenderfoot" while trying to keep up with the others. Remember that the group will only be as strong as its weakest member. Campers on extended trips should be at least twelve years old.

Every person going on a trip should first be screened by the camp health staff just prior to departing for the trip (and upon returning). It is also wise to set up a progressive set of skills in campcraft and woodcraft that campers must master before going. The list can be brief and easy for first trips, with additional skills added for succeeding, more difficult trips. Campcraft and woodcraft instruction and practice can be set up as regular parts of the program just as canoeing, arts and crafts, or swimming are. Tests may be used to determine a camper's proficiency in various skills.

A set of tests might cover such areas as the following:

A demonstrated knowledge of good manners in the out-of-doors
Use and care of knife, hatchet, and saw
Selection and use of appropriate forms of fuel
Conservation and proper extinguishing of campfires, if used
Outdoor cookery
Using or making a bedroll and having experience in sleeping out-of-doors
Knowledge of trip equipment and proper packing of duffel
Camp sanitation and proper disposal of garbage
Knowledge of weather and weather prediction
Lashing and tying various useful knots
First aid and safety
Experience in one-meal, all-day, and overnight trips
Paddling, horseback or bicycle riding, if the trip involves such methods of transportation

Such requirements impart real zest to learning and perfecting camping skills. In addition, they help insure that participants will be safe, happy, and comfortable on the trip.

The Trips Counselor

Many camps appoint one person, at least on a part-time basis, known by some such title as "trips counselor," to take charge of the entire trips program, with one or more assistants to help as needed. Such persons can set up a program of "enabling skills,' variously known as *campcraft*, *pioneering*, or *woodcraft*.

The trips counselor should be a mature, seasoned person who is thoroughly versed in the field through wide experience as well as reading and instruction in it. He or she should be levelheaded, resourceful, completely dependable, and must be a good organizer with tact and forcefulness.

One of the main responsibilities is to see that there is adequate equipment of the right type on hand and that it is kept in good repair and replenished when necessary. The trip counselor must arrange for storing equipment efficiently and safely in the equipment room and must keep careful lists as group equipment is checked out and in. Though each group is responsible for returning its gear dry, clean, and in good condition for storage, the trips counselor must check to see that this is done. He or she must know how to care for leather goods, tents, and other gear to keep them always in top condition. The person is expected to keep a complete and up-to-date running inventory of equipment, and is required to see that things are stored properly for the winter. The equipment occupies an important place in the camp budget, and the trip counselor must impart this attitude to others. Anything lost or ruined through misuse must be replaced, thus leaving that much less to buy additional equipment or develop other phases of the program. He or she also goes along on trips or at least sees that those responsible are well-prepared for their duties.

Planning the Trip

POINTS TO CONSIDER

Much of the pleasure of a trip consists in planning and anticipating it. Decisions must be made as to where to go, how to get there, what to take, and how long to stay, and they will depend upon such factors as:

1. The ages and experience of those going.
2. The probable temperature and weather conditions.
3. The means of transportation—canoe, hiking, horseback, bicycle, pack animal, covered wagon, etc.
4. The possibilities for restocking along the way.
5. The ruggedness of the terrain—hills, density of underbrush, etc.
6. Means of cooking and facilities for camping along the way. Will some areas require the use of camp stoves for cooking?
7. Availability of safe water for drinking, cooking, and washing. Will you need to purify it? Remember that thirsty campers and dehydrated food require large quantities.
8. The amount of time you want to devote to cooking and the type and variety of cooking utensils you have available and want to burden yourself with.
9. The number and length of stopovers desired to take side excursions or do special things, such as swim, visit an old mill, and so on.
10. Do some areas require you to have permits to camp, build fires, or fish?
11. Is the trail clearly marked or will you need good maps and compasses? No one should venture along an unmarked or poorly marked trail unless at least one person in the group is thoroughly versed in using map and compass.
12. Are there places convenient to the trail from which you can reach a telephone, a physician, or forest ranger in case an emergency arises? The person in charge should have complete information about this.

PLANNING WITH A GROUP

Start planning well ahead of time and elicit help from campers at every step of the way. Let it be *their* trip, not *yours,* to give them all the joy of helping to make decisions, solve problems, and make the trip a success. Only indifference, or even resentment, results from dragging them on trips someone else has planned and arranged. How much responsibility they can take will, of course, depend somewhat upon their ages and experience, but you may be pleasantly surprised by the worthwhile suggestions campers make and the amount of work their willing hands accomplish when they are given the opportunity. Ask them for their preferences but don't make the mistake of letting them make all decisions or carry too much responsibility. After all, you are ultimately responsible and supposedly have been chosen for your position because of your greater experience and maturity. The ability to guide followers into making wise decisions is the mark of a good leader, but when it becomes a question of violating principles of good judgment, safety, or good camp practices, you must

(Camp Manito-Wish, Y.M.C.A., Milwaukee, Wis.)

have the courage to come out with a big, loud "NO" and then stick to it. You will have less to regret in the future and they'll respect you much more in the long run. To avoid the unpleasantness of direct denials or confrontations, try to swing them to wise decisions so tactfully that they do not realize that the decisions were not wholly their own.

MENU PLANNING

Menus must be compiled and amounts and food lists turned in far enough ahead to allow time for measuring out or assembling stock items and ordering any necessary extras. The dietitian or person in charge of food will usually help with this and his or her knowledge and experience will be of inestimable value. Each camp usually sets up its own procedures for doing this, and you, as a counselor, should learn what they are and follow them to the letter.

Consider what cooking utensils various items will require. With how many utensils do you want to burden yourselves? You can cut down on the number by planning to cook one-pot or aluminum foil meals. Also consider how much time you want to take for cooking. Some foods require elaborate preparations and long cooking times, while others are quite simple.

GROUP EQUIPMENT

Determine what group equipment you will need, such as tents, cooking outfits, and the like. Make out duplicate lists, carrying one to check against along the way and leaving the other back at camp with the trips counselor or other person in charge to check against when you return. Assemble everything and weigh it to determine how much of it each camper will need to carry in order to have a proportionate share.

Distribute equipment equitably, taking into consideration the strength and stamina of the hikers, and don't hesitate to make changes on the road if they seem advisable. For instance, if one camper is carrying an unusually heavy piece of group equipment, someone else with less might take over some of his or her personal gear to compensate.

As with personal equipment, place related items together in ditty bags—one for fire building, one for small tools, one or more for cooking utensils and equipment, and so on. Have distinctive colors for each bag or label it conspicuously so that you can locate what you want quickly. Attach a tag securely, listing its exact contents to check against each time you pack up to move on. Select a counselor or responsible camper to make and carry a master list of who has each item. Some person should also take responsibility for the food, making a similar master list, together with menus, cooking directions, and the names of persons in charge of cooking each meal.

PERSONAL EQUIPMENT

Using the lists and information given in Chapter 28, help campers to make out their own check lists of personal equipment, completing them at least a week ahead of time. The inexperienced will probably think such concern entirely unnecessary but certain items are mandatory for everyone.

A common error in packing is to assume that the weather will stay just as it is at the moment. However, mornings and evenings undoubtedly will be chilly, and unless you have a rabbit's foot in one shoe and a four-leaf clover over your ear, you will encounter at least one cool, rainy spell. Plan for it and be prepared.

Mark each article, including clothing, with the owner's name. You can use India ink, a marking pen, or a name tape, or you can type or print your name on a piece of iron-on tape (put a bit of waxed paper beneath it) and then iron it on the article. Use a wood-burning set to burn names into wooden articles such as the handles of hatchets or shovels.

A day or two ahead of time, let each camper

(Girl Scouts, U.S.A.)

assemble all the duffel, checking it against the master list, and try it for fit by packing it into his or her pack. It's also a good idea to place everything, including the camper's pack frame and his or her share of the group equipment, on the scales and weigh it to the ounce. Take a half day or overnight hike with it to see how it rides. Does it weigh too much? Then take everything out and see how many items are actually nonessential. The mark of an experienced backpacker is the small amount of bulk and weight carried; one way to do this is by taking advantage of every saving offered by modern freeze-dried food and lightweight equipment.

An average man in good condition can carry a pack of 30 to 35 pounds, juniors and women 18 to 25 pounds, and younger children proportionately less. Around 30 pounds is suggested for trips by canoe, bicycle, or horseback. The lighter the pack the better, however, just as long as you have what you need. (See Chapter 28 for hints on packing a backpack.)

WAYS TO LIGHTEN THE LOAD

Depending on the type of outing, some camps minimize the problem of transportation on long trips by sending such heavy materials as food, clean clothing, and bedding ahead by auto, truck, or pack horse. You may also be able to replenish food supplies at stores along the way or by shipping supplies ahead by parcel post. Fresh clothing can be supplied in this way and the soiled returned to camp.

Cut down on both weight and expense by finding ways to make one piece of equipment serve several purposes and by making do at the campsite.

OTHER THINGS TO PLAN FOR

Make out a kapers chart or schedule of trip duties rotating responsibilities so that no one will feel unfairly burdened. Place different combinations of campers to work together at various times to prevent the development of cliques or personal animosities. Outline duties clearly so that no one fails to do what was supposed to be done. This also makes it easier to prevent shirking. Tempers can flare very quickly over this.

Pool all money and divide it among two or three responsible persons. Usually no money will be needed except for emergencies, for good trip country usually lies away from towns. If campers do have occasion to go into town, set a low limit on how much each can spend for sweets and other appetite spoilers. A well-planned menu includes all the sweets that are good for them, and those who are more affluent should not be encouraged to show off before the others.

Ask for volunteers to keep a trip diary or log. If they have the ability to see the funny side of things and put it into words, so much the better. Include exact times of arrival and departure and record just what you did at each stop and along the way. Official artists and photographers may also be selected. The diary will make good reading around the campfire at night, and by adding pictures, poems, souvenirs and perhaps a marked trail map, it can be made into a booklet, adorned by the trippers themselves or in the arts and crafts department and presented to each person as soon after the trip as possible. The pages can be mounted in a spiral notebook with special covers pasted on.

Work out a complete itinerary of just where you expect to be at any given time and leave a copy at the camp office so that they can locate you if it becomes necessary.

Give some thought to things to do for recreation at odd moments on the trip and take suggestions for games, songs, stunts, and poems to use as they fit in. A nature quiz or round-robin story may be just the thing for a rest stop along the trail or just before crawling into bed. Such activities help people forget how tired they are.

You should impress upon the group the importance of sticking together at all times so that no one gets lost. Counselors should have whistles with perhaps a few extra for campers who must temporarily leave the group for water or firewood. Agree upon an exact procedure for both the group and the camper if someone should become separated.

On the Road

MAKING CAMP

Begin looking for a good campsite at least an hour or two before sundown. You will be tired and thankful to have supper over, the dishes washed, and everything made shipshape

(YMCA Camp Widjiwagan, Ely, Minn.)

for the night well before dark, since camp lighting is usually something less than brilliant.*

After you have chosen your campsite, survey it carefully to decide just how to lay it out, locating the cooking area, latrine, tents, and so on. Place personal duffel in one area and group equipment in another, arranged with labels clearly in evidence so that anyone can easily find what he or she wants. Campers then start to complete their preassigned tasks as quickly as possible.

In setting up camp, remember to:

1. Put perishable supplies to cool.
2. Pitch tents fairly close for companionship and, preferably, facing north or northeast if a storm seems likely. (Most violent summer storms come from the southwest—hence the sailor's name, "Souwester," for his hat.) If fair weather seems likely, you may want to face tents southeast to catch the morning sun or vice versa if you want to sleep late.
3. Make beds, clearing away all pebbles, sticks, and clumps of grass. Have campers place their individual duffels inside their tents. Get anything needed out of the packs. If you are going to unpack or rearrange large quantities of your duffel, it is best to place it on a blanket or poncho to prevent losing or misplacing small articles.
4. Dig a latrine.
5. If you need firewood, get it and arrange your fireplace. Otherwise, set up your stove and cooking paraphernalia.
6. Get water for drinking and cooking; purify it if necessary.
7. Take care of general camping equipment, such as boats, canoes, lanterns, and so forth.

*For specific information on choosing a campsite, see Chapter 22.

DIVIDING TRIP DUTIES

It is ordinarily best to divide trippers into committees for each meal, with duties assigned somewhat as follows:

COOKS. Consult the menu and figure out methods and approximate cooking times, type of fire and fireplace needed, and so forth.

If you are going to use wood, tell the fire builders the kind of fire and fireplace you want and where and when to build them.

At the proper time, get the food out and measure out the proportions, putting the rest away so that it will not be contaminated by insects and dirt.

If cooking with wood, *soap the entire outside* of the kettles before cooking the food. Take pride in seeing that everything is palatable and well seasoned.

Get out eating utensils and set the table or arrange to serve the food cafeteria-style.

Act as hosts or hostesses and serve the plates. As soon as everyone has finished eating, put leftover food away and replace unused portions.

FIRE BUILDERS. Prepare to furnish the heat necessary for cooking in the proper manner. For a wood fire, you may or may not need an axe, knife, or saw, depending on your geographic location and the type of wood available. Have handy a fire poker, shovel, and other equipment to use in case the fire should start to spread.

Consult the cooks and prepare the type of fire and fireplace needed. Build it early enough to let it burn down to coals by the time the cooks are ready.

Gather enough wood to last through the meal, chopping or breaking it up into appropriate sizes and arranging a neat woodpile convenient to the fire but not in the way or where sparks might be blown into it.

Keep the fire going, with at least one person constantly standing by to replenish fuel, rearrange coals and so forth, at the direction of the cooks. Keep up the fire long enough to heat dishwater.

Completely extinguish the fire as soon as everyone is through with it and leave the fireplace neat and with enough fuel to start the next meal if it is to be eaten there.

If breakfast is next or there are signs of rain, gather some tinder, kindling, and firewood and put them under a tent or extra tarpaulin. (For additional information on fires, see Chapter 26.)

CLEAN UP AND SANITATION. Arrange a refrigerating or cooling system for perishable foods.

Put dishwater on to heat a soon as the cooks are through with the fire and there are large containers available for it. Heat enough for sterilizing, too.

Wash all dishes and sterilize them. Keep your dishwater clean by wiping dishes out first with dry leaves, napkins, or paper towels before immersing them in the dishwater. Fill one pan with hot soapy water, another with hot water for rinsing and sterilizing. Sand or wood ashes make good substitutes for scouring powder.

Dishes and silverware can be sterilized by placing them in a net bag or one made from a double thickness of cheesecloth and immersing them in boiling water for two minutes; then hang bag and all up to drain and dry.

Wash out dishcloths and towels and hang them out to dry. Scald them after the evening meal.

Burn out and flatten tin cans and prepare to take all garbage with you. Anything that will not burn should be carried out of the backcountry. Bring along plastic bags for this purpose. Burying is not satisfactory because the material is likely to be exposed later by animals or frost action.

Be sure there is enough properly sterilized water on hand for drinking and for taking pan baths if desired. For proper water treatment procedures, consult "Making Drinking Water Safe" in Chapter 18.

HUMAN WASTE

Fortunately, human waste is biodegradable and will return to nature. The process is speeded up when human waste is mixed with bacteria in the top four to ten inches of soil; the depth will vary depending on soil conditions. At these depths the system of biological decomposers work to quickly dispose of organic material.

For individual comfort stops while traveling, a person can select a suitable screened spot at least 100 feet from any open water. Either with the heel of the boot or with a small digging tool (a light garden trowel is good), make a small hole, taking care to dig down into the humus layer. Keep the sod intact if possible. After use, simply fill the hole with the loose dirt and then tramp in the sod. Nature will do the rest of the work in very short order.

For overnight use by a group at a campsite, it is better to concentrate all human waste in one spot rather than have each individual select his or her own area. Locate a latrine on high ground at least 300 feet from any stream, lake or marshy area so the human waste will be filtered through the soil. As noted above, do not dig below the active bacteria level. If the latrine is located in an appropriate area away from combustible fuels, burn all toilet paper in the trench. Do so only if you can avoid starting fires around the latrine.

Keep the spade handy and spread a layer of dirt over the latrine after each use. Before leaving the campsite, be sure to replace all the sod and then cover the area with a large rock or log.

Keep toilet paper nearby on a forked stick and covered with a No. 10 tin can or a 1-pound coffee can with a detachable lid as a shelter from wind and weather.

The latrine should be close enough to the campsite to be convenient and easy and safe to get to at night, yet it must be far enough away to provide privacy. If no natural screen of bushes or underbrush is available construct one with a poncho or tarp suspended on trees or bushes. Arrange facilities nearby for handwashing.

GARBAGE DISPOSAL

Disposal of waste and refuse in the backcountry must be handled carefully, since improper care of such matter can result in pollution, contamination, and unsightliness. Rubbish and waste dumped about a campsite can draw flies and other pests, and may give off offensive odors. Always leave the land clean and attractive for yourself and others to enjoy.

WASHING. Personal bathing or washing cooking utensils or clothing should not be done directly in any body of water even with biodegradable detergent. Any soap, biodegradable or not, causes pollution to streams, ponds, or lakes. To clean dishes, clothing, or yourself, carry water up on the shore and well a way from the water supply as far as is practical. Liquid wastes and soapy water should be drained on vegetation-covered soil that can filter out the soap and break it down. If you have grease left over from cooking, it can be burned on an open fire before washing pots or pans.

In some areas it may be permissible to make a grease pit for disposing of liquid wastes. If so, remove the top soil intact and set it aside. Then dig a hole and line it with small stones or gravel. Pour your dishwater and other liquids into it and burn it out each time with a quick-burning fire. Be sure to fill the hole and replace the top soil before leaving camp.

DISPOSING OF SOLID WASTES. Solid wastes normally should be placed in plastic bags and carried out of the backcountry. In some cases, however, it may be possible to dry them out on a grill or screen over an open fire and then burn them completely. Do not bury them, for some prowling animal will be sure to dig them up. Such wastes as aluminm foil, and banana, orange, and apple peelings will not burn and should be carried in a litter bag back to civilization for disposal. Remove both ends from tin cans and place them in the fire to burn out the inside contents and soften the solder so that you can mash them flat under your foot. They should also be carried home rather than buried, for it will take many years for them to disintegrate.

Twist paper to be burned tightly and burn it a little at a time, holding it down with a green stick poker so that the gases produced will not cause it to fly into the air and become a potential source of a forest fire. Tear cardboard boxes into bits and feed them to the fire a little at a time. If you do not have a wood fire, then carry out all paper.

BEDDING DOWN FOR THE NIGHT

Cache all food safely against roving animals (see Chapter 27 for techniques). Turn pots and kettles upside down and stow everything neatly away for the night. See that the campfire is comletely out and cannot spread.

Many animals like to chew on candles, soap, and the like; securely hide them or suspend them from tree limbs so that they are inaccessible. Porcupines, in particular, crave salt and consequently may chew and completely ruin articles that have been perspiration-soaked, such as axe, paddle or oar handles, saddles, shoes, belts, bridles, backpack straps, and so forth. These, too, should be suspended from ropes or taken inside the tent with you.

If you are sleeping outside, either place your boots or shoes in a plastic sack or turn them upside down as a protection against rain or heavy dew. Keep them close where they can be located quickly if needed in the night. Also, keep a flashlight nearby where it can be located instantly in the dark.

HEALTH AND CLEANLINESS ON TRIPS

Trip campers need to pay special attention to keeping themselves and their clothing clean. When necessary, it may be desirable to occasionally stay in one campsite for a half or a whole day in order to bathe and wash out clothing. Sometimes it is possible to stop at a nearby town to use public showers and a laundromat.

All the rules of health and sanitation are doubly important on a trip, where the illness or incapacity of a single person is most inconvenient. A stimulating and refreshing bath or sponge-off every day is a must, as is washing before meals. Campers should never sleep in the clothes they have worn all day, for collected body moisture will cause chilling as it evaporates. Soiled clothes, especially underwear and socks, should be washed out and hung up to dry overnight. Be sure that everyone follows the recommended procedures mentioned earlier for personal bathing and washing.

Take care of minor ailments that clearly fall within the realm of first aid; they may turn into major problems if neglected. The counselor best trained in first aid should administer all treatments and should keep an exact record of everything done.

To repeat what has already been mentioned, no trip should be taken without at least two counselors; if a camper should be seriously injured or show signs of serious illness, one counselor should take him or her to the nearest physician or back to camp while the other stays with the rest of the group.

BREAKING CAMP

Before pulling out from a temporary campsite in the backcountry, be sure that the area is in even neater condition than it was when you arrived. Make every attempt to restore it so that no one will know that you have been there. Take a last look around to see that nothing is left behind.

Unless the site had a permanent campfire area, you should see that all traces of the fire are eradicated. All charred wood should have been burned completely and the fire should be thoroughly out. The remaining gray soot and black coals can then be crushed and buried or dispersed in the least conspicuous place possible. Any rocks used for the fireplace should be dismantled and redistributed and the soil and sod groundcover replaced. Also, be sure to burn out the latrine and grease pit, if one was used, and restore any sod removed.

Back At The Main Camp

Each camper and counselor should have a physical checkup by the physician or nurse within 24 hours after arriving back in camp. All should return in good condition; cases of sunburn, indigestion, overfatigue, and the like are unforgivable since they indicate poor planning or management of the trip.

Trippers should take it easy for a day or two after returning from a hard journey, taking time to do laundry and get their personal effects in order. However, within a short time after returning, the counselor should call a group meeting to evaluate the trip, noting both the good and bad points of the preliminary planning and preparation, suitability of the food, morale of the group, and so on. The counselor should carefully make a note of all suggestions that will help to improve future trips. The counselor may also want to relay some of these ideas to the director and trips counselor for the benefit of others.

TRIPS BY WATERCRAFT

Trips by canoe, kayak, or raft are exciting and especially suited for senior campers. Long distances can be covered on water, particularly when traveling with the current of a river. To safely undertake extended trips, however, campers must be excellent swimmers and skilled boaters. They should also have toughened themselves by taking shorter excursions. Camps nearly always have rigid standards or tests that campers must pass before they can qualify; these usually include passing the American Red Cross intermediate swimming test or its equivalent as well as demonstrating a proficiency in camping and boating skills.

General Considerations

There are some general planning considerations that apply to all extended trips by water, although some alterations may be in order depending on the type of craft used and the type of water traveled. What may be appropriate equipment or procedures on calm lakes or streams may not suffice at all on more challenging whitewater.

As pointed out in Chapter 16, each person should wear a Coast Guard-approved life jacket at all times. Other appropriate clothing should be worn, including rubber sneakers while paddling. In extremely cold water and cold weather, a wet suit and neoprene booties are always a comfort. Never wear heavy or tight clothing or weigh yourself down with knives, axes, heavy shoes, or rubber boots, lest you suddenly be thrown into the water and need to swim. Dark eyeglasses should be available to protect the eyes and a safety strap to hold them on is essential.

Additional clothing, gear and food can be stored in waterproof bags or containers that are securely tied or strapped in the craft. An alternative is to place plastic bags that are tightly sealed inside of regular packs or duffle bags. Be sure to pack things on top that you might want in a hurry.

On bright sunny days, especially on water, campers should beware of suburn. It is easy to unwittingly be burned badly enough to be incapacitated, for you will probably be too far from shore to have any shade at all. Everyone should keep the exposed parts of the body well covered with a good suntan lotion. Find shady places to stop for lunch and take plenty of time to rest. On extremely hot days, it may even be necessary to confine travel to the cool of early morning and evening. When taking long voyages it is best to plan layovers every three or four days for rest and relief from the constant physical strain.

When putting in to shore and disembarking, make sure your craft is properly fastened by its painter to a tree, rock, or stake so it won't be washed away or lost. If there is a strong wind or waves, the boat can be damaged by lashing about on pebbles or rocks, therefore it is often best to carry the craft well back from shore and turn it upside down.

On large bodies of water, stay close to shore. Learn to anticipate changes in the weather (in some circumstances you might even want to carry a small portable radio for getting weather

(Camp Kooch-I-Ching, International Falls, Minn.)

reports) and get off the water if a storm is approaching. It is particularly dangerous to remain on the water during squalls, when it is lightning or in high winds.

The general rule when capsized is to stay with your craft, since the boat should be properly constructed or adapted so that it will support the passengers, even when it is filled with water. The main thing is to catch hold and stay with the craft rather than try to swim to shore. Hang on with one hand and paddle to shore with the other. If there is a wind or current, it will probably carry you there without any effort.

Another general rule is never boat alone. There should be a minimum of three boats and boaters must maintain a visual communication system. An experienced and prudent person should be in the lead craft and another in the sweep position in the rear boat. All other craft should stay between these two boats. Work out a system of hand signals to convey messages and see that everyone understands that they are to be obeyed instantly and exactly.

Before setting out with a group of campers on an extended trip, test any new and unfamiliar equipment and be sure it is in good repair. Make sure you have strong, adequately sized paddles or oars and carry sufficient spares for the length of the trip. Also be certain that there is absolutely nothing to entangle boaters if they must free themselves from an upset craft, *i.e.,* canoe seats that lock on shoe heels, baggage that dangles in an upset, loose rope in the craft, and so forth.

Provide ropes that allow you to hold onto your craft in case of an upset. Kayaks should have 6-inch diameter grab loops attached to bow and stern, while open canoes should have 8- to 10-foot bow and stern lines (painters) securely attached. Rafts should have taut perimeter grab lines threaded through the loops usually provided.

Be sure to take along an adequate amount of appropriate repair materials for the craft. Tape (heating duct tape) is popular for short trips with canoes or kayaks. More complete repair kits are necessary for longer trips.

Essentials for River Paddlers

The leader should know the river or obtain the services of an experienced person who does. It is also wise to walk the bank to determine how to run difficult rapids that may be encountered. When in doubt, don't gamble, carry craft around the rapids. Remember the old Indian saying, "No Indian ever drowned on a portage." Portaging gives you a chance to stretch your legs and insures your safety. It is also better to portage or line the craft than to try to run through rock-strewn water where it is easy to do irreparable damage to your boat.

Respect the river. Know river classifiations and learn why and how rivers are classified. For the open-canoe paddler, cold water, cold weather, remote areas, and rising rivers increase the degree of difficulty.

Whether going by canoe, kayak, or raft, there are certain basic paddling skills that will enable you and your followers to proceed down a stretch of easy rapids with confidence. It cannot be stressed too strongly that beginners and novices should learn and practice these skills under competent supervision.

Since some flatwater skills are not applicable to river situations, those people who have been trained on lake or quiet stretches of water only are not ready to venture down a river until they have been through some kind of basic river course. In such a course newcomers should be taught proper stroke techniques for rivers, how to ferry from point to point, how to brace, and how to properly use eddies to the paddler's advantage. In addition, and just as important, they should learn and practice proper rescue and safety techniques. If you are the designated leader and do not feel competent of your skills, they easily can be acquired by enrolling in a formal course of instruction or by joining a paddling club. For further information, check with your local office of the American Red Cross or consult the sources listed in the Additional Readings at the end of this chapter.

Canoes

A canoe is, for its size, one of the safest means of water travel since it won't capsize if used properly, and even if it should, you are in no danger if you hang on, for even when filled with water a canoe will support three or four people.

A 16-foot cruising canoe seems to be the general favorite for camp trips. These are made of canvas, fiberglass, plywood, aluminum, or one of the new materials now being used. The important thing is to choose a trip canoe for strength, stability in the water, and lightness if you will need to portage. For lake travel, choose a canoe with a slightly rounded bottom and a width that continues well out to the ends. A flat-bottomed, shoe-type curved keel, giving higher and slim ends, is better. Though long, tapered ends give more speed, a flat-bottomed boat gives more stability in the water. Put your canoe in first class repair and equip it with a painter and proper thwarts. When paddling, most people like to remove the seat and kneel on the bottom of the canoe with knees well apart and buttocks resting against a thwart; others prefer to leave the seats in so they can change position in calm water. Kneeling is the safest position since it keeps the center of gravity low; it also helps you to travel more rapidly and keeps the canoe steadier and well under control. You will need a light, waterproof kneeling pad that will float so that it can serve as a life preserver in an emergency; it will also serve as a pillow for sleeping or a seat for sitting on damp ground around the campfire. Buy one or make it from two layers of sponge rubber inserted inside an inner tube.

The sternman's paddle should reach up to his or her chin when it is placed on the ground; the bowman's is about three inches shorter. Label your paddle with a piece of adhesive tape on which you have printed your name in India ink so that you can always use the same paddle and get accustomed to it. Carry an extra paddle on the floor of each canoe in case one is lost or broken, and take a repair kit suitable for mending your type of canoe.

On a trip, a canoe usually holds two people and their duffel, though a large craft can carry three. The sternman should be experienced and a master of the "J" stroke, for he or she is responsible for steering. The bowman, paddling on the opposite side, sets the rhythm of the stroke and keeps a sharp lookout for half-hidden rocks or snags. He or she must be able to use the "draw" stroke to pull the canoe away from suddenly revealed obstacles in the path. Keep the canoes about two or three canoe lengths apart for companionship and for help if one gets into trouble.

Assemble all the gear for the canoe and pack it while it is entirely afloat, keeping it in shallow water and wading along the side. It is very important to *trim your load,* keeping the weight balanced crosswise and toward the center of the canoe so that the bow and stern are kept as light as possible. Place heavy things on the bottom and leave three to four inches of *freeboard,* or clear space, below the gunwales. Pack your duffel under the thwarts, if possible, and tie it so it can't slip about and throw the canoe off balance and so you won't lose it if you should capsize. Distribute the weight so that with passengers and duffel aboard the bow rides about an inch or two higher than the stern; take the canoe, loaded with both duffel and crew, out a little distance from shore and test it before you start on the trip.

When you are ready to take off, the bowman steadies the bow between his or her legs while the sternman walks down the *exact center* of the canoe, keeping the body weight low and both hands on the gunwales. When the stern is reached, the sternman's weight raises the bow so that the bowman can push off as he or she enters to send the canoe out into the clear and set it in motion.

One of the nice things about canoe travel is that the craft is easy to portage. For a two-person portage, invert the canoe, with one person supporting the bow on the shoulder, the other supporting it over his or her head. The person at the bow chooses the path, while the other follows. For a short portage you can carry a canoe upright; with one person grasping it underneath at each end. Counselors and senior campers will probably prefer the one-person carry.

> Thus the Birch Canoe was builded
> In the valley by the river,
> In the bosom of the forest;
> And the forest's life was in it,
> All its mystery and its magic,
> All the lightness of the birch tree,
> All the toughness of the cedar,
> All the larch's supple sinews;
> And it floated on the river
> Like a yellow leaf in Autumn
> Like a yellow water lily.
>
> —LONGFELLOW, *The Song of Hiawatha.*

Kayaks

It is well beyond the scope of this book to treat kayaks and kayaking in detail, but these sporty little boats are becoming popular as a means of transport for trip camping. The major drawback to their use in camp programs is that they take a bit more instruction and practice in order to master the basics. Also, most kayaks are designed to hold only one person and the amount of equipment that can be stored on board in special waterproof bags is somewhat limited. Whitewater kayaks are most common and therefore this discussion is centered on them.

Kayaks generally are of two types, rigid and collapsible. The collapsible kayak, or foldboat, has a framework of wood or tubular metal that is fitted into a rubberized canvas skin. The craft can be collapsed and carried quite easily by hand or in the trunk of an automobile. These boats do not have the durability of rigid fiberglass or plastic kayaks.

The paddler sits on a molded seat inside the cockpit of the boat and braces against hip, knee, and foot braces. To prevent water from coming into the boat, a tight-fitting waterproof device called a spray cover or skirt is worn around the paddler's waist and an outer elasticized edge is then stretched over the convex lip (coaming) around the cockpit. Whitewater kayakers also wear helmets for protection in case of a spill. Since the boat is watertight, the kayaker can quickly right the craft by using the paddle in a special maneuver called the Eskimo roll.

Paddles used for kayaking are double bladed rather than single bladed as in canoe paddles, yet most of the basic canoe strokes can be applied to kayak paddling, including the forward stroke, back stroke, and sweep (Fig 17-2).

Rafts

In recent years inflatable rafts have become more accessible and are now quite popular for river floating. Rafts come in a variety of sizes and their quality varies considerably. They usually are constructed of some combination of canvas, nylon, vinyl, neoprene, and rubber.

All inflatable craft should have multiple air chambers and should be test inflated before starting any trip. Usually the smallest acceptable rafts for river trips are between 12 and 15 feet and hold from two to five people, depending on the amount of additional equipment and gear carried. They are either rowed or paddled. Paddling has its advantages since everyone can participate,while rowing requires only one person. On the other hand, a raft mounted with a solid oar frame is easier to control and maneuver.

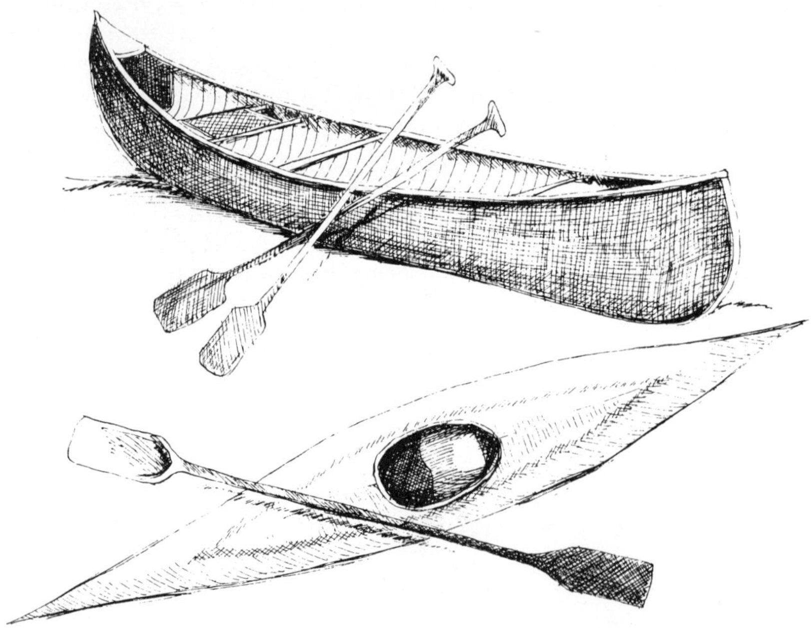

Figure 17-2 Canoe and kayak.

Figure 17-3 Inflatable rafts are popular for river trips.

INITIATIVE GAMES, TRUST EXERCISES, AND ROPES COURSES

Many problems and tasks confront any group of campers, but this is especially true on an extended wilderness excursion where everyone must learn to make and accept decisions, work together, and trust one another in order to accomplish desired goals. This does not necessarily happen automatically, since a group consists of individuals with varying backgrounds, skills, and personalities. If just one person is hard to get along with or is uncooperative in any way, a very difficult situation can arise for everyone else. In fact, the inability to trust others or cooperate with them in an adventure program can create a very dangerous situation for all.

A good way of unifying a group and developing useful physical skills is to use initiative games, trust exercises, and ropes courses. These activities can help overcome a group's problems by breaking down individual inhibitions, introducing campers to one another, enhancing each member's ability to interact and serve effectively in the group, and increasing each person's awareness of and need for mutual support. In addition, problem-solving competencies are refined and feelings of trust, responsibility, and competence are enhanced.

Just what are initiative games, trust exercises, and ropes courses? Before answering the question it should be pointed out that many of the activities to be discussed in this section might require the participant to demonstrate *both* initiativc and trust if they are to be completed sucessfully. In some cases at least, the elements of initiative games, trust exercises, and ropes courses can be merged together into one and the same element. Consequently, as will be seen in some of the examples on the following pages, it is not always possible to make a clear-cut distinction among the three terms.

This is also a good spot to mention that almost all of the concepts and activities presented here were first developed, tested, and described either by the staff of Project Adventure* or Benjy Simpson of Encounter Four.** These people deserve great recognition and praise for their contributions in this exciting area of adventure programming.

INITIATIVE GAMES. An initiative game is a group problem-solving task that requires mental and sometimes physical effort to resolve. Usually teamwork and cooperative planning by the entire group are necessary to complete the task. The counselor or leader presents a clearly defined question or problem and the group is required to solve it. There are no right or wrong ways to perform the task as long as the problem or situation is resolved within the guidelines and restrictions imposed by the leader. The important thing is for the entire group to participate as a unit.

---

*Karl Rohnke: *Cowstails and Cobras*, Project Adventure, 1977, 157 pp.

**Benjy Simpson (ed.): *Initiative Games*, Encounter Four, 1974, 67 pp.

TRUST EXERCISES. A trust exercise, on the other hand, is an activity that requires the participants to place trust and confidence in the hands of either one other person or a whole group of people. The activity usually takes a bit of courage to perform, such as falling backward from a low platform into the waiting arms of fellow campers, but through proper instruction and training the activity is really quite safe. Such activities are great confidence builders. As indiiduals learn to cope with uncertainty they also begin to understand the importance of sensitivity, cooperation, responsibility and dependence on their fellows.

ROPES COURSES. A ropes course is essentially an obstacle course designed to present a series of graduated challenges to participants as they climb, swing, jump and balance on rope and log structures. The various structures are built at progressively higher elevations in order to develop individual and group confidence. As with initiative games and trust exercises, the ropes course requires both individual and group effort and support. A great advantage to most of the exercises in this section is that they can be performed at just about any time and in any place. The various tasks can be performed individually or they can be combined into a series of progressive events. They can vary in their level of difficulty with some that are simple to solve and others that are more complex. Many are suitable for the maturity and age level of most campers; however, the leader must always give special consideration to factors such as age, fitness, and maturity when deciding which activity to choose (Fig. 17-4).

Figure 17-4 Ropes course high element: walking the two-line bridge. (D. Improta, Outdoor Program, University of Montana, Missoula, Mont.)

Leadership Considerations

Before getting into the activities themselves, let's first take a look at some specific leadership hints.

VOLUNTARY PARTICIPATION. Participation should always be voluntary and no person should ever be forced to take part in any of the activities. The courage and willingness to participate must come from the individual alone. This does not mean, however, that the leader and the group should not attempt to encourage those who are reluctant, but, if someone decidedly does not choose to take part, respect should be shown for his or her rights and decision.

USE APPROPRIATE ACTIVITIES. Use only those activities that are appropriate for the age, ability, and number in the group. In cases where you have a large number of people, it may be advisable to split the participants into several smaller groups. Also be sure to use only those activities that provide every individual with an opportunity to succeed. This can be done by following a progression, starting with simple tasks and then moving to more challenging ones.

INSTRUCTION IN FALLING. To avoid unnecessary risk of injury, all participants should first receive instruction and practice in falling correctly. This also helps to increase one's physical ability and psychological confidence. Each person should learn to absorb the impact of a fall primarily with the legs, and a lesser amount with the hands and arms. This is done while tucking up and rolling either forward or backward, depending on the momentum and the direction of the fall. Campers can practice this maneuver by jumping off of a two or three foot high object, with the counselor serving as the spotter.

SPOTTING. There are some activities that require good spotting technique in order to help break potential falls. This is especially so when someone is jumping, balancing, or attempting other maneuvers from several feet off the ground. As a general rule, spotting is mandatory for any activity taking place 6 feet from the ground or lower. Spotting involves having an individual (or a whole group, if necessary) ready to help support someone who is falling in order to reduce his or her impact. A spotter should be attentive, and should stand a few feet away with hands up, ready to support the upper part of the person's body.

DEBRIEFING. Following completion of each activity, it is important to take time to discuss with the group what has happened. How was the problem solved? What were its strengths and weaknesses? What other methods could have been used? Who took the leadership role? Was there group cooperation and involvement? What analogies can be made between the campers' solution and real life situations? Asking these and other questions during the debriefing can help to focus on the values of the exercise and can draw the group's attention to their own actions and behavior.

MIX IT UP. In order to provide variety and to reduce monotony, try to offer a good mixture of activities. Also, don't attempt to use all of the activities at once. Save some good ones for later.

Description of Activities

The initiative games, trust exercises, and ropes course activities that follow are among the more popular ones and have been used successfully for years. There are many more contained in the resources listed in the Additional Readings section at the end of this chapter and, for that matter, it isn't all that hard to develop some additional ones yourself—just use your imagination.

ALL ABOARD. Construct a platform, locate a flat rock, or find a stump several feet tall and ask everyone to get on it at the same time. They must hold the position for at least 8 seconds, with everyone's feet being off the ground. Be sure to pick a platform that has just enough room for everyone, insuring that they hold on to each other and work cooperatively. Ten or so people should be able to fit on a space 12 to 15 inches in diameter.

To make the activity more fun and interesting, tell the group that there has been a volcanic explosion and within 30 seconds boiling hot lava will encompass the area. Everyone must be on the platform before the lava reaches them.

UNTANGLE. Ask a group of 10 to 15 people to stand in a tight circle facing inward. Each person then raises his or her right arm and grabs someone's right hand. The same is done with the left hand, being sure it belongs to someone different. Without letting go, the group must now untangle the human knot to form a circle. On most occasions the group will unwind to actually form the circle, but sometimes they end up in a figure eight, which is also all right. If the group is unable to solve the problem within a reasonable period of time, you can help them out by breaking one couple's handhold and rejoining it in a different position.

FOUR POINTER. The object of this activity is to get seven cooperative persons to travel together for a distance of 30 feet using only four simultaneous points of contact (hands, feet, or whatever) with the ground at any one time. If your group is large, divide them into several teams.

GET UP. Have everyone sit in a circle with their feet touching. The group then has to stand up together by working out a system of grabbing hands and pulling or whatever other method they may choose. Let them figure it out.

CIRCLE STAND. As a follow-up to the previous exercise, have everyone turn around and sit with their backs to the circle, interlocking arms with the person on each side. Again, the object is for the entire group to move from a sitting to a standing position together. After the group has worked out cooperative method of succeding, have them try to do the same thing without locking arms.

BOIL WATER. Working in groups of four, or whatever number seems appropriate, provide each team with one match and a pot of water. They are then given 15 minutes in which to search out wood, start a fire, and bring the water to a boil. To add interest, campers can pretend that one member of their party is coming down with hypothermia and they must treat him or her with a hot drink as soon as possible.

TRUST CIRCLE. Everyone sits shoulder to shoulder in a tight circle with knees bent and feet touching. One at a time each takes a turn at standing in the middle of the circle and performing a trust fall. The person who falls is instructed to stand erect and stiff with arms folded in front of the body. The group forming the circle serves as catchers, holding their arms up with palms out. When ready, the person in the middle falls stiffly backward onto the outreached hands of a catcher, who then passes the faller on to another person. The object is to see if the faller can be passed all the way around the circle at least once.

TRUST FALL. This trust activity is conducted by having the faller stand on a sturdy platform (tree trunk, ladder rung, etc.), then fall stiffly backward into the arms of the waiting group. At least eight to ten individuals standing on level ground act as catchers and they, as well as the faller, should adhere closely to the special instructions necessary for safely carrying out this event.

The trust fall is one of the most popular and more exciting adventure activities, but it also can be dangerous if not conducted properly. First,

Figure 17–5 The trust fall.

Figure 17–6 The board walk. (D. Improta, Outdoor Program, University of Montana, Missoula, Mont.)

Figure 17–7 The climbing wall takes teamwork. (Outdoor Program, University of Montana, Missoula, Mont.)

you must find a suitable location with flat ground that is free of sharp objects such as sticks or rocks. Also, the platform must be sturdy and of proper height. For adults, 5 to 6 feet would be maximum height, while a much lower height should be used for youngsters. A good way to judge desirable height is according to the following rule established by Project Adventure: If the head and shoulders of the falling participant reaches the line of catchers before the feet, then the platform is too high. Yet another important precaution is to have everyone remove eyeglasses, watches, or any other sharp or breakable objects.

The catchers are instructed to stand with shoulders touching in two separate, facing lines that consist of at least four persons each. To form a safe landing area, hands are extended palms up so that they alternate with the hands of the people in the other line and extend almost to their elbows. Note that it is recommended that catchers do *not* grasp hands since it is better to have them free, allowing for flexibility and give of the arms. Just prior to the fall, all should pull their head well back and keep their eyes on the faller. Figure 17–5 shows the proper technique.

In order to distribute the force of the fall and to make catching easier, the faller should be instructed to hold the body rigid until caught. There should be no bending at the waist or knees. Also, the person should fold the arms in front of the body to avoid hitting someone in the face accidentally.

Figure 17–8 Getting the tire over the vertical log. (D. Improta, Outdoor Program, University of Montana, Missoula, Mont.)

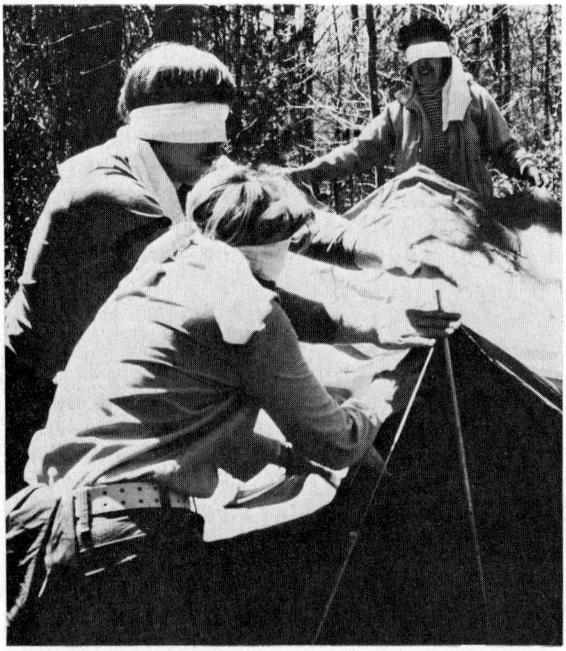

Figure 17-9 Pitching a tent while blindfolded takes initiative, teamwork and cooperation. (A. Cosgrove, Camp Spalding, Spokane, Wash.)

Have everyone alternate positions in the line after each catch and encourage each to participate in the fall. For those who are hesitant, the height of the platform can be lowered and then progressively raised as the camper gains confidence.

ELECTRIC FENCE. For this activity you will need a long rope and a small diameter log or sturdy pole about 8 feet in length. The rope is used to create an enclosure large enough to contain the group. This is done by tying it to several trees or posts at about chest height. The object is to get everyone outside the enclosure without going under the rope or touching it. To accomplish the task, the 8 foot pole can be used by the group in any manner desired, as long as it does not touch the rope.

To add interest, tell the group that the rope represents a high voltage electric fence with an impenetrable electric field extending from the fence to the ground. Anyone who goes under or comes in contact with the fence is automatically electrocuted and must attempt the crossing again. Similarly, if the pole touches the fence, all those in contact with it are "zapped" and must attempt another crossing. A time limit can be established for completing the game by telling the group that within a specified period of time the entire enclosure will be inundated with tons of poisonous jelly (or whatever) and everyone must be out of the area by then.

BOARD WALK. Using the given props, a group of 7 to 12 people must move together over a 50-foot space of ground. As can be seen in Figure 17-6, the props consist of two lengths of lumber (2 × 4 or 4 × 4 boards), with enough short ropes attached for some of the participants to hang on to.

To add interest, have the group pretend that the ground is covered with an invisible electric field. If anyone falls or steps off the boards, the group must start over.

BEAM OR WALL. Get the entire group over a 7- or 8-foot high beam. As can be seen in

Figure 17-10 Good spotting technique is important on the balance beam. (A. Cosgrove, Camp Spalding, Spokane, Wash.)

Figure 17-11 The tension traverse. (Outdoor Program, University of Montana, Missoula, Mont.)

Figure 17-12 The tire traverse. (D. Improta, Outdoor Program, University of Montana, Missoula, Mont.)

Figure 17-7, the same exercise can be done using a 9-foot high wall constructed of boards.

VERTICAL LOG AND TIRE. Have the group remove and then replace a tire that encircles a 12- to 14-foot high vertical pole or log, as seen in Figure 17-8.

STRANDED. The group is "stranded" on an island with two ropes and must find a way to each shore without swimming. Be sure everyone has on a life vest for this activity.

TREE LUNCH. A flash flood of poisonous yogurt is coming. To escape, everyone must climb into the same tree and eat lunch together.

CHAOS. Blindfold the group and, without talking or using hands or arms, they must line up by height along a wall.

BLIND PITCH. With everyone blindfolded, have them put up a tent (Figure 17-9).

BALANCE BEAM. The participant simply walks across a beam that is attached between two trees or posts. The beam can be constructed of a log 10 to 12 inches in diameter and should be 15 to 20 feet in length. Several different beams can be established at varying heights that range from a foot off the ground to up to 6 feet.

SWINGING LOG. This activity is similar to the previous one, except that the person must walk across a log that is suspended about a foot off the ground by ropes that permit it to swing freely (Figure 17-10).

Figure 17-13 High element ropes course activity. (D. Improta, Outdoor Program, University of Montana, Missoula, Mont.)

TENSION TRAVERSE. Hanging onto a support rope for assistance, the person walks the full length of another rope secured tightly between several trees. One end of the support rope is attached to a limb of one of the trees while the other end hangs free (Figure 17-11). An alternative method for establishing a hand hold is to tightly stretch a horizontal rope about 5½ to 6 feet above the lower rope.

PARALLEL ROPES CRAWL. Using trees or posts, two parallel ropes about 15 to 20 feet in length are tied horizontally about 15 to 20 inches apart. The participant must then negotiate from one end to the other by crawling on all fours.

TIRE TRAVERSE. Using a series of suspended tires (Figure 17-12), the entire group must traverse from one end of the course to the other without touching the ground. The start and finish lines should be several feet beyond the first and last tires. Anyone touching the ground must return to the starting line and begin again.

As an extension of this activity, provide the group with a pail of water and have them pretend that the water is nitroglycerin. The group must transport the "nitro" bomb from one end to the other without spilling any of the liquid. If any spillage takes place, the entire group must start over.

HIGHER ELEMENTS OF ROPES COURSES

In addition to these ropes course activities, there are a number of higher courses (*i.e.*, those above 6 feet in elevation) that can be used (Figures 17-4 and 17-13). Because of the height involved, participants are required to be on a belay in order to stop a fall. For the belay, one end of the rope is attached to the person performing the activity while another person braces the rope around his or her body or a fixed object such as a tree, boulder, or artificial aid. There are very precise ways of doing this, just as there are specific techniques involved in building the high elements of the course itself. Anyone who is responsible for either constructing high ropes courses or for conducting activities that require a belay should first consult the appropriate sources to become familiar with and skilled in these techniques.

ADDITIONAL READINGS

(For an explanation of abbreviations and abbreviated forms used, see page 13.)

Bicycling

Adshead, Robin: *Bikepacking for Beginners.* Order from Bikecentennial, 1978, 85 pp.

Armstrong, Diana: *Bicycle Camping.* Dial, 1981, 154 pp.

Asa, Warren: *North American Bicycle Atlas.* Am. Youth Hostels, Inc., 20 West 17th Street, New York, New York 10011, 1969, 127 pp.

Bicycling Magazine (ed.): *Best Bicycle Tours, Vol. 2.* Rodale, 1981, 92 pp.

Bridge, Raymond: *Freewheeling: The Bicycle Camping Book.* Order from Galloway, 192, p.

Bridge, Raymond: *Bike Touring.* Sierra Club, 1979, 456 pp.

Browder, Sue: *The American Biking Atlas and Touring Guide.* Workman, 1974, 320 pp.

Cardwell: *America's Camping Book,* ch. 43 to p. 459.

Coles, Clarence W., and Harold T. Glenn: *Glenn's Complete Bicycle Repair Manual.* Crown, 1973, 339 pp., paper.
Cuthbertson, Tom: *Anybody's Bike Book: An Original Manual of Bicycle Repairs.* Ten Speed, 1971, 176 pp., paper.
Cuthbertson, Tom: *Bike Tripping.* Ten Speed, 1972, paper.
Cycling (No. 3330). Boy Scouts, 1971, 48 pp., paper.
Frankel, Lillian and Godfrey: *The Bicycle Book.* Cornerstone.
Henkel, Stephen C.: *Bikes: A How-To-Do-It Guide to Selection, Care, Repair, Maintenance, Decoraton, Safety, and Fun on Your Bicycle.* Bantam, 1972, 189 pp., paper.
Joslin, Mandy: *How Do You Bicycle Across Canada? Slowly, Very Slowly.* Mandy Joslin, P.O. Box 16348, Seattle, Washington, 1978, 85 pp.
Macfarlan, Alan A.: *Boy's Book of Biking.* Stackpole, 1968, 160 pp.
MacGonagle, S.: *Bicycle.* Barnes.
McIntyre, Bibs: *The Bike Book: Everything You Need to Know About Owning and Riding a Bike.* Harper & Row, 1972.
Rakowski, John: *Cooking On The Road.* Anderson, 1980, 202 pp.
Savage, John H.: *The Gold Medal Bicycle Handbook.* Fawcett, 274 pp., paper.
Shaw, R.: *Teach Yourself Cycling.* Dover.
Sherman, Steve: *Bike Hiking.* Backpacker Books, 1974, 160 pp.
Sloane, Eugene A.: *The New Complete Book of Bicycling.* Simon & Schuster, 1974, 531 pp.
Thiffault, Mark: *Bicycle Digest.* Digest Books, 288 pp.
Tobey, Peter W.: *Two Wheel Travel: Bicycle Camping and Touring.* Dell.
Wagenvoord, James: *Bikes and Riders.* Van Nostrand, 1972, 157 pp.
Wilhelm, Tim and Glenda: *The Bicycle Touring Book.* Rodale, 1980, 303 pp.

MAGAZINE ARTICLES

Camping Journal:
Camping Journal, Mar., 1974 (Several articles)
Franey, Joseph: "Cross-Country Bicycle Tour: Washington State to Washington, D.C." June, 1972, p. 50.
Millar, Randall: "Cycle Care and Maintenance." July, 1974, p. 30.
Thomas, Bill: "Cycling the Backroads of America." July, 1974, p. 29.
Camping Magazine:
Stein, Bernard: "Bikecology." Mar., 1974, p. 16.
Wilderness Camping:
Hayes, Chuck: "Bicycling Camping—The Only Way to Fly." Mar./Apr., 1974, p. 39.
Moran, Margot: "Island Hopping by Bicycle." Mar./Apr., 1974, p. 34.
Spadaro, Tony: "Gear Right for Touring." Mar./Apr., 1974, p. 43.
Sumner Lloyd: "Two-Wheel Freedom." May/June, 1973, p. 31.
Walters, Bill: "1400 Mile Summer—A Northeastern Cycling Tour." Mar./Apr., 1974, p. 28

Boat and Canoe Camping

(See also related material and the bibliography in Chapter 16.)

Angier: *Skills for Taming the Wilds,* ch. 11.
Bearse, Ray: *The Canoe Camper's Handbook.* 1974, Winchester.
Berger: *Program Activities for Camps,* pp.93–97.
Better Homes & Gardens Family Camping Book, ch. 21.
Cheney, Theodore A.: *Camping by Backpack and Canoe.* Funk & Wagnalls, 1971, 210 pp.
Evans, Jay and Robert R. Anderson: *Kayaking.* Greene, 1975, 192 pp.
Fieldbook for Boys and Men, pp. 274–277.
Germain: *When You Go Canoe Camping.*
Handel, Carle W.: *Canoe Camping.* Ronald, 1953, 192 pp.
Huser, Verne: *River Running.* Regnery, 1975, 294 pp., paper.
Malo, John W.: *Malo's Complete Guide to Canoeing and Canoe Camping.* Collier, 1969, 278 pp., paper.
Malo, John W.: *Wilderness Canoeing.* Macmillan, 1971, 176 pp.
McGinnis, William: *Whitewater Rafting.* Quadrangle, 1975, 361 pp.
Merrill: *All About Camping,* ch. 5.
Ormond: *Complete Book of Outdoor Lore,* ch. 3.
Riviere: *Backcountry Camping,* ch. 2 to p. 37.
Riviere: *The Camper's Bible,* ch. 14.
Riviere, Bill: *Pole, Paddle and Portage.* Van Nostrand, 1969, 260 pp.
Ruck, Wolf: *Canoeing and Kayaking.* McGraw-Hill, 1974, 95 pp.
Schafer, Ann: *Canoeing Western Waterways; The Mountain States.* Harper and Row, 1978, 279 pp., paper.
Shivers: *Camping,* pp.288–294.

MAGAZINE ARTICLES

Camping Journal:
McKeown, William: "Boat Camping." Apr., 1970, p. 23.
Morrow, Les: "Canoe Portage Rig." Apr., 1973, p. 56.
Richards, Blaine: "How to Pack a Canoe." Mar., 1967, p. 42.
Camping Magazine:
Walbrige, Charles C.: "White Water Canoeing." May, 1978, p. 8.
Canoe Magazine:
Bearse, Ray and Mark Bryant: "Choosing a Tripping Canoe." Feb./March, 1981, p. 38.
Wilderness Camping:
Burrell, Bob: "Canoe Back Packing." July/Aug., 1973, p. 20.
Corbeille, Roger L.: "The Canoe Cargo Box." May/June, 1974, p. 28.
LeBrant, Howie, and Harry N. Roberts: *On Canoe Design.* Aug./Sept., 1976, p. 16.

Camping with Children

Bridge: *America's Backpacking Book,* ch. 23.
Langer: *The Joy of Camping,* pp. 125–132.
Manning: *Backpacking One Step at a Time,* ch. 18.
Silverman, Goldie: *Backpacking with Babies and Small Children.* Backpacker Books, 175 pp.
Stout, James and Ann: *Backpacking With Small Children.* Funk & Wagnalls, 1976.
Wood: *Pleasure Packing,* ch. 12.

MAGAZINE ARTICLES

Backpacker:
Clark, Michael J.: "You're Taking . . .Who? . . .Where?" *Backpacker-3,* Fall, 1973, p. 29.

Wallace-Brodeur, Ruth: "How To Get Your Children To Hike With You." Apr./May, 1980, p. 46.

Camping with Horse and Burro

Brower: *Going Light—With Backpack or Burro.*
Cardwell: *America's Camping Book,* ch. 47.
Merrill: *All About Camping,* chs. 11, 21, 22.
Merrill: *The Hiker's and Backpacker's Handbook,* ch. 9.
Ormond: *Outdoorsman's Handbook,* Part 7.
Shivers: *Camping,* pp. 294–295.

Desert Camping

Bridge: *America's Backpacking Book,* ch. 19.
Merrill: *All About Camping,* ch. 7.
Merrill: *The Hiker's and Backpacker's Handbook,* ch. 10.
Merrill: *The Survival Handbook,* ch. 14.

Initiative Games, Trust Exercises and Ropes Courses

Darst, Paul W. and George P. Armstrong: *Outdoor Adventure Activities for School and Recreation Programs.* Burgess, 1980, 307 pp., paper.
Erickson, Susan and Buck Harris: *The Adventure Book.* The Wilderness School, Dept. of Children and Youth Services, P.O. Box 2243, Goshen, Connecticut 06756, no date, 111 pp., paper.
Kudlas, John: *The Rock Climbing Teaching Guide.* AAHPERD, 1979, 104 pp., paper.
Loughmiller, Campbell: *Wilderness Road.* Order from ACA, 1965, 139 pp.
Meier, Joel F., et al. (ed.): *High Adventure Outdoor Pursuits: Organization and Leadership.* Brighton, 1980, 232 pp., paper.
Rohnke, Karl: *Cowstails and Cobras.* Project Adventure, 1977, 157 pp., paper.
Rohnke, Karl: *Project Adventure.* Project Adventure, 1974, 120 pp., paper.
Simpson, Benjy (ed.): *Initiative Games.* Benjy Simpson, Encounter Four, Butler County Community College, College Drive, Oak Hills, Butler, Pennsylvania 16001, 1974, 67 pp. paper.
van der Smissen, Betty and Oswald H. Goering: *A Leader's Guide to Nature-Oriented Activities.* Iowa State U., 1977, 3rd ed., chs. 3 and 6, paper.
Wood, David E. and James C. Gillis, Jr.: *Adventure Education.* National Education Association, 1979, 56 pp., paper.

Mountaineering

Bridge: *America's Backpacking Book,* c. 18.
Cardwell: *America's Camping Book,* ch. 27.
Casewit, Curtis: *The Hiking-Climbing Handbook.* Hawthorn, 1969, 182 pp., paper.
Ferber, Peggy (ed.): *Mountaineering: The Freedom of the Hills.* The Mountaineers, Seattle, Washington, 3rd ed., 1974, 478 pp.
Greenbank, Anthony: *The Book of Survival.* Order from Backpacker Books, 250 pp., paper.
Kelley, Dennis: *Mountain Search for the Lost Person.* Order from the author, P.O. Box 153, Montrose, California 91020, paper.
Kudlas, John: *The Rock Climbing Teaching Guide.* AAHPERD, 1979, 104 pp.
Mendenhall, Ruth and John: *Introduction to Rock and Mountain Climbing.* Stackpole, 1969, 192 pp.
Merrill: *All About Camping,* ch. 10.
Merrill: *The Survival Handbook,* ch. 11.
Paulicke, Wilhelm, and Helmut Dumler: *Hazards in Mountaineering.* Oxford U.
Petzoldt, Paul: *The Wilderness Handbook.* Norton, 1974, 286 pp.
Wilderness Pocket 'n Pack Library.

Survival, First Aid, etc.

Angier: *How to Stay Alive in the Woods.*
Angier, Bradford: *Living off the Country.* Stackpole, 1956, 241 pp.
Angier: *Skills for Taming theWilds.*
Angier: *Survival with Style.*
Angier: *Wilderness Cookery.*
Bale, Robert O.: *Outdoor Living.* Burgess, 1961, 199 pp., spiral.
Berglund, Berndt: *Wilderness Survival,* Scribner, 1974, 175 pp., paper.
Bevan, Dr. James: *The Pocket Medical Encyclopedia and First Aid Guide.* Simon and Schuster, 1979, 144 pp.
Bridge: *America's Backpacking Book,* chs. 15, 16.
Cardwell: *America's Camping Book,* chs. 32, 34.
Dalrymple: *Survival in the Outdoors.*
Fear, Gene: *Surviving the Unexpected Wilderness Emergency.* Survival Education Association, 9035 Golden Given Road, Tacoma, Washinton 98445, 1972, 196 pp.
Fieldbook for Boys and Men, ch. 16 and pp. 550–551.
Greenbank, Anthony: *The Book of Survival.* Signet, 265 pp., paper.
Hamper: *Wilderness Survival.*
Johnson, James R.: *Anyone Can Live off the Land.* McKay, 1961, 121 pp.
Kodet, Dr. E. Russel and Bradford Angier: *Being Your Own Wilderness Doctor.* Stackpole, 1975, 127 pp.
Learn and Tallman: *Backpacker's Digest,* ch. 16.
MacInnes, Hamish: *International Mountain Rescue Handbook.* Scribner's, 1972, 218 pp.
Medicine for Mountaineering. Order from Backpacker Books, 350 pp.
Merrill: *All About Camping,* chs. 23–25.
Merrill: *The Hiker's and Backpacker's Handbook,* ch. 11.
Merrill: *The Survival Handbook.*
Mountaineering First Aid. Backpacker Books, 96 pp., paper.
Olsen, Larry: *Outdoor Survival Skills,* BYU, 1976, 188 pp., paper.
Outdoor Living—Problems, Solutions, Guidelines. Mountain Rescue Council, P.O. Box 696, Tacoma, Washington 98401, 103 pp.
Outdoor Survival: A Game About Wilderness Skills. Stackpole. (A game for 2, 3, or 4 players testing the player's knowledge about what to do when lost away from civilization).
Rethmel: *Backpacking,* ch. 7 and Appendix H.
Shivers: *Camping,* pp. 261–267.
Shockley and Fox: *Survival in the Wilds.*

MAGAZINE ARTICLES

Camping Journal:
Haddon, E. P.: "Make You Own Pocket Survival Kit." Nov., 1970, p. 20.

Johnson, E. C.: "Camp Chef." Apr. and May, 1974.
"Survival Seminar—C. A. P. Style." Apr., 1970, p. 36.

Trip Camping

Abel, Michael: *Backpacking Made Easy*. Naturegraph, 1972, paper.
Angier: *Home in Your Pack*, chs. 1, 8.
Angier: *Skills for Taming the Wilds*, chs. 6, 10, 13.
Bridge: *America's Backpacking Book*, chs. 3, 5, 21.
Cardwell: *America's Camping Book*, chs. 22, 42.
Colwell: *Introduction to Backpacking*, chs. 6, 10.
Dalrymple: *Survival in the Outdoors*, ch. 6.
Fletcher: *The Complete Walker*, pp. 270–295.
Guide to Group Backpacking. Backpacker Books, 45 pp., mimeographed.
Johnson, James Ralph: *Advanced Camping Techniques*. McKay, 1967, 149 pp.
Langer: *The Joy of Camping*, pp. 133–143.
Learn and Tallman: *Backpacker's Digest*, ch. 19.
Macfarlan, Allan A.: *The Boy's Book of Hiking*, ch. 10.
Manning: *Backpacking One Step at a Time*,chs. 2, 3, 18.
Meier, Joel F.: *Backpacking*. Brown, 1980, 109 pp., paper.
Merrill: *All About Camping*, ch. 9.
Merrill: *The Hiker's and Backpacker's Handbook*, ch. 3.
Miracle and Decker: *Complete Book of Camping*, chs. 1, 17–21.
Ormond: *Complete Book of Outdoor Lore*, chs. 8–11.
Ormond: *Outdoorsman's Handbook*, Parts 3, 5, 8.
Primitive Camp Sanitation. Girl Scouts. (Caches, latrines, garbage disposal, and dishwashing) (Flip charts).
Rethmel: *Backpacking*, chs. 7–10.
Riviere: *Backcountry Camping*, ch. 9.
Van Lear, Denise (ed.): *The Best About Backpacking*. Sierra Club, 1974, 384 pp., paper.
Whelen and Angier: *On Your Own in the Wilderness*.
Winnett: *Backpacking for Fun*, chs. 7, 10.
Wood: *Pleasure Packing*, chs. 8, 10, 14.

MAGAZINE ARTICLES

Camping Journal:
Lockwood, Daniel: "A Low Budget Plan for Building a Unique Program for Pioneering." Feb., 1973, p. 12.
Camping Magazine:
Jambro, Thomas A.: "Visual Aids Spark Tripping Calendar." Feb., 1969, p. 21.

Where to Go

Bridge: *America's Backpacking Book*, ch. 25.
Cardwell: *America's Camping Book*, ch. 21.
Colwell: *Introduction to Backpacking*, ch. 11.
Colwell, Robert: *Introduction to Foot Trails in America*. Stackpole, 1972, 224 pp.
Colwell, Robert: *Introduction to Water Trails in America*. Stackpole, 1973, 221 pp., paper.
Johnson, J. R.: *Everglades Adventure*. McKay.
Learn and Tallman: *Backpacker's Digest*, ch. 20.
Makens, James C.: *Maken's Guide to U.S. Canoe Trails*. La Voyageur Publishing Co., 1319 Wentwood Dr., Irving, Texas 75061, 1971, 86 pp., paper.
Meier, Joel F.: *Backpacking*. Brown, 1980, ch. 1.
Merrill: *All About Camping*, chs. 2, 3, 12.
Merrill: *The Hiker's and Backpacker's Handbook*, chs. 2, 12, 13, Appendix.
National Scenic and Recreation Trails. Produced by Dept. of Interior, Bureau of Outdoor Recreation and U.S. Forest Service, Supt. of Documents, 1970.
Nickels, Nick: *Plan Now, Paddle Later*. Order from the author, P.O. Box 479, Lakefield, Ontario, Canada, paper.
Rethmel: *Backpacking*, pp. A–9 to A–12.
Riviere: *Backcountry Camping*, ch. 15.
Sutton, A. and M.: *Appalachian Trail: Wilderness on the Doorstep*. Lippincott, 1967.

MAGAZINE ARTICLES

Camping Journal:
"Best Trails Known and Unknown." June, 1974, p. 26.
Wilderness Camping:
Hixson, Robert: "20,000 Miles of Walking—the National Trails System." Sept./Oct., 1973, p. 14.

Winter Camping

Angier: *Survival with Style*, pp. 30–42, chs. 6, 7.
Bennett, Margaret: *Crosscountry Skiing for the Fun of It*. Order from Backpacker Books, 206 pp.
Bridge: *America's Backpacking Book*, ch. 20.
Bridge, Raymond: *The Complete Snow Camper's Guide*. Scribner's, 1973, 39 pp., paper.
Caldwell, John: *The New Crosscountry Ski Book*. Order from Backpacker Books, 144 pp., paper.
Curtis, Sam: *Harsh-Weather Camping*. McKay, 1980, chs. 9–12.
Goode, Merlin: *Winter Outdoor Living*. Brighton, 1978, 86 pp., paper.
Langer: *The Joy of Camping*, pp. 192–226, 261–270.
Manning: *Backpacking One Step at a Time*, ch. 19.
Merrill: *All About Camping*, ch. 8 and pp. 367–372.
Merrill: *The Survival Handbook*, ch. 12.
Mohney, Russ: *Wintering*. Stackpole, 1976, 224 pp., paper.
Osgood, William E., and Leslie J. Hurley: *Ski Touring: An Introductory Guide*. Charles E. Tuttle Co., Inc., Rutland, Vermont 15701, 1969, 148 pp.
Osgood, William E., and Leslie J. Hurley: *The Snowshoe Book*. Order from Backpacker Books, 127 pp., paper.
Rethmel: *Backpacking*, Appendix I.
Riviere: *Backcountry Camping*, ch. 11.
Rossit, Edward A.: *Snow Camping and Mountaineering*. Funk & Wagnalls, 1970, 276 pp.
Rutstrum, Calvin: *Paradise Below Zero*. Macmillan, 1968, 244 pp., paper.
Tapely, Lance: *Ski-Touring in New England*. Stone Wall Press, Lexington, Massachusetts 02173, 1973, paper.
Winter Activities (No. 26-092). Boy Scouts.
Wood: *Pleasure Packing*, ch. 11.

MAGAZINE ARTICLES

BACKPACKER:
"How to Build a Campfire in Deep Snow." *Backpacker-8*, Winter, 1974, p. 33.
Curtis, Sam: "How to Track Wildlife on Skis." *Backpacker-8*, Winter, 1974, p. 40.
Frisch, Bob: "Silence and Magic." *Bacpacker-4*, Winter, 1973, p. 30. (Snowshoeing).
Henley, Thomas: "How to Build an Igloo." *Backpacker-8*, Winter, 1974, p. 54.
Nourse, Alan E., M.D.: "Cold Weather Killers: Hypothermia & Frostbite." *Backpacker-4*, Winter, 1973, p. 36.

"Snowshoeing and Skis." *Backpacker-4,* Winter, 1973, pp. 30–35.

Waterman, Laura and Guy: "How to Keep Warm in Winter Without a Campfire." *Backpacker-8,* Winter 1974, p. 32.

Camping Journal:

Bridge, Raymond, "Go-Shoes for Snow." Dec., 1971, p. 30.

Grant, Ken: "Make Yourself Freeze-Proof." Dec., 1972, p. 23.

Roberts, Harry: "How to Choose a Ski." Feb., 1974, p. 90.

Seeghers, Carroll II: "Winter Camping."Feb., 1974, p. 23.

Stebbins, J. Ray: "Backpack Into Snow Country." Dec., 1971, p. 22.

Wilderness Camping:

Dayton, Gene: "Night Touring." Nov./Dec., 1973, p. 41. (Ski touring).

Foster, John R.: "Snowshoeing the Rugged Belts." Nov./Dec., 1973, p. 41.

Hatcher, C. L.: "Cold Weather Canoeing." Sept./Oct., 1973, p. 24.

Martin, Emilie: "A Killer for All Seasons—Hypothermia." Jan./Feb., 1973, p. 38.

Neuwirth, Joseph G., Jr.: "Principles of Cold Weather Adaptability." Nov./Dec., 1973, p. 26.

"Ski-Touring Potpourri." Jan./Feb., 1974, p. 42.

Wood, Robert S.: "Pleasure Packing—The Great Breathability Myth." Part I, Sept./Oct., 1973, p. 10; Part II, Nov./Dec., 1973, p. 18.

four

Camping and Trail Skills

eighteen

Safety and Emergency Skills

So why do we do it?
What good is it?
Does it teach you anything?
Like determination? invention? improvisation?
Foresight? hindsight?
Love?
Art? music? religion?
Strength or patience or accuracy or quickness
  or tolerance or
Which wood will burn and how long is a day
  and how far is a mile
And how delicious is water and smoky green
  pea soup?
And how to rely
On your
Self?*

—TERRY and RENNY RUSSELL

*Reprinted by permission of Sierra Club Books from *On The Loose* by Terry and Renny Russell.

SAFETY IN OUTDOOR LIVING

Many people forego the pleasures of outdoor adventure because of the horrible tales they have heard of dangers that threaten the unwary. With proper knowledge, training and supervision, however, there are probably few problems that confront those who take part in organized camping. In fact, they are probably much safer in camp than they would be in a city environment.

Throughout the text, we have stressed safety. In this chapter we will briefly discuss certain kinds of emergency situations that might cause concern, since we feel that, as in many other things, it is better to be aware of possible problems and ways to avoid them rather than to try to remedy problems after they occur. In this chapter, we have provided some basic information you will need about potential dangers campers may encounter and recommended treatments; however, this subject is more extensively discussed in the references listed at the end of the chapter. Also included here is a discussion of the characteristics of many of the so-called "dangerous" plants and animals, in order to help the reader become more familiar with their unusual features and habits as well as their importance in the balance of nature. Information on "staying found," what to do if you become lost, and on danger and distress signals is not presented here, although these are appropriate concerns in emergency situations. The reader should refer to discussions of these topics in Chapter 21.

DEALING WITH EMERGENCIES

Training in first aid is helpful for all camp personnel, but at least one member of every group taking a trip out of the central camp should be qualified in first aid. The group also should carry a suitable first aid kit and an instruction manual to take care of possible emergencies. The camp nurse or physician usually supervises any first aid training and the assembly of the first aid kit. If someone is injured in the woods, you cannot simply call a doctor; you must rely on your own common sense and what resources you have at hand. Some injuries result from failure to identify problems in time and to take appropriate action. Consequently, you should be familiar with the more common safety concerns and emergency situations presented here as well as being trained in first aid.

FIRST AID KIT

By observing safety precautions you can cut down on the number of injuries and accidents. However, no expedition, even a very brief one, should leave camp without the necessary supplies for emergencies. Campers should not take individual first aid supplies and try to treat themselves but should go to the trained person or persons designated to take care of first aid. Although you can buy first aid kits designed for camper use, many camps prefer to assemble their own.

A lightweight, aluminum fishing tackle box with compartments or a special kit with pockets makes a good container. You will need only small quantities of many supplies, which can be placed in small plastic vials available at a drug store. Any glass bottles should be wrapped in corrugated cardboard, sponge rubber, or several layers of paper towels or toilet tissue. Some medications are available in ampules just large enough for a single treatment. Here are some suggestions for supplies, but the final decision should be made by your local health personnel.

- Instruction book
- Triangular bandage (a clean bandanna will do)
- Absorbent cotton
- Adhesive tape (2″ roll)
- Ace bandages
- Adhesive bandages
- Alcohol swabs
- Gauze squares—roller gauze
- Aromatic spirits of ammonia—for bites, stings, and fainting
- Eye ointment—for minor eye irritations
- Aspirin
- Baking soda—for bites, stings, indigestion, or sunburn
- Oil of cloves—for toothache
- Disinfectant
- Sunburn ointment
- Treatment for burns
- Tweezers—sharp pointed
- Treatment for poison ivy or oak
- Snake bite kit
- Small scissors
- Safety pins
- Needle
- Insect repellent
- Moleskin—for preventing blisters

BLISTERS

Of all the ailments to confront a hiker, blisters on the feet are usually the most common. Although they may first seem to be a minor problem, they can, in fact, lead to complete incapacitation in the backcountry. Blisters are caused by the friction of the skin rubbing against a tough surface such as a boot. Moisture, temperature, and friction are the three major factors in blister formation. Hot damp skin will blister much quicker than cool dry skin. Rubbing causes the tough outer layer of the skin to separate from the sensitive inner layers, and fluid then fills the space between.

Both shoes and socks contribute to the formation of blisters. To prevent problems, shoes should fit well and should be thoroughly broken in before going on a long trip. In order to keep the feet cool and dry, coat them with powder and wear two layers of socks. A nonabsorbent nylon, silk, or polyester sock next to the foot will allow moisture to move away from the skin and also may reduce fricton. The outer sock should be a thicker wool one. Friction is thus dissipated between the socks rather than against the skin. Boots also should be laced tightly in order to prevent the foot from slipping. Frequent changing of socks is recommended.

For chronic blister problems, potential blister areas may be covered with moleskin or adhesive tape prior to beginning a hike. If, in spite of all these precautions, you still develop a blister, there are several ways of treating it. If you are away from the central camp it is probably best not to remove the skin, although the blister should be drained by inserting a sterilized needle under the loose skin just beyond the edge of the blister. First wash the foot with soap and water and then, after draining, coat the area with an antiseptic and cover with adhesive tape or bandage. Use felt tape or moleskin around the blister, not on it, to relieve the pressure and to prevent rubbing of the area while walking.

SUNBURN

Sunburn can be a serious as well as painful condition, and there can be a relationship between repeated overexposure to the sun's rays and skin damage, including skin cancer. Campers who have not already acquired a deep tan must do so gradually, beginning with a maximum of 15 or 20 minutes of exposure the first day and increasing it by that amount each succeeding day. The use of a good sun-exposure skin product also is recommended. When going out for long periods, as on a canoe trip or hike, the best protection is clothing—a wide-brimmed hat, long sleeves and pant legs, and a turned-up collar. Sunglasses also should be used to protect the eyes.

After a sunburn occurs, zinc-oxide ointment will protect the burn from more ultraviolet rays. Aspirin and over-the-counter local anesthetics also can be used for pain. Severe sunburn, with blisters, may require a doctor's attention.

HEAT EXHAUSTION

When people participate in vigorous activities, especially during the heat of hot summer days, they must be wary of heat exhaustion. This is the most common heat ailment; its symptoms are extreme fatigue, nausea, headache, and faintness. The skin becomes clammy and moist and the eye pupils dilate. Treatment is relatively simple and includes allowing the victim to rest quietly in a cool area. Also, lightly salted water should be swallowed in moderate amounts at frequent intervals.

DEHYDRATION

Dehydration can be prevented by consuming adequate amounts of liquids throughout the day. Adults normally require at least 2 quarts of water daily, while up to 4 quarts or more might be needed if one is involved in strenuous activity such as backpacking or canoeing. A loss of 1½ quarts of water without replacement will result in a 25 percent loss of stamina. In order to avoid dehydration, simply drink often.

ALTITUDE SICKNESS

Altitude sickness (or mountain sickness) can result from a rapid ascent to altitudes over 7,000 feet, especially for those who are not accustomed to being this high. The sickness is not serious, but it can cause a great deal of discomfort. Symptoms can include headaches, loss of appetite, nausea, vomiting, and even insomnia. Unsteady breathing, shortness of breath and pounding of the heart also may be noticed. These problems are caused by a lack of oxygen in the body's central nervous system, but they disappear once the victim has adapted to the altitude, usually within 24 to 48 hours.

The best treatment for altitude sickness usually is rest, although those who are more seriously affected probably should descend to a lower elevation for a day or so. Be sure that the person drinks at least 2 or more quarts of liquid daily as this seems to help.

HYPOTHERMIA

Perhaps the most dangerous problem facing inexperienced campers is hypothermia—more commonly called exposure. This is simply the loss of one's body heat at a rate greater than it can be produced, causing a drop in the body's internal temperature. If a person's internal temperature is lowered far enough, it can result in mental and physical collapse. What most people fail to realize is that hypothermia often occurs well above freezing temperatures, and even in summer months. It is caused by exposure to cold, but it is also aggravated by moisture, wind, and exhaustion.

Wet clothes can be a real problem since they lose insulating value when damp. Wind adds yet another problem since it drives cold air through the clothing and produces a refrigeration effect. These factors, combined with exhaustion, are apt to lead to a serious situation. Someone who is tired and who has already depleted most of the body's energy is in poor condition to fight off hypothermia.

Hypothermia affects the individual slowly and subtly at first, but sometimes can be recognized, since it produces lapses in memory, error in judgment, clumsiness, and loss of body coordination. However, because of the victim's mental state, he or she is unaware that these things are happening and usually will deny that there is any trouble. Therefore, it is better to believe the symptoms rather than the sufferer.

The three sequential stages of hypothermia are: (1) uncontrollable shivering of the body, (2) loss of judgment and reasoning power, resulting from cold numbing the brain, and (3) stupor or collapse and death.

At the first signs of any problem, immediate treatment should be applied. This consists of getting the victim out of the wind or rain and removing all wet clothing. The person should then be placed in warm clothes and a warm sleeping bag. If the victim is only mildly impaired, administer warm drinks and apply external heat. This can be done by making an emergency hot water bottle out of a canteen or plastic bottle filled with hot water and wrapped in a towel or flannel shirt.

If the victim is in a semiconscious state or worse, it may be necessary to place him or her in a sleeping bag with another person. This is necessary since the victim is no longer capable of generating body heat to warm the bag. If the person is able to eat, administer foods containing high levels of carbohydrates and sugars.

To prevent hypothermia, dress appropriately to ward off cold, wind and wetness. Plenty of rest as well as adequate consumption of good energy foods are also important.

STOMACH PROBLEMS

Digestive disturbances can be very upsetting, and usually they account for a camper's stomach problems. Observing the principles of moderation and good nutrition will go a long way toward preventing this sort of discomfort. Many such cases can be traced to rancid food and germs left on dishes not thoroughly washed and sterilized. It's a good idea to see that campers use their own individual drinking cups and water bottles rather than pass them among friends. Prevention also includes treating all unknown water either chemically or by boiling it.

If a person shows symptoms of appendicitis (nausea and vomiting, abdominal pains that may be general at first but eventually become localized, inability to straighten the leg comfortably while lying down or to stand up straight) do not apply heat or give a laxative under any circumstances. Seek medical help with all speed.

MAKING DRINKING WATER SAFE

The only way to be absolutely sure a natural water supply is safe for drinking and cooking or washing dishes is to have it tested by qualified personnel. If this has not been done, you must sterilize it, no matter how clear and sparkling it looks, for it may carry serious diseases such as typhoid fever. Even in remote wilderness areas, giardiasis has now become a serious problem caused by drinking infected water from streams or lakes in the high mountains. It is best to bring water from camp in clean canteens or plastic bottles or fill them from safe sources along the way. When that is impossible, use one of the following methods to purify water:

1. Boil it for 10 minutes (time it from when it actually starts to boil). This causes the water to taste flat because the air has been removed, but you can restore the oxygen and the good flavor by stirring it vigorously with a spoon or pouring it back and forth several times from one container to another.
2. Use iodine or Halazone tablets according to the directions printed on the container. Iodine from the first aid kit (2 percent tincture of Iodine) can be used by adding 20 drops per gallon of water. Let it stand for 30 minutes. A few drops of lemon juice will improve the taste.
3. Use household chlorine bleach (5.25 percent sodium hypochlorite, Clorox, or Purex), adding 8 drops to one gallon of raw water. Let it stand 30 minutes before using.

When water is available at an outpost or frequently used campsite, it is worthwhile to send a sample to the state board of health for testing so that you won't have to bother to sterilize it.

Directions for doing this can be secured from your state or county board of health or the camp director.

POISON IVY, POISON OAK, AND POISON SUMAC

Source of the Poisoning

Poison ivy, poison oak, and poison sumac cause much distress, for it is estimated that at least two out of three people are allergic to at least one of them, and they are so common and widespread that campers always run the danger of encountering them. Since all three have common characteristics, they will be discussed together.

The allergic reaction results when an oily substance from these plants comes in contact with the skin; susceptible persons vary in the severity of their reaction. Although poisoning is ordinarily caused by direct contact with the leaves, it is also possible to contract it from contact with the stems, roots, or even soot and smoke from burning plants in a brush fire or campfire. People can also get the oil on their skin indirectly by contact with things on which the oil has been deposited, such as clothing, tools, or even the hair of dogs or other animals that have been running through the brush. Poisoning is possible at any time of the year, but it occurs most commonly in spring and summer when the sap is more abundant and people are more likely to be outdoors. Individuals differ greatly in their susceptibility, some apparently being quite immune while others need only be in proximity to the plants. No one can ever be sure of immunity, however, for, as with certain other allergies, one previously immune can suddenly become susceptible.

Identifying the Plants

POISON IVY. *Poison ivy* is probably the most widespread of the three, with some variety being found in almost every area of the United States, except certain southwestern states. Although there are many varieties, they all have the same characteristic arrangement of leaves, which always grow in clusters of three on a single stem, as shown in Figure 18–1. Thus the old saying, "Leaflets three, let be" is still a good rule to follow, although it may make you unduly suspicious of certain harmless plants.

The leaves are roughly oval, from 1 to 4 inches long, and vary somewhat in appearance, even on the same plant, for some are quite irregular, sometimes even lobed like oak leaves. They are a glossy, bright green in summer and turn to attractive shades of red or russet in the fall (the uninformed have been known to gather them to use in fall decorations). The inconspicuous greenish-white flowers are borne in loose clusters on slender stems and are followed by waxy white or ivory pea-sized fruit that are segmented somewhat like a peeled orange. *Poison ivy* is often confused with harmless *Virginia creeper* or *woodbine* but it is quite easy to distinguish between them since the latter has five leaflets (the

Figure 18–1 Poison ivy.

Figure 18-2 Variations of poison oak and poison ivy.

friendly hand) whereas poison ivy has only three leaflets (the maimed hand).

The plant growth takes many forms, most commonly appearing as a vine twining about trees, fences, houses, and even rock piles; it may also appear as a low, leafy shrub, growing out in the open. As it matures, it sometimes resembles a small tree with a trunk several inches thick. It sometimes grows along the ground, blending with other plants to form an attractive green carpet.

POISON OAK. *Poison oak* is a misnomer, for it is not a member of the oak family at all, but simply another form of poison ivy (Fig. 18-2) whose characteristic three leaves are lobed somewhat like oak leaves. It is most commonly found in the states of California, Washington, and Oregon and ordinarily grows as an upright shrub, although it sometimes climbs on other objects like a vine. The leaves are usually glossy and uneven with a somewhat leathery appearance. The greenish-white flowers are about ¼ inch across and are followed by greenish-white berries in mid-October.

POISON SUMAC. *Poison sumac* (Fig. 18-3) is found chiefly in swampy areas east of the Mississippi River. It never grows as a vine, but rather as a coarse, woody shrub or small tree from 5 to 25 feet tall that is frequently asymmetrical, often leaning to one side. It is commonly confused with certain harmless varieties of sumac that serve such useful purposes as furnishing tannin for treating leather, controlling erosion on waste hillsides, or growing as ornamental plants. The classification in Table 18-1 should help you to distinguish between them.

Prevention of Poisoning

Several methods have been tried to produce immunity to these plants, but so far none has proved entirely successful. Prevention is far better than treatment in the case of these noxious plants, and it is wise to eradicate them from frequently used areas by using a good chemical preparation to kill them, following up as necessary to curb new growth. Only adults should participate in this procedure, however, and they

Figure 18-3 Poison sumac.

Table 18–1

CHARACTERISTICS OF THREE VARIETIES OF SUMAC

	POISON SUMAC	*SMOOTH SUMAC*	*STAGHORN SUMAC*
Branches	Smooth.	Smooth.	Covered with fuzz.
Leaflets	7 to 13, arranged in pairs; oval-shaped with smooth or untoothed margins. Mid-ribs are scarlet.	Many leaflets; slender, lance-shaped leaves with toothed margins.	Many leaflets; slender, lance-shaped leaves with toothed margins.
Berries	White or greenish: arranged in loose clusters 10 to 12 inches long at the *sides* of the branches.	Red; arranged in seed heads at the *ends* of the branches.	Red; arranged in seed heads at *ends* of branches.
Location	Usually in bogs or swampy areas.	Dry uplands.	Dry uplands.

should get complete information from such sources as the United States Department of Agriculture* before attempting it.

Since it is usually impractical—and improper—to try to eradicate the plants over all areas where campers hike, they should learn to recognize them and keep an eye out to avoid direct contact. When hiking, protect skin areas by wearing long sleeves, long trousers, and even gloves. It also helps to cover exposed skin surfaces with such protective ointments as those recommended by the United States Department of Agriculture* or with a thick lather of strong yellow laundry soap, which you can later wash off. Upon returning to camp, immediately remove your clothing and avoid touching it again until after it has been laundered; this is to prevent contact with any oil that may have gotten on it. Scrub your skin with several applications of strong laundry soap, rinsing well after each, then apply rubbing alcohol. This is designed to remove any oil that may have accidently adhered to the skin.

Symptoms

Symptoms may appear from within an hour or two up to seven days after exposure, beginning with redness, burning, and itching in a localized area that may then spread. This is followed by a breaking-out or rash, swelling, and watery blisters, with possible fever, major itching, and general discomfort.

Poison Ivy, Poison Oak and Poison Sumac. Farmers' Bulletin No. 1972, Supt. of Documents, U.S. Govt. Printing Office, rev. 1963, 30 pp.

Treatment

Consult a doctor for severe cases. Do not scratch, for although it may not spread the poison, it will increase the discomfort and can cause a dangerous secondary infection. Although there is no quick cure, certain measures may relieve the itching and intense discomfort. Recommended are applications of compresses of very hot or very cold water, followed by a drying agent such as calamine lotion or compresses dipped in a solution of Epsom salts or cornstarch in water or in a solution of one level teaspoon of boric acid mixed with two glasses of water.

PESKY CREATURES OF THE WILD

There are actually few dangerous animals roaming about in backcountry areas of the United States where campers are likely to go. Although many of nature's creatures can prove bothersome or possibly even dangerous on occasion, most merely want to live and let live as

Figure 18–4 Common garter snake.

far as humans are concerned. Nonetheless, it is wise to learn something about them and their habits.

The probabilities are that you can spend weeks or even months in the wilds without ever so much as seeing a poisonous snake or dangerous animal, since, even if present, they are usually shy and even less anxious than you to foster a close acquaintance. After all, a wild creature's very existence depends upon its ability to hunt natural foods and to escape being hunted or killed. An animal's senses are usually much keener than ours, thus making it aware of our presence long before we can detect it. An animal will not usually bite or otherwise cause harm unless surprised or frightened; then, like any living thing in similar circumstances, it may fight back in self defense.

Snakes

FACT AND FANCY

There are probably no more feared or despised creatures in the world than snakes, yet of the several hundred varieties in the United States, only four are poisonous—the corals, the rattlers, the copperhead, and the cottonmouth. It is estimated that about 7,000 people in the United States are bitten by poisonous snakes each year and, of these, not more than 10 to 15 will die from the effects.* For instance, for every person in Missouri who dies from snake bite, there are 3,100 who die from falls, 735 from drowning, and 5,975 from automobile accidents.** It therefore seems ridiculous to let fear of snakes keep us from taking to the woods.

A snake wants most of all just to be let alone and will almost never bite unless someone comes upon it by surprise or teases it. A snake's usual reaction upon detecting human presence is to slither away to safety or to lie still to avoid being noticed. Hence, for every snake you see, there are probably countless others that detected you first and crept silently and unobtrusively away.

Snakes play an important part in the balance of nature and are especially useful to campers and farmers, since they eat large quantities of bothersome insects as well as rats and mice that would soon overrun the countryside if not curtailed by their natural enemies. The large majority of snakes are nonpoisonous. All should be protected rather than killed. They are another example of how even commonly disliked creatures have a role to play in keeping nature in balance (Fig. 18–4).

Snakes have long been the subjects of high-powered imaginations and unfounded folk tales that attribute to them such uncanny powers as the ability to charm animals and birds, to milk cows, or to grasp their tails in their mouths and roll along the ground, and to inject poison into a victim through the "stingers" in their tails. They don't swallow their young to protect them from threatened danger, they are not vicious by nature, and they don't chase people about in order to bite them.

Snakes are not slimy and cold to the touch

*Bushnell, Richards: "Warning: Some Snakebites May Be Hazardous to Your Health," *Mariah*, Mar. 1977, p. 35.

**Keefe, Jim: "Snakebite," *Missouri Conservationist*.

but acquire their temperature from the atmosphere around them. Their skins, with a covering of scales, feel almost like soft kid leather. Most of them lay eggs, although a few bear their young alive. They have no legs but draw themselves along by means of the sharp edges of the scales on their undersides; this enables them to move quite rapidly over rough ground (one variety is called "racers"). Some in particularly smooth areas, such as deserts, propel themselves along by throwing loops of their bodies forward, first on one side, then the other, and so are called "side-winders." Some can swim, others can climb trees and shrubbery, and most have a protective coloration that makes them blend in with their native haunts. Snakes have long, slender tongues that are forked near the end and serve as sensory organs or antennae. By darting them in and out rapidly they can detect ground vibrations and movements near them. They swallow their food whole, having jaws that unhinge so that they can ingest and swallow almost unbelievably large prey.

THE PIT VIPERS

Three of the four poisonous snakes (rattlesnakes, copperheads and cottonmouth moccasins) are known as *pit vipers* (Fig. 18–5) because of the deep pits located on each side of their head about halfway between nostril and eye. The pits are sensitive organs that detect temperature changes and so warn them of an approaching warm-blooded animal and guide them to strike accurately to kill or immobilize it. Their two sharp, hollow fangs are located in the upper jaw and normally lie flat against the roof of the mouth. When the snake strikes, it erects its fangs, which pierce the flesh and act like hypodermic needles to inject poison or venom. If a snake's fang is extracted or broken off, it will be replaced by another within a few days.

The other variety of poisonous snake, the coral snake, has no pits and differs in other important ways, so it will be discussed separately. Distinguishing characteristics of the pit vipers are given in Table 18–2.

Miraculous tales abound as to the ability of some snakes to leap through the air and fasten their fangs into their victims, but a snake's tail always remains on the ground and, even from a coiled position, it cannot strike for more than one-third to one-half of its length. When not coiled, it cannot strike even that far or with any degree of accuracy. A snake's strike is so rapid that it appears as a blur and it is doubtful that any creature is quick enough to dodge it.

Although, as mentioned previously, there are only four main types of poisonous snakes in the United States, there are several varieties of each, bringing the total to 30 or 40 different kinds that are so widespread that there is probably no state without at least one kind.

WATER OR COTTONMOUTH MOCCASIN. The *water* or *cottonmouth moccasin* is usually found in swampy territory or in the trees and bushes overhanging streams and marshes in southern states, as indicated in Figure 18–6. It is 3 to 6 feet long and has a dark muddy or olive-

Bone structure of poisonous front fangs

Figure 18–5 Head of a pit viper.

Table 18-2

DISTINGUISHING CHARACTERISTICS OF PIT VIPERS

	PIT VIPERS (POISONOUS)	*NON-POISONOUS SNAKES*
Pits	Have characteristic pits.	Have no pits.
Head	Triangular, when viewed from above. It is broader than the neck and so makes a definite angle where they join. (See the diamondback rattler in Figure 18-8.)	Head not angular and not much broader than the neck so that it tapers off to join it smoothly.
Pupil of Eye	Upright and elliptical.	Round.
Underside of Tail	Scales in uninterrupted rows around the snake for all or most of its length.	There is a line that goes up the middle of the underside of the snake and divides the scales into two rows.
Teeth or Fangs	Have both teeth and fangs.	Have teeth but no fangs.

brown color with 11 to 15 inconspicuous darker bars on its short, thick body. It is somewhat pugnacious and inclined to stand its ground and fight back when threatened. There are several varieties of harmless water snakes that resemble it and are often mistaken for it. It usually threatens before striking by opening its mouth wide to show its ugly white interior; this explains its name, "cottonmouth."

THE COPPERHEAD. The *copperhead* (also called the *Northern moccasin* or *pilot snake*) is found chiefly in the eastern and southern states as indicated in Figure 18-7. It is usually 2 to 4 feet long and of a hazel or pinkish-brown color, with cross markings of darker reddish-brown blotches that are shaped somewhat like an hourglass or a short-handled dumbbell. A copperhead has the *narrow* part of the hourglass on its back, unlike several harmless varieties that somewhat resemble it but have the *broad* part of the hourglass on their backs. The name "copperhead" comes from the distinctive copper coloring of its head. It usually prefers rocky, wooded terrain.

RATTLESNAKES. It is estimated that there are 16 to 26 varieties of rattlesnakes in the United States, distributed so that there is at least one variety in nearly all of the 50 states. They

Figure 18-6 Water moccasin (cottonmouth).

Figure 18-7 Copperhead.

range in size from the little eight-inch pygmy rattlers to the giant diamondbacks (Fig. 18-8). They are variously marked and colored, but all have one common characteristic—the rattles on the end of their tails with which they usually warn their victims before striking. The tail and rattles vibrate so rapidly that you can scarcely see them and they make a unique sound somewhat like the ticking of an alarm clock or the sound of a locust. A rattler sheds its skin as many as two to five times a year, leaving a bit of skin each time to harden into another "rattle." Some of the rattles are subsequently lost through wear and accident, so it is not true that you can tell the age of the rattler by counting the number of rattles.

THE CORAL OR HARLEQUIN SNAKE

The *coral snake* is southern, as indicated on the map in Figure 18-9, and exists in several varieties, each potentially quite dangerous, since

Figure 18-8 Diamondback rattlesnake.

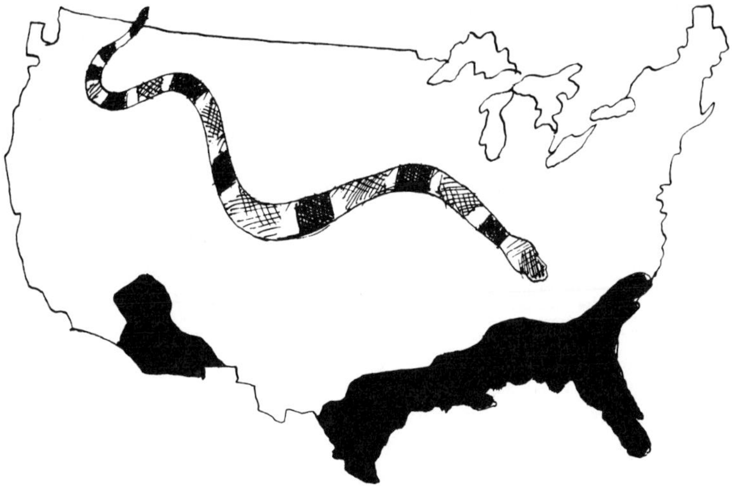

Figure 18-9 Coral snake.

their venom is even more toxic than that of the pit vipers. Fortunately, coral snakes prefer darkness and so tend to stay burrowed beneath the soil in daytime. You are not likely to encounter one except at night or after a flood or hard rain. Their heads resemble those of nonpoisonous snakes in that they have no pits and are not angular but taper off gradually to join their necks. They have short fangs that are permanently erect. Instead of striking to inject their poison in one or a few quick jabs as the pit vipers do, they try to catch hold and hang on to chew and thus inject their venom in a number of places. The venom affects the nervous system and tends to paralyze the victim, instead of traveling through the circulatory system as does that of the pit vipers.

The coral snake is long, slender, colorful, and attractive. It closely resembles some harmless varieties of the king snake (Fig. 18-10) and the milk snake. The only sure way to distinguish between them is to note the color of the nose and the exact arrangement of the red, yellow, and black bands, as indicated in Table 18-3.

Figure 18-10 King snake.

PREVENTING SNAKE BITES

Snakes are ordinarily shy and prefer to avoid contact with anything potentially dangerous except when frightened or threatened. With proper precautions, you may well camp in many areas for days or even weeks without ever meeting a single poisonous snake or even one of the much more plentiful harmless varieties. To minimize chances of an encounter, watch where you step, sit, and place your hands. Be especially careful when stepping over logs or reaching into holes or underbrush where you cannot see clearly, and be cautious when placing your hands and feet while climbing ledges, for snakes frequently hide out or sun themselves in crevices or on rock surfaces. Although they have no ears and cannot hear, they are quite sensitive to ground vibrations. Therefore, make plenty of noise when you walk in order to apprise the snake of your coming so that it will move out of your way. Since 98 percent of snake bites are on the extremities, with 68 percent on the foot or leg, it may be advisable to wear leather leggings or high-topped boots when in country known to be snake infested.

TREATMENT OF SNAKE BITES

As already indicated, not many cases of poisonous snake bite are reported each year in America, and very few of these prove fatal, even when the bite goes untreated. The poison is somewhat slow to act so that there is always time to get medical treatment in ordinary situations. Someone has said that there is more danger of choking to death from eating popcorn in a movie than of dying from snake bite, and many more people die annually from the stings of bees and wasps than from snake bite. The seriousness of the bite depends upon such factors as the size and kind of snake, the potency and amount of venom present in the snake at the particular time, the size and physical condition of the victim, and whether or not the venom was injected into or near a vital organ.

If someone is bitten, try to identify the snake or at least determine whether or not it is poisonous. The bite of a nonpoisonous snake appears as two rows of teeth marks and should be treated like any other puncture wound. If the snake is one of the pit vipers, there will be one or two deep fang marks or punctures and an immediate painful, burning sensation, quickly followed by discoloration and swelling, with later symptoms of general weakness, nausea, breathing difficulty and possibly unconsciousness. This bite calls for immediate action.

Be aware that emergency treatment for snakebite has undergone a lot of critical medical analysis in recent years. There was a time when everyone carried a snakebite kit with suction cups, a scalpel blade, and two constricting bands. But as research continues, the cross-cut and suction treatment is losing favor, since a person can be seriously cut or infected in the process of snakebite treatment. In fact, the treatment could be even more serious than the poison from the snake. If this is so, then what can be done to give first aid for a bite? If medical aid can be obtained within an hour, hurry to get it, for the most helpful treatment is a prompt injection of antivenom to counteract the poison and minimize pain and discomfort. Transport the victim by ve-

Table 18–3

DISTINGUISHING CHARACTERISTICS OF THE CORAL SNAKE

	CORAL SNAKE	*HARMLESS VARIETIES*
Nose	Black.	Pink or yellow.
Bands	Broad red bands lie next to narrow yellow bands. It may help you to remember this to recall that red, symbolizing danger, touches yellow, which symbolizes caution. The black bands lie between the yellow bands.	The red bands are broader and are separated from the narrower yellow bands by the black bands. Thus the red and yellow never touch each other.

hicle or on a stretcher improvised by buttoning up two coats, inserting two saplings or poles and lashing in spreaders to keep them apart. A blanket and safety pins can be used the same way. Keep the victim quiet and at rest, for any physical activity will speed up the person's circulation and spread the poison more rapidly. Fright and shock often do almost as much harm as the actual bite, so try to be reassuring.

In the meantime, direct your efforts toward (1) slowing down the spread of the poison, and (2) treating the victim for shock. Start these measures immediately, even while waiting for medical attention, for every second counts. Immobilize the affected limb and, using a bandana or strip of cloth, apply a constricting band directly above and below the bite site. Do not twist the bands with a stick, for you are not trying to apply a tourniquet to stop circulation but are merely trying to slow it down in order to retard the swelling and spread of the venom.

The next step is to apply a cooling agent to the bite area. Use crushed ice in a plastic bag or chemical ice packs* If neither is available, immersion in very cold water would be beneficial in decreasing the activity of the venom. Do not give stimulants of any sort, particularly alcohol, for they do no good whatsoever and are actually likely to do harm by speeding up the circulation and thus spreading the poison faster.

You can use the same treatment for the bite of a coral snake, but it is less effective. Here, the most important thing by far is to get medical treatment and an injection of antivenom serum as soon as possible.

Insects and Other Unwelcome Guests

Insects can be a nuisance since their bites can cause discomfort. More serious complications can occur in some people, especially if they are particularly allergic to stings. In fact, 60 percent of all the deaths from venomous animals in the United States are caused by insects with flying insects accounting for 40 percent of the total. Not only do insects kill more people, they also do it quicker. A snakebite victim can survive 6 to 48 hours before receiving medical treatment, while the victim of a flying insect can die within an hour. Bees, wasps, hornets, and yellowjackets are the winged, stinging insects responsible for most fatalities. Fortunately, there is some definite protection available.

BITE PREVENTION

It is no longer necessary to resort to such unpleasant, old-fashioned repellents as smudge fires and "dopes" containing citronella and creosote. A number of commercial products are quite effective, smell better, and do not irritate the skin or stain and damage clothing, except for certain man-made fabrics such as rayon. The United States Department of Agriculture** recommends repellents containing adequate amounts of "deet" (diethyltoluamide) as best for all purposes, since they protect effectively for several hours against a large number of pests, such as leeches, spiders, ticks, chiggers, biting flies, gnats, and mosquitoes. Such repellents can be applied directly to the skin or sprayed on clothing and around the tent for sleeping comfort as well as for protection when on the move.

Discourage unwelcome insects by choosing your campsite carefully. Keep garbage and debris cleaned up by placing it, as well as food, in covered containers or plastic sacks. Examine clothes, campsites and shelters for crawlers. When traveling where insects are plentiful, campers can cover themselves well with clothing and perhaps even wear a head net of cheesecloth or nylon fabric that can be tucked into the shirt or fastened at the neck with a drawstring. Apply a good repellent as directed to all exposed skin areas and to the edges of such openings in clothing as cuffs, waistbands, collars, and the tops of socks. Upon returning to camp, scrub thoroughly several times with generous applications of soap in order to remove many of the tiny insects. If "buzzed" by such insects as hornets or bees, walk slowly away from them.

*An alternative to ice is the snakebite freeze kit that contains two chemical bags that are activated by breakage. An inner bag of liquid mixes with a dry chemical to create a chemical cold of approximately 18° F. The kit, including latex constriction bands, is available from Amerex Laboratories, P.O. Box 3227-M, San Antonio, Texas 78216.

***U.S. News and World Report*, July 5, 1965.

Avoid moving rapidly or slapping at them frantically, for this frightens them and makes them more likely to bite.

TREATMENT OF INSECT BITES

When insects bite or sting they usually inject an acid that causes redness, itching, swelling, and pain. Avoid scratching the bite and apply an antiseptic to minimize the danger of infection. A compress of some neutralizing agent such as a solution of household ammonia, baking soda, or vinegar in water will help to relieve local symptoms, and cold applications in the form of ice or ice water may minimize the pain. When a bee stings, it often leaves its stinger in the wound. Use tape, tweezers or a knife blade to carefully get it out. The stinger is a hollow tube that may still contain poison so avoid squeezing it lest you force the poison into the wound.

For those individuals allergic to many insects, a sting can cause a response known as *anaphylactic shock.* This occurs rapidly, usually within a few minutes. The small air passages in the lungs close and the patient suffocates. Such persons should carry a doctor-prescribed insect sting allergy kit that contains antihistamine and an epinepherine adrenalin-loaded hypodermic.

CHIGGERS (CHIGOES, JIGGERS, OR RED BUGS)

These orangish-red, spider-like creatures are the larvae of a tiny mite and are so small that they cannot be seen without a microscope. They usually get on you while you walk through grass, and they often wander about a person's skin for an hour or more until they find a suitable place to bite. They can best be avoided by the methods previously mentioned.

WOODTICKS

These blackish or reddish-brown parasites cling to tall grass or shrubs and transfer themselves to people and animals as they pass by. They cause much discomfort and are sometimes even dangerous, since certain varieties can transmit Rocky Mountain spotted fever and other serious or even fatal diseases. Preventive injections are effective, but are not routinely recommended by public health and medical authorities. Fortunately, ticks tend to wander around on the body before settling down, and usually they are attached to the carrier several hours before feeding, providing an opportunity to find and remove them before they have done any harm. Have a regular tick inspection at least twice a day when in tick country. When undressing for bed at night, particular attention should be given to areas providing good concealment, such as the head, the back of the neck, and the genital region.

Reasonable precautions should prevent acquiring ticks on the body when visiting infested areas. Wearing clothing in such a manner as to prevent ticks from reaching the body is a recommended practice, such as keeping clothes buttoned and trouser legs tied or tucked into the boots. Lying on the grass or in the brush with uncovered long hair is an invitation for acquiring ticks.

If a tick becomes attached, the simplest method of removal is a slow, steady pull that will not break off the mouthparts. If the mouthpiece is broken and left in the wound, infection may result. Since there is no specific way to avoid detaching the mouthparts, other methods of removing the tick can be used. Do not crush a tick between your fingers lest you get some of the infective material on you. Try to make the tick detach itself by applying a bit of alcohol, kerosene, gasoline, vaseline, or fingernail polish to it. The use of benzene or chloroform is also recommended. An antiseptic should always be applied to the bite as to any open wound. Individuals who have handled ticks should wash their hands, since tick secretion may be infective. Should attempts to remove the entire tick fail, or should there be any other problems, it is important that the person see a physician.

SPIDERS

The bites of several spiders are quite painful but few are actually dangerous. One bite that is dangerous is that of the female *black widow spider* (Fig. 18–11). She can be identified by her shiny black body, which has a bright red hourglass-shaped spot on the underside of the distended, round, oversized abdomen. She is about one-half inch long.

If you are bitten, seek professional medical

treatment just as soon as possible for, although only about one bite in a hundred proves fatal, bites can cause severe illness that can be minimized by prompt medical attention. You may not even feel the bite, or it may cause severe pain. Although the result may be only a local redness and swelling, some victims have severe systemic reactions, including shock (paleness, weakness, rapid pulse, cold skin, anxiety, and sometimes unconsciousness), nausea, vomiting, labored breathing, great thirst, and cramps, especially in the abdominal region. While waiting for medical attention, use the same measures recommended for snake bite.

Another dangerous spider is the *brown recluse spider* (Fig. 18–11), which can be recognized by the dark brown fiddle-shaped area on the front portion of its back. Its body varies in color from a light grayish to dark reddish-brown and it is about one-fourth of an inch long. As its name implies, the brown recluse tends to hide during the day in obscure places, such as under rocks, in woodpiles, in decayed logs, or in dark closets or other dry remote areas in buildings, coming out only at night to feed. Its bite causes severe pain that may be delayed for as long as one-half to two hours. The bite area grows red and warm and a white spot appears over the bite and later becomes indented as the tissues eventually die and slough off after about a week or so. The patient becomes restless and feverish and may break out in a rash with weakness, numbness, and a tingling sensation in the limbs. In rare cases, jaundice occurs with bloody urine and convulsive seizures. Get professional help as soon as possible to prevent serious complications and minimize scarring.

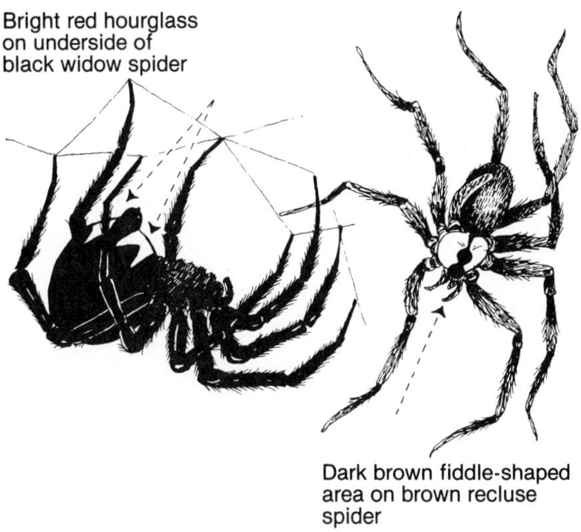

Figure 18–11 Poisonous spiders.

CENTIPEDES AND SCORPIONS

These are particularly dangerous in the Southwest. The scorpion stings with its poisonous tail and the centipede bites with its poisonous fangs. Be sure to thoroughly inspect your bedding before retiring and your shoes and clothing before putting them on. If someone is bitten, give first aid treatment as for a spider bite and get the patient to a doctor as soon as possible.

CATERPILLAR (LARVA) OF LO MOTH

This beautiful, showy specimen can be identified by its light green coat with two pink and white stripes zigzagging down each side. Its back is a wilderness of spines that give off a substance poisonous to the touch. The sting causes pain, irritation, and swelling. The imbedded hairs are best removed with cellophane tape. Wear gloves when doing this.

ADDITIONAL READINGS

(For an explanation of abbreviations and abbreviated forms used, see page 13.)

Camp Pests

Angier: *Survival With Style,* ch. 12.
Arnold, Robert E., M.D.: *What To Do About Bites and Stings of Venomous Animals. Collier, 1973, paper.*
Better Homes and Gardens Family Camping Book, ch. 16.
Boy Scout Handbook, pp. 138–143.
Cardwell: *America's Camping Book,* ch. 33.
Glass, Thomas G. Jr., M.D.: Snakebite First Aid. Available from author, Suite 112, San Antonio, Tex., 78217, 28 pp., paper.
Hillcourt: *New Field Book of Nature Activities and Conservation.*
Johnson: *Anyone Can Camp in Comfort,* pp. 79–82; chs. 9, 10, 11.
Langer: *The Joy of Camping,* pp. 242–250.
Learn and Tallman: *Backpacker's Digest,* chs. 14, 16.
Manning: *Backpacking One Step at a Time,* ch. 5.
Meier, Joel F.: *Backpacking.* Brown, 1980, ch. 6.
Miracle and Decker: *Complete Book of Camping,* ch. 29.
Reptile Study (No. 3311). Boy Scouts, 1967, 96 pp., paper.
Riviere: *Backcountry Camping,* ch. 14.
Riviere: *The Camper's Bible,* ch. 13.

Shockey and Fox: *Survival in the Wilds*, ch. 2.
Sunset Camping Handbook, pp. 76–77.
Whelen and Angier: *On Your Own in the Wilderness*, ch. 15.
Winnett: *Backpacking for Fun*, ch. 8.

MAGAZINE ARTICLES

Backpacker Magazine
Arnold, Dr. Robert: "Bug Bites." Apr./May, 1980, p. 57.
Boys' Life:
Pryce, Dick: "Living With Insects." July, 1971, p. 24.
"World Famous Snakes." Aug., 1972, p. 50.
Camping Journal:
Laycock, George: "Beat the Bugs." July–Aug., 1966, p. 49.
Rutherford, Jim: "Coping With the Camp Bugs." July, 1970, p. 26.
Camping Magazine:
Hamessley, Mary Lou, R.N.: "The Hazardous Brown Recluse." Apr., 1974, p. 14.
"Rid Camp of Poison Ivy." June, 1966, p. 23.
Mariah Magazine
Bushnell, Richards: "Warning: Some Snakebites May be Hazardous To Your Health!" Mar., 1977, p. 35.

First Aid, Health and Safety

Angier: *How to Stay Alive in the Woods*, chs. 21–25.
Better Homes and Gardens Family Camping Book, ch. 20.
Bevan, Dr. James: *The Pocket Medical Encyclopedia and First Aid Guide*. Simon and Schuster, 1979, 144 pp.
Boy Scout Handbook, pp. 121–147.
Bridge: *America's Backpacking Book*, chs. 15, 16.
Brower: *Going Light—With Backpack or Burro*, ch. 8.
Camp Physicians's Manual. Thomas, 1967, 192 pp.
The Camp Nurse. ACA Health and Safety Committee, ACA, 26 pp., paper.
Cardwell: *America's Camping Book*, Part IV; p. 347; chs. 32, 33.
Casey, Mary I.: *The Nurse and the Health Program At Camp*. Canadian Camping Assoc., 1978, 52 pp., paper. (Available from ACA)
Corbin: *Recreation Leadership*, ch. 9.
Emergency Preparedness (No. 3366). Boy Scouts, 1972, 64 pp., paper.
Fear, Gene: *Surviving the Unexpected Wilderness Emergency*. Survival Education Ass'n. Tacoma, Wash. 1972, 196 pp.
Fieldbook for Boys and Men, ch. 13.
First Aid. ARC.
First Aid (No. 3276). Boy Scouts, 1972, 64 pp., paper.
Hafen, Brent O., Alton L. Thygerson, and Ray A. Peterson: *First Aid—Contemporary Practices and Principles*. Burgess, 1972, 214 pp., paper.
Hamessley, Mary Lou, R.N.: *Handbook for Camp Nurses and Other Camp Health Workers*. Tiresias, 1973, 159 pp.
Henderson, John, M.D.: *Emergency Medical Guide*. McGraw-Hill, 2nd ed., 1969.
Johnson, Loren A., M.D.: *Survivit Manual*. Survivit Company, Lake McQueeney, Tex., 1973.
Kodet, Dr. E. Russel, and Bradford Angier: *Being Your Own Wilderness Doctor*. Stackpole, 1968, 127 pp.
Lehman, Charles A.: *Emergency Survival*. Medical and Technical Books, Inc., 11511 Tennessee Ave., Los Angeles, Calif. 90064, 1979, ch. 11.
MacInnes, Hamish: *International Mountain Rescue Handbook*. Scribner's, 1972, 218 pp.
Merrill: *All About Camping*, chs. 23, 24.
Merrill: *The Hiker's and Backpacker's Handbook*, ch. 11.
Merrill: *The Survival Handbook*, ch. 10.
Miracle and Decker: *The Complete Book of Camping*, ch. 30.
Mitchell, Dick: *Mountaineering First Aid*. The Mountaineers, Seattle, Wash., 1972, 92 pp., paper.
Nourse, Alan E.: *The Outdoorsman's Medical Guide*. Harper & Row, 1974, 128 pp.
Rethmel: *Backpacking*, ch. 7.
Rodney and Ford: *Camp Administration*, Appendix A.
Safety (No. 3347). Boy Scouts, 1971, 64 pp., paper.
Schmidt, Ernest F.: *Camping Safety*, ACA, 1971, 44 pp., paper.
Shivers: *Camping*, pp. 247–256.
Suggested Policies and Standing Orders for Camp Nursing Services. ACA, rev., 1968, paper.
Wilderness Pocket n' Pak Library. Life Support, 1969–1972. (Pocket-size, accordian-fold vinyl package of 5 booklets: "Survival in the Wilderness," "Edible Plants in the Wilderness" (Vols. I and II), "Poisonous Plants in the Wilderness," and "Primitive Medical Aid in the Wilderness.")
Wood: *Pleasure Packing*, ch. 11.

MAGAZINE ARTICLES

Adventure Travel Magazine:
Houser, Dave G.: "Could You Survive a Wilderness Emergency?" May, 1980, p. 24.
Backpacker Magazine:
Athanasiou, Bob: "Blisters." June/July, 1980, p. 50.
Dannen, Kent: "Burnt Offerings." June/July, 1981, p. 78. (How to deal with sunburn)
Eastman, Peter, M.D.: "Advanced First Aid for Sprains and Fractures." Oct./Nov., 1980, p. 58.
Houston, Dr. Charles: "High Altitude Sickness." June/July, 1978, p. 38.
Linsky, Martin: "How to Avoid Hypothermia." Feb., 1976, p. 52.
Camping Journal:
Kowalski, Julius M., M.D. and Pete Czura: "First Aid for Campers." Sept., 1971, p. 26.
Camping Magazine:
Andzel, Walter: "How to Handle Heat Illnesses." June, 1973, p. 25.
"14 Camp Accidents Which Could Have Been Avoided." Jan., 1970, p. 16.
Means, Elizabeth, R.N.: "Helpful Hints From a Camp Nurse." Apr., 1970, p. 20.
Putt, Arlene M.: "The Most Important Element in Camping Must Be Our Concern for Camper's Health and Safety." Feb., 1973, p. 20.
Stevenson, Dr. Jack L.: "Safety Is a Never-Ending Job." Apr., 1972, p. 22.
Wilderness Camping Magazine
McCartan, C. B.: "Son of Iodine, Out of Halazone." Dec./Jan., 1979, p. 56. (Water purification methods)
Meyers, Gary: "Heat Stress." Aug./Sept., 1976, p. 37.

nineteen

Knots and Lashing

The healing fragrance of the wood; the beauties of the lake and of coastline; the open air; the clean blue skies—these belong to all people, and the right to enjoy them is the heritage of every child.

—*Camping for Crippled Children**

*Published by permission of The National Society for Crippled Children and Adults, Inc.

Humans have, no doubt from their earliest existence, wanted to fasten things together, and they have used such natural materials as vines and thin strips of bark or hide to fulfill this need. Some American Indians used thongs or dried strips of leather from the skins of animals, applying them wet so that they would contract into tight fastenings as they dried.

The use of knots and lashings for various construction projects is still a popular aspect of the overall program of organized camps. However, when doing this sort of activity, we must act responsibly and should understand and follow sound environmental practices. The "frontier mentality" no longer has a place in the modern camp. Campers should learn when and where it is appropriate to build structures and that it is inappropriate to damage trees and other vegetation. Of course, anything that is constructed should always be disassembled after use.

ROPES

Until recent years, rope was made of such natural materials as jute, cotton, sisal, manila, or hemp. It is interesting to note that our native marijuana is a form of hemp; its seeds were probably broadcast as the hemp was being transported across the country to rope factories. It early became a problem when it sprouted and grew among the grass in pastures; ranchers called it "loco weed" because it made the mustangs and livestock "loco" and useless after they ate large quantities of it.

These original sources of rope have now been largely replaced by such synthetic or manmade materials as nylon, Dacron, and polyethylene which, although more expensive, are improvements. They have these points of superiority: (1) they are as much as 50 to 100 percent stronger for their size and weight; (2) they are easier to handle and do not swell and kink when wet; (3) they suffer little if any damage from mildew and moisture; (4) they float on water; and (5) they add color since they are available in a variety of shades. Their one major disadvantage is that they are often more or less slick and therefore fail to hold well in some knots. However, a few extra turns or a combination of two knots usually gives security.

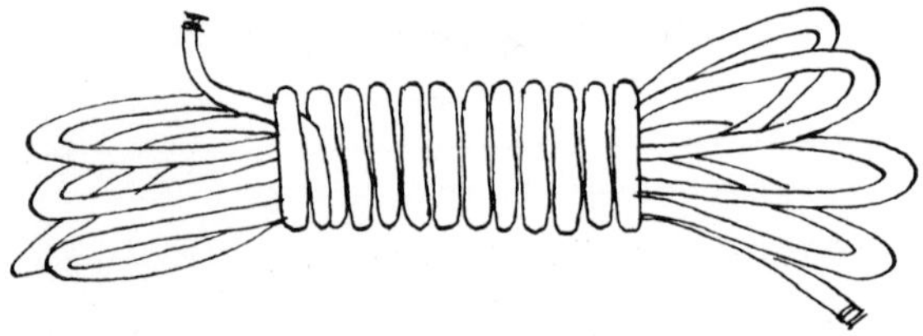

Figure 19-1 Hanking a rope.

Your Camp Rope and Its Care

Ropes are useful in dozens of ways around camp, as when pitching tents, flying a flag, hanging laundry out to dry, or mooring a boat. For ordinary camp use, a rope 5 to 6 yards long and ⅜ inch in diameter is most useful.

If your rope is made of a nonsynthetic material dampness will greatly weaken it, so avoid getting it wet whenever possible and dry it out quickly and thoroughly if it does get wet. These ropes also shrink and swell when wet, so you will need to loosen tent guy ropes and other ropes under stress if rain seems imminent or a heavy dew is expected, for otherwise, they may break under the extra strain.

Avoid walking on a rope or otherwise grinding dirt into it for the particles will gradually cut the fibers. Sharp bends and kinks weaken it so untie knots when you are through with them. When your rope is not in use, arrange it as shown in Figure 19-1 by gathering it up in even loops, circling the loops with an end, then passing the end through one of the loops (called *hanking* it); then hang it up or wear it strung on your belt.

Like axe handles, canoe paddles, or oars, ropes collect salt from hand perspiration and may attract such animals as porcupines. They may gnaw the rope to get the salt, so store it where they can't get to it, especially when on trips.

ROPE TERMS

End—short part of the rope.

Standing Part—remainder or long part of the rope.

Bight—made when an end is laid back parallel to its standing part (Fig. 19-2).

Underhand Loop—made by crossing one end *under* its standing part.

Overhand Loop—made by crossing one end *over* its standing part.

Overhand Knot—made by pulling an end through a loop.

Hitch—used to fasten a rope to something, such as a post or ring.

WHIPPING THE END OF A ROPE

The ends of a rope will untwist or fray unless they are fastened in some way. There are several different methods that can be used to do this. If the rope is made of synthetic material, fuse the fibers at each end by applying heat from a match or trench candle. Two simple methods of fastening the ends of a rope made of nonsynthetic material are tying an overhand knot in each end or wrapping the ends with electric tape. The best method, however, is whipping each end with a two-foot length of string, twine, or thin nylon cord, as shown in Figure 19-3.

Step 1. Lay a length of string in an overhand loop along the rope end.

Step 2. While holding down the string ends along the rope, begin winding the loop tightly around the rope, and back along its standing part.

Step 3. When about one inch has been wound, each end of the string is pulled tight from opposite ends of the winding. By doing this, both ends will pull under the whipping and the remaining loop will be pulled free.

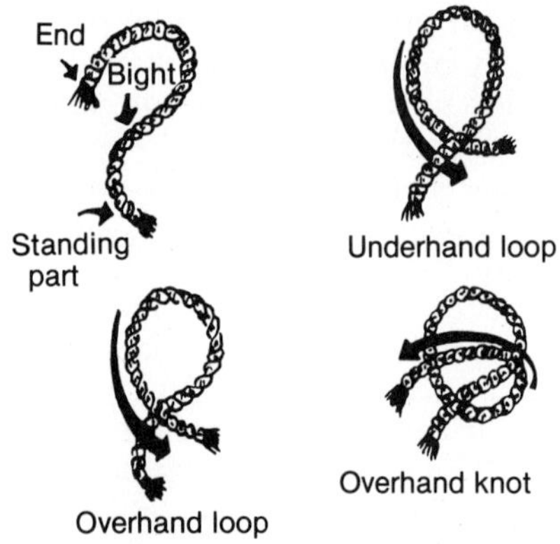

Figure 19-2 Basic terms used in knot tying.

Step 4. Now cut off the remaining string so that both ends are snug against the whipping.

KNOTS

There are literally hundreds of types of knots, but you need know only a few to meet ordinary needs in camp. Learn to tie these knots so well that you can even do it in the dark, and know what each is used for and why. You may want to learn others to meet special needs or even to use mainly for decoration or for such projects as knotting belts or lanyards.

You will need two ropes of the same or different size to practice some of the knots, but most of them can be tied with the ends of the same rope. It will help in teaching others if you give each end a different appearance by dipping one or both in ink of contrasting colors or by painting them. You can then instruct by saying, "Now cross the red end over the white," or "Pass the blue end under its standing part." It also helps when teaching others if you fasten to a knot board samples of the progressive steps in tying a knot, labeling them as needed.

Characteristics of a Good Knot

1. It is simple and easy to tie.
2. It performs well in the job for which it is intended.
3. It will not jam and is easy to untie. This is particularly important around camp where rope is usually scarce and must be used over and over.

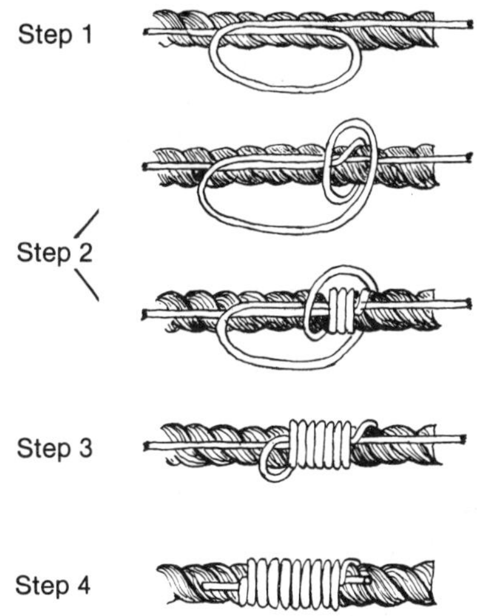

Figure 19–3 Whipping the end of a rope.

To Enlarge the End of a Rope

Stopper or *end* knots are used to enlarge the end of a rope to keep it from pulling through a ring, such as a tent grommet, or to provide a good hand grip on the end of the rope.

OVERHAND KNOT (FIG. 19-2). This knot tends to jam after stress has been applied so that it is hard to untie. To make it larger, double the end or pass it through the loop several times before tightening it.

(Forty Knots)

FIGURE EIGHT KNOT (FIG. 19-4A). This knot is slightly larger and easier to untie. Among other uses, you can attach a fishhook to a line with it. Make an underhand loop and bring the end over around the standing part and pull it up through the loop. Now pull it tight.

To Join Two Ropes

SQUARE OR REEF KNOT (FIG. 19-4B). This is used to join together two ropes of equal size or the two ends of a rope.

Form a bight with one rope and bring the end of the other rope up through it, around behind both the end and standing part, and down through the bight again. Pull it tight. To untie it, give a hard pull sideways on both the end and standing part of one rope and pick it apart.

It is easy to tie a *granny* instead of a square knot, but it is not effective since it will pull apart when stress is applied. Note in Figure 19-4C that this knot results from bringing the end of the white rope around in such a way as to have

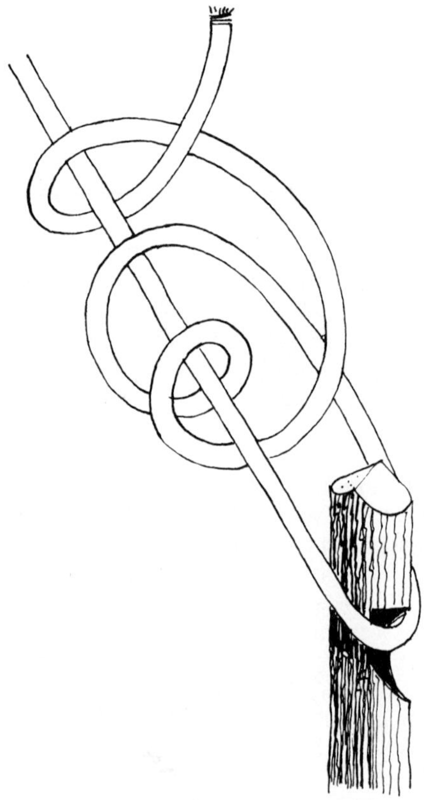

Figure 19-5 Taut line hitch.

A Figure eight knot

B Square knot

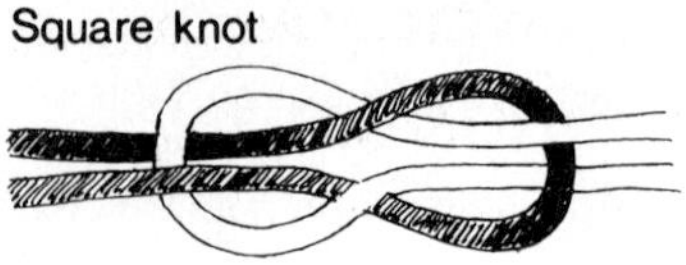

C Granny knot

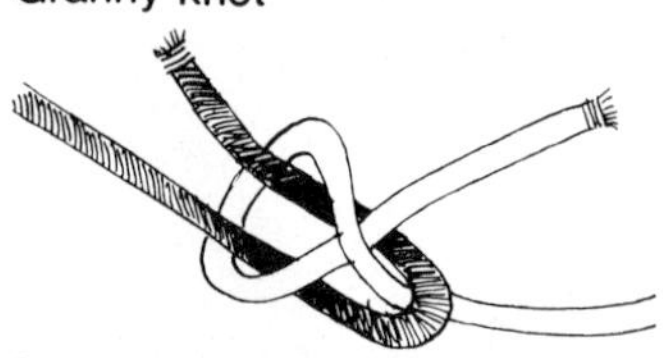

D Sheet bend knot

Figure 19-4 Figure eight, square, granny and sheet bend knots.

the end and standing part on *opposite* sides of the bight in the black rope instead of on the *same* side as in the square knot in Figure 19-4*B*.

SHEET BEND (WEAVER'S KNOT OR BECKET BEND) (FIG. 19-4*D*). A square knot will not hold when joining two ropes of unequal size, but a sheet bend will. Make a bight in the black rope and bring the end of the white rope up through it, around behind both the end and standing part of the black rope, across and around under its own standing part and pull it tight. Be sure to leave both ends somewhat long so that the knot will hold. For greater security, after bringing the end of the white rope across and under its standing part, take two or more turns around its bight and pull it under its standing part again (not shown).

To untie it, pull on the end of the black rope and its standing part to loosen the knot and then pick it apart.

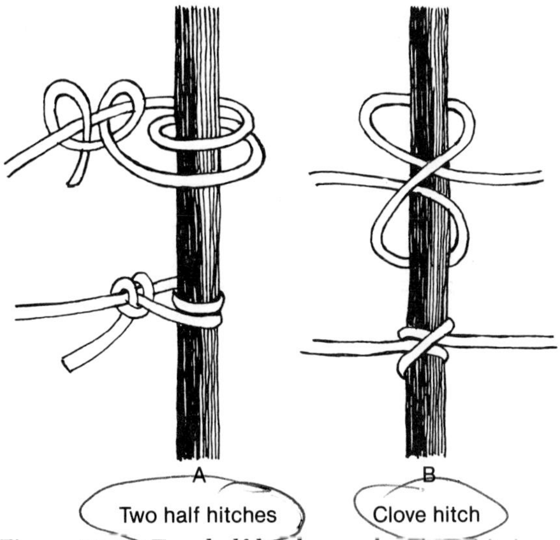

Figure 19-6 Two half hitches and a clove hitch.

To Attach a Rope to an Object

TAUT LINE HITCH (FIG. 19-5). This knot can be used to anchor a tent guy rope, to secure a rope to a ring, or for lifesaving purposes. This knot will not slip, yet you can tighten or loosen the rope merely by pushing the knot up or down on the standing part. This makes it particularly appropriate for a nonsynthetic tent guy line, for you can quickly slide the knot toward the peg to loosen it when rain threatens, then slide the knot back up the standing part to tighten it again after the rope has dried.

Pass the end of the rope around the peg, and, starting away from the peg and working back toward it, take three turns around the standing part and finish with an overhand knot around the standing part above the turns. Pull it tight.

CLOVE HITCH (FIG. 19-6*B*). This knot is used to start and finish lashing, put up a clothesline, or anchor a rope to a tree or other object. Do not use it for anything that moves about, such as a horse or boat, for movement may loosen it.

Bring one end of the rope around the post in an overhand loop and continue around the post again and tuck it under the turn just made. Pull it tight.

HALF HITCHES (Fig. 19-6*A*). This knot is used to attach a rope to a post, as when stringing a clothesline, or to a ring, as in the painter of a boat. Use two or more hitches for greater security.

Wrap the end of the rope once or twice around the post in an overhand loop and tuck it up through the loop (one half hitch). Then make a second half hitch by making an overhand loop and bringing the end up through.

SLIPPERY HITCH OR HIGHWAYMAN'S HITCH (FIG. 19-7). This is a novelty or "fun" knot that provides a temporary fastening that you can *cast off* (untie) in a hurry.

Step 1. Gather up the standing part of the rope and bring it around behind the post to make a bight.

Step 2. Gather up the standing part again and bring it in front of the post and up through the bight just made to make a second bight.

Step 3. Pull on the end to tighten.

Step 4. Now gather up the end and bring it around in front of the post and up through the second bight to make yet a third one.

Step 5. Pull the standing part to tighten all; the hitch will now hold.

To untie it in a jiffy, give a quick jerk on the end.

The name *Highwayman's Hitch* supposedly came from the fact that in olden days a highwayman could use it to tether his horse and make a quick getaway after staging a hold-up.

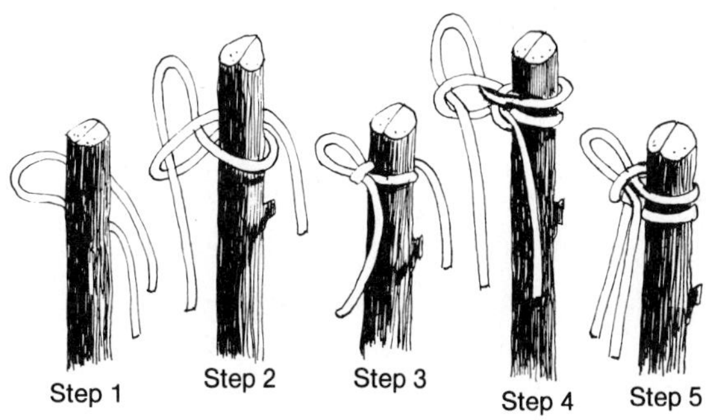

Figure 19-7 Slippery or highwayman's hitch.

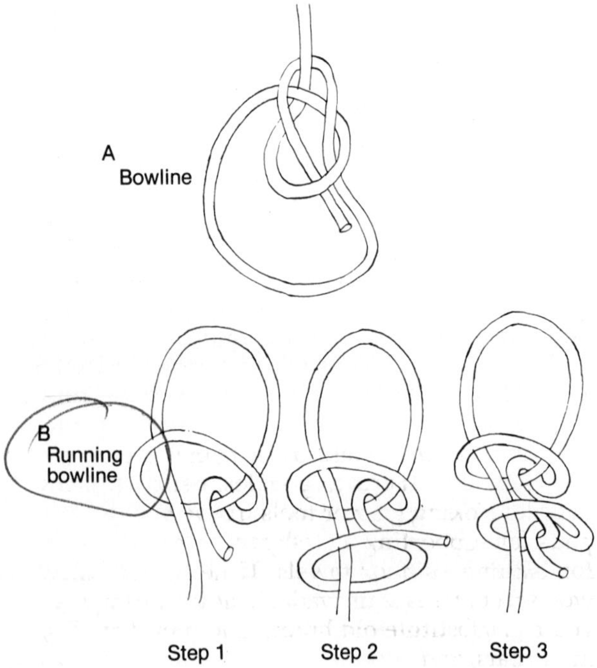

Figure 19-8 Bowline and running bowline or slip knot.

To Make a Loop in a Rope

BOWLINE* (FIG. 19-8*A*). This is used to make a permanent loop in a rope that will stay the same size even when stress is applied. It is useful for anchoring a boat, when tied in the end of its painter or bowline (hence the name) and slipped over a post, for emergency use as when lowering a person during a fire, and also for making a bedroll, tying around the waist of a mountain climber, leading or tethering an animal, or throwing out in the water to someone in trouble.

This little saying may help your campers to remember how to tie this knot

> The rabbit jumped out of its hole,
> Ran round the tree and
> Jumped back in its hole again.

Make a small overhand loop with the standing part far enough down to allow for the size noose you want. Bring the end up through the loop (rabbit jumped out of its hole), around behind the standing part (ran around the tree), and down through the loop again (rabbit jumped back in its hole again). Hold onto the end as you pull the standing part to tighten the knot.

Sailors learned to tie this knot with one hand while clinging to the rigging with the other. Could you do it?

RUNNING BOWLINE OR SLIP KNOT (FIG. 19-8*B*). This forms a noose that pulls tight when stress is applied and, therefore, it should never be used on a living person or animal. Use it to retrieve an object floating in water, tie up a package or bedroll, suspend an object from a tree, or whenever you need to fasten a rope tightly around an inanimate object.

Step 1. Use the end to tie an overhand knot around the standing part.

Steps 2 and 3. Use the end to tie a second overhand knot around the standing part and pull the knot tight. Note that since both overhand knots are tied around the standing part, they will slip up and down on it and so adjust the noose tightly about the object.

To Shorten a Rope or By-Pass a Weak Spot

SHEEP SHANK (FIG. 19-9).

Step 1. Fold the rope twice as shown to get the length you want or to by-pass the weak spot.

Step 2. Use each end to tie an overhand knot around the folded portion adjacent to it.

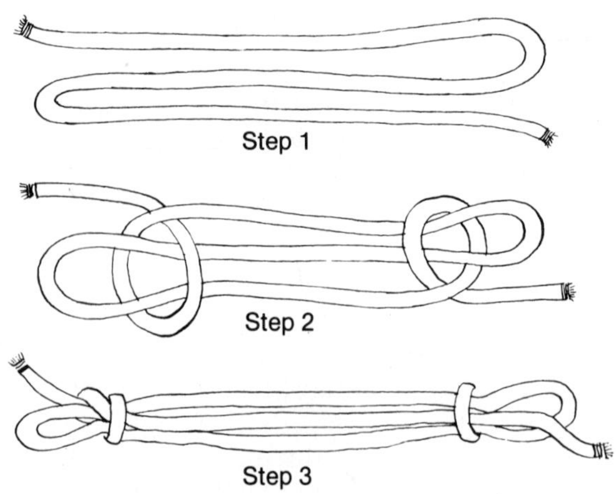

Figure 19-9 Sheep shank.

*Pronounced bō'-lin.

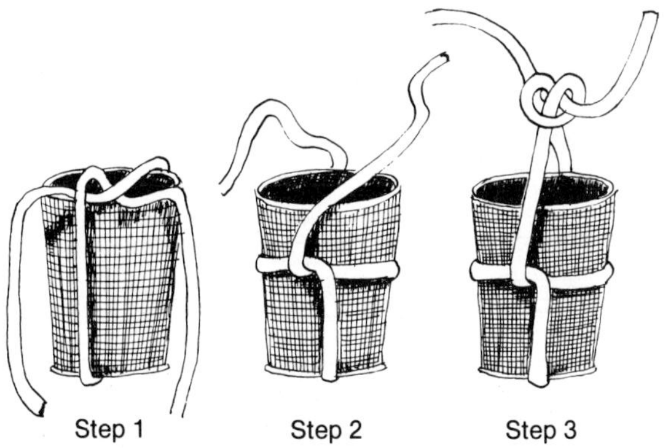

Figure 19–10 Barrel hitch.

Step 3. Tighten the knots. For more permanency, pass each end down through the loop next to it. (Not shown.)

To Suspend an Object

BARREL HITCH (FIG. 19-10). This can be used to suspend a handleless object.

Step 1. Place the object on the rope, leaving one end long enough to complete the hitch. Bring that end and the standing part of the other up above the object and complete a half knot.

Step 2. Pull the half knot open sideways to form two bights and pull them halfway down on opposite sides of the object.

Step 3. Bring both the end of the rope and the standing part up above the object and use the end to tie a slip knot about the standing part. Draw the slip knot tight around the object and suspend it by the standing part.

LASHING

Lashing is used to join sticks or poles together using cord, light rope, or *binder twine* which is cheap, strong, and readily available at most hardware or farm supply stores. Lashing is quite secure when properly done and can be applied and removed without damaging either poles or cord. It looks "campy" and substitutes well for nails, which can inflict permanent damage if driven into living trees.

Lashing can be useful in many camp projects, such as constructing tables, benches, racks to hold cooking gear or tools, rustic bridges, tripods for supporting a washpan, or drying racks for bathing suits or towels. If dead and fallen wood from trees is unavailable at your campsite, you can substitute old broom and mop handles, metal bars, and such.

Practice in lashing, using grocery string and lead pencils or small sticks, provides a good "program" for use on rainy days or at night, and campers can later transfer the skills mastered to actual camp situations.

Though it is not absolutely essential, a more finished and sturdier result is achieved by using a knife or hand axe to notch the pieces being lashed to make them dovetail together where they join (Fig. 19–15). Use enough cord to make as many turns as are necessary to do a solid, neat job.

The secret of a tight, solid job of lashing is

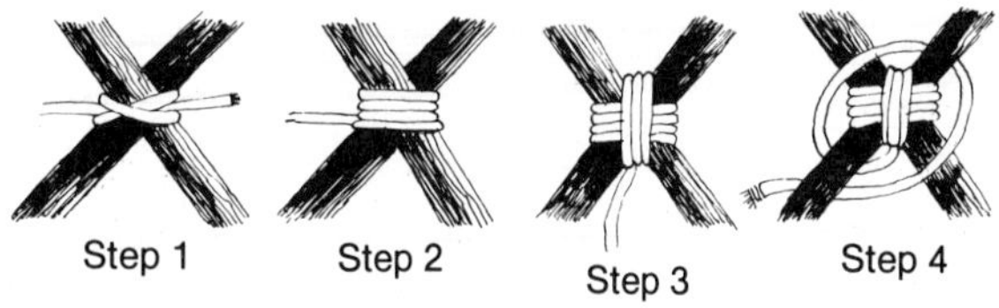

Figure 19–12 Diamond or diagonal lashing.

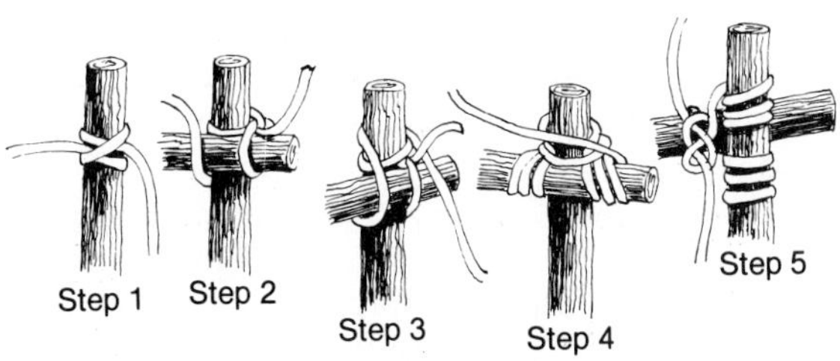

Figure 19–11 Square lashing.

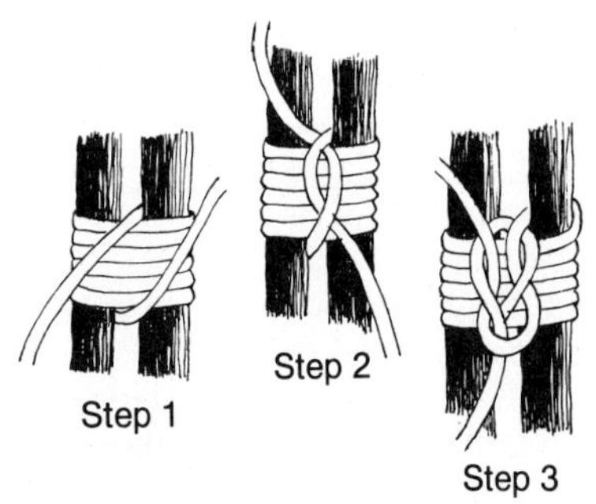

Figure 19–13 Round or shear lashing.

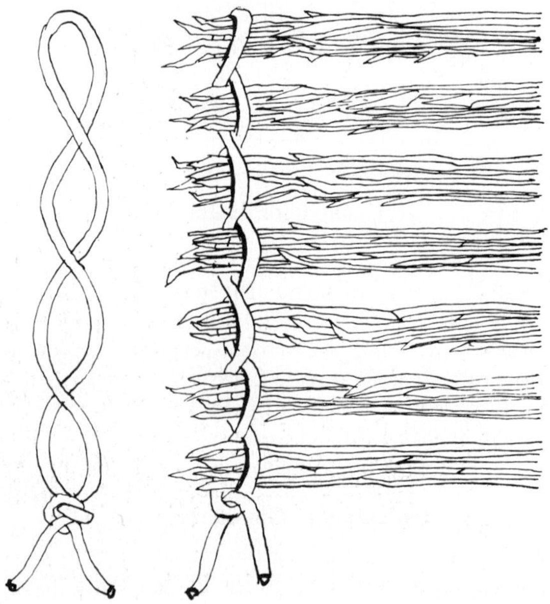

Figure 19–14 Malay hitch.

found in the final step, *frapping* (Fig. 19–11). This is done by winding the cord tightly between the sticks and the turns of lashing you have previously made.

It is customary to use the standing part of your cord when lashing instead of the end as done when tying knots.

To Join Sticks at Right Angles

SQUARE LASHING (FIG. 19-11).

Step 1. Cross two sticks at right angles and use the end of the cord to make a clove hitch around one of them, leaving enough of the end to complete a square knot when you have finished.

Step 2. Bring the standing part down across the horizontal stick, around behind the vertical stick, up across the horizontal on the other side, and then around behind the vertical stick again.

Step 3. Continue this process until you have made at least four or five complete turns around both sides of each stick.

Step 4. Frap with four or five tight turns between the lashing and the sticks.

Step 5. Tie a square knot or clove hitch with the two ends, then cut off any excess twine and tuck the ends in under the lashing.

To Join Two Sticks at an Angle

DIAMOND OR DIAGONAL LASHING (FIG. 19-12).

Step 1. Anchor one end of the rope with a clove hitch around both sticks, leaving enough of the end to complete a square knot when finished.

Step 2. Use the standing part to make three to five turns around both sticks.

Step 3. Repeat the same process in the opposite direction.

Step 4. Frap tightly and finish with a square knot (not shown) with the ends of the rope.

To Join Sticks into a Base

TRIPOD LASHING. This type of lashing is used to join three sticks that can then be spread apart and stood upright to form a base.

Step 1. Lay the three sticks parallel and tie them together with a clove hitch.

Step 2. Weave the cord over the first stick, under the second, over the third, etc., until you have made four or five turns around them.

Step 3. Frap somewhat loosely between the sticks, allowing enough slack to stand the sticks up and spread them apart as a base. Finish with the usual square knot or clove hitch.

To Join Poles Parallel with Each Other or to Lengthen a Pole

ROUND OR SHEAR LASHING (FIG. 19-13). This is used to join two poles together side by side or to make one long pole by lashing two poles together. To lash two poles together:

Step 1. Place them parallel and wind the rope around them five or six times, as shown. Leave the ends long enough to make a square knot when completed.

Step 2. Frap at least once tightly between the poles and tighten with a single knot.

Step 3. Finish off by tying a square knot with the two ends. Lash in at least two other places along the joining.

To lengthen a pole by splicing another to it, lay poles with their ends overlapping and do shear lashing with tight frapping at three or four places along the overlapping parts.

To Make Table Tops and Other Objects

A MALAY HITCH (FIG. 19-14). This is used to join sticks or boards together to make a shelf or table top. You can also use it to convert wisps of long grass, straw, or other suitable materials into a mattress, a mat for your cabin floor, a fence, or a screen in front of a latrine or outdoor shower.

Step 1. Use a cord slightly over twice as long as your completed object is to be. Space out the sticks or portions of grass at appropriate distances. Loop the middle of the cord around the stick and continue by tightly bringing one end of the cord alternately over and under each succeeding stick or wisp of grass. Then circle the top stick and bring the cord down again, passing on the opposite side of each stick until the end is down where you started. Join the two ends with a square knot.

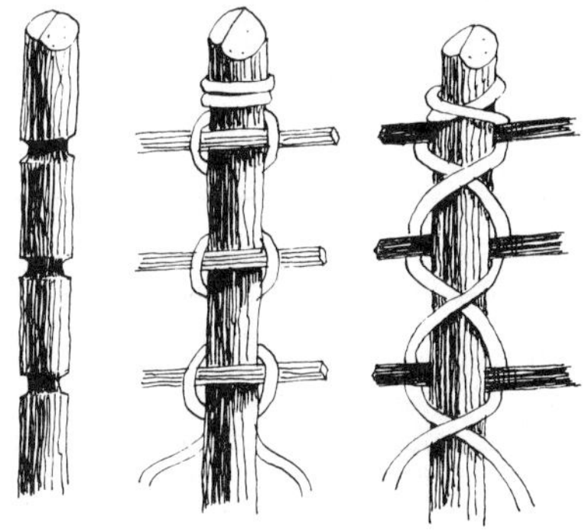

Figure 19-15 Continuous lashing.

(Camp Nahelu, Ortonville, Mich.)

Step 2. Repeat this process as many times as you wish at various places along the length of the sticks. You can gain extra security by circling each stick with the cord before going on to the next one.

CONTINUOUS LASHING (PALING HITCH) (FIG. 19-15). This is used to lash several small sticks, lengths of bamboo, or laths along one long stick or pole or between two or more sticks. You can use it for making a table top that can be rolled up for easy storing or transporting, a tie or belt rack, or a ladder for a climbing plant.

Step 1. Although not absolutely necessary, it will add more stability if you notch both long poles and crosspieces to make them dovetail snugly together. Elevate the long poles by resting their ends on objects such as rocks or chair seats so that you can work freely.

Step 2. Use a piece of string or cord about four times as long as one of the long poles and use a clove hitch to fasten the middle of the cord near the end of one of the long poles.

Step 3. Place the crosspieces at desired intervals along the long pole, then bring both ends of the cord tightly across the top of the first crosspiece, then around behind the long pole, and bring them up over the next crosspiece. Continue on to the end. Keep the cord just as tight as possible. Now make a few turns with each end around the long pole and join them with a square knot.

Step 4. Fasten the other ends of the crosspieces to the other long pole in the same manner.

ADDITIONAL READINGS

(For an explanation of abbreviations and abbreviated forms used, see page 13.)

Ashley, Clifford W.: *The Ashley Book of Knots.* Doubleday, 1944.

Boy Scout Handbook, pp. 225–229.

Cardwell: *America's Camping Book*, Part VIII, chs. 36–41.

Day, Cyrus L.: *The Art of Knotting and Splicing.* U.S. Naval Institute, 2nd ed., 1955, 224 pp.

Fieldbook for Boys and Men, ch. 7, pp. 84–111.

Gibson, Charles E.: *Handbook of Knots and Splices.* Emerson, 1963, 152 pp.

Glass, Walter: *The Key to Knots and Splices.* ACA, 1959, 94 pp., paper.

Graumont, Raoul M.: *Handbook of Knots and Splices.* Cornell Maritime Press, 1954, paper.

Harvey, Virginia I.: *Macrame: The Art of Creative Knotting.* Van Nostrand, 1972, 128 pp., paper.

Hensel, John: *The Book of Ornamental Knots.* Scribner's, 1973, 160 pp.

Knots and Lashing. Girl Scouts, rev. (Flip charts)

MacFarlan, Allan and Paulette: *Knotcraft: The Art of Knot Tying.* Ass'n Press, 1967, 186 pp.

Mason, Bernard S.: *Roping.* Ronald, 1940, 138 pp.

Mason, Bernard S.: *Woodcraft and Camping.* Dover, 1974, 580 pp.

Merrill: *All About Camping*, pp. 322–329.

Miracle and Decker: *Complete Book of Camping*, ch. 31.

Montgomery, Edward: *Useful Knots for Everyone.* Scribner's, 1973, 128 pp.

Ormond: *The Complete Book of Outdoor Lore*, ch. 12.

Pesch, Imelda M.: *Macrame.* Sterling, 48 pp. (Creative knotting)

Pioneering (No. 3382). Boy Scouts, 1967, 64 pp., paper.

Sea Exploring Manual (No. 3229). Boy Scouts, 1966, 448 pp.

Severn, Bill: *Rope Roundup.* McKay, 1960, 237 pp.

Shaw, George Russell: *Knots: Useful and Ornamental.* Collier, 1972, 194 pp., paper.

Smith, Hervey Garrett: *Arts of the Sailor.* Van Nostrand, 1953, 233 pp.

Strom, Nils, and Enestrom, Anders: *Big-Knot Macrame.* Sterling, 48 pp.

twenty
The Weather

"Whatever the weather may be," says he,
"Whatever the weather may be,
It's the songs ye sing, an' the smiles ye wear,
That's a makin' the sun shine everywhere."

—James Whitcomb Riley*

*From *Pipes O' Pan at Zekesburg*. The Bobbs-Merrill Co.

THE IMPORTANCE OF WEATHER

Although it is easy to see why the weather was so important to the people of early America, it seems of only casual interest to most of us today, except when some spectacular phenomenon such as a blizzard brings it to our attention. We are ordinarily content to flip on the radio or television or consult a daily newspaper to determine how to dress or whether to go ahead with our plans for a picnic or trip to the golf course. However, the weather is of vital interest to campers who spend most of their time in the out-of-doors with only a minimum of rather primitive equipment for shelter. When on a trip away from the main camp, your group will have no official Weather Service report to rely on, and campers will have to depend on their own knowledge and powers of observation to tell what is in store and what must be done to prepare for it. If a group is on the water, individuals' lives, as well as the safety of their boat and gear, may depend on an early start for shore. Many lives are needlessly lost each year because of lack of weather knowledge and proper respect for the hazards of rough water, mountain storms, lightning, and flash floods.

Studying the rudiments of weather prediction and the conditions that cause and foretell weather changes is interesting in itself, and it also deepens our knowledge of nature and the world around us. Many people are completely oblivious to the everchanging patterns of the sky and atmosphere around them. For instance, how often do we take time to just relax and enjoy the calmness and beauty of a blue, cloudless sky? Have you paused recently to observe the spectacular pageant as the clouds undergo a complete metamorphosis in the building-up of a storm? Have you watched "scud" clouds scurrying across the sky in a wild, turbulent scramble and wondered what force was driving them and where they were going and why? And have you watched lazy, occasional clouds gradually build up into high, spectacular mountains of a grandeur unsurpassed by the land mountains that tourists drive hundreds of miles to see?

WEATHER FORECASTING

Amateur weather forecasters cannot equal the long-range forecasts of the National Weather

Service, with its highly trained personnel and elaborate equipment for observing and measuring conditions and collecting data. The Service maintains a number of weather stations throughout this country as well as in neighboring ocean and land areas. Each observes and reports conditions in its own area that, when combined with the data from other stations, satellites, radar, airplanes, ships at sea, and cooperating foreign countries, make it possible to construct a huge worldwide weather map as it would appear from a point high enough to look down on the whole world. Since weather travels from one place to another, this master picture enables the Weather Service to predict with considerable accuracy what is coming and when it will arrive; however, many of the forces affecting the weather interact in unpredictable ways, necessitating constant revisions and liberal sprinklings of "probablies" or "possibilities."

Campers may find it interesting to learn more about the operations of the Weather Service as it constantly tries to improve its instruments and better its performance. Sources for further study can be found in some of the references listed at the end of this chapter. Also, daily weather maps can be obtained from the National Weather Service. Their forecasts cover a period of 24 to 36 hours or longer and include large areas.

Campers can, after some study and with the aid of a few simple instruments, do a creditable job of forecasting on a short-term basis of from 2 to 12 hours. Although an occasional summer storm may give as little as an hour's warning of its approach, their predictions should be accurate enough to meet your ordinary camp needs, for even young campers often attain an accuracy of from 60 to 80 percent. However, they will first need to learn something about atmospheric conditions. Weather is "made" by the interaction of such factors as temperature, pressure, moisture, and wind, which can be observed or measured and then the combinations interpreted properly to arrive at worthwhile predictions.

THE ATMOSPHERE

The study of the air or atmosphere is called *meteorology* and those professionally trained in this area are known as *meteorologists.*

Composition of the Atmosphere

The earth is a globe suspended in space, which extends outward for countless miles in all directions. The *atmosphere* or that portion of space that exerts an appreciable amount of pressure occupies an area approximately 50 miles wide around the earth. Invisible gases fill this space, gradually thinning out away from the earth until they eventually become so thin and scattered as to approach "nothingness." Gases constantly try to expand in all directions as much as the outward pressure on them will allow and, of course, they are also subject to the laws of gravity. Consequently, each layer of air presses down on all the layers below until almost 97 percent of all the gases are concentrated within 18 miles of the earth, 50 percent within the last 3½ miles. The atmosphere near the earth consists of about 20 percent *oxygen* (necessary for animal life), 0.3 to 0.03 percent *carbon dioxide* (necessary for plant life), some 78 percent *nitrogen,* 0.5 percent water in the form of vapor, and minute quantities of other gases.

The clouds and what we call "weather" are contained in the comparatively narrow band 5 to 8 miles above the earth. This explains why an airplane can often escape bad weather by flying above the clouds and turbulence we are experiencing on earth.

Air Currents

The sun's rays pass through the atmosphere without heating it appreciably until they meet the earth's surface, which they do heat. The earth then reflects this heat back to warm the air immediately above it. When the gases in the air are heated, they expand and become lighter and less dense, and hence rise. The cooler air above these gases rushes in to take their place and be warmed in turn. As the warm air rises into the increasingly thinner air, it comes under less and less pressure and so continues to expand and rise as more cool air comes down to take its place. This process of expanding and rising cools the gases at the rate of about 3.5 degrees for each 1,000 feet of altitude, so that a temperature of about 50 degrees at sea level would be near 42 degrees below zero 5 miles up. This explains why high mountains are always capped with snow regardless of the season.

The motion of the earth on its axis and the constant up-down movements of the warm and cool air exchanging places cause what are known as *air currents* or *updrafts* and *downdrafts.* Since gases under increasingly less pressure are able to expand in all directions, the rising air also expands sideways, producing horizontal movements we know as *breezes* or *winds.* We note the effect of these air currents in the capricious antics of a piece of paper, thistle-down, or winged seed that has been picked up and borne aloft. Spiders on their silken threads have been observed as high as 5 miles up where air currents have carried them. These air movements, however, are unpredictable for, in addition to other variable factors, the earth, and consequently the air above it, is not warmed uniformly. For instance, dark, plowed soil absorbs heat from the sun's rays much more readily than does a grassy meadow, and almost any sort of land absorbs it faster than does a body of water; consequently, the air above is correspondingly heated to different temperatures and at different rates. At night, when there are no longer any sun's rays to warm it, the earth continues to heat the air above from its retained heat, but again at different rates; bodies of water and meadows retain their heat longer and consequently heat the air above them less rapidly. These variations in heating cause the air to expand and move at varying speeds so that while the air is almost motionless in one spot, it may be a seething froth of activity in the form of a good breeze or stiff gale only a short distance away.

Air Pressure

The familiar expression "light as air" would lead us to believe that air is weightless, but such is not the case. Air becomes more and more compressed and consequently heavier as it nears the ground owing to the continuing attempt of the gases to expand, the pull of gravity, and the weight of all the air above pressing downward. Consequently at sea level the air ordinarily exerts a downward pressure of 14.7 pounds per square inch. This is what makes it possible to drink liquid through a straw. As you suck upward on the straw, you draw the air out of it, creating a *vacuum.* The air, pressing downward on the liquid, then forces a column of it into the straw and up into your mouth.

Humidity

Air contains moisture in the form of invisible *vapor.* Although you are ordinarily unaware of it, you have noted it as steam rising from a pan of boiling water or as your warm breath condensed in the cold air of a winter morning. The amount of moisture in the air is expressed as its *humidity.* Most of the moisture comes by evaporation from rivers, lakes, oceans, soil, and trees and other forms of vegetation. A perpetual interchange of moisture takes place between the earth and the atmosphere: the air draws or evaporates moisture in the form of vapor from the earth's surface; this vapor forms clouds and the moisture is eventually returned to the earth as rain, snow, or some other type of precipitation.

On a hot muggy day, the air is so full of moisture that it has almost reached the *saturation point* (has absorbed all the moisture it can hold at its present temperature). Consequently, it cannot adequately evaporate the perspiration from your skin, and since that is one of the best ways to rid yourself of excess body heat, you feel uncomfortable. We speak of such a day as a *humid* one. A *barometer* is a device for measuring the humidity, or amount of moisture in the air, by determining the amount of weight or pressure it exerts. By taking successive readings, we can note not only the amount of humidity but also whether it is increasing or decreasing and how rapidly. All three of these factors are quite important in weather prediction. Dry air (low humidity) is heavier and hence exerts more pressure than moist air (high humidity).

Although several types of barometers are available, the commonest is the *aneroid barometer* (meaning "without liquid"). It consists of a box that is sensitive to air pressure and a needle that moves around a marked dial to register changes in pressure. It is relatively inexpensive and is convenient since it can easily be moved about; however, it is not the most accurate type of barometer.

A *mercury barometer* acts on the same principle as drawing liquid through a staw. It consists of a graduated tube of mercury, closed at the top with an open bottom filled with mercury (Fig. 20-1). There is a vacuum above the mercury in the tube. When the air presses down on the surface of the mercury it forces some of it up into the tube, just as the liquid was forced up into the

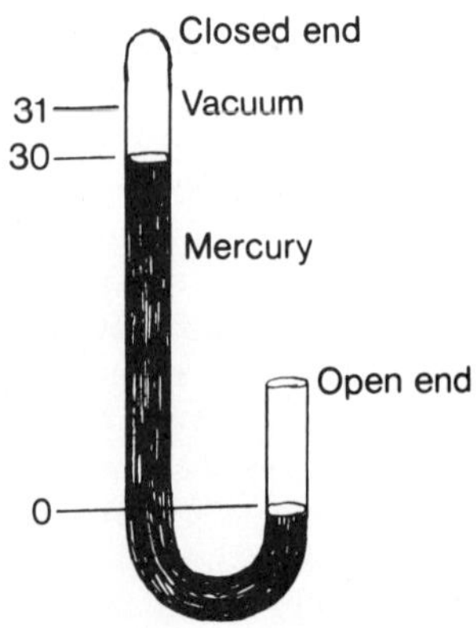

Figure 20–1 Mercury barometer.

vacuum you created in the straw. A graduated scale on the tube registers the height of the column of mercury. A square inch of air of average humidity weighs 14.7 pounds at sea level and will support a column of mercury 30 inches high. Very dry air is heavier and consequently pushes the mercury up higher; this indicates fair weather. Moist air is lighter and so lets the mercury drop; this is usually a sign of bad weather. In general, the higher tbe barometer reading, the finer the weather.

At higher altitudes above sea level, the air is thinner and lighter, as we have noted, and the normal or average barometer reading is therefore lower. At 3,000 feet above sea level, the average reading is about 27. In areas below sea level, the readings are correspondingly higher. In order to use barometer readings for weather prediction, you will need to learn what the average readings are for your particular area.

Temperature

Air temperature is measured by the familiar *thermometer.* The usual variety consists of a closed tube of mercury that expands when heated and so rises in the tube; you read its height on the graduated scale. Conversely, cooler air causes the mercury to contract, resulting in a correspondingly lower reading on the scale.

Water Condensation

The warmth of the air causes the moisture from the earth to evaporate or change into *water vapor,* an invisible gas that is light enough to be picked up and carried about in the air. The amount of moisture air can absorb and carry varies with its temperature and, in general, the warmer the air, the more it can carry. Thus, a 20 degree rise in temperature at ground level approximately doubles the amount of moisture the air can bear. When it is carrying all it can at its present temperature, we say the air has reached its saturation point, or its humidity is 100 percent. A change in temperature thus alters the saturation point. When the amount of moisture is below the saturation point, it is called the *relative humidity,* expressed as a percentage of the saturation point. Thus, theoretically, humidity could range from 0 to 100 percent.

We have noted that as the warm air near the earth expands and rises, it gradually cools. Its saturation point becomes lower and lower and its ability to hold moisture in the form of vapor decreases correspondingly. When the air passes the saturation point at its current temperature, it reaches what is known as *dew point,* and since it is also contracting as it cools, it squeezes out the excess moisture it can no longer hold in the form of minute droplets. These droplets are so tiny and light that they continue to be airborne and, under certain conditions, join together into larger and larger droplets and finally become visible as *clouds. Fog* is similar to a cloud near the earth; we have difficulty in seeing through fog because our eyes cannot penetrate these millions of droplets. The droplets reflect back automobile lights or the rays from a flashlight as effectively as millions of tiny mirrors. *Smog* results when fog is combined with smoke or other airborne particles found near industrial or otherwise polluted areas.

When the humidity is high as night comes on, the moist air is cooled as it comes in contact with the rapidly cooling trees and grass and, if it reaches dew point, its excess moisture condenses on them as *dew.* We observe this same phenomenon on a warm day when the dampness in the air condenses as beads of moisture on a pitcher of ice water.

Precipitation and Other Weather Phenomena

You have no doubt noticed minute bits of dust floating about in the air when a ray of sunshine strikes them in a certain way. Similar dust particles are distributed throughout the atmosphere and on a clear day they make the sky look blue; when especially numerous, they give the sky a gray or hazy appearance. These dust particles are the nuclei about which moisture collects as droplets when the ascending air cools to dew point. As the air continues to rise and cool, it squeezes out more and more moisture in the form of droplets that eventually take on electrical charges that attract them to each other. As they unite into larger and larger droplets, they eventually become too heavy to be airborne and fall to earth as raindrops, each consisting of from one to seven million droplets.

Snow results when the droplets freeze into tiny ice crystals in the cold, upper regions of the atmosphere, with hundreds or thousands of them uniting into the beautiful designs of single snowflakes.

Sleet occurs when snow partially melts as it falls through a layer of warmer air just above the ground. If the half-melted snow freezes just as it hits the ground, it is called *glaze.*

Hail results when rain from a rather low-lying cloud is caught in a strong updraft of air and tossed back up into a high, freezing area where it is coated with snow and ice. It then falls back down through the low-lying cloud, acquires more moisture, and again falls down into the strong updraft that may throw it back up to acquire another layer of ice and snow. This process may be repeated several times until the ice-covered pellet finally becomes so heavy that it pierces the updraft and crashes to earth as hail. It is claimed that hailstones as big as baseballs, with 25 layers of ice and snow, fell at Annapolis, Maryland on June 22, 1915. Hail is a freakish weather phenomenon that can occur even in balmy surface temperatures if other conditions are right, for as we have seen, there are always freezing temperatures high in the atmosphere. In fact, hailstorms are said to occur most frequently in June.

Frost occurs when the temperature drops below freezing under conditions that would ordinarily produce dew.

We see a *halo* or *ring* around the sun or moon when we see its light shining through ice crystals in the atmosphere.

Mythology explained *lightning* as bolts of fire sent by the War God, Thor, to paralyze the earth's people, but since the observations of Benjamin Franklin, we have known that it is actually a form of electricity. Electrical charges in the atmosphere usually pass harmlessly from one cloud to another, but a bolt of lightning occasionally comes down to earth with enough power to kill men or animals, start fires, or uproot trees. Lightning follows the line of least resistance as it leaps from one handy electrical conductor to another on its way to the ground. Therefore, to prevent it from striking you, you must avoid becoming the most convenient conductor in its path by taking care not to be the most prominent object in the area or near something else that is. Some of the most dangerous places to be are near a fence or clothesline, at the top of a hill, in a boat, on the beach, riding a horse or bicycle, on a golf course or meadow, or under an especially tall tree or one standing alone. Among the safest places are in an automobile (the metal body conducts the bolt to the ground), in a ravine between two hills, or in a grove of trees. If you are caught out in the open, lie flat on the ground or in a ditch. If you are indoors, stay away from plumbing and electrical appliances and don't use the telephone or take a bath. Since water is a good conductor of electricity, anyone swimming or boating should get on land as quickly as possible.

Thunder, although often alarming, is perfectly harmless; it is believed to be caused by the rapid expansion of the air as it is heated by the passage of lightning through it. To roughly estimate the distance of lightning in miles, count the number of seconds between the time you see the bolt and hear the thunder and divide by five. (You can roughly estimate seconds by counting a-thousand-and-one, a-thousand-and-two, etc.) This method is based on the fact that, while light travels at 186,000 feet per second, sound travels only about 1,100 feet per second. Since there are 5,280 feet in a mile, sound travels at approximately ⅕ mile per second; therefore, an interval of 5 seconds would indicate that the lightning was about a mile away.

A *rainbow* occurs when we see the sun's rays through rain that is falling opposite the sun. The water, like a prism, breaks the rays into the colors of a rainbow.

CLOUDS

The sky, nature's roof, forms a backdrop for the clouds. Cloud names are of Latin derivation

Figure 20-2 Cirrus clouds. (National Oceanic and Atmospheric Administration)

and there are four basic types of clouds, with nine combination of these four types.

Basic Forms or Families of Clouds

1. *Cirrus* are the "lock" or "curl" clouds and are the highest of all (5 to 10 miles) (Fig. 20-2). They are always white, being composed entirely of ice crystals, and are sometimes called "witch's broom" or "mare's tail." If the sky is bright blue above and the wind is from the north or northwest, cirrus clouds indicate fair weather for 24 to 48 hours. However, if the sky is gray-blue and the clouds are moving swiftly, especially from the west, they will likely turn to *cirrostratus* clouds (Fig. 20-5) and rain or snow may follow.

2. *Stratus* or "spread sheet" clouds (Fig. 20-3) are a horizontal overcast of "fog" high (up to 20,000 feet) in the air. These clouds are always a shade of gray and are sometimes dark enough to practically conceal the sun or moon. Rain usually follows.

3. *Cumulus* (Fig. 20-4) are the billowy, puffy "heap" or "wool pack" clouds with flat, grayish bottoms that rise to a high, dome-shaped mass of white. They are the lowest clouds of all, being only about a mile above the earth. They are often quite active and usually indicate fair weather, except on a hot, muggy day when, if massed near the horizon or increasing in size, they may indicate rain.

4. *Nimbus* clouds are the low-lying "umbrella" clouds. They are dark, with ragged edges and no definite shape, and usually indicate steady rain or snow. *Scud* clouds are the small, ragged pieces frequently seen traveling rapidly across the sky below the nimbus clouds.

*VARIATIONS AND COMBINATIONS**

5. *Cirrostratus* clouds (Fig. 20-5) are very high (about 5½ miles up). They veil the sky, giving it an uneven, whitish, film-like color pro-

* *Alto* means high; *fracto* means ragged or broken by the wind.

Figure 20-3 Stratus clouds. (National Oceanic and Atmospheric Administration)

Figure 20-4 Cumulus clouds. (National Oceanic and Atmospheric Administration)

duced (like the halo phenomena) by an abundance of ice crystals. They sometimes mean nothing in the morning, but when they persist or appear in the afternoon, they are likely to be a forerunner of rain or snow within 24 hours, particularly if they started as *cirrus* clouds and are coming from the west.

6. *Cirrocumulus* clouds ("mackerel" sky) have a rippled appearance somewhat like sand on the seashore (Fig.20-6). They are very high, puffy clouds about 4 miles up. They usually indicate fair weather, but may bring high winds.

7. *Altocumulus* (Fig. 20-7) are small, high, white clouds that may lie close together in rows or lines, giving a dappled appearance to the sky. They are also called "sheep" clouds and they usually indicate fair weather.

8. *Stratocumulus* (Fig. 20-8) are the dark-colored, twist-shaped clouds (about 1 mile up) that ordinarily thin to cumulus or *fractocumulus* later on and seldom bring the rain they threaten. They are likely to be accompanied by high winds, especially in the fall.

9. *Altostratus* (Fig. 20-9) are thin, gray, curtain-like clouds (about 3 miles up) that often show a bright patch when the sun or moon hides behind them. They are sometimes followed by squally weather.

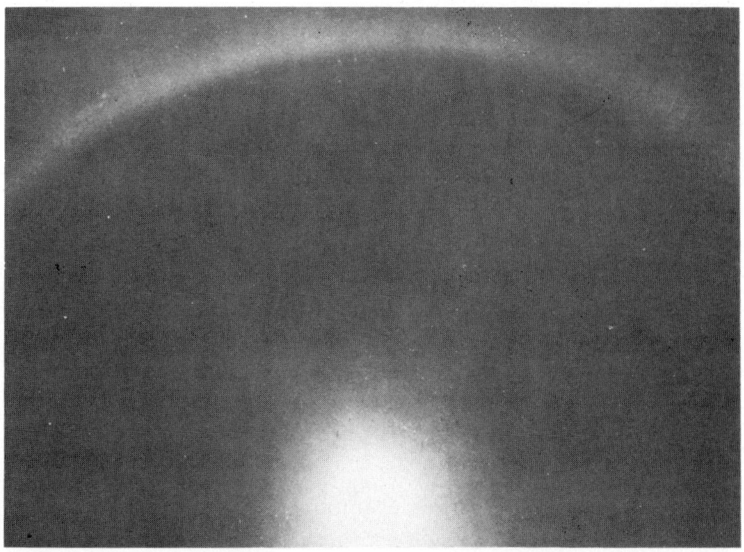

Figure 20-5 Cirrostratus clouds. (National Oceanic and Atmospheric Administration)

Figure 20-6 Cirrocumulus clouds. (National Oceanic and Atmospheric Administration)

10. *Fractonimbus* clouds follow nimbus and generally break up to disclose patches of blue sky indicating clearing weather.

11. *Fractostratus* clouds follow on the heels of fractonimbus and commonly clear into a blue sky with cirrus tufts scattered about.

12. *Fractocumulus* are cumulus clouds that have been broken up into somewhat thinner clouds of irregular appearance. They usually indicate clear weather.

13. *Cumulonimbus* (Fig. 20-10) are the "thunderhead" clouds that are the most spectacular of all. They have dark bases and light tops and tower into the air like mountains. When they appear in the west, a storm will likely occur within a few hours, often accompanied by thunder and lightning.

Clouds moving in different directions at various levels foretell rain.

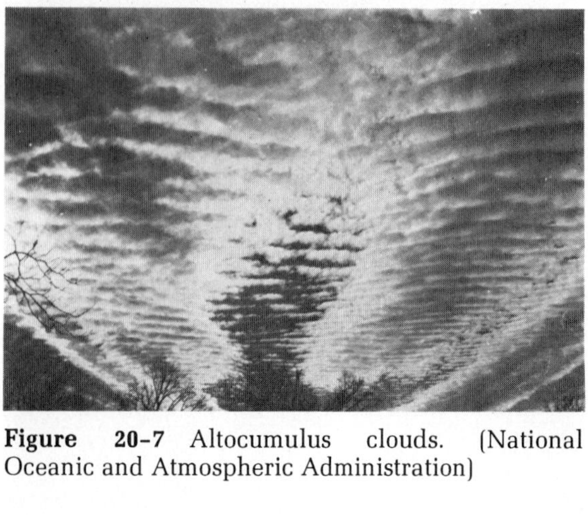

Figure 20-7 Altocumulus clouds. (National Oceanic and Atmospheric Administration)

WEATHER INSTRUMENTS YOU CAN MAKE*

There are several weather instruments that campers can make. It is advisable to have at least one good commercially made instrument of each kind by which to check their accuracy.

A Clipper Ship Barometer

A *clipper ship barometer* works on the same principle as a mercury barometer and will roughly indicate rises and falls in the humidity and how rapidly they are taking place. Fill a bot-

*Further directions for making weather instruments are contained in sources listed in the bibliography for this chapter, such as Harty's *Science for Camp and Counselor*, the Boy Scout booklet, *Weather*, and Bachert and Snook's *Outdoor Education Equipment*.

Figure 20-8 Stratocumulus clouds. (National Oceanic and Atmospheric Administration)

tle two-thirds full of colored water and fit it with a tight cork or rubber stopper. Drill a hole through the stopper and insert a 10-inch length of rubber tube through it so that one end extends into the water as shown in Figure 20-11. Use melted paraffin or candle wax to make a seal around the tube so that it is air and water tight. Invert the bottle carefully so that no air enters and anchor it securely in the shade and out of direct winds. Turn the outer end of the tube up as shown and support it in place. Some of the water will run down into the tube, leaving a vacuum in the top of the bottle above the water line. Watch the bottle for a few days to determine what the normal water level is, then mark it on the bottle and extend a graduated scale on either side of it for recording changes in the water level and, consequently, changes in the humidity or air pressure. (Water may even drip out of the end of the tube when it is rainy.)

A Weather Vane (Wind Vane)

One of the oldest weather instruments is the weather vane or wind vane. It can be built very easily (Fig. 20-12). Use light wood or a large tin can flattened into a sheet and cut into any form desired, such as an arrow, rooster, fish, or boat. Make the tail large and broad enough to

Figure 20-9 Altostratus clouds. (National Oceanic and Atmospheric Administration)

Figure 20-10 Cumulonimbus clouds. (National Oceanic and Atmospheric Administration)

catch the wind so that it will always keep the longer, lighter head pointing directly into the wind. Place a pole out in the open where the wind has free access to it and fasten direction indicators on as shown, lining them up with true, not magnetic, north. Find the balance point of the vane and drill a hole just in front of it and glue one end of a round shaft or dowel into it. Drill another hole in the top of the pole deep enough to hold the other end of the dowel securely and large enough to let it turn freely when used with a pair of washers.

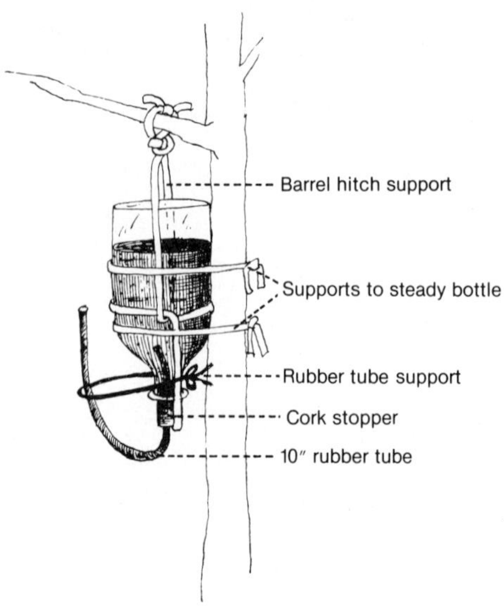

Figure 20-11 Clipper ship barometer.

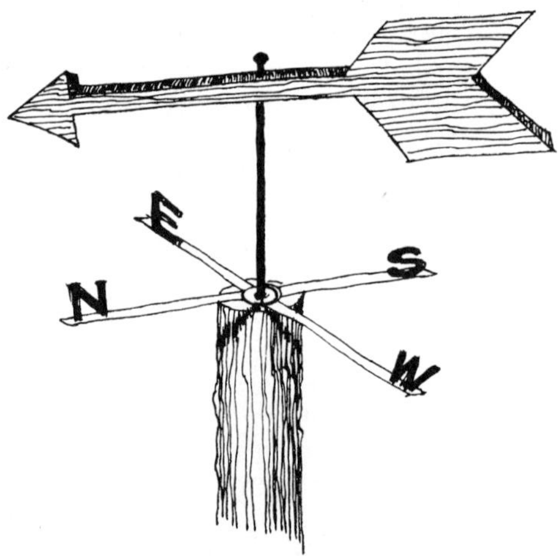

Figure 20-12 Weather vane.

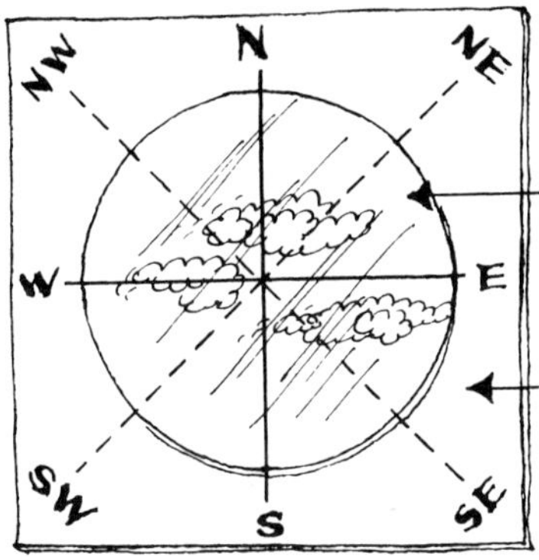

Figure 20–13 Nephoscope.

A Nephoscope

A *nephoscope* lets you watch cloud movements without having to look directly into the sun. Mark the compass directions on a flat piece of cardboard, wood, or metal and fasten it in a convenient spot out in the open, orienting it with true, not magnetic, north (Fig. 20–13). Paint the back of a fairly large mirror or piece of glass with black, shiny enamel and place it on top of the direction indicator. The glass will reflect the sky so that you can watch the clouds and their movements in the mirror.

Nature's Thermometer

Although you may prefer the conveniences of a commercial thermometer, you can estimate the temperature when it is between 45° and 80° F. by counting the chirps of a cricket. Count them for 15 seconds and add 35. The sum will closely approximate the true temperature, for a cricket varies his rate of chirping with the temperature.

A Hygrometer

A *hygrometer* measures relative humidity. You can make a wet-and-dry bulb thermometer by mounting two identical thermometers side by side (Fig. 20–14). Convert one to a wet bulb thermometer by wrapping one end of a cloth, a shoelace with the plastic or metal tip removed, or a piece of lamp wicking around the bulb and extending the other end down into a vessel of water so that it will draw up enough moisture to keep the bulb constantly damp. As the water evaporates around the bulb, it cools it so that the thermometer registers the temperature at 100 percent humidity (saturation point). The other dry-bulb thermometer registers the temperature at the true atmospheric humidity level, so that by subtracting the dry bulb reading from that of the wet bulb and consulting Table 20–1 you can learn the approximate relative humidity (percentage of saturation).

An Anemometer

To make an *anemometer* for measuring wind speed, cross two sticks at right angles (Fig. 20–15) and fasten four lightweight cups or cones across them parallel to the ground. Paper or plastic cups can be used temporarily, but for more permanent cones, plug the ends of small funnels with tight-fitting pieces of cork or whittled wood, or make a paper pattern and cut the cones from flattened tin cans or other light metal and solder them together. Give them a coat or two of paint for protection, making one a contrasting color to make it easy to count the number of revolutions as they spin around. Mount

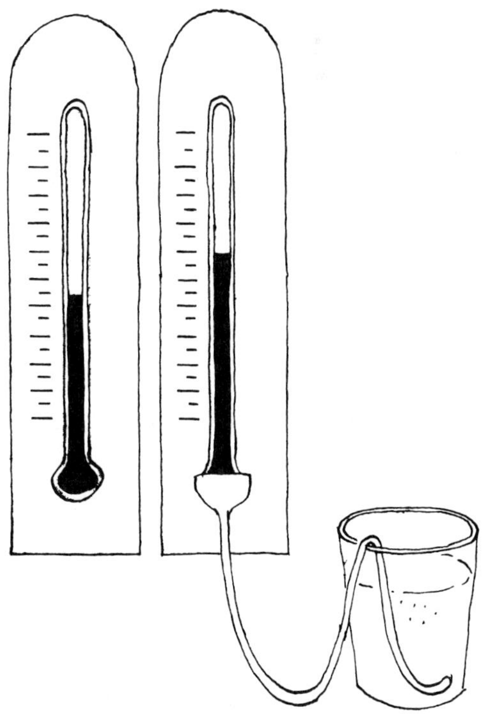

Figure 20–14 Dry and wet bulb hygrometer.

Table 20-1

HYGROMETER READINGS AND RELATIVE HUMIDITY

DEGREES OF DIFFERENCE BETWEEN WET AND DRY BULB READINGS	*DRY BULB READING (°F)*							
	30°	*40°*	*50°*	*60°*	*70°*	*80°*	*90°*	*100°*
	(The figures below indicate the relative humidity in per cent.)							
1°	90	92	93	94	95	96	96	97
2°	79	84	87	89	90	92	92	93
3°	68	76	80	84	86	87	88	90
4°	58	68	74	78	81	83	85	86
6°	38	52	61	68	72	75	78	80
8°	18	37	49	58	64	68	71	74
10°		22	37	48	55	61	65	68
12°		8	26	39	48	54	59	62
14°			16	30	40	47	53	57
16°			5	21	33	41	47	51
18°				13	26	35	41	47
20°				5	19	29	36	42
22°					12	23	32	37
24°					6	18	26	33

the crossed sticks on a dowel, then make a hole in a pole deep enough to hold the dowel securely and large enough so that the dowel can turn freely. Insert the dowel into the pole using a pair of washers, then place the anemometer out in the open where even a slight breeze will turn it. To roughly estimate the wind speed in miles per hour, count the number of revolutions in 30 seconds and divide by 5.

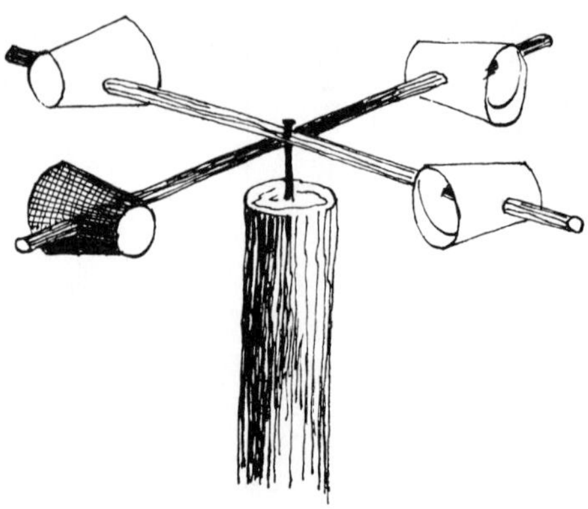

Figure 20-15 Anemometer.

SETTING UP A CAMP WEATHER BUREAU

It is both educational and fun for campers to make their own weather bureau so they can take readings from the instruments. Individuals then can be assigned to prepare daily weather reports and predictions that can be posted on a central bulletin board each day or announced at breakfast to the rest of the group.

Instruments Needed

Although you can achieve some success with a minimum of instruments or even none at all, it is desirable to have as many of the following as possible.

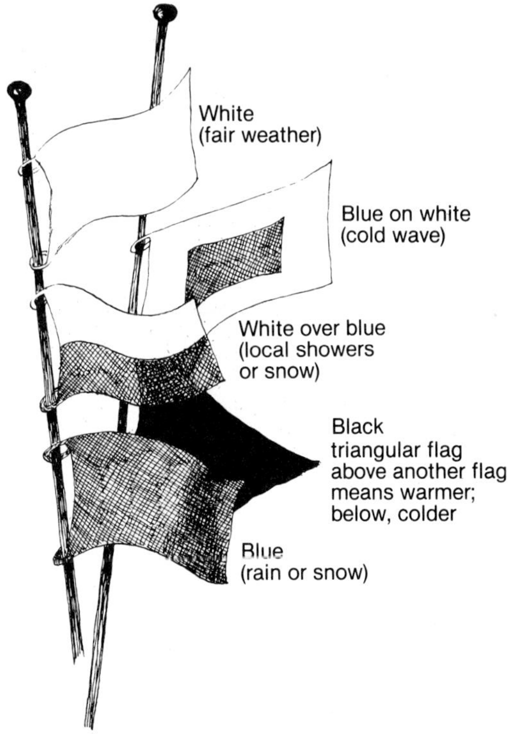

Figure 20–16 Weather flags.

1. A weather vane (wind vane) to determine wind direction. Place it on a pole 15 to 20 feet in the air and away from any obstructions, such as hills, woods, or tall buildings. Without a vane, you can observe the direction of smoke or toss a light piece of paper up into the air.

2. An anemometer for determining wind speed. Place it like the wind vane.

3. A barometer for determining humidity. Place it out of the direct sun and wind.

4. A thermometer to determine temperature. Place it facing north and where it will be shielded from wind, sun, and rain. The best way to protect it is to build a shelter with well-ventilated sides and a wide, overhanging, solid top. Paint the shelter white to give further protection from the sun's rays.

5. A hygrometer to determine the relative humidity. Protect it like the thermometer or place it in a similar shelter.

6. A nephoscope to watch cloud movements.

7. A poster of cloud forms, in color if possible.*

8. A protected outdoor bulletin board on which to post such things as pictures of cloud forms, tables, general weather information, and your observations and predictions.

9. Weather flags to use in flying predictions (Fig. 20–16).

10. Mimeographed or printed forms for recording your observations and predictions (Fig. 20–17).

Making Observations

Make your first weather observation as early in the morning as possible and make a second about 12 hours later; a third observation about

*An inexpensive poster titled "Cloud Code Chart" (S/N 003-018-00050-4), can be obtained from the Superintendent of Documents, U.S. Government Printing Office, Washington, D.C. 20402.

		WIND			CLOUDS				
DATE	*REL. HUMID.*	*DIR.*	*VEL.*	*TEMP.*	*TYPE*	*MOVE-MENT*	*OTHER SIGNS*	*FORE-CAST*	*WHAT IT WAS*
A.M. P.M.									
A.M. P.M.									
A.M. P.M.									
A.M. P.M.									

Figure 20–17 Form for recording weather data and predictions.

Table 20–2

BEAUFORT SCALE FOR ESTIMATION OF WIND FORCE*

BEAUFORT NUMBER	*EFFECTS ON LAND*	*MILES PER HOUR*	*TERMS USED BY U.S. WEATHER BUREAU*
0	Smoke rises straight up.	0–1	Calm
1	Smoke drifts slowly but wind vane does not move	1–3	Light
2	Wind felt on face; leaves rustle, wind vane moves.	4–7	Slight breeze
3	Leaves and small twigs move constantly.	8–12	Gentle breeze
4	Raises dust and loose paper: small branches move.	13–18	Moderate breeze
5	Small trees begin to sway: whitecaps form on inland waters	19–24	Fresh breeze
6	Large branches move: wind whistles in telephone wires: hats blow off.	25–31	Strong breeze
7	Whole trees in motion: hard to walk in wind.	32–38	Moderate gale
8	Breaks twigs and small branches from trees: trees in violent motion.	39–46	Gale
9	Small trees knocked down and shingles torn from roofs.	47–54	Strong gale
10	Rare inland: large trees uprooted; walls blown down.	55–63	Whole gale
11	Very rare; telephone poles and houses knocked down.	64–75	Storm
12	Impossible to stand against.	Over 75	Hurricane

*This scale was devised by Sir Francis Beaufort in 1805. The strength of the wind is indicated by numbers from 0 to 12.

midway between is desirable if convenient. Record your observations, predictions and what actually happened on a form such as that in Figure 20–17.

Interpreting Your Observations

There are practically no weather signs that universally hold true for every area of the United States, for many factors, such as the topography of the country and the presence of lakes, hills, and woods, cause variations. To compile a set of reliable relationships and signs for your particular area, make and file careful observations, recording them on forms such as that shown in Figure 20–17, study them over a period of time until you can detect a consistent pattern of causes and results.

Weather forecasters usually consider the relative humidity reading, particularly whether

Table 20–3

WIND-BAROMETER RELATIONSHIPS*

WIND DIRECTION	*BAROMETER REDUCED TO SEA LEVEL*	*WEATHER INDICATED*
SW to NW	30.1–30.2, steady	Fair, slight temperature changes for 1 to 2 days
	30.1–30.2, rising rapidly	Fair, followed within 2 days by rain
	30.2 and above, stationary	Continued fair, no decided temperature change
	30.2 and above, falling slowly	Slowly rising temperature, fair for 2 days
S to SE	30.1–30.2, falling slowly	Rain within 24 hours
	30.1–30.2, falling rapidly	Wind increasing in force, rain within 12–24 hours
SE to NE	30.1–30.2, falling slowly	Rain in 12–18 hours
	30.1–30.2, falling rapidly	Increasing wind, rain within 12 hours
	30.0 or below, falling slowly	Rain will continue 1–2 days
	30.0 or below, falling rapidly	Rain, with high wind, followed within 36 hours by clearing
E to NE	30.1 and above, falling slowly	Rain may not fall for several days
	30.1 and above, falling rapidly	Rain probably within 12–24 hours
S to SW	30.0 or below, rising slowly	Clearing within a few hours, fair several days
S to E	29.8 or below, falling rapidly	Severe storm imminent, followed within 24 hours by clearing, colder
E to N	29.8 or below, falling rapidly	Severe NE gale and heavy rain
Going to W	29.8 or below, rising rapidly	Clearing and colder

**Weather Forecasting*. U.S. Department of Commerce, p. 39.

it is rising or falling and how rapidly, as the single most important indicator of the weather. Humidity and information about the wind constitute the most important pair of indicators. Table 20–3 will help you to interpret your observations about these two factors.

Another fairly reliable combination is wind direction and cloud formations (Table 20–4). It is especially useful when on a trip because the only instrument you need is a compass to determine wind direction.

There are countless proverbs about the weather, some of them based on mere superstition. Others, however, have value since they describe atmospheric conditions that actually "cause" the weather to be whatever it is. The following seem to be somewhat reliable. Can you explain why?

Red sky (or rainbow) in the morning, sailors take warning.
Red sky (or rainbow) at night, sailor's delight.

Evening red and morning gray,
Sets the traveler on his way;
Evening gray and morning red,
Brings down rain upon his head.

A red sky has water in his eye.

Table 20-4

WIND AND CLOUD RELATIONSHIPS

DIRECTION WIND IS FROM	*CLOUD FORMS*	*FORECAST*
NE, E, SE or S	Cirrostratus (with halo) coming from SW and becoming thicker	Rain within 24 hours; warmer
NE, E, SE or S	Altostratus (hiding sun), getting lower, darker and thicker	Steady rain within 6 hours; will last 6–24 hours.
S or SW (very gusty)	Cumulonimbus clouds on horizon, approaching from W	Heavy rain showers within 2 hours; last less than 1 hour; cooler
Light, variable wind	Towering, cumulus clouds before noon; sky hazy	Rain showers (or thunderstorms) in late afternoon
NW or W	Scattered clouds	Good weather will continue

(Raindrops are caused by the condensation of water around a grain of dust, and humidity allows the red rays of the sun to pass through and be seen more clearly.)

Rain before seven, clear before eleven.

(Rain seldom lasts longer than five hours anyway.)

When dew is on the grass
Rain will never come to pass.

When grass is dry at morning's light,
Look for rain before the night.

When the stars begin to huddle,
The earth will soon become a puddle.

(Mist forms over the sky and causes the smaller stars to cease to be visible. The brighter ones shine through dimly with a blur of light about them, each looking like an indistinct cluster of stars. This, therefore, indicates an increase in humidity.)

Sound traveling far and wide.
A stormy day will betide.

The higher the clouds, the finer the weather.

Mackerel scales and mare's tails
Make lofty ships carry low sails.

When the wind's in the south, the rain's in his mouth.
When the smoke goes west, good weather is past.
When the smoke goes east, good weather is next.

The weather will clear when there is enough blue sky to make a pair of Dutchman's breeches.

The ring around the moon means rain;
The larger the ring, the sooner the rain.

(Cirrostratus clouds are around the moon and are the forerunners of unsettled weather.)

INDICATIONS OF STORMY WEATHER

Rainbow in the morning.
Wind lacking to moderate, and from southeast or east.
No dew at night.
Atmosphere muggy and sticky.
Temperature 70°F. or above, especially if rising.
Falling barometer.
Smoke not rising straight up in the air.
Crickets, birds, and other noises seem extra loud.
Odors are especially noticeable.
Breeze causing underside of leaves to show.
Rapidly moving cirrus clouds, especially from the west.
Dark clouds gathering on the horizon to the west.
Stratus, nimbus, altostratus, cirrostratus, or cumulonimbus clouds.
Clouds moving in different directions at various heights.
Clouds becoming more numerous and nearer the earth.
Red or rosy morning sky.

Gray or dull sunset.
Insects are especially obnoxious and hang about screens, tents, etc.
Smoke beats downward.
Birds fly lower; it is hard for them to fly in the higher rarefied air.

INDICATIONS OF FAIR WEATHER

Rainbow in late afternoon or evening.
Gentle winds, especially from the west or northwest.
Heavy morning dew, fog, or frost.
Temperature below 70° F., especially if falling.
Steadily rising barometer.
Smoke rising straight up.
Cloudless skies or only clouds high in the sky.
Cumulus clouds or stationary cirrus clouds.
Night sky full of bright stars.
Stratocumulus, altocumulus, cirrocumulus, fractonimbus, fractostratus, or fractocumulus clouds.
Red sunset (sun goes down like a ball of fire).
Spiders spin long, widespread webs and scurry busily over them.

No one sign is infallible when predicting the weather; note all and take an average when making a prediction.

ADDITIONAL READINGS

(For an explanation of abbreviations and abbreviated forms used, see page 13.)
Adler, Irving: *Weather in Your Life.* Day, 1960, 122 pp.
Angier: *Skills for Taming the Wilds,* ch. 2.
Angier: *Survival With Style,* ch. 5.
Bachert, Russel E. and Emerson L. Snooks: *Outdoor Education Equipment.* Interstate, 1974, ch. 4.
Basic Outdoor Boating, pp. 87–89.
Bell, Thelma Harrington: *Thunderstorm.* Viking, 1960, 128 pp.
Bonsall, George: *The How and Why Wonder Book of Weather.* Grosset and Dunlap, 1960.
Brown: *The Amateur Naturalist's Handbook,* chs. XII, XIII.
Cocannouer, Joseph A.: *Water and the Cycle of Life.* Devin-Adair, 143 pp.
Dalrymple: *Survival in the Outdoors,* ch. 12.
Fenton, Carroll Lane, and Mildred Adams Fenton: *Our Changing Weather.* Doubleday, 1954.
Fieldbook for Boys and Men, ch. 22, pp. 503–511.
Harty: *Science for Camp and Counselor,* ch. 2.
Laird, Charles and Ruth: *Weathercasting, A Handbook of Amateur Meteorology.* Prentice-Hall, 1955, 163 pp.
Langer: *The Joy of Camping,* pp. 251–268.
Lehr, Paul E., R. Will Burnett, and Dr. H. S. Zim: *Weather.* Golden, 1962, 160 pp., paper.
Merrill: *All About Camping,* pp. 121–125.
Mooers: *Finding Your Way in the Outdoors,* ch. 13.
Riviere: *Backcountry Camping,* ch. 13.
Sager, Raymond M.: *The Sager Weathercaster,* October House, Inc., 55 West 30th Street, New York, N.Y. 10011, 1969, 26 pp.
Schaefer, Vincent J. and John A. Day: *A Field Guide to The Atmosphere.* Houghton Mifflin, 1981, 359 pp.
Scharff: *The Collier Quick and Easy Guide to Motor Boating,* ch. 8.
Schneider, Herman: *Everyday Weather and How It Works.* McGraw-Hill, rev., 1961, 189 pp.
Shivers: *Camping,* pp. 217–222.
Shuttlesworth: *Exploring Nature With Your Child.*
Uman, Martin A.: *Understanding Lightning.* Sterling, 166 pp.
van der Smissen, Betty and Oswald H. Goering: *A Leader's Guide to Nature-Oriented Activities,* pp. 154–158.
Viemeister, Peter E.: *The Lightning Book.* MIT, 1972, 316 pp., paper.
Weather (no. 3274). Boy Scouts, 1963, 64 pp., paper.

MAGAZINE ARTICLES

Backpacker Magazine
Childs, Geoffrey: "Lightning Almost Always Strikes Twice," Summer, 1973, p. 28.
Boy's Life:
Jackson, Harold: "Rain or Shine." Mar., 1961. (Directions for making a weather station)
Changing Times:
"A Ring Around the Moon Means Rain." June, 1973, p. 10. (Old-time ways of predicting weather are a curious mixture of fact and fancy)

The United States National Weather Service and other federal agencies handle a number of free or inexpensive publications in this field. For a complete listing, write the Superintendent of Documents (United States Government Printing Office, Washington, D.C. 20402) for a free copy of Subject Bibliography #234—*Weather.* Some of the most useful include the following. (Order by stock numbers and name, and include payment.):

Climates of the United States (S/N 003-017-00211-0). 1973, 113 pp., $2.50.
Cloud Code Chart (S/N 003-018-00050-4). 1972, $1.00. (poster suitable for bulletin board)
Owlie Skywarn's Lightning Book: A Booklet for Boys and Girls (S/N 003-018-00086-5). 1978, 16 pp., $1.00.
Psychrometric Tables for Obtaining the Vapor Pressure, Relative Humidity, and Temperature of the Dew Point, From Readings of the Wet- and Dry-Bulb Thermometers (S/N 003-005-00003-8). 1941, reprinted 1980, 87 pp. $3.25.
Tornado (S/N 003-018-00085-7). Rev. ed., 1978, 7 pp., $1.00.

twenty-one

Finding Your Way in the Out-of-Doors

The buffalo trail became the Indian trail, and this became the trader's "trace"; the trails widened into roads and the roads into turnpikes and these in turn were transformed into railroads.

—F. J. TURNER, *The Frontier in American History* *(1893).*

Campers or hikers often travel off the beaten path on trails or poorly constructed back roads with no signs to point the way. Much of the charm of hiking and backpacking is the feeling that you are out where others seldom go, seeing things others do not see. However, for such voyaging, you will need to develop special skills, such as being able to use a compass and read *topographic* maps (often referred to as "topos" or "quads"). These maps are truly wonderful, often beautiful enough to frame, and good ones are so accurate that they show exactly where the hiker is, how to get to the desired destination, and what will be seen along the way.

THE COMPASS

There are three main types of compasses: (1) the *needle compass,* which has a fixed dial and a moveable needle, (2) the *revolving card compass,* where the needle is fixed and the card revolves under it, and (3) the *Orienteering* compass, with a moveable needle and rotating dial mounted on a base plate. Each type can be used for cross-country exploring, but those in organized camping usually prefer the Orienteering compass because it gives directions directly without having to figure degrees and it holds the bearing you have set.

The Parts of a Compass

There are many types of compasses, but we will describe here the *Silva Polaris Type 7, Orienteering Compass,* an inexpensive model manufactured by the Silva Division of Johnson Camping, Inc., which enjoys great popularity for camp use. The Orienteering Compass has three main parts: a magnetic needle, a revolving compass housing, and a transparent base plate, each with its own function. Working together they make an efficient and highly practical instrument. The plastic base plate has a *direction-of-travel arrow* imprinted on it that points in the direction you want to go. The base also has a metric scale along one side and a scale in inches across one end for measuring distances on maps. The transparent base lets you see the map through the compass. Just above the base is a freely moveable circular *housing* containing a circle called the *azimuth circle* on which 360 degrees or *azimuths* are marked

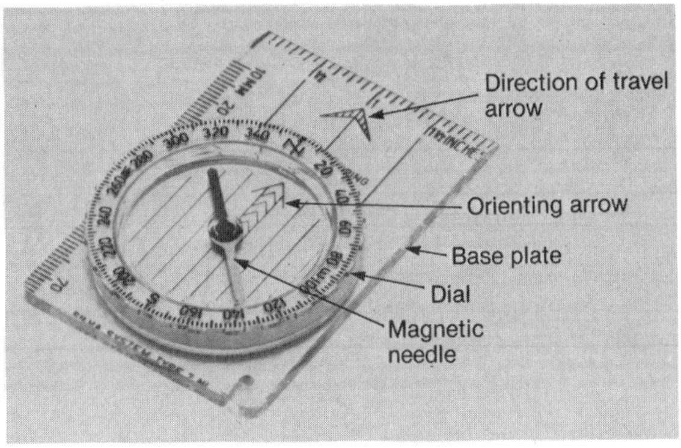

Figure 21-1 A Silva type-7 Polaris compass (Silva, Division of Johnson Camping Inc., Binghamton, N.Y.)

in a clockwise direction. The Circle is divided into *quadrants* with N (north) at 0° or 360°, E (east) at 90°, S (south) at 180°, and W (west) at 270°. The letters for the quadrants and the degrees are engraved on the top of the plastic housing.

Printed inside the housing is a stationary *orienting arrow* that points to N (0° or 360°) and a *magnetic needle* that is mounted on a pin so that it moves freely. The end of the needle is painted red and is magnetized so that when you hold the compass level so the needle can move freely, it always points to magnetic north, no matter how you turn the compass.

Using a Compass

Since the tip of the compass needle is magnetized, metal or steel near it will deflect it, resulting in an inaccurate reading. Therefore, avoid using the compass near such things as a metal belt buckle, knife blade, hatchet, outboard motor, metal bridge, or telephone or power line.

To read directions from your compass, you must first *orient* it, or turn it so that the magnetic needle is aligned with north as printed on the dial. Turn the dial so that the orienting arrow (N) is pointing in the same direction as the direction-of-travel arrow. Hold the compass level about waist high so that the needle will swing freely. Now turn yourself around until the needle lies along the orienting arrow and the red end points to N (0° or 360°). You are now facing magnetic north; your right shoulder is toward the east, south is behind you, and west is at your left shoulder.

Now, suppose you want to travel in a certain direction—let's say 60°. Orient your compass and set it by turning the dial to bring the figure 60 directly above the direction-of-travel arrow. Hold the compass level and turn yourself around until the red end of the needle is lined up with the orienting arrow and pointing to N on the dial. The direction-of-travel arrow is pointing in the direction you want to go. To take a *bearing* or *azimuth reading* on some distant object, point the direction-of-travel arrow toward it, and turn the dial until the needle lines up with the orienting arrow. Now read your bearing in degrees where the direction-of-travel arrow intersects the dial.

To follow a compass direction, pick out two conspicuous landmarks, such as trees or rocks, in line with the arrow and start out, picking out another landmark in line with the arrow as you approach the first so that you always have two landmarks to walk toward. This frees you from having to keep your eyes glued on the compass. Stop occasionally to recheck the compass bearing to make sure you are still on course.

A simple game to test your ability to follow compass directions is called the "Silver Dollar Game." To play it, place some inconspicuous object such as a can lid on the ground. Select a compass bearing of less than 120° and walk 100 steps in that direction; then add 120° to the original bearing and again walk 100 steps; add an additional 120° and walk another 100 steps. Place a marker where you finish; if your readings and measurements have been accurate, you have walked around an equilateral triangle and are back exactly where you started. You can make this into a game for campers by giving each a card with a set number of degrees and distances and seeing who can return nearest to his or her starting point.

True North and Magnetic North

A compass needle points to *magnetic north,* which over most of the United States is not the same as *true north,* the direction of the North Pole. Magnetic north is the direction of the northern magnetic pole, which is a region about a 1,000 miles south of the geographic North Pole. The only place where true north and magnetic north coincide, and where the compass needle will actually point to true north, is along a curving imaginary line called the *zero* or *agonic line*, which passes diagonally downward across the United States as shown in Figure 21-2. As the map indicates, the needle points increasingly east of north in regions west of this line and west of north in eastern regions. The angle between true north and magnetic north in any given area is called the *angle of declination* and it increases the farther we go from the agonic line, until it is as much as 20° or more in the extreme northeastern and northwestern sections of the United States. It is usually indicated at the bottom margin of a map by means of two arrows, one pointing toward the top of the map to true north, the other to magnetic north as you would read it on your compass; the angle of declination is the angle between these arrows. For further information on using the compass with a map, refer to the section in this chapter titled "Using a Map and Compass."

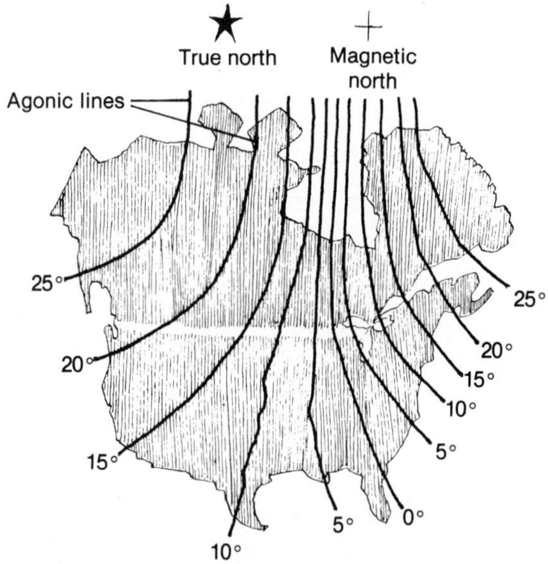

Figure 21-2 Agonic line and compass declination.

MAPS

Sources and Kinds of Maps

A map is a vertical view of an area as it would appear from the air. There are many kinds of maps, ranging from detailed printed ones to crude, homemade sketch maps for guiding a person through relatively rough and unsettled country.

The most useful maps for a hiker or backpacker are the *topographic* maps that are published by the United States Geological Survey (USGS). They are inexpensive and are excellent for anyone travelling on foot, on horseback, or by canoe, for they give a graphic picture of what can be seen on a particular trip. Each of these maps covers a relatively small area in great detail. They tell where hills are located and how steep and high they are; they show streams, and you can even determine the direction of their flow since water always flows downhill from small tributaries into larger bodies of water; in fact, by reading the changes in elevation as the stream progresses, you can even estimate how swiftly the water will be flowing. They show canoe routes and places where it will be necessary to portage; marshlands are indicated so that you can avoid camping near them and their mosquito inhabitants. Timber areas and every valley and lake, as well as such man-made "improvements" as houses and bridges, are depicted.

Topographic maps usually can be purchased in local sporting goods stores or map shops. If not available locally, an index map of any state can be obtained by writing to the USGS. You will receive the index of your chosen state that has a grid overlay showing the names for the maps that are represented. You also will receive a free booklet entitled "Topographic Maps," which explains the various sizes of maps available and information on map symbols. If you want to order maps of areas east of the Mississippi River, address your request to U.S. Geological Survey, Branch of Distribution, Eastern Region, 1200 S. Eads Street, Arlington, Virginia 22202. Mail orders for map areas west of the Mississippi River should be sent to U.S. Geological Survey, Branch of Distribution, Central Region, Box 25286, Denver Federal Center, Denver, Colorado 80225. Maps of Canada can be obtained from the National Topographical Series by contacting the Department of Mines and Technical Surveys, Map Distribution Office, 615 Booth Street, Ottawa, Ontario, Canada.

The United States Coast and Geodetic Survey* supplies similar maps for water travel, each showing about 40 miles of seacoast. They also have maps of some of the larger inland bodies of water such as the Ohio and Mississippi rivers.

Useful maps are also available from the United States National Park Service** and the Forest Service,*** as well as from state conservation agencies, state parks, and state highway departments.

Learning to Read a Map

A map usually contains a *legend,* or summary of information, in the lower right-hand corner that includes such items as the following:

1. *Name* or *title* of the region depicted.
2. *Name of the person or firm* who made the map and *date* made. The date is important, particularly for maps of well-settled regions where construction and land use or disuse may entirely change the appearance of a locality within a few years.
3. *Compass direction.* Maps are ordinarily laid out with north at the top, but the particular contour shown or the shape of the area sometimes makes it more convenient to do otherwise. Most maps use two arrows to indicate true north and magnetic north, and the arrows are joined to form the angle of declination.
4. *A scale of distances.* A map is drawn to a certain *scale,* which is the proportional relationship between the distance as represented on the map and the actual distance over the ground. For instance, backpacking maps are usually drawn to large scale, such as letting 1 unit of measure on the map represent 24,000 of the same units on the ground. For instance, the USGS topographic maps most popular among backpackers are at a scale of 1:24,000, which is about 2.6 inches to a mile (1 inch equals 2,000 feet). Scales on maps may be expressed: (1) in words and figures (1 inch = 24,000 inches); (2) as a ratio (1:24,000); or (3) as a fraction ($\frac{1}{24,000}$). The scale is usually given also as a graphical scale or measuring bar, which is convenient because you can readily measure it off on paper for use in measuring distances between points on the map.
5. A *key* to the meaning of the various symbols used on the map.

MAP SYMBOLS (FIG. 21-3). Certain map symbols are in general use and enable one person to understand maps made by others. These symbols are of four types:

1. *Culture,* or works of man, such as bridges, houses, dams, and so forth are shown in black.

However, red is used to emphasize important roads or to show urban areas.

2. *Relief,* or relative elevations and depressions above or below sea level (hills and valleys), are shown in brown. Hills are indicated by *contour lines.* All points on a single contour line are the same elevation, or height, above sea level so that, if you walked along the line you would not go up or down. Contour lines are often arranged in groups of five with the fifth index line somewhat heavier and with the height printed along it. Each line indicates a rise or fall of a certain number of feet (from 5 to 250 feet, as stated in the map legend). Widely spaced lines indicate a gradual slope; those close together, a steep one. Lines falling practically on top of each other represent a cliff or steep mountainside. Contour lines spread widely over the countryside signify that the whole region is rolling. It may help you to better visualize the actual appearance of the land if you think of the contour lines as rings left by water that once covered the hill and slowly receded, leaving a ring at each stopping point.
3. *Water features,* such as lakes or rivers, are shown in blue.
4. *Vegetation,* such as woods or crops, is shown in green, with black or blue overprints sometimes showing type.

Using a Map and Compass

Although skilled map readers may not often need to use a compass for navigation, they should always have one with them and know how to use it. There are occasions when compass skills become important, especially if you should ever become disoriented or caught in a situation where visibility is poor.

*United States Coast and Geodetic Survey, Washington, D.C. 20025.

**National Park Service, United States Department of Interior, Washington, D. C. 20240.

***Forest Service, United States Department of Agriculture, Washington, D. C. 20250.

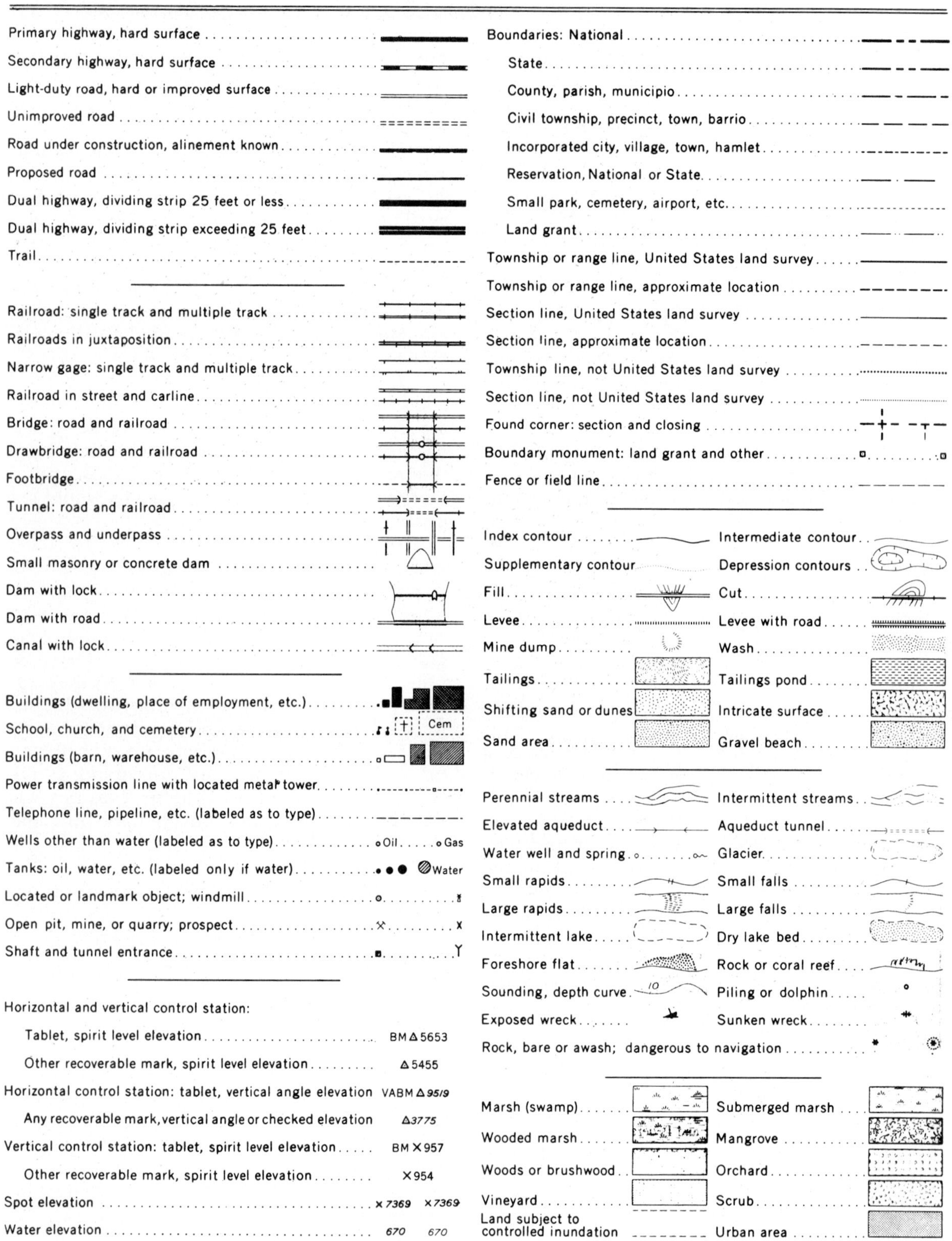

Figure 21-3 Common map symbols.

When using a map and a compass to plan a trip, first locate your present position and intended destination on the map. Study the symbols of what lies between and try to form a mental picture of the intervening terrain. Remember that the shortest route is not always best for it may lead through difficult or even impassable terrain. Plan your route carefully, making appropriate *doglegs* around obstacles, and trace on the map or a sheet of paper the exact route you plan to follow. To mark your route without permanently marring your map, laminate it with clear Contact Paper® and trace on the plastic with a wax crayon or marker pen. Calculate compass bearings at each turn and use the map scale to estimate distances between them.

Remember that directions on commercial and government maps are usually given in terms of true north, whereas your compass readings will be in terms of magnetic north. You must take the difference into consideration, especially when in an area where the declination is great, for if it is 14°, for example, you can stray as much as ¼ of a mile off course for each mile you travel. One way to compensate for this difference is to add or subtract the angle of declination each time you take a compass bearing. For instance, if the declination is 15 degrees west, you would rotate the map (simultaneously with the compass) 15 degrees east of magnetic north. Essentially what you are doing is to subtract 15 degrees from 360 degrees. Conversely, if the declination is 15 degrees east, you would turn the map that many degrees in order to add the 15 degrees to magnetic north.

An even easier technique is to place a series of magnetic north-south lines across your map, making the first one an extension of the half arrow on the map that indicates magnetic north and drawing the others parallel to it at 1-inch in-

(Cheley Colorado Camps, Estes Park, Colo.)

tervals. By simply aligning the compass along one of the lines you can automatically orient the map in the right direction.

To take an azimuth or bearing on the first leg of your trip, you must first orient your map by laying it flat on a table or the ground, placing your compass above it, and turning the map until the magnetic N-S lines you have drawn lie parallel to N-S as indicated by the needle on your compass. Now place the bottom of the base of your compass at your present location and rotate the base so that the direction-of-travel arrow lies parallel to the path of the first leg of your route. Read off the azimuth or bearing where the direction-of-travel arrow intersects the housing. Measure the length of the line, and using the distance scale on the map, estimate the length of the first leg. Determine the directions and distances of other legs in the same way and record the information on your map. Note which landmarks on the map you can use as check points as you follow the trail.

When you are ready to start out, place the direction-of-travel arrow at the degree reading of the first leg and orient your compass. Then place yourself directly behind the arrow, pick out two distinct landmarks ahead and start toward them. Once the first leg has been completed, determine the new direction and pick out landmarks to walk toward as before.

Using similar principles, you can use the *triangulation method* to find out where you are on the map when out in the field. Pick out two visible distant landmarks that can also be located on the map. Orient the map, take a bearing on the two landmarks, and draw lines through them at these degrees. You are located at the point where the lines intersect.

Making a Map

A person who draws or makes maps is known as a *cartographer.* You may want to have your campers make maps just for the fun of it as well as for the learning experience. Knowledge of mapmaking also allows you to plan and participate in many enjoyable orienteering games.

ROUGH-SKETCHING. When making a map, it is more interesting to choose a cross-country route, not more than a mile or two in length. You will need a compass, a pencil, and a notebook or a few sheets of paper on a clipboard to make the preliminary rough-sketch map as you walk along the route. Quadrille or graph paper is convenient since each square can represent a certain number of feet or paces. Jot down degrees and distances at every turn and make notes about the terrain and landmarks so that you can later convert the rough sketch into an accurate and attractive finished map. For convenience, it is suggested that you use magnetic compass readings, ignoring the compass declination in your area; this simplifies the problem for both the person making the map and the one following it. If you prefer to use true north, you will have to adjust each compass reading for declination.

A *pace* consists of two *steps.* Therefore, to count your paces you need only take note of how many times your left foot contacts the ground. To determine the length of your pace, use a string or rope exactly 20 or 25 feet long to lay off a distance of 100 yards, preferably over mixed terrain such as you might find on a trail. Beginning at the starting line, count each pace as you proceed with a normal stride; walk it several times and take the average. Now divide 3,600 (the number of inches in 100 yards) by the number of paces to determine the length of your stride in inches.

One way to avoid having to count in high numbers is to start with a counted number of pebbles and throw one away at the end of a predetermined number of paces, say 25 or 50. You then need only count the stones you have left to find the total number of paces. Another way is to tie knots in a string to represent so many paces. Distances can be estimated by determining the time it takes to cover already measured distances. In estimating distances, you should allow for travel over difficult terrain, such as steep slopes, where your step normally shortens.

When you are ready to rough-sketch the map, mark your starting point on the paper. Pick out a landmark some distance away, take a compass bearing on it, and start out, counting paces as you go. When you encounter features or landmarks that you want to include, jot them down on your sketch map, making notes as needed. When you reach the first landmark, jot down the number of paces, pick out another landmark, take a new compass bearing and proceed as before.

If you want to show a landmark that is off

at one side of the trail, such as an old deserted house (Fig. 21–4), take a compass bearing on it from some distance away *(A)*, then count the paces to another point *(B)* and take another bearing. By projecting the two angles on the map and properly plotting distance *AB* to scale, the house will be located at *C* where the lines intersect. If you want to know how far away from the path the old house is, you can measure perpendicular distance *CD* on the map and use the map scale to find the actual distance.

For convenience, self-made maps are often drawn entirely in black instead of colors. Common map symbols are simple and usually roughly resemble what they depict. You may have to invent symbols for unusual objects on your map; make them bear a likeness to what they represent and explain them in your legend.

When you have completed your rough-sketch map, translate it into a completed trail map as soon as possible, while the details are still fresh in your memory. Use a ruler, compass, and protractor to insure accuracy and draw it to scale of between 200 and 2,000 feet to the inch. Don't worry if the point where you finish on the map doesn't exactly coincide with your starting point; such deviations are common when using rather crude instruments and measurements and are called *errors of closure.* Keep your symbols small and use black India and colored inks.

Keep the purpose of your map in mind. If others are to use it as a guide, too many details will be confusing. Just for fun you can give the map a parchment-like appearance by daubing it lightly with a bit of linseed oil or yellow shellac.

Protecting a Map

Although you can carry a rolled-up map, it is usually preferable to fold it to a convenient size. Fold it once or twice lengthwise and six or eight times across accordion-fashion, like a road map. Turn it so the part you want to travel over is on the outside and place it in a vinyl map case, a plastic sheet such as the refill sheet for a photograph album, or press a piece of Contact Paper® over it.

You can add still more durability by mounting the map. Since the folds are particularly vulnerable to wear, protect them by cutting the map

(Cheley Colorado Camps, Estes Park, Colo.)

into sections at the fold marks and mounting each piece, leaving a ⅛-inch space between them. Use a warm iron to press the sections onto a special adhesive-backed material called "chartex," available at most art supply stores, or use rubber cement or wallpaper paste to fasten the pieces to unbleached muslin, linen, or sheeting, smoothing them out to eliminate wrinkles and air bubbles. Place the whole map under a heavy weight and leave it overnight.

To waterproof both sides of your map, apply two or more coats of clear shellac or spray it with a clear acrylic.

Making a Relief Map

A *papier-mâché* relief map is quite decorative and provides a more realistic view of an area. Start with a large piece of thin board, plywood, or stiff cardboard and lay off the area to scale, indicating the locations of rivers, woods, houses, and other things you want to show. Tear up a quantity of old newspapers or paper towels into small scraps and soak them for several hours in hot water. Knead and manipulate them until they become quite "gooey", then press out as much water as possible and mix in a quantity of library paste. Use the mixture to cover the base, building it up to the proper height and contour for hills and scooping it out for rivers, valleys, and other depressions. When it is dry, draw in details and paint it with appropriate shades of tempera paint or colored inks. Make "trees" of twigs and bits of sponge; "grass" of sawdust dyed green and placed on a thin layer of glue. Sand sprinkled over glue makes good bare ground and buildings may be fashioned from twigs or cardboard and finished in appropriate colors. Making such a model of your camp site is a good project and will provide hours of pleasure for your campers.

STAY FOUND

Prevention Pays

Don't be deluded into thinking that you are an expert after studying this brief treatise on compasses and maps. Before you go forth into strange territory, you will need to study carefully some of the excellent sources given at the end of this chapter and then practice many hours with the tools of your trade. A miscalculation of just a short distance or a few degrees can set you up for a truly harrowing experience. Never venture into unfamiliar territory alone and always tell some responsible person where you are going, the exact route you plan to take, who will be in the party, and when you expect to return.

Never start without your compass, and if possible, take along a detailed map of the region on which to mark your trail. It is also wise to jot down walking time as well as distances between various points. Two essential things to do are to *look back* occasionally to see how things will look on your return and to *write things down* instead of relying on memory. Remember that you must use your compass as you go, for it is of almost no use *after* you are lost. Take an initial reading and jot down additional ones each time you change directions.

Although some people claim to have a "sixth sense" of direction, experiments have shown that it simply is not true, for even those experienced in the out of doors become quite confused when blindfolded and told to walk in a straight line. Their seemingly uncanny ability to find their way without benefit of compass or map can probably be attributed to their highly developed habits of observation that cause them to unconsciously note such things as the position of the sun, the direction of prevailing winds, details about the terrain, and distinguishing landmarks along the way. You will do well to emulate them.

If you are hiking in a group, stay together. It is wise to provide each member with a whistle to use if he or she inadvertently strays, for a whistle blast carries a long way through the silent woods.

If You Become Lost

If you should suddenly realize that you are lost or stranded, don't panic; stay calm and think back over past events to see if you can retrace your travel patterns. There is probably no real emergency, for the chances are that you are not far off route and can reason your way out. Climb a tree or hill to get a long view and to try to spot some landmark that is familiar or that can be located on your map. Try to remember the exact route traveled since you were last oriented.

If none of these help, it may be best to just sit down, conserve energy, and wait for someone to find you. Members of your group will soon come looking and there are always other people available to form a search party if needed. The chances are that you'll be found within a few hours, and even if you have to stay out overnight, the experience will probably not amount to much more than an unpleasant inconvenience. If you have brought the minimum essentials, including a knife, matches, and flashlight, you can spend several days without coming to any real harm, for people have survived as long as 30 days without food, provided they had water to drink. If you have a survival kit and know how to use it, you are in good shape for you can find nourishing food in the wilds. Send out signals of your whereabouts to possible rescuers as described later on in this chapter. In most cases, it is best to stay right where you are for you are probably not too far off route and searchers will therefore know the general area in which to look.

In most civilized areas there are regular air patrol flights that usually will spot you if you choose an open area and spell out SOS in letters 6 to 10 feet high, well-spaced against a contrasting background.

If night is approaching or a potential storm is brewing, prepare to spend the night by finding the best shelter possible and making yourself comfortable until morning. Clear a space and build a fire for warmth and cheer. Remember that even warm days are often followed by uncomfortably cool nights, so lay in an adequate supply of fuel to keep the fire going as long as needed. If you leave the site for any reason, such as to look for water or more fuel, be sure to mark the path so that you can readily find your way back.

If it is fairly early in the day and you decide

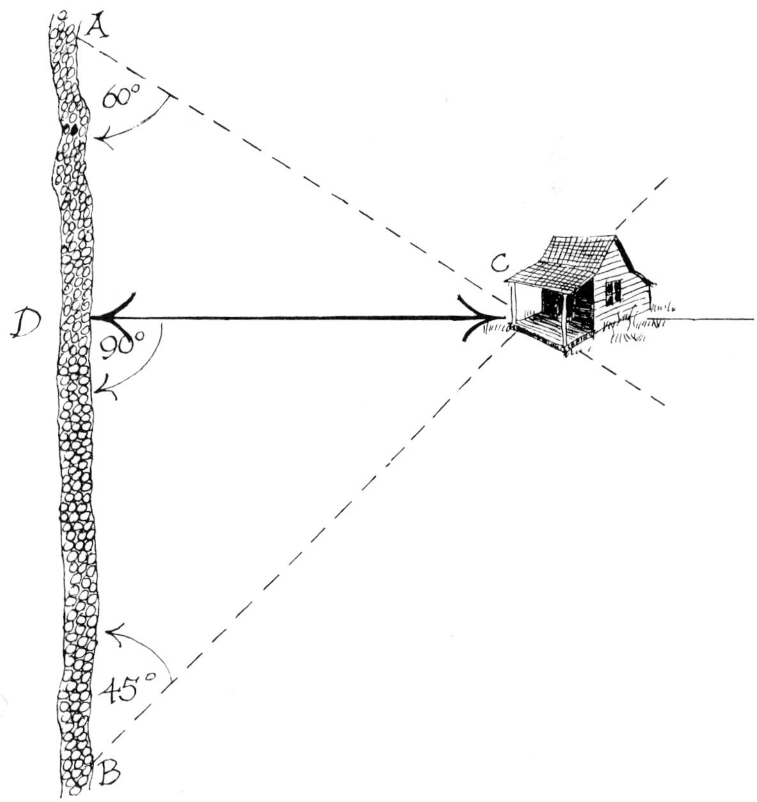

Figure 21–4 Locating an object at the side of a trail.

to seek a way out, keep in mind that every unguided person tends to travel in a more or less circular path, usually to the right but occasionally to the left. You are no exception, and unless precautions are taken to prevent it, you will probably travel in a wide circle that will eventually bring you back very close to where you started. It is best to choose one direction, then pick out two landmarks in line with it and start out, picking out another landmark as you near the first, as previously discussed. If you have a compass, things will be much simpler.

It is wise to mark your path so that you can return if you wish and so searchers will know the trail. Tear off strips of cloth and tie them about head high at intervals or use one of the methods for marking a trail discussed later on in this chapter.

A railroad track, a telephone or electric line, or a wall or fence will eventually lead you to civilization. Also, it is usually best to travel downhill along water drainages rather than uphill. Listen for human sounds and look for signs of smoke.

Danger or Distress Signals

Three of anything has been long and widely recognized as a signal of danger or distress. Three rocks placed on top of each other, three clumps of grass tied in knots, three blazes on trees, three smudge fires, three whistle blasts, or three gunshots are examples (Fig. 21–10). Note that the Morse code applies this principle in its call for help, SOS, which consists of three dots, three dashes, and three dots.

Three smudge fires can be used as signals for help in the daytime, placing them just far enough apart to be distinguishable at a distance. Build a good fire and get it going well, then pile nonflammable materials such as green or rotten wood or wet leaves on it to make it "smudge" or smoke. Use a blanket or coat to smother the smoke momentarily so it collects into larger, more noticeable puffs. A bright fire shows up better at night, but be careful not to make it large enough to set the forest on fire.

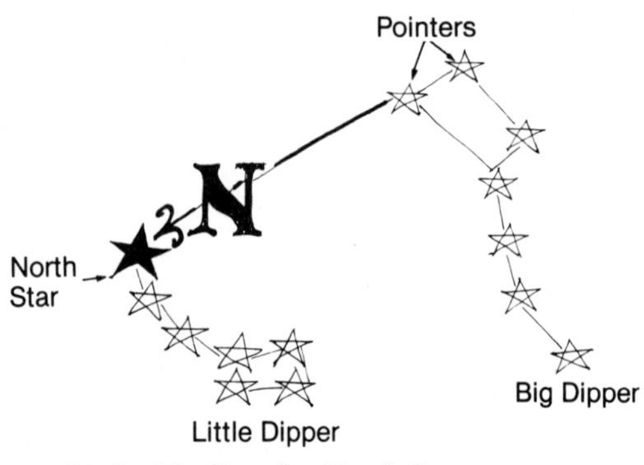

Figure 21–5 Finding the North Star.

TELLING DIRECTIONS WITHOUT A COMPASS

Some methods of using Mother Nature's signs to tell directions are not very dependable or consume so much time that you would hesitate to use them. However, the following methods are quite helpful, although they should not be considered as routine substitutions for the valuable compass that should always be a part of your standard gear.

Telling Directions by the Stars

The stars are our oldest and most faithful guides to direction. When ancient literature speaks of "being guided by a star," it refers to the *North Star* (also called *Polaris* or the *Pole Star*), which is an even more accurate guide to direction than a compass, for it never varies more than one degree from true north no matter where you are in the United States.

To locate the North Star (Fig. 21–5) find the *Big Dipper* and the *Little Dipper* in the sky. The two stars opposite the handle that form the front edge of the Big Dipper are known as the *pointers* because they point directly to the North Star in the tip of the Little Dipper's handle. Although the Big Dipper circles around the Little Dipper every 24 hours, the pointers never cease to point to the North Star. The bowls of the two Dippers constantly face so that they always seem to be pouring into each other.

There are many interesting myths about the stars. One version tells us that many years ago a tribe of Indians was living happily in the midst of good hunting until the coming of an extremely large mother bear and her cub who frightened away all the small game. This brought famine to the Indians and they decided to send out their best hunters to kill the bears. After being hotly pursued through many miles of wilderness, the bears finally fled to the top of a tall mountain where the mother leaped into the sky in desperation and was followed by her cub. The hunters began to shoot and finally pierced the cub's tail with an arrow, fastening it in the northern sky. This arrow is the North Star. The cub began running around its tail, making a complete circuit each day. The mother bear's wounds appear as the seven stars of the Big Dipper and she remains in the sky, making a complete circle each day around her cub. The Indians called the Big Dipper the Big Bear (Ursa Major) and the Little Dipper the Little Bear (Ursa Minor).

Using Your Watch as a Compass

Some people advocate a method of telling directions using the sun and a watch. Here's how to do it. Stand with your left shoulder toward the sun, hold your watch flat in your palm, and point the hour hand directly toward the sun. South is now located halfway between the hour hand and 12 o'clock, using the shorter distance between the two as shown in Figure 21-6. To find the sun on a cloudy or hazy day, stand a knife blade or match up against the watch and adjust it until the shadow of the match lies directly over the hour hand: the hour hand will now be pointing directly toward the sun. If you are on Daylight Saving Time you will have to set your watch back one hour. Many claim this method isn't accurate. Try it and check it with your compass, adjusting for declination, to see what results you get.

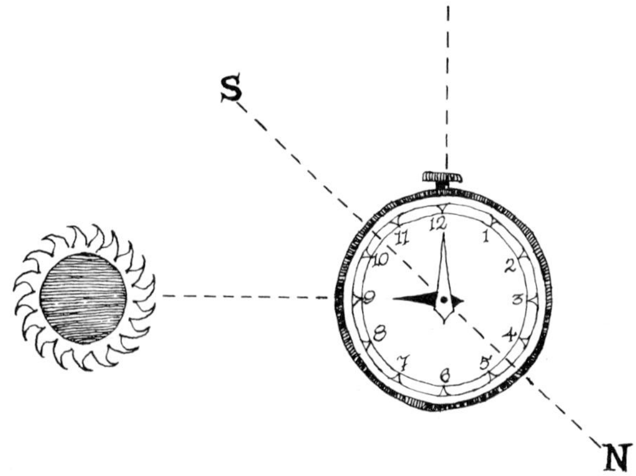

Figure 21-6 Finding south by your watch.

The Shadow Compass*

Select a place where the sun is shining and drive a stick from 2 to 5 feet tall into the ground and mark the tip of the stick's shadow with a stone or other object. Wait at least 15 minutes, or until the shadow has moved to a new location, and again mark its tip. If you have time, do this several times. Connect the tip marks with a line; it will lie roughly true east-west with the first mark pointing west. A line exactly perpendicular to the east-west line will consequently lie approximately north-south. This method is most accurate around noon and decreases in accuracy the further away from noon the time. Check your directions with your compass to find out how accurate they are, remembering to allow for compass declination. Incidentally, when your own shadow is so short that you can almost step on the tip of it, you can be sure it is about noon.

*This method is attributed to Robert Owendoff. (Robert S. Owendoff: *Better Ways of Pathfinding*. Stackpole, 1964, pp. 73–80.)

MEASURING INACCESSIBLE DISTANCES

Here are some simple principles of geometry to use for measuring inaccessible distances.

Estimating the Height of a Tree, Cliff, or Building

Cut a pole and stick it in the ground some distance from a tree or other object you want to measure (Fig. 21-7). With your eye to the ground *(C)*, sight over the top of the pole *(B)* to the top of the tree *(E)* and mark your location on the ground. The distance between *C* and *A* is to the height of the pole as the distance between *C* and *D* is to the height of the tree. In other words, *CA* equals *AB* and *CD* equals the height of the tree.

An Indian method (Fig. 21-8), not quite so accurate but giving as exact a figure as is usually needed, is to walk away from the object to be

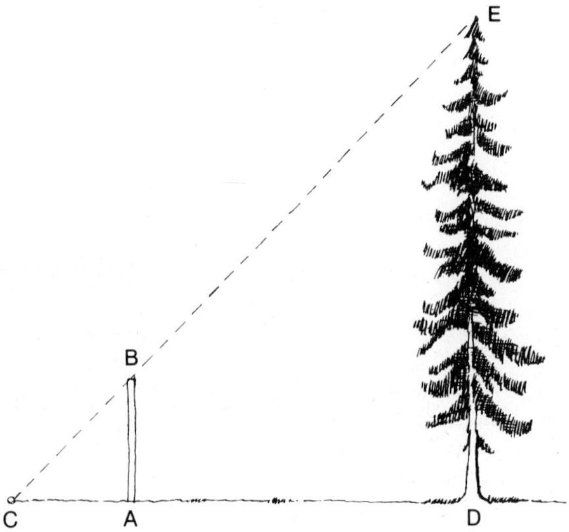

Figure 21-7 Measuring height of tree.

measured until you can just see the top of it when you bend over, clasp your ankles and look through your legs. The height of the tree in Figure 21-8 is roughly equal to the distance you are from it.

Estimating the Width of a River

To measure the width of something such as a river or gorge (Fig. 21-9), select an easily distinguishable landmark on the other side *(B)*, and

Figure 21-8 Indian method of measuring height of tree.

mark a spot *(A)* directly across from it. Next, fasten three poles of the same length into a triangle. Walk down the river bank some distance and place the triangle at *X* so that one side of it is in line with *A* and the other with *B*. Mark the spot *(X)*, then move the triangle up the river bank to *Y* and sight the same way. The width of the river *(AB)* will be ⅞ of the distance from *X* to *Y*.

Another method that can be used is to mark a spot on your side of the river that is directly across from an identifiable landmark on the other side. Next, walk down the bank until the object on the other side is at a 45° angle to you and mark that spot. You have now outlined an isosceles triangle and therefore the width of the river can be determined by measuring the distance back to your original spot.

Estimating Depth

To determine the approximate depth of a river, lake, or chasm, drop a rock from just above the water's surface and time it until it hits bottom. Square the number of seconds that elapsed and multiply the result by 16 to get the approximate depth in feet.

Learning to Estimate Measurements

Many youngsters are notoriously poor at judging distances and heights, probably owing more to lack of practice than to any innate inability to do so. Being able to make such estimates often comes in handy and the best way to acquire the skill is to practice estimating objects that you can actually weigh or measure afterward to check your accuracy. With practice, you should be able to get within 10 percent of the correct answer most of the time.

In judging long distances, it sometimes helps to mentally divide them into short, familiar distances, such as 100 yards, 3 feet, or 12 inches, and then estimate the number of shorter distances in the long one.

In making rough estimates, it is useful to know some of your own measurements, such as:

1. The length of your ordinary hiking pace and stride.
2. The length of your foot in the type of shoe you ordinarily wear.

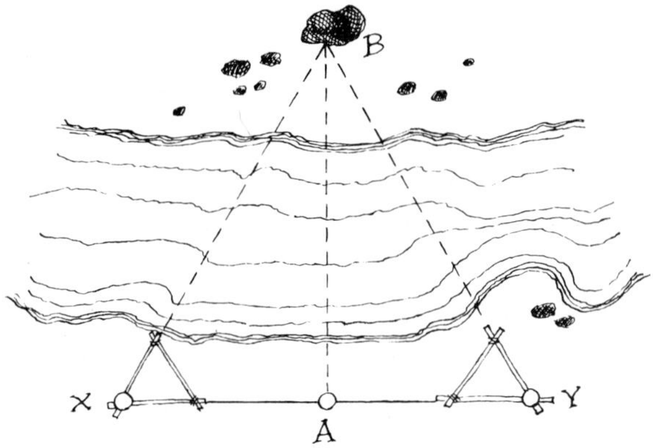

Figure 21-9 Estimating the width of a river.

3. Your exact height and the distance from finger tip to finger tip with both arms outstretched. (These distances are usually about equal so you can use one for measuring heights and the other for widths.)

4. A finger joint that is exactly an inch long.

5. The length of your forearm.

6. The length from the ground to the tips of your outstretched hands.

TRAILS AND SIGNALS

Trails are as old as mankind, for it is impossible for any creature to go through wooded territory without leaving some trace. Such obscure signs as a track in the mud or sand, a branch accidentally broken off, or a vine carelessly torn by the foot, though easily overlooked by the tenderfoot, are quite meaningful to one skilled and practiced in woodland ways.

The first trails were made by the big game animals in going to and from their favorite feeding grounds, water holes, or salt licks. The Indians, then pioneer trappers and explorers on foot or on pack horses, and finally covered wagons and stagecoaches followed these same trails, making them ever wider and easier to follow. Many of them became the bases of the routes of our railroads and highways.

Early paths seldom passed through valleys but instead kept to the ridges in hilly or mountainous country where there were few streams to ford and where travelers could command a wide view of the surrounding countryside, to protect themselves from ambush.

Methods of Laying Trails (Fig. 21-10)

BLAZING. The favorite pioneer method of marking a trail through the wilderness was *blazing*, or using an axe or sheath knife to take a chip out of a tree to expose the white surface that could be easily spotted from a distance. Of course this method is unthinkable today, for trees are far too precious to mutilate. We know that a wound in the bark of a tree is just as serious as a cut or break in our own skin, for it makes an opening for parasites and diseases to initiate their damaging, perhaps even fatal, attacks.

BRUSH BLAZES. The brush blaze was a favorite Indian method of trail marking. It consists of breaking a shrub branch every hundred yards or so, leaving it still attached but with the lighter undersides of its leaves exposed to attract attention. The branch was left pointing in the direction to be taken. To indicate an abrupt change in direction, the branch was completely broken off and supported in a crotched stick with its butt end pointing in the new direction.

This method may still be permissible in regions where the underbrush is very heavy and a few broken branches will never be missed but this is unlikely to be true near any organized camp.

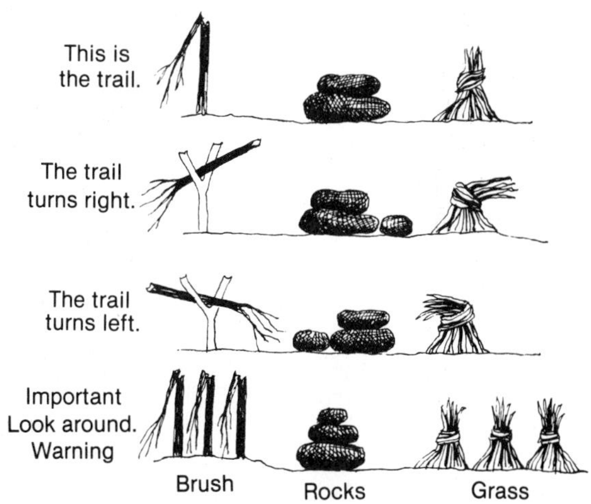

Figure 21-10 Common trail signs.

GRASS. In prairie regions where fairly long grass is abundant, a wisp of grass can be used as a cord to tie other clumps together, leaving the heads upright when the trail lies straight ahead and lopping them over to point in the direction of any turn made.

ROCKS. Use rocks to mark the trail along the seashore or in barren regions. A small rock on top of a large one is called a *cairn* and indicates "this is the trail"; a smaller rock placed to one side means turn in this direction. Pebbles can also be laid out in the form of a "V" to show directions.

OTHER METHODS. Paper weighted down with stones or bits of colored cloth or tape tied to twigs can be used, but since your trail should show no evidence that you have been over it, those following it should gather these up as they come along. You can also scratch direction arrows in bare dirt.

SIGNALING

The Morse Code (Fig. 21–11)

The most universally used and understood code is the *international Morse code* that uses dots and dashes to spell out messages. You indicate a dot by a short flash or sound (held while you count "one") and a dash by a long one (held while you count "one, two, three").

Alphabet

A	.-	N	-.
B	-...	O	---
C	-.-.	P	.--.
D	-..	Q	--.-
E	.	R	.-.
F	..-.	S	...
G	--.	T	-
H	....	U	..-
I	..	V	...-
J	.---	W	.--
K	-.-	X	-..-
L	.-..	Y	-.--
M	--	Z	--..

Numerals

1	.----	6	-....
2	..---	7	--...
3	...--	8	---..
4	....-	9	----.
5	.....	0	-----

Figure 21-11 International Morse code.

The Morse code is adaptable to many forms of communication; you can use a lantern, flashlight, automobile horn, flag, torch, whistle, drum, or a mirror held to reflect the sun's rays. When using a smudge fire to transmit smoke signals in Morse code, two persons can hold a blanket above the fire, removing it at proper intervals to allow large billows of smoke to rise and spell out the message. At night, hold a blanket in front of a blazing campfire.

Pause and count three at the end of each letter; count five at the end of a word and pause still longer for the end of a sentence. Strive for accuracy and clearness rather than speed. When first practicing at receiving the Morse code, use two persons, one to call out the dots and dashes as received, the other to write them down for later decoding. Practice signaling from short distances at first, then gradually move away until you are finally so far away that you need field glasses to read the message. Morse code is not only fun, but it may save steps or get help in an emergency when you need to communicate with a group far away.

GAMES TO MAKE LEARNING MORE ENJOYABLE

Map Symbol Relay

Teams of 4 to 10 players line up in relay formation. Each team has a set of cards bearing map symbols stacked in front of it and a similar set with names of what the symbols stand for spread out nearby. On signal, the first player on each team runs forward, picks up the top symbol card, places it on top of its matching name card and runs back to touch off the second player who repeats with the second symbol card, and so forth. The first team placing all of its cards correctly wins.

Variation. Supply each person with a paper and pencil. Hold up the symbol cards one by one and have each player write down what the symbol stands for. The winner is the individual or team with the most nearly correct list.

Compass Circle Relay

Two teams of 8 to 16 players line up in relay formation. Each team has a circle in front of it with N marked conspicuously and straight marks to indicate the positions of the other directions (NE, E, SE, S, SW, W, NW; or NNE, NE, ENE, E, ESE, SE, SSE, S, SSW, SW, WSW, W, WNW, NW, NNW). Stack a set of cards, each bearing a direction, near each circle but not arranged in order. At a given signal, the first player on each team runs up, takes the top card and places it in its correct position in the circle and comes back to touch off the second player who places the second card, and so on. The first team to place all the cards correctly wins.

Compass Change

One player is "it" while eight others distribute themselves around the circle in the positions of the different directions (N, NE, E, and so forth). A prominent sign marks N on the circle but no other positions are marked. "It" calls out two directions (as NE and S) and these two players try to change places before "it" can slip into one of their positions. The person left out is "it" and the game continues.

What Is It?

Each person has a topographic map. Pick out two base points on the map and give compass bearings from them. Each participant uses a compass to locate the base points and to determine where lines drawn at the compass bearings would intersect and what would be seen there. Give several base points and compass bearings. The person with the most nearly correct answer wins.

Beeline or Crow-Flight Hike

Pick out a compass bearing and follow it as closely as possible on a map or outdoors to find out where it will lead and what you will see along the way.

Buried Treasure

Give each person a card with a set of directions, such as "Go 25° for 75 yards, then 120° for 100 yards, and 75° for 150 yards." Each participant uses a compass and estimates distances to try to find the correct destination. Sets of directions can vary as long as all end up at the same spot. The person most nearly correct wins the "buried treasure." This can also be a "trip" over a topographic map.

Progressive Supper Hike

Half of the group take food and equipment for a cookout and lay a trail, distributing themselves at four spots along the trail. The first group prepares the first course, the second the main dish, the third dessert, and the fourth presents the evening program. The rest of the group follow with their eating utensils and try to follow the trail to get their suppers.

Decoding Messages

Use teams of four players and station one member of each at the four corners of a large building. Give a 100-word message to the first player of the first team to transmit by Morse code (using flashlight, flags, lantern, etc.) to his or her teammate at the next corner, who then sends it on to the third, and so forth. The last player decodes the message and whispers it to the leader. The second team is given a different 100-word message to transmit in the same way. The team with the most nearly correct decoded message wins.

ORIENTEERING

*Orienteering** is a sport that originated in Sweden many years ago and still flourishes there, providing fun, good exercise, and valuable experience with map and compass for many thousands of young and not-so-young people who compete annually for proficiency pins. It is also gaining well-deserved popularity in North America and other places all over the World. In fact, Orienteering is now an international sport. There are many variations to accommodate everyone from the youngest and greenest beginner to the rugged expert. In the most common type of competition, called point-to-point, the object is to cover an unfamiliar route in the shortest possible time, using a map and compass

*Orienteering is the trademark and service mark of Silva, a Division of Johnson Company, Inc.

and good judgment to pick out the best way. The route can cover from ½ to 10 miles and includes at least five or more landmarks or *control points* that are each prominently marked in the center by a 10″ × 10″ nylon bag so that they are clearly visible to anyone coming reasonably near. Individuals or buddies (two people working together) start out at several minute intervals, trying to find each of the control points and complete the course in the least possible time. Each is given a clue sheet describing the controls and is allowed a certain amount of time to study the clues and the map to determine the best way to go. To insure that a contestant passes each control point, a punch or marking device is attached to the control bag for marking a card carried by the contestant.

Types of Orienteering

Among the types of Orienteering are:

CROSS-COUNTRY ORIENTEERING. Point-to-point or cross-country Orienteering, as previously described, is the classic form of Orienteering. Each participant must visit a set number of controls or "check points" in a prescribed order, and winners are determined strictly on a time basis, providing they have completed the course properly. This is the form of Orienteering used in all major championships.

SCORE ORIENTEERING. The object in score Orienteering is to accumulate points by visiting as many control points as possible in the time allowed. The event area contains more controls than could possibly be visited within the allotted time. Those nearest the start have a low point value while controls farther away or which require a higher degree of skill to find carry a high point value.

LINE ORIENTEERING. In cross-country Orienteering the control points are given out at the start and route choice is left to the individual. However, in line Orienteering, no control locations are given to the competitor. Instead, the exact route is shown on a master map and the individual must copy the route onto his or her own map and then follow the course. The winner is determined on the basis of time and mapping accuracy. When the participant finds a control point along the route, the exact spot must be marked on the individual's map.

(Girl Scouts, U.S.A.)

ROUTE ORIENTEERING. In this form of Orienteering, speed and accuracy again determine the winner. Route Orienteering is actually a simpler version of line Orienteering, since participants simply follow a course already marked out on the ground with flags or some similar device. The location of the control markers must be marked on the map when they are found.

TEAM AND RELAY ORIENTEERING. Teams can consist of from two to six members. Everyone starts and finishes at the same place, but each individual in succession must complete the course. An alternative to this is to have all team members compete simultaneously over different sections of the course. In both cases the combined times of all persons on each team are added together to determine the outcome.

OTHER VARIATIONS. Any of the previously mentioned forms of Orienteering may be done at night. Normally, the course would be shorter than in day Orienteering and the controls would be more numerous. Dim lights or reflective material can be used to improve the visibility of the control points. Contestants would also carry flashlights to help them find the way. Additional variations might include Orienteering by bicycle, cross-country skis, snowshoes, or canoe.

Your campers may enjoy the following Orienteering game referred to as *Bringing Home the Bacon.* Lay out separate routes of equal length and difficulty for each team and station one team member at each of its control points. Give the first member of each team a compass and a key to his or her route. At a given signal, the person proceeds as rapidly as possible to the next teammate stationed at the first control point and passes on the compass and key sheet to take on to the third teammate at the next control point. The game progresses in like manner until the last person reaches the end point. Players must wait inconspicuously at control points without speaking or giving any other signal to help their teammate find them. The first team to complete its route wins.

Winning at Orienteering games requires several essential skills in path finding: (1) ability to follow instructions; (2) skill with map and compass; (3) an understanding of map symbols and how to choose the best route; (4) speed. For further information about Orienteering games, maps, and other materials, see the bibliography at the end of this chapter or write to one of the following organizations:

1. United States Orienteering Federation, P.O. Box 1039, Ballwin, Missouri 63011.
2. Orienteering Services, USA, P.O. Box 1604, Binghamton, New York 13902.
3. Canadian Orienteering Federation, 333 River Road, Vanier, Ontario, Canada.

ADDITIONAL READINGS

(For an explanation of abbreviations and abbreviated forms used, see page 13.)

Maps, Compass, and Pathfinding

Angier: *How to Stay Alive in the Woods,* chs. 16–18, 20.
Angier: *Skills for Taming the Wilds,* ch. 7.
Angier: *Survival With Style,* ch. 4.
Angier: *Wilderness Gear You Can Make Yourself,* ch. 11.
Bale: *What On Earth,* pp. 37–47, 54–55, 108–111.
Bengtsson, Hans, and George Atkinson: *Orienteering for Sport and Pleasure.* 1977, 224 pp., available from Orienteering Services, USA.
Boy Scout Handbook, pp. 184–197 and 574, 575.
Bridge: *America's Backpacking Book,* ch. 14.
Brower: *Going Light With Backpack or Burro,* ch. 7.
Brown, L.: *Map Making: The Art that Became a Science.* Little, Brown.
Cardwell: *America's Camping Book,* chs. 31, 35.
Compass and Maps. Girl Scouts, rev. (Flip charts)
Dalrymple: *Survival in the Outdoors,* ch. 5, pp. 84–91.
Darst, Paul W. and George P. Armstrong: *Outdoor Adventure Activities for School and Recreation Programs.* ch. 10.
Disley, John: *Orienteering.* Stackpole, 1973, 192 pp.
Disley, John: *Your Way With Map and Compass.* American Orienteering, 1971, 61 pp.
Eggert: *Backpack Hiking: The First Steps,* ch. 7.
Fieldbook for Boys and Men, ch. 3, pp. 62–63, 301–307, 530–533.
Fletcher: *The Complete Walker,* pp. 239–248.
Garrison: *Outdoor Education,* ch. X.
Gatty, Harold: *Nature Is Your Guide: How to Find Your Way on Land and Sea by Observing Nature.* Dutton, 1958.
Greenhood, David: *Mapping.* U. of Chicago, 1964, 289 pp., paper.
Harty: *Science for Camp and Counselor,* pp. 149–150, 259–260, 263–266.
Hathaway, J.: *Maps and Map Making.* Western.
Kjellstrom: *Be Expert With Map and Compass.*
Langer: *The Joy of Camping,* pp. 229–241.
Learn and Tallman: *Backpacker's Digest,* chs. 7, 17.
Macfarlan: *The Boy's Book of Hiking,* ch. 7.
Manning: *Backpacking One Step at a Time,* pp. 54–57; ch. 16.
Mason: *The Junior Book of Camping and Woodcraft.*
Meier: *Backpacking,* ch. 4.
Meier, Joel F., et al.: *High Adventure Outdoor Pursuits: Organization and Leadership.* Brighton, 1980, ch. 5.

Merrill: *All About Camping*, chs. 18, 19, 20.
Merrill: *The Hiker's and Backpacker's Handbook*, ch. 8.
Merrill: *The Survival Handbook*, chs. 2, 3.
Miracle and Decker: *Complete Book of Camping*, chs. 26, 27.
Mohney: *The Master Backpacker*, chs. 7 and 8.
Mooers, Robert L., Jr.: *Finding Your Way in the Outdoors.*
Orienteering. A Boy Scout Merit Badge pamphlet, 1981, 32 pp.
Ormond: *Complete Book of Outdoor Lore*, ch. 4.
Ratliff, Donald E.: *Map, Compass and Campfire.* Binfords and Mort, Portland, Ore., 1964, 63 pp.
Rethmel: *Backpacking*, pp. 8–3 to 8–8.
Rinkoff, Barbara: *A Map is a Picture.* Crowell, 1965, 40 pp.
Riviere: *Backcountry Camping*, ch. 12.
Riviere: *The Camper's Bible*, ch. 12.
Rutstrum, Calvin: *The Wilderness Route Finder.* Macmillan, 1973, 214 pp., paper.
Shockley and Fox: *Survival in the Wilds*, ch. 3.
van der Smissen, Betty and Oswald H. Goering: *A Leader's Guide to Nature Oriented Activities*, ch. 3.
Whelen and Angier: *On Your Own in the Wilderness*, ch. 17.

MAGAZINE ARTICLES

Backpacker:
Benedict, Jim: "Shouldn't We Be There By Now?," Aug./Sept., 1980, p. 22.
Braasch, Gary: "An Orientation to Map Making." Fall, 1973, p. 32.
Wilderness Camping:
Richards, Dean: "Compasses For Wilderness Travel." Jan/Feb, 1972, p. 19.
Boys' Life:
"Maps and How to Use Them." Dec., 1969, p. 64.
Marshall, Joe: "Compass Skill Games." Aug., 1971, p. 52.
Camping Journal:
Duffey, Dave: "Duffel Bag." June, 1967, p. 14. (How to estimate distances when hiking)
Martenhoff, Jim: "Wilderness Direction-Finders." Jan., 1968, p. 30.
Ormond, Clyde: "On the Trail." June, 1968, p. 14.

Orienteering

Disley, John: *Orienteering.* Stackpole, 1973, 192 pp., paper.
Kjellstrom: *Be Expert With Map and Compass.*
Learn Orienteering. Orienteering Services, U.S.A., 1973 (Instructional pamphlet—single sheet of 14 panels)
So You Want to Know About Orienteering. Silva, 1979, 12 pp.
Teaching Orienteering. Silva, 1975, 56 pp.

MAGAZINE ARTICLES

Boys' Life:
Halter, Jon G.: "Orienteering." Mar., 1973, p. 44

FILMS

These films may be rented or purchased from International Film Bureau, Inc., 332 South Michigan Avenue, Chicago, Illinois 60604:

By Map and Compass. 27 min. or 14 min. (condensed), color.
Orienteering. 10 min., color.
The Invisible Force of Direction. 21 min., color.
What Makes Them Run. 20½ min., color.

Signaling

Angier: *How To Stay Alive in the Woods*, ch. 19.
Angier: *Skills for Taming the Wilds*, ch. 22.
Angier: *Survival With Style*, ch. 14.
Cardwell: *America's Camping Book*, ch. 34.
Coggins, Jack: *Flashes and Flags: The Story of Signaling.* Dodd, Mead, 1963.
Dalrymple: *Survival in the Outdoors*, ch. 11.
Merrill: *The Survival Handbook*, ch. 4.
Shockley and Fox: *Survival in the Wilds*, ch. 4.
Signaling (No. 3237). Boy Scouts, 1940, 56 pp., paper.

twenty-two

Hiking and Trail Skills

WHERE TO HIKE

There is no shortage of places for hiking. In the high country, backpackers can encounter alpine forests and snow fields as well as deserts, tundra, and wildlife galore. Also available for our pleasure at lower elevations are river bottoms, marshes, prairies, hardwood forests and the edge of the seas. One need not travel long distances from home or the campsite to find a suitable environment since some very fine hiking country exists close to urban areas. In fact, about two-thirds of all hiking is probably done on state, county and private lands, while only 10 to 15 percent takes place in established wilderness areas and another 10 to 15 percent on national forest trails lying outside these areas.

The importance of providing hiking opportunities is increasingly being recognized at all levels of government, for today there are about 135,000 miles of existing footpaths and trails in the United States. For additional information on suitable places to hike, refer to "How and Where to Go" in Chapter 17 and also write to some of the addresses listed in Appendix C at the back of this book. General recreation maps and materials also are available from various state park departments as well as from land management agencies such as the U.S. Forest Service, the National Park Service, and the Bureau of Land Management.

CARE FOR YOUR FEET

Have you ever thought about what the word "tenderfoot" means? Since each of your feet comes down and momentarily bears your weight about a thousand times each mile, they deserve maximum care and attention. Hikers and backpackers should never start on a long trip without having gradually toughened themselves by a series of shorter hikes, wearing the same footwear that would be used on longer hikes.

As mentioned in Chapter 18, blisters result from friction between your shoes and skin, and they are much easier to prevent than to cure. Avoid wearing darned socks and ill-fitting or new shoes or boots. Also, at the first signs of redness or soreness to the skin, apply a piece of ad-

(Camp Kingsmont, West Stockbridge, Mass.)

hesive tape or moleskin (a thin layer of felt with an adhesive backing that is available at drug stores) to absorb the friction. Toenails should be kept fairly short and they should be cut straight across with rounded corners so they won't dig into the skin. If the scree shield on top of the boot irritates the back of your heel, protect it with a piece of adhesive tape or moleskin or leave the top two holes of the boot unlaced until they are well broken in. To prevent a buildup of perspiration on the feet, which also contributes to the formation of blisters, it is common practice to wear clean socks and to change them several times a day. Other considerations for footcare are discussed in the section on "Blisters" in Chapter 18.

Figure 22-1 Running shoes can be used for hiking with light loads on good trails. High-topped work boots with good cleats or corrugated soles work well for most hiking.

FOOTWEAR

Nothing is so important to a serious hiker as footwear, for one's enthusiasm wanes quickly as that little hole in the sock or the mildly tight spot in the shoe brings torture with each step. Soon the person lags behind and reaps the displeasure of companions.

Boots (Figs. 22-1 and 22-2)

TYPES. There are literally hundreds of brands and models of boots from which to choose, many of which are imported from other countries in addition to those made in the United States. We include only a brief discussion here, but more detailed information can be found in the references listed at the end of this chapter.

Before getting too deep into this subject it should be pointed out that one of the myths we

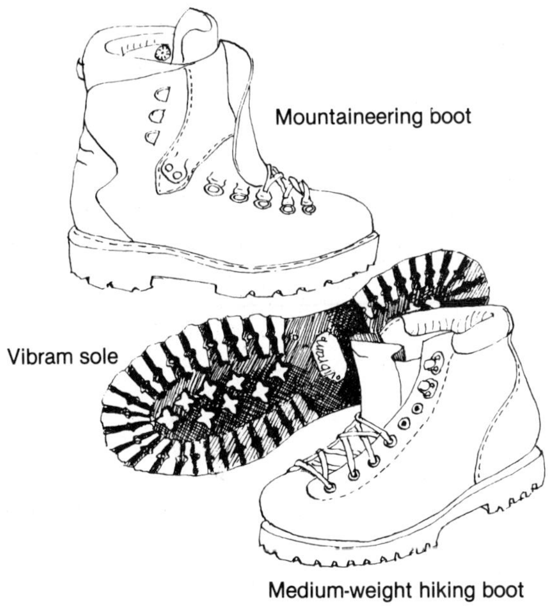

Figure 22–2 Boots for the wild country.

have been led to believe is that hiking boots must be heavy monstrosities if they are to hold up under rugged conditions in the woods and mountains. Although this may still be true for mountaineers who travel off the trail in rough country or in snow, it's hard to ignore the growing number of people who are wearing running shoes and lightweight boots into the backcountry today. The many new varieties of running shoes and lightweight hiking boots coming out on the market may be quite satisfactory for your own use. To meet the demand for these shoes, bootmakers are trimming their models while running shoe manufacturers are coming out with reinforced shoes that work well for day hiking and even for extended trips in moderate terrain. In addition to shoes made of leather, lightweight materials (synthetics such as nylon, Gore-Tex, Klimate, Thinsulate, and the like) are being added for additional comfort and weight reduction. For that matter, many people still hike in old-fashioned tennis shoes, which may prove satisfactory for short jaunts over smooth trails and with a light load, but continued use will likely produce sore soles and possibly bruised or sprained ankles.

High shoes that reach above the ankles and that have cleated or corrugated soles are recommended. Well-fitting, sturdy work boots with cleats or corrugated soles give good support and are satisfactory for most people. Shoes such as *waffle stompers* and *campus boots* are light, comfortable, and easy to break in, but they prove quite unsatisfactory for serious hiking.

Trail boots are tougher and stiffer and so are preferable for the hiker who follows longer trails or travels cross-country where running streams or rock slides will occasionally be crossed. Their sturdy construction and thicker soles support the feet well, and they can be made water repellent. *Mountaineer boots* are heavier and more rugged and have thicker soles. Although they are too heavy and stiff for general hiking, they may be desirable for expeditions into heavy brush or where the user is likely to encounter rocks, ice, or snow. For those who will be sloshing around in very wet areas, there are boots with rubber bottoms and leather tops.

WHICH TYPE FOR YOU? It is very important to select a boot that is suited to the type of travel you will engage in and then see that the pair you buy is exactly fitted to your feet. Tell the clerk in the outfitting store exactly how you expect to use the boots and approximately what price you are willing to pay. Will you need special protection against sharp rocks, stinging insects, cold, snow, or desert sand? Will the toes need to be stiff enough to kick steps in snow and ice while climbing? Will you just be traveling along easy forest trails with only a light pack? As a general rule, the more rugged the travel conditions, the sturdier the boot should be, but choose the lightest shoe that will do the job, for it is estimated that each pound carried on your foot is equivalent to 5 pounds carried on your back. Therefore, if your shoe weighs a mere pound over what is necessary, you are carrying the equivalent of an extra 10 pounds in your pack. That's a lot of wasted effort and can take the fun out of hiking. A fairly light, flexible shoe that fits comfortably and is reasonably priced will, for ordinary purposes, give all the protection the average hiker needs. The important thing is to choose what's right for you and the situation.

SOME FEATURES. Leather uppers can "breathe" and so are preferable for ventilation and can also be made quite water repellent. Some uppers are made with the smooth side of the leather out, but "rough outs," which can also be made water repellent, are becoming more popular because of their superior resistance to abrasion from rough surfaces and underbrush. Suede leather results when leather has been split, and although it is lighter than regular leather, it naturally will not hold up as well under rough usage. Lined and insulated boots are available for use in extremely cold weather.

Boots that lace to the toe can be tied tightly to keep the feet from sliding about unduly. Boots can lace with eyelets, rings (swivel eyelets), hooks, or a combination of these. Lacing and unlacing is faster with hooks, but they sometimes catch on underbrush or get broken or twisted, making them unusable; this is indeed unfortunate on a trip, but they can later be replaced at a boot repair shop. Leather laces stretch and loosen when wet and have been largely supplanted by nylon laces that wear well and, if made of soft-woven unwaxed material, are not likely to come untied. To tie your shoestrings, moisten them and then pull one loop through the knot a second time before tightening it. This prevents the strings from coming untied along the trail.

Soles should be sufficiently thick and hard to protect the feet on rough terrain and are usually made of corrugated synthetic rubber that provides good traction. Vibram (Fig. 22–2) is the trade name of the most popular type of sole, but beware lest they leave black scuff marks when worn on home floors. Softer soles offer little protection from rough surfaces and wear out rapidly. Leather soles are not at all satisfactory since they slip on pine needles and wet surfaces commonly encountered on a trail.

Boots should have as few seams as possible because they are difficult to waterproof, and what seams there are should be double or triple stitched. Boots should reach just above the ankle to give good support and protection from rough underbrush and outcroppings along the path. The average hiker will not want boots higher than this since they are hot, hard to put on and take off, and inclined to bunch and buckle around the ankle, irritating the Achilles tendon along the back of the heel. Some boots have a scree shield to keep out water, rocks, or snow; this is located at the top of the boot and is usually made of some type of elastic fabric. If your boots don't have one or if you want more extensive protection, gaiters are available to slip on as needed. These are waterproof fabric sleeves, usually about 7 to 9 inches high, which zip closed around the ankle and are held down by a strap or thong that slips under your instep. The toes of your boots should be fairly firm to prevent injury to your toes when banging up against rocks.

SELECTING THE PROPER SIZE. When trying on boots wear the two pairs of socks you expect to hike in. You will probably need a hiking shoe a size or a size and a half larger than your usual street shoe; this is because your feet spread out owing to the weight of your pack and the extra blood that accumulates as you hike along. In addition, the two pairs of socks take up extra room. Solicit help from a knowledgeable outfitter when making your selection. Since nearly everyone has one foot larger than the other, try the boot on this one first. Everyone's feet are different and shoes are made on different lasts and to different specifications, so you should try on many pairs in the search for one that feels exactly right.

Here are some tests for a proper fit. With the boot still unlaced, slide your foot as far forward as possible in it and try to slip one finger down behind your heel as far as the sole of the boot. It should fit snugly; if there is room for two fingers, the shoe is too big. Now kick the back of the heel against the floor to push your foot back in the boot and lace it tightly. There should now be enough room to curl your toes slightly. Next, kick the toe. The foot should not slide forward enough to touch the front of the boot. Do some knee bends; your foot should move about very little in the shoe. Have someone hold your foot down to the floor and try to move your foot sideways inside the boot; if much movement is possible, the boot is too loose. Walk around the store for several minutes with a shoe from each of two pairs on your feet. Remove the shoe that feels least comfortable and substitute another from a third pair; keep repeating this process until you finally locate the pair that feels most comfortable. If possible, try climbing up and down stairs or up and down an incline; this is the acid test for comfort. Some outfitters will lend a pair of boots to wear indoors at home for several hours if you are careful not to scuff them, other outfitters rent out boots, which is another way to try out several models and sizes before making a final selection.

It is possible to buy boots by mail, if you are

careful to follow the specific directions given by the outfitter for determining the correct size. Although this is probably not as satisfactory as being fitted in a shop, you can usually return them for a new selection if they don't fit.

Some people find that arch supports and/or one or more inner soles improve both fit and comfort.

CHILDREN'S BOOTS. Getting good hiking boots for children is sometimes difficult. However, there are now strong work shoe and outing types available in shoe stores, and a few manufacturers now make regular hiking boots in children's sizes. One drawback to buying an expensive pair is that children's feet grow so rapidly that the shoes are likely to be outgrown before they are worn out. Some outfitters will allow a generous trade-in on a new pair if the old ones are still in good condition, and some camps, as well as outfitters, have found a solution by keeping an assortment on hand to rent out.

BREAKING IN BOOTS. In caring for boots, bear in mind that most are made of leather that has pores to "breathe" and so ventilate both foot and boot. In order to preserve this quality, strive for water repellency rather than waterproofing, which would necessitate actually plugging up the pores. Also, avoid applying anything that will stretch and soften the leather so that it no longer gives firm support. A new pair of boots needs an application of something to condition the leather and make it water repellent. Among the several good preparations available is one with a silicone dressing and wax base called Sno Seal. Warm it right in the container

(Girl Scouts, U.S.A.)

to liquefy it and use a brush or piece of cloth to paint it on the leather. Then rub it in vigorously with your fingers and work it in especially well around the seams and the welt, for these are the places where moisture tends to enter. Now put the boots on and go for a short walk about town or along an easy trail. Gradually increase the length of your walks as you continue to break in the boots. Some people advocate breaking in boots by soaking them in water and walking about in them until they are dry, but we do not recommend this because of the damage soaking does to the leather.

BOOT CARE. A good pair of boots represents a sizeable investment, but if properly cared for, they will serve you well for many years. Heat is probably the worst enemy of leather so never place boots on a radiator, in the oven, or near a campfire, or leave them in the trunk of a car on a hot summer day. If they accidentally get wet, wipe them clean and stuff them with crumpled newspapers, then let them dry out gradually at room temperature. When dry, treat them with a good leather conditioner as previously described.

Occasionally during use, brush the dirt off your boots and use a small brush and a bit of saddle soap with a small amount of water to wash them; then apply a good conditioner. This keeps the leather from drying out and becoming stiff and also restores the water repellency.

SOCKS

It is customary to wear two pairs of socks when hiking; a heavy pair on the outside and thinner ones next to the foot. Socks absorb perspiration as well as moisture from the outside, cushion the feet, and minimize the blister-causing friction between boot and foot. A "wick dry" sock is recommended for the inner pair; it claims to "wick" perspiration from the feet and is made of 50 percent Orlon acrylic, 30 percent wool, and 20 percent nylon. Other popular inner socks include those made of thin wool, silk, or polypropylene. An outer pair with padded soles should be wool. A blend containing wool is superior because it stays cushiony and warm even when wet, but it can be mixed with other fibers such as Orlon or nylon for longer wear. Cotton socks are not at all satisfactory since they absorb and hold perspiration and outside moisture. The outer socks should be a full size larger than those you ordinarily wear.

On a trip, carry several pairs of socks and change to fresh ones at rest stops or at noon, fastening the soiled pair to the outside of your pack to dry. Soiled socks should be washed each night so that you have a fresh supply for the next day. Never wear darned socks or those with holes in them and avoid those with a rough texture that might prove irritating.

LOADING AND CARRYING A PACK

Modern backpacks such as those described in Chapter 28 allow us the freedom and independence to carry all of our needs with us in the backcountry, wherever we may go. To do so with a reasonable degree of comfort, however, we need to know something about how much weight to carry, how to load the pack and how to carry it properly.

Once a camper learns what equipment (Chapter 28) and food (Chapter 27) are necessary for an extended trip into the backcountry, there should be no reason that the weight and bulk of all the supplies cannot be carried without undue strain on the person's back and legs. Unfortunately, no one has yet been able to accurately measure the maximum amount of weight an individual should carry for efficiency and enjoyment; however, a common rule of thumb is to carry no more than one-third of your body weight if you are in good physical condition, and no more than one-fourth if you are not. Keep in mind that this formula is for *maximum* weight of the pack, which would be much heavier than needed for most wilderness trips of seven days or more. In fact, a more realistic weight range is for the pack to weigh no more than one-fifth of your body weight.

An additional consideration pertains to how the pack is actually loaded. In order to align the heavy items more closely with your center of gravity and to keep the pack from pulling back on your shoulders, it is generally best to place the heavy objects near the top of the pack and close to your back. Of course, you will also want to be sure to keep items that are frequently needed, such as maps, rain gear, and snacks, where you can get to them.

It is helpful to pack various items of like need together in nylon or plastic stuff sacks before placing them in the pack. Each sack can then be labeled for easy identification, eliminating the need to open each one while looking for a specific item. It is also a good idea to always place each item in the same location in the pack, since this saves time when you are attempting to find the article in a hurry.

Most hikers now tend to favor the modern backpack that is mounted on a frame, where the weight is distributed so that most of it rests on the hips rather than on the neck and shoulders. This is possible because of the waist strap attached to the lower end of the frame. To wear the pack properly, however, you must first place it on your back and then tighten the shoulder straps until the pack is held comfortably against your back. The next important step to to hunch up your shoulders and then cinch and fasten the waist belt tightly before relaxing the shoulders. This holds the weight of the pack on the hips once the shoulders are lowered to their normal position. From this point on, the shoulders simply lend stability to the pack by holding it in a vertical position against the back.

HIKING TECHNIQUES

General Hints

Just before starting out on the day's hike, make any last-minute clothing adjustments, since a change in your body temperature can soon be expected. It is usually best to start a little on the cool side for within a few minutes of going along the trail you will feel just fine. This practice eliminates the need for frequent group stops, especially after only being on the road for a short time.

Remember that perspiration-soaked clothing is just as dangerous as rain-soaked clothing insofar as hypothermia is concerned. This is an important reason for removing outer garments before overheating occurs. When on a trip of any length, always carry a change of clothing with you and slip into it immediately if you get wet. If no change is possible, it may be necessary to stop and build a fire in order to dry out.

When hiking, relax your whole body and swing the arms and legs along rhythmically as you walk. Keep your body erect or, if carrying a pack, lean forward slightly from the hips to counter balance it. The length of stride and walking tempo should be consistent on flat ground. That same tempo should be maintained when going up or down hills, although the stride must be adjusted, that is, use a shorter stride when going uphill and a longer one when going down.

Do not make a hike a speed or endurance contest, for what you do and see along the way is as important as how far you go. Like a machine, your body works most efficiently at a moderate rate of speed, so strike a steady pace that can be maintained indefinitely by everyone in the group. Three miles an hour is a good speed to maintain for most people and this pace eats up miles steadily without causing undue fatigue. Whatever the pace, it should allow you to have a controlled, rhythmic movement that keeps the heartbeat and breathing rate even. Also, in order to avoid fatigue an experienced hiker never steps on anything, such as a rock or log, that can be stepped over or around.

It is advisable to rest a few minutes every hour or so on a long hike, but avoid staying immobile too long lest your leg and back muscles stiffen. When stopped, relax completely by sitting against a tree or lying flat on your back with feet propped up to let the blood that has collected in your legs and feet drain away.

Group Considerations

When hiking with campers, one counselor should head the line as a pacesetter, striking a moderate pace that all can maintain without undue hardship, and a second counselor should bring up the rear. Everyone else should stay between, with each individual separated at least 10 to 15 feet from the person in front and behind. This allows each person to set his or her own rhythm and length of stride. Also, there is less likelihood of someone being hit in the face by a branch or bush that might snap back if caught on the person in front.

The most successful hiking groups are composed of individuals of approximately the same age and physical stamina so that the strong do not have to wait for the slow or the slow overwork in an effort to keep up. Even when the group is moderately well matched, there will al-

(Pacific Peaks Girl Scout Council, Olympia, Washington)

ways be those who tend to fall behind. This can often be remedied by putting slower walkers near or at the front of the line.

Thirst and Hunger

Thirst often results from a drying out of the tissues lining the mouth rather than from general dehydration; consequently, this kind of thirst is best relieved by merely rinsing the mouth instead of gulping down large quantities of liquid. If you have been perspiring freely, however, you will need to replace the salt as well as the fluid your body has lost, so add some extra salt to your food or put a little in the drinking water. Eating candy bars along the way will make you thirsty, so munch on raisins or other dry fruit or suck on a fruit pit, a piece of hard candy, or a clean pebble instead.

Vigorous hiking soon uses up the fuel readily available in the blood stream, so it is a good idea to take along a trail snack, such as a plastic bag of "gorp" to eat along the way. Although the variation and recipes for this are endless, a popular blend consists of salted peanuts and mixed nuts, raisins, and small candies such as M & Ms. Any other haphazard mixture of nuts, seeds, dried fruits, and granola cereal will likely be just as enjoyable. Such a mixture will furnish a good balance of protein, carbohydrates, and fats that will keep any hungry tramper going throughout the day.

Each person in the party will usually want to carry a canteen of water unless there are safe sources on the way. You can refill it at a suitable stream, and by following the procedures recommended in Chapter 18 you can purify the water as you hike.

If the Trail Disappears

There is usually no problem in finding your way on a designated trail. However, there are times when even well-marked paths may tend to disappear, especially when they lead into meadows, marshy areas, downed timber, or rock slabs. This is probably due to hikers who wander through the open space of the meadow or are forced to pick a route around fallen trees or rocks. If you should have difficulty locating where the trail resumes, the best procedure is to establish a search pattern and then have your group fan out to look for signs of the trail. Keep everyone within hearing distance during the search and also establish a time limit for everyone to return in case the trail is not located. Chances are you'll soon find the lost route and will be off on your way again with little lost time.

Off-Trail Travel

Should your party be traveling cross-country or off the trails, additional knowledge is needed beyond simple map and compass techniques. To determine the best route to take, you must study the terrain and elevation changes and then travel in areas that have gradual slopes. This prevents unnecessary gain or loss in elevation and expenditure of valuable energy. Also keep in mind that it is often easier to travel on ridge tops than in valley floors, which may be thick with vegetation, down timber and other hazards. Of course, each situation is different and consideration must therefore be given to such factors as the type of groundcover, your distance from drinking water and the like. Sometimes it is simply best to choose a longer route with easy going in order to avoid problems later on. Whatever you do, keep as many route options open for as long as possible before committing yourself to any of them. By doing so you can always alter your plans if the going gets too rough.

Estimating Distance

In Chapter 21 we discussed how to use pacing to determine distances traveled. This method works well on short jaunts, but it is really not practical on long hikes when one needs to estimate how long it will take to travel several miles or more. *Time/distance estimating* is a more useful method for long hikes. Experienced backpackers come to know their hiking speed; most allow about 1 hour for every 3 miles traveled on flat terrain and they add an additional hour to this for every 1,000 feet of steep ascent or descent. To apply this technique to a hypothetical example, let's assume your map shows that there are 5 miles of trail to the next campsite. The contour lines on the map also show that the trail to the camp climbs 2,000 feet and then descends 1,000 feet. The formula reveals that it will take your group 4 hours and 40 minutes to reach the camp (5 miles = 1 hour and 40 minutes + 3,000 feet of ascent and descent = 3 more hours). Depending on the physical condition and age of your party, however, you may need to adjust these figures slightly. Also be

(Cheley Colorado Camps, Estes Park, Colo.)

sure to allow for time taken on rest stops and lunch breaks.

Etiquette

When hiking, there are some common courtesies that should be extended to other persons and to the property of others. Respect no trespassing signs; in all likelihood they have been put up because of damage done by previous travelers and may be assumed to mean just what they say. Close gates behind you if they were found that way and avoid climbing fences, for it is easy to break them down and do permanent damage. Do not walk across cultivated fields but stay close to the edges where no crops have been planted. Pick fruit or flowers only when given express permission to do so.

When meeting other parties on a trail, those coming downhill should have the right of way and your group should step aside and let them pass. If going the same way as a faster group, you should always let the faster hikers go by. Groups on horseback or with pack animals should be given plenty of room. Your party should move to the side of the trail and remain quiet to avoid exciting the animals.

(Columbine Girl Scouts Council, Inc., Pueblo, Colo.)

As a common courtesy to resource managers and property owners we should always respect their rules and regulations and do everything possible to make their work easier for them. Doing such things as avoiding cutting corners on the trail and picking up and carrying out others' litter will help to maintain a clean landscape and will set a good example for others to follow.

CAMPSITE SELECTION AND SET-UP

It is always wise to allow plenty of time to establish a campsite, so plan on stopping your hike early enough in the day to complete all necessary tasks before dark. There is plenty of work to be done by everyone, so teamwork is the order of the day. In addition to selecting an appropriate area and setting up the tents or shelter, your group must also get water, prepare the evening meal, wash up after eating, and get everything stored away while there is still daylight.

In choosing a campsite, there are a number of points to consider. It probably will be impossible to find one combining all of them, but you can at least look for one that meets as many requirements as possible. Choose a spot that has good drainage and is well above high-water marks so that there will be no danger of inundation from flash flooding of a nearby creek or runoff of water from a neighboring hillside. If possible, find a spot that is slightly higher than the surrounding area and with a natural windbreak to provide shelter from strong winds and rain. Avoid pitching tents directly under trees, and inspect those nearby to see that they are sound and not likely to drop dead limbs or blow over in a storm. Although trees may give some shelter during a deluge, they will continue to drip on your tent for a time after the rain is over. Also, beware of pine, birch, and maple trees, which tend to drop substances damaging to tent fabrics.

Select a level area with no sharp rocks, twigs, or other rough objects that may damage your shelter floor and disturb your sleep. Be sure to pitch the back of your tent toward prevailing high winds and rain and secure all ties and stakes properly. The tent should be taut but not overly so. When there is a high wind, tighten the ropes and close all openings, for wind inside a tent can cause ballooning and possibly severe damage to the tent itself. Once the shelter has been established, the next step is to prepare your quarters for the night by rolling out the ground pad and unpacking and fluffing your sleeping bag in order to allow time for it to gain maximum loft before bedtime.

LOW-IMPACT HIKING AND CAMPING TECHNIQUES

Those who hike or backpack generally do so in order to find solitude and be in close contact with the natural environment. As a result, the less we see of other groups and their impact on the land, the better the experience will be for everyone. Unfortunately, inexperienced youngsters and many adults have little awareness of the adverse impact they may have on such vulnerable ecological systems as those found in the backwoods or wildlands. Consequently, as is mentioned many times throughout this text, it is important for camp counselors and trip leaders to adopt and then demonstrate a low-impact camping ethic that is based on proper ecological attitudes toward the natural environment. This means that we must respect the fragility of wild areas and must make a personal commitment to treat these areas with loving care. It should be the goal of every hiker or backpacker to practice minimum-impact camping by leaving the fewest traces of his or her presence as possible, no matter how far or where the hiker travels. Those who are truly skilled in the ways of the outdoors never leave signs such as aluminum foil, cut boughs, scarred trees, fire rings, or anything else other than a few blades of bent grass to show where they have been. Everything they carry into the wilderness they also carry out. Many good ideas for practicing low-impact camping are presented in Chapter 17, including a discussion of how to keep a campsite clean, how to handle human waste and garbage, and bathing and washing techniques. The following are additional environmental practices that should be considered:

1. In order to protect the scenic view and to prevent pollution, camps should be at least 100 feet from water.
2. No permanent structures should be built in the campsite and trenching of tents should be discouraged. If a trench is dug around a tent, it should be filled in after use. Remember that a trench destroys part of the ground cover.
3. Using green boughs for a bed is a thing of the past. Keep your campsite as primitive and natural as possible.
4. Use established camps whenever possible rather than destroy the groundcover in a new area. If you come across an undesignated campsite that shows scars from overuse, find an alternative place to bed down.
5. When selecting a campsite, look for a sturdy or rocky spot rather than camp on lush but delicate soils of meadows or streamsides. Use areas that are covered with sand, fallen tree needles or leaves and be sure the area is on high elevation and dry.
6. Cook with a mountain stove if at all possible and avoid having a campfire unless absolutely necessary. If a fire is used, build it in a shallow pit dug in the earth (in an appropriate, safe place). Set the turf aside and keep it moist so that it can be replaced prior to breaking camp. Scatter any fireplace stones and spread the extra wood around the area so there is no telltale sign left.
7. Do not build big or unnecessary fires. Use only fallen timber since even the standing dead trees are part of the natural scene. If there is no wood on the ground, then the area cannot produce enough wood for people to burn, so use a stove. Do not chop down trees or remove dead branches unless absolutely necessary. If you don't carry an axe, you won't be tempted! Wood found near timberline takes several hundred years to be produced, so plan on using a stove in such areas.
8. Garbage should be burned, not buried, and unburnable materials should be packed out. Do not throw aluminum foil into a fire since the aluminum will remain behind for many years without decomposing.
9. Picking flowers causes unnecessary damage in timberline and alpine tundra regions since these areas are very delicate and the ecological systems are easily upset.
10. Stay on existing trails and hike in single file to avoid creating multiple lanes. Also avoid cutting across switchbacks even though it may save time and energy. Switchbacks are graded to prevent erosion and cutting across them only increases the problem.

11. Pick up any litter along the route; have one pocket of your pack available for trash or carry a plastic bag for this purpose.

12. When traveling cross-country or off the trail, the group should spread out rather than follow one another. A group of people tramping in a row can crush fragile plant tissues beyond recovery and create channels for erosion.

13. Limit your group size to ten or less in order to minimize your impact. Also be sure the appearance and sounds of your party are low keyed in order to avoid disturbing other campers or wildlife.

These are just a few of the things that can be done to reduce our impact on the land. There are many more ideas that could be added to the list but, in the final analysis, using common sense is all that is necessary.

HIKING VARIATIONS FOR ADDITIONAL FUN

Even old, familiar trails can take on a new glamour when there is a definite purpose for following them. Usually we have a certain objective or distination in mind, but we should not be in such a hurry that there is not time to stop for the unusual. Here are some possible hiking variations that can add interest to normal outings.

1. *Orienteering and Map and Compass Hikes.* (These are discussed in Chapter 21.)

2. *Heads and Tails Hike.* Flip a coin at each fork in the road to determine whether to turn right or left.

3. *Carefree Hike.* Hike to some interesting or beautiful spot to cook an outdoor meal, hold a program, sing, or play nature games.

4. *Breakfast Hike.* Go to a good vantage point to watch the sun rise and cook breakfast. Start at daybreak if you want to see and hear the birds at their best.

5. *Star Hike.* Go to a hill on a clear evening to study the stars and their legends. Take blanket rolls or sleeping bags and plan to stay overnight.

6. *Fishing Trip.* Hike out to fish in a nearby stream or lake. Take a lunch to supplement the fresh fish you *hope* to catch.

7. *Historical Hike.* Brief yourself by reading and consulting others about nearby historical spots, then hike out to visit them.

8. *Moonlight Hike.* Go out to note nature's completely different night life.

9. *Camera Hike.* See who can snap the most interesting photographs along the way.

10. *Nature Hike.* Give each hiker a list of nature specimens (flowers, trees, animals, or insects) to collect or identify, or see who can collect the most interesting pieces of driftwood, sea shells, or other items to use in the craft shop or add to the nature display.

11. *Rain Hike.* Waterproof yourselves completely and splash along, watching how animals and plants behave in the rain.

12. *Creek's or River's End Hike.* Follow a creek or river to its origin or mouth.

13. *Overnight Hike.* Find a good place to spend the night; cook breakfast and return to camp.

14. *Sealed Orders Hike.* Give the group a set of sealed directions with a new one to open at each spot along the way or distribute them along the route so the group will find a new one as soon as they have successfully followed the old. Give instructions in compass points and distances such as "Go 50 paces at 75° and look under the three rocks piled below the big pin oak tree; then go straight E and look inside the big hollow oak tree off at the left." For variety, give clues in rhymes, riddles, or codes. Make the clues challenging but not so difficult as to discourage the campers. A group is best limited to five or six.

15. *Hold the Front.* The participants draw for positions in line and arrange themselves in single file. The object is to get and maintain the head position. As they hike along, the counselor picks out some nature specimen and asks the head player to identify it. If the person cannot do so, each person behind is in turn given a chance to try. The first to succeed advances to the head of the line. The counselor then asks a question of the person behind the one who has just advanced and the question is repeated down the line as before until someone answers it correctly and advances up ahead of the one who first missed it. The winner is the person at the head of the line when the game ends.

16. *Bus or Camp Truck Hike.* Ride out by bus or camp truck and hike back or let the vehicle meet you at the halfway point on your return. This gives you a chance to venture farther from camp.

17. *"What Is It?" Hike.* Give each member a list of objects that might be seen along the way, such as a particular kind of bird, tree, moss, or flower. Assign points to each object according to its rarity. The hiker who first sees and correctly identifies an item on the list scores the specified number of points. Penalize the person in points if his or her identification is incorrect.

No matter what kind of a hike you take, do not let it degenerate into a prosaic walk or you will end up with a group of bored, disgruntled campers on your hands. Some of the activities mentioned here help to add additional interest to a regular hike. You must, of course, adapt your methods to the age of the group. *Plan* your hike, no matter how short it is. It is best to meet as a group to decide where to go, what to do, what to wear and what equipment to take, how to pack it and how to divide up the jobs on the way. It also is best to return by a different route if you can.

ADDITIONAL READINGS

(For an explanation of abbreviations and abbreviated forms used, see page 13.)

Footwear

Angier: *Home In your Pack,* pp. 80–90.
Bridge: *America's Backpacking Book,* ch.8.
Cardwell: *America's Camping Book,* pp. 94–97.
Colwell: *Introduction to Backpacking,* ch.4.
Fletcher: *The Complete Walker,* pp. 26–37.
Learn and Tallman: *Backpacker's Digest,* ch. 2.
Manning: *Backpacking One Step At A Time,* ch. 8.
Meier: *Backpacking,* pp. 30–34.
Merrill: *The Hiker's and Backpacker's Handbook,* ch. 7.
Rethmel: *Backpacking,* pp. 3–3 to 3–7.
Riviere: *Backcountry Camping,* pp. 110–117.
Wood: *Pleasure Packing,* ch. 2.

MAGAZINE ARTICLES

Backpacker
Barker, James: "Bootery Snobbery." Winter, 1973, pp. 65–67.
"Boots for Backpackers." Feb./Mar., 1980, p. 63.
Bryant, Mark: "Outfitting—The New Age of Lightweight Delights." Aug./Sept., 1981, p.75.
Masia, Seth: "You and Your Gear—Breaking in Boots." Winter, 1973, p. 16.
Micholas, Howe: "Boots Roots." Oct./Nov., 1978, p. 45.
"The Best of the Boots." Winter, 1973, pp. 49–72.
Camping Journal:
"Boots and Rainwear." Feb., 1973. ('73 Buyers' Guide)
Wilderness Camping:
Wood, Robert S.: "Pleasure Packing—Buying Boots." May-June, 1973, p. 12.

Hiking

Angier: *Home in Your Pack, chs. 1, 8.*
Angier: *Skills for Taming the Wilds,* ch. 1.
Berger: *Program Activities for Camps,* pp. 88–92.
Boy Scout Handbook, pp. 191–203.
Bridge: *America's Backpacking Book, chs. 1, 4, 17.*
Cardwell: *America's Camping Book,* ch. 42.
Colwell: *Introduction to Backpacking,* ch. 6.
Corbin: *Recreation Leadership,* ch. 25.
Eggert: *Backpack Hiking: The First Steps,* chs. 1, 2, 3, 9, 10.
Fieldbook for Boys and Men, ch. 2.
Fletcher: *The New Complete Walker,* 490 pp.
Kujoth: *The Recreation Program Guide,* pp. 144–160.
Langer: *The Joy of Camping,* pp. 186–191.
Macfarlan: *The Boy's Book of Hiking.*
Mohney: *The Master Backpacker,* chs. 3, 4.
Manning: *Backpacking One Step at a Time,* chs. 1, 17.
Meier: *Backpacking,* ch. 5.
Musselman, Virginia: *Learning About Nature Through Games.* Stackpole, 1967, 128 pp., ch. 13.
Ormond: *Complete Book of Outdoor Lore,* ch. 1.
Ormond: *Outdoorsman's Handbook,* part 5.
Rutstrum: *New Way of the Wilderness.*
Sussman, Aaron, and Ruth Goode: *The Magic of Walking.* Simon and Schuster, 1969, 410 pp., paper.
Whelen and Angier: *On Your Own in the Wilderness,* ch. 3.
Winnett: *Backpacking for Fun, ch. 6.*
Wood: *Pleasure Packing,* ch. 9.

MAGAZINE ARTICLES

Backpacker
Nordstrom, Frank: "Shaping Up." Spring 1974, p. 61.
Wilderness Camping:
Aune, Michael: "Backpack Loading." Aug./Sept., 1977, p. 24.
Ross, Robert N.: "The Merchanics of Walking." May-June, 1973, p. 28.

Where to Go

Bridge: *America's Backpacking Book,* ch. 25.
Bridge, Raymond: *Tourguide to the Rocky Mountain Wilderness.* Stackpole, 1975, 160 pp.
Fletcher: *The Complete Walker,* Appendix III. (Organizations that promote walking)
Kujoth: The Recreation Program Guide, pp. 160–164.
Learn and Tallman: *Backpacker's Digest,* ch. 20.
Macfarlan: *The Boy's Book of Hiking,* chs. 1, 3.
Meier: *Backpacking,* ch. 1.
Merrill:*AllAbout Camping,* ch. 1,2.
Ryback, Eric and Tim: *The Ultimate Journey: Canada to Mexico Down the Continental Divide.* Chronicle Books, San Francisco, 1973, 207 pp.
Sterling, E.M.: *Western Trips and Trails.* Stackpole, 1974, 351 pp.

MAGAZINE ARTICLES

Readers' Digest:
Farney, Dennis: "Walk the Wild Applachian Trail," Oct., 1972, p. 208.

twenty-three
Using Knife, Axe and Other Tools

The Yankee boy, before he's sent to school,
Well knows the mysteries of that magic tool,
The pocket-knife. To that his wistful eye
Turns while he hears his mother's lullaby;
His hoarded cents he gladly gives to get it,
Then leaves no stone unturned till he can whet it;
And in the education of the lad
No little part that implement hath had.
His pocket-knife to the young whittler brings
A growing knowledge of material things.

—John Pierpont

A WORD ON THE ENVIRONMENTAL ETHIC

Before getting into a discussion on knives, axes and other tools we should first say a few words on their use and proper relationship to the camping ethic. Out of necessity, the old frontier ethic of the pioneers and early campers in America was to subdue nature and civilize the wilderness. In earlier times there existed unlimited natural resources and therefore there was no need to worry about their consumption. Camping in those days was more a matter of survival rather than recreation. Unfortunately, that same attitude still motivates far too many modern campers who continue to destroy the very qualities they are seeking. An inexperienced camper must therefore learn the importance of an awareness and sensitivity to the environment that leads to responsible behavior. There is no better way to teach this than when instructing campers on how, when, and where to use knives, axes, and other camp tools. The days when we could indiscriminately carve up trees or chop them down are long past. Campers should be aware of these facts before they are allowed to handle camp tools.

THE CAMP KNIFE

The knife, along with the gun and axe, was an important tool of the pioneer, and the modern camper engaged in campcrafts finds it equally important. It is useful for performing many camp kitchen chores and for making utilitarian items, such as fuzz sticks to start a stubborn fire and handy gadgets to use around the campsite, and decorative articles, such as totem poles and lapel pins. Young children may lack the hand-eye coordination necessary to use a knife skillfully and safely, but older girls and boys (age 11 and up) soon become quite adept with it when taught carefully and enthusiastically. All of us have been dismayed upon seeing initials and other designs carved in public places, but they do bear mute testimony to the fascination that using a knife holds; therefore, in camp, let us concentrate on teaching youngsters to channel this seemingly irresistible impulse into constructive rather than destructive uses.

Selecting a Knife

A knife with multi-purpose blades, such as a Boy or Girl Scout knife or Swiss Army knife, is usually best for general camp use. It probably will have a cutting blade, a combination screwdriver and bottlecap opener, an awl or reamer for making holes in leather and other materials, and a can opener. Whatever model is chosen, it should be sturdy and fit well in the user's hand. A knife with a bright-colored handle is easier to find if you mislay it or drop it in the duff on the ground.

Trying to economize on a knife will prove to be poor economy in the long run, since a cheap one is likely to be poorly constructed with a blade composed of such soft material that it won't hold a sharp edge. A blade of good quality carbon steel is best. Stainless steel should be avoided since it can't be sharpened to a keen edge and it won't hold what little edge it has.

Caring for a Knife

A knife should be treated like the high-class tool it is. Wipe the blade off after each use and never put it away wet. Remove any rust or stains with fine steel wool, scouring powder, or dampened ashes from your campfire, and occasionally put a drop of oil on the spring and blade joints. When storing it for any length of time, protect the blade by applying a coating of oil or petroleum jelly. Never carelessly leave a knife lying about; stow it away in a safe place or keep it in your pocket, anchored to your belt or pants by a chain, leather thong, or strong cord long enough to permit it to be used without detaching.

A knife should not be used to stir hot food or to poke around in the fire, for heating the blade excessively destroys its *temper* so that it will never again hold a sharp edge. On a cold day, hold the blade in your hands for a few moments to warm it, for an extremely cold blade chips easily.

Opening and Closing a Knife

To open the blade, hold the knife in your left hand, insert your right thumbnail in the notch in the blade, and pull it open. Never allow the fingers of your left hand to rest across the blade slot at any time lest the strong spring snap the blade shut on them with disastrous results. To close the blade, again hold the knife in your left hand and push the back of the blade with your right, being careful, of course, not to place your fingers across the blade slot.

If the blade of a new knife seems stiff and hard to open, apply a few drops of lubricating oil to the spring and use a metal pry to open and close it several times; it will loosen up with continued use.

Sharpening a Knife

Manufacturers sometimes leave a knife blade dull so the new owner can sharpen it to suit his or her own particular taste. For general camp use, extend the *bevel* or sharpened area back only a short distance. If thinned back too far, the blade will be weakened and may chip. If left too rounded, it will be dull. A sharp blade cuts fast and clean and with less effort. It is also much safer, since it bites into the wood instead of sliding off and possibly cutting you or a bystander.

When a knife has been neglected and is quite dull, use a file or handturned grindstone to rough-shape it. Avoid using a power grindstone unless you are quite experienced, for when improperly used, it cuts away too rapidly, overheating the blade and spoiling its temper and thus damaging it permanently. A nick in the blade can be removed by using a file or hand grindstone to cut down the whole edge even with the nick before you put a sharp edge on it.

An *oilstone* or *carborundum stone (whetstone)* is used for the fine edge. The latter is more convenient since water is applied instead of oil to lubricate it to reduce friction and avoid overheating the blade. These stones usually have a coarse side for preliminary fast grinding and a fine one for putting on the finishing touches (*honing* the blade).

If you use a rectangular stone, hold it in your left hand and keep it well lubricated with water or oil. With the knife in your right hand, turn the edge of the blade away from you and elevate the back slightly (about 20°). Using a circular motion, draw the edge of the blade toward you across the stone. Reverse the blade and repeat on the other side, always drawing the blade away from the edge. Continue alternating sides until the blade is sharp. When using a round stone, hold the knife steady and move the stone across the blade with the same circular motion. Now finish by stroking each side of the blade a few times on a piece of leather such as an old belt or leather shoe sole. This removes the *wire edge* or hooked roughness left by the stone.

Test the sharpness of the blade by trying to cut a sheet of paper held between your thumb and forefinger. If the blade is really sharp, it will sever the paper cleanly and easily. If not, repeat the whole sharpening process.

A knife can be kept in good condition by giving it a few strokes on the fine side of the sharpening stone and on a piece of leather after each use. If this is done, you should never have to use the file or coarse side of the carborundum again, unless you are so unfortunate as to get a nick in the blade. Campers should take pride in always keeping their knives sharp and should observe the unwritten law of never lending or borrowing a knife.

Using a Knife

Youngsters can practice whittling on a bar of soap (save the shavings to use later) or a piece of soft wood such as basswood or white pine. Remember that a knife is potentially very dangerous and should never be used carelessly. Always direct your strokes so that you can't possibly cut yourself or anyone else if the knife should slip. Keep your thumb and fingers around the handle, never on the back of the blade where they would close the blade on your fingers if your knife should slide off what you are cutting. Although expert whittlers sometimes violate this rule when doing intricate work, their long practice has given them skill and control a novice does not possess.

Cut with a sliding stroke *straight* down the wood and away from you; never use diagonal strokes that may carry the blade off the wood to cut you. Take your time, and work slowly and deliberately, since haste, carelessness, and overconfidence result in accidents.

If your fingers become red or sore, apply a piece of adhesive tape, an adhesive bandage, or a leather fingerstall to prevent further irritation that would eventually result in a blister.

A knife should be closed whenever you move about, even for a few steps; serious accidents have occurred from tripping while carrying an open knife. When passing a knife to someone else, close it or hand it to them handle first.

After some preliminary practice, you and your campers will be ready to try making such simple, utilitarian items as those descirbed under "Wood Carving" in Chapter 14.

THE SHEATH KNIFE

A *sheath* or *hunting knife* (Fig. 23–1) was indispensable to the pioneers and served them well in many ways. However, a large-bladed knife is heavy and too large for most tasks. Unless it is essential, why not leave it at home and use a pocketknife instead.

Sheath knives come in many styles, sizes, and shapes. If one must be used for camping it is best to choose a rather small one with a fairly narrow, thin blade, 4 to 6 inches long, that slopes gradually from the back of the blade to the sharp edge. Such a blade takes a keen edge and is easy to manipulate. Most modern handles are made of some sort of composition material, although the older types made of horn, hair, or leather still exist. The upright guard just back of the blade serves to prevent your forefinger from slipping onto the blade.

To sharpen and care for a sheath knife, use the same methods described previously for a pocketknife. Place it in its protective sheath when not in use, and when traveling, keep it in your pack or wear it on your belt at the side of your hip where it won't be in the way when you sit down or bend over. When handing it to

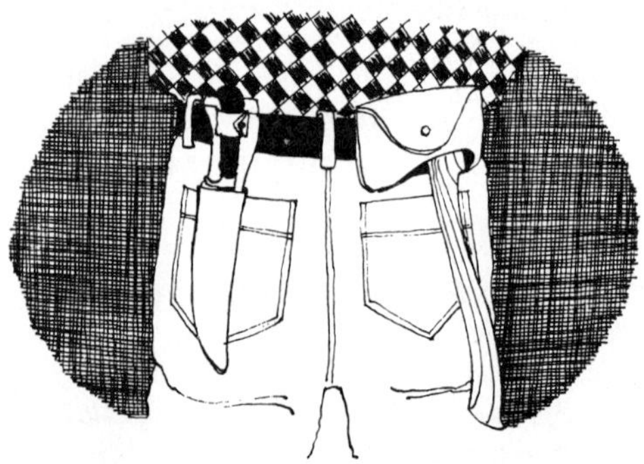

Figure 23–1 Wearing a sheath knife and belt axe.

someone else, extend it handle first with the blade turned upward.

AXES

The need for axes in a camp, like sheath knives, has often been overplayed. They do serve their purpose when actually needed, but many times they should be left at home. This is especially so on extended overnight hiking trips in some areas where there are ample amounts of small dead branches on the ground or fallen trees that can be broken and used for firewood. However, since the axe does serve a purpose in some cases, all campers should learn how to use it properly.

Types of Axes

The axe also was indispensable to the pioneer and played an important role in the settlement of our country. Nearly every area had its own blacksmith who fashioned his product to suit his own preference or that of his customers. Each type of axe was consequently unique to the particular region it came from and so was known as the Maine axe, the Hudson's Bay axe, the Kentucky axe, and so on. The designs of the several types now available are therefore the result of both tradition and adaptation to the purposes they served in various areas. Axes range in length from the little 10 to 13 ½-inch scout axe to the 33-inch axe of the lumberjack and experienced woodsman; they vary in weight accordingly.

DOUBLE-BITTED AND POLE AXES

There are two basic types of axes. The *double-bitted axe* is usually full size and has a *bite* or *blade* (cutting edge) on each side of the head. One edge is usually ground thin and sharp for felling trees while the other is left thicker and stronger for splitting wood. This type of axe is attributed to that legendary hero of the Northwoods, Paul Bunyan, who of course wasn't content to chop like ordinary people but had to have an axe with which he could chop "both coming and going." The champions of the double-bitted axe claim that it is better-balanced and easier to handle than the single-bladed axe,

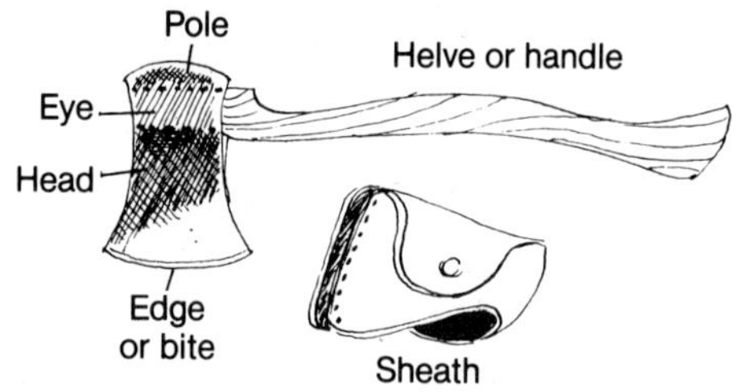

Figure 23–2 Hand axe and sheath.

called a *pole axe.* However, it has little if any place in the usual organized camp, for it is too dangerous for anyone but a mature and experienced person to use.

The head of a *pole axe* has an edge on one side and a flattened area called the *pole* or *poll* on the other. This gives it an advantage over the double-bitted axe because the flattened area can be used as a hammer for such tasks as pounding in tent pegs. The pole axe comes in a wide variety of styles and weights, but we will confine our discussion to the two types most commonly used in organized camps.

THE SCOUT OR HAND AXE

This short 10- to 13½-inch axe weighs from 8 ounces to 1¼ pounds and is recommended for general light camp use. It is sturdy and rugged, inexpensive, light, easy to handle, and will meet your ordinary needs.

It is known by a variety of names, such as *scout axe* or *hatchet,* and since it is held in one hand, it also is called a *hand axe.* It has a protective leather sheath that permits it to be worn on your belt; hence another of its names, the *belt axe.*

SELECTION. Don't try to economize on an axe, for like a knife, a cheap one will likely be poorly balanced and have a blade of inferior steel that won't take or hold a sharp edge. The parts of an axe are indicated in Figure 23–2.

Most handles are made of tough hickory and may be bonded into the eye of the head with epoxy, which usually will hold tight for a long time. Handles also are secured by either (1) a series of screws; (2) a wedge of hard wood; or (3) a wedge of metal driven into the end of the handle to spread it to fit tightly in the eye. Another type of handle consists of a thick layer of composition material or leather over a strip of metal that continues on down to form the head; this type has an advantage in that it can never work loose.

If the handle is made entirely of wood, the grain should be fine and run parallel with the handle. Hold the axe up and sight along the handle to make sure that it is aligned directly with the head. Avoid choosing an axe with a gaily painted handle, for the paint may conceal flaws in the wood or it may irritate your skin as you use the axe. The bump at the end of the handle is to keep it from slipping out of your hand as you use it.

THE CAMP AXE

A *camp* or *three-quarter axe* is smaller and lighter than a full-sized axe, but is sturdy enough to turn out large amounts of work and so is a favorite with counselors and experienced older campers. It has an 18- to 22-inch handle and a slightly larger and heavier head than that of a scout axe, which gives it more power. It should be fitted with a protective sheath with metal rivets or a tough leather buffer strip that fits across the edge.

The *Hudson's Bay axe* is a slightly longer, heavier model that finds favor with many who have heavy work to do.

Taking Your Axe on Trips

As already mentioned, many hikers consider it unnecessary and even inadvisable to take any type of axe along on short trips, for there are usually ample amounts of down wood that can be broken by hand or under your foot. However, if it is necessary to take a scout axe, place it in its sheath and keep it handy in your pack or wear it on your right hip with the blade pointed toward the rear, as shown in Figure 23–1.

A camp axe turns out so much work with so little time and effort that many prefer to take it on extended trips even though its longer handle makes it somewhat inconvenient to handle. If this axe is chosen, place it in its sheath and strap it on the outside of your pack with the blade pointed toward the rear.

Caring for an Axe

Treat your axe like any other fine tool and always keep it in good condition, sharp and ready to go. As with any prized tool, a camper should neither lend nor borrow an axe; you will learn why after going through the painful experience of having to renew the edge on an axe that has been misused.

In cold weather, warm the blade in your hands before using it, since cold metal is brittle and may chip or break.

Inspect the handle of your axe frequently to make sure that it is still tight, for it is easy to see the danger of a loose head on a swinging axe. No matter how tightly a head held in by screws or wedges fits at first, it will probably eventually work loose as the wood dries out. Some may advise you to tighten it by soaking the axe overnight in a pail of water, but this will tighten it only temporarily and it will be looser than ever when the handle dries out. Soaking it in oil will tighten it for a somewhat longer period, but the only really satisfactory method is to drive another wedge into the handle. Use a hacksaw to cut off any portion of the wedge that protrudes.

Never leave an axe lying about where it might cut or trip someone. Drive it firmly into a chopping block, a dead log, or a stump, or replace it in its sheath and put it away.

When carrying an unsheathed axe for even a short distance, turn the blade down and grasp the handle close to the head to keep it from cutting you if you should trip or catch it on underbrush. When handing it to another, hold it by the handle and extend it head first and do not let go until the other person has a firm grip on it.

Sharpening an Axe

Manufacturers often leave an axe dull to allow the new owner to sharpen it to his or her own taste. If the axe is extremely dull or has a nick in the blade, it may need to be rough-shaped with a hand grindstone. Hold the axe so that the stone turns into the blade and keep the stone moist to avoid overheating the blade and ruining its temper.

Follow with the 7- to 10-inch *flat* or *mill file*. Use a large metal washer or use the reamer of your knife to make a wooden guard to slip over the tip of it (Fig. 23–3) to keep your fingers from slipping down onto the edge of the axe. Clamp the axe in a vise or use your hand, foot, or a peg to hold it firmly against a log or block of wood (Fig. 23–3). Kneel on one knee, hold the file in

Figure 23–3 Using a flat file.

one hand, and place the fingers of the other near the tip to keep it at the correct angle. Take long strokes away from the edge and extend the edge back about an inch, tapering it enough to produce a sharp edge but not enough to weaken it so that it will chip or break. Leave the corners of the blade a little thicker since they enter the wood first and so must be strong.

After you have finished with one side, turn the axe over and proceed with the other. Now repeat the whole procedure with the fine side of the file. Finish off by holding the axe between your knees or in one hand and using a carborundum or sharpening stone in circular fashion over both sides to *hone* them (remove the *burr* or *wire* edge).

When an axe is sharp, it does a much faster job, biting in to remove sizeable chips of wood instead of chewing it out in small bits. It is also less likely to glance off the wood and injure you or a bystander. Frequently take a few moments to hone your axe and keep it in tip-top shape, so that you will never again need to use the coarse side of the file or grindstone unless the blade gets a nick.

Using an Axe

Get a solid, broad chopping block, 1 to 2 feet high, and level off the top, making a small depression in the middle to hold the wood. If the block tends to roll, drive stakes in solidly against it on both sides.

Before beginning, look carefully about to make sure there is no one near and no brush or overhanging branches to deflect your axe on the backswing. Wipe the perspiration from your hands frequently, for wet hands are slippery, and keep your hands and legs well out of the way in case your axe should miss or slide off the wood. Chop at a 45-degree angle (Fig. 23–4), never directly across the grain of the wood since this makes little progress and quickly dulls the axe. Aim so that the axe will enter the chopping block after you have severed the stick instead of striking you or the ground, where contact with sand or pebbles will dull or chip it.

When using a scout axe, grasp it close to the end of the handle and kneel on one knee. With a camp axe, stand with your feet comfortably spread and solidly planted on cleared ground. Grasp the axe with your left hand up near the end of the handle and your right fairly well down toward the head. Take a good backswing to get momentum and slide your right hand down to join the left as the axe bites into the wood. Slide your right hand back up the handle again to help lift and control the axe on the backswing, then repeat. Learn to coordinate your whole body in a rhythmic swing, using many muscles, especially the powerful ones in your back, shoulders, and hips. Skilled and powerful chopping, however, depends more on skill and timing than on muscle power. A long backswing creates good momentum that when combined with the pull of gravity and the weight of your axe head, produces power. Work steadily but don't rush; keep your eyes focused constantly on the spot you want to hit and try to score a bull's-eye every time. Rest whenever you get tired, for fatigue lessens coordination and leads to bad accidents. With an axe, a slight miscalculation or a moment of carelessness can re-

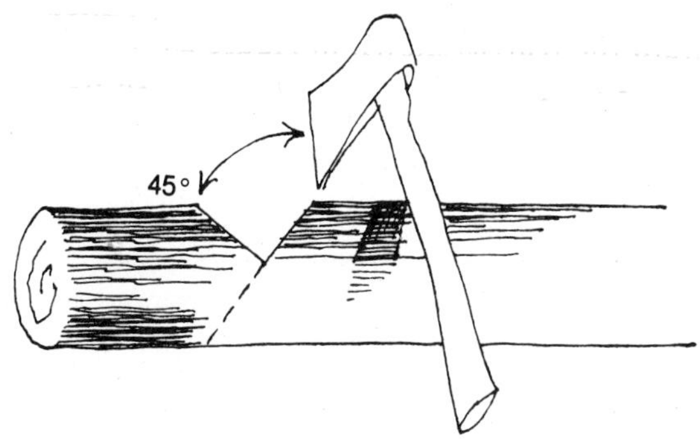

Figure 23–4 Cut at an angle of 45°.

sult in a very serious, disabling injury, so err on the side of being overly cautious.

CUTTING A LOG IN TWO

If the log you want to cut has a tendency to roll, anchor it by driving several stakes in along the sides. If it is small enough to be turned over easily, make a "V" halfway through it on the top side with the top of the "V" as wide as the log is thick. Cut at a 45-degree angle and chop alternately from right and left, using well-aimed, decisive strokes that take out chips frequently. You may need to twist your axe slightly to free them. If your axe sticks in the wood, loosen it by pressing down on the handle slightly. Avoid using a short backswing and timid strokes that merely peck out the wood in fine bits instead of sizeable chips. Remember that "the better the axeman, the fewer the chips." When you have finished the "V" on one side, turn the log over and make another on the other side to meet it. If the log is to be cut into several pieces, complete all the "V's" on one side before turning it over. This leaves the weight and length of the log to steady it as you chop.

If the log is too large to turn over, stand on one side of it and cut fairly wide "V's" across from you, keeping the log between you and your axe for protection. Then step across the log and repeat from the other side. Make your "V's" wide enough to almost meet so that you can complete the job with a few well-aimed blows.

FELLING A TREE

Never cut a standing tree if you can avoid it. Even dead standing trees have their purpose, providing hole nesting birds and other animals a place to live and feed, and helping to maintain a sense of beauty in the natural environment. If it is absolutely necessary to cut a live tree, choose one that is diseased, crooked, or crowded, for you destroy something it will take nature many years to replace. Also be sure this is acceptable with the policies of the land owner or manager.

To sever a small sapling with one stroke, bend it over until the fibers are strained, then give it a sharp blow on top of the bend. For a larger tree (Fig. 23–5), determine in which direction it can fall with the least danger of getting entangled with other growth. Then cut a small *kerf (A)* on the opposite side. Cut another kerf *(B)* a little over halfway through and slightly farther down on the opposite side of the trunk. Slope the tops of the kerfs downward and cut them straight across at the bottom so that they will leave a stump that is flat on top. Push gently on side *A*, and if the tree doesn't fall, take a few more strokes in kerf *A* and try again.

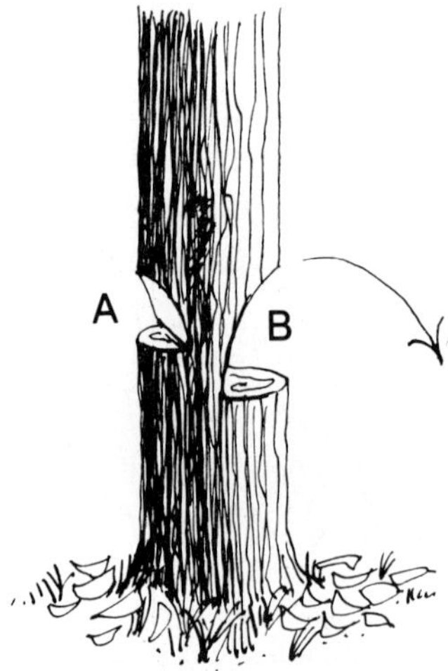

Figure 23–5 Felling a tree.

Kerf *B* acts as a hinge to pull the tree over in the direction you want and it should keep the butt from sliding back to injure you. Nevertheless, play it safe and step quickly out of the way when the tree starts to fall just in case you have miscalculated.

Felling a tree with a saw is even easier and leaves a perfectly flat stump. Use the same principles to direct the fall, sawing a short slit on side *A* and a longer, lower one opposite it at *B*. Then deepen the slit on side *A* until a slight push will send the tree over.

LOPPING OFF BRANCHES

To trim the branches from a fallen tree, stand on one side of it, and starting at the butt end, lop off the lowest branch on the opposite side of the trunk. Sever it as close to the trunk as possible. Continue on up the trunk always keeping the trunk between you and your swinging axe. Then step across the trunk and clear the branches from the other side.

CUTTING SMALL STICKS IN TWO WITH A SCOUT AXE

When cutting small sticks in two, avoid the dangerous practice of simply laying the stick loose on the block and hitting it. This leaves both ends free to fly dangerously through the air.

The *contact method* is one of the safest. Use your left hand to hold the stick crosswise on the block (Fig. 23-6), place your axe on it and bring both axe and stick down simultaneously against the outside edge of the block. If necessary, continue to bring both axe and stick down against the block until the stick is severed. Be sure to direct your strokes so that the axe will enter the block after the stick is severed. With a larger stick, use several strokes, giving the stick a quarter or half turn between each.

SPLITTING KINDLING

Since split wood burns much better than whole sticks with the bark on, it is wise to keep some fine kindling and larger split wood on hand. To use the *contact method*, stand at one side of the chopping block, grasp the piece of wood in your left hand, place your axe on top of it, and bring both wood and axe down simultaneously against the edge of the chopping block (Fig. 23-7*A*). Repeat as many times as necessary to complete a split across the top. Then, turning your axe to face downward in the split, stand the stick upright on the block, remove your left hand and

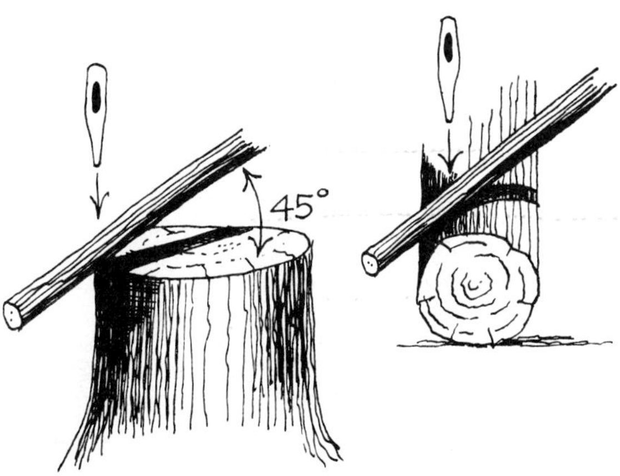

Figure 23-6 Chopping small sticks in two.

Figure 23-7 Contact method of splitting kindling.

bring both axe and wood down against the chopping block. Repeat as many times as necessary to complete the split. To get still finer kindling, split the segments.

If your stick is too large to split by this method, stand it upright on the chopping block,

Figure 23-8 Sharpening a stake.

place your axe on top of it and drive it into the stick with another piece of wood (Fig. 23-7*B*). Never use another axe for this purpose for it is likely to break one or both of them.

You should never use your foot to hold the stick against the chopping block for it is extremely dangerous.

SHARPENING A STAKE

To sharpen a stake, hold it upright on the chopping block and sharpen it on four sides (Fig. 23-8). A four-sided point can be made more quickly and will drive into the ground more easily.

SAWS

Campers often prefer to use a saw to cut large pieces of wood. In comparison with using an axe, it is safer, especially for the inexperienced, wastes less wood, and does the job more quickly and easily. It also leaves the pieces with flat ends, a decided advantage when using them for camp construction or arts and crafts.

A *crosscut saw* or *bucksaw* (Fig. 23-9*A*) is an old favorite for use in camp and there are even some folding types so light and compact that they are suitable to take on trips. Two people use it, one at each side, with each taking turns pulling; no one ever pushes. Keep the frame perpendicular to the wood and do not bear down on it but let the weight of the saw do the biting.

Figure 23-9*B* is a *jackknife saw* featuring a blade that folds into the handle like the blade of a jackknife and is held in place by a wing-nut when in use. It folds to a length of about 12 inches and weighs about 11 ounces.

Figure 23-9*C* is a one-handed *Swede* or *bow saw* with a tublar metal frame curved over the blade like an archer's bow. Several sizes are available, and some weigh as little as 2 pounds and can be dismantled and fitted into a case 12 to 18 inches long.

Figure 23-9*D* shows another popular model that works well for most purposes. The *cable saw* (Fig. 23-10) is the lightest and smallest of all. It consists of a thin, wire-like flexible blade with a handle at each end that can be rolled up into a small coil for carrying. One person can use it for light cutting by holding onto both handles, or two can use it with each holding a handle and standing on opposite sides of the piece to be cut. Unfortunately, this saw is simply too inefficient for cutting a considerable amount of wood.

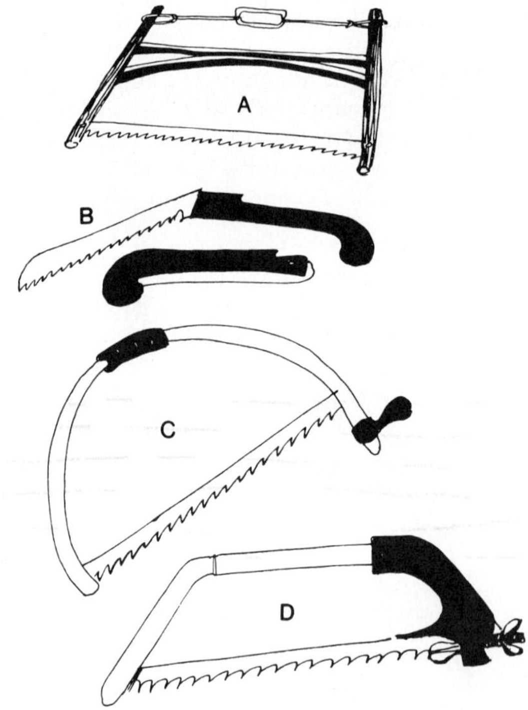

Figure 23-9 Some types of saws.

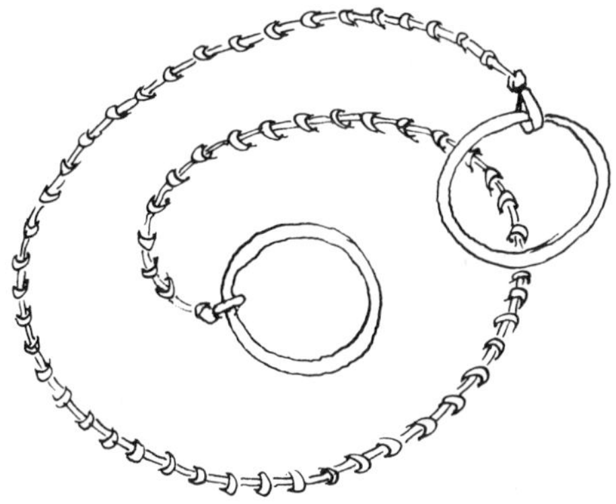

Figure 23-10 Cable saw.

The Sawbuck

If you expect to do much sawing, it will pay you to construct a *sawbuck* or *sawhorse* (Fig. 23-11). Cut and sharpen four sturdy stakes, about 3 to 4 inches thick and 3 feet long, and drive them firmly into the ground in pairs to form "X's." Steady the joints as shown by lashing them with wire or strong cord. Lash or wire a short stick across the bottom of each "X," placing one end inside and the other outside the crossed sticks. Lay the stick or log across the two "X's," stand on the far side, and rest your knee on the stick to steady it. The piece to be sawed off rests just outside the sawbuck; this keeps the saw from binding in the wood.

Figure 23-11 Saw buck.

OTHER TOOLS

When simple tools are readily available, most campers enjoy using them. It is an imposition to ask the caretaker to lend tools; therefore, each living unit should have its own basic set, each painted with a distinguishing color or design so that straying tools can be instantly recognized. Other special or more expensive tools should be kept available at some central place where they can be checked out when needed.

When many people use the same tools, some will invariably be lost or mislaid. A tool board helps to prevent this and allows you to arrange them in an orderly fashion so they can be quickly located. Use a peg board and pegs or make a tool board from any suitable piece of lumber. Lay it flat and place your tools on it in desired locations, then trace the outline of each tool on the board and paint it in solid. Insert nails, hooks, or other suitable holders to suspend each tool and stand or hang the board upright and put the tools in place. Make a card for each tool, with its name and a rough drawing of the tool on it. Punch a hole in the card for hanging it on the board, and file the cards in a box near the board. When borrowing a tool, the user removes its card from the box, signs his or her name on it, enters the date and time, and hangs it on the board in place of the tool. When replacing the tool, the person enters the time and date on the card and refiles it in the box. The outlines of the tools on the board show each person where to replace them and also reveal at a glance which tools are missing. Since people are not always familiar with the correct name of a tool, you may find it advantageous to number as well as name them and file the cards by number.

Hold each user responsible for returning a tool in good condition and occasionally set aside a rainy day or other convenient time to thoroughly recondition them. It is valuable for youngsters to learn to respect good tools and to understand the need to keep them in top condition as well as how to do so.

Provide as large an assortment of tools as possible and add to it as finances permit. Remember that cheap tools are usually inferior and prove to be a poor investment in the long run.

Here is a suggested minimum list for a camp:

(Columbine Girl Scout Council, Inc., Pueblo, Colo.)

Claw hammer
Shovels
Saw and saw files
Cold chisel (⅝″)
Machine oil in a can
Camp axes (20″)
Jigsaw
Rope and nylon cord for lashing
Assortment of nails, tacks, screws, brads, etc.
Strong shoe thread
Bucksaw and sawbuck
Plane
Hand drill
Files (assorted types)
Sandpaper (assorted grades)
Rakes
Brace and bit
Screwdrivers (assorted sizes)
Hand grindstone
Wheelbarrow
Thin copper or picture wire
Tin snips
Post hole digger
Plastic wood
All-purpose cement
Sharp rasp
Binder twine
Pliers with wire cutter (6″ or 8″)
Ice pick
Needles (assorted sizes)
Level
Square
Steel tape measure
Yardstick

ADDITIONAL READINGS

(For an explanation of abbreviations and abbreviated forms used, see page 13.)

Knife, Axe, Etc.

Aller, Doris: *Sunset Wood Carving Book.* Lane, 1964, 95 pp.
Angier: *Skills for Taming the Wilds,* ch. 8.
Ball, A.: *Wood Carving For Fun and Profit.* Exposition.
Better Homes and Gardens Family Camping Book, ch. 15.
Cardwell: *America's Camping Book,* ch. 8.
Jaeger: *Wildwood Wisdom.*
Knife and Axe (no. 19-6318). Girl Scouts, 1953, 40 pp., paper.

Langer: *The Joy of Camping*, ch. 6.
Mason: *The Junior Book of Camping and Woodcraft.*
Miracle and Decker: *The Complete Book of Camping*, chs. 8, 9.
Riviere: *Backcountry Camping*, ch. 8.
Riviere: *The Camper's Bible*, ch. 6.
Rutstrum: *The New Way of the Wilderness.*

Tools, Whittling, Camp Construction

Anderson, (H.S.) Andy: *How to Carve Characters in Wood.* U. of New Mexico, 77 pp.
Beard, D. C.: *Shelters, Shacks and Shanties.* Scribner's, 1972, 243 pp.
Carlson, Bernice W.: *Make It and Use It.* Abingdon, 1958, 160 pp., paper.
Fun With Tools (No. BL-25). Boys' Life. (Articles reprinted from Boys' Life)
Furniture You Can Make. Lane, 2nd ed., 1971, paper.
Gottshall, Franklin: *Wood Carving and Whittling Made Easy.* Bruce, 1963, 128 pp.
Gross, Chaim: *The Technique of Wood Sculpture.* Arco, 1964, 136 pp.
Gross, Fred (ed.): *How to Work with Tools and Wood.* Pocket Books, 1955.
Hoppe, H.: *Whittling and Woodcarving.* Sterling, 1969, 48 pp.
Hunt, W. Ben: *Ben Hunt's Big Book of Whittling.* Bruce, 1970, 182 pp.
Hunt: *Golden Book of Crafts and Hobbies*, pp. 108–111.
Ickis: *Book of Arts and Crafts*, chs. I, X.
Jeffrey, Harry R.: *Wood Finishing.* Bennett, 1957, 112 pp., paper.
Leavitt, Jerome E.: *Carpentry for Children.* Sterling, 1959, 96 pp.(Grades 2–6).
Leeming, Joseph: *Fun With Wood.* Lippincott, 1942, 111 pp.
Maintenance and Care of Hand Tools (No. WI 35:9–867). Supt. of Documents.
Miracle and Decker: *The Complete Book of Camping*, ch. 10.
Ormond: *Complete Book of Outdoor Lore*, ch. 13.
Ormond: *Outdoorsman's Handbook*, pp. 119–150.
Peterson, Harold A.: *American Knives.* Scribner's, 1958 (A history of knives)
Pioneering (No. 3382). Boy Scouts, 1967, 64 pp., paper.
Rood, John: *Sculpture in Wood.* U. of Minn., 1950, paper.
Rowlands, John J.: *Cache Lake Country.* Norton, 1947.
Rutstrum, Calvin: *The Wilderness Cabin.* Macmillan, rev., 1972, 194 pp., paper.
Sunset Ideas for Building Barbecues. Lane, 1971, 72 pp.
Tangerman, E. J.: *Whittling and Woodcarving.* Dover, 1962, 293 pp., paper.
Toolcraft, Girl Scouts, rev., (Flip charts)
van der Smissen, and Goering: *A Leader's Guide to Nature-Oriented Activities*, pp. 44–49.
Waltner, Elma: *Carving Animal Caricatures.* Dover, 1972, paper. (Grades 7 –12.)
Woodcarving (No. 3315). Boy Scouts, 1966, 48 pp., paper.
Woodcraft Techniques and Projects (by Sunset Editors). Lane.
Woodwork (No. 3316A). Boy Scouts, 1970, 64 pp., paper.

MAGAZINE ARTICLES

Backpacker Magazine:
Blumenfeld, Jonathan, and Lionel Atwill: "Backpacking Blades." Dec./Jan., 1981, p. 52.
Boys' Life:
Green, Bar Bill: "Time for Pioneering." Oct., 1965, p. 30. (How to construct a monkey bridge).
Wagner, Glenn: "Start a Home Workshop." Aug., 1963.
Wagner, Glenn: "The Adirondack Lean To." Sept., 1962, pp. 72–73.
Wheeler, Alan: "Wilderness Engineering." June, 1972, p. 36.
Camping Magazine.
Cassel, Sylvia: "Make Whittling Worthwhile." June, 1954.
Cassel, Sylvia: "Try Hiking Sticks," Mar., 1952.
Jaeger, Ellsworth: "Making Belts and Necklaces From Twigs." Jan., 1950.
Melamed, Monte: "Easy-to-Make Bench Using Chimney Blocks as Base." June, 1965, p. 27.
Melamed, Monte: "Easy-to-Make Small Parts Bin." June, 1964, p. 13.
Wilderness Camping:
Dodd, Harvey: "The Cutting Edge." Feb./Mar., 1977, p. 14. (Knives)

twenty-four
Tents and Shelters

Aloft I raise my Shield; the pelting Rain
And rattling Hail assault my Slope in vain.
The burning Sun, the Weight of Winter Snow
Alike I scorn—then rest secure below.

—From Mottoes*

*Published by permission of Western Brick Company.

THE IDEAL SHELTER

Campers sometimes go on overnight or even longer trips and at night merely curl up in their jungle hammocks, sleeping bags, or blankets. You may, in fact, prefer to lie out in the open under a star-spangled sky where you can enjoy to the fullest the sounds, sights, and smells of nature. This is fine in good weather or when there is shelter nearby to flee to when a storm threatens; however, on extended trips or when the forecast calls for possible thunderstorms, you will need to carry some sort of shelter. Don't be misled into thinking that in bad weather you can remain snug, dry, and happy for long with only a sleeping bag and ground cloth for protection. In addition, when working with youngsters, remember that they feel great excitement at the mere idea of living in a tent, for to them it is the very essence of camping.

An ideal tent would be quick and easy to set up and take down, be lightweight and compact to carry, offer absolute protection against rain, insects, and forest creatures, provide privacy, and be cool and well-ventilated in summer, yet warm on cool nights. Unfortunately, such a combination of virtues just isn't possible. This explains the several hundred varieties of tents now on the market, as each manufacturer attempts to produce one that is superior to those of the competition.

TYPES OF TENTS

Some modern tents are merely variations on old ideas, while others use refreshing new approaches. Most tentmakers now take advantage of a recent wave of new materials and technologies to produce tents that are lighter, roomier, and sturdier than ever before. Many now feature light flexible tubular poles made of fiberglass and aluminum alloys. Some tents have folding aluminum or plastic frameworks that you can erect in as little as 90 seconds. Others, such as free-standing tents (Figs. 24–4 and 24–5) are suspended from a framework, thus eliminating the need for pegs and guy lines, and are stable enough to pick up and move about. *Pop-up tents* usually have a light, collapsible, compact framework of aluminum that springs into an igloo-shaped structure almost as quickly as you can open an umbrella. *Wing tents* give added room through flies that extend like wings from two or more of the corners.

In addition to the large tents most suitable for a permanent resident camp, there are a vast number of newer *alpine tents* (also called *timberline, mountaineering,* or *backpacking* tents) that are more suitable for trip camping with backpack or canoe. These are made of very lightweight material but are strong enough to hold up in severe weather conditions, such as extreme cold, snow, blizzards, and winds up to 100 miles an hour. They must be very rugged and constructed to conserve heat while providing adequate ventilation for living and even cooking. Also, there must be enough room to shelter the people and their gear, yet compact and light enough to carry in a backpack.

Tents Classified by Shape

In general, we can roughly classify tents into four or five basic types according to shape, but there are many hybrids that combine characteristics of the various types.

CONICAL AND PYRAMIDAL TENTS. These tents (Fig. 24–1), which are usually tall, were formerly erected with a center pole that was always in the way like a sore thumb; however, they now feature other means of support. Their steeply sloped sides shed rain very quickly, which makes them especially well suited to open-plains country where there are often sudden and severe storms. They are sturdy and serve nicely in a permanent or semi-permanent camp, since, in the large sizes, several campers can bed down, lying with their feet toward the center and their bodies arranged like the spokes of a wheel. However, the bulk and weight of these tents usually make them impractical for light-trip camping.

Tepee. The *tepee* (Fig. 24–2) of the plains Indians has no bothersome pole in the center and features smoke flaps that adjust to let the smoke escape when you want to build a small fire inside for warmth or cooking. Not too much waterproofing is required, since the steep walls quickly shed water.

Miner's Tent. (Fig. 24–1, Top). This tent, once a favorite, is seldom seen now. It is supported by either a center pole or a rope attached to the peak and thrown across a tree limb. It accommodates two or three campers and is tall enough to stand up in.

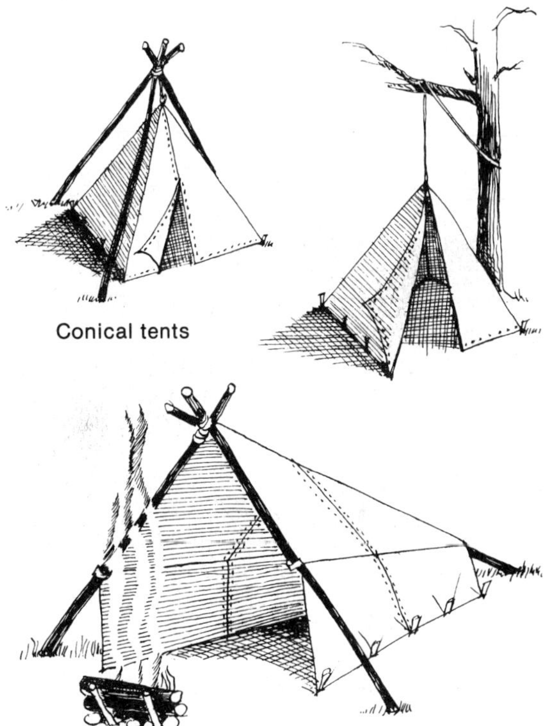

Figure 24-1 Tents.

Umbrella Tent. This rather heavy, bulky tent is sometimes used for family camping or for

Figure 24-2 The tepee is a popular tent for a permanent or semi-permanent campsite.

long trips where transportation is not too much of a problem and the occupants expect to stay put for some time. It is easy to erect, has ample headroom and has a front porch for light cooking. The usual sizes accommodate three to five campers and flaps can be added at the sides of the canopy to house two or three more. Early models were supported by a center pole with side supports that spread out like the ribs of an umbrella, but some of the newer models are suspended from a frame or have side poles that leave the center unobstructed.

WEDGE OR "A" FRAME TENTS. *Wedge or "A" tents* are favorites for light-trip camping, since they are relatively light, are easy to pitch, and furnish adequate shelter for the average summer backpacker. The steep roof sheds rain well and some models are tall enough to permit standing.

Pup Tent. The familiar *pup tent* design has long been a standby for short-term camping. It is just large enough to provide a crawl-in type shelter for two people and their duffel. However, the cramped quarters may prove a bit frustrating during a prolonged rainy spell unless supplementary facilities are available. Many modern backpacker tents are variations of the pup tent and, when made of light materials, they may weigh as little as 2 or 3 pounds. When poles are required, collapsible ones made of lightweight aluminum can be used. In wooded country the smaller models need no poles, since they can be supported on a rope strung between two trees or bushes.

Explorer Tent. The *explorer tent* is amazingly roomy and has enough headroom to permit standing. You can pitch it by stringing ropes from loops on top of the tent and throwing them across the limb of a tree or by using an inside "T" pole. This tent is easy to pitch and strike and sometimes has a screened window in the rear to improve ventilation. It is well adapted to winter camping, since you can build a fire in front of the open door. It is a favorite for canoe, pack animal, or automobile camping, but it is not light enough for backpacking. Some types reduce weight and bulk by sloping and narrowing toward the rear.

Wall Tent. (Fig. 24-3). This ever-popular tent is most commonly used for permanent sleeping quarters at the main camp or when a party expects to remain in the same place for

Figure 24-3 Wall tent.

Figure 24–4 Low-profile dome tent with flexible poles.

several weeks. It provides ample headroom and the sides can usually be rolled up for free ventilation. It comes in a variety of sizes, but it is usually too bulky and heavy for light-trip use.

LEAN-TO TENTS. Lean-to tents, which can be used in summer, are also suitable for cold-weather camping, because the canopy over the open front will catch the heat from a reflector fire and reflect it inside onto the sleepers. A small fire for cooking can also be built in front of the opening. The walls slope toward the rear to reduce weight and they shed rain well.

Camper Tent. The *camper tent* has a short ridge and a front porch, and requires two poles for pitching.

Baker Tent. This is a great favorite for a permanent or semi-permanent camp. It is adaptable to both summer and cold-weather use but cannot withstand the high winds characteristic of some areas. It is especially suitable for automobile or station wagon camping, because the canopy can be suspended from the vehicle to provide added privacy and space. It is really like half a wall tent, with a versatile flap that can be used as an awning in sunny weather or lowered over the front to shut out rain.

DOME, BOX AND TUNNEL TENTS. Increasing interest is now being focused on the new lightweight *dome, box* and *tunnel tent* designs that are especially popular for backpacking. Most of these are free standing, with a canopy hung from a self-supporting frame (Figs. 24–4 and 24–5) so they can be set up anywhere with a minimum of stakes and guy lines. Recent advances in flexible pole materials have simply revolutionized the market. Their primary advantage is that there is nearly 50 percent more volume than in an "A" frame tent with the same floor space because the sidewalls are more vertical. This makes them more comfortable to live in when the occupants become stormbound.

TENT FEATURES

Size and Weight

Tents vary in size from the huge summer-cottage varieties intended to be transported by automobile or truck to the small crawl-in types suited primarily for overnight sleeping or protection during a downpour. Campers can usually

(Boy Scouts of America, North Brunswick, N.J.)

save both weight and money by buying tents that are only large enough for their specific needs. A floor size of at least 5 × 7 feet is needed for two or more adults.

Since only the larger outfitters carry a complete line of tents and have enough room to set them up, you may want to consult the catalogues of some of the dealers listed in Appendix E to find out what is available. To help you to visualize the actual size of a tent, use string or rope to make a mock-up of it; then get in it with your sleeping bag and duffel. How does it feel?

Waterproofing vs. Water Repellency

Since one of the most important functions of a tent is to protect its occupants and their equipment from rain and heavy dew, we need to understand the difference between a waterproofed and a water repellent material. A *waterproofed* material is impervious to rain because the individual fibers have been treated with a waterproofing substance or because the material has been coated with one.

Although a waterproofed material may sound ideal, it has certain disadvantages. Waterproofing makes the material heavier and stiffer, and in time the treatment may crack and lose its effectiveness, necessitating a retreatment. In addition, it is obvious that a surface that won't let moisture in won't let it out either. Therefore, in a tightly closed tent, the pint or more of moisture that each occupant gives off during the night through breathing and perspiration remains in the tent. As the evening progresses and the air cools off, this moisture condenses upon contact with the cooler tent walls and ceiling and can eventually drop down on the sleepers below, making them and their gear almost as wet as if they had been out in a rain.

Water repellent materials, on the other hand, are made of coated fibers or of fibers that are very closely woven. A tent made of water repellent material may prove satisfactory during a light rain, especially if it has a steep roof to drain the water off rapidly and is pitched tautly, leaving no wrinkles or folds to collect and hold moisture. However, in areas that frequently have heavy or steady rains, water repellent materials alone will not prove satisfactory.

Ventilation and Insect Screening

Another problem with a tightly closed waterproof tent is that it will not freely admit oxygen. As the night wears on, a sleeper uses up much of the available oxygen, replacing it with carbon dioxide; the result may well be a severe headache, nausea, and general malaise. Inadequate ventilation can have much more serious consequences when a camper succumbs to the temptation to avoid foul weather and cooks inside the tent with a portable stove. This is extremely dangerous, because the burning process creates the insidious killer, carbon monoxide, which can make the camper feel drowsy and, in extreme cases, may eventually cause unconsciousness. Records show that this fatal result has occurred in all too many cases.

Figure 24-5 Free-standing dome tent with netted door and rain fly (partially rolled up).

Fabrics that do allow the passage of air are said to be "breathable." It is obvious that a tent has breathability in inverse proportion to how waterproof and airtight it is, so that even one which is merely water repellent will need some means of ventilation. There are various ways to provide this.

At one extreme are the tarpaulin shelter and the time-honored pup tent, which, being open at both ends, obviously admit plenty of air as well as numerous unwanted flying and crawling creatures. Don't consider going on a trip without adequate protection from blood-thirsty pests, for no trip can be fun with them as tent mates. The better tents have screened doors, which usually open with one or more zippers, as well as vents or windows. There should be rain shields to adequately cover them, preferably ones you can manipulate from inside.

The Tent Fly

A *tent fly* (Fig. 24-5) consists of a separate piece of waterproofed material that is suspended above the tent itself, and it solves the problem of protecting a tent that is only water repellent. The advantage of this is that the fly keeps out the rain, but condensation of body moisture and carbon dioxide is allowed to escape through the breathable inner walls of the tent and dissipate in the space between the roof and the fly. Should any moisture condense on the inside of the fly, it will run down the sides to the ground outside the tent. Yet another advantage of the fly is that it keeps a tent warmer in the winter by helping to hold heat in and shed the wind and it also keeps the tent cooler in summer if it is pitched in the sun.

The fly should always be pitched steeply enough to shed water quickly and it should extend well out beyond the tent eaves and walls so that a slanting rain will not blow in and the dripping from the rain will be well outside the tent walls. The fly should be constructed so that it never touches the tent walls or ceiling.

Shelter Fabrics

COTTON. Prior to World War II, cotton was used in nearly all tents and shelters, usually in such forms as canvas, drill, duck, twill, or poplin. Now, however, it is rarely used except in heavy tents for family or long-term camping or in tents for those who value economy above lightness and compactness. In addition to its heaviness, cotton has other disadvantages: it has a low tear strength and it tends to mildew or rot when exposed to moisture and not promptly dried out. On the positive side, however, cotton is cheaper than most synthetics and can be tightly woven into a water repellent fabric whose fibers swell when wet to further close up the air spaces between them. Its fibers also readily accept and retain waterproofing.

NYLON. Shelters made of some form of nylon are now chosen by most light-trip campers. Although more expensive than cotton, it is ultra-light and can be compressed into a very small bundle for packing. Two forms are common: a smooth fabric called *nylon taffeta* and *ripstop nylon,* which has heavier fibers interspersed at quarter-inch intervals to give it added strength and to prevent tears from spreading farther down the fabric. Nylon has good tear strength, will not rot or mildew, and dries out quickly when wet. Tightly woven nylon is water repellent and will prove satisfactory in a light rain, but in a heavy or continuous downpour, the rain will sift through the material as a fine mist. Therefore, a waterproof fly should be used over the roof of the tent, as described earlier. Manufacturers usually treat the flooring of the tent and the fly cover with polymer, polyurethane, or vinyl in order to keep the rain out. This, of course, adds weight but the nylon will still be lighter than cotton. Unfortunately, the coating may eventually crack and disintegrate, necessitating a retreatment.

NEW MATERIALS. New materials constantly appear under various trade names, such as Gore-Tex or Klimate, as manufacturers vie with each other to find the "perfect" material that is breathable but won't let water in. Investigate these but don't embrace them too enthusiastically until they have stood the test of time, for continued hard usage will often reveal drawbacks that weren't apparent at first.

You can buy various shelter materials from outfitters (see Appendix E) to make a tent or shelter on your own sewing machine. You will find directions in some of the references listed in the bibliography at the end of this chapter. Kits also are available from some outfitters.

COLOR. Tent color is largely a matter of personal preference. White and light colors reflect rather than absorb the sun's rays and so are cooler in summer, but they also soil easily, attract insects, and tend to silhouette the occupants at night to provide an impromptu movie for the neighbors. Although some people prefer the cheery and flamboyant blues, yellows, oranges, and reds now available, true nature lovers are likely to stick to more somber hues, such as khaki, olive-drab, soft brown, or green, which blend in better with woodland surroundings.

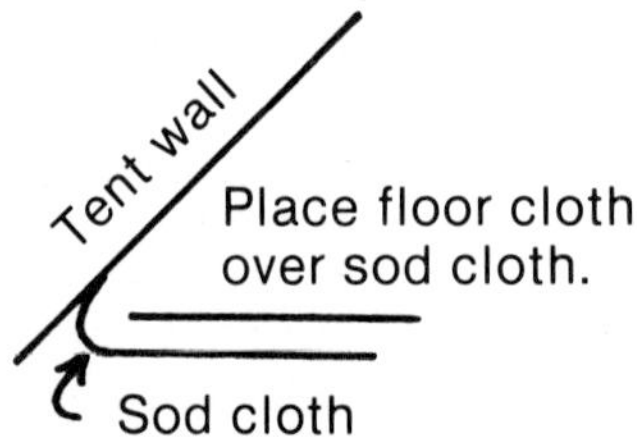

Figure 24–6 Sod cloth in place inside tent wall.

Flooring

Some large tents and almost all alpine or backpacking tents come with a waterproof tent floor already sewn in. This should be a *tub floor,* so called because it extends 6 to 18 inches up the tent wall to form a shallow "tub" that prevents ground water from entering the tent.

Tents without sewn-in floors should have a *sod cloth* (Fig. 24–6), which is a strip of material 6 to 18 inches wide that extends inward from the bottom of the tent wall. You can then overlap it with a waterproof *ground cloth* to produce a floor that is impervious to ground water and things that fly, crawl, and creep. A tarp of waterproof nylon serves nicely, or you can even use a piece of polyethylene, although it won't last as long. Dirt and abrasion are the arch enemies of a tent floor, so take off your hiking shoes before you enter and clean the floor daily (a small whisk broom is ideal for this). One advantage of the detachable floor cloth is that it is easier to clean and replace when necessary.

Tent Poles

For backpacking, tent supports must be light and simple and quick to erect in case of sudden rain. Some poles telescope; others come apart and nest together for easy packing. Still others come in sections that are held together by *shock cords* (bands of rubber sheathed in nylon running up through the hollow centers), which make the poles easy to assemble and help to prevent loss. Light poles are made of tubular aluminum, duraluminum, fiberglass, or a still lighter material, magnesium, and each weighs 2 ounces or less.

Tent Pegs

Tents often come without tent pegs so that the owner can select the proper type for the conditions under which the tent will be used. Because of the urgent need for forest conservation, the day is gone and should be forgotten when campers could simply go out and use a knife and axe to cut and shape their own tent pegs; if your tent needs stakes, plan to take them with you. Figure 24–7*A* shows a variety of tent pegs that can be purchased or made. Some manufactured ones are of the twisted skewer type and are available in aluminum or chrome alloy steel. They are strong and drive easily, and are especially suited for use in pebbly ground, although they will hold well almost anywhere. Others nest together for compactness and can be held together with a rubber band. Lightweight plastic T-pegs are inexpensive but quite durable and will not bend as aluminum sometimes does.

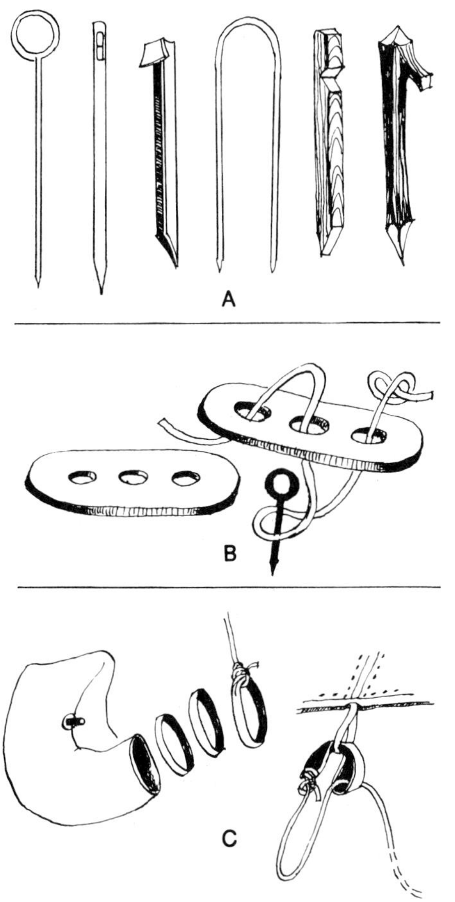

Figure 24-7 A) Tent pegs, B) tent adjusters and C) rubber bands from an inner tube.

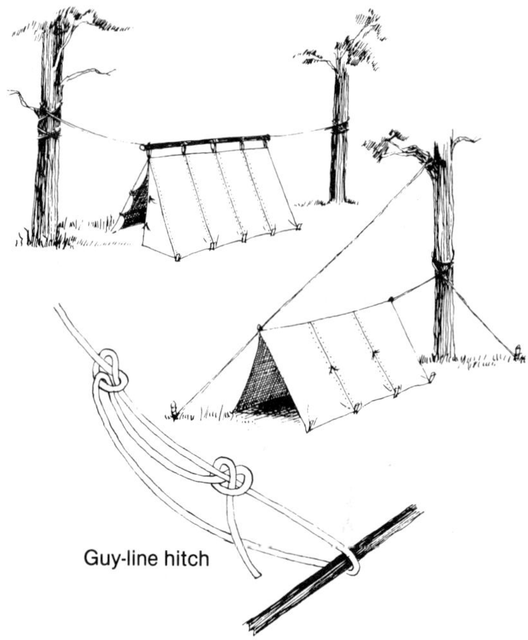

Figure 24-8 Ways to use trees in tent or tarp pitching.

Modern stakes are inexpensive and extremely light, but of course, in backpacking every ounce counts, so travelers in woodland areas usually take as few as possible, anchoring their tarp or tent lines to rocks, trees, or even bushes. Figure 24–8 shows some ways to do this. By using a *guy line hitch*, the rope may be adjusted by sliding the lower knot up and down. The hitch also can be used when tying guy ropes to tent pegs.

Figure 24–7*B* shows some tent adjusters. These are available in nylon or aluminum and are used to adjust tent lines to the proper degree of tension. Each adjuster has three holes in it and the line is threaded up through one end hole, down through the center hole, around the tent peg, up through the other end hole, and then tied or knotted. To adjust it, pull the guy line slack and slide the adjuster to a new position.

The adjuster takes the place of the time-honored taut line hitch that is used for this purpose. Each adjuster weighs only 1 ounce and costs very little.

Tent Lines

A roll of 100-pound test nylon cord provides the best tent lines, for it is quite strong, does not shrink when wet and resists mildew and rotting. Parachute cord, number 5 manila rope, and window sash cord are also acceptable. You can make the lines waterproof by periodically rubbing them with beeswax or melted paraffin. Be sure your rope is strong enough to withstand high winds and storms. A 1- to 1½-inch wide strip of strong automobile inner tube added to your rope and passed through the tarp or tent grommets or beckets (Fig. 24–7C) will give extra flexibility for protection against damage from high winds.

SELECTING A TENT

When choosing a tent, consider such factors as means of transportation, the duration of your camping trips, how often and how long you expect to use it, what seasons you will be using it in, such climatic conditions as rainfall, winds, and temperatures, the need for protection from insects, and the *state of your finances.*

As with many other purchases, you will usually get just about what you pay for, so buy the best tent you can afford. When properly cared for, a quality tent will give you many years or even a lifetime of satisfactory service. Before making a final choice as to size, shape, and other features, you may want to rent or borrow several models to try out.

Select a tent made of good-quality fabric that is lightweight and closely woven. The tent should have wide felled seams, and all seams should have two rows of double stitching, with at least 8 or 10 stitches to the inch. The thread should be nylon or Dacron. There should be reinforcement at points of friction or strain, such as corners and peaks, where loops are attached, and where poles or pegs come in contact with the material. Be sure there is adequate ventilation and insect protection. Zippers should be heavy duty and made of noncorroding material. Check to see that all specified pegs, poles, guy lines, and the stuff bag and other extra equipment are actually included in the package.

An extremely inexpensive tent is likely to become an expensive headache in the long run, since it will probably wear out quickly and perform poorly. Such a tent is often made of leaky, nondurable material and is not cut squarely, so that you can never pitch it quite right. The seams may be so poorly constructed that they pull out or fail to brace the material to give it the added strength needed. They may be sewn with that abomination, the "chain stitch," which pulls out completely as soon as you break one thread. *Grommets,* or the metal rings inserted for attaching lines may be so poorly anchored in the material that they quickly pull out as soon as they are subjected to the strain of strong winds. *Beckets* are the loops along the bottom of the tent walls that are slipped over pegs when pitching the tent; be sure they are well made and strongly reinforced. Although it is occasionally possible to get an inexpensive tent that will fulfill your ordinary camp needs, don't trust your own judgment unless you know tents or can get expert advice. It is wise, if you can afford it, to buy a tent made by a reputable tent maker who takes pride in the product and is willing to stand behind it.

USE AND CARE OF TENTS

Care of Your Tent in Camp

Air out your tent thoroughly on sunny days and roll up the flaps with the edges inside where they won't catch and hold dew. Keep your tent floor clean; dirt, leaves, and other debris are messy and can damage the fabric and promote mildew. During wet weather it is helpful to place a doormat of old burlap outside to use as a "shoe scraper." Keep an extra pair of soft shoes just inside the door to slip into as you enter the tent. A little warm water on a cloth or sponge will remove mud, pitch or sap, or other dirt from inside the tent.

Packing

Your tent will repay you with a longer life and better service if you care for it properly. To pack your tent, fold it neatly, but avoid creasing

(Columbine Girl Scouts Council, Inc., Pueblo, Colo.)

it repeatedly in the same places or the fabric will eventually break down there. Roll the folded tent into a narrow, compact bundle, using your knee to exert pressure, and shape it to fit into your tent stuff bag. This bag simplifies carrying the tent and also protects it from dirt and wear. For a small tent, you can make your own stuff bag or you can use a gunny, flour, or feed sack with a drawstring at the top.

TARP AND PONCHO SHELTERS

A *tarp (tarpaulin)* is a versatile piece of equipment that is almost worth its weight in gold; you can cover your duffel with it, use it as a ground cloth for your tent or bedroll, convert it into almost any type of shelter desired, erect it as a dining porch or cooking area, use it as a fly over your tent, or string it between two trees to serve as a windbreak. You can use it as an emergency stretcher by pinning it with blanket pins or lashing it through its grommets to two long poles and you can even use a light tarp as a sail.

For summer camping in mild climates, many backpackers prefer a tarp or poncho shelter to a tent. A tarp usually has grommets or tie tapes along all four sides for attaching it to guy lines and tent pegs, and the variety known as a poly tarp has five additional tie tapes strategically located on the center area to offer additional possibilities. Some tarps have snaps along the sides, allowing you to snap two of them together to form one large surface.

Several ways to construct a tarp or poncho shelter are shown in Figure 24-9, and an ingenious camper can devise dozens of others. You can use one end as a ground cloth, stretching the other above you as a shelter. You will not actually need tent pegs since you can weight the edges down with rocks. Since tarp shelters are particularly vulnerable in high winds, keep them low to minimize wind ballooning.

Tarps are available in most tent materials and come in a variety of sizes, weights, and colors. A popular choice is one 9 × 12 feet, that is made of waterproofed ripstop nylon. This type will shelter two adults, weighs only about a pound, and folds into a small, compact package that can be carried in an outside pocket of your packsack. A tarp should be lap felled and double stitched around the edges with nylon or Dacron thread. Since a tarp shelter is open at both ends, you will have no trouble with condensation or lack of ventilation, but you will need some form of protection in insect country.

A still lighter and cheaper tarp is a sheet of thin, transparent *plastic* or *polyethylene,* such as painters use for dropcloths and farmers use for various purposes. It is available in 2 mil (.002 inch) or 3 mil (.003 inch) thicknesses at paint and hardware stores. Outfitters carry a superior translucent type in a 4 mil thickness. Although easily torn, it is stronger than it looks, is completely waterproof, and is so inexpensive that campers consider it expendable and often take along several sheets to use as a ground cloth, to keep the wood for their campfire dry, or to shelter themselves and their gear. It can be converted into an emergency poncho by cutting a hole in the center. The cheapest way to buy it is in rolls of 100 feet, which you can then cut to the size you need. Since exposure to flame will "wilt" or burn it, use care around an open fire.

Ely* suggests reinforcing the sheet by means of a 150 foot length of ½-inch wide adhesive filament tape (sometimes called acetate-backed, glass-reinforced strapping tape). Place strips of tape around the four edges of the plastic and both ways across the center. Add three or four strips across the piece in both directions and finish with two strips running diagonally between opposite corners.

Since holes made in plastic will quickly tear out, you will have to devise some other way to attach lines for pegs and guy lines. A special device called a *Visklamp* (Fig. 24–10) works nicely. It consists of a small rubber ball and a clamp with two holes in it. To use it, pick the spot to attach a guy line, gather up the plastic, twist it a few times around the ball to secure it, and pass both ball and plastic up through the larger hole in the Visklamp. Now slide both ball and plastic down to the smaller hole and attach the guy line to the larger hole.

Figure 24–10 also shows simple, do-it-yourself "buttons" for attaching guy lines. To make these, place a bit of the plastic around a small stone or a wad of paper, grass, or dirt, and secure it with a bit of string or twine. Tie these buttons at the corners and at frequent intervals along the edges of the plastic, then use a slip knot to attach the guy lines to the buttons. Since poly tents tend to balloon in the wind, stabilize them by tying ropes diagonally across between the corners, as shown in Figure 24–10.

If you want to add ends to your shelter, use pieces of plastic, or a poncho, tarp, or raincoat. To make a door in a piece of plastic, place strips of adhesive filament tape along the edges of the opening or turn back the edge around a small stick and fuse the materials together with a little gentle heat.

Since plastic is so fragile and easily torn, avoid walking on it or laying it over sticks, stones, or rough surfaces. Even with great care, it will probably last only a week or two, but it does provide a cheap emergency shelter. Its very inexpensiveness and expendability, however, have created a serious problem. Travelers now report that the landscape is marred by bits and pieces of plastic discarded by selfish or ignorant campers that clutter up the landscape and create eyesores for all who follow. Never be guilty of this serious breach of outdoor etiquette—take every scrap you brought out back with you and take time to remove fragments left by others.

A *plastic tube tent* (Fig. 24–11) is a popular variation of the plastic sheet shelter and is commonly used by backpackers. You can buy such tents or make your own from rolls of tubing available from outfitters in 3-foot diameters and 3 or 4 mil thicknesses. You can suspend the tent across a line tied between two trees. It provides its own ground cloth and no tent pegs are necessary since the weight of your body and duffel will hold it down. The tent has the same advantages and disadvantages found in the plastic tarp shelter. With care, it will last a week or two.

*Ely, Ron: "The Polytarp." *Boy's Life,* Mar., 1967.

Figure 24-9 Tarp and lean-to shelters.

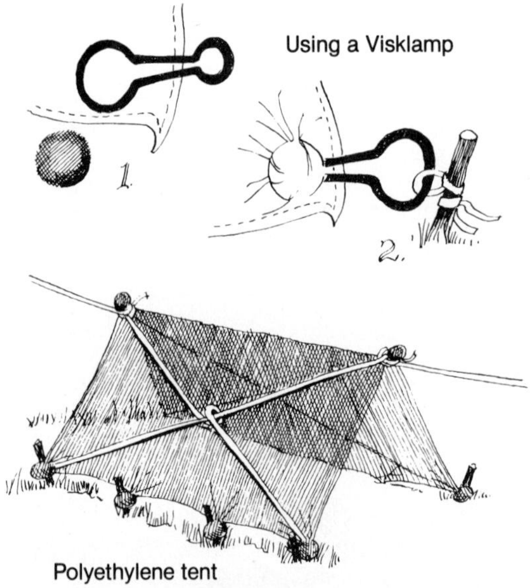

Figure 24–10 Constructing a tarpaulin shelter.

Carry a few plastic spring clothespins with you to keep the tube in place on the supporting line and to pin up the ends to keep out ground water and blowing rain. You can also make a doorsill by propping up a few inches of the plastic across some of your gear. Since plastic is airtight, you must be careful not to completely close off both ends. Tube tents can be erected in just a few minutes, weigh only about a pound per person, and cost very little; these qualities probably account for their popularity. Tube tents are also available in coated nylon, which lasts much longer but weighs and costs more. You can add beckets of doubled-over cloth or adhesive tape.

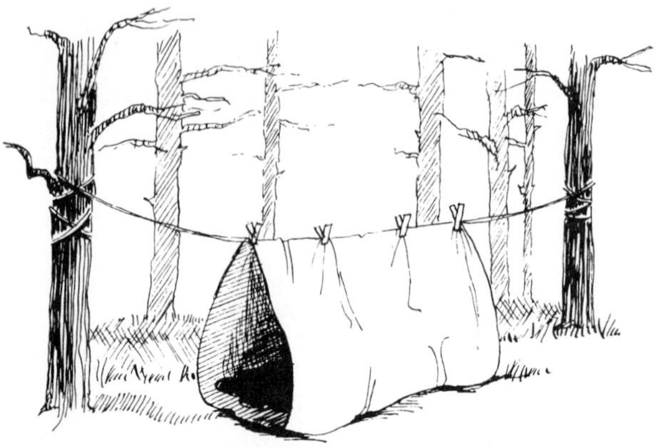

Figure 24–11 Plastic tube shelter.

BUILDING SHELTERS

Campers often like to construct Indian tepees (Fig. 24–2) by lashing the tops of 5 to 20 poles together and then spreading them out at the bottom in a large circle to serve as a base for a hand-decorated cover of waterproofed canvas or other tent material. (The Indians used birch bark, buffalo hides, or deer skins.) You can find directions for making tepees in some of the references listed in the bibliography at the end of this chapter.

Older campers may find it challenging to build a *lean-to*, an *Adirondack shack*, or a log cabin, and these make welcome additions at outpost camps or other frequently used sites where such structures are permitted.

For winter camping, building snow shelters, including snow caves and igloos, is fun. They take time to construct but, once finished, they provide excellent protection and comfort.

CAMPSITE SELECTION AND SET-UP

When picking a campsite and a location for your shelter, be sure to observe the regulations of the resource management agency or land owner. For general considerations on how to select a proper area, follow the recommended procedures discussed under "Campsite Selection and Set-Up" in Chapter 22.

ADDITIONAL READINGS

(For an explanation of abbreviations and abbreviated forms, see page 13.)

Angier: *Home in Your Pack*, ch. 4 (Includes directions for making several types of tents).
Angier: *Skills for Taming the Wilds*, ch. 12.
Angier: *Survival With Style*, ch. 2.
Angier: *Wilderness Gear You Can Make Yourself*, ch. 2.
Better Homes and Gardens Family Camping Book, chs. 6, 7.
Boy Scout Handbook, pp. 230–232.
Bridge: *America's Backpacking Book*, ch. 11.
Bridge: *The Complete Snow Camper's Guide.* Scribners, 1973, 390 pp.
Cardwell: *America's Camping Book*, chs. 4, 12. (Includes directions for making your own tent).
Colwell: *Introduction to Backpacking*, ch. 7 to p. 108.

Cunningham and Hansson: *Lightweight Camping Equipment and How to Make It*, chs. I, V.
Dalrymple: *Survival in the Outdoors*, ch. 10.
Davis, Skye: *Trailside Shelters*. Stackpole, 1977, 224 pp.
Fieldbook for Boys and Men, pp. 38–41.
Fletcher: *The Complete Walker*, pp. 137–176.
Johnson: *Anyone Can Camp in Comfort*, ch. 2.
Lamoreaux: *Outdoor Gear You Can Make Yourself*, ch. 7 (Making tents).
Langer: *The Joy of Camping*, pp. 3–28.
Laubin, Reynold and Gladys: *The Indian Tipi*. Order from N.R.P.A., 208 pp.
Learn and Tallman: *Backpacker's Digest*, ch. 15.
Litepac Camping Equipment. Boy's Life, (Articles reprinted from Boy's Life).
Macfarlan: *The Boy's Book of Hiking*, ch. 10.
Manning: *Backpacking One Step at a Time*, ch. 12.
Mason: *The Junior Book of Camping and Woodcraft*.
Meier: *Backpacking*, ch. 2.
Merrill: *All About Camping*, pp. 87–102.
Merrill: *The Survival Handbook*, ch. 5.
Miracle: *Sportsman's Camping Guide*, pp. 15–22 and 46–48.
Olsen: *Outdoor Survival Skills*, ch. 2.
Ormond: *The Complete Book of Outdoor Lore*, ch. 6.
Ormond: *Outdoorsman's Handbook*, pp. 178–181. (Tepees and wigwams).
Rethmel: *Backpacking*, ch. 4.
Riviere: *Backcountry Camping*, ch. 3.
Riviere: *The Camper's Bible*, chs. 1, 2, and 4.
Rutstrum: *The New Way of the Wilderness*.
Shockley and Fox: *Survival in the Wilds*, ch. 11.
Tents and Simple Shelters. Girl Scouts. (Flip charts).
Wood: *Pleasure Packing*, ch. 7.

MAGAZINE ARTICLES

Backpacker:

"Backpacker's Equipment Section." Fall, 1973, pp. 57–59.
Bentley, Judy: "You and Your Gear—Care and Repair of Tents." Fall, 1973, p. 16.
Hastings, Honey C.: "Make and Fix It." Fall, 1973, p. 18. (How to make a tent)
"The Revolution In Three-Season Tents," June/July, 1978, p. 54

Camping Journal:

"Buyer's Guide." (Current year)
Clark, Fred: "New Tents and Tarps." July–Aug., 1966, p. 30.
Forshee, John H.: "You Build It Backpack Tent." Jan., 1972, p. 26.
Gibbs, Jerry: "Take a Tarp." Jan., 1973, p. 26.
Laycock, George: "How to Pitch a Tent." June, 1967, p. 26.
Ormond, Clyde: "On the Trail." Feb., 1970, p. 16. (Plastic sheets)
Ormond, Clyde: "On the Trail." Apr., 1970, p. 18. (Tent pegs for different situations)
Ormond, Clyde: "On the Trail." May, 1971, pp. 22. (Emergency shelters)
"Pop and Prairie Schooner Tents." Apr., 1967, p. 66.
Reynolds, Judith L.: "How to Repair Your Tent." Oct., 1973, p. 24. (Cotton tents)
White, Robin: "The Versatile V-Fly." Oct., 1971, p. 26. (Directions for making a fly that pitches 12 ways, sleeps 6, and costs under $30)

twenty-five
Sleeping Out-of-Doors

Night is a dead monotonous period under a roof; but in the open world it passes lightly, with its stars and dews and perfumes, and the hours are marked by changes in the face of nature.

—ROBERT LOUIS STEVENSON,
in Treasure Island.

Since a third or more of our time is spent sleeping, the camper's bed deserves much thought and attention. A good night's rest with at least eight hours of sleep for adults and even more for youngsters is necessary at any time and especially so when undergoing the rigors of a trip.

If campers are traveling by covered wagon or have other means of transporting their heavy baggage, the bulk and weight of bedding are not of tremendous importance, but when they are traveling on foot with all equipment on their backs, it really becomes a problem to provide a comfortable bed that is lightweight and not too bulky. Canoe bedding, too, should be light and compact, although it is possible to take a little more than when backpacking.

REQUIREMENTS FOR SLEEPING COMFORT

A good outdoor bed should provide warmth, for even in summer nights are cool and the ground is always more or less cold and damp. The bed should be light and compact for carrying, should provide a reasonable amount of softness and smoothness with freedom from bumps, and should provide protection from the cold, damp ground.

SLEEPING BAGS

Most people who expect to do much outdoor sleeping will invest in some sort of sleeping bag. A good-quality bag, properly cared for, will last for years and will provide convenience, comfort, warmth, and maximum lightness and compactness. In the long run, it may actually save you money, since continued use of home bedding under trip conditions is hard on it and necessitates frequent cleaning.

Shapes

Sleeping bags come in four basic shapes, and the shape you choose will have a definite effect on your warmth.

RECTANGULAR BAGS. These are roomy, square-cut bags (Fig. 25–1*B*) with plenty of room for restless sleepers, but their ample

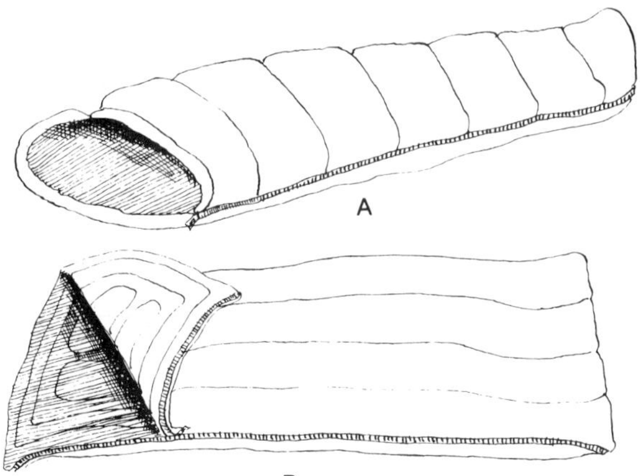

Figure 25-1 A) Mummy and B) rectangular sleeping bags.

proportions add bulk and weight, making them more suitable for car camping than backpacking. They are also not as warm as the other types since there is excess space inside to absorb body heat.

MUMMY BAGS. Mummy bags (Fig. 25-1*A*) represent the opposite extreme in shape. They follow the shape of the body, and this reduces bulk and weight and increases warmth. Although some find a mummy bag too confining, its advantages are so great that most backpackers prefer it.

BARREL BAGS. This variation on the mummy bag has, as the name suggests, a rounded portion in the middle to permit bending the knees and maneuvering about a bit more freely.

SEMI-MUMMY BAGS. These are a cross between the mummy and the rectangular bag.

For comfort, all bags should have an oval enlargement or "box" at the foot to permit room for the sleeper's feet.

Bag Construction

A sleeping bag consists of an *inner* and an *outer shell* with a filler (a rather thick layer of insulating material) in between. Neither shell should be waterproof or even extremely water repellent, since it is essential that the bag "breathe" to allow the pint or more of body moisture given off each night to evaporate. Various materials are used for the shells, the commonest being nylon. This is especially so for bags filled with down since they require an especially closely woven material to confine the down, which tends to migrate and drift through ordinary materials. All nylon should be the ripstop kind to keep little rips and holes from becoming big ones.

It is desirable for the shell to have a *differential cut.* This means that manufacturers cut the inner shell so that it is smaller than the outer one. This makes the bag warmer because it prevents the inner shell and the insulation from being compressed against the outer shell by various parts of the user's body.

INSULATION (MIDDLE LAYER OR INSULATION)

Although warmth may seem like the thing you want least as you pack up your gear on a warm sunny day, bear in mind that when the sun goes down the air will likely become quite chilly before morning. This is especially true at high altitudes.

When sleeping, our muscles relax and our metabolism slows down markedly, causing a corresponding drop in the production of body heat. When we get cold, our muscles automatically contract (perhaps even to the point of causing shivering) to step up heat production. In such a situation we sleep fitfully, if at all, and arise stiff, tired, and decidedly unenthusiastic about starting out for another hard day on the trail.

Bedding cannot, of course, supply any heat in itself, but it serves as insulation to keep out cold air and prevent the loss of body heat by conduction and convection. In a sleeping bag, insulation is provided by the thick filler between the shells, which is usually a loose, fluffy material containing countless minute air pockets that trap and render motionless large amounts of warm air generated by the body. This still or "dead" air provides excellent insulation.

Many materials insulate well, but none to date can perfectly meet the backpacker's need for a light, compressible, resilient, "breathable," fireproof, nonallergenic, yet inexpensive material. Of the many materials tried, only three are currently used in modern sleeping bags: the down of waterfowl, polyester fiberfill, and forms of polyurethane foam. However, new materials continue to appear as manufacturers attempt to find a more nearly perfect filler.

The thickness, or *loft*, of the insulation is all important in determining how well it will insulate, and it is customarily measured by zipping up the bag, fluffing it up as full of air as possible, and measuring the height from the floor to the top of the bag. Of course, you must remember that half of the loft will be above you and the other half below when you are in the bag. Therefore, when a manufacturer says that a bag has a loft of 6 inches, the effective amount of insulation around you is actually 3 inches.

The Army Quartermaster Corps has developed a guide for rating the insulation value of sleeping bags according to their thickness. However, experienced outdoorsmen say that these figures are only minimums, especially at the colder temperatures, and you will need more for real comfort.

TEMPERATURE IN DEGREES	*TOTAL LOFT IN INCHES*
40	1.5
20	2.0
0	2.5
−20	3.0
−40	3.5
−60	4.0

MATERIALS USED FOR INSULATION

GOOSE DOWN. Although many new materials are now competing with goose down, it is still a popular choice of the cold-weather backpacker. It is extremely light, can be compressed into a small bundle for carrying, yet is so resilient that it quickly springs back into shape as soon as pressure is released. Ounce for ounce, it provides more insulation than any of the synthetic materials yet devised. The best quality of down is found under the regular feathers on the breasts of mature northern geese and is plucked in the fall or winter when it is most luxuriant.

High-quality goose down is becoming increasingly scarce and expensive, because the geese are being raised commercially for food and are killed at a younger age before the down has reached its prime. The down from northern ducks is sometimes used, and although it is not as soft and warm as goose down, it is often superior to some of the inferior-grade and "reconditioned" goose down on the market. Down bags first came into extensive use after World War II and are now widely used.

A major drawback of down is its tendency to clump together and lose nearly all its insulating value when wet. It is also quite difficult to clean.

POLYESTER FIBERFILL. Recently there has been a great improvement in the quality of polyester synthetic fibers used for insulating purposes. Although sleeping bags filled with such material are a little heavier than down bags and not quite so compressible, they have become popular because they are much less expensive and work well. Another advantage over down is their resistence to wetness. Polyester bags will absorb less than 1 percent moisture and will maintain loft even when wet. The fact that they dry out quickly also is a real advantage in damp climates. In addition, they are nonallergenic and easy to wash. Hollowfil II and Polarguard are the most widely used polyester fiberfill insulation products, although other trademarked fills are quickly expanding the market.

POLYURETHANE FOAM. *Polyurethane foam* is another entrant in the field and shows promise as improvements continue to be made. It is a spongelike material that, although heavier than down, is cheaper and provides much better insulation when wet. It both breathes and is nonallergenic, but, unlike down, it does not drape closely about the body and so leaves air spaces that absorb body heat. It also has a tendency to turn with the body, creating air currents that carry away still more heat. For these reasons, this type of insulation is not too satisfactory for use in extremely cold weather.

Polyurethane foam is not as compressible as either down or polyester fiberfill, so a bag cannot be compressed into a small space but must be rolled up and carried on the outside of the pack. However, this very incompressibility is at the same time an advantage, because it provides a softer cushion and better insulation under the sleeper. It also gives good protection from ground dampness, although you may want to use the customary ground cloth under it for protection from dirt and abrasion.

Most foam bags open only at the top and have a drawstring to pull them close about the neck; this makes them rather hard to get into and out of. They can be washed out by hand and squeezed almost dry. Like polyester fiberfill bags, their chief appeal lies in their low cost.

WAYS OF STABILIZING INSULATION

Down is composed of thousands of units called *pods,* each consisting of a center with many branching filaments that create numerous small air pockets to trap dead air; this gives down its superior insulating ability. As previously mentioned, down has a tendency to migrate or move about, so that if it is simply placed loose in a large area, such as that between the inner and outer shells of a sleeping bag, it will wander about and eventually collect in a few areas, leaving the rest of the bag devoid of down and, consequently, of insulation. Therefore, some method must be used to stabilize the down and keep it evenly distributed throughout the bag. The simplest method is called *quilting* (Fig. 25–2*A*), which is done by stitching straight through the shells and the down. This is not satisfactory for anything but hot-weather bags, since each row of stitching compresses the down to almost nothing, resulting in a series of cold spots. *Double quilting* (Fig. 25–2*B*), is better because it uses two layers of quilted down, placed so that the stitching or thin part on one is opposite to the thick part on the other.

Still better than double quilting are baffles, which are strips of material placed vertically between the inner and outer shells to form tubes that contain the down. The *box* type of baffle is inserted at right angles; the *slant wall* baffle (Fig. 25–2*C*) is placed at a 45-degree angle. The *chevron* or *overlapping* V baffle is made by sewing a strip of material continuously along between the inner and outer shells to create interlocked triangular compartments that form the overlapped *V* tubes. This is considered the best method of all for retaining uniform distribution of down.

Various materials are used for the baffles, with ripstop, downproof nylon being best for down. The tubes formed by the baffles usually run horizontally around the bag to counteract the tendency of the down to drift toward the bottom of the bag and there are usually some cross baffles in the tubes to further stabilize the down. Installing the baffles and distributing the down properly in them requires much painstaking, skilled work, and this partially accounts for the high cost of a good down bag.

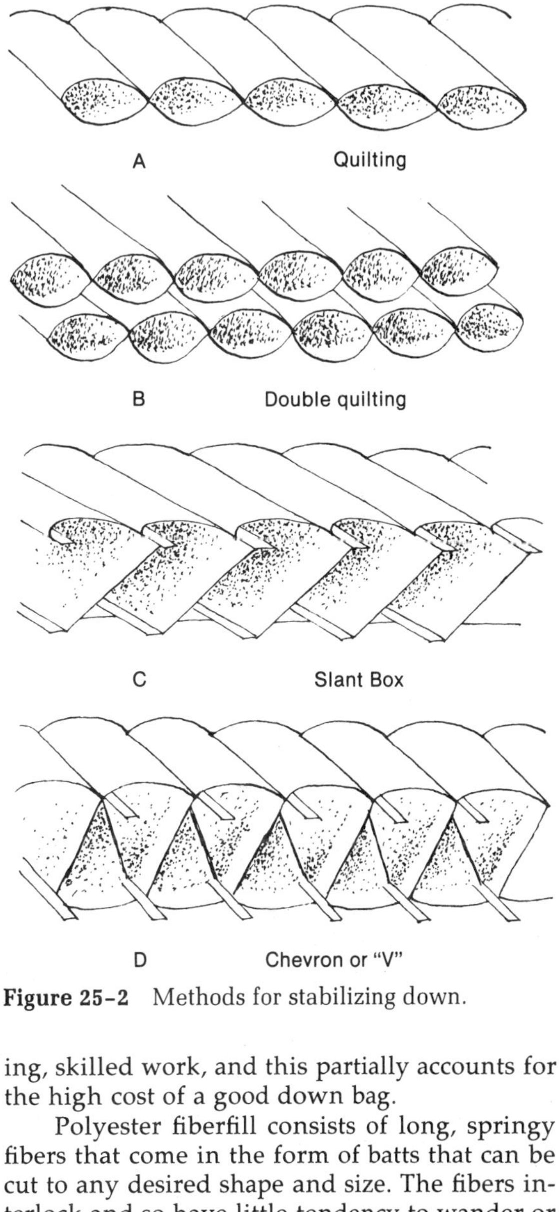

Figure 25–2 Methods for stabilizing down.

Polyester fiberfill consists of long, springy fibers that come in the form of batts that can be cut to any desired shape and size. The fibers interlock and so have little tendency to wander or drift, making an intricate system of baffles unnecessary. The filler can be kept in place merely by sewing straight through both it and the shells, although this will, of course, result in the usual cold spots. For this reason, double quilting is usually recommended. With this type of filler, cheaper materials such as nylon taffeta can be used for the shells.

Polyurethane foam needs neither baffles nor quilting, but can simply be cut to the desired proportions and enclosed in appropriate inner and outer shells.

BAG OPENINGS

Some bags, particularly the warmer mummy types, have an opening at the top and a zippered opening extending most of the way down one side. Another arrangement is a zipper that runs all the way down the side and across the bottom. This allows the bag to be completely opened for ventilation. Some are designed so that two different bags can be zipped together for double sleeping.

Metal zippers are seldom found in modern bags since they transmit cold and are more likely to jam. They have been largely supplanted by those made of nylon or plastic, which are lighter, work more smoothly, and have less tendency to jam. If a zipper does become balky, apply a little wax or Zip-Eaze and work it up and down several times.

Double zippers with slides at both the top and bottom are superior since they permit opening the bag from either end to provide a greater choice in ventilation. They should be workable from either the inside or the outside, especially for cold-weather camping.

Since the zipper opening is the prime source of cold from the outside and loss of heat from the inside, it should be completely faced with a good *zipper draft tube* filled with insulating material and extending all the way to the bottom and slightly beyond. It must be attached so that it can't possibly foul the zipper or cause it to jam.

HEAD AND NECK PROTECTION

Rectangular bags are usually left open at the top or have a drawstring to draw them close about the neck. This makes it necessary to carry some sort of supplementary protection for the head and neck in cold weather. Separate hoods are available for this purpose, and some bags have detachable hoods that can be left at home during warm weather. Mummy bags and their variations usually have an extension at the top that can be pulled tight about the face and neck in cold weather, leaving only the nose and eyes exposed, and some have an extra drawstring around the shoulders to make them fit even more snugly.

REMOVABLE LINERS

Some bags come with removable liners to protect the inside of the bag from dirt and abrasion, and these can be taken out for laundering. They come in a variety of materials, such as cotton shirting, outing flannel, or ripstop nylon, and are anchored in place with tapes or snaps to keep them from twisting or rolling up as the occupant turns.

If your bag has no such liner, you can easily make one from material of your choice. A twin-bed size sheet or cotton "bed blanket" works well in summer and is about the right size for an adult bag, but you may want a warmer material for cold weather. The problem of fitting the liner to the bag is simplified if your bag is the type that opens down one side and across the bottom. Open the bag and measure the length along one side, across the bottom, and up the other side, and buy a piece of snap tape or Velcro of this length. To fit the liner into the bag, carefully sew one strip flat along the inside of the bag opening, just inside the zipper where it won't foul it or interfere with opening or closing it. Attach the other half of the tape to the liner, sewing along one side, across the bottom, and up the other side. You are now ready to snap the liner in place inside the bag.

THE USE AND CARE OF A DOWN BAG

A down bag usually comes with its own *stuff sack* into which you literally stuff it, handful by handful, being sure to work at least half of the bag down into the bottom half of the sack. As soon as you arrive at your campsite, remove the sleeping bag from the stuff sack (handle it carefully to avoid damaging the delicate system of baffles inside). With the zipper closed, pick up the bag by the edges and shake it with a sort of whip-like motion to get as much air as possible into the down. Do this at least an hour before retiring to give the down time to attain its full loft. Leave the zipper closed until you are ready to crawl into the bag to prevent the down from collecting moisture. Always keep the bag well away from any open flame, for a stray spark can burn a hole in it.

Air out your bag every day if possible, turning it inside out and placing it outside on sunny days. This will prevent mildew and odors.

Before storing it, fasten a plastic dress bag such as cleaners use around it and suspend it in a dry, clean room or otherwise store it loosely so the down can maintain its loft.

Make every effort to keep the sleeping bag clean, for it is difficult to wash satisfactorily without damage occurring. Some people advise against doing anything other than simply using a damp cloth to wipe the surface of the bag. Others claim to have good results by hand washing the bag with mild soap, but natural oils and loft of down can be reduced by soap and water. Care must also be taken not to cause interior structrual damage while washing, since baffles can be torn easily from the pressure caused by lifting a water-soaked bag.

Dry cleaning should only be done by an expert who has the proper "know how" and equipment. Do not attempt to dry clean it yourself unless you have received complete instructions from a reliable source. After dry cleaning, do not sleep in the bag until it has been thoroughly aired out for several days, for noxious fumes often linger and can cause severe illness or even death to someone sleeping in it.

Selecting a Sleeping Bag

A sleeping bag is a highly personal item and there is no one bag that will suit everyone's tastes and needs. In selecting the particular one that is right for you, consider such factors as the season of the year, the altitude and probable minimum and maximum temperatures to be encountered, the prevalence of winds, the likelihood of rain or other precipitation, your own personal characteristics (some people sleep much "warmer" than others), how extensively it will be used, how much bulk and weight you are willing to carry, and how much you are willing to spend.

Despite its cost and the difficulty of cleaning it, a good down bag may well be a wise purchase in the long run, especially if you will be camping out frequently in all kinds of weather, for when properly cared for, it will give years of dependable service and will have a good resale value if you should decide to sell it. However, a down bag might well be a foolish luxury for someone who camps out only occasionally in the summer, when the bag might often be too warm. A lightweight bag made of synthetic materials costs less and would probably adequately meet the needs of the occasional summer camper.

So-called three-season bags are satisfactory in all but the coldest weather. Some of them come with an extra-warm inner bag that zips inside, and this can sometimes be used separately to provide an extra bag. A serious camper who goes out in all types of weather may want to invest in two bags, a light one for summer and a heavy one for winter.

Since there are now so many bags on the market, you should delay making a final choice until you have looked at several different types. Study the catalogs of outfitters (see Appendix E), visit stores, and talk to experienced campers. If possible, borrow several bags from friends or rent them from outfitters so that you can test them in actual use. It is usually best to avoid buying so-called "bargains" made by relatively unknown manufacturers; stick to reputable companies who are willing to stand behind their products.

If you want a bag for cold weather, be sure there is a hood that will give good protection for your head and neck. Bags come in several lengths with corresponding variations in width. Buy the smallest one you feel comfortable in; it will save you money, bulk, and weight and will even be warmer.

Note the quality of workmanship throughout the bag; this is usually one of the best measures of its overall quality. Turn the bag inside out to check the inside too. Is the stitching even, and are there from 8 to 10 stitches per inch (neither more nor less)? Is there adequate backstitching or tacking (made by stitching back and forth over the same spot several times) at all points of stress and at the ends of the rows of stitching, and are there double rows of stitching at such points of stress as seams, zippers, and the place where the hood is attached? Is good thread used and is it of Dacron or cotton with a nylon core for strength?

Read all the labels on the bag, for the government requires that the manufacturer disclose such information as (1) the amount and type of filling used (be wary of reprocessed materials that may be some manufacturer's castoffs or the leftovers from some other product), (2) the type of outer covering, and (3) the cut and size of the bag (these dimensions usually are given in terms of the uncut material with no allowance for hems and seams).

Some bags feature a pocket for inserting an air mattress, but these are not usually satisfactory since it is difficult to inflate the mattress inside the bag and, when it is inflated, there isn't much space left inside for the sleeper.

It is often difficult to buy suitable bags for children, since many manufacturers do not make them and others use inferior materials (this is particularly true of down bags). Fortunately, there is now a greater selection of bags made from synthetic materials and these are generally inexpensive and serve quite well for summer camping.

BLANKET BEDS

In this day and age of ultra-lightweight camping gear, most people prefer a sleeping bag. However, since it is one of the more costly camping items, blankets can still provide reasonable warmth for those with limited resources or those who sleep out so seldom that they can scarcely justify buying a bag. We should not look down on the idea of sleeping in blankets, for they served adequately for hundreds of years before sleeping bags were even invented. In fact, they have some advantages, because they can be easily altered to suit weather conditions and are easy to wash. Dark, strong blankets that won't show soil are preferable.

Cold weather calls for blankets of 100 percent virgin wool; their loose weave and long nap trap dead air, making one wool blanket equivalent in warmth to several part-wool or cotton ones. Two relatively thin blankets are better than one thick one, since they are easier to manipulate and trap a layer of dead air between them to provide extra insulation. Quilts and comforters are too bulky and fragile to merit consideration.

Making a Bedroll. Some people simply roll up in their blankets and claim to sleep in perfect comfort throughout the night. This seems unlikely, however, since the average person changes position many times during the night. If you want to try it, wrap yourself in an *envelope bed;* spread a blanket on the ground, bring the two sides up over you, tucking one edge of the blanket under you, then lift your feet and tuck the blanket under them. To use two blankets, place the edge of one blanket at the center of the other, lie down and proceed as before.

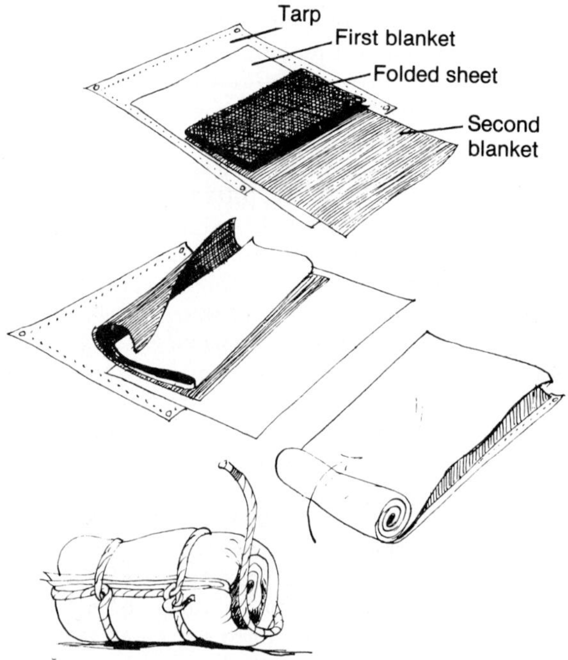

Figure 25-3 Making and tying a bedroll.

When using two blankets, it is usually best to pin them together in some way. A *Klondike bedroll* (Fig. 25–3) is easy to make. The one illustrated is made from two blankets and four 3-inch horse blanket pins. First place a tarp or ground cloth on the ground and spread one blanket over about half of it. Add as many blankets as you want, placing the edge of each at the center of the one below. Finish with a folded sheet or light cotton blanket that will be next to you. Now begin folding the blankets over, starting with the top one and working your way down to the bottom blanket. Insert two blanket pins along the outside edge and two along the bottom (make sure that the pins go through all thicknesses). For carrying, fold or snap your poncho or ground cloth around the outside and roll and tie it for carrying as shown in Figure 25–3. Be sure to make the bedroll wide enough to allow some movement, for most people dislike a feeling of confinement and find that it interferes with their rest.

MATTRESSES

Some hikers still sleep with only a sleeping bag and ground sheet for a mattress, but most of us would find this pure torture. Although this type of bedding cuts down on a backpacker's load, even Pollyanna would have to admit that softness is not one of its virtues and that it may well have been the source of the expression "making mountains out of mole hills."

As we have noted, the weight of your body will compress the bottom of your sleeping bag, particularly if it has a down filler, until very little thickness or loft remains, thus reducing softness and insulation. Although campers of the past cut branches or gathered leaves, grass, or hay to supply a comfortable "mattress," such practices cannot be sanctioned today. Therefore, the modern backpacker must carry some sort of ground pad or mattress. For the ultimate in lightness and compactness, they usually settle for a "shorty" pad that is just long enough to support the body from shoulders to hips or mid thighs. For a pillow, simply stuff soft clothing into a stuff sack or other bag.

Types of Mattresses

Three types of outdoor mattresses are in current use: (1) air mattresses, (2) open cell foam pads, and (3) closed cell foam pads (Fig. 25–4).

AIR MATTRESSES. Air mattresses, although favorites for many years, are now seldom used by backpackers for several reasons. Although they provide softness when properly used, they take some time to get used to and have other more serious drawbacks. They make for cold sleeping since they confine quantities of air in relatively large air spaces; this air moves about with every movement of the sleeper and as we have seen, moving air carries away body heat. This characteristic, of course, might be welcome in hot weather. Perhaps their worst feature is that they will eventually develop leaks, all too often in the middle of the night when they really let you down with a bump.

There currently is one brand of air mattress that has much better insulating properties than others. It combines the advantages of open cell foam mixed with air inside a durable, airtight, waterproof nylon covering. An air valve allows the pad to be deflated and rolled for easy backpacking.

The main advantage of air mattresses is that they can be deflated and compressed into a very small package for transporting. To carry one, roll it up and place it vertically in your pack; don't fold it because repeated folding in the same place will cause the material to deteriorate, resulting in leaks.

Mattresses of rubberized materials are heavy and cold to sleep on, and the cheap, plastic variety are not worth buying for they wear out very quickly and are totally undependable, even developing pin-prick holes while not in use. Vinyl is more satisfactory and, with care,

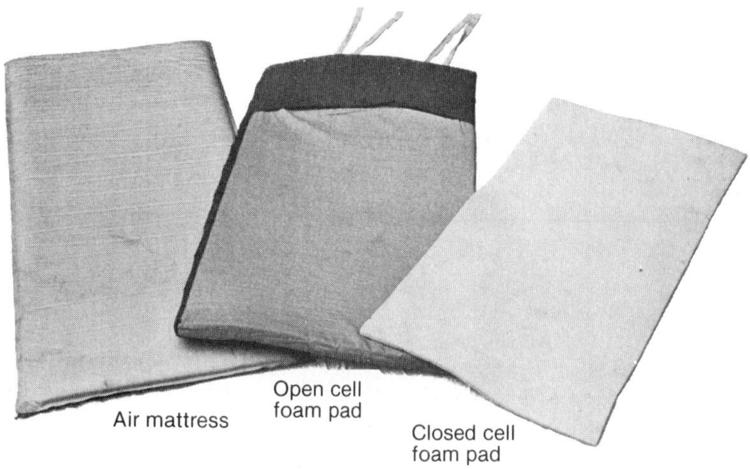

Figure 25–4 Sleeping pads or mattresses. The open cell foam pad is enclosed in a protective nylon shell with a cotton upper surface. (J. Meier)

will last an appreciable length of time, and nylon is probably best of all.

The secret of sleeping comfortably on an air mattress is to underinflate it so that you sleep *in* and not *on* it. Inflate the mattress fully, then lie down on your side on it and slowly let out air until your hip almost touches the ground.

To save time when deflating the mattress in the morning, open the valve when you first get up and let it deflate while you eat breakfast and pack.

OPEN CELL FOAM PADS. An open cell foam pad, as the name suggests, has cells that open into each other like cells of a sponge. The pad is soft to sleep on if it is at least 1½ inches thick. Like a sponge, it absorbs dampness, therefore it must be enclosed in a waterproof nylon covering. If the covering has cotton on the upper surface it will be less slick, reducing the tendency for the sleeper to slide off in the night. In addition, the cotton reduces the build-up of body heat and moisture.

CLOSED CELL FOAM PADS. A closed cell is much warmer to sleep on since the cells are completely separate and so confine the air in small spaces. Since it does not absorb moisture, it needs no covering, although you may want to use a ground sheet or a washable cover to protect it from soil and abrasion. Although the closed cell pad may not be as soft as other types of mattresses, it is quite washable, smooths out ground bumps nicely, and provides good insulation. As a result, it is used by many backpackers. These pads are sold under various trade names, such as Ensolite, Thermobar, and Voltek, and come in sheets from ¼ to ½ inch thick (the ⅜-inch size is probably the most popular). A pad can be purchased ready to use or can be cut from a sheet of the material. This type of pad is less bulky and expensive than the open cell pad and can be rolled up into a compact package to attach to your pack.

GROUND SHEET OR TARP

The ground is always more or less cold and damp, and since neither a blanket roll nor a sleeping bag is or should be completely waterproof, you will need a waterproof tent floor, a sleeping pad, and a good tarp or ground sheet to protect your bedroll from dampness, dirt, and abrasion. Even if you do use a tent, it is still a good idea to place a ground sheet under it for additional protection. Since any material used for this purpose will eventually develop tiny tears and even larger holes from contact with the rough ground, many people use only an inexpensive, lightweight sheet of plastic (polyethylene), considering it expendable and easily replaceable. Although coated nylon costs more, it will last several times as long as polyethylene. Carry a roll of plastic or ripstop tape along to mend holes as they appear.

ADDITIONAL READINGS

(For an explanation of abbreviations and abbreviated forms, see page 13.)

Bridge: *America's Backpacking Book*, ch. 12.
Cardwell: *America's Camping Book*, ch. 5.
Colwell: *Introduction to Backpacking*, pp. 108–122.
Eggert: *Backpack Hiking: The First Steps*, pp. 51–61.
Fletcher: *The Complete Walker*, pp. 165–196.
Langer: *The Joy of Camping*, pp. 29–43.
Learn and Tallman: *Backpacker's Digest*, ch. 3.
Manning: *Backpacking One Step at a Time*, ch. 11.
Meier: *Backpacking*, pp. 16–22.
Merrill: *The Hiker's and Backpacker's Handbook*, pp. 85–95.
Mohney: *The Master Backpacker*, pp. 37–41.
Rethmel: *Backpacking*, pp. 2–1 to 2–5.
Riviere: *Backcountry Camping*, ch. 4.
Scout Handbook, pp. 234–235.
Sunset Camping Handbook, pp. 21–26.
Wood: *Pleasure Packing*, ch. 4.

MAGAZINE ARTICLES

Backpacker:
"Backpacker's Equipment." *Backpacker-2*, Summer, 1973, pp. 45–51, 64–76.
Kutik, William: "You and Your Gear—Cleaning your Bag." *Backpacker-2*, Summer, 1973, p. 12.
Packer, Nelson: "How to Buy a Duck Down Sleeping Bag." *Backpacker-8*, Winter, 1974, p. 59.
"The Pick of the Polyester Bags." *Backpacker-6*, Summer, 1974, pp. 73–85.
Boys' Life:
Cost, Rick: "Sleeping Comfort at Camp." July, 1971, p. 66.
Camping Journal:
Heyl, Frank: "Bag a Good Night's Sleep." Jan., 1971, p. 22.
Consumer Reports 1974 Buying Guide;
"Warm Weather Sleeping Bags." p. 342.
"Down-Filled Sleeping Bags." p. 343.
Wilderness Camping:
Wood, Robert S.: "Outdoor Insulation; Down vs. Dacron vs. Foam." Part I, Jan./Feb., 1973, p. 8; Part II, Mar./Apr., 1973.

CONSERVATION AND ECOLOGICAL CONSIDERATIONS

One of the penalties of an ecological education is that one lives alone in a world of wounds. Much of the damage inflicted on land is quite invisible to the layman.

—ALDO LEOPOLD

If our first settlers could return today, they would no doubt be utterly astounded at our concern for conserving our remaining wilderness areas and other places still imbued with outstanding natural beauty. To them, the supply of natural resources must have seemed inexhaustible. The dense forests provided wood for their many needs, as well as fruit, herbs, fish, and wild game for their tables. "Chop and burn" was a way of life to them, for the trees had to be cut and cleared to make room for growing crops.

As the farming industry grew, people soon discovered that there was a ready market for excess wood products in England and other countries that could supply the cash Americans needed to buy the manufactured products that the young country was not yet equipped to produce. Consequently, lumbering became a major industry, and soon thereafter our country experienced a rapid expansion in the use of other natural resources.

Fortunately, we have undergone a belated awakening to the need to conserve at least part of what was once our great natural heritage. One important step has been the development of the science of natural resources management, which seeks means to use our lands in ways most beneficial to both present and future generations. These well-managed natural areas now serve us in many ways, but of special interest to campers is the fact that they provide the environment for organized camping, where youth can live simply, surrounded by plants and animals in their natural habitats. These same benefits also are available to the many people who are discovering the joys of taking to the woods for such pastimes as backpacking, hiking, swimming, boating, fishing, hunting, and family or group camping. However, such large numbers of people are placing increased pressure on the capa-

twenty-six

Camp Stoves and Wood Fires

Then after a day filled with pleasure and work,
As you trudge back to camp with your trout,
The smell of bacon that's cooking up there,
Is the sweetest of odors, no doubt.

—E. K. BERRY, Cooking in Camp.

bility of the environment to withstand the demands placed upon it. If we hope to preserve the naturalness of the great outdoors as well as the accompanying values and benefits derived from it, we must act responsibly and do everything possible to reduce our impact on these lands.

One of the biggest problems facing resource managers who work to maintain our outdoor recreation areas is the impact of campfires. Far too many campers and backpackers leave behind an assortment of ugly, pock-marked fire sites as each apparently feels compelled to build a fire in a new spot. In many backcountry campsites, all of the available wood has long since been burned, and some neophytes have even chopped down green saplings, little realizing that green wood will not burn satisfactorily anyway. As a result of all this, campers are now either discouraged or prohibited from building wood fires in many of our wilderness and backcountry areas, especially in those that are frequently used. Some areas that still permit controlled wood fires have compromised by establishing fire sites and requiring that all fires be built in them using only dead wood provided or available nearby.

The awakened interest in and understanding of ecology teaches us that burning wood not only causes those problems already mentioned, but it also disrupts nature's balance by permanently destroying a natural resource instead of leaving it to decay and return its nutrients to the soil as nature intended. Yet another cause for concern is the numerous disastrous forest fires that have been started by careless campers that annually burn over thousands of acres of woodlands, destroying valuable timber and undergrowth and ruining the homes of countless wild creatures.

Although wood fires can no longer be widely encouraged for general camp use, there are some situations in which they are still permissible. This is particularly true in certain resident camps that have extensive woodlands, especially those that practice scientific methods of forest management, promote the health of all trees, and systematically replace those that are used. In fact, such a practice may well provide valuable conservation lessons as youngsters observe what is being done and learn to be selective in choosing what wood to use and how to use it. For this reason and for the benefit of those who feel that all campers should attain some proficiency in building wood fires, we are including a discussion in this chapter on some of the principles of this skill.

THE CASE OF THE DISAPPEARING WOOD FIRE

Whereas the sight of a backpacker using a camp stove was a rare thing only 20 to 25 years ago, it is now quite commonplace. There are several reasons for this, including reducing the impact of wood fires, as mentioned earlier. One of the other primary advantages of using a stove is that it is simply more convenient, for you can unpack, assemble and put it into operation in a matter of minutes; you don't have to scamper about searching for suitable dry wood, then arrange it carefully in the type of fire you want, and wait for it to burn down to the good bed of coals so essential for successful cooking. Stoves produce an even heat of any intensity desired while leaving your pots and pans shiny bright, for there is no smoke or soot to coat them. When handled properly, a stove will not explode and offers little chance of starting a destructive forest fire. When through with it, you can simply turn it off; you don't have to wait for it to burn down and then carefully extinguish each ember and partially burned stick. A modern backpacking stove is so light, compact, and easy to use that experienced campers never hesitate to carry one along wherever they go.

SOME ALTERNATE SOURCES OF HEAT

Several substitute sources of heat have enjoyed various degrees of favor.

Canned Heat

Jellied fuel such as that found in Sterno canned heat and heat tabs is relatively safe for use by even young campers but, unfortunately, gives out so little heat that it is scarcely useful for anything beyond heating a bowl of soup or stew or cooking such a simple things as an egg. To use jellied fuel, place the can of fuel between two rocks to support the pan or use the portable folding wind screen and kettle support that is available.

Charcoal

Cooking with charcoal is a backyard activity familiar to almost all children and is a fairly safe and satisfactory method for them to use in the main campsite or on short jaunts. Charcoal briquettes are relatively light and easy to carry and you can extinguish them when through and save them for future use. It is best to use some sort of charcoal starter, and you will need some type of grill to contain the fire and support cooking utensils. Several types are available commercially that fold up to fit in a carrying case. Grills can also be handmade; the one shown in Figure 14–14C is made of a 5-gallon tin can in which ventilator holes are punched in the sides with a juice can opener. If needed, a metal grate can be placed on top to support the pan, and the charcoal can be supported on a metal disc or screen inserted about half way up the side of the can. A fire pan can also be constructed by cutting diagonally across two opposite corners of a large rectangular can and placing a metal grate on top to support cooking utensils. Instructions for working with metal are found in Chapter 14.

One of the most serious drawbacks of most homemade grills is that they cannot be folded up, so they are somewhat cumbersome to take on a trip. Materials for making the grill, as well as the necessary metal rods and pieces of wire screening, usually can be found in trash heaps or you can buy a piece of gravel screening to use as a pan support.

Gasoline and Kerosene

Gasoline is more volatile than kerosene, making it a more convenient fuel for backpacking stoves because of the greater ease of operating the stove as well as the greater efficiency of the fuel itself. Although slightly more dangerous than kerosene stoves if not properly handled, gas stoves are preferred by most experienced campers. Kerosene stoves were once more popular but they are both sooty and smelly, and necessitate carrying a volatile priming fuel for preheating the vaporizing tube to get it going.

Gasoline stoves use white, unleaded appliance gas, which is relatively inexpensive and available at most outfitters, often under some trade name such as Coleman or Blazo fuel. Although many ordinary gasoline stations carry white gasoline, it is often too dirty to burn satisfactorily and will eventually damage your stove. Ordinary automobile gasoline is quite unsuitable, for even though unleaded, it contains additives that destroy its usefulness. Although it takes a little time to get the hang of lighting and using gasoline stoves, they are efficient and maintain a steady heat as long as any fuel remains in the tank. Gasoline's very volatility, however, makes careful handling mandatory, since any spilled on the hands, clothing, or surroundings or even escaping vapors can go off like a torch when exposed to open flame or even a hot surface such as a stove or lantern.

A gasoline or kerosene stove should NEVER be used in a small, enclosed area such as a tent or cabin unless absolutely necessary, and then only if the area is well ventilated. Like all fuel-burning stoves, they produce carbon monoxide, which, if inhaled, can cause serious illness or even death from asphyxiation or carbon monoxide poisoning. They also give off vapors from unburned and partially burned fuels that are highly flammable and can easily build up to dangerous proportions. These, together with the carbon monoxide, gradually displace the oxygen, resulting in a vicious circle wherein the stove burns less and less efficiently and gives off more and more carbon monoxide and vapors from improperly burned fuel, thus intensifying the danger of fire and explosion. Using a stove in cramped quarters also increases the danger of upsetting it or having something flammable come in contact with it.

Carry your extra fuel in a conspicuously marked, leakproof round or flat container, preferably of aluminum and with a tightly fitting rubber gasket and screw-on lid. These are available at outdoor equipment stores. It is also desirable to carry a small funnel with a fine mesh filter to sift out dirt when the fuel is poured. Fill the stove only ¾ full to allow room for the gasoline to expand, as is necessary for proper burning (Fig. 26-1).

Never fill a stove when it is hot, for escaping fumes or any liquid spilled on the hot surface may burst into flame. To avoid the danger of a flashback or explosion when lighting the

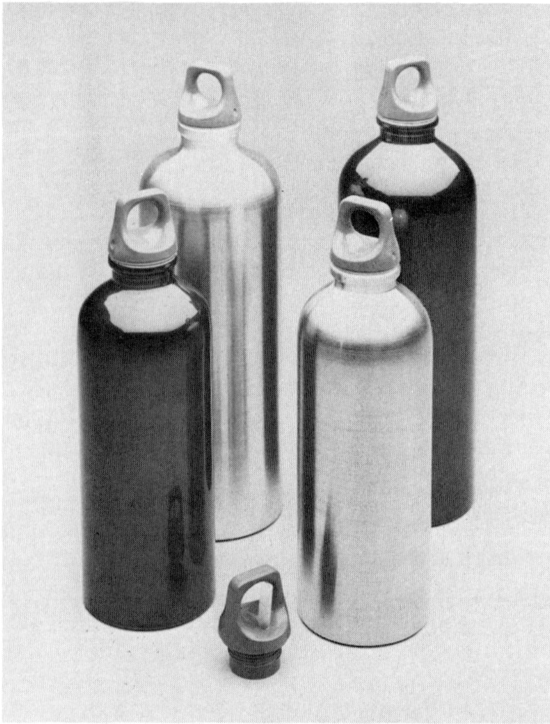

Figure 26-1 Aluminum fuel bottles with screw lids. (Eastern Mountain Sports, Inc., Peterborough, N.H.)

stove, strike the match and apply it to the burner *before* turning on the gas. If your first attempt fails, turn off the gas immediately and wait a short time to let the vapors dissipate before trying again.

Since both stoves and fuel containers give off unpleasant odors, they should be placed in the outside pocket of your pack. Gasoline weighs about 1.5 pounds per quart and two persons on a 7-day trip should need no more than 2 quarts. However, consideration must be given to what kinds of foods are being prepared as well as your altitude—the higher you are, the longer the cooking time. Stoves weigh from 1 to 3 pounds and there is a variety of choices available among several different types.

One of the greatest advantages of a gasoline or kerosene stove is the ease with which you can determine the amount of fuel left in the stove and add any needed before starting to cook. As we will see, that is not possible with propane or butane stoves, and in using them you may run out in the middle of cooking and have to wait until the stove is cold before adding a new cylinder of fuel.

Propane and Butane

Although relative newcomers to the field, propane and butane stoves are now quite popular. Propane and butane are gases compressed under low pressure (LP) and contained in a thin metal cylinder or cartridge that attaches directly to the stove. This eliminates the danger and messiness of having to pour a flammable liquid. They are clean burning and soot free and as easy to light and regulate as a kitchen stove. They require no priming or preheating, and a new cylinder of fuel is easy to attach. Although both fuels burn well in warm weather, only propane is recommended for use in cold weather. When used with caution, there is little danger of starting a forest fire or causing an explosion; however, you should never crush or puncture a used cartridge since it may still contain enough fuel to cause an explosion. Instead, place the used cartridge in your pack to carry out and dispose of properly; too many ignorant or lazy campers have cast away their old cartridges, leaving be-

(Youth Services Section, Los Angeles, California City Schools)

hind a cluttered landscape, which has brought disfavor to the whole field of camping.

Since the cartridges for different stoves are not usually interchangeable, you may have to search around to find the particular type you need. This is not usually too much of a problem, however, since good outfitters usually stock a fairly wide selection of the more popular types.

A variety of sizes and types of stoves are now on the market, and some popular backpacker models are so small and compact that an entire outfit consisting of a burner, a couple of pots, a frying pan, and a windscreen all nest into a package that weighs only 2 to 3 pounds and is small and compact enough to fit into the pocket of an ordinary rucksack. Such small stoves, however, have only one burner, so you will need to either carry more than one stove or cook your meal in courses. Larger 2- or 3-burner stoves are available for larger groups, but they are too bulky to carry on a backpacking trip.

Propane and butane stoves have several disadvantages. These fuels are less efficient than gasoline or kerosene, and cooking therefore takes more time. They are also slightly more expensive, although the difference is negligible. They weigh more per unit of heat, largely because of the weight of the nonrefillable cartridge. Another disadvantage is that both pressure and heat decrease during the last 10 minutes of burning of a cartridge. As previously mentioned, there is also no way to accurately determine the amount of fuel remaining in a partly used cartridge so that you may run out in the middle of cooking and have to wait until the stove gets cold before adding a new cartridge.

Use a windscreen to concentrate the heat under the cooking vessel, and turn off the fuel supply before you extinguish the stove. As with all fuel-burning stoves, avoid using a stove in a small, poorly ventilated area such as a tent or cabin.

Some of the more popular types of backpacking stoves are shown in Figure 26–2.

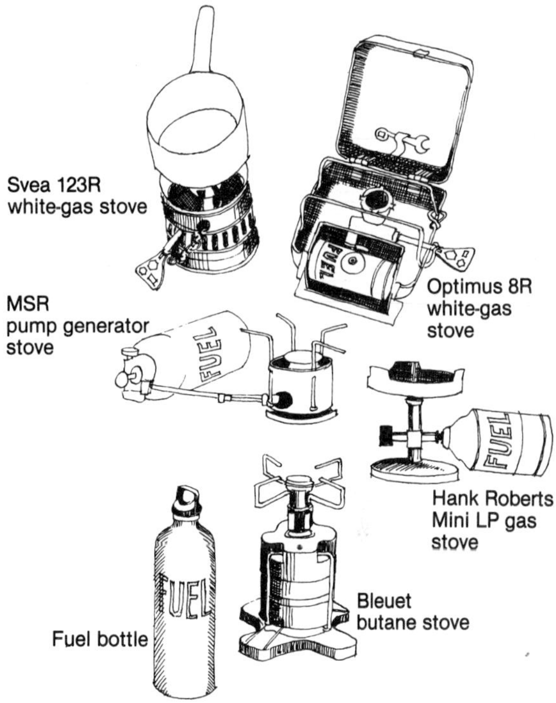

Figure 26–2 Backpacking stoves.

WOOD FIRES

Each color or tint that a tree has known
  In the heart of a wood-fire glow.
Look into the flames and you will see
  Blue dusk and the dawn's pale rose,
The golden light of the noonday sun,
  The purple of darkening night.
The crimson glow of the sunset, The
  sheen of the soft moonlight,
Fire brings forth from the heart of a
  tree
Beauty stored there in memory.

MARY S. EDGAR*

Among the fondest memories of older campers is that of sitting in peaceful camaraderie with good friends around a blazing camp fire. Nothing else is so cheerful, has such an enchanting aroma, is so attractive to watch, imparts such a delicious taste to food, dries out wet clothing so well, or warms you so pleasantly when it is chilly.

Although, as we have stated, wood fires can no longer be widely encouraged for general camp use, there are probably some situations in which they are still permissible.

*From *Wood-Fire and Candle-Light.* Permission by The Macmillan Company, Ltd., of Canada.

Choosing a Fire Site

When choosing a fire site, you must be sure, above all, to choose one that will offer little chance for your fire to spread. No matter how pleasant and romantic a fire in a deeply wooded area sounds, it is always dangerous, for there are usually low-hanging dry branches to catch on fire, and even green ones may dry out enough to burn if the fire is hot. It is best to choose one spot and confine all fires to it to avoid destroying any more of the natural environment than necessary. In fact, if you are in an area where no previous fire rings or scars exist, do everything possible to build your fire in such a way that no signs of it will remain once you are through.

Use a small shovel or hand spade to remove the top layer of sod, set it aside carefully, and keep it moist for replacement after your fire is out and the ground has cooled. Prior to replacing the sod, however, be sure to douse the ashes and scatter them so they will not be noticed by others.

The floor of the forest is usually covered with a litter of dead leaves, broken branches, and other debris called *duff*, with some underlying organic matter such as leaf mold and decomposing branches, which is called *humus.* These are combustible, and a fire may smolder in them and break out in an open blaze several hours after you have left the vicinity and forgotten all about it. Therefore, you will need to clear away all this material down to hard ground for an area of at least 6 to 10 feet in diameter. Be especially careful with the soil known as "peat" or "muck," for it is itself combustible and may burn underground for several days before breaking out. Find a sandy area if possible, since there is no worry about spreading the fire and less likelihood of showing a fire scar once you are through.

A ring of rocks placed around the fire site is traditional, especially if the rocks are needed to brace pots or pans, but avoid doing this if you can since they blacken from the smoke and leave signs of your presence. If rocks are already blackened from previous campfires, use them instead of new ones. Avoid shale and limestone,

(Camp Kooch-I-Ching, International Falls, Minn.)

for they may crack and fly like shrapnel when heated. Rocks near water or in a creek bed are often so waterlogged that they create enough steam to burst when heated. If you dry them out *gradually* by gentle heat, they may eventually prove satisfactory.

Never build a fire against a tree, for if dead, it might catch on fire; if green, you will injure or even kill it.

Controlling Your Fire

Keep an orderly campsite with everything in its place and dispose of all debris promptly to minimize the danger of having your fire spread.

Before lighting the fire, be prepared to handle it quickly if it should start to spread and to put it out when through with it. Certain tools are useful for this purpose. A small, compact shovel or hand spade comes in handy for clearing off combustible debris before building your fire and for smothering it with dirt if it starts to spread. Keep water nearby to use for an emergency or to extinguish the fire when through with it.

A campfire should never be left unattended for even a few minutes.

IF A FIRE STARTS TO SPREAD

If a fire starts to run wild, immediate action is imperative, for a situation that you alone could easily control at its start can get completely out of hand in moments. Get help unless you are *absolutely certain* you can handle it yourself.

To extinguish a fire, you must cut off the supply of oxygen or combustible material. To deprive it of oxygen, douse it with water, beat it with a wet burlap bag or other heavy material saturated with water, or cover it with sand, dirt, or gravel. Beat *toward* the wind so that you will not simply fan the fire and spread sparks ahead of you. To deprive it of fuel, go up far enough ahead on the windward side to allow time to dig a trench 12 to 18 inches wide and deep enough to reach mineral soil; throw all flammable material *away* from the path of the fire so that it will simply burn itself out for lack of anything to burn. Watch over the area long enough to make sure that it does not blaze up again.

Fuel for Your Campfire

The disappointment and discomfort of campers when no one in the group can produce more than a smudge fire is enough to disenchant them with camping forever. Your expertise at building the right fire in the right place at the right time tells a great deal about how good a camper you are.

The kindling's dwindling
  The log won't catch,
The only blaze
  Is the new-struck match.
The flames are low,
  The smoke is high.
The wood is green
  And so am I.

—AUTHOR UNKNOWN

TINDER, KINDLING, AND FIREWOOD. Three components are necessary for successful firebuilding: (1) good *tinder* that will catch immediately when you apply the match and burn long enough to ignite (2) the *kindling,* which, in turn, sets fire to (3) the *firewood,* which burns with enough force to provide the heat, light, or atmosphere you want. You must select, prepare, and arrange each of these exactly right to get a fire going. Select and arrange each bit of fuel for a definite purpose. A balky fire that burns sluggishly or coughs spasmodically and finally dies results from choosing the wrong kind of wood or from arranging it incorrectly.

Tinder. Many things will serve satisfactorily as tinder, that highly inflammable material that ignites at the touch of a match. Curls of white birchbark are excellent, since they burn well, even when wet or rotten. Look for them on a dead or fallen tree or where quantities of them are hanging loose or have peeled off a live tree and fallen to the ground. Dry pine needles, dry evergreen cones, last year's dry weed stalks, dried goldenrod, grape, and honeysuckle vines, Queen Anne's lace, old birds' or squirrels' nests, milkweed silk, sagebrush, dried cactus, corn stalks, and dry corncobs are also excellent. Small pieces of dry pitch from the trunk or branches of pine trees are volatile. Only a few pieces added to the tinder will assure a good fire start.

Three fuzz clumps or fuzz sticks, pyramided

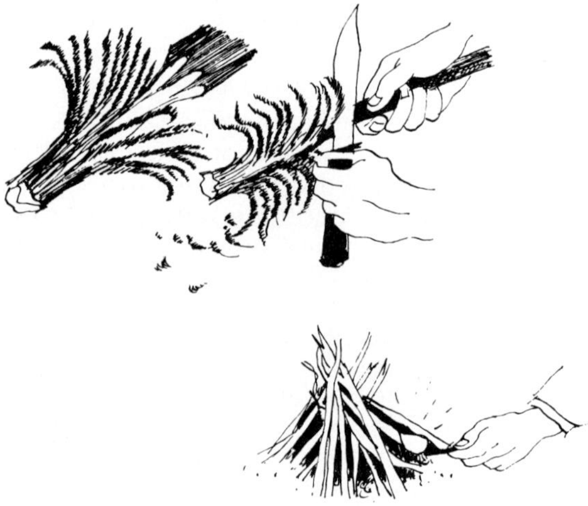

Figure 26-3 Fuzz sticks.

together as the base of a fire (Fig. 26–3), make good timber. Thin, curly shavings or a handful of twigs, each hardly bigger than a match, split and broken in the middle, also serve adequately.

Such things as waxed bread paper, waxed milk cartons, and crumpled up newspapers are fine, but don't bring them just to build fires for there are too many other things available almost anywhere you go.

Don't depend on dry grass and leaves, for although they blaze brightly, they burn out too quickly to set fire to anything else.

Never use gasoline or aerosols not specifically intended for starting fires.

Kindling. You will need kindling that will catch readily from the tinder and burn strongly enough to ignite the firewood. Split it for best results and keep it small in size, ranging from the size of a matchstick to about the length of your little finger or longer. Fat pine, cedar, or paper birch are best, but all the birches are satisfactory and you can also use evergreen, basswood, tulip, sumac, white pine and nearly all other kinds of pine, spruce, balsam, or box elder, as well as the frayed bark of cedar or hemlock.

Firewood. Firewood is divided roughly into hard woods and soft woods, each with its own special uses for camping. Kinds of wood vary in different sections of the country, so study your own particular region to determine what it provides. It isn't enough to be able to glibly recite the names of trees in full leaf, for campers use dead, dry wood with no leaves; you must identify firewood by its bark and the character of the wood itself.

SOFT WOODS. The lumbering industry regards as soft woods only the *evergreens* or *conifers,* while the broad-leaved trees (*deciduous,* or those that shed their leaves annually) are considered hard woods. Campers, however, consider as soft woods any that are actually softer and weigh less for their size. This includes the evergreens as well as some broad-leaved trees.

To distinguish between soft woods and hard woods, pick them up and weigh them in your hand; since hard woods are more compact, they weigh more. Soft woods burn quickly and briskly, making them good for kindling, providing quick flames for rapid boiling or baking, and blazing brightly for a campfire gathering. They are inclined to be somewhat smoky and sooty, however.

Good soft woods include alder, quaking aspen (poplar), balsam, basswood (linden), the birches, chestnut, cottonwood, soft or silver maple, pine (jack or Labrador and white or loblolly), pitch pine (fine for kindling, but even when burning brightly, emits a resin that taints foods and coats utensils), and spruce.

HARD WOODS. Hard woods are preferable for extended cooking and a long-lasting fire. They kindle slowly, so soft wood must be mixed with them to get them started, but once ablaze, they last a long time and provide a good bed of glowing coals that remains hot indefinitely. Hickory, oak, and maple are usually considered best; however, apple, white ash, beech, dogwood, hornbeam (ironwood), locust, mulberry, yellow pine, and larch (tamarack) are also good.

SPITFIRE WOODS. These are woods that in general, burn well enough, but tend to spit, make alarming noises, and, worst of all, throw sparks that may start forest fires or burn holes in tents or blankets. Soft woods in this category are the conifers (pine tree type), basswood (linden), box elder, chestnut, sassafras, spruce, tamarack, tulip (yellow poplar), and willow (which is also undesirable because it imparts an acrid taste to food cooked over it).

SLOW-BURNING GREEN WOODS. These are woods that, when green, will scarcely burn at all and so are worthless for either cooking or warmth. However, this very quality makes them valuable as fire dogs, backlogs, and fire banks.

The following belong in this class: black ash, balsam, basswood (linden), box elder, buckeye, butternut (white walnut), chestnut, cypress, hemlock, red (scarlet) maple, red and water oak, persimmon, pine (black or white and pitch), poplar (aspen), sassafras, sourwood, sycamore (plane tree or buttonwood), tamarack, tulip (yellow poplar), and tupelo (sour gum).

MAKING A SELECTION. You must use discrimination when selecting firewood. Green wood, because of its moisture content, seldom burns well. On the other hand, wood that is extremely old has lost much of its valuable heat-producing qualities. A little intelligent experimentation will help you select wisely.

The forest floor tends to hold moisture, so that even in comparatively dry weather, branches lying on it may be somewhat damp and questionable as firewood. As each tree in a crowded forest grows, it constantly struggles with its neighbors to reach up and absorb as much sunlight as possible. As the tree grows, its bottom limbs get so little sunlight that they often die. Their position under the tree keeps them quite dry except during a severe storm. Their value as fuel seems to have been recognized even in feudal times. Then, all of the land belonged to the lord of the manor and the peasants were not allowed to cut trees or use any wood except what they could find on the ground or reach in the trees with their pruning hooks and shepherd's crooks (an ingenious way for the lord to keep his woodlands clean and neat). It is easy to imagine what devious methods they invented to get more than was rightfully theirs—thus, the expression "by hook or by crook." Branches extending upward from downwood, driftwood, dry weathered roots, and knots also make excellent, long-lasting fuel.

Break wood to test it for dryness. Small, dry sticks snap and break cleanly, whereas wet or green ones bend and finally break with jagged edges. Large, dry sticks feel firm and heavy in the hand and will usually snap if you hit them sharply against the edge of a rock, and if you tap two of them together, they emit a clear, sharp sound instead of the dull, muffled sound of wet or green sticks. Sticks that crumble or break up too easily when you give them a sharp blow are rotten and would only smolder and smoke if put on a fire. Wood picked up from the ground is called *squaw wood* and, if perfectly dry, should be used rather than dead wood still on a standing tree. The Indians probably used little else, for they had no implements comparable to our sharp hatchet for chopping and splitting.

Modern campers differ as to how much to use a hatchet for preparing firewood. It is only common sense and not at all unwoodsman-like to break sticks by hand or under your foot if you can do it easily. You can also avoid chopping by laying long pieces of wood across the fire to burn apart. On the other hand, skill in using a hatchet is a big asset for splitting large pieces of wood. Walt Whitman said, "We are warmed twice by wood, once when we cut it and again when we burn it." You should ordinarily split pieces of wood over 2 inches thick before placing them on the fire.

YOUR STOCKPILE OF WOOD. If you are going to stay at a campsite for any length of time, arrange your wood in piles, ranging in size from large sticks for extensive cooking and council fires down to kindling and tinder. Place the wood conveniently near but not in the way of activity around the fire site. Throw a tarpaulin or poncho over your woodpile to keep it dry.

Building the Fire

LAYING THE FIRE. Collect a big handful of tinder, about twice as much kindling, and quite a supply of firewood before you start, for no self-respecting camper should have to scamper about getting more fuel to keep a fire going after it once starts. Place these materials within easy reach.

Make a fire foundation by crossing three small sticks with an end of each resting on one of the others to provide good air circulation. Pile the tinder loosely within this framework, leaving a little tunnel at the bottom on the *windward side* (side from which the wind is blowing). Now pile on a quantity of kindling in a loose pyramid. This completes what is known as a *basic fire lay* and forms the basis of any kind of fire you want to build.

Now add some larger pieces of wood, preferably split, in pyramid fashion. Burning consists of *combustion*, or the uniting of fuel with oxygen, and when you apply a match through the tunnel to the bottom of the tinder, this loose structure permits the flame to travel upward and soon sets the whole thing ablaze. Most fire fail-

(Columbine Girl Scout Council, Inc., Pueblo, Colo.)

ures result from piling the fuel on too compactly or in such a way as to let it fall down as it burns so that it smothers itself, resulting in a dead fire or at best one that is smoky and balky. Remember that fire burns upward and only materials directly in its path will ignite. Keep cautiously adding still larger pieces of wood until your fire is as big as you need.

STARTING THE FIRE. It is best to use *kitchen* or *torch matches* to start your fire since safety or book matches can be practically worthless for camp use.

CARRYING MATCHES. Matches are so essential to comfortable camping that you should pack them in several different waterproof containers and keep them in a well-protected spot in your pack. Also, it is handy to carry a small emergency supply in your pocket.

There are several varieties of containers available for protecting the matches. A metal box, such as a film cannister, works well, as does a plastic pill bottle. A common and inexpensive metal case, available at most supply houses and equipment stores, is watertight and its screw-on top is attached so that you can't lose it.

WATERPROOFING MATCHES. Individual matches can be waterproofed with paraffin. Simply place the paraffin in an old No. 10 tin can, immerse the can in a pan of water, and heat the water until the paraffin melts. Do not cover the paraffin or place it directly over the fire for it is quite flammable and can ignite into a ball of fire in a matter of seconds. Use tongs or pliers to remove the can of hot paraffin from the water. Tie your matches in bundles of six to eight, leaving a piece of string attached to *each* bundle with which to manipulate it. Dip each bundle of matches into the melted paraffin to coat them. When you are ready to use a match, pick it out of its paraffin bed and scrape off any excess paraffin; what little remains will make the match burn better.

Only counselors or older, very responsible campers should handle paraffin because of the fire danger and the fact that hot paraffin causes nasty burns. Never pour paraffin down a sink, for it will clog it as it hardens.

You can also waterproof matches by dipping them in a thin solution of shellac, varnish, or fingernail polish, or by dripping wax on them from a candle.

Lighting the Fire. Pride yourself on laying your fire so well that you will need only one match to start it. Only greenhorns arrange their fire materials so poorly that they must strike enough matches to make the surroundings look like a game of pick-up-sticks.

Grasp the match well down its shaft to

avoid breaking it, strike it, and hold it downward so the flame burns up the shaft. Cup your hands to shield the match from the wind and, as soon as it is burning well, cautiously insert it through the tunnel to the *bottom* of the tinder. If your fire lay is good, it will blaze up immediately and you need only stand by to add more fuel as needed. Place it on loosely to avoid smothering the fire. If your fire doesn't catch after two or three matches, the fault obviously lies in your fire lay and you'll save time in the long run by tearing it down and starting all over.

GENERAL HINTS ABOUT FIRES. One of the commonest errors in building fires is to build one much bigger than you need. Indians expressed disdain for this practice by saying, "White man big fool; make big fire, can't go near; Indian make little fire and sit happy."

A very small fire will cook a simple meal. Big fires take more work, are hot, waste fuel, burn the food or cook it too rapidly, create greater fire hazards and are more apt to scar the landscape.

Let your fire burn down to coals before you start to cook. This cooks the food slowly and clear through instead of leaving it charcoaled on the outside while the inside remains raw. Coals are also more comfortable to cook over and do not leave your kettle with a black, sooty mask. To get good coals, light a good hardwood fire well in advance and keep it going until there is a thick bed of glowing embers.

Figure 26-4 Tepee fire in hunter-trapper design.

To burn large, heavy sticks, raise them on a pair of green stick *fire dogs* (large sticks) to improve the draft. This is especially important on a damp, muggy day.

Smoke follows a vacuum. To keep from having smoke in your face, create a vacuum on the other side by building your fire in front of a cliff, placing your canoe on its side, or suspending a poncho or blanket on a framework of sticks.

The *inspirator* is an indispensable device for encouraging stubborn fires. Use a piece of surgical hose 1 ½ to 2 feet long. Place one end at strategic points at the *bottom* of the fire and blow gently through the other end to supply the extra oxygen needed to set it ablaze.

Kinds of Fires

WIGWAM OR TEPEE FIRE. (Fig. 26–4). An 18-inch wigwam or tepee fire burns quickly, with enough heat to boil water or cook a quick, one-pot meal or provide light and cheer for a small group meeting. Its rapid flame renders it a good foundation for getting more long-lasting fires going.

HUNTER-TRAPPER FIRE. (Fig. 26–4). This is one of the most thoroughly satisfactory cooking fires. Lay rocks in the form of an open V with the wide end toward the wind and about 15 to 16 inches wide, tapering to the small end, which is just wide enough to support your smallest kettle. Build a wigwam fire inside and keep it going until you have a good bed of coals to distribute along under your kettles. Keep a brisk fire going at one end to produce coals to replenish those under your kettles. This fire is cooler to cook by and conserves fuel, since the rocks reflect all the heat up onto your kettles.

KEYHOLE FIRE. (Fig. 26–5). This is somewhat similar in technique to the hunter-trapper fire, the difference being that rocks are laid in a keyhole pattern that provides a corridor in which the burning wood and hot coals can be separated at one end for warmth and for cooking at the other. Two green logs can be used in place of the rocks.

LOG CABIN OR CRISSCROSS FIRE. (Fig. 26–6). This is a good cooking fire, especially when you need a good bed of coals for continued heat. It also makes a good council ring fire.

Figure 26-5 The Keyhole fire provides warmth on one end and cooking on the other.

Use sticks an inch or less in diameter if you want it to burn briskly. Build the structure loosely and light a small tepee fire underneath to set the whole thing going quickly.

REFLECTOR FIRES. (Fig. 26–7 and 26–8). Reflector fires give steady heat for baking in a reflector oven or for throwing heat into an open tent. Place the reflector on the leeward side of the fire so that it will draw the smoke and flames and reflect back only the heat.

You can make a *fire bank* by piling up stones or stacking green logs (Fig. 26–8) against uprights driven into the ground at a 75° angle. Dirt also can be piled in front to keep it from catching on fire. Figure 26–7 shows an aluminum foil reflector oven made by wrapping the foil around two forked sticks that are separated by another stick placed behind the "V" of the forked ones.

ALTAR FIRES. Altar fires are labor-saving devices for permanent campsites since you do not have to stoop either to tend the fire or to stir your food. They also minimize the danger of having the fire spread through the duff. Cement rocks together or notch logs and fit them together to form a hollow base and fill it with some nonflammable material such as flattened tin cans, sand, or rocks. Build it to a convenient height for those using it—1 ½ to 2 feet high for children, 2½ to 3 feet high for adults. If you extend one side of the base up a foot or two, it will make an excellent reflector fire.

COUNCIL FIRES. When a group meets for a summer campfire program, they want a maximum of light and cheer with a minimum of

Figure 26-6 Log cabin fire.

Figure 26-7 Foil reflector oven.

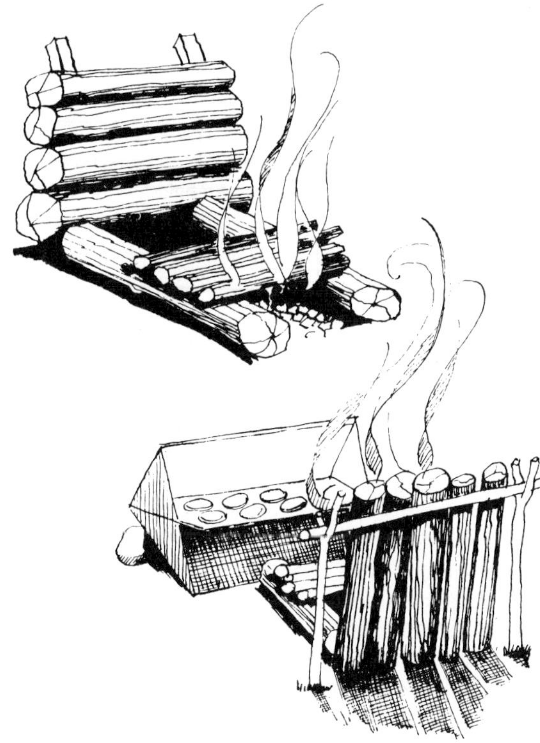

Figure 26-8 Reflector fireplaces.

heat. Adapt the size of your fire to the size of your group and avoid using varieties of wood that crackle and pop, for they are dangerous and distract attention from the program. Use a plentiful supply of tinder and kindling as a base and intersperse larger split kindling among your logs so that the fire will get underway quickly. A mixture of soft and hard woods usually gives best results. It is a hazardous practice to use kerosene or gasoline to produce a spectacular blaze, for such fires can easily get out of hand. Since the average campfire program seldom lasts more than an hour, you should be able to lay a fire that will last that long without having to replenish it, but you should have fuel available in case it is needed.

Log Cabin Fire. (Fig. 26–6). This cooking fire is also a favorite for campfire programs. Start the base with two logs about 3 feet long and 5 to 6 inches thick, placed about 2½ feet apart. Then build up five or six layers of successively smaller and shorter sticks, laid parallel, leaving small spaces between. Build a foundation fire on top that will burn brightly and soon drop enough hot embers down to set the whole thing ablaze.

Tepee or Wigwam Fire. (Fig. 26–4). As previously mentioned, a small wigwam fire is excellent for a small group. Although a tall bonfire towering high in the air is spectacular, it is not appropriate for camp use, for it is extremely hazardous since no matter how well you wire or otherwise fasten it together, there is always a danger that the long poles will work loose or burn in two and fall perilously close to those around it or set fire to the surroundings. It is also usually too hot for comfort in summer.

Extinguishing Your Campfire

Water is the best thing to use for extinguishing a campfire. Scatter all the embers that remain and douse them thoroughly, making sure that every bit of living fire is thoroughly drenched. Carefully pull aside all blazing pieces for a special dousing, saturating them or immersing them in a nearby stream or lake. Stir the fire bed repeatedly and keep sprinkling it with water. Place your hand at various spots on and in it to search for any remaining heat. Make sure it's *dead out;* it's not safe to leave it if there is even a trace of heat, flame, smoke or steam.

If water is unavailable, smother the fire with sand, gravel or dirt, but choose the soil carefully, for some types contain enough vegetable matter to smolder for days before breaking out into a full-fledged flame. If you have to move

(Willamette Council of Camp Fire, Salem, Oreg.)

hot ashes, wet them down thoroughly and deposit them at a fireproof spot.

Wet Weather Fires

The novice at fire making has enough trouble producing a bright, steady flame in clear, dry weather, but that is nothing compared to the difficulty of building a fire when it is damp or raining. Then comes the real test, for now a fire is more necessary than at any other time. It is quite important psychologically as well as physically to send everyone to bed with warm, dry clothing, hot food in their stomachs, and memories of fun and fellowship around a cheerful blaze. Bedding down on a dismal night without these comforts is enough to quell anyone's ardor for camping.

Whenever you are in camp, always keep a supply of dry tinder, kindling and firewood under a tent or tarpaulin. If caught without it, search under overhanging rocks or fallen trees or on the dead bottom limbs of standing trees. Even wet wood is usually damp only on the top layers and dry wood can be found by stripping off the bark or shaving off a few layers. Splitting large sticks also will reveal an inner core of dry wood to use as kindling or to make fuzz clumps or fuzz sticks.

TRENCH CANDLES. *Trench candles* carried in a plastic bag or waterproof tin box, are excellent for starting a fire anytime, but especially on a rainy day. To make them, lay a strip of cloth, twine, or thick cord in the center of six to ten sheets of newspaper and roll and twist them into a tight cylinder. Tie pieces of string snugly about the roll at intervals of 2 to 4 inches, leaving an end of the string on each section long enough to handle it by. Sever the roll midway between the strings and pull out the center cloth or cord of each segment far enough to serve as a wick. Dip each piece several times in melted paraffin or old candle wax, letting it harden a few minutes in between so that the paper becomes thoroughly saturated with the wax.

Trench candles are almost impervious to rain and wind and will burn long enough to start a fire under almost any conditions. By themselves, they will provide enough heat to cook on a hobo stove or give a fairly adequate light when burned flat in a dish or other container.

A plain candle stub or, even better, a plumber's candle will serve the same purpose, although not nearly so well.

FLASHLIGHT BATTERIES AND STEEL WOOL. Number 00 (very fine) steel wool will burn. Take a length of it and place the two ends in contact with flashlight batteries that are in contact with one another. Hold the steel wool over your tinder and drop it in when it begins to glow. Now blow on it until it becomes red hot and bursts into flame; then push it under your prepared fire lay. Use fresh batteries from your flashlight or extras carried in a plastic bag.

PEAS. Barbara Ellen Joy and Jeanne Bassett* describe a method for making "peas," which are good to start wet weather fires. Mix ashes from a soft wood fire with kerosene and roll them into small balls about the size of large peas. Let them dry out and carry them in a tin box. A match will set them burning brightly enough to start any stubborn fire.

LAYING A WET WEATHER FIRE. A fire built on sopping-wet ground can produce enough steam to smother itself. To avoid this, build a little platform of aluminum foil, stones, or sticks as a base.

A wigwam fire works best on wet ground. Lay it with even more than usual care, using fuzz sticks, peas, or trench candles and good tinder and kindling at first, adding other fuel gradually as your fire gains momentum. Damp fuel dries out with surprising rapidity when leaned gingerly up against already flaming sticks and you can place an additional supply close to the fire to gradually dry out.

An inspirator is especially helpful for wet weather fires.

If rain is falling, suspend a piece of tarpaulin or an extra poncho on a framework of sticks at least 5 feet above the fire to shield it until you have it going well. If it is windy, anchor the corners with guy ropes. Since this is rather hard on good material, some camps set aside a few special pieces for this purpose. If the wind is especially strong, erect a tarpaulin windbreak on the windward side.

---

*Barbara Ellen Joy and Jeanne Bassett: "Wet Weather Fires." *Camping Magazine*, April, 1939.

ADDITIONAL READINGS

(For an explanation of abbreviations and abbreviated forms used, see page 13.)

Camp Stoves

Angier: *Wilderness Gear You Can Make Yourself,* pp. 65–66. (Instructions for grills)
Bridge: *America's Backpacking Book,* pp. 86–89, 206–209.
Eggert: *Backpack Hiking: The First Steps,* pp. 90–94.
Fletcher: *The Complete Walker,* pp. 105–114.
Langer: *The Joy of Camping,* pp. 56–64.
Manning: *Backpacking One Step at a Time,* pp. 224–237.
Meier: *Backpacking,* pp. 23–25.
Mohney: *The Master Backpacker,* pp. 49–52.
Riviere: *Backcountry Camping,* pp. 132–135.
Riviere: *Family Camper's Cookbook,* chs. III, IV.
Sunset Camping Handbook, pp. 29–31.
Whelen and Angier: *On Your Own in the Wilderness,* ch. 10.
Wood: *Pleasure Packing,* pp. 55–62.

MAGAZINE ARTICLES

Backpacker:
"The Best of Stoves," June/July, 1981, p. 51.
Camping Journal:
Bigwood, Steve: "How to Prevent Fuelish Accidents," Aug./Sept., 1975, p. 32.
"Buyer's Guide." Mar., 1973.
Consumer Reports:
"Camp Stoves." June, 1969, p. 338.

Fire Without Matches

Angier: *How to Stay Alive in the Woods,* pp. 109–116.
Angier: *Survival with Style,* pp. 45–52.
Angier: *Wilderness Gear You Can Make Yourself,* pp. 21–26.
Bale: *What On Earth,* pp. 31–36.
Boy Scout Handbook, pp. 179–181.
Dalrymple: *Survival in the Outdoors,* pp. 207–223.
Fieldbook for Boys and Men, pp. 310–312.
Hamper: *Wilderness Survival,* pp. 19–21.
Merrill: *The Survival Handbook,* pp. 81–86.
Olsen: *Outdoor Survival Skills,* ch. 3.
Shivers: *Camping,* pp. 240–241.
Shockley and Fox: *Survival in the Wilds,* ch. 6.
Wood: *Pleasure Packing,* ch. 5 to p. 64.

Wood Fires

Angier: *Home in Your Pack,* ch. 9.
Angier: *How to Stay Alive in the Woods,* chs. 10, 11.
Angier: *Skills for Taming the Wilds,* ch. 5.
Angier: *Survival with Style,* ch. 3.
Bridge: *America's Backpacking Book,* pp. 83–86.
Cardwell: *America's Camping Book,* chs. 16–18.
Dalrymple: *Survival in the Outdoors,* pp. 195–207.
Fieldbook for Boys and Men, ch. 8.
Fire Building. Girl Scouts (Flip charts)
Firemanship (No. 3317). Boy Scouts, 1968, 64 pp., paper.
Garrison: *Outdoor Education,* ch. IV.
Gould: *The Complete Book of Camping,* pp. 32–44.
Langer: *The Joy of Camping,* pp. 67–72.
Learn and Tallman: *Backpacker's Digest,* ch. 10.
Manning: *Backpacking One Step at a Time,* pp. 29–33, 223–224.
Meier: *Backpacking,* pp. 62–63.
Merrill: *All About Camping,* ch. 13.
Merrill: *The Survival Handbook,* ch. 6.
Michaelson, M.: *Firewood.* Gabriel Books (A division of the Minnesota Scholarly Press, Inc., P.O. Box 224, Mankato, Mn. 56001), 1978, 157 pp., paper.
Miracle and Decker: *Complete Book of Camping,* ch. 22.
Ormond: *Complete Book of Outdoor Lore,* ch. 7.
Riviere: *Backcountry Camping,* ch. 6 to p. 132.
Riviere: *The Camper's Bible,* ch. 5.
Riviere: *Family Camper's Cookbook,* ch. II.
Shivers: *Camping,* pp. 238–247.
Whelen and Angier: *On Your Own in the Wilderness,* ch. 11.

MAGAZINE ARTICLES

Camping Journal:
Duffey, Dave: "How to Choose Campfire Wood." Jan., 1968, p. 32.
Camping Magazine:
Clark, E. W.: "Organization Guide for Camp Fire Safety." Mar., 1962, p. 20.

twenty-seven

Food and Outdoor Cooking

We may live without friends,
We may live without books,
But civilized man
Cannot live without cooks.*

—NESSMUK

*Nessmuk (George W. Sears): *Woodcraft.* Dover Publications, Inc., 1963.

PLANNING AND PACKING FOR TRIPS

Planning Menus

No matter how much other fun there is in camp, nothing can quite take the place of good, nourishing meals, tastily prepared and attractively served. With the variety of mixes and dehydrated and freeze dry foods now on the market, there is no excuse, even on long trips, for serving dull, monotonous meals. All that is required is a little imagination, a pinch of good common sense, some forethought and planning, and a good outdoor recipe book. Then even the inexperienced can turn out a tasty meal.

Young beginners should start out by planning simple *nosebag* or *poke* lunches, such as sandwiches, fruit, and a cold drink to be packed at the main camp and taken out and eaten. The next step might be cooking a one-pot meal for a supper cookout, then an aluminum-foil menu with meat and vegetables all cooked together in a package, followed by cooking in hot coals, and so on through the whole category of wonderful cooking methods available in primitive surroundings. It is usually best to add only one new item at a time so that the whole meal won't be ruined if the new technique doesn't turn out as anticipated. Such shake-down ventures give experience in gauging appetities and preparing food before longer trips are taken.

Some of the more elaborate dishes and methods of cooking may prove quite challenging when you are near camp and have ample time and when carrying out extra utensils won't be a burden, but on trips you will want to stick to simple substantial meals that can be prepared in jig time and require only a minimum of utensils to be carried and washed out after each meal. This explains why stews and other one-pot meals are so popular.

Above all, shun the inevitable and indigestible picnic menu of wieners, buns, potato chips, pickles, and marshmallows, which apparently constitutes the average American's idea of the only possible outdoor menu. It is important from a psychological as well as a health standpoint to have meals that are just as nutritious, well cooked, and attractively served as those indoors. The fact that vigorous exercise and breathing large quantities of fresh air produces ravenous appetites isn't an adequate excuse for serving half-raw, unappetizing conglomerations.

Let campers share in planning and cooking their own meals, learning the principles of good nutrition and imaginative food selection and preparation as they do so. Toward this end, many camps make it possible for campers and counselors to work closely with the dietician or a well-trained trip counselor. If you wish, you can include a consideration of costs, giving them a budget and letting them figure costs per meal, per day and per week. They will soon realize that those in average financial circumstances can't afford steak for every meal but can have good, tasty food all the time, with enough money left over for an occasional splurge.

There are now many excellent outdoor recipe books, so that anyone who can read and follow directions can plan and prepare a variety of delicious, nutritious meals. After some experience in outdoor cooking, you may even want to adapt regular recipes for out-of-doors use.

Planning Meals

On the trail, breakfast is usually simple but must be substantial enough to stick to the ribs throughout a morning of activity. Lunch is also hearty and likewise simple, often consisting of sandwiches and other cold foods, possibly supplemented by hot soup or a hot drink if the weather is rainy or chilly. A cold lunch enables you to get back on the trail quickly without having to consume time in building and putting out a fire or unpacking your stove. Supper can be more leisurely, with a hot, filling stew or other one-pot dish along with a hot bread, perhaps some side dishes, and dessert.

Vitamins and minerals consumed through normal meals are usually sufficient to meet our daily needs, but when hiking or backpacking, it is important to provide plenty of proteins, carbohydrates and fats—the essentials for energy. Proteins maintain the body in good working order, while carbohydrates and fats allow quick replenishment of lost energy to meet the increased demands on the body. Fats provide a long-term reserve, while carbohydrates give quick energy for work beyond the normal level.

Because of the body's continual need to replenish itself with calories, most trippers carry some sort of snack food to munch along the trail or at brief rest stops. These may consist of a combination of such items as dried fruits, hard candy, nonmelting chocolate or candy bars, unsalted peanuts or other nuts, and sugar-coated cereal. (Such snacks are commonly called *gorp.*

(Columbine Girl Scout Council, Inc., Pueblo, Colo.)

(Boy Scouts of America, New Brunswick, N.J.)

Several suggested mixtures are presented in Chapter 22.) Each camper carries his or her own supply in a plastic bag, secured at the top with a twist-'em or pipe cleaner.

Including enough roughage in the diet to prevent constipation is often a problem, but it can be remedied by including plenty of dried fruit (prunes, figs, dates, and so on); put them to soak the night before if you want them soft for breakfast.

Plan each meal in detail, following recipes exactly and putting down the exact amount of each ingredient needed. In selecting recipes consider such things as: (1) ease of preparation, (2) time required for cooking, (3) number and type of utensils needed (these add bulk and weight to the pack), (4) amount of fuel required, (5) amount and type of weight to be disposed of or carried back with you, (6) age, and personal preferences of those going on the trip, and (7) religious and cultural characteristics of the group. If possible, try out each recipe before using it on a trip.

Most camps furnish blank trip forms to be filled out before the trip. These ask for such information as the names of those going, the date and time of departure, destination, date and time of return, number of days and meals planned for, the actual menus planned for each meal, the exact quantities of each foodstuff needed, and a summary of the total number of utensils needed for the trip. After your plans have been approved, it is well to copy the menu for each meal on a 3- by 5-inch card, stating the exact quantities of foodstuffs required, cooking utensils needed, type of fire required, and complete directions for preparing everything; give the card to the head cook well ahead of the meal so that he or she can study it and make plans for preparing it. After your plan has been approved, representative campers, with one or more counselors, serve as *marketers,* working with the dietician or trips counselor to assemble and pack the supplies requisitioned.

When a group is large, it is usually best to divide it into small groups of six to eight, each cooking and perhaps even planning its own meals, for coping with large numbers sometimes proves quite overwhelming to inexperienced youngsters.

New Lightweight Foods

Serious backpackers today seldom take ordinary foods on a trip of any duration, for in addition to the danger of eating certain foods that have been kept for even a few hours without refrigeration, they are simply too bulky and heavy for comfortable carrying. From 70 to 90 percent of such foods are just plain water, which weighs a pound for each pint (2 cups). Modern methods of food preparation seek to remove much of this water, leaving foods that are dry, light, and compact and that, when properly packed, will keep a year or more without refrigeration. They can usually be reconstituted in from 10 to 30 minutes by adding water and cooking quickly, and they produce a finished product that closely resembles the original food in taste, eye appeal, and nutritional value.

Various methods are used to make these lightweight foods, such as puff drying and vacuum drying, which produce foods that are commonly called dehydrated foods, and actual freeze drying, which involves rapidly reducing the temperature to 40° to 50° below zero and then placing the foods in a near vacuum where the water comes off as vapor. Freeze drying is superior for many foods since it removes as much as 97 percent of the water content, but it is the most expensive method because of the large investment in plant and equipment that is required. After being freeze dried, a pound of meat weighs only 2 ounces, 10 pounds of potatoes only 1.7 pounds, and a pound of peaches that will serve four only 3 ounces. A whole cooked meal can be freeze dried and then reconstituted merely by adding boiling water. Many foods carelessly referred to as freeze dried are actually dehydrated by one of the methods previously mentioned, and although not as much of the water is removed, they are less expensive and often quite satisfactory.

The increasing popularity of camping has created a brisk demand for these foods, and a number of specialized firms have been established to produce them. Their constant experimentation and efforts to produce something better have resulted in the availability of well over 200 imaginative products, including all kinds of fruits, puddings, stews, breads, eggs and egg products, applesauce, milk shakes, fruit juices, hamburger, casseroles, beefsteak, chicken, pork chops, pizza, chow mein, and even ice cream. You will find the names of several such firms in Appendix E and you may want to write to them to learn more about their products and prices.

In addition to individual foodstuffs, whole meals are available in 1-person, 2-person, 4-person, and 8-person packets. However, some users find the portions in some brands too skimpy to satisfy appetites, so you may want to do a little experimenting before starting out on a long trip. An active teenager or adult will burn up 3,000 to 6,000 calories a day, and growing children may surprise you with what they can tuck away. Daily rations per person usually weigh from 1¾ to 2 pounds.

Each item in a prepackaged meal usually comes packed in its own individual lightweight plastic (polyethylene) waterproof bag, and those for the whole meal are then assembled in a larger bag, clearly marked with the name of the meal and the contents. Some items come in a bag in which you can soak, cook, or even eat them. You can then burn the bag, leaving no garbage to carry back or dishes to wash.

As mentioned, individually packaged items also are available so you can make up your own menus. Foods can also be bought in bulk, which allows individuals or camps expecting to take several trips during the summer to save money by measuring out and repackaging what is needed for meals.

Although buying these special lightweight foods and prepackaged meals from suppliers does cost a little more, the difference is not as great as it might seem and the fact that there is absolutely no waste and the convenience afforded may well make it seem like a very good investment.

Some people involved in camping object to using such foods exclusively, feeling that campers thereby miss out on valuable experience in planning nutritious, well-balanced meals and in learning to budget. Preplanned meals also fail to allow for individual tastes and for giving experience in using various outdoor cooking methods.

(Pacific Peaks Girl Scout Council, Olympia, Wash.)

LIGHTWEIGHT FOODS AVAILABLE AT YOUR GROCERY

An increasing variety of dehydrated and freeze dried foods, often called "dried," "instant," or "minute" foods, can be found on the shelves of your local supermarket. They are usually cheaper than those purchased from specialized suppliers. If you are planning substantial purchases, ask the manager to help you find what is available. You also will find suitable foods at Oriental and health food stores. Here are some possibilities:

- Bread, biscuit, muffin, cornbread, and pancake mixes
- Cake, cookie, brownie, and gingerbread mixes
- Oatmeal, grits, cornmeal, farina, Granola, Grapenuts and other cold cereals
- Dried peas, lentils, and beans of all types
- Instant rice
- Skillet dinners
- Dried soups
- Dried fruits (apricots, raisins, apples, prunes, dates, figs, fruit cocktail)
- Macaroni, spaghetti, noodles, pizza
- Hard cheese
- Pream and other nondairy products
- Instant pudding, Jello (cool in a stream)
- Dried milk (a pound makes a gallon of milk)—this is usually skim milk, but dried whole milk is available
- Instant potatoes
- Bread sticks or hard crackers
- Powdered fruit juices
- Parsley, onion, and carrot flakes
- Instant cocoa, coffee and tea, malted milk tablets, Ovaltine
- Popcorn (excellent for campfire nibbling)
- Peanuts and other nuts, hard candy, and non-melting chocolate
- Dried beef, codfish flakes and cakes
- Pemmican (dried meat pounded to a pulp and then mashed with fat and sometime raisins and sugar and formed into cakes or bars)
- Beef jerky (thin, brown strips that you can suck on)
- Wilson bacon bar
- Hard cookies, such as ginger snaps
- Bouillon cubes, dried mushrooms, and gravy mixes (excellent for adding flavor to soups and casseroles)
- Pie and cobbler mixes
- Herbs and spices—choose a few favorites, such as ground cummin, oregano, thyme, herb mixtures, cinnamon, cloves, bay leaves, dried dill, rosemary, and sage

PACKING FOOD

Any kind of trip, particularly one on foot, offers a challenge to plan menus using foods that require no refrigeration and are not too bulky and cumbersome. Many items purchased at the grocery store come in packages too fragile to stand the wear and tear of a trip or have sharp corners that may gouge into other things in your pack. They also do not contain the exact amounts you will need, so that you would be carrying excess bulk and weight; why carry ten pounds of flour when you need only six or a whole jug of molasses when you need only a cupful? Measure out and package exactly what you need for each meal, being careful to detach any essential directions for preparations.

Pack semiliquids such as oleo, syrup, peanut butter, jams, jellies, or honey in refillable wide-mouthed squeeze tubes or in plastic (poly) bottles that are available at outfitting shops. Lightweight aluminum cans such as baking powder cans also can be used. Other packing possibilities are Tupperware, old plastic prescription bottles, and plastic containers intended for home freezing.

Place dry materials in strong plastic bags

available from suppliers or in those intended for home freezing, squeezing out excess air and fastening them at the top by pressing with a warm iron or using plastic twist-'ems or half of a pipe stem cleaner, crimping back the ends with pliers so they won't puncture other things. Double bag (one inside the other) fine-particle foods such as flour and sugar. Be sure the bags are strong enough to hold up under trail use, and label them with a felt tip pen before you fill them. Include the name of the contents, the amount, and the meal they are to be used in. If there are printed directions for preparations, place them inside so they can be read through the clear plastic. When planning such things as flapjacks, biscuits, soups, and cakes, mix all the dry ingredients at home and pack them in a labeled plastic bag; this cuts down on the number of bags necessary and saves having to measure out and mix ingredients on the trail.

Glass bottles are heavy and breakable, so remove the contents and place them in wide-mouthed plastic bottles or light aluminum cans with screw-on or press-in tops, saved from commercial products or purchased from outfitters.

Hard cheese (not processed) in chunk form will keep quite well without refrigeration if properly packed. Package it in meal-size quantities, wrapping each portion in two or three layers of cheesecloth, pressed lightly against the cheese. Dip each package quickly into melted paraffin so that it acquires a good coating, then place the packages in a rigid metal container to prevent other objects from breaking the paraffin shield. Although a little mold may form around the edges of the cheese, it is merely a harmless form of penicillin, which can be scraped off if you find it objectionable.

Fresh eggs will not keep well for long without refrigeration; it is better to depend on the several dried egg products available from outfitters. If you prefer to take fresh eggs for use early in the trip, wrap them in paper to make them fit snugly in a plastic container designed specifically for this purpose and available from local outfitters.

Spices and other flavorings do wonders in perking up prosaic foods, so include a few well-chosen favorites. Large quantities of salt will be needed to replace that lost through perspiration. Since salt draws moisture, it will eventually rust out tin containers, so carry it in a plastic bottle or bag or in one of the poly shakers for both salt and pepper that are available from suppliers. Fasten doubtful corks and lids with adhesive tape.

For a one-meal cookout, you can simply carry your food in your cooking kettle or in a No. 10 tin can hobo stove (see Figure 27–7). For longer trips, assemble all the bags for a single meal into a larger bag, carefully labeled as to the meal for which it is intended. Place all your bags for a day (breakfast, lunch, and supper) into a larger bag, labeled with the day for which it is intended, and place these bags in your food duffel bag, arranged in the order in which they will be used, with that to be used first on top. Although it may be advisable occasionally to substitute one meal for another, as when rainy or cool weather makes a warm meal seem more desirable than the cold meal that was planned, do it rarely lest you end up with all the less attractive meals for the end of the trip. Confine portions allowed to what was planned; your extra snack foods should take care of any lack. Keep a running diary of comments and observations on each meal regarding such things as amounts, preparation, palatability, and so forth. Use this to help you plan better for each succeeding trip.

When going on an extended trip, investigate the possibilities of lightening your load and adding fresh supplies by purchasing from groceries and roadside stands along the way. You may also be able to arrange a rendezvous with the camp truck at some point en route to get fresh clothes and food or arrange with some supplier to make a drop shipment to you at some post office along the way. You may also be able to add variety to your diet by picking fruit or catching fish along the way, but don't count too much on it or you may end up hungry.

OUTDOOR COOKING

Since camps often have cookout sites near their cabins or the main camp or take short trips involving only one or two meals, we have included some recipes and cooking methods that are especially suitable for use with wood fires in such situations. For additional recipes and cooking methods, consult the references at the end of the chapter.

(P. Parker, Girl Scouts, U.S.A.)

Some General Notes About Cooking

For general cooking over wood fires, ordinary kettles with wire handles that can be hung over lug poles or on pot hooks (see Figure 27–9) are recommended.

When cooking over a wood fire, coat the outside surfaces of your kettles with a thick paste of detergent and water or rub a moistened bar of laundry soap over them. When you wash the kettle, the soap washes off easily, taking the smoke and soot with it. Not all campers are agreed on this, however; some feel that kettles heat better and more evenly if you leave the coating of smoke and soot on them, and in that case, you will need to carry each kettle in it's own carrying bag so that the soot won't rub off on other things in your pack.

When preparing fresh vegetables, do not leave them standing in water longer than necessary, for it removes some of their precious vitamins. Add them to rapidly boiling salted water and cook quickly, using as little water as possible. Avoid overcooking, keeping them on just long enough to tenderize them without destroying their crispness. Add them to water below the boiling point only if you want to extract their flavor, as in making soups or stews.

You can skin tomatoes quickly by scalding them with boiling water or holding them over the flames until their skins crack. However, it is more healthful to wash the skin well and eat it too.

Use a glass bottle or tin can when you need a rolling pin.

Grease the vessel in which you melt chocolate or measure molasses to keep it from adhering to the sides.

Test eggs for freshness by dropping them into water. If they sink quickly, they are fresh; if they sink slowly, proceed with caution, for they are doubtful; if they float, don't use them at all, for they are ancient.

Put a container of water over the fire when you first light it and you'll have hot water all ready for your main cooking by the time the fire burns down to coals.

When a recipe calls for sour milk, you can produce it immediately by adding two tablespoons of lemon juice or a few drops of vinegar for each cup of sweet milk.

You can improvise double boilers for cooking rice and other cereals by supporting the food vessel on three or four small stones inside a larger vessel partly filled with water.

Line your frying pan with aluminum foil before cooking meat or other hard to remove food and you'll have no pans that are difficult to scrub.

A little vinegar and water boiled inside the utensils in which fish has been cooked removes the fishy odor.

When cooking meat, use low or moderate heat. This requires more time, but the meat will not shrink so much and will be much more palatable and tender. When you want to draw the juices and flavor out of meat, as in making soup or stew, start it in cold water and cook it with low heat. To seal the juices and flavor in, drop it into boiling water or sear it on all sides over a hot fire, then cook it over low or moderate heat. Do not season meat until it is nearly done, for seasonings draw out juices. Neither overcook nor undercook fresh meat, but cook pork especially thoroughly because of the danger of trichinosis.

Dried milk will taste better if you mix it and let it stand for some time before drinking it.

To test breads and cakes for doneness, stick a straw or sliver of wood into them; if it comes out clean, they are done; if doughy or sticky, they need to bake longer.

Be sure to follow recipes and directions carefully.

Long, slow cooking usually improves the flavor of food. When using a wood fire, start the fire early and let it burn down to a glowing bed of coals. You can regulate the heat by changing the distance of the food from the fire or by drawing more coals under the pot, keeping a brisk fire going over at one side to produce more coals if they are needed.

Remember to allow more time for cooking at high altitudes.

In general, keep a cover on your cook pot to conserve heat and help preserve moisture.

When preparing to cook, it is a good idea to spread a plastic sheet on the ground and place all your foodstuffs and cooking utensils on it. This will keep them readily visible and prevent misplacing some essential item.

Frying is frequently overused in camp cookery and, when incorrectly done, results in an unappetizing and indigestible dish. The chief problem comes from letting fried foods absorb too much fat as they cook. To avoid this, have the food as dry as possible and heat the grease to

(Girl Scouts, U.S.A.)

just under the smoking stage before you put the food in. The hot grease sears the food, sealing the juices in and the grease out. Drain fried foods on a paper napkin or paper towel to remove excess grease. When frying in a skillet over an open fire, avoid high flames lest they set fire to the grease in the pan.

Pan broiling is a healthful and highly recommended form of frying that uses low heat. You start with very little grease in the pan and pour off the excess as it forms, leaving barely enough in the pan to keep the food from sticking. Turn the meat several times.

Broiling is cooking by direct exposure to the heat from glowing coals. Build a fire of hard wood well in advance of cooking time and keep it going until it burns down to a good bed of coals. Place the meat over the flame to sear it quickly on both sides, then place it over the coals; watch it carefully. Beware of letting fat drip into the flame, for it may catch on fire and burn the meat. Avoid using resinous or strong-tasting woods lest they impart a disagreeable flavor to the food.

Wilderness cookery is done without utensils and includes cooking in ashes or coals, in an imu or beanhole, or on a stick or spit. It is fun to plan a whole meal using only wilderness cookery, and it is surprising what a variety of tantalizing foods you can serve.

COMMON MEASURES

3 teaspoons (tsp.) = 1 tablespoon (T)
16 T = 1 cup (C)
1 C = ½ pint (pt.)
2 pts. = 1 quart (qt.)
4 qts. = 1 gallon (gal.)
No. ½ can = 1 cup
No. 1 can = 1½ cups
No. 2 can = 2½ cups
No. 2½ can = 3½ cups
No. 3 can = 4 cups
No. 5 can = 5 cups
No. 10 can = 1 gal. (12 cups)
2 T butter = 1 oz.
2 C butter or lard = 1 lb.
4 T flour = 1 oz.
4 C flour = 1 lb.
2 C granulated sugar = 1 lb.
3–3½ C brown sugar = 1 lb.
3–3½ C powdered sugar = 1 lb.
4 C cocoa = 1 lb.
3½–4 C cornmeal = 1 lb.
2 C rice = 1 lb.
2–2½ C dry navy beans = 1 lb.

OUTDOOR RECIPES

ONE-POT MEALS

These are stews or mixtures that, as the name suggests, are cooked in one kettle and furnish a whole meal in themselves. They are usually built upon a base of macaroni, spaghetti, dumplings, rice, potatoes, or noodles with various dehydrated vegetables, broth cubes, and your favorite seasonings. They may be served hot on rice, toast, or crackers.

SLUMGULLION (SERVES 5)

6 to 10 slices of bacon
2 onions, diced
1 No. 2 can tomatoes
¼ to ½ lb. cheese, diced
2 C meat, already cooked
½ tsp. salt

Cut the bacon into small pieces and fry the onion with it; drain off part of the fat, and add the tomatoes, meat, and salt. Cook for about 20 minutes; then add the cheese and continue cooking until it is melted.

IRISH STEW (SERVES 5)

5 onions, sliced
1 lb. meat cut in 1 inch cubes
5 potatoes
Other vegetables such as carrots, as desired
Salt and pepper

Melt a little fat in a kettle and fry the onions and meat until brown. Cover them with cold water and bring to a boil. Cook slowly for 1½ hours, add the potatoes, and continue to cook slowly until they are tender. Season to taste.

RING TUM DIDDY (SERVES 5)

6 slices bacon, diced
2 onions, sliced
¼ lb. cheese, diced
1 No. 2 can tomatoes
1 No. 2 can corn
Salt and pepper

Fry the bacon and onions until brown, and pour off part of the fat. Add them to the tomatoes and corn and bring to a boil. Add the cheese and cook slowly until it is melted. Season to taste.

KOMAC STEW (SERVES 8)

1 small can tomatoes or 4 fresh tomatoes (diced)
1 green pepper
2 onions, diced
3 eggs
4 T butter
Salt and pepper

Melt the butter and fry the onions until brown. Wash and dice the pepper and add to the tomatoes and onions and cook slowly for ½ hour, stirring frequently. Season to taste and add the eggs one at a time, stirring meanwhile. Avoid cooking over a fire that is too hot, for it will make the mixture curdle and look unappetizing, although this won't impair the taste or quality.

Stick Cookery (Fig. 27–1)

For stick cookery, use a metal skewer or peel and sharpen a green stick about 2 feet long. Resinous woods and willow impart an unpleasant taste. If in doubt about the suitability of the wood, peel the end and bite it. Cook over coals, not flames. You can support the stick above the fire by laying it across a rock or forked stick and weighting the handle end down with a rock or other heavy object.

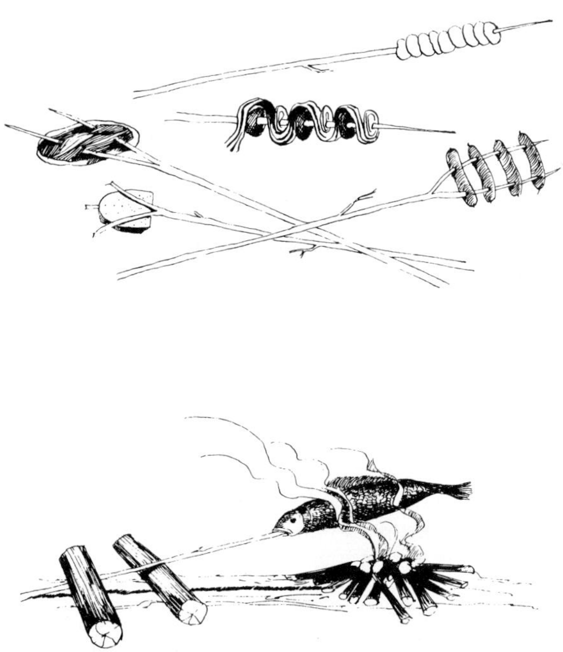

Figure 27–1 Stick cookery.

1. BREAD TWISTER OR DOUGHBOY. Use a regular biscuit mix, adding just enough water to make it sticky. Roll out flat about ¼ to ½ inch thick and cut into long strips about 2 inches wide. Remove the bark from the end of a stick about twice the size of your thumb, heat the end, flour it, and wind a strip of dough spirally around it, leaving a slight gap between the spirals. Bake for 10 to 15 minutes over coals, turning it so that all sides bake evenly. It will come off the stick in the form of a cylinder closed at one end. When filled with jam, jelly or cheese, it is known as *a cave woman cream puff.*

2. PIG-IN-A-BLANKET. Cook a wiener or long sausage on a stick, then cover it with biscuit dough and bake.

3. BACON TWISTER. Cook a piece of bacon thoroughly, cover it with dough and bake like a pig in a blanket. You can use sausage instead of the bacon.

4. PIONEER DRUMSTICKS (SERVES 5)

1¼ lbs. beef, chopped fine
¾ C cornflakes, crumbled fine
1 egg
Onion (if desired)
Salt and pepper

Thoroughly mix the ingredients and wrap a thin portion tightly around the peeled end of the stick and squeeze firmly into place. Toast it slowly over coals, turning frequently, and serve in a roll. Some prefer to put the cornflakes on after the meat has been placed on the stick, so that they form a sort of crust over the outside.

5. ANGEL ON HORSEBACK. For each serving, thread one slice of bacon on the sharpened end of a stick, and partially cook. Then wrap the bacon tightly around a 1-inch square of cheese, and hold over the fire until the bacon is done and the cheese melted. Serve with lettuce in a bun.

6. SHISH KEBABS. Lace a slice of bacon in and out among alternate 1-inch squares of steak, chops, slices of onion, oysters, small tomatoes, green peppers, and so forth, as desired, impaled on a stick. Place the pieces close together if you want the meat rare, farther apart if well done. The bacon will serve to baste them. Broil over gradual heat from coals. Shish kebab got its name from two Turkish words, "shish" meaning skewer, and "kebab" meaning "broiled meat."

7. COOKING ON A FORKED STICK. A forked stick or a wire fork may be used for cooking steaks, oysters, wieners, sausages, bacon, toast, green corn, apples, parsnips, marshmallows, or chops or for toasting sandwiches. When cooking meats, toast, and similar foods, run the tines into the food lengthwise or lace them through the food several times to hold it securely so it can be turned to cook evenly on all sides.

8. DATE DREAMS. Make these by alternating pitted dates with halved marshmallows on a stick and toasting slowly over the fire.

Cooking in Ashes or Coals

The secret of cooking in ashes or coals is to build a hardwood fire early and let it burn to coals. To keep a new supply of hot coals coming, keep a fire going at one side and draw coals over as you need them. Parsnips, fish (wrapped in clay), oysters (in the shell), squash, and hamburger (wrapped in aluminum foil) may be cooked in this way.

1. POTATOES. Scrub well Irish potatoes, sweet potatoes, or yams of medium size and without blemishes, and place them on hot coals in a single layer so that they do not touch each other; cover with coals to a depth of about 1 inch, replenishing them frequently. They are done when a sharp stick will penetrate them easily (45 to 60 minutes, depending on their size). Jab a small hole in each to let the steam escape. Some like to coat potatoes with skins on with a thick layer of wet mud or clay before roasting; both skins and mud come off cleanly when they are done. Cook fish in the same way.

2. ONIONS. Cook them as you cook potatoes.

3. EGGS. Prick a small hole through the egg shell (but not the membrane) on the large end of the egg and another through membrane and all at the small end (these holes are to let the steam escape and to keep the egg from bursting). Balance the egg carefully on its large end close to the fire where it will get moderate heat; avoid too much heat lest the egg explode. The eggs should be ready to eat in 5 to 12 minutes, depending on whether you want them hard or soft. Some prefer to wrap the egg in wet leaves, wet mud or clay before baking.

4. LITTLE PIG POTATOES. Slice the end off a potato and hollow out enough of the center to insert a small, thin sausage (cheese, bacon or raw egg may be used instead). Replace the end of the potato and fasten it with slivers of wood and bake it as previously described.

5. ROASTING EARS. Turn back the husks from young, tender roasting ears and remove the silks. Sprinkle lightly with salt, replace the husks, soak the whole thing in water a few moments, and bake in the same way as potatoes.

6. ROASTED APPLES. Core the apple and fill the cavity with raisins, brown sugar, nuts, and the like. Bake them as you bake a potato.

7. ASH BREAD. Build a hard wood fire, preferably on top of a large rock, at least a half hour before baking. Rake the embers aside and place the loaf of bread, well floured and rolled out to a thickness of ½ to ¾ inches, on the hot surface. Cover it with ashes and a layer of coals, replenishing them as they cool. It is ready to eat when a sliver of wood inserted in it comes out without dough adhering to it. Unlikely as it seems, the loaf will emerge quite clean and any adhering ashes can be quickly brushed away.

You may use any bread dough, but baking powder biscuit dough is preferred because of the short baking time necessary. If desired, raisins, nuts, berries or other fruits may be mixed with the dough.

8. POPCORN. Few things are more delightful than sitting around a blazing campfire eating popcorn. To pop properly, the kernels must be stored so they won't lose their moisture, so keep them in a moisture-proof, air-tight container, and open it only when you are ready to pop the corn. Place about ¼ cup of cooking oil in the bottom of a fairly heavy skillet or pan with a tight fitting lid and heat it over your camp stove or campfire. It is hot enough when a trial grain spins in the hot oil. Cover the bottom of the utensil with a layer of kernels, put the lid on, and start to shake it gently over the heat; continue shaking until most of the kernels have popped. Pour into a large container and mix in salt and melted oleo or butter.

Baking Potatoes in a No. 10 Tin Can

Scrub the potatoes well and wrap each in a layer of waxed paper, then in damp newspaper. Pack them in enough wet dirt or sand in a No. 10 tin can to keep them from touching each other or the sides of the can. Place the can among hot coals and leave about 45 minutes, adding additional glowing coals as needed. Keep the dirt in the can moist by adding more water if necessary.

Baking in a Reflector Oven

Reflector ovens are very useful cooking utensils and should be a part of every outdoor cooking kit, although you may hesitate to carry their two or three pounds of weight on a trip. Purchase them from outfitters or make them from tin cans as described on page 207. Commercial varieties are hinged so that they fold up and fit into a carrying case. You can also fashion an oven on the spot, as described in Chapter 26, using heavy duty aluminum foil (Fig. 26–7). Prop up the oven so the shelf is level and about 8 to 12 inches away from the fire and on the windward side, so that the ashes and flames will be blown away from the contents; it works even better if you place a reflector wall of rock or wood on the leeward side of the fire (Fig. 26–8). Use flames, not coals, and keep them brisk and about as high and wide as the oven shelf. When the shelf is hot enough to sizzle when you sprinkle water on it, place the food directly on it or use a baking pan. The sloping top and bottom reflect the heat onto the food from both above and below, insuring thorough cooking and even browning, but the metal must be kept bright and shiny to do its job well. If the surface of the shelf becomes tarnished, line it with aluminum foil to restore its brightness. Handles on the oven permit you to adjust it to a position just far enough from the fire to get the right amount of heat.

1. GENERAL BAKING. Rolls, biscuits, pies, gingerbread, cornbread, cakes, cookies, meat, and small cut up birds such as chickens can be baked to a turn in a reflector oven.

2. SWEET POTATO SOUFFLÉ. This can be baked in hollowed-out oranges (be sure to remove all the bitter lining) or in scooped-out apples.

3. EGGS BAKED IN ORANGE SHELLS. Prepare the orange as above and break an egg into it; season, and set in the reflector oven to bake.

4. POTATOES. Scrub Irish potatoes, sweet potatoes or yams. Grease their jackets with oleo or bacon fat to keep them tender. Bake them in a reflector oven for 45 minutes, turning them and testing to see when they are done.

5. SOME MORES. Make a sandwich of a marshmallow and a piece of a chocolate candy bar between two graham crackers. Press gently together and place in a reflector oven to bake.

6. BANANA BOATS. Peel back a narrow strip of peeling from the inside curve of a banana, scoop out part of the banana and fill with marshmallow, chocolate, nuts, or raisins. Replace the strip of peeling and bake in a reflector oven.

Baking in a Skillet

Support the skillet at a 45° angle against rocks on the windward side of the fire and over coals (Fig. 27–2).

1. BANNOCK. This is a traditional woodsman's bread, made by baking biscuit dough in a floured skillet. Shape the dough about one inch thick and of a form just big enough to fit the skillet. Flour it on both sides. Turn the loaf over when done on one side; both sides will be ready in about 15 minutes. Coals shoveled out and put behind the pan hasten the baking of the underside.

Figure 27–2 Baking in a skillet.

2. PANCAKES (FLAPJACKS). Grease skillet lightly and brace as described. Use only moderate heat from a small fire or from coals and heat the skillet to just under the smoking point. Drop the batter from a spoon and turn the flapjacks as soon as bubbles appear on top. Avoid too much heat for it is easy to burn them. Add blueberries or other fruit for variety. You can make your own syrup by mixing a cup of white or brown sugar with ½ cup of water, then bringing it to a boil as you stir it. Add a small amount of vanilla for a different flavor.

Cooking in a Dutch Oven

The heavy, black, cast iron Dutch oven (Fig. 27–3) of our pioneers is still an outstanding favorite, for you can bake, broil, fry, roast, or stew in it—in fact, do anything you could in your oven at home. Unlike the reflector oven, which reflects heat, it absorbs heat slowly and steadily and stays hot for a long time. Unlike indoor Dutch ovens, an outdoor oven has three stubby legs that leave enough room to rake coals under it to heat it from below, and its flat, tight-fitting lid with a turned-up edge lets you put coals on top to heat from above. It has a strong wire handle with which to manipulate it. Ovens come in diameters of 10, 12, and 14 inches. Some lighter-weight ovens are now made of heavy aluminum, which lightens them by about 2 pounds, but they are not nearly as satisfactory as those of cast iron. You won't want to carry an oven on a long trip but you will enjoy using it near camp.

"Season" a new cast iron oven before using it to keep it from rusting or having food stick to it. Scrub the inside with soap and water and dry it thoroughly. Then coat the inside with a layer

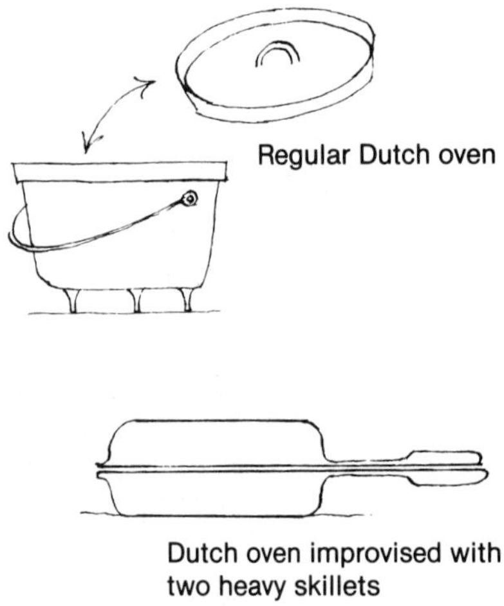

Figure 27–3 Dutch ovens.

of unsalted fat and place it in your home oven for 2 hours at 450°, swabbing the sides occasionally with the melted fat. Let it cool slowly and wipe off the excess fat. After each use, wash it out with hot, soapy water, letting it stand a little while if there are particles of food sticking to it. Never use steel wool or metal scouring pads on it, for they will destroy the effects of the "seasoning" and may cause it to rust. Dry it thoroughly and apply a light coating of grease if the oven will not be used again soon.

Its tight-fitting lid and heavy construction retain the heat and steam so that it cooks the food thoroughly without letting moisture and any of the succulent flavors escape. Be careful not to let the hot coals under the oven actually touch it or it may burn the food.

The most common error made in cooking with a Dutch oven is to use too much heat. Experience is the best teacher here. Check on progress by using a forked stick or wire hook to carefully remove the lid occasionally to see what is happening; then add or take away coals as needed.

You can improvise a Dutch oven by inverting one *heavy* skillet so it fits tightly over another one (Fig. 27–3). Support this legless oven on green sticks or rocks to provide a little space for coals underneath.

1. POT ROAST. Put bits of fat meat or other fat in the bottom of the kettle. Sear all sides of the roast over an open fire and put it in the kettle, adding such vegetables as onions, parsnips, carrots, turnips, Irish or sweet potatoes about a half hour before it is ready to serve. This provides a delicious meal in itself, and you can use the stock left in the bottom to make gravy if desired. A five-pound piece of meat requires about three hours to cook. This is a good way to cook tough meat, for it combines frying, baking, and steaming, and the long exposure to even, moderate temperature tenderizes almost any cut. If the meat is quite lean, rub it with fat or lay a few strips of bacon across it to baste it as it cooks.

2. BAKING. A Dutch oven is excellent for baking corn bread, biscuits, rolls, pies, cookies, potatoes in their skins, chicken; in fact, almost anything to be baked will come out cooked to a turn.

The Imu or Pit Barbecue (Fig. 27–4)

This is another splendid method to cook by steam with moderate even heat. It is really a variety of fireless cookery, and the excellent results obtained justify the long cooking time required. About 3 hours are necessary to cook a chicken, about a half-day for a ten-pound roast, and as much as 15 or 16 hours for anything as big as a whole sheep.

To begin the *imu,* dig a hole about two to three times as large as the food to be cooked and line the sides and bottom with nonpopping rocks; build a good hard wood fire in it and keep it going for an hour or two until the rocks are sizzling hot and there is a good bed of coals. Get all the food ready and place it in the pit as rapidly as possible so that no more heat than necessary escapes. Remove part of the coals and hot rocks, place the food in the pit, and pack the hot rocks and coals back in around and over it. Then shovel on about 6 inches of dirt to make a steamproof covering (if you see smoke or steam escaping, shovel more dirt over the leak). You can now forget the food until you dig it up, ready to eat, 3 to 20 hours later. You can cook green corn,

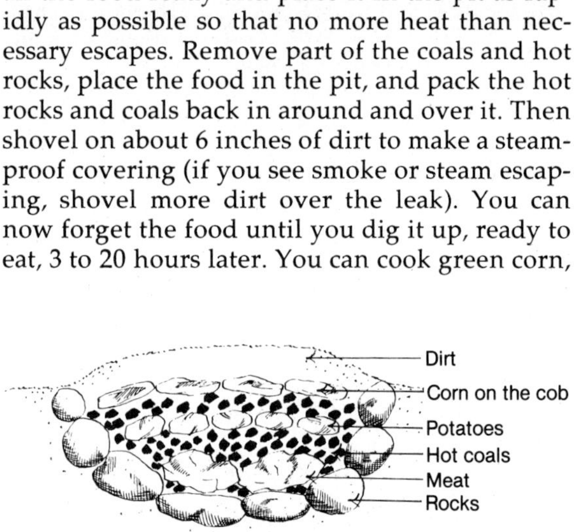

Figure 27–4 Pit barbecue or imu.

parsnips, carrots, onions, ham, clams, potatoes with meat, and many other foods in this way.

A preheated Dutch oven makes the best container for food, but if none is available you may wrap the meat and vegetables in damp butcher paper, damp paper towels, damp grass or seaweed, or damp nontasting leaves, such as lettuce, cabbage, sassafras, or sycamore. Bitter resinous leaves and burlap bags may be used if kept several layers away from the food.

BEAN HOLE BEANS

¾ lb. (2 C) dried navy beans
½ lb. salt pork or bacon, diced
1½ tsp. salt
⅛ C sugar
⅛ C molasses
2 onions, chopped fine

These are excellent when cooked in a Dutch oven inside an imu, or a bean hole made like an imu. Wash the beans and soak them overnight until their skins start to crack. Then mix all the ingredients and place them in a bean hole and let cook for six to eight hours. This cooking time can be shortened several hours by first cooking the beans in water over an open fire until they are soft, then pouring off the water and mixing in the ingredients before placing them in the imu.

Cooking on a Stone Griddle

Prop a large, flat, nonpopping rock on stones, leaving plenty of room underneath for draft. Build a fire both on and under the well-scrubbed stone, and when it is sizzling hot, clean off the top, grease it well with a swab, and fry such foods as bacon and eggs or flapjacks on it.

Barbecuing

There are several ways to barbecue meat; you can place it directly over coals (never flames) or a short distance away at the side of the fire. Barbecuing is a satisfactory method for cooking anything from a small chicken to large cuts of meat or even whole animals.

1. BARBECUING ON A SPIT OVER THE FIRE (FIG. 27-5). Dig a pit, build a good hard wood fire in it, and let it burn down to coals. Place the meat on the spit and fasten it firmly in place so that it will turn as the stick does and so cook evenly on all sides. The coals will cool off and must be replaced frequently, so keep a separate fire at one side of the pit to provide a constantly fresh supply.

Figure 27-5 Barbecuing on a spit.

When barbecuing a chicken, select a young, tender bird, commonly known as a springer or broiler. One weighing two pounds serves two people and you can cook several side by side on the same spit. Clean the chicken well and insert the spit firmly from tail to neck. Protect the wings and legs from burning by pinning them close to the body with wooden slivers. Rotate the spit slowly over the coals, and baste the bird every ten minutes with melted butter, bacon fat, or other shortening applied with a swab made by tying a cloth to the end of a stick.

Make the handle of the spit long enough to let you stay well back from the fire and place nails at varying heights on the uprights for adjusting the spit to the proper height above the heat. You can use a peeled green stick for a spit, but a metal rod with a nonheating handle does a better job, since it conveys the heat into the meat and cooks it from the inside as well as the outside. Cook roasts of beef or pork, ducks, turkeys, and small game in this way.

2. BARBECUING ON A WIRE GRILL. Fit a wire grill or piece of gravel screen on a framework of rocks, two logs, or metal poles over a pit. Build a fire of charcoal or hard wood and let it burn down to coals; place the food to be cooked (wieners, chickens, spareribs, chops, steaks, and the like) on the grill over at one side of the pit. Two persons using garden forks or similar tools can fasten them in the food-laden grill to draw it into position over the coals. Use a long-handled spatula, further lengthened by tying a long stick to the end of it, to turn the meat. Do not

Figure 27-6 Barbecuing at the side of the fire.

prick the meat with a fork, for holes allow juices to escape. Baste the meat occasionally with a cloth swab to keep it from drying out.

3. BARBECUING AT THE SIDE OF THE FIRE (FIG. 27-6). For this style of cookery, suspend the meat by a cord or wire from a lug pole 5 to 6 feet above the ground and on the leeward side of the fire. Insert a flat piece of wood or flattened No. 10 tin can about halfway down the string. Even on a seemingly still day, the tin can will catch enough breeze to keep the meat turning automatically so that it cooks evenly. Prepare the chicken as described for cooking over the fire, and reverse the lug pole and meat periodically to cook both sides. Set a pan under the meat to catch the drippings, and baste it every 10 or 15 minutes. A reflector wall on the leeward side speeds up the process.

Aluminum Foil Cooking

Aluminum foil is versatile material, for you can line cooking utensils to avoid hard scrubbing, make a reflector oven and dishes from it; you can fashion cooking utensils from it and then eat right out of the utensils. Since foil will not burn, place it in the fire to burn off the food after use, then crumple it into a ball and take it home with you. If you want to save the foil, simply wash it off and use it again.

HOW TO COOK PRESSURE-COOKER STYLE. Heavy duty foil is best for outdoor cooking, since it is about twice as thick as the ordinary variety. To prepare a meal in it, tear off a piece large enough to surround the food, allowing 2 to 3 inches of excess on the three open sides. Lay the food on one half of the piece, bring the other half over, and fold the two edges up into at least ½-inch folds and crimp them to make an airtight envelope; the all-important thing is to make it absolutely airtight so that no steam can escape, carrying with it the juices and wonderful flavor. If you have ordinary rather than heavy-duty foil, use two layers, wrapping them around in opposite directions and crimping each separately.

Cook in a good bed of coals from a hard wood fire, made well ahead of time. Round out a depression in the coals big enough for the food, place the package in it, and pull the coals back over and around it. Turn the food over halfway through the cooking process. When it is done, rake it out carefully, let it sit a minute to cool, and then make a slit down the center or open the ends and eat right from the foil.

Vegetables should be washed just before they are wrapped in the foil; the moisture will provide the necessary steam to cook them. When cooking meat that has little fat, put in a slight amount of oleo, cooking fat or oil, or a few strips of bacon. Add very little, if any, water, and salt and pepper to taste.

WHAT TO COOK. To cook a hamburger meal, place a patty in the foil along with strips of potato, green pepper, onions, carrots, and tomato. Flavor with a pinch of salt and cook 15 minutes.

Lamb or pork chops, steaks, fish, and chicken can be cooked in this way, surrounding them with such vegetables as sliced carrots, turnips, potatoes, onions, or green beans. Wet a roasting ear thoroughly, leaving it in its husks, wrap a hot dog in biscuit dough, core an apple and fill the hole with brown or white sugar, cinnamon, and raisins, and cook similarly. You can wrap the ingredients for several meals before you start out, labeling them so that you can select the right one and toss it into the coals when ready to eat. If you want to take extra foil with you, tear off a strip and roll it around a small stick; folding it might cause holes at the creases.

COOKING TIME. Cooking time will depend on such factors as the size of the package and the heat of the coals; if necessary, peep into the package to see if it is done but be sure to seal it up airtight again before replacing it in the coals. When cooking several things together, you must, of course, allow enough time for the slowest one to cook. The following are suggested cooking times:

MEATS	
Chicken (cut up)	20–30 minutes
Fish (whole)	15–20 minutes
Fish (fillets)	10–15 minutes
Shish kebab	14 minutes
Beef cubes (1 inch)	20–30 minutes
Frankfurters	10–15 minutes
Pigs-in-blanket	15–17 minutes
Lamb chops	20–30 minutes
Pork chops	30–40 minutes

VEGETABLES	
Corn (silks and husks removed)	6–10 minutes
Potatoes (Irish)	60–70 minutes
Potatoes (sweet)	45–50 minutes
Carrots (sticks)	15–20 minutes
Squash (acorn)	30 minutes

MISCELLANEOUS	
Apple (whole)	20–30minutes
Banana (whole)	8–10 minutes
Biscuits (wrap loosely in foil to allow for rising)	6–10 minutes
Stew (1-inch meat chunks, potato cubes, onions, carrots, salt, etc.)	20 minutes

OTHER COOKING DEVICES

Campers should be adaptable enough to use whatever resources they can find or can convert into cooking devices and other gadgets for use around the campsite. Ingenuity and skill will aid you in improvising cooking devices, and your satisfaction will be greatly enhanced by building your creation from scratch.

Improvised Cooking Utensils

Fashion stew pans and frying pans from a double layer of heavy-duty foil, fastening the top securely around a loop formed by lashing the tips of a forked stick together and shaping the middle portion of the foil into whatever sort of vessel you want. Let the butt end of the forked stick extend backward for a handle. Fry in it or make soup, cocoa, or anything else you want in it. You can also make a framework from a coat hanger, twisting the top into a long handle with a loop at the end to form the basis for the body of the utensil.

Campfire Paraphernalia

It is essential to take time to prepare properly for work; a camper disabled through carelessness is about as welcome around camp as a rainstorm. Canvas or other work gloves and a large bandanna are useful for handling hot objects around the fire and for keeping the hands clean for cooking. When cooking over a wood fire, a green forked-stick fire poker and a shovel are indispensable for moving hot rocks, burning embers, and glowing coals into more advantageous positions for cooking.

TIN CAN OR HOBO STOVE. A *hobo stove* (Fig. 27–7) is made from a No. 10 tin can and provides a fine little device for making toast, bacon and eggs, or other quickly cooked foods. Cut a three-inch hole at the bottom to contain the fire and use a can opener to punch several triangular holes around the top to provide ventilation and a smoke outlet. A small amount of fuel is all that is necessary; in fact, you must be careful to avoid burning the food. In the interest of ecology, it is best to use canned heat (Sterno), a warming candle, a buddy burner, or a trench

Figure 27–7 Stoves made from cans.

candle to provide the heat, but, if necessary, you can use a few small twigs. Light the fire and place the hobo stove over it, making sure that it is level so the food won't spill.

PARAFFIN STOVE OR BUDDY BURNER. A little *paraffin stove* or *buddy burner* (Fig. 27-7) is excellent for quick cooking, for it will burn for several minutes, throwing out enough heat to cook simple foods. You also can place it under a charcoal or stubborn wood fire to get it started.

Make the stove by placing about two thirds of a medium or small-sized cake of paraffin or some old candle stubs in a tuna can or a can cut down to about that height and immerse the can in boiling water, using the method described for waterproofing matches. Use extreme care in handling the paraffin, for it is flammable and can cause very severe burns if it gets on your skin. Wind a piece of cardboard or corrugated paper into a loose spiral, and insert it into the wax when it begins to harden, leaving enough of the edge extending above the wax to act as a wick. You can use the paraffin stove in your cooking fireplace for quick, simple cooking, and it will also serve as an emergency light. Placing it under a charcoal or stubborn wood fire will help to get it started quickly. When you are through with it, smother the flame by placing a lid over the can and save it to use another time.

PAN TREE. To make a handy *pan tree,* find a dead but solid branch or small tree and trim the small branches to make pegs for hanging things. Sharpen the end of the shaft and drive it into the ground near your campfire or work table. Another way to keep your pans and other paraphernalia handy and off the ground is to tie your camp rope between two trees and hang your utensils on the rope with wire pot hooks.

Supports for the Kettle

Ingenious campers find many ways to support kettles over the fire. Some sort of griddle or grate is almost a necessity for successful cooking, because it keeps things from tipping or upsetting, usually can be adjusted to bring the heat nearer to or farther from the kettles, and increases the efficiency of the fire by reflecting the heat up onto the kettles.

Figure 27-8 Stone griddles.

STONE GRIDDLES (Fig. 27-8). You can place three rocks in a triangle to support a one-pot meal or you can line up several rocks in rows, spacing them just widely enough to support your kettles and making them several rocks high if you wish. A popular variation is the *keyhole fireplace* discussed in Chapter 26 and shown in Figure 26-5. The fire is kept going in the broad end of the keyhole to furnish fresh coals to put under the kettles supported at the narrow end.

WIRE OR METAL GRATES. A number of different lightweight grills weighing less than 5 or 6 ounces are available from outfitters. They can be supported across the fire on rocks, green logs, cinder blocks, or bricks. Some come with folding legs and a carrying case. The legs can be extended and placed in the ground so no other support is necessary.

Creative campers may want to improvise, and it is usually possible to find metal bars or old pieces of flat metal in scrap heaps that will serve nicely. Other possibilities are a piece of gravel screen or even chicken wire, the shelf from an old oven, or an unpainted shelf from an old refrigerator.

THE STANDARD CRANE. Few things are more valuable around a campsite than the good old *crotched stick;* there are a thousand-and-one uses for it, including providing the supports for a standard crane. For ease in driving, sharpen the end into a four-sided point.

The *standard crane* (Fig. 27–9) has long been used to suspend several kettles over the fire simultaneously. Modern campers should not ordinarily use it, however, because it requires too much precious wood. It consists of a *lug pole* of metal or wood supported on two forked sticks about 3 to 4 feet above the fire. Pot hooks of various lengths can be hung on the lug pole for varying the distance of the kettles from the fire. After the meal is over, the lug pole can be removed and the fire built up for the evening program.

Other ways of suspending pots also are shown in Figure 27–9.

POT HOOKS. The pot hooks shown on the standard crane in Figure 27–9 include a metal one and others made of wood. The pot hook on the left in Figure 27–9 is made of strong wire or a coat hanger bent over to form two hooks, one to place over the lug pole and the other to hold the pot.

An assortment of pot hooks of various lengths is desirable so that the pot can be hung at just the right height above the fire. They also are useful for many other purposes, such as hanging pots, kitchen utensils, clothing, and other camp paraphernalia on your camp rope or even on low-hanging branches of a live tree.

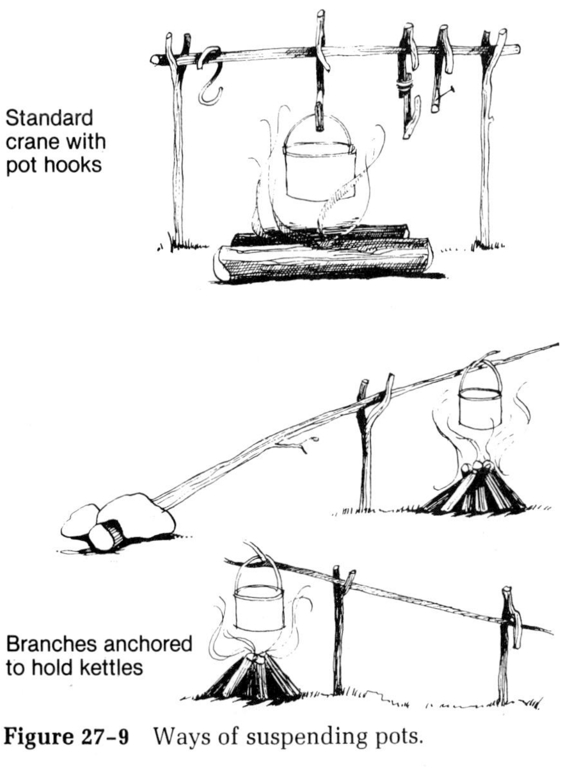

Figure 27–9 Ways of suspending pots.

Clay Ovens

The various types of clay ovens are interesting to construct and, if properly made, give excellent results when roasting meats and vegetables or baking pies, cakes, or cookies. If the ovens are to be durable and satisfactory, they must be made of clay that is cohesive and that will bake hard.

Satisfactory clay is available in most regions, and published geological surveys or persons in the neighborhood who are interested in geology may provide help in locating it. You may be able to find it in cellars, road cuttings, and other places of excavation and along the banks of streams. To test the clay for cohesiveness and workability, allow it to dry out for a little while, then knead it thoroughly and curl it around your finger. If you can curl and uncurl it without breaking or cracking it, it probably will be satisfactory.

Dig enough clay to make your oven, taking care not to mix any dirt with it. Allow it to dry for a while and then work and knead it until it is quite pliable. If it does not seem to stick together well, weave in a little hay or grass to give it added body.

To make a clay oven over a large round or rectangular metal can, cut a hole in the top for a chimney and build up a platform of clay or rocks for it to rest on. Place a layer of rocks over the sides, ends, and back of the can and cover them with clay to a depth of about a foot, making sure to leave the chimney hole uncovered. Bake the clay in the sun for a couple of days, and then build a slow-burning fire of partly green wood inside it and keep it going for two or three hours to bake it hard and firm. The fire must not be too hot or it will cause cracks to appear.

There are other forms over which you can

build a clay oven. One form consists of small sticks bound into a round bundle of the desired size and shape; another is made from a wooden packing box, and a third from half the side of a keg or a 50-gallon oil drum. Make the form for the chimney by inserting a tin can with both ends removed or a small wooden box or bundle of sticks of the appropriate size. Cover the form with clay and bake as previously described, letting the fire inside burn out the wooden form as it hardens the clay. If cracks appear, fill them with new clay and let it harden the next time you use the oven. Make the oven just large enough to accommodate the baking for your group.

When ready to bake, build a fire in the oven and keep it going until it is as hot as desired. If the wood does not burn well, place rocks or green stick fire dogs under the fuel to improve the ventilation. When the proper temperature has been reached, rake out the fire, place the food inside, and close the oven up tightly by placing a flat stone over the chimney and fitting some sort of door tightly into place. You can use a flat stone or a piece of metal for the door, or you can make one by joining a few pieces of wood together.

KEEPING FOOD COOL AND SAFE

"Oh, this is the life," you say to a handful of friends, a delicious supper under your belt, dishes all washed up and put away, and nothing to do but gather around the campfire and enjoy yourself until it is time to turn in for the night. You've escaped from civilization for a few days and there's no danger of outsiders crashing in.

You may be right insofar as human intrusion is concerned, but there are many curious creatures who will soon want to investigate this strange assortment that has established itself in the midst of their forest home. These creatures are hungry, too, and will nibble on anything and everything they can find after you have gone to bed.

Unless you are camping in true wilderness country, you are extremely unlikely to be visited by such animals as wolves, foxes, and bears, but others such as chipmunks, squirrels, mice, pack rats, and even roving dogs or cats are likely to be your neighbors. In some regions, porcupines are numerous and may prove troublesome, for their sharp teeth can be very destructive. Anything with a salty taste has an irresistible attraction for them, and perspiration-soaked paddles, axes, shoes, belts, bridles, and saddles must be kept well beyond their reach. Any food with an odor is particularly likely to draw uninvited guests.

Protection from Insects

You must anticipate the ever-present flies, ants, and other tiny crawling and flying creatures that love to sample your food. To protect food from ants and other crawling insects, you can erect a water barrier by placing the food on a table with each leg resting in a small container of water or you can make a hanger by poking a piece of stiff wire, such as a straightened out coat hanger, through the bottom of a shallow tin can and soldering it to make it watertight. Fill the can with water, then bend the ends of the wire over to make two hooks; hang the food on one and suspend the other over a limb or on your camp rope tied between two trees. Also effective is a sprinkling of common moth flakes or moth balls around the legs of a table or on the path ants would have to take to reach the food.

To keep out flying insects, place the food in jars or cans with tight-fitting suction or screw-on lids or plastic covers; wrap it in cloth, mosquito netting, cheesecloth, or waxed paper; or place it in plastic bags that can be sealed at the top.

Protection from Animals

The type of marauders you expect will, of course, determine the kind of cache or protection you must provide. Even tin cans are not safe, for some animals, including dogs, can pierce them with their teeth and suck out the contents. The usual method of caching food is to suspend it on a tree limb about 15 to 20 feet above the ground, far enough away from the tree trunk and overhanging branches that neither jumping nor climbing animals can get to it. Fasten one end of a ⅛-inch nylon rope to the food package, then tie a small rock or other small

(R. E. Smallman, Girl Scouts, U.S.A.)

heavy object to the other end and throw it over a tree limb to use as a pulley to raise the food to a safe height.

CUPBOARD CACHE. Make this convenient cupboard from an oblong box, such as an old orange crate, and insert appropriate shelves in it. Fit it with an insect-proof covering of cheesecloth or plastic and a protective front of canvas, oilcloth, or cheesecloth with tabs to tie into eyes or loops to slip over hooks placed around the bottom and sides of the crate. To attach a rope for suspending the box, anchor the rope to large screw eyes fastened in the top of the box or tie overhand or figure-of-eight knots in holes in the box. Although this cupboard is too awkward to take on a hiking trip, it is excellent for a wagon or canoe trip. It is also a practical refinement to leave at an outpost camp.

As shown in Figure 27–10, you can construct a similar cupboard that can be folded up or collapsed. Use flat plywood or other material for the shelves and suspend them with nylon cord, tying knots at the appropriate height for each shelf. Canvas, burlap, or nylon sheets work well for the sides. They should be attached to the edges of each shelf, except for the front side since it will need to be opened for access to the food.

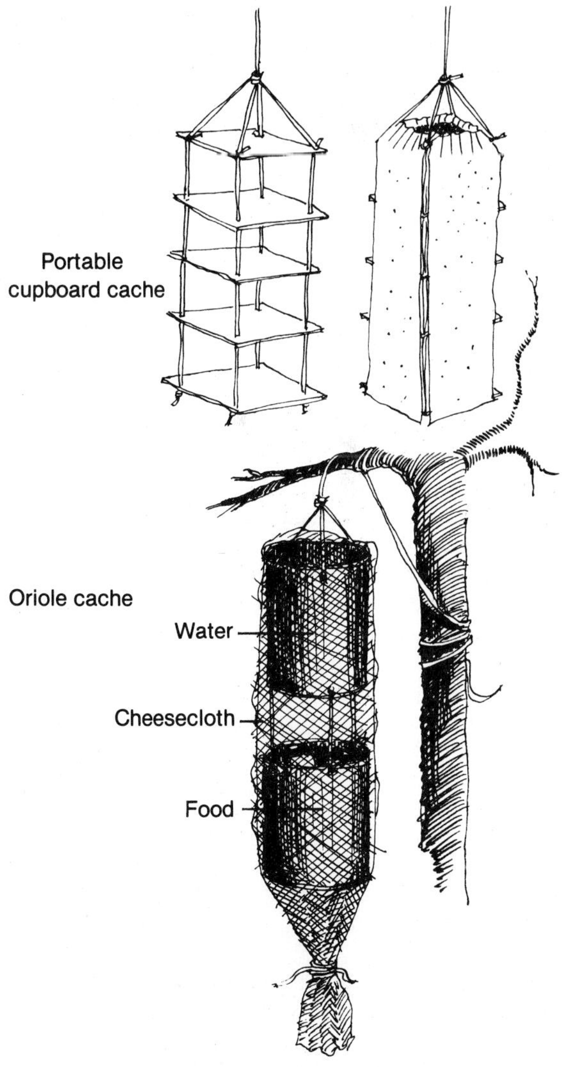

Figure 27–10 Food caches.

Keeping Food Cool

One of the main problems when trip camping is keeping such perishable foods as butter and milk cool. When stored in an airtight container, milk will keep for 24 hours or a little longer and butter will remain sweet and relatively firm for 2 weeks or more. In general, however, when going out for more than a day, it is better to take nonperishable foods or some of the multitude of dehydrated foods now available than to take chances with perishable foods, for even the most efficient refrigeration devices are too bulky to take for the kind of camping we are talking about. For short stays, you can use various methods to keep your food cool, depending upon what materials are available at your campsite.

COOLING WITH ICE

Though it isn't practicable when backpacking, it is entirely feasible to take ice for cooling when you are transporting your supplies by automobile or truck. A 50-pound cake of ice will last four days when properly cared for and a 100-pound cake will last twice as long.

As soon as possible after you arrive at the campsite, dig a hole big enough for the ice and the food you want to pack with it. Line the bottom and sides with small rocks or gravel and a layer of grass or leaves. Insulate the ice by wrapping it tightly with several layers of newspaper and an outside covering of burlap. Thoroughly moisten the insulation and place the package in an old cardboard box or tin can with holes punched in it to allow the ice water to drain off. Pack the food in close to the ice and lower the container into the pit; then shovel wet sand or gravel in all around and cover the whole thing with wet burlap or dampened newspapers.

Plan your cooking program so that you will need to open your "refrigerator" as seldom as possible and the ice will last surprisingly well.

COOLING WITH WATER

When water from a stream or lake is available, you can devise several varieties of satisfactory coolers. If the water may be disturbed by strong waves, swift currents, or boats, weight the food down with rocks or anchor it to trees or rocks on the shore so that it can't be overturned or washed away. Place the food in waterproof containers to keep impure water from contaminating it.

A SPRING BOX. A large box, can, or barrel can be sunk at the water's edge to hold food. Insert a shelf large enough to hold all the food that is not in watertight containers and leave the underpart unshelved to accommodate tall watertight containers. Make large holes near the bottom of the container to promote a free flow of water through it.

By feeling about in the water of a lake, you can often locate one or more spots that seem appreciably cooler than the rest; these are places where underground streams feed into the lake. Place your spring box in one of these spots, preferably in the shade. Weight it down with heavy rocks and cover it with newspapers or a heavy piece of burlap. This covering should either be kept constantly wet or its ends should be left dangling in the water to absorb moisture to cool the contents by evaporation.

IMMERSING DIRECTLY IN WATER Food can be placed in a large watertight container, such as a five-gallon milk can, a bucket, or a pan, and then submerged in a cool spot in the lake or stream, using rocks to weight it down if necessary. Place it in the shade and cover it with newspapers that are kept constantly wet, or with a piece of burlap or cheesecloth long enough to extend down into the water for cooling by evaporation as described for the spring box.

COOLING BY EVAPORATION

Cooling by evaporation is effective, particularly on a hot day when there is a fairly good breeze. Putting salt in the water will hasten the evaporation, making the system more efficient.

AN ORIOLE CACHE. This is one of the best methods for storing food because it cools it and at the same time protects it from animals and insects (Fig. 27–10).

Make three or four holes near the tops of two buckets or No. 10 tin cans, spacing the holes evenly so that the cans will hang straight. Join the cans with rope, as shown in Figure 27–10, leaving enough space between them to insert food into the lower one.

Take a piece of cheesecloth large enough to cover both cans and use small rocks to anchor the center of it in the upper can, which is kept about two-thirds full of water. Bring the cheesecloth down under the cans and fasten it tightly to form an insect-proof cover.

The cheesecloth absorbs water from the top can and the resulting evaporation keeps the food cool. Hang the cache in the shade in a fairly strong breeze. Swing the rope over a limb and raise the cache to a level where it will be safe from insects and animals.

The portable cupboard cache (Fig. 27–10) described earlier also can be converted into a cooling device by placing a pan of water on the top shelf and then inserting the top of the covering fabric in it, in the same fashion as for the oriole cache.

ADDITIONAL COOLING METHODS

If you dig a shallow pit in the bank close to a lake or stream, it usually will fill up quickly with underground water that is even cooler than that in the lake or stream. Place food in suitable receptacles in the pit and cover the top with wet burlap or newspapers as described previously.

Dig a hole in a shady place under a tree and line it with rocks, gravel, or leaves. Place the food in it and cover the top and sides with dampened leaves, newspapers, or burlap, and redampen them frequently.

Keep your drinking water cool by suspending it in the breeze in a desert bag; the water seeps out slowly through the canvas and cools the contents by evaporation.

ADDITIONAL READINGS

(For an explanation of abbreviations and abbreviated forms, see page 13.)

General

Angier: *Home in Your Pack,* chs. 10, 11, 12.
Angier: *Living off the Country.*
Angier: *Skills for Taming the Wilds,* chs. 14, 15, 16.
Angier: *Wilderness Cookery.*
Antell, Steve: *Backpacker's Recipe Book.* Pruett Publishing Co., Boulder, Colo., 1980, 106 pp., paper.
Bates, Joseph D., Jr.: *The Outdoor Cook's Bible.* Doubleday, 1963, 212 pp., paper.
Better Homes and Gardens Barbecue Book. Bantam, 1972.
Better Homes and Gardens Family Camping Book, chs. XI, XII, XIII, XIV.
Betty Crocker's New Outdoor Cookbook. Golden.
Boy Scout Handbook, pp. 247–251, 261–273.
Bridge: *America's Backpacking Book,* ch. 6 to p. 83 and pp. 89–111.
Brower: *Going Light with Backpack or Burro,* ch. 5.
Bunnelle, Hasse, with Shirley Sarvis: *Cooking for Camp and Trail.* Sierra, 1972, 198 pp.
Bunnelle, Hasse, with Winnie Thomas: *Food For Knapsackers.* Sierra, rev., 1970, 144 pp.
Bunnelle, Hasse, and the editors of *Backpacker* magazine: *The Backpacker's Food Book.* Simon and Schuster, 1981, 319 pp.
Cardwell: *America's Camping Book,* pp. 171–172, chs. 19, 20.
Carhart, A. H.: *The Outdoorsman's Cookbook.* Macmillan, rev., 1962, paper.
Casola, Matteo: *Successful Mass Cookery and Volume Feeding.* Ahrens, 1969, 308 pp.
Cooking (No. 3257). Boy Scouts, 1967, 96 pp., paper.
Cooking Out-of-Doors (No. 19-9842). Girl Scouts, spiral.
Dutch Oven Cooking. AAA Tent and Awning Co., 24 West 5th South, Salt Lake City, Utah 84101, paper.
Fieldbook for Boys and Men, pp. 122–123, ch. 9.
Fleming, June: *The Well Fed Backpacker,* 2nd ed. Random, 1978, 111 pp., paper.
Fletcher: *The Complete Walker,* pp. 66–137.
Friedlander, Barbara: *Earth, Water, Fire, Air.* Collier, 1972, 192 pp., paper.
Germain: *When You Go Canoe Camping,* ch. V.
Groene, Janet: *Cooking on the Go: A Camping and Galley Cookbook.* Grosset & Dunlap, 1971, 140 pp.
Holm, Don: *The Old-Fashioned Dutch Oven Cookbook.* Caxton, 1970, 106 pp., paper.
Jaeger: *Wilderness Wisdom.*
Johnson: *Anyone Can Camp in Comfort,* chs. 5, 6, 7.
Kinmont, Vikki, and Claudia Axcell: *Simple Foods for the Pack.* Sierra, 1978, 212 pp.
Langer: *The Joy of Camping,* pp. 79–99, 287–291.
Learn and Tallman: *Backpacker's Digest,* ch. 9.
Macfarlan: *The Boy's Book of Hiking,* ch. 5.
MacKay: *Creative Counseling for Christian Camps,* pp. 48–54.
Manning: *Backpacking One Step at a Time,* pp. 235–246, ch. 14.
Mason: *Junior Book of Woodcraft.*
Merrill: *All About Camping,* chs. 14, 15, 16.
Merrill: *The Hiker's and Backpacker's Handbook,* ch. 6.
Miller, Dorcas: *The Healthy Trail Food Book.* 1976, Coastal Business Center, Wiscasset, Maine, 59 pp.
Miracle and Decker: *Complete Book of Camping,* chs. 12, 13, 24, 25.
Mohney, Russ: *Trailside Cooking.* Stackpole, 1976, 176 pp.
Morris, Dan and Inez: *The Complete Outdoor Cookbook.* Hawthorn, 1970, 373 pp.
Ormond: *Outdoorsman's Handbook,* Part 4.
Pennington, Jean A., and Helen Nichols Church: *Food Values of Portions Commonly Used.* 13th ed. Harper and Row, 1980, 186 pp., paper.
Powledge, Fred: *The Backpacker's Budget Food Book.* McKay, 1977, 124 pp., paper.
Rethmel: *Backpacking,* chs. 4–6.
Riviere: *Backcountry Camping,* ch. 7.
Riviere: *The Camper's Bible,* ch. 7.
Riviere: *Family Camper's Cookbook.*
Rutstrum: *The New Way of the Wilderness.*
Shivers: *Camping,* pp. 228–238, Appendix A.

Stephens, Mae Webb, and George S. Wells: *Coping With Camp Cooking*. Stackpole, 1968, 96 pp.
Sunset Barbecue Cook Book. Lane, 1965, 159 pp., paper.
Sunset Camping Handbook, pp. 40–57, 65–67.
Sunset Ideas for Building Barbecues. Lane, 1971, 71 pp., paper.
Tarr, Yvonne Young: *The Complete Outdoor Cookbook*. Quadrangle, 1973, 308 pp.
Thomas, Dian: *Roughing It Easy*. BYU, 1974, 202 pp., paper.
Thomas, Dian: *Roughing It Easy 2*. Warner, 1977, 223 pp., paper.
van der Smissen and Goering: *A Leader's Guide to Nature-Oriented Activities*, pp. 101–125.
Walrath, Arthur J.: *Camp Cookery for Small Groups*. Walraths, P. O. Box 245, Blacksburg, Va. 24060, 1967, 84 pp., paper.
Whelen and Angier: *On Your Own In the Wilderness*, chs. 10, 27, 28, 29 and pp. 315–320.
Winnett: *Backpacking For Fun*, ch. 4.
Wood: *Pleasure Packing*, pp. 64–71 and ch. 6.

MAGAZINE ARTICLES

Backpacker:
"The Best of the Freeze-Dried Dinners." *Backpacker-7*, Fall, 1974, p. 63.
"How to Round Out Your Freeze-Dried Dinner Menu." *Backpacker-10*, Summer, 1975, p. 64.
Packer, Nelson: "How to Pick a Freeze-Dried Dinner." *Backpacker-7*, Fall, 1974, p. 65. (See also pp. 67–80.)
Saijo, Albert: "Go Light Backpacking." *Backpacker-3*, Fall, 1973, p. 86.
Van Lear, Denise: "You and Your Gear—Supermarket Substitutes." *Backpacker-6*, Summer, 1964, p. 26.
Camping Journal:
"Build Your Own Backpack Oven." Apr., 1972, p. 97.
Sibley, H.: "Jury Rigs For Cooking." Jan., 1968, p. 44.
Stebbins, J. Ray: "Food for Backpackers." Aug., 1972, p. 30.
Steindler, Gerry: "Cooking With Foil." July, 1970, p. 24.
Steindler, Gerry: "5-Minute Meals." Apr., 1973, p. 54.
Steindler, Gerry: "Trail Chow: How to Pick It, Pack It, Cook It." Mar., 1970, p. 38.
Steindler, Gerry: "Wagon Tongue." July, 1970, p. 14. (Convenience foods)
Camping Magazine:
Burkart, Audrey C.: "Dear Mom, the Food Is Great." Mar., 1974, p. 9.
"Lighten Canoe Trip Loads With Modern Food Products." May, 1965.
Proud, Dorothy M.: "Planning Nutritious Camp Meals." Feb., 1966.
Treadwell, Dawn D.: "Planning Meals for Young Campers." May, 1972, p. 18.

Wild Foods

Angier, Bradford: *Feasting Free on Wild Edibles*. Stackpole, 1972, 320 pp., paper.
Angier, Bradford: *Free for the Eating*. Stackpole, 1966, 191 pp.
Angier, Bradford: *Gourmet Cooking For Free*. Stackpole, 1970, 192 pp.
Angier: *How to Stay Alive in the Woods*.
Angier: *Living Off the Country*.
Angier: *Skills for Taming the Wilds*, chs. 17, 18, 19, 23.
Angier: *Survival With Style*, chs. 9–11.
Angier, Bradford: *We Like It Wild*. Macmillan, 1973, paper.
Angier: *Wilderness Cookery*, chs. 3–6, 10.
Barnett, Harriet and James: *Game and Fish Cookbook*. Grossman, 1968, 162 pp.
Berglund, Berndt, and Clare E. Bolsby: *The Edible Wild*. Scribner's.
Coon, Nelson: *Using Wayside Plants*, 4th ed. Hearthside, 1969, 254 pp.
Dalrymple: *Survival in the Outdoors*, ch. 8.
Edible and Poisonous Plants of the Eastern States and Edible and Poisonous Plants of the Western States. Plant Deck, 2134 S.W. Wembley Park Road, Lake Oswego, Oregon 97304. Two decks of 52 cards each, with a picture of the plant on one side of the card and its description on the other.
Ellerhoff, Kay (ed.): *Savoring the Wild*. Montana Dept. of Fish and Game, Helena, MT., 1974, 96 pp., paper.
Fernald, Merritt L., Alfred Kinsey, and Reed Rollins: *Edible Wild Plants of Eastern North America*. Harper & Row, rev., 1958.
Fieldbook for Boys and Men, pp. 322–331.
Gibbons, Euell: *Stalking the Blue-Eyed Scallop*. McKay, 1964, 332 pp., paper.
Gibbons, Euell: *Stalking the Good Life*. McKay, 1971, 247 pp.
Gibbons, Euell: *Stalking the Healthful Herbs*. McKay, 1970, paper.
Gibbons, Euell: *Stalking the Wild Asparagus*. McKay, 1962, 303 pp., paper.
Hall, Alan: *The Wild Food Trail Guide*. Holt, Rinehart, 1973, 195 pp., paper.
Hamper: *Wilderness Survival*, pp. 22–59.
Kirk, Donald: *Wild Edible Plants of the Western United States*. Naturegraph, 1970, 307 pp., paper.
Langer: *The Joy of Camping*, pp. 287–291.
Medsger, Oliver P.: *Edible Wild Plants*. Macmillan, rev., 1972, 323 pp., paper.
Merrill: *The Survival Handbook*, chs. 7, 8.
Mohney, Russ: *Trailside Cooking*. Stackpole, 1976, ch. 8.
Olsen: *Outdoor Survival Skills*, chs. 4–6, pp. 146–178.
Shockley and Fox: *Survival in the Wilds*, chs. 5, 8–10, 13.
Sweet, Muriel: *Common Edible and Useful Plants of the West*. Naturegraph, 1962, 64 pp., paper.
Wilderness Pocket 'n Pack Library, Vols. 1 and 2.

"ROUGHING IT SMOOTHLY"

Newcomers to camp usually bring along all sorts of unnecessary *duffel* or *gear* (camp jargon for your possessions), most of which lies unused, collecting dust and occupying valuable space. The secret of orderly camp living is to have everything that is needed for health, safety, and happiness without being surrounded by a collection of unnecessary claptrap. Remember that the keynote of camp living is simplicity. Your camp living quarters probably will be clean, comfortable, and quite adequate for your needs but without extra embellishments or an unlimited amount of storage space. The ultimate goal, both in camp and on the trail, is perhaps best expressed by the title of Elon Jessup's book, *Roughing It Smoothly*. However, unless you are engaging in the type of camping known as "survival camping," it is just as bad to go to the opposite extreme by trying to live too primitively.

DUFFEL FOR TRIPS

When planning for a trip, choosing what to take and how to pack it is truly an art in itself, especially if you plan to carry everything on your back, for even after traveling only a few miles over a trail that is rough or steep, perhaps in disagreeable weather, each inch of bulk seems like a foot and each ounce a pound. Transportation by canoe, pack saddle, or horseback allows a bit more latitude, but compactness and lightness are important even then, since space is still at a premium and every unnecessary thing will need to be picked up and handled many times as you search for needed items.

Sources of Equipment

Camps and counselors should not promote long expeditions into the backcountry unless a minimum of equipment of the right sort is available for doing it comfortably and safely. However, elaborate outlays suitable for going on an African safari aren't at all necessary, for campers can initially get along with little more than the things they or the camp already have, adding to them as their experience dictates and their finances permit. Camps sometimes rent or lend

twenty-eight Duffel for Camping and Trips

Look out, when you start for the day,
That your kit is packed to your mind;
There is no use going away,
With half of it left behind.

—Rudyard Kipling*

*From "A Boy Scout's Patrol Song," 1909. *In Rudyard Kipling's Verse,* Definitive Edition, 1940, Doubleday & Co., Inc. Reprinted with permission from the publishers.

pieces of personal equipment to campers and customarily furnish such group equipment as tents, tools, and group cooking and eating outfits. Campers also can make many items, perhaps as a special project before the trip begins. The references listed at the end of this chapter can be consulted for ideas and instructions on making such things as ponchos, ground cloths, tents, packsacks, and sleeping bags. Also, listed in Appendix E are some firms that sell do-it-yourself packages by mail order.

Army-Navy surplus stores are good sources of inexpensive gear and quantity discounts are often available from suppliers. Also, don't overlook those things that can be assembled at home, such as cooking utensils, mess kits, and other items.

DITTY BAGS AND STUFF SACKS

Figure 28–1 Stuff sacks or ditty bags.

A camper's pack is a series of bags within bags, with similar things, such as toilet articles or underwear, collected in small *ditty bags* or *stuff sacks;* this allows you to put your hand on just what you want without having to turn everything topsy-turvy. Articles packed singly or in disorderly fashion have a way of dropping to the bottom of your pack or being left behind at some stopping place.

The number of sacks or bags needed depends upon the length of your trip and your personal preferences. A minimum is one for toilet articles, one for clothing, one for eating utensils, and one for miscellaneous items. You may want to add others for such things as tools and repair materials, shoes, and food.

Many campers like ditty bags made of strong plastic since they are waterproof, tough, and readily reveal what is in them. Although these can be purchased from outfitters, you can collect your own assortment by saving such things as home freezer bags and bags in which food and other items are sold. For extra security when packing fine substances such as flour, place one bag inside another. Fold over the tops and fasten them with rubber bands or "twist-'ems."

Outfitters also offer zippered pouches and bags that close with drawstrings, which are usually waterproofed and made from lightweight materials. However, it is easy to make your own. The very best material to use is probably parachute nylon, which is light, compact, and strong. Other possibilities are balloon silk, Egyptian cloth, denim, and unbleached muslin, which can be waterproofed if you wish. To determine the size needed for an individual bag, assemble all the items that are to go in it and fashion a paper pattern big enough to surround them, leaving enough extra width for double-stitched seams and enough room at the top for a hem wide enough to admit a drawstring.

Broad ditty bags with round bottoms, such as those shown in Figure 28–1, will stand open and upright, although they are not as simple to construct as those made by simply sewing two rectangular pieces of cloth together. Use distinguishing colors and draw a representative picture on each bag or list the contents on the side with enamel for permanence, Mystik Tape, or a wax crayon for a temporary job. Label long, narrow bags on top so that they can be slipped into your backpack upright and removed without disturbing the rest of the contents.

CLOTHING

Clothing and outfitting stores display attractive camping outfits of almost every type and description, but the wise novice goes slowly and chooses carefully before making a large investment. Although everyone wants to look well dressed and attractive, comfort, suitability, and durability are far more important considerations.

Your choice of clothing should be influenced by such factors as the season and weather expected, the length of the trip, and the type of terrain in which you will travel. Garments should be comfortable and fit snugly, yet be cut full enough to permit freedom of movement for hiking, climbing, canoeing, working around camp, or whatever else you will be doing. They obviously need to be serviceable, snag resistant, and washable.

Layering System

Remember that the human body has a built-in thermostat with its own heating and cooling devices, so choose clothing with a view to helping it perform efficiently. Persons wise to the outdoors know that the best way to do this is to adhere to the principle of *layering*. Here's an example of how it works: On a cool summer morning, you start out wearing underwear, trousers, a shirt or two, and even a sweater and lightweight windbreaker. As the day warms up, you simply remove the garments as needed. In reverse order, clothing is added to meet the cool of the evening.

There are a number of advantages to this system. For instance, several layers of clothing provide more warmth than does a single thick garment because immobile air is trapped between the various layers. A person is also better able to make refined clothing adjustments in order to adapt readily to changing weather conditions. Yet another important consideration is one's ability to control perspiration caused by overheating. An important point was made in the discussion on hypothermia in Chapter 18 and should be remembered: The collection of moisture on clothing, whether from perspiration or any other source, can lead to a dangerous and sometimes fatal situation.

Regardless of how many piles of clothing you use for layering, the system has three primary components.

1. *Vapor Transmission Layer.* This consists of *breathable* garments next to your skin that allow body moisture to pass quickly and efficiently through them. To wick away moisture in cold weather, it is best to wear underwear made of wool, silk, or the new synthetics olefin and polypropylene. Although wool has long been the traditional standby and still works well, more and more people are now using the new space-age synthetics. Above all, in cold climates be sure to avoid garments made of cotton since they provide no insulation when wet. In fact, collected moisture in cotton fabrics actually can draw heat away from the body faster than it can be generated by your system.

2. *Insulating Layer.* A wide variety of garments work well for the insulating layer, including those made of wool or down or any of the newer synthetics such as pile, Polarguard, Hollowfil II, or Thinsulate. Shirts, sweaters, vests, jackets, or parkas commonly are used to hold the warm air around your body.

3. *Protective Layer.* The outermost layer protects the inner layers from abrasion and also shelters the wearer from water and wind. As with the insulating layer, there is a wide variety of suitable garments available, including jackets, anoraks, windshirts, cagoules, and other variations of these.

Since the moisture protecting element of the outer layer must protect against rain or even snow, a major dilemma arises in selecting proper materials. For years there has been a controversy among experts as to whether the fabric used for these garments should be waterproof or water repellent. Waterproof shells (usually made of coated nylon or plastic) are totally impervious to moisture and consequently they do not breathe. Thus, a person can become soaked from body moisture that collects inside, especially when involved in hard physical activity. This is one of the reasons why waterproof ponchos are popular, since air can circulate under them.

The other choice is to wear a breathable garment made of water repellent material that allows body moisture to escape to the outside. Materials such as 60/40 cloth (40 percent cotton, 60 percent nylon) work well, but they can only resist rain for a short duration before becoming saturated. Fortunately, the market recently has begun to offer PTFE (polytetrafluoroethylene) laminates under such registered trademarks as Gore-Tex and Klimate. Under most conditions these materials actually do keep out the rain, yet, because of microscopic pores in the laminate, body moisture is allowed to pass through in the form of water vapor molecules. The major disadvantage of clothing made of PTFE laminates is the cost. Although these garments are expensive, they do work in most circumstances, so they may well be worth the money for those who do spend a great deal of time outdoors.

Specific Garments

Certainly not all of the items mentioned earlier can be or necessarily should be part of every camper's attire. This is especially so because of their expense as well as because of the many different settings and climates in which camps operate throughout the country. Nonetheless, a helpful checklist of equipment and clothing that might be desired appears on page 443. Following is a more specific discussion of some garments that can be considered for warm summer use.

UNDERWEAR. Although almost any well-fitting, comfortable cotton underwear will do for summer wear, many experienced backpackers prefer open-weave *fishnet underwear,* which consists of a network of large diamond-shaped holes. The mesh feels quite comfortable as it soaks up perspiration and allows it to evaporate. When it is cool, the weave also provides warmth if covered with outer garments, since the open spaces between the netting trap dead air. At least one extra set of underwear is needed so that you can wash out the soiled set at night to always have a pair in reserve for an emergency.

PANTS. Pants should be of sturdy, closely woven material that will resist snagging and picking up trailside impedimenta such as burrs and nettles. Although wool is preferable for cold weather, cotton or part cotton is better for summer as long as it stays dry. When wet, however, it provides little insulation and becomes quite heavy. Therefore, it is important to have plenty of good rain protection gear. Blue jeans, once a camping favorite except during cold or rainy weather, are still a good choice if you can find a pair of the old-fashioned roomy kind; unfortunately, most of today's jeans are cut in the form-fitting Western style that fits too tightly for comfort and does not permit free movement. You will find several types of work pants at your local stores that will do nicely, and a large selection of suitable pants are available from outfitters. Look for designs that have large pockets, and for those with pocket closures. Stout whipcord, denim, khaki, drill, and corduroy are some of the more satisfactory materials.

Cuffless pants are preferable since cuffs collect dirt and catch on snags, causing tears and possibly accidents. If the pants you want to wear have cuffs, cut them off and rehem the bottoms of the legs.

Some prefer shorts for walking along country roads or on open woodland trails. They should be ruggedly constructed and comfortably cut. On most occasions, however, long pants are recommended for general hiking through the woods since they offer protection from scratches, poison ivy or oak, insect bites, chiggers, and too much sun. If the legs are cut wide enough, you can pull them up or roll them up for coolness when such protection is not needed. While walking through sand or an infestation of insects, your pant legs can be taped or tied snugly about your ankles.

SHIRTS AND SWEATERS. Cotton shirts or those of part cotton may become uncomfortably soggy and chilly when wet. For this reason, many prefer a lightweight wool shirt or a combination of wool and cotton. At least one wool shirt or sweater should be taken along.

Long sleeves discourage mosquitoes and other biting insects and protect against sunburn, scratches, and poison ivy and oak. A long shirt tail keeps the shirt inside your trousers, or it can be worn outside for better ventilation when it is hot. One or two breast pockets with button down flaps are a convenience. Also, a button down shirt is easier to ventilate than a sweater.

Take at least one extra shirt to wear for extra warmth and to allow you to wash one out at night.

WINDBREAKERS. Your summer outfit should include a lightweight windbreaker jacket. One with a hood is called a *parka.* It should be of closely woven, water repellent (not waterproof) material so that it "breathes" to keep your perspiration from being trapped inside where it will condense. Long-fiber cotton, tough nylon, or a combination of the two are satisfactory materials. The garment should be long enough to pretty well cover your hips and should be roomy enough to permit free arm movement even when worn over several layers of clothing. Most jackets have elasticized wrists or Velcro closures and there should be several large pockets. Windbreakers come in two styles: one a slipover jacket, the other opening down the front. Although a slipover is simpler and lighter, it cannot be worn open to adjust to temperature changes.

HEADGEAR. A hat with a fairly wide brim will be needed to protect you from sun glare and to keep rain water from running down your neck. It should fasten under your chin with a strap or ties so it can't blow away. There should be holes in the crown, and these should be placed high enough to permit ventilation; add some triangular ventilation holes of your own if there aren't enough. A roller-crusher type hat of soft material, which can be rolled up and stored in your pack, is good. Some prefer to wear a hat of terry cloth that can be kept wet to cool your head. Berets, although worn by some, obviously, do not meet all of these requirements. Other campers like a duckbill visored tennis, hunting, or baseball cap. For cooling your head, try knotting a bandanna into the semblance of a hat and wear it damp; it also can be used as a headband to keep perspiration from running down into your eyes.

SLEEPWEAR. Never sleep in the clothes you have worn all day, for they are likely to be perspiration-soaked and clammy. Most campers prefer to change into a fresh T-shirt and shorts, although some may even carry along pajamas.

BOOTS AND SOCKS. The choice of boots and socks and the care of the feet are discussed in Chapter 22 under "Footwear."

RAINWEAR. Keep rainwear near the top of your pack where you can find it in a hurry. As already mentioned, there is little agreement as to the best rain protection but no one disputes the inadequacy of the gossamer, oiled-silk cape with hood.

Raincoats that are too long are a pure nuisance, for they flap about at every step and constantly fly open to expose the lower part of your body to the elements. They are usually hot and binding and cause profuse sweating.

As we have previously noted, snug-fitting, waterproof garments trap perspiration and make a person wet. Therefore, unless modern "breathables" are used, you should have rainwear that fits loosely to admit some ventilation, making sure that wrists, collars, and fronts can be opened during breaks in the weather. To make garments absolutely rainproof, they must be coated with rubber, which makes them heavy, or made of some light material with a rainproof coating, such as urethane-coated nylon. Garments of thin plastic vinyl are adequate for occasional wear but will quickly disintegrate under rugged use.

Poncho. A frequently used garment for general rainwear around camp is a poncho. This is a waterproof sheet with a center hole and hood for the head (Fig. 28–2). Some types have a long flap in the back that can be draped over your pack to protect it. This loose construction provides ample ventilation. The hood can be held close about your face with a drawstring. A poncho is especially useful in a canoe, where the loose flap can be draped over your duffel on the bottom of the canoe. The garment proves rather unsatisfactory, however, when trying to walk in a strong wind, which sets it flapping, or when trying to walk through heavy brush or weeds. A poncho is particularly valuable because of its versatility—there is usually a covering for the head hole that allows you to convert it into a flat waterproof sheet to cover gear, use it as a ground cloth under your sleeping bag, or construct an improvised shelter with it. Some ponchos can be snapped together to form a larger sheet.

Rain Suits. A rain suit (Fig. 28–2) consists of a hip length jacket with a hood and full cut trousers that slip on or off easily over your shoes and are roomy enough to wear over several other garments. The suit should be well constructed and of a strong, lightweight, and durable material.

Rain Chaps. Rain chaps slip onto each leg individually and tie at the waist. Since they have no front, back, or crotch, they weigh very little. They protect your legs well and should be worn with a fairly long rain jacket to protect the rest of the body.

Cagoule. A *cagoule* is a knee-length pullover parka, usually made of coated nylon. "Cagoule" is an old French word meaning "monk's hood," so of course the contemporary models still have hoods. It is roomy, provides good protection in any but extreme weather conditions, and allows free body movement. Some are provided with snaps to shorten them when their full length is not needed.

Figure 28-2 Poncho and rain suit.

Rain Hat. As noted, many items of rainwear come with built-in or detachable head protectors. If you need a separate hat, you can either carry a rainproof cover for your regular hat or get one of the various sou'westers or light waterproof hats with medium brim and strings to tie under your chin.

Footwear. Although your boots may be made water resistant, it is practically impossible to waterproof them completely. Light rubbers are available to slip on over them if you expect to do extensive walking in wet conditions. Rubber boots are heavy and clumsy and tiring to walk in and recommended only for actually wading through water.

GLOVES. A pair of lightweight leather gloves or washable canvas work gloves are a very important part of your equipment. They are indispensable for handling hot cooking utensils and for protecting your hands from blisters, abrasions, and splinters when doing heavy work or building fires.

BANDANNA. A large-sized bandanna is another piece of equipment that adapts itself to many purposes. It can be used to handle hot pans, to tie up a homemade mess kit, to hold specimens gathered along the trail, to double as a triangular bandage or tourniquet, to shield your neck and face from sunburn and insects, to wear around your forehead to keep perspiration out of your eyes, to dampen and make into a turban to wear wet around your head for cooling, or to place folded under your tump line or the straps on your pack to keep them from cutting. Carry it in your hip pocket or an outside pocket of your pack or wear it around your neck ready for instant use.

TOILET ARTICLES

Carry a few well-chosen toilet articles in a ditty bag or in a specially constructed case. For a trip, you need to take only small quantities of toilet supplies, such as a small bar or tube of biodegradable soap, a toothbrush and small quantity of paste, dental floss, comb, toilet paper, polished steel hand mirror, and a washcloth. For a towel, a diaper makes a good substitute because of its lightness and great absorption ability. Pack all liquids in unbreakable containers. Such planning is the secret of successful *go-light* trips. You may sometimes have to pack such articles as your toothbrush, toilet soap, washcloth and towel wet, so it is best to fit them with individual waterproof ditty bags. You need to take no more than one washcloth and towel, since they can be washed out and hung up to dry overnight.

By carefully saving and washing out the plastic bottles and bags that home products commonly come in, you can soon accumulate almost all the containers and bags needed.

MISCELLANEOUS EQUIPMENT

It will be necessary to include a few tools in your trip outfit, but if several campers are going, you need not burden each member of the party with duplicates. If one axe or bow saw will serve the whole party, then share the load accordingly or take turns carrying it.

Tool Kit

Such tools as a small screwdriver and pliers with wire cutter are useful. A compact tool haft is available that consists of a hollow handle filled with various attachments for converting the tool into a screwdriver, an awl, and so on. Each party should carry at least one trowel or small shovel, preferably with detachable handle, for digging sanitary facilities and manipulating and putting out fires.

AXE, KNIFE, AND BOW SAW. If your group plans to build wood fires, you may need an axe, knife, and perhaps a bow saw, as discussed in Chapter 23. This, of course, depends on the type of wood available and the area in which you will travel. In most cases, there may be little need for most of these items since there will likely be plenty of small pieces of dead wood available on the ground.

Always keep your axe in its sheath, and carry your knife in your pocket, attached to your belt loop, or in a "catch-all" ditty bag in one of the pockets of your backpack.

OTHER ITEMS. Some lengths of strong nylon cord, thin copper or picture wire, shoe thread, canoe and tent repair kits, and a small assortment of cotter pins (for pack frame problems) will also prove helpful. You also may find many uses for ½- to 2-inch strips of old inner tube (tying packages, fastening them to your pack frame, and so on). Keep these things together in a repair ditty bag.

Mending Kit

Pack mending equipment in a tin box or ditty bag and include such items as needles (laced through a small piece of cardboard), both straight and safety pins, a few yards of thread wound on a piece of cardboard, small pointed scissors, buttons, patches of cloth and leather, assorted rubber bands, adhesive tape, and strong waxed linen thread.

First Aid Kit

Items suggested for a first aid kit are presented in Chapter 18. No expedition, even a brief one, should leave camp without the necessary supplies for emergencies.

Map and Compass

Even though you may not actually need a map to find your way, a topographical map of the region will prove interesting and will help you to choose the most intriguing path. Prepare it for hard use on the road as described on pages 335–336. A compass also is needed for following or making a trail map. It should always be a standard piece of equipment for any trip.

Protection from the Sun

In addition to a broad-brimmed hat or visored cap, long sleeves, full-length trousers, and a bandanna, you also will need a good pair of sunglasses and some suntan oil. This is especially so if you are to be much in the open while on or near water. Sunglasses not only protect your eyes from bright sunlight, but also help to keep out dust and wind.

Protection from Insects

Take a good insect repellent and, if needed, a head net to cover the face and neck. If there is no built-in insect protection for your tent, you may want to add some netting or screening for the tent door.

Sleeping Equipment

This consists of a poncho or ground cloth to place under your sleeping bag, and a mattress or sleeping pad (Fig. 25–4) for softness and additional insulation from the ground. A ditty bag filled with soft materials, such as socks and extra underwear, can be used for a pillow.

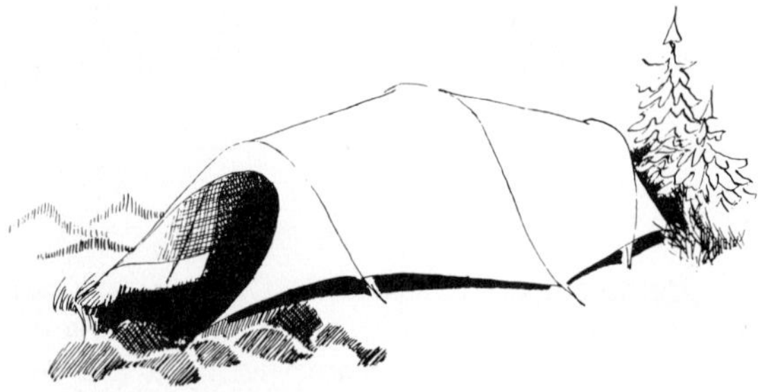

Figure 28-3 Alpine tent.

Shelter

A lightweight alpine tent (Fig. 28-3) or tarpaulin is necessary for protection against the elements. For further details on tents and other forms of shelter see Chapter 24.

Flashlight

Each person should have a small pocket-sized flashlight, such as a Mallory, with extra bulbs and batteries. When not using your flashlight, reverse the top battery so that the two negative poles meet; this will prevent any possibility of the light being turned on in your pack accidentally. A flashlight probably will be used less than you think, for when on a trip you usually will take advantage of daylight hours by stopping early to make camp, eat supper, and clean up before dark.

Candles

Short, fat plumbers' or miners' candles are best, for they burn strongly enough to start even a wet-weather fire and also give off quite a bit of light. Some prefer to use a candle in a lantern (Fig. 28-4) that has a shatterproof plastic chimney to shield the flame and a chain at the top by which to hang it. The lantern folds down compactly for carrying.

Water Supply

You will need to carry a supply of water with you, the amount depending upon your ability to replenish the supply from known safe sources along the way. When not absolutely certain of the water's purity, you will need to take equipment to purify it by one of the methods discussed in Chapter 18.

Several types of containers are available for carrying water, including the traditional aluminum, military-type canteen. Also, a wide assortment of polyethylene bottles now on the market allows ample variety from which to choose. Look for one with an attached stopper and screw-on lid in order to eliminate the possibility of leaks (Fig. 28-5). A wide-mouth bottle is easier to clean and more convenient for mixing powdered drinks. To improvise, use discarded plastic soft drink containers, since they work well if handled carefully. Different types of collapsible water bags and desert bags are available for carrying larger quantities of liquid; these usually are available in ½- to 3-gallon capacities. Individual canteens ordinarily come in 1- and 2-quart sizes.

Carrying larger quantities of water than you need becomes a real burden since water weighs 8 pounds per gallon. Therefore, it helps to find out in advance of a trip whether water will be available along the route.

Fire Starters

A small supply of matches is always a good thing to take for emergency use on a trip, and if you plan to build wood fires, you will need a

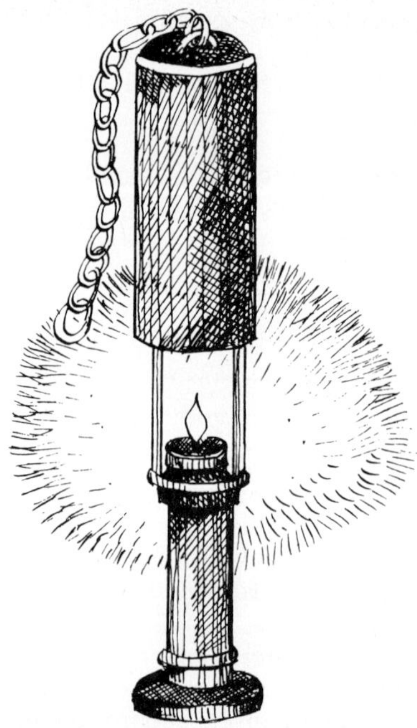

Figure 28-4 Candle lantern.

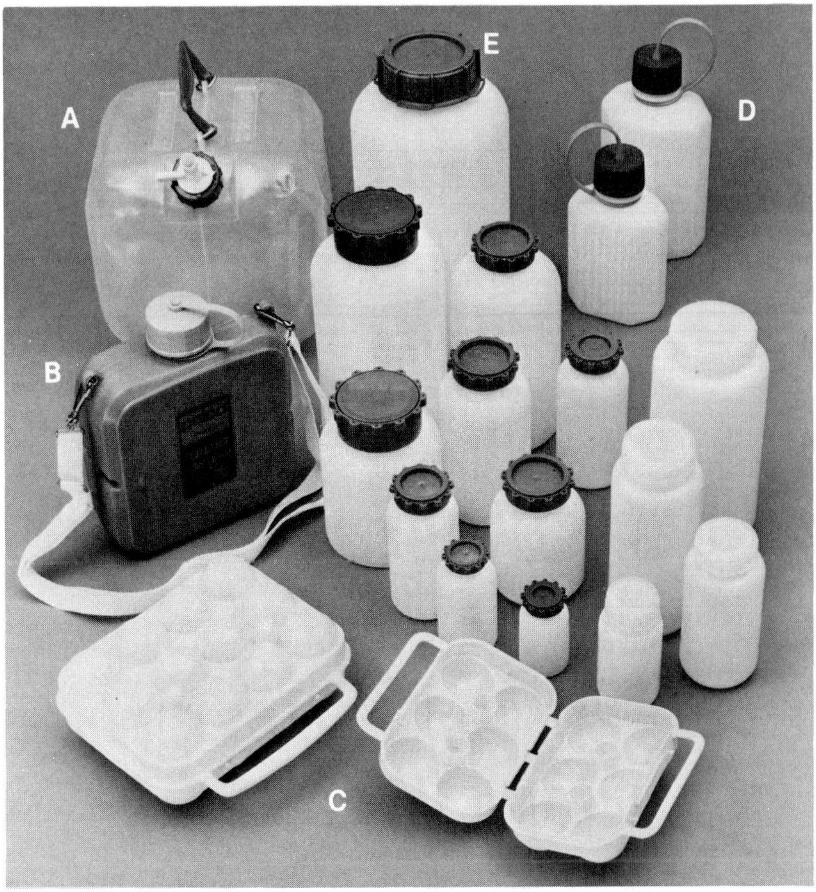

Figure 28-5 A) Collapsible water carrier, B) insulated poly canteen, C) plastic egg carriers, D) canteens with attached stoppers and screw caps and E) polyethylene bottles with screw caps. (Eastern Mountain Sports, Inc., Peterborough, N.H.)

large supply. Your matches should be waterproofed and carried in a waterproof container.

Trench candles, "peas," plumbers' candles, and bits of dry tinder help to start a fire in wet weather. An inspirator, coiled up in one of your cooking kettles, is also worth its weight in gold. All of these things are discussed in Chapter 26.

Whistles

Several whistles on lanyards should be available so that any person or group going even a short distance away from the main group can carry one. When traveling in thick woods it is easy to become confused or lost when going even a short distance, and it can turn out to be a very serious matter. A whistle blast carries much farther than the voice and, of course, the universal signal for help is three blasts on the whistle.

Cooking and Eating Outfits

If you will not be cooking on an open fire, a lightweight backpacking stove is necessary equipment for a trip. But no matter what your heating source may be, cooking utensils are a must.

Nested cooking kits are available to serve from 1 to 12 persons (Fig. 28-6). These cooking utensils usually have no handles, but instead are manipulated by a detachable handle that fits any of them. This lightens the weight of the outfit and allows the vessels to fit more compactly together. This arrangement has an added advantage in that the handle stays comfortably cool to the touch, since it is never left over the fire.

Although aluminum utensils are lightest in weight, those of lightweight steel are better since they weigh only a little more, are less likely to become dented or misshapen, and

Figure 28-6 Cookset: fry pan, clamp handle, billy pots and dishes. (Eastern Mountain Sports, Inc. Petersborough, N. H.)

spread the heat more uniformly under the food so that there is less tendency for it to stick or burn. Porcelain or enamel utensils chip too easily to be practical for continued use on the trail.

You can assemble your own mess kit by purchasing odds and ends at a variety or hardware store, using the trial and error method to find ones that nest together. Cut off the handles and buy a pot gripper to handle them by or use a pair of needle-nosed pliers. Carry this mess kit in a homemade bag with a drawstring. Fold-down rings instead of knobs on lids and shallow spouts and bail ears on pots also make for compact nesting. Pot covers should fit tightly to keep the juices in and dirt and ashes out. Low, wide utensils are less liable to be upset than tall ones and the contents also cook faster. Knives, forks, and spoons can be placed inside the kettles or carried inside a bag.

A reflector oven that folds flat is greatly enjoyed on a trip, perhaps even to the extent that you will be willing to carry the extra weight. Baking does take time, however, so many backpackers tend to leave them at home.

Nonbreakable plastic is considered by many to be superior for cups, plates, and other dishes, and sectioned plates are available. Others prefer pie tins or aluminum plates.

Most steel and aluminum cups burn your lips when filled with hot liquid. Enameled cups can also be used, especially the type with a handle that is open at the bottom so that you can hang it on your belt or pack. The Sierra Club cup, although made of stainless steel, weighs

Figure 28-7 Essentials for a backpacking trip. *Top row:* pack and sleeping bag, ground cloth, tent, sleeping pad, clothing, parka, chaps. *Middle row:* stove, fuel container, pot with lid, water bottle, cup, spoon, pocket knife, matches in waterproof container, flashlight, toilet paper, soap and toothbrush with stuff bag, boots, socks, camp shoes, towel, down jacket in stuff sack. *Bottom row:* sun glasses; first aid kit; bug lotion; candle; compass; map; camera; nylon cord; breakfasts, lunches and dinners separated into ditty bags. (J. Meier)

only 3 ounces. It is constructed so that it keeps the contents warm while staying cool at the brim so that it will not burn your lips. You can hang it on your belt or pack by means of the handle. The cup is also wide enough to be suitable for use as a dish when eating such things as soups and stews.

Each person will need a spoon and possibly a fork, but the pocket knife substitutes well for a table knife.

Careful menu planning will eliminate utensil problems. You can combine ingredients into many tasty one-pot dishes and can cook many things in ashes or in aluminum foil, as described in Chapter 27.

Incidentals

Most of the items already mentioned in this chapter should be considered as necessities for safe camping. There are a few additional things that can be taken along in order to enhance the pleasure of a trip. Carrying such items as a camera and film, fishing gear, pencil and notebook, binoculars, and extra money may be considered a sacrifice in weight, but may be worth the effort for the satisfaction and enjoyment gained.

A pencil and a looseleaf notebook are handy for taking field notes and jotting down anything that might be of help for later reference, such as interesting games, stories, songs, bits of nature lore, and so on. The notebook can also be used for recording program ideas to take on the trip. Good quality lightweight binoculars are also valuable for studying wildlife and enjoying distant scenery. Fieldbooks on birds, animals, and geology can be educational as are books of stories, songs, or poetry. You may also need a small amount of money for emergency telephone calls or supplies along the way.

CHECK LISTS FOR PACKING EQUIPMENT

To best meet your own particular needs for camping and tripping, go over the following items and then make out your own check list. Recheck your list and eliminate everything not really essential. After you return from your trip, revise your list on the basis of your experience and keep it handy for use the next time. Figure 28–7 shows all of the essentials needed for an extended backpacking trip of several days or more.

PERSONAL EQUIPMENT

ESSENTIAL	*OPTIONAL*
Wearing Apparel	***Wearing Apparel***
Trousers and belt	Insect head-net or mosquito netting
Walking shorts	Swim suit
Shirts	
Sunglasses	
Boots	
Extra shoes	
Socks (several pairs)	
Wide-brimmed hat or duckbill visor cap	
Pajamas	
Rainwear (poncho, parka, chaps, etc.)	
Leather or heavy canvas gloves	
Bandanna	
Underclothes (including long underwear)	
Windbreaker, wool shirt, jacket, or sweater	
Sleeping Gear	***Sleeping Gear***
Ground sheet or poncho	Sleeping bag liner or sheet
Pad or mattress	
Tent or tarp	
Sleeping bag or bedroll	

PERSONAL EQUIPMENT

ESSENTIAL

Toilet Articles
Biodegradable soap in plastic box or tube
Towel and washcloth
Pocket mirror (metal preferred)
Toothbrush and paste
Dental floss
Comb
Suntan lotion
Insect repellent
Sanitary napkins or tampons
Toilet paper

For Food
Fork
Canteen or water bottle
Mess kit, including cup and spoon

Tools and Other Items
Pocket knife
Waterproofed matches or matches in waterproof matchbox
Flashlight, extra bulb and batteries
Packsack
Rope or nylon cord
Stuff sacks or ditty bags
Maps
Compass
Mending kit
Pocket notebook
Pencil

OPTIONAL

Toilet Articles
Shaving kit (men)
Lotions for skin
ChapStick

Tools and Other Items
Hatchets or saws
Tump line
Fishing equipment and license
Whistle
Pedometer
Day pack
Money
Binoculars
Camera and film (in waterproof bag)
Nature books, poetry books, games
Stationery (already stamped)
Musical instrument
Songbooks
Extra eyeglasses in case
Watch
Hammock (can be rolled up to size of a fist)

GROUP EQUIPMENT

ESSENTIAL

For Food
Menus and recipes
Water purification equipment
Cooking forks, spatula, spoons
Cooking utensils
Plastic food bags
Salt and pepper in shakers (fit piece of waxed paper inside tops)
Food (carefully checked against check list)
Stoves and fuel containers
Can opener

OPTIONAL

For Food
Hobo stoves, reflector oven, Dutch oven
Paper towels
Grates
Aluminum foil
Water pail (plastic or canvas folding)

PERSONAL EQUIPMENT

ESSENTIAL	*OPTIONAL*
Tools	***Tools***
Repair kit for mending tents, air mattresses, etc.	Extra paddles for canoe or kayak trip
Tarpaulins or tents for sheltering equipment	No. 10 tin can buckets, etc.
Spade or shovel	Candles
String, wire, etc.	25 or 50 feet of strong cord
	Camp lantern
	Axes or saws
	File and sharpening stone
Fires and Sanitation	***Fires and Sanitation***
Extra supply of waterproofed matches	Inspirator, "peas," trench candles, etc.
Toilet paper	
Insect repellent	
Wash pan or canvas wash basin	
Dishcloths, towels	
Biodegradable soap or detergent	
Metal or plastic sponge for cleaning pans	
Steel wool	
Miscellaneous	***Miscellaneous***
Check list of equipment	Extra shoelaces (twine or nylon cord will do)
Mending kit (buttons, thread, shoelaces, etc.)	
First aid kit and instruction book	
Tents or tarps and accessories	
Maps of area	

BACKPACKS

Traveling on foot with your bedding, food, and clothing on your back offers the ultimate in freedom, for only when you leave the beaten path and learn to walk unobtrusively through the backcountry do you experience the true wonders of nature. All equipment for such a trip must obviously be stored in some form of pack-sack, even when you are only going on a day hike. Packs of almost any size and description are available to suit your needs, no matter what sort of trip you take.

Belt, Waist, or Fanny Packs

The pack known as a *belt, waist,* or *fanny pack* is the smallest of all, consisting simply of a small container attached to a nylon or web belt that is worn around the waist. It will hold from 3 to 5 pounds of supplies, including your lunch, a camera and film, and a water bottle. These packs are made of the same materials as larger packs and they usually open by means of a zipper on top that is covered by a protective rain flap. Some packs also have one or two zippered pockets on the side. The belt is worn with enough slack so that you can turn it around to extract the contents without having to remove the belt.

Rucksacks and Frame Packs

Rucksack is a term of German origin and literally means "back sack." Rucksacks or backpacks come in many sizes and designs, varying from those just large enough to carry a lunch to others more suitable for extended overnight excursions of several days or more. To avoid confusion in discussing packs, it becomes necessary to classify them by their size or intended use. They may be classified into three types: (1) day packs, (2) overnight packs, and (3) expedition packs.

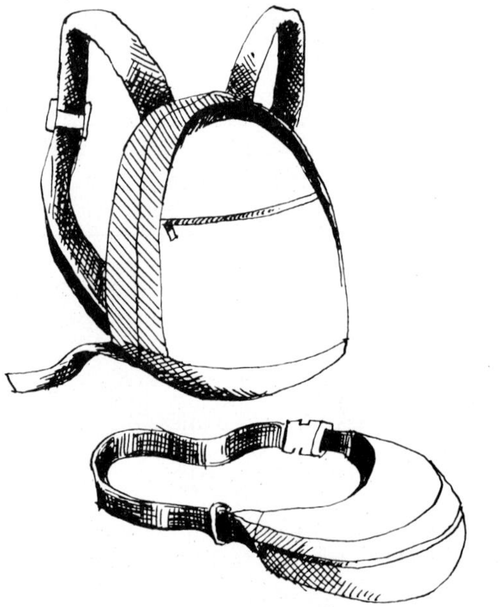

Figure 28–8 *Top:* day pack. *Bottom:* fanny pack.

DAY PACKS. These are the smallest of the choices and, as the name implies, their uses generally are limited to day trips or brief excursions away from the central camp area. One kind of day pack is the *knapsack,* which is just large enough to carry a lunch and possibly a garment or two. Another, the *haversack,* is slightly larger and more suitable for daylight jaunts and cookouts. With careful packing, adolescents might even be able to manage with such a pack on a light overnight trip; however, this would necessitate attaching the bedroll or sleeping bag in an inverted U across the top and sides of the pack. (See Fig. 28-8.)

OVERNIGHT PACKS. A midsize pack is the overnight pack, which is big enough for limited food and clothing as well as a sleeping bag. The user must plan very carefully if this pack is to serve satisfactorily for anything more than a night or two in the woods.

EXPEDITION PACKS. These are obviously the largest packs of all and are intended primarily for carrying loads on extended trips of up to a week or longer. Many are designed to carry 40 pounds or more, but such quantities of camping gear are usually more than is desired or necessary.

In addition to size or intended use, packs can also be grouped by the types of suspension systems used to support them. Of course, there are always a few hybrids that don't fit into any grouping, but most can be classified as either a frameless pack or one with a frame. Frame packs are further divided into those with external frames and those with built-in frames (sometimes called internal frame packs). The following description of each will explain the differences.

FRAMELESS PACKS. These packs have been around for as long as anyone can remember. They have shoulder straps and often a waist strap that holds the pack close to the wearer's body to prevent excessive swaying and bouncing. The shoulder straps usually are made of padded nylon webbing or leather, and they usually can be adjusted for size by means of buckles. The pack hugs the back well, which is helpful for those climbing over rocks, scrambling through brush, or traveling in other close quarters. The primary disadvantage of a frameless pack, on the other hand, is that most of the weight is borne on the shoulders, which forces the pack's center of gravity away from the body and causes the hiker to compensate by leaning forward. The softness of the bag also can create an additional problem since, when loaded, the heavy items placed on top often cause the pack to sag. There are two common bag shapes available: straight-sided or rectangular bags and teardrop-shaped bags that are narrow at the top and broad toward the bottom to permit free arm action.

BUILT-IN FRAME PACKS. Packs with built-in or internal frames have all the advantages of the frameless bags but are sturdier and distribute the weight more evenly on the back. Those that have good hip belts will also transfer much of the weight to the hips. Rucksacks with built-in frames usually have stays made of steel or plastic slats, aluminum tubing, or fiberglass rods. Some frames are flexible while others are not. In order to allow the pack to be stored in a small space, some frames are removable.

The disadvantage of built-in frame packs, like soft frameless ones, is their tendency to hug the back. This allows no space for air circulation, making them hot and uncomfortable, especially in warm weather. Nonetheless, both the frameless and the built-in frame packs are popular among mountaineers and Nordic skiers because they have a low center of gravity and do not hinder elbow and arm movements along the side of the body.

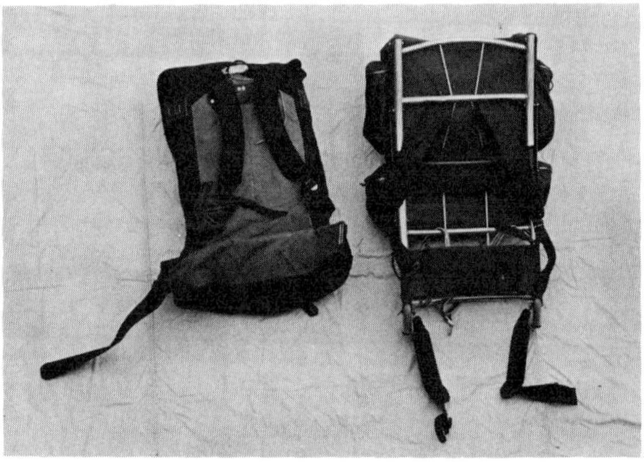

Figure 28-9 Expedition packs. *Left:* the frameless pack. *Right:* external or rigid frame pack.

Figure 28-10 The frameless pack hugs the back and allows for free arm movement.

EXTERNAL FRAME PACKS. Packs of this classification are attached to the back of a rigid frame made usually of aluminum tubing or plastic. Various devices are used to make the attachment, but usually clevis pins are extended through holes in the frame to grommets in the bag. These same type of pins also are used to attach the shoulder straps, backband, and hip belt to the front of the frame. A typical external frame pack is shown in Figures 28-9, 28-11 and 28-12. The advantage of a properly fitted rigid external frame is that it can shift as much as 75 percent of the pack's weight from your shoulders to the back, hips and powerful muscles of the legs. This not only relieves the burden on the shoulders, but also allows you to stand or walk in a nearly erect position. Other benefits of the pack frame are that it prevents the pack from bulging out of shape, keeps its contents from gouging into your back, and provides air space to cool the back, thus allowing perspiration to evaporate.

As mentioned, a pack frame consists of a metal or plastic framework, shoulder straps, a

Figure 28-11 The external frame pack transfers weight from the shoulders to the hips and legs. (J. Meier)

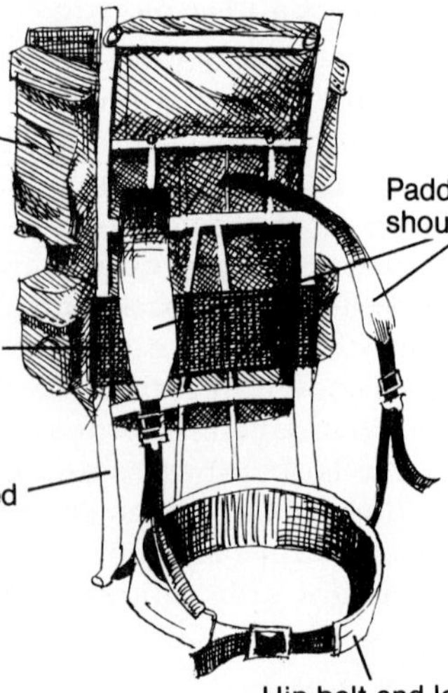

Figure 28-12 Parts of the external frame pack.

hip belt, and at least one back band (some have both an upper and a lower one). The frame is shaped roughly like a shallow **S,** which follows the contours of the body when properly fitted and slants forward slightly over the shoulders at the top. Some manufacturers have also come out with models that have flexible joints in the frame that allow the upper and lower sections to flex in the same direction as the hiker's shoulders and thighs as they move.

The padded shoulder straps stabilize the pack and hold the top of it close to the hiker's body. The upper and lower pack bands are positioned about even with the shoulders and waist and are taut enough to keep the middle part of the pack from coming into contact with the body. These bands usually are made of strong webbing, nylon, or several layers of other strong material and can be adjusted up or down to coincide with your own physique. The hip belt is worn cinched tight so that it can perform its important function of holding the bottom of the pack close to the body while transferring most of the weight to the strong hip region (Fig. 28-12).

The pack bag is ordinarily supported on the top two thirds of the pack frame, leaving room below for strapping on a sleeping bag or bed roll. The bag's various pockets and compartments allow you to be quite selective when packing and distributing the weight of the gear.

When a good pack is properly loaded, the average healthy person who is accustomed to it can walk comfortably while carrying a load of 35 pounds or more. For a more detailed description of how to use the frame pack, refer to the section titled "Loading and Carrying the Pack" in Chapter 22.

Specialized Packs

There are several specialized packs that have been used for years and still have their place today in camping and tripping. For many persons of the Northeast, as well as across the continent, the *Duluth Packsack* has become legendary. This packsack served early fur traders, the trapper and the Indian, and has probably transported more tonnage of freight and trade goods than any other nonrigid container. It is one of the variety of big sacks or bags capable of holding a very large supply of food and clothing. Since it is a frameless soft pack made of water repellent canvas, it is popular for canoe trips. The bag fits easily into the boat and also can be used for hauling equipment for short distances, as at a canoe portage. However, this packsack is simply too heavy for inexperienced or adolescent campers to handle and it would not be at all suitable for a long backpack trip.

Another specialized pack is the *Adirondack pack basket,* which is a part of our heritage from the Indians of the Northeast. Though it is almost

Figure 28-13 Adirondack pack basket.

a thing of the past, some campers still prefer it. However, it really serves best as a heavy-duty carrier for odd jobs, such as lugging firewood, picnic goodies, canned goods, and collecting driftwood. What makes it suitable for doing these things is that it is constructed of oak or ash splints that protect the contents and keep sharp objects inside from gouging into the back. It is shaped to fit the back and has carrying straps. The Adirondack pack basket is available in several sizes (Fig. 28-13).

Selecting a Pack

Your pack should, of course, be selected to meet your own particular needs. There are many models from which to choose, and new ones are constantly appearing on the market. In general, select the smallest pack that will carry your needs. If you will be taking trips of various lengths, especially in different seasons or by various means, you may even want to invest in several models and sizes.

The first thing to look for in a pack is good workmanship. Stitches should be close together and there should be reinforcements at all points of strain. Seams should be well sewn and reinforced where necessary so that they can't pull or ravel out. All zippers should be strong, operate smoothly, and be protected by rain flaps. Hardware on the pack should be well constructed, and if attached to a frame, there should be an adequate number of contact points.

Since larger packs are designed to carry heavy loads, be sure the materials used in their construction will hold up under the expected strain. A favorite material is tough, closely woven nylon, which bears up well under the rough use the pack receives. Although most packs are nearly waterproof, they often have a tendency to develop leaks, especially at the seams and along the zippers, so it is advisable to cover the pack with a waterproof rain cover or poncho when out in a rain.

Large packs usually have one or two main compartments. In addition to these, there is a growing tendency to add more and more outside pockets, and a modern pack may have as many as five or more, with two on each side and one or two across the back. The better packs will have protective flaps to keep out dirt and moisture. These pockets increase carrying space and provide a place for things needed quickly.

If you are selecting a pack with a frame, there are additional things to look for before making a purchase. The most important consideration in buying a pack frame is to get one that fits, otherwise it will hit on your body at all the wrong places. If it is too small, it will bind at the shoulders, and if too large, it will teeter and wobble about above your head in a most distressing manner.

Pack frames usually come in four sizes: small, medium, large, and extra large, but these classifications are actually of little value since a proper fit really depends mostly upon the actual size and shape of your own torso. Although back bands, shoulder straps, and hip belt are all adjustable, they cannot satisfactorily compensate for a frame that is not basically of the right proportions for you. Fortunately, there are some companies that make frames that are adjustable to fit anybody, which is a real advantage to a growing youngster. This also allows the pack to be used by several different people.

A final suggestion when choosing a pack is to pick out a few that appeal to you, pack them with an approximation of the gear you will take on a trip, and then walk around with each one to see how comfortably it rides. Most of today's backpacks are made according to high standards so you probably can't go wrong too often as long as the one you select fits well.

Improvised Packsacks

The following information is intended for camps that cannot afford to purchase backpacks or for those individuals who don't have their own. A lack of resources to obtain manufactured equipment doesn't necessarily mean you can't include tripping as a part of your program. Some of the improvised packsacks discussed here may not always work or look like manufactured models, but at times they will do just fine.

BLANKET ROLL. A youngster may enjoy rolling gear in a blanket, securing it with 3-inch horse blanket pins and a short rope, and wearing it in a **U** that is draped around one shoulder after tying it together near the opposite hip. This works well enough for a short trip, but the roll will make the hiker hot and sweaty and can catch on every tree and branch along the way, making it ill-adapted for any but short excursions. A poncho or ground cloth should be used as the outside layer to render it waterproof.

BLUE JEANS OR SLACK PACK. Another novel way to make a pack is to use blue jeans or slacks. This is done by slipping your duffel into the body and legs of the slacks and securing it by cinching a rope through the belt loops and running it around your waistline. The legs are converted into pack straps by bringing them up across your shoulders and under your arms. Fasten them to the waistline rope about 2 inches apart near the center so the legs hug your shoulders snugly in order to center the weight of the pack well down on your back.

BURLAP BAG PACK. A large burlap bag or something similar can be converted into a pack. Four pebbles and two lengths of nylon webbing or strong rope about 3 feet long will also be needed. To make shoulder straps, place one pebble in a lower corner of the sack and tightly fasten one rope around it with a clove hitch. Place another pebble in the upper corner on the same side and fasten the long end of the rope around it. Repeat on the other side of the bag using the other rope. Since these ropes serve as carrying straps, be sure to leave enough slack to slip your arms through them. Foam rubber, old socks, or other improvised materials can be used to pad the ropes where they cross the shoulders.

ADDITIONAL READINGS

(For an explanation of abbreviations and abbreviated forms, see page 13.)

General References

Bridge: *America's Backpacking Book*, chs. 2, 7, 9, 13, 22.
Cardwell: *America's Camping Book*, chs. 9–11, 51.
Colwell: *Introduction to Backpacking*, chs. 4, 5, 9.
Eggert: *Backpack Hiking: The First Steps*, chs. 1–5.
Fieldbook for Boys and Men, pp. 33–37, 272–273.
Fletcher: *The Complete Walker*, pp. 13–43, 197–220, 221–269, 325–327.
Langer: *The Joy of Camping*, pp. 44–55.
Learn and Tallman: *Backpacker's Digest*, chs. 6, 8.
Lightweight Equipment for Hiking, Camping and Mountaineering. Potomac, 1972, paper.
Macfarlan: *The Boy's Book of Hiking*, chs. 6, 9.
Manning: *Backpacking One Step at a Time*, chs. 7, 9, 15.
Meier: *Backpacking*, ch. 2.
Merrill: *The Hiker's and Backpacker's Handbook*, ch. 5.
Rethmel: *Backpacking*, chs. 1–3, 5, 10.
Riviere: *Backcountry Camping*, ch. 5.
Boy Scout Handbook, pp. 218–221.
Sunset Camping Handbook, pp. 26–29, 31–37.
Winnett: *Backpacking for Fun*, chs. 2, 3, 5, 11, and Appendix II.
Wood: *Pleasure Packing*, ch. 3.

MAGAZINE ARTICLES

Backpacker:
"Autumn Trailwear . . . For More than Hiking." Aug./Sept., 1980, p. 39.
Hastings, Honey C.: "Make & Fix It." *Backpacker-6*, Summer, 1974, p. 30. (Repairing equipment)
"Rainwear." Aug./Sept., 1979, p. 67.
Saijo, Albert: "Go-Light Backpacking." *Backpacker-3*, Fall, 1973, p. 86.
Tabor, James: "Layering: The Inside Story." Aug./Sept., 1981, p. 63.
Camping Journal:
Hamft, Martin: "Backpacking—What to Pack and How to Pack It." June, 1974, p. 24.
Heyl, Frank: "How to Choose and Use Rainwear for Camp." Oct., 1971, p. 22.
Wilderness Camping:
Coggeshall, Almy D.: "The Old Woodchuck's Winter Closet." Dec./Jan., 1977, p. 260.
Strong, Steve: "Gadgets of Back Packing—Essential Materials or Trivial Frills." Jan./Feb., 1974, p. 28.

Making and Repairing Your Own Equipment

Angier: *Wilderness Gear You Can Make Yourself*.
Bridge: *America's Backpacking Book*, pp. 118–128, 167–172.
Burch, Monte: *Outdoorsman's Fix-It Book*. Harper & Row, 1972, 274 pp.
Cardwell: *America's Camping Book*, Part III (pp. 115–169).
Cunningham, Gerry, and Margaret Hansson: *Lightweight Camping Equipment and How to Make It*. Gerry, 3rd ed., 1964, 130 pp.
Fieldbook for Boys and Men, pp. 540–549.
Lamoreaux: *Outdoor Gear You Can Make Yourself*, chs. 1–7.
Learn and Tallman: *Backpacker's Digest*, ch. 5.
Litepac Camping Equipment. Boy Scouts, paper.
Ormond: *Outdoorsman's Handbook*.
Spielman, Patrick E.: *Make Your Own Sports Gear*. Bruce, 1970, 154 pp.

MAGAZINE ARTICLES

Backpacker:
Hastings, Honey C.: "Make & Fix It." *Backpacker-1*, Spring, 1973, p. 14. (Miscellaneous)
Hastings, Honey C.: "Make & Fix It." *Backpacker-2*, Summer, 1973, p. 14. (Belt pouch)
Hastings, Honey C.: "Make & Fix It." *Backpacker-3*, Fall, 1973, p. 18. (Tents)
Hastings, Honey C.: "Make & Fix It." *Backpacker-4*, Winter, 1973, p. 18. (Mittens, boots)
Hastings, Honey C.: "Make & Fix It." *Backpacker-5*, Spring, 1975, p. 22. (Ponchos)
Williams, Lee A.: "How to Make A Laminated Backpack Frame." June/July, 1979, p. 28.
Camping Journal:
Bolton, Dick: "Make Your Own Pack Frame." Aug., 1971, p. 20.

Collier, Ed J., Jr.: "Backpacker's Delight." Nov., 1973, p. 54. (Lightweight simple-to-construct cot just right for backpackers)
Engerbretson, Dave: "Kits for Campers." Mar., 1974, p. 68.
Richards, Chuck: "Sew Your Own Sleeping Bag." Mar., 1972, p. 40.
"You Built Backpacker Tent." Jan., 1972, p. 26.

Packs

Bridge: *America's Backpacking Book*, ch. 10.
Cardwell: *America's Camping Book*, ch. 7.
Colwell: *Introduction to Backpacking*, ch. 3.
Fieldbook for Boys and Men, pp. 42–47.
Fletcher: *The Complete Walker*, pp. 53–66.
Langer: *The Joy of Camping*, pp. 110–124.
Learn and Tallman: *Backpacker's Digest*, chs. 4, 5, pp. 266–284.
Manning: *Backpacking One Step at a Time*, ch. 10.
Meier: *Backpacking*, pp. 7–10.
Merrill: *The Hiker's and Backpacker's Handbook*, ch. 4.
Rethmel: *Backpacking*, chs. 2, 10.
Riviere: *Backcountry Camping*, ch. 1.
Wood: *Pleasure Packing*, ch. 1.

MAGAZINE ARTICLES

Backpacker:
"The Best of the Weekend Packs." *Backpacker-5*, Spring, 1974, pp. 49–61.
"Byers Guide: Day Packs." June/July, 1980, p. 77.
"Children's Packs—A Survey of Packs Made Just for Kids." Feb., 1978, p. 48.
"Internal Frame Packs." Oct./Nov., 1979, p. 63.
Packer, Nelson: "How to Pick a Pack." *Backpacker-1*, Spring, 1973, p. 57.
"Pick of the Extended Trek Packs." Oct., 1977, p. 58.
"The Pick of the Packs." *Backpacker-1*, Spring, 1973, p. 48.
"The Pick of the Polyester Bags." *Backpacker-6*, Summer, 1974, pp. 73–85.
Shepard, Bill: "The Wrap-Around Controversy—One Man's Opinion." *Backpacker-1*, Spring, 1973, p. 61.
"This Year's Gear: Packs and Stoves." Apr./May, 1979, p. 65.
Wilderness Camping:
Aune, Michael: "Backpack Loading." Aug./Sept., 1977, p. 24.
"Tempest in a Backpack." Mar./Apr., 1973, pp. 38–43.
Wood, Robert S.: "Pleasure Packing." Mar./Apr., 1974, p. 21. (The birdcage pack and a new awareness)

appendix A
Selected General Bibliography

Note: This listing of books includes only those that are deemed to be of special interest to the readers. Other excellent sources can be found in the bibliography in each chapter. For an explanation of abbreviations and abbreviated forms used, see page 13.

Angier, Bradford: *Home in Your Pack.* Collier, rev., 1972, 202 pp., paper.

Angier, Bradford: *How to Stay Alive in the Woods.* Macmillan, 1966, 286 pp., paper.

Angier, Bradford: *Living Off the Country.* Stackpole, 1965, 241 pp.

Angier, Bradford: *Skills for Taming the Wilds.* Stackpole, 1967, 288 pp.

Angier, Bradford: *Survival with Style.* Stackpole, 1972, 256 pp.

Angier, Bradford: *Wilderness Cookery.* Stackpole, rev., 1970, 256 pp., paper.

Angier, Bradford: *Wilderness Gear You Can Make Yourself.* Macmillan, 1973, 115 pp., paper.

Bale, R. O.: *What On Earth.* ACA, 1969, 160 pp., paper.

Basic Outboard Boating Textbook. ARC, 1964, 98 pp., paper.

Berger, H. Jean: *Program Activities for Camps.* Burgess, 2nd ed., 1969, 179 pp., paper.

Better Homes and Gardens Family Camping Book. Meredith, 1961, 160 pp.

Bloom, Dr. Joel: *Camper Guidance—In the Routines of Daily Living.* ACA, 1965, 16 pp., paper.

Bloom, Dr. Joel W., et al.: *Camper Guidance—A Basic Handbook for Counselors.* ACA, 1961, 24 pp., paper.

Bridge, Raymond: *America's Backpacking Book.* Scribner's, 1973, 417 pp.

Brower, David R. (ed.): *Going Light—With Backpack or Burro.* Sierra, 1972, 152 pp.

Brown, Vinson: *The Amateur Naturalist's Handbook.* Little, Brown, 1948, 475 pp.

Camp Job Descriptions. ACA, 20 pp., paper.

Camping (No. 3256). Boy Scouts, 1966, 96 pp., paper.

Camping is Education. ACA, 1960, 24 pp., paper.

Camp Standards with Interpretation for the Accreditation of Organized Camps. ACA, 1980, 78 pp., paper.

Cardwell, Paul, Jr.: *America's Camping Book.* Scribner's, 1969, 591 pp.

Catalog of Selected Camping Publications. ACA, published annually, paper.

Chappell, Wallace: *When You Go Trail Camping.* ACA, 1969, 96 pp., paper.

Colwell, Robert: *Introduction to Backpacking.* Stackpole, 1970, 192 pp.

Convention Highlights. ACA, 1962, 106 pp., paper.

Corbin, H. Dan: *Recreation Leadership.* Prentice-Hall, 3rd ed., 1970, 418 pp.

Cunningham, Gerry, and Margaret Hansson: *Lightweight Camping Equipment and How To Make It.* Colo. Outdoor Sports, 1964, 131 pp.

Dalrymple, Byron: *Survival in the Outdoors.* Dutton, 1972, 309 pp.

Danford, Howard G., and Max Shirley: *Creative Leadership in Recreation.* Allyn and Bacon, 2nd ed., 1970, 398 pp.

Darst, Paul W., and George P. Armstrong: *Outdoor Adventure Activities for School and Recreational Programs.* Burgess, 1980, 307 pp., paper.

Disley, John: *Orienteering.* Stackpole, 1973, 192 pp.

Edginton, Christopher R., David M. Compton, and Carol J. Hanson: *Recreation and Leisure Programming.* Saunders, 1980, 419 pp.

Eggert, Richard: *Backpack Hiking: The First Steps.* Stackpole, 1977, 224 pp., paper.

Eisenberg, Helen and Larry: *Omnibus of Fun.* Ass'n Press, 1956, 625 pp.

Ensign, John and Ruth: *Camping Together as Christians.* Knox, 1958, 148 pp., paper.

Farrell, Patricia, and Herberta M. Lundegren: *The Process of Recreation Programming.* Wiley, 1978, 313 pp.

Fieldbook for Boys and Men (No. 3201). Boy Scouts, 1967, 576 pp., paper.

Fletcher, Colin: *The Complete Walker.* Knopf, 1972, 353 pp.

Fletcher, Colin: *The New Complete Walker.* Knopf, 1974, 490 pp.

Ford, Phyllis M.: *Principles and Practices of Outdoor/Environmental Education.* Wiley, 1981, 348 pp.

Gabrielson, M. Alexander, Betty Spears, and Bramwell W. Gabrielson: *Aquatics Handbook.* Prentice-Hall, 2nd ed., 1968, 224 pp.

Garrison, Cecil: *Outdoor Education: Principles and Practice.* Thomas, 1966, 239 pp.

Germain, Donald L.: *When You Go Canoe Camping.* ACA, 1968, 69 pp., paper.

Gould, Heywood: *The Complete Book of Camping.* Signet, 1972, 156 pp., paper.

Hammerman, Donald R., and William M. Hammerman (eds.): *Outdoor Education: A Book of Readings.* Burgess, 2nd ed., 1973, 412 pp., paper.

Hammerman, Donald R., and William M. Hammerman: *Teaching in the Outdoors.* Burgess, 2nd ed., 1973, 144 pp., paper.

Hammett, Catherine T.: *Your Own Book of Campcraft.* Pocket Books, 1950, 197 pp., paper.

Hamper, Stan: *Wilderness Survival.* Order from ACA, 1963, 97 pp., paper.

Harbin, E. O.: *The Fun Encyclopedia.* Abingdon, 1940, 1008 pp.

Hartwig, Marie D., and Bette B. Myers: *Camp Leadership: Counseling and Programming.* Mosby, 1976, 224 pp.

Harty, William T.: *Science for Camp and Counselor.* Ass'n Press, 1964, 320 pp.

Hillcourt, William: *New Field Book of Nature Activities and Conservation.* Putnam, 1971, 420 pp.

Jaeger, Ellsworth: *Wildwood Wisdom.* Macmillan, 1966, 228 pp.

Kjellstrom, Bjorn: *Be Expert with Map and Compass.* Scribner's rev., 1972, 136 pp.

Kraus, Richard G.: *Recreation Leader's Handbook.* McGraw-Hill, 1955, 299 pp.

Kraus, Richard, Gay Carpenter, and Barbara J. Bates: *Recreation Leadership and Supervision.* Saunders, 2nd ed., 1981, 382 pp.

Kujoth, Jean Spealman (compiler): *The Recreation Program Guide.* Scarecrow, 1972, 437 pp.

Lamoreaux, Marcia and Bob: *Outdoor Gear You can Make Yourself.* Stackpole, 1976, 160 pp., paper.

Langer, Richard: *The Joy of Camping.* Saturday Review, 1973, 320 pp.; Penguin, 1974, paper.

Learn, C. R., and Anne S. Tallman: *Backpacker's Digest.* Digest Books, 1973, 288 pp., paper.

Ledlie, John A., and Francis W. Holbein: *Camp Counselor's Manual.* Ass'n Press, rev., 1969, 128 pp., paper.

Lightweight Equipment for Hiking, Camping and Mountaineering. Potomac Appalachian Trail Club Equipment Co., Washington, D.C., 13th ed., 1972.

Macfarlan, Allan A.: *The Boy's Book of Hiking.* Stackpole, 1968, 159 pp.

MacKay, Joy: *Creative Counseling for Christian Camps.* Scripture, 1966, 129 pp., paper.

Mand, Charles L.: *Outdoor Education.* Pratt, 1967, 192 pp., paper.

Manning, Harvey: *Backpacking One Step at a Time.* Recreational, 1972, 356 pp.

Mason, Bernard S.: *The Book of Indian Crafts and Costumes.* Ronald, 1946, 118 pp.

Mason, Bernard S.: *The Junior Book of Camping and Woodcraft.* Ronald, 1943, 120 pp.

Meier, Joel F.: *Backpacking.* Brown, 1980, 108 pp., paper.

Meier, Joel F., et al. (eds.): *High Adventure Outdoor Pursuits: Organization and Leadership.* Brighton, 1980, 232 pp., paper.

Merrill, Bill: *The Hiker's and Backpacker's Handbook.* Winchester, 1971, 320 pp.; Arco, paper.

Merill, Bill: *The Survival Handbook.* Winchester, 1972, 312 pp.

Merrill, W. K.: *All About Camping.* Stackpole, 1970, 399 pp., paper.

Miracle, Leonard, and Maurice H. Decker: *The Complete Book of Camping.* Harper & Row, 1961, 594 pp.

Mohney, Russ: *The Master Backpacker.* Stackpole, 1976, 287 pp., paper.

Mohney, Russ: *Trailside Cooking.* Stackpole, 1976, 176 pp., paper.

Mooers, Robert L., Jr.: *Finding Your Way in the Outdoors.* Dutton, 1972, 275 pp.

Moser, Clarence G.: *Understanding Girls.* Ass'n Press, 1957, 252 pp.

Mountaineering: The Freedom of the Hills. The Mountaineers, Seattle, 1967.

Mulac, Margaret E.: *Fun and Games.* Macmillan. 1963, 350 pp., paper.

Olsen, Larry Dean: *Outdoor Survival Skills.* BYU Press, 1976, 188 p., paper.

Ormond, Clyde: *Complete Book of Outdoor Lore.* Harper & Row, 1965, 498 pp.

Ormond, Clyde: *Outdoorsman's Handbook.* Dutton, 1971, 336 pp.

Outdoor Tips. Remington, 1972, 190 pp.

Parents Guide to Accredited Camps. ACA, published annually.

Rethmel, Robert C.: Backpacking. Burgess, rev., 1974, 185 pp., paper.

Riviere, Bill: *Backcountry Camping.* Doubleday, 1971, 320 pp.

Riviere, Bill: *The Camper's Bible.* Doubleday, 1960, 176 pp., paper.

Riviere, Bill: *The Family Camper's Cookbook.* Holt, Rinehart, 1965, 244 pp.; Doubleday, paper.

Rodney, Lynn S., and Phyllis M. Ford: *Camp Administration.* Ronald, 1971, 402 pp.

Rohnke, Karl: *Cowstails and Cobras.* Project Adventure, 1977, 157 pp., paper.

Rutstrum, Calvin: *The New Way of the Wilderness.* Macmillan, rev., 1973, 280 pp., paper.

Scout Handbook. Boy Scouts, 8th ed., 1972, 480 pp., paper.

Scoutmaster's Handbook. Boy Scouts, 1972, 384 pp., paper.

Shea, Thomas M.: *Camping for Special Children.* Mosby, 1977, 244 pp.

Shivers, Jay S.: *Camping.* Appeton-Century, 1971, 424 pp.

Shivers, Jay S.: *Recreational Leadership.* Princeton, 1980, 268 pp.

Shivers, Jay S., and Clarence R. Calder: *Recreational Crafts.* McGraw Hill, 1974, 440 pp.

Shockley, Robert O., and Charles K. Fox: *Survival in the Wilds.* Barnes, 1970, 150 pp.

Shuttlesworth, Dorothy E.: *Exploring Nature with Your Child.* Hawthorn, 1952, 448 pp.

Smith, Julian W., et al.: *Outdoor Education.* Prentice-Hall, 2nd ed., 1972, 335 pp.

Strean, Herbert S. (ed.): *New Approaches in Child Guidance.* Scarecrow, 1970, 313 pp.

Sunset Camping Handbook. Lane, 1970, 96 pp., paper.

Thomas, Dian: *Roughing It Easy.* Warner, 1976, 246 pp.

Todd, Floyd and Pauline: *Camping for Christian Youth.* Harper & Row, 1968, 198 pp., paper.

van der Smissen, Betty, and Oswald H. Goering: *A Leader's Guide to Nature Oriented Activities.* Iowa State U., 3rd ed., 1977, 253 pp., spiral.

Van Krevelan, Alice: *Children in Groups: Psychology and the Summer Camp.* Brooks/Cole, 1972, 136 pp.

VanMatre, Steve: *Sunship Earth.* ACA, 1979, 265 pp., paper.

Vinal, Dr. William: *Nature Recreation.* Dover, 2nd ed., 1963, 310 pp., paper.

Vinton, Dennis A., and Elizabeth M. Farley (eds.): *Camp Staff Training Series.* (A joint publication of Project REACH, ACA, and Hawkins and Associates.) Available from ACA, 1979. Six modules individually bound: (1) *An Orientation to Camping and the Camp,* (2) *Knowing the Campers,* (3) *Camp Program Planning and Leadership,* (4) *Camp Health and Safety Practices,* (5) Dealing with Camper Behavior, (6) *Evaluating the Camp Experience.*

Vinton, Dennis A., et al.: *Camping and Environmental Education for Handicapped Children and Youth.* Hawkins, 1978, 170 pp., paper.

Webb, Kenneth B. (ed.): *Light From a Thousand Campfires.* ACA, 1960, 384 pp., paper.

Webb, Kenneth B.: *Summer Camps—Security in the Midst of Change.* ACA, 1968, 52 pp., paper.

Wells, George and Iris: *Handbook of Wilderness Travel.* Harper & Row, 1956, 294 pp.

Whelen, Townsend, and Bradford Angier: *On Your Own in the Wilderness.* Stackpole, 1958, 330 pp.

Wilderness Pocket'n Pack Library. Life Support, 1969–1972, five pocket-sized books. (*Survival in the Wilderness, Edible Plants in the Wilderness* [2 Volumes], *Poisonous Plants in the Wilderness,* and *Primitive Medical Aid in the Wilderness.*)

Wilkinson, Robert E.: *Camps: Their Planning and Management.* Mosby, 1981, 291 pp.

Winnett, Thomas: *Backpacking for Fun.* Wilderness, 1972, 131 pp., paper.

Wood, Robert S.: *Pleasure Packing.* Condor, 1972, 211 pp., paper.

appendix B Magazines

American Forests. Published monthly by The American Forestry Association, 919 17th St., N.W., Washington, D.C. 20006.

American Whitewater Journal. Published bimonthly by the American Whitewater Affiliation, Box 1483, Hagerstown, Md. 21740.

Audubon. Published six times a year (Jan., Mar., May, July, Sept., Nov.) by the National Audubon Society, 950 Third Ave., New York, N.Y. 10022.

Backpacker. (Including *Wilderness Camping.*) Published bimonthly by Ziff Davis Publishing Co., P.O. Box 2784, Boulder, Colo. 80321.

Boys' Life. Published monthly by the Boy Scouts of America, North Brunswick, N.J. 08902.

Camping Magazine. Published monthly Jan.-June and bimonthly Sept.-Dec. by the American Camping Association, Martinsville, Ind. 46151. ACA membership includes subscription.

Canoe Magazine. Published six times a year by Voyager Publications Inc., 1204 Main St., Fort Wayne, Ind. 46808.

Currents. Published monthly March through August, by the National Organization for River Sports, Box 6847, Colorado Springs, Colo. 80934.

Journal of Experiential Education. Published semiannually by the Association of Experiential Education, Box 4625, Denver, Colo. 80204.

J.O.P.E.R.D. (Formerly *J.O.H.P.E.R.*) *Journal of Physical Education, Recreation and Dance.* Published monthly except July and August, with November–December combined, by the American Alliance for Health, Physical Education, Recreation and Dance, 1900 Association Drive, Reston, Va. 22091. AAHPERD membership includes subscription.

The Living Wilderness. Published quarterly by The Wilderness Society, 729 15th St., N.W., Washington, D.C. 20005.

National Wildlife. Published bimonthly by the National Wildlife Federation, 1412 16th St., N.W., Washington, D.C. 20036.

Parks and Recreation. Published monthly by the National Recreation and Park Association, 3101 Park Center Drive, Alexandria, Va. 22302. NRPA membership includes subscription.

Wilderness Camping. Now included in *Backpacker.*

appendix C

Organizations Promoting Outdoor Activities

Note: This list is necessarily selective; the names and addresses of many other organizations promoting outdoor activities can be found in the latest annual issue of the *Conservation Directory,* published by the National Wildlife Federation (see address in this appendix).

American Alliance for Health, Physical Education, Recreation and Dance, 1900 Association Drive, Reston, Va. 22091.

American Camping Association, Bradford Woods, Martinsville, Ind. 46151.

American Canoe Association, Box 248, Lorton, Va. 22079.

American Forestry Association, 1319 18th Street, N.W., Washington, D.C. 20036.

American National Red Cross, 17th and D Streets, N.W., Washington, D.C. 20006.

American Water Ski Association, P.O. Box 191, Winterhaven, Fla. 33880.

American Whitewater Affiliation, Box 1483, Hagerstown, Md. 21740.

American Youth Hostels, Inc., National Campus, Delaplane, Va. 22025.

Appalachian Mountain Club, 5 Joy St., Boston, Mass. 02108.

Appalachian Trail Conference, P.O. Box 236, Harpers Ferry, W.Va. 25425.

Association of Experiential Education, Box 4625, Denver, Colo. 80204.

Association of Private Camps, 55W. 42nd St., New York, N.Y. 10036.

Bikecentennial, P.O. Box 8308, Missoula, Mont. 59807.

Boy Scouts of America, North Brunswick, N.J. 08902.

Boys' Clubs of America, 771 First Ave., New York, N.Y. 10017.

Camp Archery Association, 200 Coligni Ave., New Rochelle, N.Y. 10801.

Camp Fire, Inc., 4601 Madison Ave., Kansas City, Mo. 64112.

Canadian Camping Association, 1806 Avenue Rd., Suite 2, Toronto, Ontario, Canada M5M 3Z1.

Christian Camping International, Box 400, Somonauk, Ill. 60552.

Federation of Western Outdoor Clubs, 512½ Boylston East, #106, Seattle, Wash. 98102.

Friends of the Earth, 124 Spear St., San Francisco, Calif. 94105.

Funds for the Advancement of Camping, Suite 1126, 19 S. La Salle St., Chicago, Ill. 60603.

Girl Scouts of the USA, 830 Third Ave., New York, N.Y. 10022.

League of American Wheelmen, 19 South Bothwell St., Palatine, Ill. 60067.

National Archery Association, 1951 Geraldson Drive, Lancaster, Pa. 17601.

The National Audubon Society, 950 Third Ave., New York, N.Y. 10022.

National Campers and Hikers Association, P.O. Box 182, 7172 Transit Road, Buffalo, N.Y. 14221.

National Camping Association, 353 West 56th St., New York, N.Y. 10019.

National Organization for River Sports, Box 6847, Colorado Springs, Colo. 80934.

National Parks and Conservation Association, 1701 18th St. N.W., Washington, D.C. 20009.

National Recreation and Park Association, 3101 Park Center Drive, Alexandria, Va. 22302.

National Trails Council, P.O. Box 1042, Saint Charles, Ill. 60174.

National Wildlife Federation, 1412 16th St., N.W., Washington, D.C. 20036.

Nature Conservancy, 1800 North Kent St., Suite 800, Arlington, Va. 22209.

The New England Trail Conference, 26 Bedford Terrace, Northampton, Mass. 01060.

Orienteering Service U.S.A., P.O. Box 1604, Binghamton, N.Y. 13902.

Project Adventure, P.O. Box 157, Hamilton, Mass. 01936.

The Sierra Club, 1050 Mills Tower, 270 Bush St., San Francisco, Calif. 94108.

Student Conservation Association, Box 550, Charlston, N.H. 03603.

United States Canoe Association, 617 South 94th St., Milwaukee, Wi. 53214.

United States Lifesaving Association, P.O. Box 1286, Twain Harte, Calif. 95383.

United States Orienteering Federation, P.O. Box 1039, Ballwin, Mo. 63011.

United States Ski Association, The Broadmoor, Colorado Springs, Colo. 80906.

Isaak Walton League of America, 1800 North Kent St., Suite 806, Arlington, Va. 22209.

The Wilderness Society, 1901 Pennsylvania Ave., N.W., Washington, D.C. 20006.

appendix D
Directory of Publishers and Other Organizations

Note: Publishers and organizations are listed by the abbreviations and contractions used throughout this book.

AAHPERD: American Alliance for Health, Physical Education, Recreation and Dance, 1900 Association Drive, Reston, Va. 22091.

Abingdon: Abingdon Press, 201 Eighth Avenue, Nashville, Tenn. 37203.

ACA: American Camping Association, Bradford Woods, Martinsville, Ind. 46151.

Allyn & Bacon: Allyn & Bacon, Rockleigh, N.J. 07647.

Amer. Orienteering: American Orienteering Service. (Now named Orienteering Service U.S.A, P.O. Box 1604, Binghampton, N.Y. 13902).

Anderson: Anderson World, Inc., Mountain View, Calif. 94040.

Appleton-Century: Appleton-Century-Crofts, Educational Division, 440 Park Ave. S., New York, N.Y. 10016.

ARC: American National Red Cross, 17th and D Sts., Washington, D.C. 20006. (Books may usually be purchased from local chapters).

Arco: Arco Publishing Co., Inc., 219 Park Ave. S., New York, N.Y. 10003.

Ass'n Press: Association Press. (Now Follett Publishing Co., 1010 W. Washington Blvd., Chicago, Ill. 60607).

Atheneum: Atheneum Publishers, 122 E. 42nd St., New York, N.Y. 10017.

Augsburg: Augsburg Publishing House, 426 S. 5th St., Minneapolis, Minn. 55415.

Backpacker Books: Backpacker Books, Main St., Orwell, Vt. 05760.

Baker: Baker Book House, 1019 Wealthy St., S.E., Grand Rapids, Mich. 49506.

Ballantine: Ballantine Books, Inc., 201 E. 50th St., New York, N.Y. 10022.

Bantam: Bantam Books, Inc., 666 Fifth Ave., New York, N.Y. 10019.

Barnes: A. S. Barnes & Co., Forsgate Dr., Cranbury, N.J. 08512.

Barnes & Noble: Barnes & Noble, Inc., 10 E. 53rd St., New York, N.Y. 10022.

Basic Books: Basic Books, Inc., 10 E. 53rd St., New York, N.Y. 10022.

Bennett: Charles A. Bennett Company, Inc., 809 West Detwiler Dr., Peoria, Ill. 61614.

Better Homes and Gardens. See Meredith Press.

Bikecentennial: Bikecentennial, Inc., P.O. Box 8308, Missoula, Mont. 59807.

Boy Scouts: Boy Scouts of America, National Council; North Brunswick, N.J. 08902.

Branford: Charles T. Branford Co., 28 Union Street, Newton Centre, Mass. 02159.

Brighton: Brighton Publishing Co., P.O. Box 6235, Salt Lake City, Utah 84106.

Brooks/Cole: Brooks/Cole Publishing Co., 540 Abrego St., Monterey, Calif. 93940.

Brown: Wm. C. Brown & Co., 2460 Kerper Blvd., Dubuque, Iowa 52001.

Bruce: Bruce Publishing Co., 2642 University Ave., St. Paul, Minn. 55114.

Burgess: Burgess Publishing Co., 7108 Ohms Lane, Minneapolis, Minn. 55435.

BYU: Brigham Young University Press, 209 University Press Building, Provo, Utah 84601.

Chilton: Chilton Book Co., Chilton Way, Radnor, Pa. 19089.

CLC Press: Covenant Life Curriculum Press. See John Knox Press.

Cokesbury: Cokesbury, Southwestern Regional Service Center, 1910 Main St., Dallas, Tex. 75221.

Collier: P. F. Collier, Inc., 886 Third Ave., New York, N.Y. 10022.

Condor: Condor Books, 1000 Mariposa, Berkeley, Calif. 94707.

Consumer Reports: Consumer Reports, P.O. Box 1000, Orangeburg, N.Y. 10962.

Coop. Rec. Service: Cooperative Recreation Service, Publishing Department, Radnor Rd., Delaware, Ohio 43015.

Cornell: Cornell University Press, 124 Roberts Place, Ithaca, N.Y. 14850.

Cornell Maritime: Cornell Maritime, P.O. Box 109, Cambridge, Md. 21613.

Coward-McCann: Coward-McCann & Geoghegan, Inc., 200 Madison Ave., New York, N.Y. 10016. (Carried by Putnam)

Crowell: Thomas Y. Crowell Co., 666 Fifth Ave., New York, N.Y. 10019.

Crown: Crown Publishers Inc., 1 Park Ave. S., New York, N.Y. 10016.

Davis: Davis Publications, Inc., 50 Portland St., Worcester, Mass. 01608.

Day: The John Day Co., Inc., 257 Park Ave. S., New York, N.Y. 10010.

Dell: Dell Publishing Co., Inc., 1 Dag Hammarskjold Plaza, 245 E. 47th St., New York, N.Y. 10017.

Delta: Delta Education, Inc., Box M, Nashua, N.H. 03061.

Denison: T. S. Denison and Co., Inc., 5100 W. 82nd St., Minneapolis, Minn. 55431.

Devin-Adair: The Devin Adair Co., 1 Park Ave., Old Greenwich, Conn. 06870.

Dial: The Dial Press, 1 Dag Hammarskjold Plaza, 245 E. 47th St., New York, N.Y. 10017.

Digest Books: Digest Books, 540 Frontage Rd., Northfield, Ill. 60093.

Dodd, Mead: Dodd, Mead & Co., Inc., 79 Madison Ave., New York, N.Y. 10016.

Doubleday: Doubleday and Co., Inc., 501 Franklin Ave., Garden City, N.Y. 11530.

Dover: Dover Publications, Inc., 180 Varick St., New York, N.Y. 10014.

Drake: Drake Publishers, Inc., 381 Park Ave. S., New York, N.Y. 10016.

Duke: Duke University Press, Box 6697, College Station, Durham, N.C. 27708.

Dutton: E. P. Dutton & Co., Inc., 2 Park Ave., New York, N.Y. 10016.

Eerdmans: William B. Eerdmans Publishing Co., 255 Jefferson Ave., S.E., Grand Rapids, Mich. 49502.

Emerson: Emerson Books, Reynolds Lane, Buchanan, N.Y. 10511.

Encounter Four: Encounter Four, Butler County Community College, College Drive, Oak Hills, Butler, Pa. 16001.

Exposition: Exposition Press, Inc., 50 Jericho Tpk., Jericho, N.Y. 11753.

Fawcett: Fawcett Publications, Inc., Fawcett Place, Greenwich, Conn. 06830.

Fearon: Fearon Publishers, Inc., 6 Davis Dr., Belmont, Calif. 94002.

Fell: Frederick Fell, Inc., 386 Park Ave. S., New York, N.Y. 10016.

Fleet: Fleet Press Corp., 156 Fifth Ave., New York, N.Y. 10010.

Follett: Follett Publishing Co., 1010 West Washington Blvd., Chicago, Ill. 60607.

Forest Service: Forest Service, U.S. Department of Agriculture, Washington, D.C. 20250.

Fox: Sam Fox Publishing Co., 1540 Broadway, New York, N.Y. 10023.

Funk & Wagnalls: Funk & Wagnalls, 666 Fifth Ave., New York, N.Y. 10019.

Galloway: Galloway Publications, 5 Mountain Ave., North Plainfield, N.J. 07060.

Gerry: Gerry, Inc., 5450 North Valley Highway, Denver, Colo. 80216.

Girl Scouts: Girl Scouts of the U.S.A., 830 Third Ave., New York, N.Y. 10022.

Golden: Golden Press, Educational Division, Western Publishing Co., Inc., 850 Third Ave., New York, N.Y. 10022.

Greene: The Stephen Greene Press, Fessenden Road, Indian Flat, P.O. Box 1000, Brattleboro, Vt. 05301.

Grosset & Dunlap: Grosset & Dunlap, Inc., 51 Madison Ave., New York, N.Y. 10010.

Hallmark: Hallmark Cards, Inc., 25th and Magee Trafficway, Kansas City, Mo. 64108.

Hammond: Hammond, Inc., 515 Valley St., Maplewood, N.J. 07040.

Harcourt: Harcourt Brace Jovanovich, Inc., 757 Third Ave., New York, N.Y. 10017.

Harper & Row: Harper & Row Publishers, Inc., 10 E. 53rd St., New York, N.Y. 10022.

Harvey: Harvey House, Inc., Publishers, South Buckout, Irvington-on-Hudson, N.Y. 10533.

Hawkins: Hawkins and Associates, Inc., 729 Delaware Ave., Southwest, Washington, D.C. 20024.

Hawthorn: Hawthorn Books, Inc., 260 Madison Ave., New York, N.Y. 10016.

Hoffman: Hoffman Publications, Inc., P.O. Box 7196, Fort Lauderdale, Fla. 33304.

Holt, Rinehart: Holt, Rinehart and Winston, Inc., 383 Madison Ave., New York, N.Y. 10017.

Horizon: Horizon Press, Inc., 156 Fifth Ave., New York, N.Y. 10010.

Horn: Horn Books, Inc., 585 Boylston St., Boston, Mass. 02116.

Houghton Mifflin: Houghton Mifflin Co., Educational Division, 1 Beacon St., Boston, Mass. 02107.

Int'l Textbook: International Textbook Co., Scranton, Pa. 18515.

Interstate: The Interstate Printers and Publishers, 19-27 North Jackson St., Danville, Ill. 61832.

Iowa State U.: Iowa State University Press, South State St., Ames, Iowa 50010.

Knopf: Alfred A. Knopf, 201 E. 50th St., New York, N.Y. 10022.

Knox: John Knox Press, 341 Ponce de Leon Ave., N.E., Atlanta, Ga. 30308.

Lane: Lane Magazine and Book Co., Menlo Park, Calif. 94025.

LaSiesta: LaSiesta Press, Box 406, Glendale, Calif. 91209.

Lea & Febiger: Lea & Febiger, 600 S. Washington Sq., Philadelphia, Pa. 19106.

Libra: Libra Publishers, Inc., 391 Willets Rd., Box 165, Roslyn Heights, N.Y. 11577.

Life Support: Life Support Technology, Inc., P.O. Box 16, Manning, Ore. 97125.

Lion: Lion Books, 111 E. 39th St., New York, N.Y. 10016.

Lippincott: J. B. Lippincott Co., E. Washington Sq., Philadelphia, Pa. 19105.

Little, Brown: Little, Brown & Co., 34 Beacon St., Boston, Mass. 02106.

Longman, Green: Longman, Green and Co., Inc. See *David McKay Company, Inc.*

Luce: Robert B. Luce, Inc., 2000 North St., N.W., Washington, D.C. 20036.

McGraw-Hill: McGraw-Hill Book Co., Princeton Rd., Hightstown, N.J. 08520.

McKay: David McKay Co., Inc., 750 Third Ave., New York, N.Y. 10017.

McKnight: McKnight Publishing Co., Box 2854, Bloomington, Ill. 61701.

Macmillan: The Macmillan Publishing Co., 866 Third Ave., New York, N.Y. 10022.

Meredith: Meredith Corporation—Better Homes & Gardens Books, 1716 Locust St., Des Moines, Iowa 50303.

Morrow: William Morrow and Co., Inc., 105 Madison Ave., New York, N.Y. 10016.

Mountain Press: Mountain Press Publishing Co., 1600 North Ave. West, Missoula, Mont. 59801.

Nat'l Audubon: National Audubon Society, 950 Third Ave., New York, N.Y. 10022.

Nat'l Ed. Ass'n: National Education Association Publications, 1201 16th Street, N.W., Washington, D.C. 20036.

Nat'l History: Natural History Press. See *Doubleday and Company, Inc.*

Nat'l Park Service: National Park Service, Department of the Interior, Washington, D.C. 20240.

Nat'l Press: National Press Books, 850 Hansen Way, Palo Alto, Calif. 94304.

Nautilus: Nautilus Books, 5 Mountain Ave., North Plainfield, N.J. 07060.

N.R.P.A.: National Recreation and Park Association, 3101 Park Center Drive, Alexandria, Va. 22302.

Nat'l Safety Council: National Safety Council, 425 North Michigan Ave., Chicago, Ill. 60611.

Nat'l Wildlife Fed.: National Wildlife Federation, 1412 16th Street, N.W., Washington, D.C. 20036.

Nature Study: Nature Study Aids, Inc., 411 Dakota St., Red Wing, Minn. 55066.

Nature Study Guild: Nature Study Guild, P.O. Box 972, Berkeley, Calif. 94701.

Naturegraph: Naturegraph Publishers, 8339 Dry Creek Rd., Healdsburg, Calif. 95448.

Nelson: Thomas Nelson and Sons, 407 Seventh Ave. S., Nashville, Tenn. 37203.

New Am. Library: The New American Library, 1301 Avenue of the Americas, New York, N.Y. 10019.

Norton: W. W. Norton and Co., Inc., 55 Fifth Ave., New York, N.Y. 10003.

Oak: Oak Publications, Inc., 165 W. 46th St., New York, N.Y. 10036.

Outdoor Ed. Ass'n: The Outdoor Education Association, Inc., 606 S. Marion Ave., Carbondale, Ill. 62901.

Owen: F. A. Owen Publishing Co., Danville, N.Y. 14437.

Oxford: Oxford University Press, Inc., 16-00 Pollitt Dr., Fairlawn, N.J. 07410.

Peek: Peek Publications, 164 E. Dana St., Mountain View, Calif. 94040.

Phoenix: Phoenix Publishing, Dept. 112, Woodstock, Vt. 05091.

Plant Deck: Plant Deck, Inc., Dept. W. C., 2134 S.W. Wembley Park Rd., Lake Oswego, Ore. 97034.

Plays: Plays, Inc., 8 Arlington St., Boston, Mass. 02116.

Pocket Books: Pocket Books, Inc., 630 Fifth Ave., New York, N.Y. 10020.

Popular Library: Popular Library, Inc., 600 Third Ave., New York, N.Y. 10011.

Praeger: Praeger Publishers, Inc., 111 Fourth Ave., New York, N.Y. 10003.

Pratt: J. Lowell Pratt, 15 East 48th St., New York, N.Y. 10017.

Prentice-Hall: Prentice-Hall, Inc., Englewood Cliffs, N.J. 07632.

Presscraft: Presscraft Papers, Benzonia, Mich. 49616.

Princeton: Princeton Book Co., 20 Nassau St., P.O. Box 109, Princeton, N.J. 08540.

Project Adventure: Project Adventure, P.O. Box 157, Hamilton, Mass. 01936.

Putnam: G. P. Putnam's Sons, 200 Madison Ave., New York, N.Y. 10016.

Quadrangle: Quadrangle/The New York Times Book Co., 10 East 53rd St., New York, N.Y. 10022.

Rand McNally: Rand McNally and Co., P.O. Box 7600, Chicago, Ill. 60680.

Random: Random House, Inc., 201 East 50th St., New York, N.Y. 10022.

Recreational: Recreational Equipment, Inc., Box C-88127, Seattle, Wash. 98188.

Regnery: Henry Regnery, 114 West Illinois St., Chicago, Ill. 60601.

Remington: Remington Arms Co., Inc., Bridgeport, Conn. 06602.

Revell: Fleming H. Revell Co., Old Tappan, N.J. 07675.

Rodale: Rodale Press, Emmaus, Pa. 18049.

Ronald: The Ronald Press, 79 Madison Ave., New York, N.Y. 10016.

Rubin: Louis D. Rubin, Box 8615, Richmond, Va. 23226.

Saturday Review: Saturday Review Press. See *E. P. Dutton and Co., Inc.*

Saunders: Saunders College Publishing, West Washington Sq., Philadelphia, Pa. 19105.

Scarecrow: Scarecrow Press, Inc., 52 Liberty St., P.O. Box 656, Metuchen, N.J. 08840.

Schocken: Schocken Books, Inc., 200 Madison Ave., New York, N.Y. 10016.

Scholastic Book Service: Scholastic Book Service, 50 West 44th St., New York, N.Y. 10036.

Science Research: Science Research Associates, Inc., 1540 Page Mill Rd., Palto Alto, Calif. 94304.

Scott, Foresman: Scott, Foresman and Co., 1900 East Lake Ave., Glenview, Ill. 60025.

Scribner's: Charles Scribner's Sons, 597 Fifth Ave., New York, N.Y. 10017.

Scripture: Scripture Press Publications, Inc., 1825 College Ave., Wheaton, Ill. 60187.

Sequoia: Sequoia, 300 Kalamazoo Ave., Kalamazoo, Mich. 49006.

Sierra: Sierra Club Books, 530 Bush St., San Francisco, Calif. 94108.

Signet: See *New American Library*.

Silva: Silva, Inc., Box 966, Binghamton, N.Y. 13902.

Silver-Burdett: Silver-Burdett Co., 250 James St., Morristown, N.J. 07960.

Simon & Schuster: Simon and Schuster, Inc., 1230 Ave. of the Americas, New York, N.Y. 10020.

Sing Out: Sing Out, 589 Broadway, New York, N.Y. 10012. (Publishers of *Sing Out! The Folk Song Magazine*)

Stackpole: Stackpole Books, Cameron and Kelker Sts., Harrisburg, Pa. 17105.

Sterling: Sterling Publishing Co., Inc., 2 Park Ave. S., New York, N.Y. 10016.

Supt. of Documents: The Superintendent of Documents, U.S. Government Printing Office, Washington, D.C. 20402.

Syracuse: Syracuse University Press, 1011 E. Water St., Syracuse, N.Y. 13210.

Tenspeed: Tenspeed Press, Box 4310, Berkeley, Calif. 94704.

Thomas: Charles C Thomas, Publisher, 301 East Lawrence Ave., Springfield, Ill. 62703.

Tiresias: Tiresias Press, Inc., 116 Pinehurst Ave., New York, N.Y. 10033.

Trail-R-Club: Trail-R-Club of America, 3211 Pico Blvd., Santa Monica, Calif. 90405.

Tudor: Tudor Publishing Co., 221 Park Ave. S., New York, N.Y. 10003.

U. of Chicago: University of Chicago Press, 5801 Ellis Ave., Chicago, Ill. 60637.

U. of Mich.: University of Michigan Press, 615 East University, Ann Arbor, Mich. 48106.

U. of Minn.: University of Minnesota Press, 2037 University Avenue, S.E., Minneapolis, Minn. 55455.

U. of Neb.: University of Nebraska Press, 901 N. 17th St., Lincoln, Neb. 68588.

U. of Okla.: University of Oklahoma Press, 1005 Asp Ave., Norman, Okla. 73069.

U. of Ore.: University of Oregon, Eugene, Ore. 97403.

U. of Wash.: University of Washington Press, Seattle, Wash. 98195.

U. of Wis.: University of Wisconsin Press, Box 1379, Madison, Wis. 53701.

U.S. Coast and Geodetic Society: U.S. Coast and Geodetic Society, Washington, D.C. 20025.

U.S. Geological Survey: U.S. Geological Survey, Department of the Interior, Washington, D.C. 20242.

U.S. Naval Institute: U.S. Naval Institute, Naval Institute Press, Annapolis, Md. 21402.

Van Nostrand: Van Nostrand-Reinhold Co., 135 W. 50th St., New York, N.Y. 10020.

Vantage: Vantage Press, Inc., 516 West 34th St., New York, N.Y. 10001.

Viking: The Viking Press, Inc., 625 Madison Ave., New York, N.Y. 10022.

Wadsworth: Wadsworth Publishing Co., Inc., Belmont, Calif. 94002.

Walck: Henry Z. Walck, Inc., 3 East 54th St., New York, N.Y. 10022.

Warner: Warner Books, Inc., 75 Rockefeller Plaza, New York, N.Y. 10019.

Washington Square: Washington Square Press, 630 Fifth Ave., New York, N.Y. 10020.

Watts: Franklin Watts, Inc., 730 Fifth Ave., New York, N.Y. 10019.

Welch: G. R. Welch Co., Ltd., 222 Evans Ave., Toronto 18, Ontario, Canada.

Western: Western Publishing Co., Inc., 1220 Mound Ave., Racine, Wis. 53404.

Westminster: The Westminster Press, Witherspoon Bldg., Philadelphia, Pa. 19107.

Whitman: Whitman Publishing Co., 1220 Mound Ave., Racine, Wis. 53404.

Whittlesey: Whittlesey House, 330 West 42nd St., New York, N.Y. 10036.

Wilderness: Wilderness Press, 2440 Bancroft Way, Berkeley, Calif. 94704.

Wildlife: Wildlife Management Institute, 709 Wire Blvd., 1000 Vermont Ave., N.W., Washington, D.C. 20005.

Wiley: John Wiley and Sons, Inc., 605 Third Ave., New York, N.Y. 10016.

Winchester: Winchester Press, 460 Park Ave., New York, N.Y. 10022.

Workman: Workman Publishing Co., Inc., 231 E. 51st St., New York, N.Y. 10022.

World: The World Publishing Co., 110 East 59th St., New York, N.Y. 10022.

Y.M.C.A.: National Board of the Y.M.C.A., 600 Lexington Ave., New York, N.Y. 10022.

Y.W.C.A.: National Board of the Y.W.C.A., Bureau of Communications, 600 Lexington Ave., New York, N.Y. 10022.

Zondervan: Zondervan Publishing House, 1415 Lake Dr., S.E., Grand Rapids, Mich. 49506.

appendix E Where to Get Equipment and Supplies

ARTS AND CRAFTS

American Handicrafts, 1011 Foch St., Fort Worth, Tex. 76107.

Bersted's Hobby-Craft, Inc., 521 W. 10th Ave., Monmouth, Ill. 61462.

Boin Arts and Crafts Co., 87 Morris St., Morristown, N.J. 07960.

Customade Leather Goods, 265 Highway 55, Hamel, N. Mex. 55343.

Economy Handicrafts, 50-21 69th St., Woodside, N.Y. 11377. (Kilns)

Grey Owl Indian Craft Co., Inc., 150-02 Beaver Road, Jamaica, N.Y. 11433.

Lily Mills Co., Shelby, N.C. 28150.

Magnus Craft Materials, Inc., 109 Lafayette St., New York, N.Y. 10013.

Rit Dye, Best Foods Div., CPC International, International Plaza, Englewood Cliffs, N.J. 07632.

S and S Arts and Crafts, Colchester, Conn. 06415.

School Products Co., 312 E. 23rd St., New York, N.Y. 10010.

Signature Graphics, Box 125, Nevada, Iowa, 50201.

Tandy Leather Co., 1001 Foch St., Fort Worth, Tex. 76107.

BOATS, CANOES, KAYAKS, RAFTS, WATERFRONT

Adventurer Canoe Co., P.O. Box 296, Wilton, Conn. 06897.

Alumni-Span, 122 N. Main St., Pittsford, Mich. 49271.

Aqua/matic Lifeguard Mfg. Corp., 7173 Northern Blvd., East Syracuse, N.Y. 13057.

Aqua-matic Piers, Inc., 3238 W. Pierce St., Milwaukee, Wis. 53215.

Canhan Whitewater Accessories, 7815 S.E. Luther Rd., Portland Ore. 97206. (Rafting equipment)

Extrasport, Suite 603, 3050 Biscayne Blvd., Miami, Fla. 33137. (Life vests and accessories)

Flaghouse, 18 W. 18th St., New York, N.Y. 10011.

Grumman Boats, 7 South St., Marathon, N.Y. 13803.

IPCO Inc., 541 W. 79, Minneapolis, Minn. 55420.

Klepper America, 35 Union Square West, New York, N.Y. 10003. (Folding boats and kayaks)

Lifeguard Mfg. Corp. 1224 W. Genessee, Syracuse, N.Y. 13204.

Mad River Canoe, P.O. Box 610 L, Waitsfield, Vt. 05673.

Northwest River Supply, P.O. Box 9186, Moscow, Idaho, 83843.

Old Town Canoe Co., 58 Middle St., Old Town, Me. 04468.

Ouachita Marine & Industrial Corp., P.O. Box 420, Arkadelphia, Ark. 71923.

Perception, Inc., P.O. Box 686, Liberty S.C. 29657. (Kayaks, canoes and accessories)

P.Z.P. Associates, Inc., 396 Sharon Drive, Cheshire, Conn. 06410.

Rocky Mountain Kayak Supply, Inc. Box 8150, 611 East Durant, Aspen, Colo. 81612.

Rolf Godon Co., 15 California St., San Francisco, Calif. 94111.

Salmon River Boatworks, Box 1804, Salmon, Idaho 83467. (Kayaks)

Seda Products, P.O. Box 997, Chula Vista, Calif. 92012. (Canoes, kayaks and accessories)

Select Service and Supply Co., 180 Allen Road N.E., Atlanta, Ga. 30328.

United Flotation, United McGill Corp., 2400 Fairwood Ave., Columbus, Ohio 43216.

We.no.nah, Box 247, Winona, Minn. 55987. (Canoes)

Wildwater Designs, 230 Penllyn Pike, Pennllyn, Pa. 19422. (Kayak and canoe accessories and self-made kits)

CAMPING AND TRIP EQUIPMENT

(Most of these firms furnish catalogues that are excellent sources of information, even if you intend to shop in person locally.)

Alpine Designs, 6185 E. Arapahoe, Boulder, Colo. 80303.

Alpine Hut, 4725 30th Ave., N.E., Seattle, Wash. 98105.

Eddie Bauer, 5th and Union, P.O. Box 3700, Seattle, Wash. 98124.

L. L. Bean, Inc., 4641 Main St., Freeport, Me. 04033.

Bell Manufacturing Co., 25 Bell Bldg., Lewiston, Me. 04240. (Name tapes)

The Camp & Hike Shop, 4674 Knight-Arnold Rd., Memphis, Tenn. 38118.

Camp and Trail Outfitters, 21 Park Place, New York, N.Y. 10007.

Camp Supply Co., 1151 S. 7th St., St. Louis, Mo. 63104.

Camp Trails, Box 966 O, Binghamton, N.Y. 13902.

Class 5 Mountaineering Equipage, 2010 Seventh St., Berkeley, Calif. 94710.

Coleman Company, Inc., 250 N. Francis St., Wichita, Kan. 67201.

Colorado Outdoor Sports Corp., P.O. Box 5544, Denver, Color. 80217.

Early Winters, Ltd., 110 Pre-Fontaine Place South, Seattle, Wash. 98104.

Eastern Mountain Sports, Two Vose Farm Rd., Peterborough, N.H. 03458.

Eureka Tent Inc., P.O. Box 966J, Binghamton, N.Y. 13902.

Gerry, 5450 North Valley Highway, Denver, Colo. 80216.

Don Gleason's Campers Supply, 21 Pearl St., Northampton, Mass. 01061.

Hi-Camp, P.O. Box 17602, Charlotte, N.C. 28211.

Highland Outfitters, 3579 University Ave. (8th St.), P.O. Box 121, Riverside, Calif. 92502.

Himalayan Industries, 807 Cannery Row, P.O. Box 950, Monterey, Calif. 93940.

Hirsch-Weis/White Stag, 5203 S.E. Johnson Creek Blvd., Portland, Ore. 97206.

Holubar Mountaineering, Ltd., Box 7, Boulder, Colo. 80306.

JanSport, Plain Field Industrial Park, Everett, Wash. 98204.

Kelty Pack, Inc., Box 639, Sun Valley, Calif. 91352.

Optimus, Inc., 12423 E. Florence Ave., Santa Fe Springs, Calif. 90670. (Backpacking stoves)

Paul Petzoldt Wilderness Equipment, P.O. Box 489, Lander, Wyo. 82520.

Recreational Equipment, Inc., P.O. Box C-88127, Seattle, Wash. 98188.

Sierra Designs, 247 Fourth St., Oakland, Calif. 94607.

Silva Compass, Box 966, Binghamton, N.Y. 13902.

Ski Hut, 1615 University Ave., Berkeley, Calif. 94703.

The Smilie Co., 575 Howard St., San Francisco, Calif. 94105.

DO-IT-YOURSELF KITS

Carakit Outdoor Equipment Kits, P.O. Box 1153, Boulder, Colo. 80302.

Country Ways, 3500 Highway 101 South, Minn. 55343.

Eastern Mountain Sports, 12402 Vose Farm Rd., Peterborough, N.H. 03458.

Frostline Kits, Frostline Circle, Denver, Colo. 80241.

Holubar Mountaineering, P.O. Box 7, Boulder, Colo. 80302.

Lightweight Wilderness Fabrics, 2511 Latch, Nampa, Idaho 83651.

Mountain Adventure Kits Co., P.O. Box 571, Whittier, Calif. 90608.

Vermont Tubbs Snowshoe Kits, Wallingford, Vt. 05773.

LIGHTWEIGHT FOODS

Bernard Food Industries, Box 487, St. James Park Station, 222 S. 24th St., San Jose, Calif. 95103. (Kamp Pack Foods)

Chuck Wagon Foods, Micro Drive, Woburn, Me. 01801.

Dri-Lite Foods, 11333 Atlantic, Lynwood, Calif. 90262.

Eastern Mountain Sports, Inc., Two Vose Farm Rd., Peterborough, N.H. 03458.

Freeze-Dry Foods Ltd., 579 Speers Rd., Oakville, Ontario, Canada L6K 2G4. (HarDee Food)

S. Gumpert Co., 812 Jersey Ave., Jersey City, N.J. 07302.

Natural Food Backpack Dinners, P.O. Box 532, Corvallis, Ore. 97330.

National Packaged Trail Foods, 18607 St. Clair Ave., Cleveland, Ohio 44110. (Seidel's)

Oregon Freeze Dry Foods, Inc., P.O. Box 1048, Albany, Ore. 97321. (Mountain House Foods)

Perma-Pak Camping Foods, 40 East 2430 So., Salt Lake City, Utah 84115. (Camplite Foods)

Rich-Moor Corp., P.O. Box 2728, Van Nuys, Calif. 91404.

Stow-A-Way Sports Industries, Inc., 166 Cushing Hiway (Rt. 3A), Cohasset, Ma. 02025. (Stow-Lite Food)

RIFLERY PROGRAM AND SUPPLIES

Benjamin Air Rifle Co., 826 Marion St., St. Louis, Mo. 63104.

Daisey Division, Victor Comptometer Corp., Box 220, Rogers, Ark. 72756.

National Rifle Association, 1600 Rhode Island Ave., N.W., Washington, D.C. 20036.

National Shooting Sports Foundation, Inc., 1075 Post Rd., Riverside, Conn. 06878.

National Target Co., Inc., 4960 Wyconda Road, Rockville, Mo. 20853.

Remington Arms Co., Inc., 939 Barnum Ave., Bridgeport, Conn. 06602.

appendix F
Suggestions for Conducting Courses in Camp Counseling

This book has been designed particularly to be used by those in college courses in camp counseling, but it will be equally useful for participants in C.I.T. (counselor-in-training), precamp, and in-training courses as well as for those already employed in a camp situation. The purposes of the four sections of this book and the persons for whom it is intended have been discussed in the Preface. Since successful camp counselors must be well rounded, understand people, maintain proper attitudes, and possess specialized skills, it seems obvious that if they are to do an adequate job, a number of methods of training and preparing them will be necessary. Like the children with whom they expect to work, counselors will profit most from a lively and varied course that seems meaningful to them. The theoretical aspects of the course can be covered with the usual lectures, discussions, testing, and such, but something more is needed. There must also be some provision for laboratory periods to give practice in camping skills, including the use of equipment and tools and working effectively with groups. There should be at least a few excursions to practice camping, outdoor cooking and other trail skills. Ideally, these will culminate in an extended camping trip of 6 days or more, which is needed if participants are to catch the real flavor of living in the out-of-doors. If some actual work with children can also be included, so much the better.

Since we know that some learn best by *seeing,* others by *hearing,* and still others by *doing,* it seems logical to use all of these methods of instruction, just as our prospective counselors will be doing later on a modified basis with their own campers. Use variety to spark interest and develop a sense of what being a counselor means. Here are some suggestions that may prove helpful:

1. Study the text, supporting it with lectures, class discussions, demonstrations, testing, and the like.
2. Assign supplementary reading. No student can be prepared adequately who has not been exposed to different opinions and methods, as well as to some, at least, of the excellent publications available in the field. In addition to requiring certain readings from everyone, it is also wise to permit choices from diverse fields such as ecology, aquatics, and dramatics to allow for personal interests and to help counselors prepare for the specific jobs they may hold.
3. Hold discussions—round table, panel, or led by a group member—about topics of general interest, perhaps chosen by the class. Also have class members make oral presentations and/or write special reports concerning some phase of camping. Encourage them to be innovative and seek ways to present material in a dynamic manner that will challenge them and appeal to several of the senses. The class can evaluate the methods used.
4. Individuals should take turns at instructing their classmates on chosen topics, such as how to lead a discussion, plan a campfire program, lay a fire, pitch a tent, use and care for a knife, and so on. Discuss methods of presenting such material to campers.
5. Assign special projects—collecting songs suitable for camp use, making articles for camp or personal use, etc.
6. Use visiting speakers or consultants—a scouting leader, camp director, first aid instructor, conservation agent, forest ranger, and the like. Also invite persons from related teaching fields such as psychology, sociology, elementary education, or home economics.

7. Use some of the many good slides and movies now available on camping and related topics.

8. Collect, circulate, or display such materials as camp bulletins, pamphlets published by the American Camping Association and other organizations, selected books about camping, arts and crafts materials, small models of various fires and their uses, and the like.

9. Schedule laboratory periods for practicing campcraft skills, perhaps inviting a group of youngsters to receive instruction from members of the class.

10. Have students prepare an annotated bibliography or card file of literature on camping. They will find such a compilation invaluable later as it enables them to quickly locate needed information.

11. Have class members plan and participate in cookouts, overnights, and longer backcountry trips. This gives experience in using a committee system, delegating responsibility, and working democratically with others to put into practice some of the theories that were discussed.

12. Individual class members can plan and make sets of flip charts or lesson cards to use when explaining techniques to others.

13. Tape record or video tape students as they lead sessions or discussions, and let them evaluate the playback.

14. Slide photographs or motion pictures can be taken and used to arouse interest or to present a special topic.

15. Use various group methods, such as role playing, circular discussion, and others described in the text.

16. Study various types of camping equipment available, using the catalogues of various outfitters (see Appendix E). Visit supply stores or arrange to borrow items of equipment for study and comparison.

17. Attend meetings and workshops sponsored by the ACA or related organizations and encourage student memberships.

18. Sponsor a camp staff job mart or placement day, and invite various camps to send representatives. Provide areas for various displays and private interviews.

Although camp leadership training courses continue to grow in both number and quality, the supply of those completing them still lags far behind the demand. Anyone who contemplates offering such training is urged to contact the American Camping Association about their leadership courses which are conducted by instructors approved by the Association. Appropriate certificates are available for those who satisfactorily complete these programs. It would be wise for you to become qualified to conduct such courses yourself.

appendix G
Suggestions for Conducting Camp CIT (Counselor-In-Training) Courses

INTRODUCTION

A number of camps conduct their own Counselor-In-Training (CIT) programs. These are essentially incamp leadership training courses with strong emphasis on inservice experiences designed to prepare older youth for their future role as camp counselors. The participants in such a program are referred to as "CITs." Although they are still campers, they are in a specific category and therefore, in addition to their own specific training program, they also usually have their own separate living quarters apart from the younger campers.

There are some basic guidelines that should be applied to any CIT program, including the development of specific learning activities for the individuals who participate. On a regularly scheduled basis, CITs should be assigned outside readings as well as responsibility for leading discussions and giving reports. These experiences should be intermixed with chances for observation and opportunities to acquire certain basic skills. In addition, followup and evaluation must be a continuous part of the program so that CITs can recognize their growth and judge the progress of their own performance.

For the first year of a two-year course, CITs are usually more involved in observation and skill development rather than actual leadership. After they have been exposed to a variety of skills and principles of leadership, they are given more opportunity to practice and demonstrate their knowledge during the second year. This is also the time for more indepth exploration of the total workings of the camp.

The nature of the CIT course, and its implementation, will, of course, depend upon such factors as the philosophy of the camp, the number of CIT personnel involved, and the facilities available. The following two-year course outline is therefore intended to serve merely as a guideline for those who are responsible for organizing and leading the program. This text should serve as a valuable resource for trainees as well as for leaders of CIT courses.

SUGGESTED CIT PROGRAM FOR A TWO-YEAR COURSE

I. First Summer

A. *Philosophy and objectives.* What are the objectives of camping generally and specifically of your own camp? Develop a program of learning that includes information and understanding to be gained about these objectives, including:
   1. Skills and habits to be developed.
   2. Attitudes and interests to be encouraged.

B. *History and current trends in camping.* Examine the following:
   1. The background of the camping field.
   2. Types of camps and their sponsors.
   3. Issues and problems, campers' needs, and various camp programs.

C. *Leadership skills in program areas.* Emphasis should be on observation and discussion for the first year in order to help trainees develop knowledge and leadership abilities in various camp activities. Discuss and demonstrate the teaching-learning process and teaching methods, including proper activity progression. Limited opportunities should be available for CITs to gain experience by functioning as aids and assistants to counselors and other staff. Opportunities should be provided in some of the following areas:

1. Land sports—tennis, archery, riding, etc.
2. Music—songs and song leading.
3. Creative activities—arts and crafts, dramatics, story telling, dance, etc.
4. Special activities—campfire and evening programs, rainy day activities, and other special programs.
5. Campcraft, trip camping, and outdoor living skills.
   (a) Basic skills—hiking, backpacking, canoeing, kayaking, toolcraft, ropecraft, firecraft, map and compass skills, food and menu planning, outdoor cooking.
   (b) Conservation, nature, and ecology.
   (c) Waterfront activities—swimming, life saving, sailing, canoeing, kayaking, waterskiing, etc.
   (d) Health, safety, and first aid.

D. *Leadership skills in social aspects of camp life.* Provide opportunities for observation of groups in camp, including factors leading to their success or failure.
   1. Methods and techniques of leadership.
      (a) Leadership of both individuals and groups.
      (b) Analysis of skills.
   2. Serve as aids to counselors while working with youngsters of various ages in a variety of activities and settings.
      (a) Observe campers during activities in living quarters and on trips.
      (b) Develop an understanding of camper behavior and age group characteristics.
   3. Assist in organizing specific camp activities and special events.

E. *CIT evaluation.*
   1. Several times throughout the summer (beginning, middle, end), review and discuss with each trainee such matters as background, attitude, experience, strengths and weaknesses, leadership potential. (See Chapter 4.)
   2. Counselor evaluations.
   3. Self evaluation.
   4. Recommendations concerning each CIT's continuation in the course the following summer.

II. Second Summer

A. *Continue the development of skills, techniques, and knowledge of camping activities.*

B. *Further experience in assisting and serving as an aide to counselors and other staff.*

1. Live in different age group units for several weeks to acquire a variety of experiences and assume various camp roles.
2. Practice teaching and leading camping activities under the direction of various counselors.
3. Assist on trips and other camp activities.

C. *Group interaction and discussion concerning campers.*
1. Backgrounds and needs.
2. Means of assessing individual abilities and problems.
3. Discussions of specific situations.

D. *Observe and learn about other camp functions and responsibilities.* This could include maintenance, business procedures, records and reports, supplies and inventory, administration, food service, ACA camp standards, etc.

E. *CIT evaluation* (as in I-E). The trainee program should end with each person receiving a recommendation concerning future employment as a member of the camping staff.

Index